When the Lights Go Down

Also by Pauline Kael

I Lost it at the Movies
Kiss Kiss Bang Bang
Going Steady
The Citizen Kane Book
Deeper into Movies
Reeling

Pauline Kael

WHEN THE LIGHTS GO DOWN

Holt, Rinehart and Winston □□ New York

Library of Congress Cataloging in Publication Data
Kael, Pauline
When the lights go down.
Includes index.
1. Moving-pictures—Reviews. I. Title.
PN1995.K254   791.43'7   79–19067
ISBN Hardbound: 0-03-042511-5
ISBN Paperback: 0-03-056842-0

All material in this book originally appeared in *The New Yorker*.

Designer: *Joy Chu*

Printed in the United States of America
2   4   6   8   10   9   7   5   3

Acknowledgments

I want to thank the checkers of *The New Yorker,* where these pieces first appeared, and William Whitworth, who is the most patient and scrupulous of editors. And once again I must express my deepest thanks—thanks, with bonds of love—to William Shawn, Editor of *The New Yorker,* and to William Abrahams, now of Holt, Rinehart and Winston, who has been the editor of all the books I've published, and to my daughter, Gina James, the critic's critic.

Contents

Part One

Part Three

PART ONE

The Man from Dream City

"**Y**ou can be had," Mae West said to Cary Grant in *She Done Him Wrong*, which opened in January, 1933, and that was what the women stars of most of his greatest hits were saying to him for thirty years, as he backed away—but not too far. One after another, the great ladies courted him—Irene Dunne in *The Awful Truth* and *My Favorite Wife*, Katharine Hepburn in *Bringing Up Baby* and *Holiday*, Jean Arthur and Rita Hayworth in *Only Angels Have Wings,* Ingrid Bergman in *Notorious*, Grace Kelly in *To Catch a Thief,* Eva Marie Saint in *North by Northwest*, Audrey Hepburn in *Charade*. Willing but not forward, Cary Grant must be the most publicly seduced male the world has known, yet he has never become a public joke—not even when Tony Curtis parodied him in *Some Like It Hot*, encouraging Marilyn Monroe to rape. The little bit of shyness and reserve in Grant is pure box-office gold, and being the pursued doesn't make him seem weak or passively soft. It makes him glamorous—and, since he is not as available as other men, far more desirable.

Cary Grant is the male love object. Men want to be as lucky and enviable as he is—they want to be like him. And women imagine landing him. Like Robert Redford, he's sexiest in pictures in which the woman is the aggressor and all the film's erotic energy is concentrated on him, as it was in *Notorious*: Ingrid Bergman practically ravished him while he was trying to conduct a phone conversation. Redford has never been so radiantly glamorous as in *The Way We Were*, when we saw him through Barbra Streisand's infatuated eyes. But in *The Great Gatsby,* when Redford needed to do for Mia Farrow what Streisand had done for him, he couldn't transcend his immaculate self-absorption. If he had looked at her with desire, everything else about the movie might have been forgiven. Cary Grant would not have failed; yearning for an idealized love was not beyond his resources. It may even be part of his essence: in the sleekly confected *The Philadelphia Story*, he brought conviction to the dim role of the blue blood standing by Katharine Hepburn and waiting on the sidelines. He expressed the very sort of desperate constancy that Redford failed to express. Grant's marital farces with Irene Dunne probably wouldn't have been as effective as they were if he hadn't suggested a bedevilled constancy in the midst of the confusion. The heroine who chases him knows that deep down he wants to be caught only by her. He draws women to him by making them feel he needs them, yet the last thing he'd do would be to come right out and say it. In *Only Angels Have Wings,* Jean Arthur half falls apart waiting for him to make a move; in *His Girl Friday,* he's unabashed about everything in the world except why he doesn't want Rosalind Russell to go off with Ralph Bellamy. He isn't weak, yet something in him makes him hold back—and that something (a slight uncertainty? the fear of a commitment? a mixture of ardor and idealism?) makes him more exciting.

The romantic male stars aren't necessarily sexually aggressive. Henry Fonda wasn't; neither was James Stewart, or, later, Marcello Mastroianni. The foursquare Clark Gable, with his bold, open challenge to women, was more the exception than the rule, and Gable wasn't romantic, like Grant. Gable got down to brass tacks; his advances were basic, his unspoken question was "Well, sister, what do you say?" If she said no, she was failing what might almost be nature's test. She'd become overcivilized, afraid of her instincts—afraid of being a woman. There was a violent, primal appeal in Gable's sex scenes: it was all out front—in the way he looked at her, man to woman. Cary Grant doesn't challenge a woman that way. (When he tried, as the frontiersman in *The Howards of Virginia*, he looked thick and stupid.) With Gable, sex is inevitable: What is there but sex? Basically, he thinks women are good for only one thing. Grant is interested in the qualities of a particular woman—her sappy expression, her non sequiturs, the way her voice bobbles. She isn't going to be pushed to the wall as soon as she's alone with him. With Grant, the social, urban man, there are infinite possibilities for mutual entertainment. They might dance the night away or stroll or go to a carnival—and nothing sexual would happen unless she wanted it to. Grant doesn't assert his male supremacy; in the climax of a picture he doesn't triumph by his fists and brawn—or even by outwitting anybody. He isn't a conqueror, like Gable. But he's a winner. The game, however, is an artful dodge. He gets the blithe, funny girl by maneuvering her into going after him. He's a fairy-tale hero, but she has to pass through the trials: She has to trim her cold or pompous adversaries; she has to dispel his fog. In picture after picture, he seems to give up his resistance at the end, as if to say, What's the use of fighting?

Many men must have wanted to be Clark Gable and look straight at a woman with a faint smirk and lifted, questioning eyebrows. What man doesn't—at some level—want to feel supremely confident and earthy and irresistible? But a few steps up the dreamy social ladder there's the more subtle fantasy of worldly grace—of being so gallant and gentlemanly and charming that every woman longs to be your date. And at that deluxe level men want to be Cary Grant. Men as far apart as John F. Kennedy and Lucky Luciano thought that he should star in their life story. Who but Cary Grant could be a fantasy self-image for a President and a gangster chief? Who else could demonstrate that sophistication didn't have to be a sign of weakness—that it could be the polished, fun-loving style of those who were basically tough? Cary Grant has said that even he wanted to be Cary Grant.

And for women, if the roof leaks, or the car stalls, or you don't know how to get the super to keep his paws off you, you may long for a Clark Gable to take charge, but when you think of going out, Cary Grant is your dream date—not sexless but sex with civilized grace, sex with mystery. He's the man of the big city, triumphantly suntanned. Sitting out there in Los Angeles, the expatriate New York writers projected onto him their fantasies of Eastern connoisseurship and suavity. How could the heroine ever consider marrying a rich rube from Oklahoma and leaving Cary Grant and the night spots? Los Angeles itself has never recovered from the inferiority complex that its movies nourished, and every moviegoing kid in America felt that the people in New York were smarter, livelier, and better-looking than anyone in his home town. The audience didn't become hostile; it took the contempt as earned. There were no Cary Grants in the sticks. He and his counterparts were to be found only in the imaginary cities of the movies. When you look at him, you take for granted expensive tailors, international travel, and the best that life has to offer. Women see a man they could have fun with. Clark Gable is an intensely realistic sexual presence; you don't fool around with Gable. But with Grant there are no pressures, no demands; he's the sky that women aspire to. When he and a woman are together, they can laugh at each other and at themselves. He's a slapstick Prince Charming.

Mae West's raucous invitation to him—"Why don't you come up sometime and see me?"—was echoed thirty years later by Audrey Hepburn in *Charade*: "Won't you come in for a minute? I don't bite, you know, unless it's called for." And then, purringly, "Do you know what's wrong with you? Nothing." That might be a summary of Cary Grant, the finest romantic comedian of his era: there's nothing the matter with him. Many of the male actors who entered movies when sound came in showed remarkable powers of endurance—James Cagney, Bing Crosby, Charles Boyer, Fred Astaire—but they didn't remain heroes. Spencer Tracy didn't, either; he became paternal and judicious. Henry Fonda and James Stewart turned into folksy elder statesmen, sagacious but desexed. Cary Grant has had the longest romantic reign in the short history of movies. He might be cast as an arrogant rich boy, an unscrupulous cynic, or a selfish diplomat, but there was nothing sullen or self-centered in his acting. Grant never got star-stuck on himself; he never seemed to be saying, Look at me. The most obvious characteristic of his acting is the absence of narcissism—the outgoingness to the audience.

Cary Grant was a knockout in his dapper young days as a Paramount leading man to such suffering sinners as Sylvia Sidney, Carole Lombard, Tallulah Bankhead, Marlene Dietrich, Nancy Carroll. He appeared with this batch in 1932; Paramount threw him into seven pictures in his first year. In some two dozen roles in four years, he was a passable imitation of Noël Coward or Jack Buchanan, though not as brittle as Coward or as ingratiatingly silly as Buchanan. He played a celebrated javelin thrower in *This Is the Night,* a rotten rich roué in *Sinners in the Sun,* the husband of a diva in *Enter Madam* and of another diva in *When You're in Love.* He was a flier who went blind in *Wings in the Dark*; he wore a dinky mustache and was captured by the Kurds in *The Last Outpost*; he used a black bullwhip on the villainous Jack La Rue in *The Woman Accused.* But that's all a blur. He didn't have a strong enough personality to impose himself on viewers, and most people don't remember Cary Grant for those roles, or even much for his tall-dark-and-handsome stints with Mae West. He might never have become a star if it had not been for the sudden onset of screwball comedy in 1934—the year when *The Thin Man* and *Twentieth Century* and *It Happened One Night* changed American movies. His performances in screwball comedies—particularly *The Awful Truth*, in 1937, his twenty-ninth picture—turned him into the comedian-hero that people think of as Cary Grant. He was resplendent before but characterless, even a trace languid—a slightly wilted sheik. He was Mae West's classiest and best leading man, but he did more for her in *She Done Him Wrong* and *I'm No Angel* than she did for him. She brought out his passivity, and a quality of refinement in him which made her physical aggression seem a playful gambit. (With tough men opposite her, she was less charming, more crude.) Sizing him up with her satyr's eyes and deciding he was a prize catch, she raised our estimate of him. Yet Grant still had that pretty-boy killer look; he was too good-looking to be on the level. And although he was outrageously attractive with Mae West, he was vaguely ill at ease; his face muscles betrayed him, and he looked a little fleshy. He didn't yet know how the camera should see him; he didn't focus his eyes on her the way he learned to use his eyes later. No doubt he felt absurd in his soulful, cow-eyed leading-man roles, and tried to conceal it; when he had nothing to do in a scene, he stood lunged forward as if hoping to catch a ball. He became Cary Grant when he learned to project his feelings of absurdity through his characters and to make a style out of their feeling silly. Once he realized that each movement could be stylized for humor, the eyepopping, the cocked head, the forward lunge, and the slightly ungainly stride became as certain as the pen strokes of a master cartoonist. The new element of romantic slapstick in the mid-thirties comedies—the teasing role reversals and shifts of mood—loosened him up and brought him to life. At last, he could do on the screen what he had been trained to do, and a rambunctious, springy side of his nature came out. Less "Continental" and more physical, he became funny and at the same time sexy. He was no longer effete; the booming voice had vitality.

It was in 1935, when the director George Cukor cast him as a loudmouthed product of the British slums—a con man and strolling player—in the Katharine Hepburn picture *Sylvia Scarlett,* that Grant's boisterous energy first broke through. He was so brashly likable that viewers felt vaguely discomfited at the end when Brian Aherne (who had given an insufferably egotistic performance) wound up with Hepburn. Grant, on loan from Paramount to RKO, doesn't play the leading-man role, yet his con man is so loose and virile that he has more life than anything else in the picture. Grant seemed to be enjoying himself on the screen in a way he never had before. Cukor said that Grant suddenly "felt the ground under his feet." Instead of hiding in his role, as usual, he expanded and gave his scenes momentum. *Sylvia Scarlett* was a box-office failure, but Grant knew now what he could play, and a year later, free to pick his own projects, he appeared in *Topper* and his fan mail jumped from two hundred letters a week to fourteen hundred. A few months after that, he got into his full stride with *The Awful Truth.*

What makes Grant such an uncannily romantic comedian is that with the heroine he's different from the way he is with everybody else; you sense an affinity between them. In *The Awful Truth,* he's a hearty, sociable businessman when he's with other people, but when he's with Irene Dunne you feel the tenderness that he conceals from others. The conventional bedroom-farce plot (filmed twice before) is about a couple who still love each other but have a tiff and file for divorce; during the period of the interlocutory decree, the husband has visiting rights to see their dog, and this cunning device enables Grant to hang around, romping affectionately with the dog while showing his (unstated) longing for his wife. Grant is a comic master at throwaway lines, and he turns them into a dialogue, as if he were talking to himself. The husband can't quite straighten out his marriage, yet every muttered, throwaway word expresses how badly he wants to. Grant's work with Irene Dunne in *The Awful Truth* is the most gifted stooging imaginable. She was betrayed by the costume designer: she's shrilly dressed. And though she is often funny, she overdoes the coy gurgles, and that bright, toothy smile of hers—she shows both rows of teeth, prettily held together—can make one want to slug her. The ancestor of Julie Andrews, Irene Dunne has a bad habit of condescending to anything oddball her character does—signalling the audience that she's really a lady playacting. But Grant stabilizes her and provides the believability. He's forceful and extroverted, yet he underplays so gently that his restraint enables her to get by with her affectations. Grant uses his intense physical awareness to make the scenes play, and never to make himself look good at the expense of someone else—not even when he could waltz away with the show. He performs the gags with great gusto, but he never lets us forget that the character is behaving like an oaf because he doesn't want to lose his wife, and that he's trying to protect his raw places.

Henry Fonda played roles similar to Grant's, and it isn't hard to imagine Fonda as the husband in *The Awful Truth* or as the paleontologist hero of *Bringing Up Baby,* but Fonda would have been more of a hayseed, and lighter-weight. And if Grant had played Fonda's role in *The Lady Eve* Grant wouldn't have been the perfect, pratfalling innocent that Fonda was: Fonda, with his saintly bumpkin's apologetic smile and his double-jointed gait, could play bashful stupes more convincingly than any other romantic star. However, it's part of the audience's pleasure in Grant that he isn't a green kid—he's a muscular, full-bodied man making a fool of himself. There were other gifted urbane *farceurs.* The best of them, William Powell, with his skeptical, tolerant equanimity, was supremely likable; he got the most out of each blink and each twitch of his lips, and he had amazing dimples, which he could invoke without even smiling. But Powell and the others didn't have romantic ardor hidden inside their jokes. And although there were other fine romantic actors, such as Charles Boyer, their love scenes often turned mooshy, while Grant's had the redeeming zest of farce.

Perfection in drawing-room comedy was almost certainly Grant's dream of glory (it appears to have remained so), but he had, as a young vaudeville comedian, acquired the skills that were to turn him into an idol for all social classes. Drawing-room-comedy stars—no matter how artful—don't become that kind of idol. When we in the audience began to sense the pleasure he took in low comedy, we accepted him as one of us. Ray Milland, Melvyn Douglas, and Robert Young acted the screwball-comedy heroes proficiently, but the roles didn't release anything in their own natures—didn't liberate and complete them, the way farce completed Grant. Afterward, even when he played straight romantic parts the freedom and strength stayed with him. And never left him: he gave some embarrassed, awful performances when he was miscast, but he was never less than a star. He might still parade in the tuxedos and tails of his dashing-young-idiot days, but he was a buoyant, lusty performer. The assurance he gained in slapstick turned him into the smoothie he had aspired to be. He brought elegance to low comedy, and low comedy gave him the corky common-man touch that made him a great star. Grant was English, so Hollywood thought he sounded educated and was just right for rich playboys, but he didn't speak in the gentlemanly tones that American moviegoers think of as British; he was a Cockney. In the early sixties, when he was offered the role of Henry Higgins in the big movie version of *My Fair Lady,* he laughed at the idea. "The way I talk *now*," he said, "is the way Eliza talked at the beginning." Cary Grant's romantic elegance is wrapped around the resilient, tough core of a mutt, and Americans dream of thoroughbreds while identifying with mutts. So do moviegoers the world over. The greatest movie stars have not been highborn; they have been strong-willed (often deprived) kids who came to embody their own dreams, and the public's.

Archibald Alexander Leach, born in Bristol on January 18, 1904, was the only child of Elias James Leach and Elsie Kingdom Leach, their firstborn son having died in infancy. Elias Leach was tall, and in photographs he seems almost reprehensibly handsome, with a cavalier's mustache, soft, flashing dark eyes, and a faintly melancholy look of resignation. He is said to have been convivial and fond of singing—a temperament his wife definitely did not share. There wasn't much they did share. He came, probably, from a Jewish background, but went along with his wife's Anglicanism. He couldn't live up to her middle-class expectations, however. Elias Leach pressed men's suits in a garment factory, and although he worked hard in the first years of the marriage, he never rose far or made much of a living. Mrs. Leach pampered their protesting child, keeping him in baby dresses, and then in short pants and long curls. A domineering woman with an early history of mental instability, she was married to a pants-presser but she wanted her son to be a cultured, piano-playing little gentleman. The parents were miserable together, and the boy was caught in the middle. When Archie was nine, he returned home from school one day to find that his mother was missing; he was led to think she had gone to a local seaside resort, and it was a long time before he learned that she had broken down and been taken to an institution. In a series of autobiographical articles published in the *Ladies' Home Journal* in 1963, he wrote, "I was not to see my mother again for more than twenty years, by which time my name was changed and I was a full-grown man living in America, thousands of miles away in California. I was known to most people of the world by sight and by name, yet not to my mother."

After Mrs. Leach's removal, Leach and his son took up quarters in the same building as Leach's mother, but the boy was left pretty much on his own, fixing meals for himself most of the week, and trying to live up to his absent mother's hopes for him. He went to Boy Scout meetings, studied hard, and won a school scholarship; he planned to try for a further scholarship, which would take him to college, but found out that even with a scholarship college would be too expensive. From early childhood, he had been going to the children's Saturday movie matinées, and he later said that the sessions with Chaplin, Ford Sterling and the Keystone Cops, Fatty Arbuckle, Mack Swain, John Bunny and Flora Finch, and Broncho Billy Anderson were the high point of his week. When his mother was still at home, he had a party (the only children's party he remembers attending) that featured a candle-powered magic lantern with comic slides, to which he added his own joking commentary. His first contact with music hall came quite by chance. At school, he liked chemistry, and he sometimes hung around the lab on rainy days; the assistant science teacher was an electrician, who had installed the lighting system at the Bristol Hippodrome, and one Saturday matinée he took Archie, just turned thirteen, backstage.

It was probably the only free atmosphere the boy had ever experienced. He wrote later that backstage, in a "dazzling land of smiling, jostling people," he *knew*. "What other life could there *be* but that of an actor? . . . They were classless, cheerful, and carefree." He was lonely enough and had enough hustle to start going to the Hippodrome, and another theatre, the Empire, in the early evenings, making himself useful; he helped with the lights, ran errands, and began to pick up the show-business vernacular. When he learned that Bob Pender, a former Drury Lane clown, had a troupe of young knockabout comedians that suffered attrition each time a boy came of military age, he wrote, in the guise of his father, asking that Archibald be taken for training. Pender replied offering an interview and enclosing the railway fare to Norwich, and Archie ran away from home to become an apprentice. He was so tall that Pender accepted him, not realizing that he wasn't yet fourteen—the legal age for leaving school. It took a few days before Leach noticed that his son was gone. Earlier that year, Archie had taken a spill on an icy playground and broken an upper front tooth. Rather than tell his father, he had gone to a dental school and had the remainder of the tooth pulled out. His other teeth had closed together over the gap (giving him his characteristic upper-lip-pulled-down, tough-urchin grin) without his father's ever noticing. But, whatever Leach's failings, he appears to have meant well, and when it registered with him that the boy had run off, he tracked him down and brought him back. He might as well have saved himself the effort. Having given up his dream of college, Archie no longer cared about school, and he concentrated on acrobatics, so he'd be in shape to rejoin Pender as soon as he could. It was soon. Just after he turned fourteen, he and another boy attempted to explore the girls' lavatories, and he was expelled from school. Three days later, with his father's consent, he was a member of Pender's troupe. Only three months passed before he returned to Bristol in triumph—on the stage at the Empire, his old schoolmates in the audience.

Archie Leach found his vocation early and stuck to it. He studied dancing, tumbling, stilt-walking, and pantomime, and performed constantly in provincial towns and cities and in the London vaudeville houses. In the Christmas season, the troupe appeared in the traditional entertainments for children—slapstick musical-comedy versions of such stories as

"Cinderella" and "Puss in Boots." Living dormitory-style, exercising and rehearsing, Archie had left his parents' class-ridden world behind. Once he'd joined up with Pender, he never lived with his father again, and he lost track of him over the years. The music-hall theatre became his world; he has said that at each theatre, when he wasn't onstage, he was watching and studying the other acts from the wings. In July, 1920, when Pender selected a group of eight boys for an engagement in New York City, the sixteen-year-old Archie was among them. They sailed on the S.S. Olympic, which was also carrying the celebrated honeymooners Douglas Fairbanks, Sr., and Mary Pickford. More than forty years later, Cary Grant described his reaction to Fairbanks: "Once even I found myself being photographed with Mr. Fairbanks during a game of shuffleboard. As I stood beside him, I tried with shy, inadequate words to tell him of my adulation. He was a splendidly trained athlete and acrobat, affable and warmed by success and well-being. A gentleman in the true sense of the word. . . . It suddenly dawns on me as this is being written that I've doggedly striven to keep tanned ever since, only because of a desire to emulate his healthful appearance." He and Fairbanks had much in common: shattered, messy childhoods, and fathers who drifted away and turned to drink. It appears that they were both part Jewish but were raised as Christians; and they both used acrobatics in their careers—though Fairbanks, a narrowly limited actor but a fine acrobat, was a passionate devotee, while Grant used acrobatics only as a means of getting into theatrical life. And, though they represented different eras, they were loved by the public in similar ways—for their strapping health and high spirits, for being *on* and giving out whenever they were in front of an audience, for grinning with pleasure at their own good luck. Grant's later marriage to Barbara Hutton—Babs, the golden girl, "the richest girl in the world"—had a fairy-tale resemblance to the Fairbanks-Pickford nuptials.

In New York City, the Bob Pender boys were a great success at the Hippodrome, which was considered the world's largest theatre. After the engagement was over, they got booked in the major Eastern cities and wound up back in New York at the top—the Palace. When the American tour ended, in 1922, and it was time to go home, Archie Leach and several of the other boys decided to stay. He had four solid years of performing behind him, but he had never actually been in a play, and though he'd been singing on the stage, he'd never spoken dialogue. The Pender troupe had been big time, but on his own he wasn't even small time—he had no act. In the first summer of job-hunting in New York, his savings went and he ate into the return fare Pender had given him for an emergency retreat. He must, however, have been an incredible charmer (it isn't hard to imagine), because, although he was only eighteen, he was invited to fill in at dinner parties, where he sat among the wealthy and famous—on one occasion, he was delegated to be the escort of the great soprano Lucrezia Bori. By day, after he finally landed work, he was a stilt-walker on the boardwalk at Coney Island, advertising Steeplechase Park. (It was many years before his status in life was commensurate with the regard people had for him.) In the fall, he shared quarters with a young Australian, who later became known as the costume designer Orry-Kelly; in those days, Kelly made and tried to sell hand-painted neckties, and Archie Leach peddled them along Sixth Avenue and in Greenwich Village. Around the same time, Leach and other ex-members of the Pender troupe got together in the new Hippodrome show, and joined up with some Americans and organized a vaudeville act. After trying it out in small towns in the East, they played the lesser vaudeville circuits through Canada and back across the country from California to New York. In 1924, having saved enough money to go their separate ways, the boys disbanded, some of them returning to England, Archie Leach to job-hunting in New York again.

He worked in juggling acts, and with unicycle riders, and with dancers; he was the audience plant with a mind-reading act. As a straight man for comics, he got one-night stands at churches and lodges, and brief engagements in the stage shows that movie theatres used to put on before the film. As his timing improved and he became more experienced, he got more bookings; he says that eventually he played "practically every small town in America." Then, when he was working in New York, a friend who was a musical-comedy juvenile suggested that instead of going on with his vaudeville career he should try to get into Broadway musical comedy, and introduced him to Reggie Hammerstein, who took him to his uncle, the producer Arthur Hammerstein. At the end of 1927, Archie Leach appeared in the role of an Australian—the second male lead—in the Otto Harbach–Oscar Hammerstein II show *Golden Dawn,* which opened the new Hammerstein's Theatre and ran there until the late spring. He'd got onto Broadway, all right—and Broadway was then in its frivolous heyday—but he hadn't got into musical comedy. It was operetta he was caught in, and, having signed a contract with the Hammersteins, that's where he stayed. Marilyn Miller wanted him as a replacement for Jack Donahue, her leading man in the Ziegfeld hit *Rosalie,* but Arthur Hammerstein and Ziegfeld were enemies, and instead (despite his pleas) his contract was turned over to the Shuberts—for three full years of operetta.

Archie Leach's first Shubert show was *Boom Boom,* a 1929 hit, starring Jeanette MacDonald. (*The New Yorker*'s reviewer, Charles Brackett, wrote that "*Boom Boom* can teach one more about despair than the most expert philosopher.") During its run, he and Jeanette MacDonald were both tested at Paramount's Astoria studio. She was immediately signed up to be the bubbly Maurice Chevalier's petulant, coy co-star in Ernst Lubitsch's *The Love Parade*; he was rejected, because he had a thick neck and bowlegs. Had he been signed as a singing star, he might have been stuck in a Mountie's hat, like Nelson Eddy. He did become a singing star on the stage. He played a leading role in a lavish and, apparently, admirable version of *Die Fledermaus* called *A Wonderful Night,* but it opened on October 31, 1929, two days after the stock-market crash, and it crashed too; for months it was performed to near-empty houses. In the summer of 1931, the Shuberts sent him to St. Louis for the open-air Municipal Opera season, where he was a great success in such shows as *Irene, Rio Rita, Countess Maritza, The Three Musketeers,* and the Broadway casualty *A Wonderful Night.* After that, he got a temporary release from the Shuberts and appeared on Broadway in the role of Cary Lockwood, supporting Fay Wray (who was already a popular movie actress) in *Nikki,* a musical play by her husband, John Monk Saunders, which flopped.

In 1931, Leach also appeared in *Singapore Sue,* a ten-minute movie short, starring Anna Chang, that Casey Robinson made for Paramount in Astoria; Leach, Millard Mitchell, and two other actors played American sailors in an Oriental café. Leach is striking; he grabs the screen—but not pleasantly, and he does have a huge neck. He's rather gross in general—heavy-featured, and with a wide, false smile. His curly-lipped sailor is excessively handsome—overripe, like the voluptuous young Victor Mature. Some of the early-thirties Hollywood publicity photographs of Grant are like that, too; the images have the pop overeagerness one often sees in graduation and wedding poses in photographers' shopwindows. Self-consciousness and bad makeup must have overcome him on that first bout with the movie camera, because photographs of him in his stage performances show a far more refined handsomeness, and the Leach of *Singapore Sue* doesn't fit the image of him in accounts by his contemporaries.

Although Leach didn't appear in the smart shows, he was something of a figure in the New York smart set, and he was known to the Algonquin group in that period when the theatrical and literary worlds were one. Some people considered him an intellectual and a powerhouse talent of the future. Moss Hart later described him as disconsolate in those years; Hart and Leach were among a group of dreamers talking of changing the theatre (the circle also included Edward Chodorov and Preston Sturges) who met daily in the Rudley's Restaurant at Forty-first Street and Broadway. It was a hangout where one got leads about possible jobs, and many performers frequented the place—Jeanette MacDonald, George Murphy, Humphrey Bogart. But Archie Leach was the only actor who was a regular at the Rudley rebels' table. The Anzac role he'd played in *Golden Dawn* must have clung to him, or perhaps, since he never talked much about his background, some of the others mistook his Cockney for an Australian accent, because they called him Kangaroo, and sometimes Boomerang. "He was never a very open fellow," Chodorov says, "but he was earnest and we liked him." "Intellectual" was probably the wrong word for Leach. They talked; he listened. He doesn't appear to have been much of a reader (except later on, during his marriage to Betsy Drake, when he became immersed in the literature of hypnotism and the occult), but there's no indication that anyone ever doubted his native intelligence. It's a wide-awake intelligence, though this may not be apparent from his public remarks of the sixties, which had a wholesome Rotarian tone he adopted during LSD treatments with a medical guru. In his youth, Leach liked to hang around people who were gifted and highly educated; always looking for ways to improve himself, he probably hoped that their knowledge would rub off on him. But there must have been more to it than that; he must have looked up to the brilliant young Rudley's group because the theatre he worked in didn't fully satisfy his mind. Uneducated outside the theatre, he was eager for spiritual leadership—for wisdom. In Hollywood, he was to sit at the feet of Clifford Odets, the leading wisdom merchant of the theatrical left (the sagacity was what marred Odets' plays). And during his many years of LSD sessions he was euphoric about how the drug had enabled him to relax his conscious controls and reach his subconscious, thus making him a better man—less selfish, fit at last for marriage, and so on. Obviously, he felt that he'd found a scientific route to wisdom.

When *Nikki* closed, on October 31, 1931, Leach decided to take a "vacation," and set out with a composer friend to drive to Los Angeles. He knew what he was after; many of the people he'd been working with were already in the movies. He had the situation cooled: he'd been earning from three hundred dollars to four hundred and fifty dollars a week for several years, and the Shuberts were eager to employ him if he returned. He had barely arrived in Hollywood when he was taken to a small dinner party at the home of B. P. Schulberg, the head of Paramount, who invited him to make a test (*Singapore Sue* had not yet been released), and after seeing it Schulberg offered him a contract. The studio executives wanted his name changed, and his friends Fay Wray and John Monk Saunders suggested that he use "Cary Lockwood." He proposed it when he went back to discuss the contract, but he was told that "Lockwood" was a little long. Someone went down a list of names and stopped at "Grant." He nodded, they nodded, and the contract went into effect on December 7th. He wasn't ever "discovered." Movies were simply the next step.

*I*f Archie Leach's upward progress seems a familiar saga, it is familiar in the rags-to-riches mode of a tycoon or a statesman. What is missing from his steady climb to fame is tension. He became a performer in an era in which learning to entertain the public was a trade; he worked at his trade, progressed, and rose to the top. He has probably never had the sort of doubts about acting which have plagued so many later performers, and he didn't agonize over choices, as actors of his stature do now. A young actor now generally feels that he is an artist only when he uses his technique for personal expression and for something he believes in. And so he has a problem that Archie Leach never faced: When actors became artists in the modern sense, they also became sellouts. They began to feel emasculated when they played formula roles that depended on technique only, and they had to fight themselves to retain their belief in the audience, which often preferred what they did when they sold out. They were up against all the temptations, corruptions, and conflicts that writers and composers and painters had long been wrestling with. Commerce is a bind for actors now in a way it never was for Archie Leach; art for him was always a trade.

He was unusually long-sighted about his career, and prodigiously disciplined, and so he got into a position in which he didn't have to take any guff from anybody. The Hammersteins had sold him to the Shuberts when he wanted to go to Ziegfeld; and to get movie roles he had to commit himself to a five-year contract with Paramount. But that was the last time he let others have the power to tell him what to do. He was twenty-seven when he signed the contract—at a starting salary of four hundred and fifty dollars a week. Paramount didn't know what it had. It used him as a second-string Gary Cooper, putting him in the pictures Cooper was too busy for—or, even worse, in imitations of roles that Cooper had just scored in. In between, Paramount lent him out to other studios and collected the fees. He was no more than a pawn in these deals. M-G-M requested him for one of the top roles in *Mutiny on the Bounty,* a role he desperately wanted, but Paramount refused, and Franchot Tone won the part. A little later, Paramount lent him to M-G-M to support Jean Harlow in the piddling *Suzy.*

When that contract ended, in February, 1937, Cary Grant, just turned thirty-three, was raring to go. He never signed another exclusive contract with a studio; he selected his scripts and his directors, and this is probably what saved him from turning into a depressingly sentimental figure, like the later, tired Gary Cooper, or a drudge, like the big M-G-M stars. It was in his first year on his own, free of studio orders, that he became a true star. In comedy, Cary Grant just might be the greatest straight man in the business, and his specialty is to apply his aplomb as a straight man to romance.

The "lunatic" thirties comedies that made him a star are still enjoyed, but their rationale has dropped from sight. In essence, they turned love and marriage into vaudeville acts and changed the movie heroine from sweet clinging vine into vaudeville partner. Starting in 1934, when things were still bad but Roosevelt and the New Deal had created an upswing spirit, the happy screwball comedies were entertainment for a country that had weathered the worst of the Depression and was beginning to feel hopeful. Yet people had been shaken up. The new comedies suggested an element of lunacy and confusion in the world; the heroes and heroines rolled with the punches and laughed at disasters. Love became slightly surreal; it became stylized—lovers talked back to each other, and fast. Comedy became the new romance, and trading wisecracks was the new courtship rite. The cheerful, wacked-out heroes and heroines had abandoned sanity; they were a little crazy, and that's what they liked in each other. They were like the wisecracking soldiers in service comedies: if you were swapping quips, you were alive—you hadn't gone under. The jokes were a national form of gallantry—humor for survival. Actual lunatics in these movies became enjoyable eccentrics, endearing nuts who often made better sense than anybody else (or at least as much sense), while the butts of screwball humor were the prigs and phonies, the conventional go-getters, the stick-in-the-mud conformists. Ralph Bellamy, the classic loser and opposite number to Cary Grant in *The Awful Truth* and again in *His Girl Friday,* still thought in the strict, stuffed-shirt terms of the Babbitty past. The word "square" wasn't yet in slang use, but that's the part Bellamy played—the man who didn't get the joke. Obliging and available, always around when you didn't want him (there was really no time when you did), he was the man to be jilted.

The comedies celebrated a change in values. In the movies of the twenties and the early thirties, girls who chased after riches and luxury learned the error of their ways, but after 1934 sin wasn't the big movie theme it had been. Adultery was no longer tragic; the unashamed, wisecracking gold diggers saw to that. Glenda Farrell, one of the toughest and most honestly predatory of the millionare-hunters, put it this way in *Gold Diggers of 1937*: "It's so hard to be good under the capitalistic system." Impudence became a virtue. Earlier, the sweet, archly virginal heroine had often had a breezy, good-hearted confidante; now the roles were reversed, and the lively, resilient heroine might have an innocent kid sister or a naïve little friend from her home town who needed looking after. What man in the Depression years would welcome a darling, dependent girl? Maybe the hero's shy buddy, but not the hero. He looked for the girl with verve; often she was so high and buoyant she could bounce right over trouble without noticing it. It was Carole Lombard's good-hearted giddiness that made her lovable, Jean Arthur's flightiness, Myrna Loy's blithe imperviousness—and in *Bringing Up Baby* Katharine Hepburn was so light-headed, so out of it, that she was unbeatable. The mistreated, masochistic women who had been moping through the confessional movies, pining for the men who had ruined them and looking tenderly at their fatherless offspring, either faded (like Ann Harding, Ruth Chatterton, and Helen Hayes) or changed their styles (like Constance Bennett in *Topper,* Lombard in *Twentieth Century,* and, of course, Claudette Colbert in *It Happened One Night* and Irene Dunne in *Theodora Goes Wild* and

The Awful Truth). The stars came down to earth in the middle and late thirties—and became even bigger stars. Marlene Dietrich, who had turned into a lolling mannequin, reëmerged as the battling floozy of *Destry Rides Again*. Just as in the late sixties some of the performers loosened up and became hip, thirties performers such as Joel McCrea and Fredric March became lighter-toned, gabby, and flip. An actor who changes from serious to comic roles doesn't have problems with the audience (the audience loves seeing actors shed their dignity, which has generally become a threadbare pose long before it's shed); it's the change from comic to serious that may confound the audience's expectations.

The speed and stylization of screwball humor were like a stunt, and some of the biggest directors of the thirties had come out of two-reel comedy and had the right training. Leo McCarey, who directed *The Awful Truth,* had directed the Marx Brothers in *Duck Soup* and, before that, Laurel & Hardy comedies for Hal Roach. George Stevens, who directed Grant in *Gunga Din,* was also a Hal Roach alumnus—cameraman on Laurel & Hardy and Harry Langdon shorts, and then a Roach director. *Topper,* with its sunny hocus-pocus and Grant as a debonair ghost, was actually a Hal Roach production; it was considered Roach's most ambitious project. Movies in the thirties were still close to their beginnings. Wesley Ruggles, who directed Grant in *I'm No Angel,* had been one of Mack Sennett's Keystone Cops; Howard Hawks, who directed Grant in several of his best thirties films, had started as a director by writing and directing two comedy shorts. The directors had graduated from slapstick when sound came in and Hollywood took over Broadway's plays, but after a few years all that talk without much action was becoming wearying.

The screwball movies brought back the slapstick tradition of vaudeville and the two-reelers, and blended it into those brittle Broadway comedies. When it was joined to a marital farce or a slightly daring society romance, slapstick no longer seemed like kid stuff: it was no longer innocent and was no longer regarded as "low" comedy. The screwball movies pleased people of all ages. (The faithful adaptations of stage plays had often been a little tepid for children.) And the directors, who had come out of a Hollywood in which improvising and building gags were part of the fun of moviemaking, went back—partly, at least—to that way of working. No longer so script-bound, movies regained some of the creative energy and exuberance—and the joy in horseplay, too—that had been lost in the early years of talkies. The new freedom can be seen even in small ways, in trivia. Grant's screwball comedies are full of cross-references, and gags from one are repeated or continued in another. In *The Awful Truth,* Irene Dunne, trying to do in her (almost) ex-husband—Grant—refers to him as Jerry the Nipper; in *Bringing Up Baby,* Hepburn, pretending to be a gun moll, tells the town constable that Grant is the notorious Jerry the

Nipper. And the same dog trots through the pictures, as Mr. Smith in *The Awful Truth,* as George in *Bringing Up Baby* (and as Mr. Atlas in *Topper Takes a Trip* and Asta in the *Thin Man* movies). That dog was a great actor: he appeared to adore each master in turn.

Once Grant's Paramount contract ended, there seemed no stopping him. As long as the screwball-comedy period lasted, he was king. After *The Awful Truth,* in 1937, he did two pictures with Katharine Hepburn in 1938—*Bringing Up Baby* and *Holiday.* It was a true mating—they had the same high-energy level, the same physical absorption in acting. In 1939 he did *Gunga Din* and *Only Angels Have Wings,* and in 1940 *His Girl Friday, My Favorite Wife,* and *The Philadelphia Story.*

During those peak years—1937 to 1940—he proved himself in romantic melodrama, high comedy, and low farce. He does uproarious mugging in the knockabout jamboree *Gunga Din*—a moviemakers' prank, like *Beat the Devil.* Ben Hecht and Charles MacArthur stole the adolescent boys' fantasy atmosphere from *Lives of a Bengal Lancer,* then took the plot from their own *The Front Page,* mixed it with a slapstick *The Three Musketeers,* and set it in a Hollywood Kipling India. Douglas Fairbanks, Jr., plays the Hildy Johnson role—he plans to leave the British Army to get married and go into the tea business—and Victor McLaglen, in the Walter Burns role, and Grant, as the Cockney bruiser Archibald Cutter, scheme to get him to reënlist. When the three comrades fight off their enemies, they're like three Fairbankses flying through the air. Grant looks so great in his helmet in the bright sunshine and seems to be having such a marvellous time that he becomes the picture's romantic center, and his affection for the worshipful Gunga Din (Sam Jaffe) becomes the love story. The picture is both a stirring, beautifully photographed satiric colonial-adventure story and a walloping vaudeville show. Grant's grimaces and cries when Annie the elephant tries to follow him and Sam Jaffe onto a rope bridge over a chasm are his broadest clowning. (The scene is right out of Laurel & Hardy.) And he's never been more of a burlesque comic than when he arrives at the gold temple of the religious cult of thugs and whinnies with greedy delight at the very moment he's being shot at. The thug guru is shaven-headed Eduardo Ciannelli (the original Diamond Louis of *The Front Page*), who wears a loincloth and chants "Kill! Kill! Kill for the love of Kali!" Perhaps because the picture winds up with a bit of pop magic—an eye-moistening, Kiplingesque tribute to Gunga Din, shown in Heaven in the British Army uniform he longed to wear—the ·press treated it rather severely, and George Stevens, the director, was a little apologetic about it. He may have got in over his head. He had replaced Howard Hawks as director, and when he added his Stan Laurel specialties to the heroic flourishes Hawks had prepared, and after the various rewrite men (William Faulkner and Joel Sayre were among them) built on to the gags, the result was a great, bounding piece of camp. Grant has always claimed that he doesn't like to exert himself, and that his ideal role would be a silent man in a wheelchair, but his performance here tells a different story. (All his performances tell a different story.) The following year, when Grant played Walter Burns in *His Girl Friday* (this time an acknowledged remake of *The Front Page,* and, with Charles Lederer's additions, a spastic explosion of dialogue), he raised mugging to a joyful art. Grant obviously loves the comedy of monomaniac egotism: Walter Burns' callousness and unscrupulousness are expressed in some of the best farce lines ever written in this country, and Grant hits those lines with a smack. He uses the same stiff-neck, cocked-head stance that he did in *Gunga Din*: it's his position for all-out, unsubtle farce. He snorts and whoops. His Walter Burns is a strong-arm performance, defiantly self-centered and funny.

When Grant was reunited with Irene Dunne in *My Favorite Wife,* they had another box-office smash, but his playing wasn't as fresh as in *The Awful Truth.* This marital farce was really moldy (it was based on Tennyson's *Enoch Arden,* filmed at least a dozen times, starting in 1908), and Grant's performance as the rattled husband is a matter of comic bewilderment and skittish double takes. The presence in the cast of his close friend Randolph Scott (they shared a house for several years) as the rival for Irene Dunne's affections may have interfered with his concentration; he doesn't provide an underlayer of conviction. He's expert but lightweight, and the role and the bustling plot don't bring anything new out of him.

The Hollywood comedy era was just about over by then. The screwball comedies, in particular, had become strained and witless; the spoiled, headstrong runaway heiresses and the top-hatted playboy cutups had begun to pall on the public, and third-rate directors who had no feeling for slapstick thought it was enough to have players giggling and falling over the furniture. Right from the start, screwball comedy was infected by the germ of commercial hypocrisy. The fun-loving rich, with their glistening clothes, whitewall tires, mansions in the country, and sleek Art Deco apartments, exalted a carefree contempt for material values. The heroes and heroines rarely had any visible means of support, but they lived high, and in movie after movie their indifference to such mundane matters as food and rent became a self-admiring attitude—the attitude that is still touted in *Travels with My Aunt* and *Mame.* Like Mame, the unconventional heroines of the thirties were beloved by their servants. Irene Dunne in white fox and a trailing evening gown would kick her satin train impatiently to tell us that it was not money but love and laughter that mattered. The costume designers often went in for sprightly effects: Irene Dunne and Katharine Hepburn would be put into pixie hats that clung on the side of the head, dipping over one eye, while on top there were pagodas that shot up six or seven inches to a peak. All too often, the villains were stuffy society people or social climbers (as in *Mame*), and the heroes and heroines just too incorrigibly happy-go-lucky. Love seemed to mean making a fool of yourself. The froth hung heavy on many a screwball comedy, and as the pictures got worse and the Cary Grant parts began to be played by Lee Bowman and David Niven the public got fed up. The movement had already run down before the war started. In the forties, there were still some screwball comedies, but they were antic and shrill, except for a few strays: some of the Tracy-Hepburn pictures, and the comedies in which Preston Sturges reinvented slapstick in a more organic form—creating an image of Americans as a people who never stopped explaining themselves while balling up whatever they were trying to do.

*T*hough he remained a top box-office star, Cary Grant fell on evil days. After 1940, he didn't seem to have any place to go—there were no longer Cary Grant pictures. Instead, he acted in pictures that nobody could have been right for—abominations like the 1942 anti-Nazi romantic comedy *Once Upon a Honeymoon,* in which he was an American newsman in Warsaw trying to rescue the American stripper Ginger Rogers from her Nazi husband (Walter Slezak). From the first frame, it was as clammily contrived as anything that Paramount had shoved him into, and in one pathetically insensitive sequence Grant and Rogers are mistaken for Jews and held in a concentration camp. His performance is frequently atrocious: he twinkles with condescending affection when the nitwit stripper develops a political consciousness and helps a Jewish hotel maid escape from danger. Mostly, he acted in stock situation comedies—comedies with no comic roots, like *The Bachelor and the Bobby-Soxer* (1947), in which Myrna Loy is a judge who works out a deal. Grant, a philandering artist, will go to jail unless he dates her schoolgirl sister (Shirley Temple) until the teen-ager's crush on him wears off. Escorting Shirley Temple—wearing his shirt open and acting like an adolescent—Cary Grant is degradingly unfunny. There's no core of plausibility in his role. Grant doesn't have the eyes of a Don Juan, or the temperament. When Grant is accused of being a skirt-chaser, it seems like some kind of mistake.

In the thirties, Grant would sometimes appear in a role, such as the despondent husband of a mercenary, coldhearted woman (Kay Francis) in the 1939 *In Name Only,* that suggested that he had unexplored dimensions. They remained unexplored. In 1941, when he departed from comedy, it was in just the sort of sincere tearjerker that Hollywood was always proudest of—*Penny Serenade,* with Irene Dunne again. The unrealistic casting of this inert, horribly pristine film is the trick: the appeal to the audience is that these two glamorous stars play an ordinary couple and suffer the calamities that do in fact happen to ordinary people. When tragedy strikes Cary Grant and Irene Dunne, it hurts the audience in a special way—*Penny Serenade* is a sweet-and-sour pacifier. Grant, who got an Academy Award nomination, could hardly have been better. Using his dark eyes and his sensuous, clouded handsomeness as a romantic mask, he gave his role a defensive, not quite forthright quality, and he brought out everything that it was possible to bring out of his warmed-over lines, weighting them perfectly, so that they almost seemed felt.

Nearly all Grant's seventy-two films have a certain amount of class and are well above the Hollywood average, but most of them, when you come right down to it, are not really very good. Grant could glide through a picture in a way that leaves one indifferent, as in the role of a quaint guardian angel named Dudley in the bland, musty Goldwyn production *The Bishop's Wife* (1947), and he could be the standard put-upon male of burbling comedy, as in *Every Girl Should Be Married* (1948) and the pitifully punk *Room for One More* (1952)—the nice-nice pictures he made with Betsy Drake, who in 1949 became his third wife. He could be fairly persuasive in astute, reflective parts, as in the Richard Brooks thriller *Crisis* (1950), in which he plays a brain surgeon forced to operate on a Latin-American dictator (José Ferrer). He's a seasoned performer here, though his energy level isn't as high as in the true Grant roles and he's a little cold, staring absently when he means to indicate serious thought. What's missing is probably that his own sense of humor isn't allowed to come through; generally when he isn't playing a man who laughs easily he isn't all there.

He was able to keep his independence because he had a good head for business. Within a short time of leaving Paramount, he could command a hundred and fifty thousand dollars a picture, and that was only the beginning. Later, he formed partnerships and produced his pictures through his own corporations—Grandon, Granart, Granley, and Granox. He didn't do what stars like Kirk Douglas did when they gained control over their productions: he didn't appear in Westerns, for the virtually guaranteed market. He was too self-aware for that; he was a lonely holdout in the period when even Frank Sinatra turned cowpoke. From the thirties on, Grant looked for comedies that would be mass-oriented versions of the Noël Coward and Philip Barry and Frederick Lonsdale drawing-room and boudoir farces that Broadway theatregoers admired in the twenties. And so he settled for Sidney Sheldon (*The Bachelor and the Bobby-Soxer, Dream Wife*), or Stanley Shapiro (*Operation Petticoat, That Touch of Mink*), for Norman Panama and Melvin Frank (*Mr. Blandings Builds His Dream House*), or for Melville Shavelson and Jack Rose (*Room for One More, Houseboat*). He sought the best material and got the second-rate and synthetic, because good writers wouldn't (and couldn't) write that way anymore. His taste didn't change, but he didn't do the real thing—not even the real Lonsdale. His friends say he believes that the world doesn't understand fine language. With *People Will Talk* and *The Talk of the Town,* he was probably reaching toward Shaw. He got the loquacity without the wit.

Considering that he selected his roles, these choices indicate one of the traps of stardom. When actors are young, they're eager for great roles, but when they become stars they generally become fearful that the public won't accept them in something different. They look for roles that seem a little more worthwhile than the general run. With one exception—*None but the Lonely Heart*—Cary Grant appeared to be content throughout his career to bring savoir-faire to pratfalls, romantic misunderstandings, and narrow escapes. It seems reasonable to assume that he attained something so close to the highest aspirations of his youth that, as far as acting was concerned, he had no other goals—and no conflicts. Moss Hart said that Archie Leach's gloom vanished when he became Cary Grant.

*T*he only trace of gloom in Grant's movies is in *None but the Lonely Heart,* which he made in association with Clifford Odets (as writer and director) in 1944. The film was an ironic interlude in Grant's career, coming, as it did, between the cloying whimsey of *Once Upon a Time,* in which he was a Broadway sharpie exploiting a boy who had a pet dancing caterpillar, and *Night and Day,* the ten-ton Cole Porter musical bio, in which he skittered about as a youthful Yalie before facing life with stoic courage and inscrutable psychic hangups. In *None but the Lonely Heart,* set in the East End of London, he plays Ernie Mott, a young Cockney—a restless drifter who lacks the will to leave the ghetto for good. Ernie grew up in oppressive poverty, but he wants to make life better for his mother, who runs a grubby antiques and secondhand-furniture shop. Made at Grant's instigation (he acquired the rights to the book), the film was a gesture toward the ideas he shared with the other dissidents at Rudley's, and, even more, a gesture toward his own roots—toward the grimness of his life before he apprenticed himself to the theatre. His mother was released from confinement in 1933 (that same year, his father died of "extreme toxicity"), and he established a surprisingly close relationship with her. Eccentric but hardy and self-sufficient, she had a whole new life after that twenty-year incarceration. She lived into her mid-nineties, and until she was in her late eighties she did all her own shopping and housework, and occupied her days with antiquing—driving fierce bargains when she spotted something she wanted. Grant has described her as "extremely good company." He wrote that "sometimes we laugh together until tears come into our eyes." In the thirties, he went to England several times a year to see her, and he took the English beauty Virginia Cherrill (Chaplin's leading lady in *City Lights*) to meet his mother before they were married, in London, in 1934—his first marriage, which was dissolved the following year. The outbreak of the Second World War must have brought his English past even closer to him; he was still a British subject, and in 1939 he became involved in activities to aid the British. Later, when the United States was in the war, he went on trips to entertain the troops and on bond-selling tours. (In one routine, he played straight man to Bert Lahr.) In June, 1942, less than two weeks before his marriage to Barbara Hutton, he legally changed his name and became an American citizen.

Grant's old name had long been a joke—to the public and to him. He had named his pet Sealyham Archibald, and when the dog ran away from his Los Angeles home (it is said that the dog ran out the door while Grant was carrying Virginia Cherrill over the threshold), he took large ads in the papers giving the dog's name. In *Gunga Din,* when Grant, as the soldier Cutter, receives an invitation to a regimental ball, he reads the salutation aloud—"Arch-i-bald Cutter"—chewing the syllables and savoring their preposterousness. As the editor in *His Girl Friday,* when Grant is threatened with prison by the mayor and the sheriff, he yammers out, "The last man to say that to me was Archie Leach, just a week before he cut his throat."

Yet when he played Ernie Mott in *None but the Lonely Heart* he became Archie Leach again; even the names are similar. *None but the Lonely Heart* was the first movie Clifford Odets had ever directed, and although the original material was not his but a best-selling novel by Richard Llewellyn, Odets gave it the rich melancholy of his best plays. Too much of it, however: the dirgelike, mournful, fogged-up atmosphere seemed fake and stagy. Odets worked up each scene (almost as one develops scenes in the theatre) and didn't get them to flow thematically, but he went all out. He brought off some hard-earned effects with an élan that recalled Orson Welles' first films, and there were unexpected crosscurrents. (Ernie's girl, played by June Duprez, was plaintive and distressed, and turned out not to be Ernie's girl at all.) It was an extraordinary début film, and it is an indication of the movie industry's attitude toward talent that Odets got only one other chance to direct— fifteen years later (*The Story on Page One,* in 1959). The complicated texture of *None but the Lonely Heart* made a pervasive, long-lasting impression. What can one remember of such Grant films as *Room for One More* or *Dream Wife* or *Kiss Them for Me* or *Houseboat*? But from *None but the Lonely Heart* one retains June Duprez's puzzlingly perverse face and voice; a scene of Grant and a buddy (Barry Fitzgerald) drunk in a tunnel, letting out their voices and teasing their echoes; and—especially— Grant and Ethel Barrymore together. She played his mother, and her great, heavy eyes matched up with his. In her screen roles, this statuesque, handsome woman usually substituted presence and charm and hokum for performance; she wasn't tedious, like her brother Lionel, but she was a hollow technician. Not this time, though. In a few scenes, she and Grant touched off emotions in each other which neither of them ever showed on the screen again. When Ernie, who has become a petty racketeer, is told that his mother has been arrested for trafficking in stolen goods, he has an instant's disbelief: "They got her inside, you mean—pinched?" Grant says that line with more fervor than any other line he ever delivered. And there are viewers who still—after three decades—recall the timbre of Ethel Barrymore's voice in the prison hospital when she cries, "Disgraced you, Son."

Grant is not as vivid in the memory as Ethel Barrymore is. Of the profusion of themes in the film, the deeply troubled bond of love between the mother and the son must have been a strong factor in his original decision to buy the book. Yet he didn't fully express what had attracted him to the material. His performance was finer than one might have expected, considering that in all his years on the stage he'd never actually done a play without music, and that he couldn't use the confident technique that made him such a dynamo in screen comedy, or the straightforward, subdued acting he depended on in the war film *Destination Tokyo*. Grant was always desperately uncomfortable when he played anyone who wasn't close to his own age, and though he may have felt like the Ernie of the novel (a dreamy nineteen-year-old, an unformed artist-intellectual), as an actor he was too set in his ways. The slight stylization of his comic technique—the deadpan primed to react, the fencer's awareness of the camera, all the self-protective skills he'd acquired—worked against him when he needed to be expressive. Cary Grant acts from the outside; he's the wrong kind of actor to play a disharmonious character, a precursor of the fifties rebel-hero. Grant isn't totally on the surface: there's a mystery in him—he has an almost stricken look, a memory of suffering—but he's not the modern kind of actor who taps his unconscious in his acting. Part of his charm is that his angers are all externally provoked; there are no internal pressures in him that need worry us, no rage or rebelliousness to churn us up. If he reacts with exasperation or a glowering look, we know everything there is to know about his reaction. When we watch Brando, the dramatic stage is *in* him, and the external aggressions against him are the occasions for us to see the conflicts within; the traditional actor's distance and his perfect clarity are gone. Life seemed simpler with Cary Grant's pre-Freudian, pre-psychological acting-as-entertaining. But he couldn't split Ernie Mott apart effectively, and he couldn't hold him together, either. And—it was nobody's fault—one reason Ernie wasn't as vivid a character as he needed to be was that it was Cary Grant trying to be grubby Ernie Mott. A movie star like Cary Grant carries his movie past with him. He becomes the sum of his most successful roles, and he has only to appear for our good will to be extended to him. We smile when we see him, we laugh before he does anything; it makes us happy just to look at him. And so in *None but the Lonely Heart*, in the role that was closest to Grant's own buried feelings—the only character he ever played that he is known to have consciously identified with—he seemed somewhat miscast.

It's impossible to estimate how much this failure meant to him, but more than a year passed before he plunged into the inanities of *Night and Day*—the only year since he had entered movies in which he made no pictures, and a bad year in other ways, too, since his marriage to Barbara Hutton broke up. However, Cary Grant appears to be a profoundly practical man; after the dissapointing box-office returns from *None but the Lonely Heart* (he did get an Academy Award nomination for it, but the award was given to Bing Crosby for *Going My Way*), he never tried anything except Cary Grant roles. As far as one can judge, he never looked back. He remained a lifelong friend of Clifford Odets; he was proud to be accepted by Odets, and Odets was proud that the handsome, tanned idol was there at his feet. But Odets' passion no longer fired Cary Grant to make business decisions. When Odets was trying to set up picture deals and needed him as a star, he didn't return the calls. This didn't spoil their friendship—they had both been living in Los Angeles a long time.

No doubt Grant was big enough at the box office to have kept going indefinitely, surviving fables about caterpillars, and even such mournful mistakes as hauling a cannon through the Napoleonic period of *The Pride and the Passion*. But if Alfred Hitchcock, who had worked with him earlier on *Suspicion*, hadn't rescued him with *Notorious*, in 1946, and again, in 1955, with *To Catch a Thief* (a flimsy script but with a show-off role for him) and in 1959 with *North by Northwest*, and if Grant hadn't appeared in the Stanley Donen film *Charade* in 1963, his development as an actor would have essentially been over in 1940, when he was only thirty-six. In all four of those romantic suspense comedies, Grant played the glamorous, worldly figure that "Cary Grant" had come to mean: he was cast as Cary Grant, and he gave a performance as Cary Grant. It was his one creation, and it had become the only role for him to play—the only role, finally, he *could* play.

Had he made different choices, had he taken more risks like *None but the Lonely Heart,* he might eventually have won acceptance as an actor with a wide range. He might have become a great actor; he had the intensity, and the command of an audience's attention. But how can one tell? One thinks of Cary Grant in such a set way it's difficult even to speculate about his capacities. Yet, considering his wealth and his unusually independent situation, it's apparent that if he was constricted, it wasn't just Hollywood's doing but his own. Working within the framework of commercial movies, James Mason, who at one time also seemed a highly specialized star, moved on from romantic starring roles to a series of deeper character portraits. However, Mason had to move away from the sexual center of his movies to do it, and it's doubtful if Grant would have sacrificed—or even endangered—the type of stardom he had won. His bargaining power was probably more important to him than his development as an actor; he *was* a tycoon. Whatever his reasons were, they're concealed now by his brisk businessman's manner. He doesn't seem to know or to care whether his pictures were good or bad; he says that if they did well at the box office, that's all that matters to him, and this doesn't appear to be an affectation. He made a gigantic profit on the gagged-up *Operation Petticoat*, which he produced in 1959; his friends say that he makes no distinction between that and *Notorious*.

Cary Grant always looks as if he'd just come from a workout in a miracle gym. And it's easy for audiences to forget about his stinkers (they're not held against him), because he himself isn't very different in them from the way he is when he has a strong director and a script with some drive. It's his sameness that general audiences respond to; they may weary of him, but still he's a guaranteed product. (It's the pictures that aren't.) And if he didn't grow as an actor, he certainly perfected "Cary Grant." One does not necessarily admire an icon, as one admires, say, Laurence Olivier, but it can be a wonderful object of contemplation. (If Olivier had patented the brand of adorable spoiled-boy charm he exhibited on the stage in *No Time for Comedy,* he might have had a career much like Grant's—and, indeed, in *Sleuth* Olivier played the sort of role which would then have been all that could be expected of him.)

As a movie star, Grant is so much a man of the city that he couldn't play a rural hero or a noble, rugged man of action, and so much a modern man that he couldn't appear in a costume or period picture without looking obstreperous—as if he felt he was being made a fool of. In *The Howards of Virginia,* it wasn't just the hot-blooded fighter-lover role that threw him, it was also wearing a Revolutionary uniform and a tricornered hat, with his hair in a chignon; he waddled through the picture like a bowlegged duck.The thought of him in Biblical sackcloth or in a Roman toga or some Egyptian getup is grisly-funny. And he's inconceivable in most of the modern urban films: how could Cary Grant play a silent stud or a two-fisted supercop? Grant never quite created another character—not even in the limited sense that screen stars sometimes do, using their own bodies and personalities as the base for imaginative creations. There are no Fred C. Dobbses or Sam Spades in his career. It's doubtful if he could even play a biographical character without being robbed of his essence. As Cole Porter, he wanders around in *Night and Day* looking politely oblivious; he's afraid to cut loose and be himself, yet he's too constrained to suggest anything resembling Cole Porter, so the hero seems to have a sickly, joyless nature. Composing song after song, his Cole Porter appears to have less music in his soul than any other living creature. Grant relaxes a little just once, while singing "You're the Top" with Ginny Simms.

He sings quite often in movies—as in *The Awful Truth,* when he parodies Ralph Bellamy's version of "Home on the Range," or in *Suzy*, in which he does the number that is included in *That's Entertainment*, and he replaced Bing Crosby as the Mock Turtle in the 1933 *Alice in Wonderland*, and sang "Beautiful Soup"—but he played an actual singing role in only one movie, early in his career: the disarmingly frilly 1934 *Kiss and Make Up*, one of Paramount's many imitations of the Lubitsch musical-comedy style. A sense of fun breaks through when he shows off his vaudeville skills—a confident, full-hearted exhibitionism. He frequently plays the piano in movies—happily and enthusiastically—and he does off the screen, too. For the past decade, since the breakup of his fourth marriage—to Dyan Cannon—following the birth of a daughter (his first child), he's been in retirement from the screen, but he's been active as an executive with Fabergé, whose president, George Barrie, used to play the saxophone for a living (Barrie composed the title song for *A Touch of Class*, produced by Brut, a subsidiary of Fabergé); they sometimes have jam sessions after board meetings, with Grant playing piano or organ. It's a corporate business right out of a thirties Cary Grant movie: in *Kiss and Make Up*, he actually ran a swank beauty salon. Grant belongs to the tradition of the success-worshipping immigrant boy who works his way to the top, but with a difference: the success he believes in is in the international high style of the worldly, fun-loving men he played—he's got Rolls-Royces stashed away in key cities. He has lived up to his screen image, and then some; welcome everywhere, more sought after than the Duke of Windsor was, in his seventies he's glitteringly—almost foolishly—hale.

Grant has had an apparently wide range of roles, but only apparently. Even in the era when he became a star, his sexual attraction worked only with a certain type of co-star—usually playing a high-strung, scatterbrained heroine, dizzy but not dumb. He would have been a disaster opposite Joan Crawford. With her gash smile, thick-syrup voice, and enormous tension, she required a roughneck titan like Gable to smite her; she would have turned Cary Grant into Woody Allen. A typical fan-magazine quote from Joan Crawford in her big-box-office youth was "Whatever we feel toward the man of the moment, it is he who is our very life and soul." It hardly matters whether Crawford herself was the author of those sentiments; that was the kind of woman she represented on the screen. It's easy to visualize Cary Grant's panic at the thought of being somebody's "very life and soul." He wanted to have a good time with a girl. It was always implicit that she had something going on her own; she was a free lance. She wasn't going to weigh him down—not like Crawford, who was all character armor and exorbitant needs. Crawford actually intended to take over the man of the moment's life and soul; that was what love meant in her pictures, and why she was so effective with skinny, refined, rich-hero types, like Robert Montgomery and Franchot Tone, whom she could scoop up. She gave the same intensity to everything she did; she inspired awe. But Grant didn't want to be carried away—nobody scoops up Cary Grant—and he didn't want an electrical powerhouse. (He's unthinkable with Bette Davis.) Once Grant became a star, there was a civilized equality in his sex partnerships, though his co-star had to be not only a pal but an ardent pal. When he appeared with Myrna Loy, they were pleasant together, but they didn't really strike sparks. Loy isn't particularly vulnerable, and she isn't dominant, either; she's so cool and airy she doesn't take the initiative, and since he doesn't either (except perfunctorily), nothing happens. They're too much alike—both lightly self-deprecating, both faintly reserved and aloof.

In dramatic roles, the women stars of the thirties and forties could sometimes triumph over mediocre material. This has been one of the saving aspects of the movie medium: Garbo could project so much more than a role required that we responded to her own emotional nature. Her uniquely spiritual eroticism turned men into willing slaves, and she was often at her best with rather passive men—frequently asexual or unisexual or homosexual (though not meant to be in the course of the films). Garbo's love transcended sex; her sensuality transcended sex. She played opposite Clark Gable once, and the collision, though heated, didn't quite work; his macho directness—and opacity—reduced her from passionate goddess to passionate woman. And Garbo seemed to lose her soul when she played mere women—that's why she was finished when the audience had had enough of goddesses. But for a time in the late twenties and early thirties, when she leaned back on a couch and exposed her throat, the whole audience could dream away—heterosexual men as much as the homosexuals (whom she was, indeed, generally seducing in her movies). Something similar operated, to a lesser extent, with Katharine Hepburn. In the thirties, she was frequently most effective with the kind of juveniles who were called boys: they were male versions of sensitive waifs, all cheekbone. She was effective, but there wasn't much sexual tension in those movies. And, despite the camaraderie and marvellous byplay of her later series with Spencer Tracy, she lost some of her charge when she acted with him. She was humanized but maybe also a little subjugated, and when we saw her through his eyes there seemed to be something the matter with her—she was too high-strung, had too much temperament. Tracy was stodgily heterosexual. She was more exciting with Cary Grant, who had a faint ambiguity and didn't want her to be more like ordinary women: Katharine Hepburn was a one-of-a-kind entertainment, and he could enjoy the show. The element of Broadway conventionality that mars *The Philadelphia Story* is in the way she's set up for a fall—as a snow maiden and a phony. Grant is cast as an élitist variation of the later Spencer Tracy characters.

Cary Grant could bring out the sexuality of his co-stars in comedies. Ingrid Bergman, a powerful presence on the screen, and with a deep, emotional voice (her voice is a big part of her romantic appeal in *Casablanca*), is a trifle heavy-spirited for comedy. She was never again as sexy as in that famous scene in *Notorious* when she just keeps advancing on Grant; you feel that she's so far gone on him that she can't wait any longer—and it's funny. Although Grant is a perfectionist on the set, some of his directors say that he wrecks certain scenes because he won't do fully articulated passages of dialogue. He wants always to be searching for how he feels; he wants to waffle charmingly. This may be a pain to a scenarist or a director, but in his own terms Grant knows what he's doing. He's the greatest sexual stooge the screen has ever known: his side steps and delighted stares turn his co-stars into comic goddesses. Nobody else has ever been able to do that.

When the sexual psychology of a comedy was right for Grant, he could be sensational, but if it was wrong and his energy still came pouring out, he could be terrible. In Frank Capra's *Arsenic and Old Lace* (made in 1941 but not released until 1944, because, by contract, it couldn't open until the Broadway production closed) he's more painful to watch than a normally bad actor—like, say, Robert Cummings—would be, because our affection for Grant enters into our discomfort. As it was originally written, the Mortimer Brewster role—an acerbic theatre critic being pursued by his aggressive, no-nonsense fiancée—wouldn't have been bad for Grant, but the Capra film sweetened the critic and turned the fiancée into a cuddly, innocuous little dear (Priscilla Lane). Capra called Grant Hollywood's greatest *farceur*, but the role was shaped as if for Fred MacMurray, and Grant was pushed into frenzied overreacting—prolonging his stupefied double takes, stretching out his whinny. Sometime after the whopping success of *It Happened One Night,* Frank Capra had lost his instinct for sex scenes, and his comedies became almost obscenely neuter, with clean, friendly old grandpas presiding over blandly retarded families. Capra's hick jollity was not the atmosphere for Cary Grant, and he was turned into a manic eunuch in *Arsenic and Old Lace*.

In drag scenes—even in his best movies—Grant also loses his grace. He is never so butch—so beefy and clumsy a he-man—as in his female impersonations or in scenes involving a clothes switch. In *Bringing Up Baby,* Katharine Hepburn takes his suit away, and he has nothing to wear but a flouncy fur-trimmed negligee. When Hepburn's aunt (May Robson) arrives and demands crossly, querulously, "Why are you wearing a robe?" Grant, exasperated, answers "Because I just went gay all of a sudden." It doesn't work: he goes completely out of character. Burt Lancaster was deliriously, unself-consciously funny in a long drag sequence in *The Crimson Pirate* (a parody adventure picture roughly comparable to *Gunga Din*); he turned himself into a scrambled cartoon of a woman, as Harry Ritz had done in *On the Avenue*. That's what Tony Curtis and Jack Lemmon did in *Some Like It Hot*—only they did it by yielding to their feminine disguises and becoming their own versions of gorgeous, desirable girls. Bert Remsen does it that way in *California Split,* anxiously seeing himself as a gracious lady of quality. But Grant doesn't yield to cartooning femininity or to enjoying it; he doesn't play a woman, he threatens to—flirting with the idea and giggling over it. His sequence in a skirt and a horsehair wig in the stupid, humiliating *I Was a Male War Bride* was a fizzle. He made himself brusque and clumsy to call attention to how inappropriate the women's clothes were on him—as if he needed to prove he was a big, burly guy.

The beautifully tailored clothes that seem now to be almost an intrinsic part of the Cary Grant persona came very late in his career. Decked out in the pinstripes, wide lapels, and bulky shoulders of the early forties, Grant, with his thick, shiny black hair, often suggested a race-track tout or a hood. He was a snappy dresser, and when he was playing Ivy League gentlemen, his clothes were often kingpin flashy, in the George Raft manner. Happy and hearty, he looked terrific in those noisy clothes; he wore baggy pants in *Only Angels Have Wings* and was still a sexual magnet. But sometimes his slouch hats and floppy, loose-draped jackets seemed to dominate the actor inside. His strutting appearance was distracting, like a gaudy stage set. As he got older, however, he and his slim-line clothes developed such an ideal one-to-one love affair that people could grin appreciatively in the sheer pleasure of observing the union. In *North by Northwest,* the lean-fitting suit he wore through so many perils seemed the skin of his character; and in *Charade,* when for the sake of a dim joke about drip-dry he got under the shower with his suit on, he lost the skin of his character—even though that character was "Cary Grant."

*I*t's a peerless creation, the "Cary Grant" of the later triumphs— *Notorious, To Catch a Thief, North by Northwest,* and *Charade.* Without a trace of narcissism, he appears as a man women are drawn to—a worldly, sophisticated man who has become more attractive with the years. And Grant really had got better-looking. The sensual lusciousness was burned off: age purified him (as it has purified Paul Newman). His acting was purified, too; it became more economical. When he was young, he had been able to do lovely fluff like *Topper* without being too elfin, or getting smirky, like Ray Milland, or becoming a brittle, too bright gentleman, like Franchot Tone. But he'd done more than his share of arch mugging— lowering his eyebrows and pulling his head back as if something funny were going on in front of him when nothing was. Now the excess energy was pared away; his performances were simple and understated and seamlessly smooth. In *Charade,* he gives an amazingly calm performance; he knows how much his presence does for him and how little he needs to do. His romantic glamour, which had reached a high peak in 1939 in *Only Angels*

Have Wings, wasn't lost; his glamour was now a matter of his resonances from the past, and he wore it like a mantle.

Some stars (Kirk Douglas, for one) don't realize that as they get older, if they continue to play the same sort of parts, they no longer need to use big, bold strokes; they risk self-caricature when they show their old flash, and they're a bit of a joke when they try to demonstrate that they're as good as they ever were. But if they pare down their styles and let our memories and imaginations fill in from the past, they can seem masters. Sitting in an airport V.I.P. lounge a few years ago, Anthony Quinn looked up from the TV set on which he was watching *To Catch a Thief* and said, "That's the actor I always wanted to be"—which is fairly funny, not only because Quinn and Grant are such contrasting types but because Quinn has never learned the first thing from Cary Grant. He's never understood that he needs to dry out a little. Some actors are almost insultingly robust. If you should ask Anthony Quinn "Do you know how to dance?" he would cry "Do I know how to dance?" and he'd answer the question with his whole body—and you'd probably wind up sorry that you'd asked. Cary Grant might twirl a couple of fingers, or perhaps he'd execute an intricate, quick step and make us long for more. Unlike the macho actors who as they got older became strident about their virility, puffing their big, flabby chests in an effort to make themselves look even larger, Grant, with his sexual diffidence, quietly became less physical—and more assured. He doesn't wear out his welcome: when he has a good role, we never get enough of him. Not only is his reserve his greatest romantic resource—it is the resource that enables him to age gracefully.

What the directors and writers of those four suspense films understood was that Cary Grant could no longer play an ordinary man—he had to be what he had become to the audience. In box-office terms, he might get by with playing opposite Doris Day in *That Touch of Mink,* but he was interchangeable with Rock Hudson in this sort of picture, and the role was a little demeaning—it didn't take cognizance of his grace or of the authority that enduring stardom confers. The special charm of *Notorious,* of the piffle *To Catch a Thief,* and of *North by Northwest* and *Charade* is that they give him his due. He is, after all, an immortal—an ideal of sophistication forever. He spins high in the sky, like Fred Astaire and Ginger Rogers. He may not be able to do much, but what he can do no one else has ever done so well, and because of his civilized nonaggressiveness and his witty acceptance of his own foolishness we see ourselves idealized in him. He's self-aware in a charming, non-egotistic way that appeals to the very people we'd want to appeal to. Even when he plays Cockneys, he isn't English or foreign to us—or American, either, exactly. Some stars lose their nationality, especially if their voices are distinctive. Ronald Colman, with his familiar cultivated, rhythmic singsong, seemed no more British, really, than the American Douglas Fairbanks, Jr.; they were both "dashing" men of the world. Ingrid Bergman doesn't sound Swedish to us but sounds simply like Ingrid Bergman. Cary Grant became stateless early: he was always Cary Grant. Making love to him, the heroines of the later movies are all aware that he's a legendary presence, that they're trying to seduce a legend. "How do you shave in there?" Audrey Hepburn asks bemusedly in *Charade,* putting her finger up to the cleft in his chin. Her character in the movie is to be smitten by him and to dote on him. Actually, he had begun to show his age by that time (1963); it was obvious that he was being lighted very carefully and kept in three-quarter shots, and that his face was rounder and a little puffy. And although lampblack may have shielded the neck, one could tell that it was being shielded. But we saw him on Audrey Hepburn's terms: Cary Grant at his most elegant. He didn't need the show-stopping handsomeness of his youth; his style, though it was based on his handsomeness, had transcended it.

Everyone likes the idea of Cary Grant. Everyone thinks of him affectionately, because he embodies what seems a happier time—a time when we had a simpler relationship to a performer. We could admire him for his timing and nonchalance; we didn't expect emotional revelations from Cary Grant. We were used to his keeping his distance—which, if we cared to, we could close in idle fantasy. He appeared before us in his radiantly shallow perfection, and that was all we wanted of him. He was the Dufy of acting—shallow but in a good way, shallow without trying to be deep. We didn't want depth from him; we asked only that he be handsome and silky and make us laugh.

Cary Grant's bravado—his wonderful sense of pleasure in performance, which we respond to and share in—is a pride in craft. His confident timing is linked to a sense of movies as popular entertainment: he wants to please the public. He became a "polished," "finished" performer in a tradition that has long since atrophied. The suave, accomplished actors were usually poor boys who went into a trade and trained themselves to become perfect gentlemen. They're the ones who seem to have "class." Cary Grant achieved Mrs. Leach's ideal, and it turned out to be the whole world's ideal.

[July 14, 1975]

PART TWO

Lazarus Laughs

*H*elmut Berger has often been perversely likable, flaunting manner-isms that many other actors avoid. As Konrad in Luchino Visconti's *Conversation Piece*, Berger is of a queenly self-centeredness so garish that he becomes a comedian. A petulant little nymph, Konrad acts as if the whole world were his closet. He is being kept—lavishly—by a countess (Silvana Mangano), who enlists her teen-age daughter and the daughter's fiancé in her schemes to hang on to him; meanwhile, he and the kids play threesomes.

Visconti, not fully recovered from a stroke suffered while he was completing his last film, *Ludwig,* directed *Conversation Piece* from a wheelchair part of the time. Although it takes place entirely in the interior of a Roman house, one doesn't feel confined: Konrad and the Countess are such depraved beasties that when they start screaming insults at each other, who cares about whether there's a sun outdoors? When Berger sashays around the room, or steps out of the shower and flings a white towel around his golden nudity in a swirling movement Dietrich couldn't have improved on, there's action enough. And Mangano's Countess is never at rest; her darting eyes don't miss a thing. She's gorgeous, but with the reptilian glitter of an aging swinger. She'd crunch your heart to clean a pore. You like her, though, and you like the performer—the way you always like the actresses who play chic, ultra-neurotic witches. The Countess is so venomous, arrogant, and tantrummy she's funny, like Konrad.

The house belongs to the Professor (Burt Lancaster), a retired American scientist who is spending his declining years, secluded, in the study of art history. He collects the eighteenth-century English portraits of domestic groups known as conversation pieces, and the film itself is small-scale, intimate, and dark, as if under layers of varnish. At the opening, the Countess inveigles the Professor into renting her the top floor of his home; her lover, Konrad, moves in, and the Countess and her brood invade the Professor's life, carelessly brushing him aside. The story mechanism is much like that of those old *Kind Lady* plays in which a gang of schemers moves in on a helpless person, but this troupe has no ulterior motive. These intruders simply use the Professor the way they use everybody, and he's more than willing to be used. It is the theme of Visconti's *Death in Venice* all over again, with Lancaster playing Aschenbach to Berger's grownup Tadzio, but this time the director is in a more jovial mood and the dignified Professor isn't destroyed; on the contrary, he is recalled to life. It's a winning movie—Visconti has come back changed. When you laugh, you can't always be sure that you're meant to be laughing, but you feel certain that he wouldn't mind. He seems to have got past the point at which one minds being laughed at.

Visconti's pictures have often had an undercurrent of silliness (though the solemn pacing kept audiences respectful); this time, the silliness is so close to the surface that the Professor can ask Lietta, the Countess's daughter, if she sees him as a character in a comic opera. *We* do, because his situation is a joke. He's entranced by Konrad's scurrilous chatter; he begins to be addicted to the intrusions, wanting to experience more of the family's disorderliness. When Konrad is beaten up (by rough trade? by his fellow drug-smugglers?), the Professor nurses him and, kneeling, like a devoted slave, scrubs the blood off the stairs, so the police won't see it. The Professor is the ultimate putz—he's being cuckolded by *everybody*. Yet it's easy to empathize with him. The giddy people barging in and out are certainly more entertaining than he is. They're as irresponsible and unpredictable as figures in a dream. And as he hovers on the sidelines, watching, almost forced into voyeurism, he sees everything he has shut out of his waking life, and maybe even out of his dream life.

One keeps waiting for the Professor to make a pass at Konrad. I was profoundly grateful to Visconti that the Professor didn't—the audience might split its sides if Burt Lancaster were to be shown coming out—but part of what makes the film giggly is that it's set up as if he should. Hollywood used to go in for the polarity of the innocent, unworldly pedant versus the carefree pleasure-seeker, because it was a convenient stereotyping for the purposes of comedy. We in the audience can't help feeling superior to a bookworm: countless movies have conditioned us to expect his repressed emotions to break through. So when Lietta tells the Professor that since he is childless he should adopt Konrad, we may feel like snickering. The Professor is kindly disposed toward the suggestion, however; he takes it under advisement, the way he takes everything, with bowed head. (Selfless rectitude seems to weigh him down.) I wish that somewhere in this movie some trace of dirty sanity had crept into his character, because we miss it.

Whose idea can it have been to cast Burt Lancaster as a gentle intellectual? He is as extroverted as an actor can be. When he entered movies, in the mid-forties, he was a beautiful blank—an athlete-actor, like Jim Brown, all physical charge. A typically American star, he was best in the open air and when his desires were expressed (and fulfilled) in direct physical action. The only time he had a strong personality was when he was bounding through a swashbuckler, like his classic *The Crimson Pirate,* or selling pure energy, as in *The Rainmaker.* Acting with his whole body, he was buoyantly beautiful, and his grin—with those great white Chiclets flashing—could make you grin back at the screen. Yet when he closed his mouth there was an appealing puzzled dissatisfaction in his slightly traumatized look, and that, too, came to seem typically American—taking pleasure in action but feeling violated and incomplete. It was clear that Burt Lancaster wasn't content to be a lusty, Tarzan-jawed man of action. He was soon making it possible for a number of offbeat projects to get off the ground and giving new directors their first chance, and he himself turned to producing and directing. He appeared in such out-of-the-ordinary films as *All My Sons, Come Back, Little Sheba, The Rose Tattoo, Sweet Smell of Success, The Devil's Disciple, Birdman of Alcatraz, A Child Is Waiting,* and *The Swimmer.* Some of them were terrible, but they weren't complacent choices; they were the choices of a restless, eager hard worker, and if he didn't prove himself the world's most expressive actor, he did pretty well in several of them. Why, then, is he so hopeless as the Professor? Visconti seems to have put Smokey the Bear into the Emil Jannings role in *The Blue Angel.*

Lancaster's performance made me realize that I've watched him for almost thirty years and I don't know the first thing about him. Whatever goes on inside that man, he doesn't use it as an actor: he doesn't draw from himself. So how can he play a character whose life is all inner? Lancaster simply negates himself in the role, as if by not using any physical energy and by moving slowly, with a long face and a demure expression, he would become a thinker. He *impersonates* a contemplative scholar. In 1962, when Visconti needed a big star in order to finance *The Leopard,* Lancaster leaped at the chance, and he delivered. He held his energy in, but it was there, and his patriarchal Sicilian prince had the authority of controlled strength. At the final ball, when the old prince was overpowered by nostalgia for the life that was slipping away from him, we felt his defeat—and reluctant surrender—as our own. But in *Conversation Piece,* when the Professor talks about his waning years, he's so prosaic and inert we don't feel a thing. Burt Lancaster needs to use his body, because when he doesn't he has no intensity; when he's serious he's sexless and almost obsequiously conscientious.

Yet Visconti (and his co-scenarists, Suso Cecchi D'Amico and Enrico Medioli) seem to see this drone as a noble and sympathetic figure. Opening with electrocardiagram tape spilling out under the titles, *Conversation Piece* has a special quality, rather like an *apologia pro vita sua,* and at times, particularly toward the end, the Professor stands in for the director. The Professor is like a somnambulist, powerless to alter anything; the interlopers—the family—go on doing whatever they feel like. Yet he presides over the movie, and Visconti places the camera so that the Professor is always looming up—not part of the action but above it all. It's almost as if his scenes were shot at a different time—as if he were in a movie house, standing near the screen observing the show. This isn't the kind of show he grew up with, but he's not shocked, or even surprised, and he makes no moral judgments. He's a nice, avuncular sort of Aschenbach—cultured, reserved, isolated, but completely permissive. And, unexpectedly, a Marxist.

Visconti has often used "detached" figures (as far back as the movie director in *Bellissima*), and it may have been the theme of Meursault's detachment from his own life that attracted Visconti to *The Stranger*. But what an erratic development it is that he should combine a spinoff of Aschenbach with the idea of the detached observer. What it comes to is that the Professor doesn't need the sexual awakening we anticipate in the early part of the film—that he understands and accepts physical passion, even though he himself is a recluse. It's hardly any wonder that Lancaster has trouble with this conception: the Professor represents everything virtuous in the director. (Lancaster's unrevealing face could be an attempt to model himself on Visconti's hooded sternness.) Maybe Visconti, now that he has lost part of his mobility, actually believes that he sees the life around him—and his own past—as if he were watching a movie. As if he were an outsider to passion.

However, the inadvertent comedy of *Conversation Piece* comes from Visconti's *lack* of detachment. Audiences don't generally ask of artists that they resolve their conflicts, but political ideologues demand it of them, and Visconti seems to feel the pressure acutely. He can't seem to accept the contradictions that have always plagued him; he's still trying to find a way to prove that his "decadent" tastes and his Marxist politics are not really contradictory, and *Conversation Piece* turns into a carnival of special pleading. When Visconti has ideas he wants to get across, he simply gives the explanation to anyone at hand. We get the film's sexual rationale when Lietta recites Auden's "last poem" to the Professor, remarking airily that she learned it from Konrad: "When you see a fair form, chase it/ And if possible embrace it,/ Be it a girl or boy./ Don't be bashful: be brash, be fresh./ Life is short, so enjoy/ Whatever contact your flesh/ May at the moment crave:/ There's no sex life in the grave." (It's from Auden's and Chester Kallman's masque "The Entertainment of the Senses," where it's intended ironically.)

The political rationale comes in last-minute bursts of undramatized exposition. We have all but forgotten that there is a world outside the house when the characters begin what seems like a race against the "End" title to tell us that the Countess's Fascist-industrialist husband has been involved in a plot to kill the Communists in the government, and that

Konrad—a revolutionary—has informed on him, thus preventing a coup. Visconti turns Shavian ironist, and we learn that when Konrad sells his favors he's a victim of the ruling-class buyers. Konrad stands revealed as a saint.

There's grandeur in the silliness: one comes away with visions of Marxist dukes cruising the boys on the barricades. Fortunately, Visconti's control is so serenely relaxed that the picture seems part charade anyway—a seriously intended *opera buffa,* like Sartre on Genet (and much more fun). Somehow, the sloppiness—even the ungainly shift to a closeup almost every time an actor speaks—doesn't bother one. The film is only part dubbed; the three principals spoke in English (French and Italian versions were also recorded, which probably explains the dialogue closeups), but it isn't colloquial English. It sounds as if the Italian script had been translated literally, and it's so formal that Konrad's profanity has maximum impact; twisting his Austrian tongue over phrases like "She'll break your balls," he's the dirtiest piece of angel cake since Marilyn Monroe. The hollow ring of the dialogue contributes to the thinness of the film's sensibility; no one in it has any depth, and even the memory scenes, when the Professor recalls his mother and his long-ago bride, lack resonance. The famous beauties who play the flashback roles throw these bits slightly out of whack, but the flashbacks are abrupt and unrevealing and would be out of whack whoever was in them.

It's idiosyncratic filmmaking, all right. The film's Audenesque argument is generous, but what's it doing here? Visconti sets up one of his howlingly decadent families and then claims sweet naturalness for the daughter and fiancé who are cavorting with the mother's lover. Maybe the film's flower-child rhetoric is meant to be double-edged, but more likely Visconti is so romantic that he wants to remove the stigma from whores like Konrad and to show that the men who fall in love with them aren't the ludicrous, deceived sugar daddies they're generally taken to be. The plot about the Countess is amusing but essentially false: anybody with half an eye in his head can see that Konrad's appeal is primarily homosexual. (When the Countess first explains that he's her paid lover, she calls him her "kept boy"; it sounds wrong, of course, but how could a woman refer to Konrad as a kept man?) The politics by which Visconti tries to redeem him are the cuckoo aspect. If envy and hatred of the rich were what defined a radical, then Konrad could be called one, but only reactionaries think that's all that "radical" means. As for the victimization, Visconti seems a Marxist old dear to think that Konrad is a sensitive boy sacrificed to the lust of the industrialist class and that "society" is responsible. Konrad is too convincing a tart.

Visconti is an eccentric master who has earned the right to his follies, when he can make them as pleasurable as *Conversation Piece,* which opens the New York Film Festival this week. It has been reported that he hopes to film the "Sodom and Gomorrah" section of *Remembrance of Things Past,* with Marlon Brando as the Baron de Charlus. It's a breathtaking casting idea, and Charlus is the character that Visconti has been working toward—it should be Charlus, rather than the Professor, watching Berger wrap his thick muscles in that tentlike towel. Are there moneymen with the nerve to finance this madcap dream? Suppose that two-thirds of it is absolutely, irredeemably stinking. Imagine what the other third might be.

[September 29, 1975]

The Visceral Poetry of Pulp

*T*he hero of *Hard Times* rides into town on the rails, looking like an authentic Depression worker—a cap on his head, his face worn, narrow slits of hurting eyes. It's a lean, stoical face from the breadlines and close kin to Dorothea Lange's migratory workers, but it's also the face of Charles Bronson, the most popular movie star in the world and one of the highest-paid. And *Hard Times,* though low-key, stays completely within the conventions of pulp. It's unusually effective pulp—perhaps even great pulp, though not quite in the class of *Jaws. Jaws,* a primal-terror comedy, keeps you in a state of unconscionable, ridiculous suspense: you're waiting for the shocks, yet somehow the picture catches you on the offbeat, so that you're never quite prepared. *Jaws* tricks you in such an open way that at the same time that you're horror-struck you're laughing. *Hard Times,* the first feature directed by the young screenwriter Walter Hill, isn't as inventive in its manipulation, and it's by no means as gleeful or as bouncing. One more version of the myth of the strong, silent loner, it is close to stately in its manner—spacious, leisurely, and with elaborate period re-creations that seem almost to be there for their own sake. Hill fills in the Louisiana backgrounds—a black Pentecostal church meeting, a steamboat, a fair on the bayous—with reverent care, like the artists who painted detailed landscapes around the Christ figure. Yet by using Bronson, with superb calculation, so that he is the underdog in every situation, Hill gets our hearts pounding in fear that our hero may be hurt or vanquished. Hill gets us scared for *Charles Bronson.* When the visceral power of a film is poetic, as it is here, you may retain a sense of irony but you don't resent the film's grip on you. *Hard Times* offers excitement that makes you feel good; Walter Hill respects the loner myth.

With slight modifications, the story could be set at any time; it appears to be set in the thirties for the decorative ambience of hardship. The Depression is needed to explain Bronson's gnarled face and to ennoble it. Put him in modern clothes and he's a hard-bitten tough guy, but with that cap on he's one of the dispossessed—an honest man who's known hunger. *Hard Times* makes the actor called Il Brutto in Italy look beautiful. His face is creased by pain, and his pain is not merely personal—it is also pain he feels for others. This man—Chaney, he's called—is what Alan Ladd's Shane was trying to be. Chaney jumps off the boxcar, goes into a run-down diner, orders a ten-cent coffee, and tips the waitress a nickel. Noblesse oblige. That's the theme of the picture. Bronson's taciturn, withdrawn face is already the myth; his thoughts always seem far away. He doesn't have the vocal gifts to sustain the qualities of that stolid, sneaky face, but Chaney is a man of few words, in contrast to Speed (James Coburn), a gambler whose compulsive smart talk gets him in trouble, and a hophead unlicensed doctor named Poe (Strother Martin), who speaks in florid metaphors. Speed and Poe are no more than stereotypes vivified, but they're astutely worked out so that Speed's mobile, bright-eyed face and Poe's soft plumpness set Chaney off, and their vices add dignity to his Spartan habits. These three go into business together in New Orleans. The gambler arranges bare-knuckled, no-holds-barred fights on the docks or in warehouses—illegal fights, strictly for gambling—and the tired, small stranger (Bronson is in his fifties) goes into them reluctantly; his heart isn't in it.

There's a moment when Chaney, looking anxious and forlorn, is about to take on a powerful young giant, who calls out to him, "Hey, Pop, you're a little old fer this, ain't ya?" And we see Bronson's faint smile, his eyes flashing for an instant, before he calmly goes over and, with one punch, knocks the punk out. It's primitive, but who can resist the sense of pleasure that fills one's chest with pride and relief? When Bronson fights against the local champ, Jim Henry (Robert Tessier)—a boulder of flesh, with a dirty, ominous smile—you feel the way you did as a kid at the movies. Tessier is frightening the way Ernest Borgnine was frightening in *From Here to Eternity,* and next to him Bronson seems almost as defenseless as Frank Sinatra. But the cords in his neck could hold up Madison Square Garden. He's a bull-headed Christ with a punch.

Hill's staging of the fight with Jim Henry makes it a titanic battle—the walloping fists sound like rhinos crashing into trees—but this climactic bout comes too early. The director and his co-scenarists (Bryan Gindorff and Bruce Henstell) couldn't figure out how to top it later on, so the picture slumps a little. They also couldn't figure out a plausible reason for Chaney and the wounded, saint-whore type he loves (Jill Ireland) to part; it sounded to me as if they split because she didn't like him to go off home after sex—she wanted him to commit himself by spending the whole night, and he was too proud and dedicated a loner for that. But maybe there was something I missed. Chaney doesn't find happiness—only obligations—and sometimes it seems as if his mission in life were to be disappointed in people. (I wish he hadn't taken in a stray cat.) The details may be unconvincing, but it's all consistent. The literary, too colorful dialogue and a scene with a caged black bear—the emblem of the writer-director John Milius—suggest that Hill is declaring himself of the neo-commercial school of Milius, but Hill has a steadier hand. Milius tries to evoke visceral poetry in *The Wind and the Lion,* but he doesn't establish the necessary simple context, and since his nostalgic flourishes seem only half-believed, the film's childish view of heroism turns into macho camp. Hill tells his story single-mindedly, showing his appetite for ostentation mostly in those background crowds. The hero is presented formally: he comes out of the darkness—a king among men—and goes back into the darkness, like any good loner. On its own pulp terms, *Hard Times* is a triumph.

□ □ □

Sydney Pollack doesn't have a knack for action pulp. He has directed the spy thriller *Three Days of the Condor* in his earnest, inimitably expensive style, trying to elevate the material, and has succeeded only in taking the charge out of it. Robert Redford plays a researcher for a C.I.A. front who accidentally turns up a clue to the existence of a renegade conspiratorial network within the C.I.A. and becomes everybody's target. After a long stretch of chasing and killing, with Max von Sydow running around as a high-toned hit man and Cliff Robertson, as a C.I.A. official, skulking about, with ugly black hair that looks like a tam-o'-shanter, the picture gets some tension going, but there's no real fun in it. As in *The Parallax View,* the enemy is omnipresent and essentially invisible. There's no solution to the mystery. The message is that the past was corrupt and there may not be a future. In a concluding political dialogue, Robertson speaks, Nazi-fashion, for the cynical forces of darkness, and Redford defends democratic processes. But where can he go for help? Who isn't part of the conspiracy? He has only one hope: the *New York Times.* And the film leaves Redford, refrigerated, asking himself, Will the *Times* print the story, or is it, too, the enemy? Films like *Parallax* and *Condor* don't merely not give you anything—they seem to take away from you. *Condor's* heroine, Faye Dunaway, is a photographer who shoots bare, wintry scenes and is meant to be half in love with death. In the film's high point of flossy artistry, Redford and Dunaway go to bed together, and their coitus is visualized for us in a series of her lonely, ghostly pictures. Ah, the beauty of sexual desolation. If this death-rattle sex is intended to be a variant of the old romantic scene "Kiss me as if it were for the last time," it fails. All it does is sustain the film's gloom, which gradually begins to seem like the director's guilt taking visible form.

□ □ □

*S*mile, a comedy set in Santa Rosa during the Jaycee-sponsored California final of the national "Young American Miss" pageant, is about the American smile that certifies likability. It's about the booster spirit, and optimism as a way of life. There hasn't been a small-town comedy in so long that this fresh, mussy film seems to be rediscovering America. Though we laugh at the gaffes of the rawboned teen-age girls, the laughter isn't cruel. When the girls are interviewed, or when they have to perform in public, they look dumb, but they're not. They stumble and blurt out idiocies because what they're saying isn't what they feel at all. They're cued to talk cant about "helping others" by the chief judge of the contest—Big Bob Freelander (Bruce Dern), a mobile-home salesman and the biggest booster in town. He's a civic-minded man who lives by the beaming banalities that Bert Parks celebrates. Dern has a furtively hip style of comedy, and he's built for this part. He isn't tall and lanky in the heroic Western tradition—you don't think of that body in open spaces. His Big Bob is tall in a graceless, sexless way—he's one of those American men who haul their height around. Big Bob speaks in homilies that express exactly how he feels. He's a donkey, but he doesn't have a mean bone in his body. When Big Bob is attacked by his closest friend and forced into a moment of self-recognition, he's so shaken his face gets squinched up, like a pouting infant's. The film—a cousin to *Lord Love a Duck*—is an affectionate satirical salute to the square. (*Smile* has already opened around the country, though it's getting its first New York showing at the Film Festival.)

Are beauty contests too easy a target, as some of the film's negative reviews have charged? I don't think so. As a student at Berkeley, I was initiated into a women's honor society in a ceremonial that required each girl to wear a white formal and a gardenia corsage, and to carry a lighted candle. Who doesn't get stuck in false positions? Who hasn't been through stupid rituals? If many of us can't resist turning on the TV to watch at least one or two beauty contests each year, perhaps it's because these competitions seem like pockets of the past—pure fifties—and link in with our memories, the way seeing Fred Wiseman's *High School* brings back the indoctrination we went through and makes us realize it's still called education. There's not much heft to *Smile,* but Michael Ritchie, who directed, isn't the right director for big subjects anyway; he's not a director for depth, he's the man to turn loose on marginalia and surfaces. *Smile* supplies wonderful details of frazzled behavior, though Jerry Belson's script is often too blunt. Ritchie's direction is highly variable in quality; the picture doesn't hold together, and it lacks narrative flow—the jokes and the "talent" skits seem to be cut in rather haphazardly. But nobody is better at found (and pseudo-found) moments than Ritchie is. He's a whiz at setting up situations and then catching an embarrassed splutter or a woolly stare or a performer whose eyes wander desperately, and this film has his funniest off-guard bits yet. Maybe the hit-and-run continuity was the only way to convey the unresolved mixture of affection, disbelief, comic horror, camp, and imbecile suspense which is part of why some of us watch beauty contests.

In the past, Ritchie has had trouble with his women characters. In *Downhill Racer* and *The Candidate,* the women were lacquered figurines, and Ritchie gave the impression that he didn't have any idea what went on in their heads. And at the beginning of *Smile* we feel like connoisseurs when we look at the thirty-three contestants. (Young professional actresses—some of them former beauty contestants—are salted among non-professional Santa Rosa girls.) The camera itself seems to buttress the whole rationale of beauty contests: we appraise the skinny legs and the perfect little Aryan-goddess features, and people in the audience laugh automatically at ungainly conformations and chubby bodies. But when the girls are sorted out and we see what they are going through, there's no more of this appraisal or derision. Ritchie's attitudes don't seem ready-made this time; he seems to be willing to pick up new impressions. And willing to concede that the green, gawky girls aren't necessarily going to turn into packaged commodities (like the Candidate).

Miss Antelope Valley (Joan Prather), a straight-A brunette, realizes she's been had, and she can grin, shamefaced about what a fool she's been. Miss Anaheim (Annette O'Toole), a creamy redhead, is wised-up from the start. In the talent competition, she comes on overdressed, delivers a paean to "inner beauty," and uses it as the excuse to do a zingy striptease down to her tights, clutching a small lily to each breast. Not recognizing that Big Bob is looking for sincerity, she outsmarts herself and finishes as the fourth runner-up. But she's snappy and resourceful, like the girls Joan Blondell used to play. Only one contestant is really obnoxious—Miss Salinas, a self-made witch, programmed to smile and to wring the last ounce of advantage out of her Mexican-American background. Maria O'Brien (daughter of Edmond O'Brien and Olga San Juan) makes her a rollicky ethnic caricature, completely self-absorbed. Sucking up to the judges with presents of bowls of guacamole, she's the kind of gushing phony who can stare down a saint. She can even stare down a master phony like Brenda, the girls' thirtyish den mother (Barbara Feldon), who always looks on the bright side, her chipper smile just sitting there. When Brenda's soggy-faced husband (Nicholas Pryor) gets fed up with her indefatigable cheer and complains to her, she comments "Another evening of sarcasm and self-pity!" and her inflections detonate. It was a mistake, though, to make her frigid and to use that as the reason for her husband's blubbering drunkenness. There's no wit in it. Barbara Feldon keeps trying, but Brenda lacks what Big Bob has—an essential innocence and good will. She isn't human enough to be a funny character or buggy enough to work as a cartoon. Feldon has the bad luck to be in several of the longer, broad-comedy scenes, and Ritchie doesn't pace them well. The only way he gets pace in a sequence is by editing; his longer scenes (like the Jaycees' nighttime get-together) are too schematic, and they don't develop the black-comedy hysteria that seems needed.

Smile might have been a classic American comedy if he'd been able to use the darting techniques on the Jaycees and the older townspeople which he used on the contest itself. However, I didn't mind the film's wobbling ineptness; it seems preferable to *The Candidate*'s stunningly cool, glib style, which went with its counterculture platitudes. In his earlier films Ritchie was misogynistic yet sentimental. In *Smile* he really appears to like most of the people on the screen. The film acknowledges the possibility that people can be cynical without being corrupt. Michael Kidd, the choreographer (who appeared on the screen once before, in *It's Always Fair Weather*), plays the once big-time, now fading choreographer brought in to stage the pageant. This jaded outsider is a hardboiled pro, observing the local shenanigans without surprise. He talks straight to the contestants, and when there's a petty crisis he resolves it by taking a lower fee. It's not a big thing, but he does it for the girls' sake, and it's the only clear-cut generous action I can recall in a Michael Ritchie film. Ritchie is no longer dividing the world between the manipulators and the manipulated. He has responded to the confusion and eagerness in the girls' smiles, and he's smiling back.

[October 6, 1975]   ·

Living Inside a Movie

Gene Hackman doesn't have the sexiness of a movie star; he's more like a character actor. He looks so dull and ordinary that it's almost hard to believe that he *is* a star, yet, unlike others who play mediocre men,

45

Gene Hackman is such a consummate actor that he illuminates mediocrity. That's probably what makes him a star. Jeff Bridges shares this ability to transform the commonplace. He appears to be an average, good-looking, burly, blond American boy, yet he sensitizes us to the boy's feelings to such a degree that this average kid seems like the most wonderful kid we've ever seen. His face is masculine and open—like the classic American outdoor boy's—yet totally expressive. Jeff Bridges doesn't seem to keep anything closed off. He makes us care so deeply for the commonplace mugs he plays that, of course, they stop being commonplace and we really love them. (What did Lloyd Bridges feed his sons? The only other young screen actor who gives off this intense, expressive warmth is Jeff's older brother Beau. Both of them have beatific smiles.)

Jeff Bridges is just the right actor for the role of Lewis Tater in Howard Zieff's new comedy, *Hearts of the West* (which is in the New York Film Festival and is to open in a theatre a few days later). Lewis is an upright Iowa farm boy who writes Western stories and aspires to be like his idol, Zane Grey; he leaves home, heads toward the land of his purple-prose dreams, and stumbles into a job as a bit player in Western pictures directed by Kessler (Alan Arkin). The setting is mostly Hollywood in 1930, but it's a special part of Hollywood—the Gower Street area, where Jewish peddlers with heavy Eastern European accents produce quickie Westerns on pathetic budgets. The Rob Thompson script (his first) is about the humor of bottom-level picture-making, and Zieff (this is his first feature since his début film, *Slither*) doesn't lob the jokes across. He idolizes comic characters for their own sweet sake, and he wants us to share his pleasure in the penny-pinching hysteric Kessler, the yelling in Yiddish, and the troupe of cowboy extras and stunt men, led by Howard Pike (Andy Griffith), who bargain over the price for each fall off a horse. At night, on location in the desert, they let out mock cowboy yells in order to satisfy Kessler's fantasies about what happy fellows they are, but they ration their hi-yippies so as not to spoil him.

As long as the film stays with this happy, snaggletoothed mix of cultures, it has an eccentric enchantment to it. Lewis's friendliness takes you back to the period when Americans who were good were sincere and idealistic; he embodies how we feel now about that period. A lot of what we feel about it comes from the movies. We feel that people weren't so hip in those days—that they were more gullible about simple things, that they had dumb, mail-order dreams, and the confident strength to make some of them come true. *Hearts* is a nostalgia comedy; Lewis is a mock hero who is a true hero. He has that noble-American look of early cowboy stars like George O'Brien. He's Candide in Hollywood, but a conquering Candide, and the contrasts between his high-principled spunk and the other extras' grizzled, good-natured cynicism are nicely underplayed. It's delayed-reaction slapstick, with a distinctive evocative tone; Zieff turns movie conventions around the way Buster Keaton used to. You're watching a scene and then the capper comes: a car rolling back downhill, a dummy that's alive, Howard Pike disappearing into a rattan chair, Lewis jumping onto a horse—his eyes crossing with pain as he lands. And you realize that the scene is a stylized movie gag, and that this is how movies have led us to imagine the past.

There's no condescension or caricature in Zieff's eye for faces. The Gower Gulch cowboys are true screen originals; Zieff brings back comic character actors in a new way, getting their qualities across in a few glimpses (as in a TV commercial). He knows where your eyes will go in a shot, and he knows (from directing commercials) how to get everything in. A director from the theatre might have more going on underneath a scene; Zieff doesn't have layers of texture—it's all where you can see it, and even some of the best moments are overdetailed. But his feelings for the material transforms the television techniques. He grew up in Los Angeles; he knows this gypsy atmosphere, and he doesn't want to paint it in primary colors. He's trusting, like Lewis: he wants to believe that people will respond to a comedy that doesn't punch them on the head. That's what gives *Hearts* its tone. The trouble is, we like the people and the atmosphere so much we want more of them than we get.

We certainly want more of the heroine, Trout, played by Blythe Danner. A couple of years ago, Blythe Danner starred as an independent earth-mother woman who lived with two men most of her life, in the suicidally titled *Lovin' Molly,* from Larry McMurtry's *Leaving Cheyenne.* It was crudely made, but there were suggestive spaces in it—you couldn't tie it all up. Danner's full-blown, straightforward Molly, who didn't worry about being conventional, because conventions meant nothing to her, was like a Hardy heroine—Eustacia Vye, or Tess—growing up in Texas. I thought Blythe Danner was going to become a great movie star, but *Lovin' Molly* got measly distribution and vanished, and stars aren't made by flop movies. She has appeared on television (most conspicuously as Amanda in the "Adam's Rib" series), but Trout, in *Hearts of the West,* marks her return to the screen, and this time as a skinny comedienne. She looks startlingly different: her radiant, strong face has narrowed down, and, with less to her physically, one is far more aware of her husky, changeable voice. That voice has levels in it; it's a French 75—you get the champagne through the chipped ice and cognac. Trout, Kessler's script girl, is the kind of girl you imagine you'd find in Hollywood, though you're not sure why she's there. She's accepted in the men's world of the movie company, but she's not really part of the easy camaraderie; she's accepted as an outsider who knows enough not to butt in. The men are an ensemble, and they spoof seriousness even when they're serious, the way people who work together and drink together often do. But Trout is more tense—she's special. She tries to wise up the inexperienced hero—like Jean Arthur in

47

Mr. Deeds Goes to Town or *Mr. Smith Goes to Washington*. Trout, however, is more matter-of-fact and grownup than the Jean Arthur heroines. There's less girlish coquetry in her manner. Wide-eyed in the sense of looking at things unblinkingly, Blythe Danner suggests a harsher-voiced, less fragile Margaret Sullavan as well as Jean Arthur; she has style.

The defects of *Hearts* are mostly a tribute to its charm. We don't need or want the rinky-dink chase plot, involving two crooks pursuing Lewis for a money box he got hold of by accident. And this plot limits the film's time span to a few days, when Lewis's story needs a longer period—time for him to adapt to places like his rooming house, with the sign outside: STERN'S HACIENDA LA CIENEGA ROOMS TO LET. We want to see what happens to Lewis Tater; he's the real plot. Chances are that no studio would have financed *Hearts* without the standard farce-chase garbage, but it limits the film's scope. It makes the picture cute in places, and it forces an artificial tempo, so that Lewis's travels in Hollywood are too hurried and the scenes don't get a chance to play out.

The viewer expects Lewis to become a cowboy star, and it's a letdown for the audience when, upon being promoted to leading man, he ill-advisedly asks Kessler for a hundred and fifty dollars a week and gets fired. That's when the picture loses its subject and is caught in plot complications involving Herbert Edelman, as a producer, and Donald Pleasence, as his brother-in-law, a Western-pulp publisher. (The moviemakers, who give Pleasence the palatial Harold Lloyd estate for his home, seem to have an inflated idea of pulp-mill profits.) We waste time at a lavish brunch at Pleasence's place, and one of the richest elements in the movie—Lewis's finding his Zane Grey father figure in Howard Pike—is slighted. The camera feasts on Andy Griffith's lined, rugged beauty, but we don't get enough insight into Pike's betrayal of the hero-worshipping kid. There are smaller flaws. Zieff tries to make the picture effective by throwing in bits that are often nifties (like Lewis's screen test, which starts before the titles) but don't quite fit. And sometimes he gives a scene the wrong emphasis (at Lewis's home in Iowa, his family laughs at the wording of a letter he gets from a correspondence school, when it is his aspirations that would be the target). There are slips, too: Kessler gives a smoker for "Sid," and the Gower Gulchers all attend, but we don't know who Sid is, or what the smoker sequence is doing in this movie. What I'm asking for is smooth perfection—for *Hearts* to be as wonderful as its best parts. But what's there plays on in the mind—maybe because we never get our fill of the characters. Kessler alone is more of a character than one meets in most movies. He's so intense he's funny; this is a specialty of Alan Arkin's, and he does vocal tricks and gestures that nobody's ever quite thought of before. When Kessler tries to be suavely relaxed, his tongue gets coated with honey, and nobody trusts him. So he's coaxing the stunt men one moment and flaring up like a madman the next. In his own way, he's as ingenuous as Lewis, and he, too, knows what he wants. The high-strung son of a bitch might even have talent. *Hearts of the West* doesn't sell anybody short.

□ □ □

*R*oyal *Flash* was adapted by George MacDonald Fraser from one of his novels celebrating the inglorious career of Captain Harry Flashman, of the 11th Hussars (Malcolm McDowell), a rotten, snivelling Victorian coward. The Richard Lester film might be a holiday, rumpus-room epic if we had any reason to feel affection for Flashman—if he were blithe or sunny, or if we could feel a driblet of complicity with him. But the characters don't care about each other, and we don't care about any of them. Lester is on his own antic wavelength, and he doesn't try to tune us in. On the dedication page of *Royal Flash,* Fraser acknowledges "Ronald Colman, Douglas Fairbanks, Jr., Errol Flynn, Basil Rathbone, Louis Hayward, Tyrone Power, and all the rest of them." The conception is a parody of movie heroics. Since most of the swashbuckler entertainments these stars appeared in were harmless half-parodies anyway, one can hardly raise this idea to the level of irreverence—impudence is surely the highest one can aspire to. *Royal Flash* is no more than a takeoff on *The Prisoner of Zenda,* plus *The Man in the Iron Mask, The Mark of Zorro,* and others of the genre. Why, then, the scathing tone? Lester keeps showing us bawdiness, blood sport, lechery—revelling in trouncing it all. No one else has ever had such a brittle hauteur toward roustabout prankishness. Are the romantics who allow themselves dreams of courage and chivalry really such a serious enemy? Richard Lester's vision of the past is surely no more accurate.

If ever there was a movie director who needed to rediscover simplicity, it's Richard Lester—even more than Ken Russell. These directors overvalue their own fertility; they don't bother timing their gags, or building up to them—they just throw everything together. You can still feel the frenzied joy of sacrilege in Russell's bombast—Russell has kept his relish for little-boy naughty jokes. Lester has no relish left—*Royal Flash* is little-boy humor gone dry. The decorative clutter of his *Musketeer* films was the best thing about them; Lester appeared to be integrating Buster Keaton's visual precision with his own love of scurrilous excess. Here the clutter seems to be merely slovenly filmmaking. The color and the imagery form an irritating pale blur in one's head. The Wagnerian passages on the track sometimes come on with an amusing whoosh of emotion, but Fraser's dialogue—undistinguished at best—is carelessly synched.

Lester uses extravagant Bavarian locations—castles out of fables—and doesn't tip us to where we're supposed to be. He can't hold an idea for more than a few frames; he's too restless to carry anything through.

Watching *Royal Flash* is like flipping the TV dial and seeing brawling and bashing and sword-sticking on every channel. Lester is inventive, all right, but a director with a quarter of his inventiveness and a little warmth would be more entertaining. Probably *Juggernaut* worked better than his other recent films because he could vent his scorn on the numbskull Grand Hotel ship-in-danger plot. He burned the story to a crisp, yet that story gave him the dramatic underpinnings he needed. He doesn't have any here, and he goes through his bag of tricks like a magician with dishpan hands.

There's an element of cruelty in the duelling horseplay. When Oliver Reed, as the Prussian statesman Bismarck, pencils in scars on McDowell's face, there's something nasty in the wait for the slashes we know are coming. And when Florinda Bolkan, as Lola Montez, fights a duel with a fat prima donna and cuts an "L" on the woman's cushy breast, the movie-joke reference to *Zorro* might be funny if we didn't see the blood dripping. Lester seems determined to take the innocence out of his games.

And they are always *his* games. Alastair Sim, the great dissembler himself, turns up (as a lawyer), is given nothing to do, and is gone; as an assassin with an iron arm, Lionel Jeffries manages a shivering, demented stare now and then, but he is barely given an identity, and by the time you spot Tom Bell or Joss Ackland or Michael Hordern they've been disposed of. (I never even noticed Roy Kinnear, though he's listed in the credits.) Richard Lester's style turns actors into objects; he uses them for their surface appearances. It isn't possible for an actor to develop a layered character in the brief gag scenes; the actors perform actions, and that is all. The figures they play may calculate or conspire or leer, but no depth or intelligence is permitted them. Lester's is the mind at work. His attitude toward the actors here seems both mocking and fond—but perhaps fond only because he has got them scaled down to subnormal size. He's carved his "L" on them.

Alan Bates is just a mustachioed villain, and as Flashman's bride, the Duchess Irma, ruler of the mythical Strackenz, Britt Ekland has only one funny bit—she becomes clenched with fright on her wedding night. The Duchess's character is supposed to undergo a transformation from zombie-like pre-marital iciness to post-marital insatiability—not such a very original comic idea, and even danker in the execution. (Madeleine Carroll was funnier in this role in *The Prisoner of Zenda,* without even intending to be.) The only actor Lester appears to respect is Oliver Reed, and maybe that's because Reed is a prize object. What a face he's got for horror films: swinish, contaminated, clammy. Moss grows on that brackish face. And that dirty smirk—he always looks as if someone off camera had just accepted one of his obscene offers and he's already wondering if he can improve on it. Oliver Reed can be lewdly funny, like nobody else, but he isn't here, though since Bismarck is the chief villain, his mean presence dominates the movie. Lester takes comedians and doesn't allow them time to be funny, and he tries to turn Malcolm McDowell and Florinda Bolkan into low comics. McDowell doesn't have the trained agility for physical comedy; his Flashman is just a squirming silly. As for Florinda Bolkan, she's stalwart, like a female Randolph Scott, and when she's trying to be bewitching, each repositioning of the muscles of her face seems to require the services of a derrick.

If anti-heroes have become a far less appealing cliché than heroes ever were, Richard Lester is one of those responsible. *Royal Flash* is so alienating because Lester has done all this carousing and pratfalling before. His inventiveness is beginning to seem desperate, compulsive—as if he kept piling on the jokes because he was bored. There are times when one would swear that he wanted the slapstick unfunny.

[October 13, 1975]

Metaphysical Tarzan

The Werner Herzog film that showed at the New York Film Festival under the title *Every Man for Himself and God Against All* opens this week as *The Mystery of Kaspar Hauser*. Herzog prefaces the images with a quotation from Georg Bücher's short story "Lenz": "Can't you hear that terrible screaming that men call silence?" Yes, I've heard/not heard that sound. It's the scream of one hand clapping. I heard/didn't hear it last at Antonioni's *The Passenger*. It's the sound of garbled, pop-abstract enigmas.

The story of Kaspar Hauser, who appeared in a German town in the 1820s, is a factually based variant of the lost-or-abandoned-child, Mowgli-Tarzan myth; Kaspar wasn't raised among wolves, bears, or apes but, rather, in isolation. In Werner Herzog's nightmare version, Kaspar is a grunting lump of a man, chained in a dungeonlike cellar from infancy. Covered with sores and welts, unable to stand, he is fed by a black-caped man who beats him with a truncheon. One day, the man carries him to a town square and, saying "Wait for me," leaves him there—a catatonic statue, with a letter in his hand. The puzzled townspeople stare at him blankly, then do their best to help him. He is a grown man who has just been born; they consider him mentally defective, but they train him in human habits and try to educate him. As he begins to learn, however, he

51

balks at what he is taught, and becomes obstinate, trying to retain his new, mesmerized pleasure in nature. Before the issues are resolved, he is struck down by the caped figure, who returns, first to maim him, then to murder him. The film is a double fable—intermingling the deadening effects of bourgeois society and the cruelty of the universe.

Werner Herzog has achieved a visionary, overcast style. The higgledy-piggledy pink and blue roofs of the town of Dinkelsbühl, where *The Mystery of Kaspar Hauser* was shot, suggest the world of a German primitive painter, or of an awkward, self-taught puppeteer who has gone a little haywire. The gentle farmlands have something ominous hovering in the atmosphere, and even normal domestic scenes are airless and oppressive. The estrangement is poignant. Herzog's images look off-balance, crooked, as if the cameraman were wincing; there are distances, large vistas, but the perspectives aren't inviting. The universe is enclosed in an invisible hand. Caught in that grip, nobody seems warm-blooded; everyone is alone, immobilized, slightly stiff. Herzog holds shots for a second or two longer than one is used to, so that a character is left with a reaction on his face when what he's reacting to is gone. You're aware of every shot, because each one suggests a visual or emotional displacement. Even the children, who are Kaspar's first teachers, are unnaturally lackluster. You're looking at a drained, dissociated world—a godforsaken world. The hand that holds it belongs to that black figure with the truncheon.

In Hollywood's versions of the Tarzan story, the point was always that the noble savage was superior to civilized man, and Tarzan was played by a handsome, athletic superman. Bruno S., who plays Kaspar, is not a professional actor; he was once believed to be a mental defective himself, and he was the subject of a documentary, *Bruno der Schwarze,* by Lutz Eisholz, in which he talked of his youth as an orphan in reform schools and homes for the retarded. Kaspar, here, is smudgy and top-heavy; he looks physically stunted by his chained-down years. But Werner Herzog is far more of a romantic than Edgar Rice Burroughs ever dared to be. Kaspar seems conceived sculpturally—man being formed out of clay. Rooting in the muck in his dungeon, he shows no fear of his guardian, and he doesn't suffer any visible pain when he's beaten: he doesn't cower, he doesn't cry out. It's not until he walks upright and has experienced the freedom of mingling with flowers and birds that he learns to suffer. At first, Kaspar's responses seem arbitrary and unconvincing, but Bruno S. is never ordinary; as an actor he's as awkward, hallucinatory, and stylized as Herzog is as a filmmaker, and he begins to take hold of the part. His Kaspar has sly, piggy eyes, like Michael J. Pollard in *Bonnie and Clyde,* and a short, piggy nose, yet he's so totally absorbed in experiencing nature, his head thrust out ecstatically, straining to grasp everything he was denied in his cave existence, that he becomes Promethean; the light dawning in that face makes him look like a peasant Beethoven. Kaspar is the only one who hasn't lost his innocent responses to the world about him, who hasn't been blighted by society. He's still got his soul. The film becomes *The Passion of Kaspar Hauser.*

Herzog is a film poet, but he's a didactic poet, and what he has to say is extremely fashionable right now. The film says that society stultifies you under the guise of civilizing you, and that education destroys your innocent, true perceptions. In Truffaut's account of a lost boy, *The Wild Child,* he regarded the boy's pain as necessary if the howling, frightened animal-child was to come into his human heritage; Truffaut cast himself in the role of the doctor who became the boy's teacher and guide. Herzog says that society puts you through the pain in order to deform you, and he makes it absolutely impossible for you to identify with anyone but Kaspar.

Incidents are devised to show how society attempts to degrade him. He is exhibited as a sideshow attraction, along with other sad, dignified figures (they are characters from earlier Herzog pictures), and he and the rest of the freaks run into the countryside to escape and are chased like runaway animals. An effete English lord makes a protégé of Kaspar in order to exhibit him, like a trained ape, to aristocratic society. The representatives of education and church and government are shown to be trapped in their systems of thought and too obtuse to respond to anything spontaneous. A logician poses a conundrum to test Kaspar's mental processes, and rejects Kaspar's perfectly logical answer, because it wasn't the textbook answer. Kaspar is a holy innocent whose wisdom stumps those dummies. (Throughout, Herzog's assumption is that philosophers don't raise the questions that Kaspar does, though they are precisely the questions that philosophers have worried over endlessly.) Typically, Herzog sets up what might be a dramatic situation and then just lets it sit there, flat on; and it can be effective in its formality. He's worst when his purposes are clearly decipherable (as with the logician, or in an even more specious scene involving Kaspar's belief that apples have feelings), because then he's pointing up the idiocy of those who can't understand Kaspar. The local churchmen urge Kaspar to acknowledge that he felt the presence of God when he was still attached to the dungeon floor, and are baffled by his refusal. The town officials make careful records of all the externals of his life but perceive nothing of how he feels. In West Germany, Herzog's folk-art jokes about bourgeois institutions must have special satiric force, but here they seem merely reflections of a popular mood.

The larger ideas come from all over. They're lying around in the pop storehouse of people's heads: ragtags of German Expressionist movies and half a hundred mystical works—the same paraphernalia of the deep which American film students draw on when they ponder the question What is man's destiny on earth? Kaspar, dying, describes the vision he has had; it's ye olde seer's chestnut about the caravan lost in the desert and the blind

Berber who tastes a grain of sand and says "Go north." You may wonder if there were stacks of the *Reader's Digest* in that dungeon. And at the close Kaspar, the outsider who could never be one of the crowd, is a cadaver in the autopsy room; his brain is poked about and dissected, and is certified abnormal. The pedantic little town clerk is overjoyed that at last the mystery of Kaspar Hauser has been solved, and the camera stays on the clerk's figure as he recedes, a limping, dwarflike creature himself, down the zigzag road out of the frame. It's ten-ton irony—Buñuel with lead feet.

Personalizing the unknown in the form of that black-caped murderer, Herzog creates a fable of a demonic universe—"Every Man for Himself and God Against All"—which is just the reverse of the faith that the churchmen want Kaspar to accept. It's Christianity turned upside down, and given a bitter, malignant tinge, but Herzog has found in Kaspar Hauser a new, uncorrupted Christ figure. And then had him martyred all over again. This film was considered by some to be the peak of the Festival, and Herzog is being compared to Buñuel and Bergman, but if it succeeds at all with audiences the reason will be, I think, that it presents a sentimental view of man's natural state. One of the oldest audience-pleasing gimmicks in mass culture is to show the simpleton outwitting the learned. Herzog has given this gimmick a metaphysical framework that could make it appeal to present-day moviegoers who want to believe that the spacey innocents have the answers.

There's something of a contradiction involved in using modern film technology to argue against learning in favor of an innocent response to nature; a filmmaker is not exactly a hewer of wood. Werner Herzog comes as close as he can, though. Like Bergman, he compares himself to the anonymous artisans of Chartres, and he even speaks of his physical relationship to cans of film. A writer-director, he has worked as an individual artist, answerable to himself only, right from the start—with shorts and then with his first feature, *Signs of Life,* in 1967. (Still in his early thirties, he raises the money he needs through scrounging, foreign sales, TV sales, and cash awards from the Bonn government.) His technique owes little to previous commercial films; it doesn't owe very much to previous films of any sort. And there are penalties for working as a self-conscious artist in movies, as there are in the theatre (where it's even less common). A movie or a play has a duration, and a director who has never served a commercial apprenticeship may rhythm his work in ways that seem punishing to an audience. Herzog's pacing may be masterly in terms of his cool, objective, controlled style, but the hour and fifty minutes of this film is a trial for anyone of a restless disposition or an agnostic temperament. You fight to keep your eyes open. Buñuel's best work draws upon irrational sources of humor; Herzog is anti-rational, in an almost self-satisfied way. In Buñuel's world, everyone is alive; there's a raucous, lewd energy in the characters. Herzog's people are unanimated; life is dormant in them. And though one could not fault this in a painter's vision, in a filmmaker's it is numbing.

A pretty fair case can be made for the idea that a little corruption is good for the soul: it humanizes you. Werner Herzog is an artist before he's a human being, and we may experience his dedication to art as a form of priggishness. Bergman may be obsessive, he may be frightfully high-toned, but he's a man of the theatre. In a corner of his mind, Bergman knows there's an audience out there. Herzog has just about everything to be a great film artist but this alchemical element: there's no theatre in his soul. As with Robert Bresson, we can admire Herzog's work abstractly, intellectually, but we may find it perversely academic. A film artist such as the ascetic mystic Bresson expresses his vision through an austere repression of the personalities of the actors, and it can make his films a freezing experience. *Kaspar Hauser* allows Bruno S. to participate creatively, and that gives the film some tension and life, but in Herzog's dedication to film art he denies us the simple pleasures of story involvement, of suspense, of interest in the people on the screen, of sexuality. His goodness saps our strength.

[October 20, 1975]

All for Love

After a two-year break to read and to write, François Truffaut has come back to moviemaking with new assurance, new elation. *The Story of Adèle H.* (the closing-night selection of the New York Film Festival) is a musical, lilting film with a tidal pull to it. It's about a woman who is destroyed by her passion for a man who is indifferent to her—a woman who realizes herself in self-destruction. The only surviving daughter of the writer Victor Hugo, Adèle was sharing his exile in the Channel Islands during the reign of Louis Napoleon when she met the English Lieutenant Pinson, with whom she had a brief affair. When Pinson was transferred to Nova Scotia, she followed him. The film, based on her journals, begins with her arrival in Halifax in 1863—at the high point in her life, when she has had the courage to defy her family and cross the ocean.

A composer as well as a writer, Adèle (Isabelle Adjani) is educated, perceptive, wily; she's not taken in by Lieutenant Pinson (Bruce Robinson). She knows that he's essentially worthless—selfish, mercenary, fickle—and that he doesn't want her. But she constructs an altar to his photograph in the rented room where she waits out months, years. "Love is my religion," she writes in her journal. It may be necessary to this neurotic conception that the love object be himself negligible, even contemptible. How else can she—the gifted daughter of the most famous man in the world—know the full grandeur of self-abasement but with a tinhorn in a flashy uniform? How better punish her father for being a man of great accomplishments than to declare that she cares for nothing but love? By throwing herself in the dirt at the feet of a good-for-nothing, she proves her moral superiority to her father and all his worldly honors. You can see the pride she takes in being the lowliest of the low. With nothing to lose (she has already lost Pinson, before the start of the picture), there's nothing she won't stoop to. He's a gambler, so she bribes him with money. He's a womanizer, so she sends him a whore. All her waking moments are given to planning the blackmailing pressures that the unloved exert on those they claim to love. "Do with me whatever you will!" she cries, but the only thing he wants to do with her is to get rid of her. Spying on him, claiming to be his wife, breaking up an advantageous match he has arranged, turning up to make a scene when he's on maneuvers with his unit, she has him surrounded.

She's an appallingly devious woman, and as it becomes clear that she doesn't care anything about him, that all that matters to her is the purity of *her* feeling toward him, you begin to relate to the hounded Pinson, not because you're concerned for his career but because you can't help recognizing that it's only an accident—a joke, really—that he is the recipient of all this unwanted passionate attention. Weakly ladylike in appearance, Adèle looks a mere maiden—the sort of frail gentlewoman that men would help across the street in bad weather. But out of nowhere some hidden spring will snap, and she'll be rude and peremptory. Truffaut has one gasping at this dainty woman's fearless outrageousness. Adèle isn't a charmer, like Jeanne Moreau's Catherine in *Jules and Jim*; she's a limp, strung-out madwoman, so obsessed with love that she isn't even very sexy. The film doesn't have the raw, playful, sensual lyricism of *Jules and Jim*; it doesn't shift moods in that young, iridescent way. *Adèle H.* is damnably intelligent—almost frighteningly so, like some passages in Russian novels which strip the characters bare. And it's deeply, disharmoniously funny— which Truffaut has never been before. This picture is so totally concentrated on one character that it's a phenomenon: we become as much absorbed in Adèle as she is in Lieutenant Pinson. And our absorption extends from the character to a larger view of the nature of neurotically willed romanticism. The subject of the movie is the self-destructive love that everyone has experienced in one form or another. Adèle is a riveting, great character because she goes all the way with it.

One never for an instant condemns her or pities her. The triumph of *Adèle H.* is that she is a heroine. And, because of that, an archetypal creation. Her unshakable conviction that this one man—Lieutenant Pinson—is the only man for her may be woman's inverse equivalent of the Don Juan, forever chasing. Woman's mania transcends sex; the male mania centers on physical conquest. The woman values the dream of what she's almost had, or what she's had and lost; the Don Juan values only what he's never had. You could draw the connections geometrically: Adèle does what a woman can do to carry her social and biological position to maniacal extremes, and that's what—in male terms—a Don Juan does. Perhaps the one obsessive could intuitively understand the other. (Victor Hugo was an insatiable sexual prodigy right up to the end—a white-bearded satyr, tumbling new women each day.) Don Juanism has often been dealt with on the screen, but no one before Truffaut has ever treated a woman's crippling romantic fixation with such understanding, black humor, and fullness. Truffaut has found an exact visual metaphor for her neurosis. Toward the end of the film, Adèle, still dogging Pinson's footsteps, has followed him to Barbados. Living in the native quarter under the name Mrs. Pinson, she's a wintry wraith, out of place, belonging nowhere. The Lieutenant, now a captain, married, and fearful that her use of his name will cause more trouble for him, confronts her on the street. And she sails by him, as if she were from another world; she seems at peace, insensible to pain, with the calm of exhaustion. She has given herself over to love so completely that the actual man doesn't exist for her anymore. She doesn't even know him. It's inevitable, perfect. She has arrived at her goal.

Only nineteen when the film was shot, Isabelle Adjani is much younger than the woman she's playing. (Adèle Hugo was in her early thirties when she took off after Pinson.) She hardly seems to be doing anything, yet you can't take your eyes off her. You can perceive why Truffaut, who had worked on the Adèle Hugo material off and on for six years, has said that he wouldn't have made this "musical composition for one instrument" without Isabelle Adjani. She has a quality similar to Jean-Pierre Léaud's in *The 400 Blows*—not a physical resemblance but a similar psychological quality. The awareness and intelligence are there, but nothing else is definite yet; the inner life has not yet taken outer form, and so in the movie you see the downy opacity of a face in process, a character taking shape. We keep staring at Adèle to see what that face *means*. She's right for the role, in the way that the young Jennifer Jones was for Bernadette: you believe her capable of anything, because you can't see yet what she is. If the planes of Isabelle Adjani's face were already set in the masklike definition of a famous movie star's face (even child stars can get it), we couldn't have this participatory excitement—the suspense of seeing what Adèle is turning into. Isabelle Adjani has been a professional actress since she was fourteen without tightening; one French director says that she's James Dean come back as a girl. Considering how young she is, her performance here is scarily smart. She knows how to alert us to what Adèle conceals; she's unnaturally quiet and passive, her blue eyes shining too bright in a pale flower face. Truffaut had the instinct not to age her with makeup in the course of the film; we can see that years are passing, but the tokens of time are no more than reddened eyes, a pair of glasses, tangled hair, a torn, bedraggled gown. Aging her would have wrecked the poetry of her final, distraught image, and it's the poetry of the whole conception— the undecorated, pared-to-the-bone poetry—that gives the movie its force. The film is concrete, simple, literal, yet it all works on a metaphorical level. It's an intense, daring vision of the passions that women have kept hidden under a meek exterior. And Isabelle Adjani's soft, plangent quality (along with her trained, outsize talent) makes it possible for Adèle's heroic insanity to seem to explode on the screen.

It's a great film, I think—the only great film from Europe I've seen since *Last Tango*. Thematic ideas that have been plaguing Truffaut have fallen into place—especially the two-sisters theme of his *Two English Girls*. In that film, the girl could not be happy with the man she loved, because he had slept with her older sister, who had died. But Truffaut couldn't seem to express what engaged him in the material, which may have been an unworked-out allusion to the deceased Françoise Dorléac, who had appeared in a Truffaut film, and her younger sister Catherine Deneuve, who subsequently starred for him. It's possible that he was attracted to the story of Adèle Hugo by the fact that Adèle also had an older sister who died. Léopoldine Hugo was drowned at nineteen, along with her young husband, who was trying to save her, and she was temporarily immortalized in commemorative poems by her father; Adèle broke off her own engagement to her sister's husband's brother when she took up with Lieutenant Pinson. This time, however, Truffaut doesn't shy away from the competitive love-hate possibilities of the subject. Adèle is so wan because her energies are spent by violent nightmares: she tosses at sea, crying out as if she were drowning, while Maurice Jaubert's slightly jangling music intensifies the turbulence. (The score is from Jaubert's unpublished compositions—he died before the Second World War.) The water imagery is very powerful throughout. Adèle wrote letters to a brother, which were then transmitted to her father, for whom they were intended, and who replied. Midway in the film, we follow the oceanic trail of these letters; there's no apparent rational motive for this break in the action, yet it's highly effective. Adèle's biggest act of independence was to cross the waters all alone—a journey in bondage to a delusion. *Adèle H.* is her trip, and her divided spirit makes the whole movie vibrate.

Truffaut quoted the Brontës in *Two English Girls*, but this is his Brontë movie—finally brought off because he has given it his own thin-skinned, analytic spirit. His Gothic heroine brought up to date might have been conceived by Edna O'Brien Brontë. Truffaut is romantic *and* ironic: he understands that maybe the only way we can take great romantic love now is as craziness, and that the craziness doesn't cancel out the romanticism—it completes it. Adèle's love isn't corrupted by sanity; she's a great crazy. She carries her love to the point where it consumes everything else in her life, and when she goes mad, it doesn't represent the disintegration of her personality; it is, rather, the final integration. *Adèle H.* is a feat of sustained acuteness, a grand-scale comedy about unrequited love, and it's Truffaut's most passionate work. There's none of the puppyish reticence of several of his recent films. You get a sense of surging happiness from the way the picture moves; the ongoingness—the feeling of being borne on a current—recalls Vigo's *L'Atalante* and the sequence in Renoir's *A Day in the Country* when the flooding river represents the passage of the years. For some time, I've thought that Sven Nykvist was a peerless cinematographer, but on the basis of this film I'd say that Nestor Almendros, who shot it, is right up there with him. Almendros' unusual consistency was memorable in Eric Rohmer's summery *Claire's Knee,* and in *The Wild Child* the radiant orderliness of the interiors was part of the theme. *Adèle H.* is in desaturated, deepened color, with the faces always clear and the bodies swathed in clothing, dark, yet distinctly outlined against the darker backgrounds. It seems to me that I wasn't aware of the sky at any time during the movie. The images are dark on dark, like a Géricault, with the characters' emotional lives brought luminously close.

Adèle gets so close that when you hear the voice of her father answering her letters (she writes home only to ask for money, and to reproach him), you may begin to fantasize about his tone. He is always considerate, obliging, loving, yet somehow the paternal solicitude begins to weigh on one. Isn't he too humane, and impersonally so, as if he were demonstrating what a blameless father he is, and writing letters for the ages? His even-tempered voice from the other side of the ocean sounds very aloof when we're watching Adèle turn into a pile of rags: it cannot be easy to be the daughter (or son, either) of a great man. The godlike constancy of his tone recalls Cocteau's famous remark "Victor Hugo was a madman who believed himself to be Victor Hugo." Adèle Hugo used false names, her sister's name, any name but her own. Maybe she wasn't sure she had a right to it: it was rumored that her godfather, Sainte-Beuve, was actually her father. All the more reason for her to prove that, unlike her mother, and unlike her father, she was pure in her love. When Victor Hugo died, at eighty-three, he was buried like a divinity. His body was exhibited at the Arc de Triomphe, which was draped in black, and the route from the Étoile to the Panthéon, where his coffin was enshrined, was hung with crêpe and with shields bearing the titles of his works. Truffaut shows us photographs of the magnificent turnout: a procession of two million mourners followed the coffin. Adèle was not among them; she spent her last forty years in an asylum, writing in her journal, in code. Victor Hugo is said to have had no equal as a poseur and a mythmaker, but, on Truffaut's evidence, his daughter, who lived to eighty-five, burning with faith to the end, may have surpassed him.

□ □ □

*D*iana Ross doesn't act the starring role in *Mahogany,* she shoots up on it. As Tracy, a secretary from the South Side of Chicago, who becomes the first black model to crack the color bar and goes on to be a whirling international celebrity as well as a terrific haute-couture designer, and then gives it all up to help her black lover, Billy Dee Williams, fight to improve conditions at home, she has an overachiever debauch. (Even her lover's fight is high-level stuff—he's running for Congress.) At the bottom of the white world, Tracy sees vicious hardhats and has to deal with her nastily prejudiced boss, Nina Foch. When she rises to the top of the white world, she finds nothing there but decadence: pawing white lesbians leching for her honest black flesh; scrawny, stiff, stupid white models; Jean-Pierre Aumont as a rich aristocrat who tries to buy her. In between, she's discovered, packaged, and renamed Mahogany by Tony Perkins, a flitting homosexual photographer so impotent with women that he's supine even with Diana Ross. (That's carrying black revenge a bit far.) From Perkins' druggie-male-hustler mannerisms we can tell that he's trying to do something complexly ghastly with the role, but really the picture would be better off if he didn't. He's all too embarrassingly convincing when he's nuzzling Diana Ross's chest, and in the agony-in-the-bedroom scene, and what for? Even in its own recycled-tinsel terms, *Mahogany* is a series of missed opportunities. When the aristocrat wants Diana Ross's ravishingly emaciated body, she goes cold, like the white high priestesses of the Hollywood past; why didn't she do what we had earlier seen her do to a black man tailing her in Chicago—give him a line of brazen filth to turn him off? Diana Ross is almost irresistible when she makes a ribald, jittery style out of high-pitched mock-pickaninny teasing; that high, shrill voice is a soul scream. But this movie thinks it's giving her class when it gives her suffering-great-lady airs. At that, it does better by her than by anybody else; Beah Richards, who plays Tracy's indispensable seamstress, seems to get mislaid—she just evaporates.

Diana Ross's actual packager, Berry Gordy, chairman of the board of Motown Records, put *Mahogany* together after firing the director Tony Richardson, some of whose work remains. Since there is not one well-directed sequence in the entire film, Gordy seems to have had some reason to object to Richardson's work, but what a pity nobody had the power to fire Gordy. The formula is to pour black experience into discarded old-Hollywood molds, hoping for a lurid, jabbing new vitality. Gordy can't get that working from a do-it-yourself kit. Diana Ross could be what many of the black women in the audience clearly want her to be: their Streisand, their Liza Minnelli, their Lana Turner and Stanwyck and Crawford. And she could hold down the movie-queen color bar that she hurtled across in *Lady Sings the Blues*. But *Mahogany* is a brutal setback to her talent. She's a cyclone blowing through this movie: her performance isn't controlled, it isn't shaped, and she has nothing to do but dress up, pose for still shots that look like album covers, and be adorable. She's got her quick, funny, spontaneous style, and that hypnotic looseness—the wriggling, flowing jive movements that no trained screen actress has ever had—but there isn't any attempt at characterization, and she has no depth. Still, Ross doesn't make you want to avert your eyes until she gets the Crawford grimaces in the scenes just before she renounces the rotten life of the white swells. The scenarist (I assume it's John Byrum, who's credited, since the earlier screenplay, by Bob Merrill, isn't credited) tries to doll things up with kicky displays of decadence, and he has her doing a masochistic, writhing strip while holding up a lighted candle and dripping hot wax on herself. Somebody should have taken the lighted wick to Byrum's ideas. The folly of *Mahogany* runs deeper than the script, though. In a movie in which Perkins does his car-wrecking number out of *Phaedra* while Ross is synthesizing shards of Katharine Hepburn in *Woman of the Year,* Audrey Hepburn in *Funny Face,* and Lana Turner in *The Bad and the Beautiful*, it was decided that Ross should be a pure actress and not sing. Instead, she designed the clothes, which seem to be inspired by Chinese-restaurant décor.

In the Broadway movie house where I saw the picture, the black women laughed, shouted, and cheered Diana Ross on, though they didn't seem so happy about her learning her lesson and going home to be a politician's submissive wife. Black women appear to want the forties glamour dazzle that they haven't had before in their image, and they may want it so badly they don't mind the garish, sleazo *Mahogany*. Some of the black men in the audience were groaning, but some of them may accept it, too. However, this regression to outmoded white kitsch is a new ghettoization in the arts. Diana Ross has a mouth with a pout built in, like Lana Turner at her prettiest, and she's got a face-splitting grin like no white star who ever lived. The funkiest beauty the screen has known deserves better than white hand-me-downs.

[October 27, 1975]

Horseplay

Rooster Cogburn, a Western shoot-'em-up produced by Hal Wallis and starring John Wayne and Katharine Hepburn, was filmed in the spectacular scenery of Oregon's Deschutes National Forest and Rogue River area, but it looks as if it had been shot by a tourist with a Brownie. The color, from Universal's back-lot Technicolor lab, is reminiscent of Cinecolor at its most vagrant; the shots don't match, and the long-distance ones are out of focus. This cheesiness might not be so noticeable if the combination of Wayne and Hepburn set up some cross fire, but when they spar it's mortifyingly blunt vaudeville, and their inevitable mutual admiration comes all too coyly soon. He acts the grumpy old dear, and she gives an overeager performance—all arch, anxious charm, and with the resolute, chin-tucked-in, tomboy perkiness made famous by the young Katharine Hepburn and the even younger Shirley Temple. (Her head is wrapped in scarves, as if she had the mumps.) The director, Stuart Millar, can't seem to find a discreet enough distance for the camera: you can tell when Wayne has shifted hairpieces, and for a while he wears one that gives him the inch-and-a-half forehead of a teen-age werewolf.

Wayne wallows in his role, grinning and slopping his big jowls around, and so the character of one-eyed Rooster Cogburn, carried over from *True Grit*, loses the bit of tall-tale fantasy it had: the suggestion that Rooster, the United States marshal feared by badmen, was a relic of a mythic era. There was a moment in *True Grit* when the old fighter galloped into battle, twirling his rifle; the rays of the sun flashed off the spinning metal, and he was a comic deity. There's no myth in *Rooster Cogburn*; it's just a belch from the Nixon era. Rooster is stripped of his badge for being too quick on the trigger (he's killed sixty-four suspects), and the whole picture is a vindication of his methods. He talks like a frontier Spiro Agnew, describing his court-appointed deputies as "them lily-livered law-bookers"; they don't show up to help when he is sent on a special mission to bring in the mean varmint Hawk (Richard Jordan), the leader of a gang of robbers who sell liquor to Indians and then murder them. Hawk kills a saintly reverend who has his mission in the Indian settlement; Hepburn, her role lifted bodily from the 1952 *The African Queen*, is Eula, the missionary's daughter, who has been teaching the Indian children. (In *The African Queen,* when she was forty-four, Hepburn played the missionary's *sister*; the troupe of screenwriters here—including Hal Wallis and his wife, Martha Hyer—who are lumped together under the face-saving pseudonym Martin Julien, seem determined to make her ridiculous.) After Eula's father is murdered, Rooster comes along and takes her with him, and the script forgets all about the orphaned schoolchildren she has shooed off into the tall grass to escape the robbers' gunfire; they may still be there. She and Rooster and a drearily virtuous adolescent Indian boy set off to track down the badmen. Eventually, Wayne and Hepburn get to a perilous river and ride the rapids on their own African Queen—a log raft loaded high with cases of nitroglycerin—while being shot at. Wayne makes goo-goo eyes at her, as the script requires, but you can see what he's really in love with: it's the Gatling gun he's got on the raft. He blasts away with it exultantly—this is lusty man's work. His bluster seems to have got to Richard Jordan, who plays Hawk as a greedy-for-gold mad dog. Popping his eyes, Jordan delivers such beauts as "Nothin's gonna keep me away from that gold! Nothin', ya hear me? Nothin'!" It's an atrocious exhibition from a generally intelligent actor. There are two performers who manage to shine even in this muck. As Breed, an outlaw with a streak of affection for Rooster, Anthony Zerbe is almost as hammy as Jordan at first, but then he pulls in a bit and shows some class. He gives his character a reflective, rueful element that keeps it from getting sticky. But in acting terms the only real hero of the piece is Strother Martin; he's onscreen for just a minute or two, but as the crusty, anti-social old geezer whose raft Rooster commandeers he gives the picture its one burst of vitality. (I began to speculate about what the movie might be like if this old coot were the man Eula was trying to charm. Those girlish wiles wouldn't win *him* over; Hepburn would have to act to hold her own with Strother Martin.) At the end, Rooster and Eula—the lovebirds—make their farewells, giving us to understand that they will soon resume their courting, though these two are hardly at a time of life to postpone romance.

The two principal subjects of the script's attempts at humor are Wayne's gut and Hepburn's age, which is to say that the film tries to make jokes of what it can't hide. This insult badinage would sit a whole lot better if the film weren't at the same time trying to cover for the debilities of the stars. Wayne is supposed to be the match for any gang of outlaws, but when he lurches toward his horse the scene cuts away just as he should be swinging up into the saddle. Hepburn is playing a steely-eyed crack markswoman, but she looks lost—frightened—and she hops about weightlessly, twittering. As it is difficult for her to remain still, or to be seen listening, Wayne is given stale jokes chiding women's talkativeness. We know what John Wayne is doing here; this role is just a further step in the career of a movie star who was never an actor. Once upon a time, he had a great, rugged, photogenic body, and his transparency as an actor—his inability to convey any but the simplest emotions—gave him a frank, American-hero manner. We got used to his gruffness and his sameness; since he's always got by on "naturalness," recently he's been trying to turn his bulk to account, using his huge, puffy face as a Wallace Beery comic mug, and going for softhearted slob effects. There's probably nothing left for him to do but this horseplay. What, however, is Katharine Hepburn doing in this movie—in essentially the same relationship to Rooster Cogburn as the little girl in *True Grit*? Hepburn's ravaged beauty doesn't connect with John Wayne's broad-beamed affability. She was once a defiantly odd actress—curt one moment, exposed the next—and not always popular; now she plays up her oddness. When she goes all breathless with determination to speak her piece and then tells Wayne he's "a credit to the whole male sex," she's drawing upon her reserves of good will, asking us to admire Katharine Hepburn no matter what she's doing.

One wants to believe that in the right roles this great actress could still surprise us—Gladys Cooper found parts that were appropriate. But it's possible that Hepburn is so mannered by now that there's nothing she can play but her younger self. Because of how she looks in *Rooster Cogburn*—shiveringly thin, with that face, which was always tight-skinned over the fine bones, now gone beyond gauntness into some form of gallantry—her performance suggests a bewildered self-parody.

Are people going to accept this movie as a happy low comedy? I suppose some will. There are films that get by because they give people a secure feeling, and people can take in *Rooster Cogburn* the way they take in TV movies—inattentively, satisfied that everything's going according to plan. What they're seeing on the screen is the saga of two rich, world-famous people who are still competing in a popularity contest. If you don't mind seeing indomitable old stars go through their most infantile tricks—snuggling into your favor at whatever cost—you can enjoy *Rooster Cogburn*. The demoralization seems to have gone very far: shouldn't the studio that produced this picture have paid a little attention to how it was mounted? When Eula pleads Rooster's case in a court hearing at the end (and persuades the judge to exonerate him for not taking any prisoners), couldn't Universal afford a few extras, so there'd be some people in the courtroom? There's practically nobody in the whole movie, and if there were, with Universal's color processing you couldn't see them anyway.

□ □ □

*I*f there was any reason for Barry England's play *Conduct Unbecoming* to be filmed, I couldn't discover it in Michael Anderson's movie. The play was a hit in London and had a moderate run on Broadway, in 1970, probably because it has the contrived tautness of a sealed-in courtroom situation, with big themes lurking around; every now and then a line of dialogue pushes a button marked military hypocrisy, or corruption of colonialism, or subterranean sex perversion. The setting is a cavalry outpost in India, in 1878. At the opening, there are troops parading, but that's just for production values; we're really at a play, and the story starts when two characters enter, let us know who they are, and then wait for the next characters to come in the doors. Millington (James Faulkner), a newly arrived junior officer—a dark, long-lashed wastrel who looks a little like Jean Simmons—is bored and wants to be sent home. He makes advances to Mrs. Scarlett (Susannah York), the promiscuous widow of a regimental hero, thinking that that will get him a discharge, but when she is sexually brutalized she says that he did it, and he's in serious trouble. His trial is held in secret so the scandal won't leak out and damage the honor of the regiment. Drake (Michael York), also a new arrival but an exemplary soldier, who has grown up idolizing this regiment, is ordered to defend him and told to make no more than a perfunctory defense. Trevor Howard, Christopher Plummer, Stacy Keach, Richard Attenborough, James Donald, and Michael Culver are in the cast, and this may suggest that the film is impressive, but actually it's a convenience to have all these famous people playing the officers, because you couldn't tell the characters apart if you didn't recognize the actors. Enunciating their stage dialogue in professional, letter-perfect fashion, they keep the film at a tolerable level, but there's not a new performance from any of them. Anderson's staging is barely functional, and the actors keep stoking the plot. It turns out that the assault was uglier than we had at first supposed. The officers have a sport—pigsticking a stuffed pig on wheels—and it seems that Mrs. Scarlett, and another regimental widow, have been jabbed with a saber as if they were the pig. We wait to find out who the assailant really was, and why Mrs. Scarlett is protecting him by accusing Millington.

Eventually, Millington is cleared, and he undergoes a character change (as people used to do in well-made plays). He's transformed from a ne'er-do-well cynic to an officer proud to be accepted by the other men, while Drake, his courageous defender (and the central character), loses his innocence about regimental honor and, clearheaded, resigns his commission. Is anybody really interested in this kind of neat dramaturgy? In *Conduct Unbecoming,* the neatness is fake anyway. We've never had a clue as to why Millington took such a cynically bored view to start with, and what exactly has soured Drake, since justice did win out? Because nothing basic about the military is actually revealed in the trial, his resignation seems no more than a wounded idealist's pique. And when Stacy Keach, as the captain in charge of the trial, shifts from heavy villainy of the no-neck, powerful-malignity variety to confused good intentions, it's as if Keach had flipped a page in the script and suddenly discovered he'd got the character all wrong. The big letdown of the film is that when, after much hocus-pocus and hushed talk and dimming of lamps, we find out who the pervert really is, we can't see why the women didn't name him to start with, or why he gave the trial testimony that he did. The only thing that held us was the promise of a logical solution, and we've been betrayed.

So what is the point? Is the attack on Mrs. Scarlett an illuminating metaphor for the rot of imperialism, or is it just a kinked-up gimmick for a courtroom-chat drama? Susannah York gives one of her lewd-mouthed, flirty performances; the invitation "You can get dirty with me" is spelled out in her lipwetting smiles. During the court-martial she pushes a women's-lib button, crying out that all the men in the regiment treat women like pigs, but this doesn't relate to anything that we can observe. The final explanation of why the psychopath has attacked her is so farfetched Gothic (involving schizophrenia and "possession" by a dead man) that it can hardly be politicized. *Conduct Unbecoming* doesn't begin to know what it's about.

□ □ □

*L*et's Do It Again is like a black child's version of *The Sting*—an innocent, cheerful farce about an Atlanta milkman (Sidney Poitier) and a factory worker (Bill Cosby) who go to New Orleans and pull off a great scam. They outwit the black mobsters (John Amos, Julius Harris, and Calvin Lockhart) and win enough money for their lodge back home, The Sons and Daughters of Shaka, to put up a new meeting hall. Nobody is hurt, and everybody who deserves a comeuppance gets it. Their con involves hypnotizing a spindly prizefighter, played by Jimmie Walker, of TV's "Good Times," in his first screen role. The elder of their lodge (it's their church, too—as if it were the Benevolent and Protective Order of Muslim Elks) is played by Ossie Davis; and the cast also includes such well-known black performers as Mel Stewart, playing the fighter's manager, Denise Nicholas and Lee Chamberlin, as the heroes' wives, and George Foreman. The film was scored by Curtis Mayfield, and the rather patchy script was written by a black scenarist, Richard Wesley.

It's apparent why Sidney Poitier set this project in motion and directed it: he's making films for black audiences that aren't exploitation films. *Let's Do It Again* is a warm, throwaway slapstick, and the two leads are conceived as black versions of Bing Crosby and Bob Hope in the *Road* series. Poitier is trying to make it possible for ordinary, lower-middle-class black people to see themselves on the screen and have a good time. The only thing that makes the film remarkable is that Poitier—who has been such a confident actor in the dozens of roles he has played under other people's direction since his first film, in 1949—gives an embarrassed, inhibited performance. As casual, lighthearted straight man to Bill Cosby, he is trying to be something alien to his nature. He has too much pride and too much reserve for low comedy.

Clearly Poitier is doing something that he profoundly believes in, and there can't be any doubt that he is giving the black audience entertainment that it wants and has never had before. Probably there was no one else who was in a position to accomplish this. One cannot simply say that he is wrong to do it. Many groups have been demanding fantasies in their own image, and if this often seems a demand for a debased pop culture, still it comes out of a sense of deprivation. But for an actor of Sidney Poitier's intensity and grace to provide this kind of entertainment is the sacrifice of a major screen artist. In a larger sense, he's doing what the milkman is doing in the movie: swindling like a Robin Hood, for the good of his lodge, his church. But it's himself Poitier is robbing. For Bill Cosby, snug in a beard, there's no sacrifice. Cosby doesn't feel that the hipster he's playing is a degrading stereotype, and so the way he plays it it isn't. He has to be a family-picture hipster, but Cosby is spaced out on his own innocent amiability anyway. He's so little-boy antsy that when he stands still he can't resist mugging; it's all right, though, because he's floating along. The format here is too repressive for him to fly, but Poitier lets him run away with the show; maybe he's allowed to be a little too disarming, too droll—which is always a danger for Cosby. As a director, Poitier is overly generous with the actors: he isn't skilled enough to shape sequences so that the actors can benefit from their closeups (nobody could benefit from all those tacky reaction shots). Jimmie Walker is used unimaginatively, but he's well cast—you can't help wanting him to win his fights, and he has a Muhammad Ali routine in his dressing room, shouting "I am the champ," that is very funny. Ossie Davis has one lush moment: at the feast celebrating the opening of the new meeting hall, he eats his chicken with ceremonial pleasure, and in his great rumbling basso announces, "I tell you, I knew this bird from another life."

It's not a disgraceful movie—I liked the people on the screen better than I liked the people in *The Sting*—but what I can't get out of my head is the image of Sidney Poitier doing primitive-fear double takes, like Willie Best in the old days, only more woodenly. For the fact is that black audiences roar in delight at the very same stereotypes that have been denounced in recent years. It's true that the context is different in these movies, but the frozen, saucer-eyed expressions when Poitier and Cosby are caught doing something naughty or something they can't explain go right back to little Farina in the *Our Gang* comedies. *Let's Do It Again* isn't the first of Poitier's two-black-buddies features: he also directed and appeared in *Buck and the Preacher* and *Uptown Saturday Night*. It amounts to a doggedly persistent skewering of his own talent. What a strange phenomenon it is that the actor who rose through sheer skill and became as elegant as a black Cary Grant should now, out of his deepest conviction, be playing a milkman, bug-eyed with comic terror, hanging outside a window by a sheet. And looking sick with humiliation. If Ralph Ellison were to found a new, black-oriented *Saturday Evening Post* and write innocuous stories for it, he might find that he had less talent for light fiction than dozens of writers who couldn't write anything else. Poitier is fighting what he's doing with every muscle of his body; he's fighting his own actor's instinct, which is telling him that this cartoon role is all wrong for him.

Poitier has always had drama going on under the surface of his roles—you could sense the pressures, the intelligence, and the tension of self-control in his characters; that's part of why he became the idealized representative of black people. Now he's trying to make himself an ordinary black man, in comic fantasies for black audiences. But in low comedy you have to abandon yourself and be totally what you are; you can't have a sense of responsibility under the character—or banked fires, either—and be funny. And so this vivid, beautiful actor casts himself as the square, because he knows that in slapstick he comes across unhip. He can't even hold the screen: he loses the dynamism that made him a star. Sidney Poitier, who was able to bring new, angry dignity to black screen acting because of the angry dignity inside him, is violating his very essence as a gift to his people.

[November 3, 1975]

A Dream of Women

The color imagery of Satyajit Ray's *Distant Thunder* is so expressive that I regretted the need to look down to the subtitles; it took precious time away from the faces and bodies, with their hint of something passive, self-absorbed—a narcissism of the flesh. The setting is a torpid Bengali village in the early 1940s. Gangacharan (Soumitra Chatterji), a newly arrived Brahmin, is the only educated man for miles around; he's the schoolteacher, the priest, the doctor. The ignorant villagers treat him with reverence. "You are the jewel in our crown," they tell him, and he agrees. His condescension is all of a piece with his umbrella, his mustache and specs, and his preoccupied manner. He strokes himself in the moist, wilting

heat; he sucks on a water pipe, inhaling wherever he goes—Gangacharan
wants every kind of gratification he can get.

Soumitra Chatterji, Ray's one-man stock company, moves so differently in the different roles he plays that he's almost unrecognizable. He
was the passionately romantic Apu in the last film of the trilogy, the
husband in *Devi,* the suitor in tartan socks and English boots in *Two
Daughters,* the guest in *Charulata,* the handsome, arrogant leader of the
four young men in *Days and Nights in the Forest.* At first, his Gangacharan
is almost physically dislikable—thin yet flabby, contemptuously pedantic;
in the course of the film, as the feudal system that sustains this contempt is
eroded, his body seems to change. The Second World War, which is so
remote from the villagers that they don't know who is fighting, destroys the
traditions that bind the community. The area is idyllically lush, but it isn't
self-sufficient. When faraway supply ports for grain fall to the Japanese,
and large shipments of food are needed for the Army, the price of rice
soars. Speculators send it higher, and starvation and cholera will shortly
follow. Famine approaches with the force of a natural disaster; the villagers
are helpless.

During the early stages, the light is so soft, and the lily pads, the flying
insects, the bathing women are so tranquil, that even when the women are
hungry and picking snails out of the mud or digging for wild potatoes, the
images are still harmonious. The film is delicately, ambiguously beautiful;
the shadowing comes from our knowledge—and Gangacharan's
knowledge—that the people we're looking at are endangered. It is a lyric
chronicle of a way of life just before its extinction, and Ray gives the action
the distilled, meditative expressiveness that he alone of all directors seems
able to give. We're looking at something that we feel is already gone, and
so the images throb. Or is it that *we* do? It comes to the same thing.

Whether intentionally or not, Ray has put something of himself into
Gangacharan—of his own sense of guilt, of weakness, and of commitment.
And something even more personal—his seeing the beauty in the Indian
past almost completely in the women. The men in this village are ignorant
and obsequious, and physically very unprepossessing; the rich ones hoard
and profiteer, the poor panic, become violent, riot. But the women are
conceived of as in a dream of the past—they might be iridescent figures on
a vase. These women are uneducated and superstitious, they know nothing
of the world outside; yet they're tender and infinitely graceful. Moving in
their thin, clinging saris, they create sensuous waves of color in the steamy
air. Gangacharan's bride, Ananga, is innocently childlike, undulant,
luscious, with a pouty ripe-pink underlip; the brilliant orange-red spot in
the middle of her forehead is like a cosmic beauty mark. Played by the
actress Babita (that should mean Baby Doll), Ananga is the Indian version
of a Hollywood darling. She seems to have been created for the pleasure of

men; she has been bred to think of nothing but her husband, and she finds her pride and her fulfillment in pleasing him. She wants to be a tempting morsel so that her husband can take a juicy bite.

Ananga is just the ornament to his existence that this preening Brahmin would have found; everything in the society appears to be designed to assuage his ego. Yet he's intelligent, and he's not a bad fellow—merely infantile. When he realizes that he can't fulfill his end of the bargain, and his wife must do demeaning work to get food for them, the whole basis of their relationship changes. Gangacharan begins to care about someone besides himself. He loves her now not because she takes care of him but because of how she feels about taking care of him. There are other actresses in the film with a fine-grained quality that goes beyond Babita's almost pornographic charm—the one who plays Moti, the Untouchable, and another who plays a woman who gives Gangacharan food to take home to his wife. They, too, are gentle and undemanding—ideal traditional women.

Ray is one of the most conscious artists who ever lived, and in this film he means to show us the subservient status of women; the children Gangacharan teaches (by rote, drumming information into them) are, of course, all boys. The women remain illiterate, and locked into the vestiges of the caste system—Ananga and Moti are friends, but if they touch each other Ananga bathes. However, I wonder if Ray realizes the degree to which he shows a deep-seated distrust of Indian men and an equally deep trust in the selflessness of women. (Even Ananga's friend Chhutki, who trades her favors for food—giving herself to a hideously scarred kiln worker—wants to share the rice she gets.) Ray is not a vulgar chauvinist, exalting subservient women; quite the contrary. While the men in his films are weak and easily flattered—dupes, self-deceived by vanity and ambition—the women have conflicts that are larger, more dignified, involving a need for love, for independence, for self-expression. They are morally stronger than the men. This may, in part, reflect a belief that the women, having always been in a subservient position, were not corrupted by English rule in the way that the men were.

Still, in *Distant Thunder,* in a village far removed from that emasculating Anglicization, Ray perceives the women with such love that they become figures in a vision, and since he sees the men without that etherealizing intensity, there's an imbalance—poetry and prose. In the Apu trilogy, the hero was the embodiment of poetry, but here it is only at the end, when Gangacharan accepts a group of famine victims as his family, that he becomes as compassionate (and as fully human) as the women were all along. For Ray, the source of their strength is humility. And although one wouldn't propose any other course of action for Gangacharan, the way Ray sees him—made whole by his passive, chivalrous acceptance of what's coming—suggests a rather attenuated attempt at universalizing his situation. Satyajit Ray has rarely before dabbled in having his characters do what he so obviously believes is symbolically right; you expect a faint white light to begin whirring around Gangacharan's head. And when, with famine victims approaching their home, Ananga, with a shy, flirtatious smile of pride, speaks of the child she is carrying, this, too, seems to be symbolic of endurance in the midst of extreme adversity.

The music, which Ray composed, is also used portentously, signalling "distant thunder." And Ray has developed an alarming affection for melodramatic angles and zoom-fast closeups; when there's a violent action—the scarred man's overtures to Chhutki, or a rapist's assault on Ananga—he wants us to feel the dislocation. But it's intrusive, pushy; his style can't accommodate this visual abrasion. When a movie director suddenly loses his tact, he can shock viewers right out of the movie: cameras are cruel to the disfigured, and when Ray forces us to look close at the enlarged burned face of the kiln worker, we don't understand why. He's introduced like a Quasimodo, and though the more we see him, the easier it is to look at him, his becoming more sympathetic—so that we notice how attractive the good side of his face is—is too pedagogic, too symbolic. The rapist appears even more abruptly; we don't see his face—all we know about him is that he smokes cigarettes, like a Westerner. He remains a plot device, an illustration of the horrors these women experience, and hide, guiltily. Ray's use of emphatic techniques to heighten the impact of his material actually lowers it. When Ananga first mistakes planes flying overhead for insects, that's naïve and halfway acceptable, but when, later, the noise of the planes drowns out her screams as she's being raped, that's ladling it on. The ironies are too charged, as in the situations that American television writers come up with; this cleverness is the dramatist's form of yellow journalism. In Ray's work, what remains inarticulate is what we remember; what is articulated seems reduced, ordinary.

Distant Thunder is not one of his greatest films, yet it's still a Satyajit Ray film, and in how many directors' films does one anticipate greatness? With Ray, you puzzle if a picture is a little less than a masterpiece. If this one lacks the undertones of a *Days and Nights in the Forest,* it's probably because he's trying to do something that sounds straightforward but isn't quite clearly thought out. Ray wants to show us how war changes people (Bergman brought it off in *Shame*), but he also wants to make an indictment. And somehow he fails on both counts. Probably he fails on the first because he doesn't endow the villagers with enough complexity. And maybe he didn't think of them in complex enough terms because he had that second, social purpose in mind. When Gangacharan learns political lessons—when he discovers that what's wrong is that "the peasants do all the work and we live off them"—it's just plain fake. Gangacharan's sponging off the peasants—in the sense that he served them with bad grace, contemptuously, demanding a little more than was fair—is hardly a factor in the starvation. When we get the closing title, telling us that five million Bengalis died in the man-made famine of 1943, Ray uses the term "man-made" because it implies that the famine was a crime. But it looks more like a horrible pileup of accidents, plus some criminal greed, and thousands of years of no planning. His statement seems forced; his whole structure is forced, and yet the film is astonishingly beautiful. The character of Gangacharan—a mixture of slothful peacefulness and a sense of dissatisfaction which he takes out on the peasants and an inquisitive, modern mind—is a fine creation, except for terminal loftiness. And there's also a character Ray can't quite get a grip on: a beggar Brahmin with a gap-toothed rabbity smile that Gangacharan calls sly. It's that, and worse. Throughout the movie, whenever he appears, he seems to suck life away. He creates the most disturbing images, maybe because Ray sees him as both the life force and as dirty Death itself. At the end, it's he who arrives with his tribe of dependents—eight in all—to join Gangacharan's household. With his rags hanging on him and his staff in his hand, he's all four horsemen rolled into one. In the final image, the silhouetted figures of this old man leading his family are extended into a procession of the starving advancing on us. It's a poster design, and yet we're also prey to unresolved feelings about that sly beggar. The film is more puzzling than it seems at first; Ray is such an imagist that even his poster art slips into ambiguities.

I don't know when I've been so moved by a picture that I knew was riddled with flaws. It must be that Ray's vision comes out of so much hurt and guilt and love that the feeling pours over all the cracks in *Distant Thunder* and seals them up.

[November 10, 1975]

Walking into Your Childhood

Since the only thing about reviewing movies that makes me unhappy is that I can't get to the opera often enough, Ingmar Bergman's film version of *The Magic Flute* is a blissful present. Filmed operas generally "open out" the action or else place us as if we were spectators at a

72

performance, looking at the entire stage. Bergman has done neither—he has moved into the stage. He emphasizes the theatricality of the piece, using space as stage space, but with the camera coming in close. We get the pixillated feeling that we're near enough to touch the person who is singing; we might be dreamers sailing invisibly among the guests at a cloud-borne party. Bergman has often delighted in including little plays (plummy satires of stage acting) within his movies, and even movies (silent slapstick comedies) within his movies. He's used them not only to comment on his characters and themes but also for the joy of re-creating different performing styles. This time, the play inside the movie has become the movie, and he's sustained his ironic juggling all the way through. He can use what he knows (and loves) about the theatre.

Although the film was actually made in a studio, it is set within the Drottningholm Court Theatre, and at the beginning we see details of the baroque décor. Bergman retains the sense of the magical theatrical machinery of Mozart's time. When the three cherubim ascend in the basket of a balloon, the ropes don't move smoothly, and all through the film he calls our attention to toy moons and suns, to trick entrances, to what's going on backstage. We get the story of the performance as well as the story of the opera. The dragon who threatens Prince Tamino prances for applause; the three flirty temptresses who compete for Tamino also compete for the audience's approval. For Bergman, who says that he usually doesn't begin to write a part until he knows who's going to play it, it must have been like a game to find the singers he did, who look the roles to perfection. He must have used everything he's learned about how to get actors to trust him, because they act as if working in front of the camera were a natural thing. They don't have the wild-eyed dislocation of so many singers—that crazed stare that seems to be their amazed response to the sounds coming out of them. Those cherubim are the most winning cast members; they're three rosy-cheeked Pucks yet three child hams, and Bergman wants us to see the conscious pleasure they take in performing. They sing as if each note marked the happiest moment in their lives; you absolutely can't not grin at them.

Unlike *Don Giovanni* or *Così Fan Tutte, The Magic Flute,* Mozart's last opera, makes a special claim on one's affections, because its libretto is high camp. It's a peerlessly silly masterpiece: sublimely lucid music arising out of a parodistic fairy tale that celebrates in all seriousness the exalted brotherhood of the Freemasons. In most of the first act, the story seems to be a conventional romantic quest—a fairy Queen of the Night sends Prince Tamino to rescue her daughter, Pamina, from the evil sorcerer, Sarastro, who is holding her by force. But by the time the second act was written, Mozart and Schikaneder, his librettist, had shifted directions, and now Sarastro is the lord of enlightenment, High Priest of the Temple of Wisdom, and he's protecting Pamina from her demonic mother. This confusion arising from the belated decision to convert a fairy tale into a story about the mystic brotherhood (Mozart was a Mason) seems to add to rather than take away from the opera; the confusion serves as an ironic comment on the tangled stories of most librettos. In Bergman's version, Sarastro is Pamina's father—which does give the conflict between him and the Queen more substance, and even a bit of logic.

One could, if one wished, see all Bergman's themes in this opera, because it is a dream play, with many of the same motifs as *Smiles of a Summer Night*, *The Seventh Seal*, *Wild Strawberries*, and *Cries and Whispers*. In *Wild Strawberries*, the doctor, Isak Borg (I.B., like Ingmar Bergman), walked into his childhood, and that's what Bergman is doing here. But he isn't doing it realistically this time. In *The Magic Flute*, the need for love, the suicidal despair of loneliness, ambivalent feelings about one's parents, the fear of death are already ritualized, so Bergman can play with them, in mythological fantasy form. *The Magic Flute* takes place in a philosophical bubble in which you recognize your love—your other half—at once, because the names are in pairs. It's heavenly simplicity, in parody: Tamino is sent to rescue Pamina, and he's accompanied by the bird-catcher Papageno, who finds his Papagena. We know that we should identify with Prince Tamino—he's the pure-at-heart hero of legend, and Bergman has found a tenor (Josef Köstlinger) who looks like the handsome knights in the storybooks of one's childhood—but in *The Magic Flute* nothing works quite the way it's meant to, and it comes out better. Tamino goes through the trials and performs all the proper deeds, but he's a storybook stiff compared to Papageno, who flubs his tests. There's a lesson implicit in Tamino's steadfastness: he accepts his responsibilities and earns his manhood. But Papageno doesn't want responsibility—he just wants pleasure. He'll never be a "man"—he's an impetuous kid, a gamin, a folk hero. I think the reason Papageno isn't tiresome, like other buffoonish-everyman squires (and I include Sancho Panza), must be that he hasn't been burdened with practical, "earthy" wisdom; he's too goosy for that. He has his own purity—he's pure, impulsive id. Although Papageno isn't initiated into the priestly brotherhood with Tamino, and so will presumably never experience the divine wisdom of the consecrated, he is forgiven for his flimsy virtue. Papageno doesn't earn his prize, but he gets it anyway: his Papagena is easy as pie, a pushover, as carnally eager as he.

The brotherhood is clearly strictly male; like Papageno, women are considered too talkative. But Bergman tries to integrate the order by including women, from nowhere, among the men at the final ceremonial, when Sarastro retires as the leader, putting his spiritual kingdom in the hands of Tamino and Pamina. Bergman's gesture is understandable but a bit specious. The opera is based on strict polarities, turning on male-female. The Queen of the Night (Birgit Nordin) is a glittering coloratura harpy, served by witches-in-training, while Sarastro, the deep, friendly bass (Ulrik Cold, whose face belies his name), and his priests stand for sunlight, justice, and reason. Not surprisingly, the Queen and her vamps are a delight, while Bergman has to use all his ingenuity to keep the solemn priests from grinding the show to a halt. This is where his cinematographer, Sven Nykvist, turns wizard; since a film of *The Magic Flute* wasn't expected to create pandemonium at box offices around the world, it had to be shot in 16-mm., yet Nykvist got such extraordinary quality that even in the 35-mm. blowup for theatres there's a tactile dimension to the contrasting forces. This saves the dignified temple scenes, which are dull stretches in most live performances. Sarastro's dark-eyed, sympathetic face looks as if it would be warm to the touch, and Bergman's emblematic composition of two overlapping faces—used here for father and daughter—adds psychological shading to Sarastro's stepping down from his office. Though Sarastro defeats the nightmare-canary Queen (whose high trilling is a wickedly funny vocal metaphor for neurosis), the ending represents a new harmony of male and female, with joint rule by Tamino and Pamina. The melodic line of this opera, with its arias of men and women yearning for each other, is one of the rare perfect expressions of man-woman love.

The Magic Flute is a fairy tale that is also a parody of fairy tales; the libretto says that when you have your counterpart you'll never be lonely again. The working out of the story is so playful that you never forget you're in an enchanted landscape, yet the music—airily poignant— expresses the passionate desire for all this seraphic happiness to be true. The music is the distillation of our giddy longing for ideal romantic consummation; when we listen, we believe that there are partners ordained for us. *The Magic Flute* is a love poem that teases love; the women's costumes, cut low, show off the plushiest soft bosoms—it's all a teasing dream. The emotional quality of the music—delirium expressed in perfectly controlled, harmonious phrasing—may perhaps be compared to the flights of language in *A Midsummer Night's Dream,* but this music bypasses the mind altogether and goes right to the melancholy, rhapsodic core. *The Magic Flute* is about love as the conquest of death—and about love of the theatre as the conquest of death.

Eric Ericson conducts the Swedish State Broadcasting Network Symphony; the voices may not have the depth of feeling—that special rounded sweetness—that Dietrich Fischer-Dieskau, as Papageno, and Fritz Wunderlich, as Tamino, bring to the Deutsche Grammophon recording, with Karl Böhm conducting the Berlin Philharmonic, but they're wonderful enough, and Håkan Hagegård, who has a bright-eyed, crooked-toothed smile, is just what one wants Papageno to look like and to act like. Bergman was able to spare us the usual views of tongues and tonsils by having Ericson record the score first (in Swedish, which sounds remarkably pleasing), then playing it bit by bit while photographing the singers, who move their mouths in a more genteel manner than is feasible in actual performance. The synchronization is as close to impeccable as seems humanly possible.

The Magic Flute uses to the fullest that side of Bergman which I missed in *Scenes from a Marriage* (and I saw the complete, six-episode TV version). The telegraphic naturalism of that film seemed condescending, as if it represented Bergman's vision of how ordinary, uncreative people live; I responded most to the few minutes when Bibi Andersson was onscreen, because she appears to be closer in spirit to Bergman—she expresses the tensions of intelligence. Bergman seems more complexly involved in *The Magic Flute,* with only one exception: in the framing device, when he goes outside ironic theatricality to documentary-style shots of the "audience." During the overture and at the break between the acts, and a few times during the opera itself, he gives us family-of-man portraits of this audience, with special emphasis on a celestial-eyed little girl. The faces tell us that people of all ages, colors, and creeds enjoy Mozart; it's fiercely banal, like his sticking those modern youths in *Wild Strawberries* so we'd have something to identify with. This production, which is apparently the consummation of a dream Bergman has had for more than two decades, was financed to commemorate fifty years of Swedish broadcasting, and was presented on both Swedish and Danish television last New Year's Day. His cutting to the reactions of that princessy little girl, whom one wants to strangle, suggests that the production is designed to introduce opera to children. Some years back, I found *The Magic Flute* a wonderful first opera to take a child to, but for Bergman to institutionalize this approach—treating *The Magic Flute* as if it were *Peter and the Wolf*—devalues the opera and what he has done with it. He's undersold himself, for, apart from this visual platitudinizing, the picture is a model of how opera can be filmed. The English translation of Bergman's adaptation (he clarifies the text) is graceful, and the titles are unusually well placed on the frame. Having the titles there in front of you, you follow the libretto without losing anything; the story comes across even more directly than when you hear the opera sung in English. Bergman must have reached a new, serene assurance to have tackled this sensuous, luxuriant opera that has bewildered so many stage directors, and to have brought it off so unaffectedly. It's a wholly unfussy production, with the bloom still on it. He recently said, "Making the film was the best time of my life. You can't imagine what it is like to have Mozart's music in the studio every day." Actually, watching the movie, we can.

□ □ □

*T*he Sunshine Boys is Neil Simon's variation on his own *The Odd Couple*; this time it's the old couple—a vaudeville team, Lewis (George Burns) and

Clark (Walter Matthau), who, eleven years back, broke up after forty-three years and haven't spoken to each other since. Decrepit, semi-senile, Lewis and Clark are brought together again to appear on a big TV special. It's a risky play to have attempted to put on the screen—a small play, no more than an extended sketch, a Broadway Jewish version of what John Gielgud and Ralph Richardson did in *Home.* Cracking jokes has become a reflex for these ancient clowns, and the play itself is written in the form of rapid-fire one-liners—snappers as routinized as the doctor-patient question-and-answer routine they did eleven thousand times on the stage. We know that they always fought in the past, we're briefed on what they fought about, and we wait for the inevitable. They're walking into their second childhood; if anything could make this situation funny, it would have to be supreme timing.

Richard Benjamin is the unlucky actor who wound up playing Matthau's agent-nephew, who arranges the TV-show reunion. His role is really that of a matchmaker, and Neil Simon (who also did the adaptation) hasn't provided even halfway plausible pretexts for his actions. Benjamin is obliged to run around in such hysterical devotion to his uncle that he gets chest pains from being upset, yet he must always take off when he's most needed, so the doddering old men can have their flareups and mishaps. Matthau is supposed to be the aggressive, energetic member of the team—the one who wanted to go on when his partner was tired of the act. But there's none of the old vaudevillian's spring to his movement, no élan to his compulsive jokes, and his chinlessness and stooped-over walk are tedious. Matthau needs his swaggering height and the forelock on his face; he needs to be sneakily adroit, scruffy yet suave. Here he seems to depend almost entirely on that bullhorn voice, which keeps blasting us.

George Burns's Lewis has the repose of a tortoise, his eyes gleaming and alert; he has a rhythmed formality in his conversation, as a trouper of his generation might. Burns creates the only character in the movie—or, at least, an impersonation of a character. He can't quite bring it to life, because Simon provides no levels for Lewis—no vitals, no insides. We're tipped that as soon as the partners start their act, Lewis will ram his forefinger into Clark's chest and spit at him. But Burns's Lewis seems so gentle and rational that we don't know where this calculated aggression comes from; it almost seems as if he were acting out Clark's paranoia. What was needed, I think, was for Lewis to turn into a different person as soon as he was rehearsing or onstage—for something wild to break out of him, some domineering, manic charge.

All along, we're cued to recognize that underneath the fraternal hatred Lewis and Clark show for each other there's fraternal love—and Clark comes right out with it: "One person, that's what we were." We imagine that when we see their act we'll feel the love between them, and not a personal love so much as a fellowship of the theatre, a glorious, idiotic joy in performance. Because if their act doesn't have the effortless snap of two people who transcend their crabbing and become a magical team onstage, what have we been watching them for? What is the meaning of the title *The Sunshine Boys* if the daily meannesses don't turn into something happy onstage? Is it no more than a sour irony? When Lewis and Clark finally do their act at a dress rehearsal at the television studios, and it's cloddishly unfunny, we feel confused, let down. What it says to us is that Neil Simon cannot believe that the show business of which he's a kingly part has any possibility of transcendence. He thinks he's being honest and authentic when he shows these famous vaudevillians to be klutzes. It's a twist on the usual show-biz sentimentality: his Pagliaccios crack jokes to hide their misery and can't even make people laugh.

The film collapses when the two men quarrel during the TV rehearsal and don't even finish their act. After that, Simon, having failed to give the material the climactic lift it needed, uses every bit of shtick he can dredge up to keep the picture going: a heart attack for Matthau's Clark, Lewis devotedly sending flowers and candy, the prospect of the two reunited in a home for old actors. It's all sentimental friendship, as if their decades of quarrelling—and Lewis's final round of poking and spitting, which causes Clark's heart attack—had been nothing but the stubborn irascibility of two dear old codgers. Simon has refused to make them talented, as if that would be sentimentalizing show business, but he has no compunction about sentimentalizing their relationship. In his "light" comedies, Simon fills a stage with soreheads who get upset over little things, and he keeps the jokes coming. When he's dissatisfied with that and wants to write a more serious play (like *The Sunshine Boys*), he makes the people despondent cranks—glum, out-of-work, moping wet blankets. And so the more serious his plays are, the worse they are. You can convert dissatisfaction, quarrelsomeness, and outright meanness into vaudeville but not into drama.

However, you can't even convert them into vaudeville with Herbert Ross directing. There's a comic tradition behind this gag material; we ought to be able to respond to *The Sunshine Boys* as if it were a berserk ballet, and Ross's background as a choreographer should have helped. But the worst thing you can do with broad stage comedy is to play it close to the camera, belting the audience, and that's what he does: he uses shouting in place of timing, and each line crashes on its own. A gag such as Matthau's repeated struggle with the lock on his hotel-room door needs to become a *number*; merely repeated, it's contemptible. As a director, Ross is an unintentional minimalist; he just doesn't seem to have many ideas, and he's negligent in handling the simplest movie setups. When Matthau yells and carries on at the Friars Club, no one in the background even looks up at him—Matthau's histrionics might be taking place in a void. When he has his backstage heart-attack scene, Ross can't summon up any reactions.

Maybe what's missing in Ross is a feeling for the craziness in vaudeville shtick; under his direction, it becomes loudmouthed New York abrasiveness.

I'm a very easy laugher, and I didn't laugh once at *The Sunshine Boys*. The only part of the movie I enjoyed was the footage during the titles—clips of vaudeville headliners from early short subjects and *Hollywood Revue of 1929*. The clips went by all too fast—dozens of old stars, and then, surprisingly, Arthur Freed. (There's a little inside joke involved here: Freed and Nacio Herb Brown wrote the song "Singin' in the Rain" for that 1929 revue, and in 1952, for the movie *Singin' in the Rain*, they wrote "Make 'Em Laugh," which is the theme song for the opening of this picture.) Why, with this opening, and with the talk all the way through of the greatness of Lewis and Clark and their place in theatrical history (the ten thousand dollars that ABC is offering them to do their old act for the special is probably the funniest joke in the movie), are they made so lousy? The meaning of the movie seems to be that show-business people aren't artists but, since they're depressed and quarrelsome, they're human, and should be loved. We're asked to identify with their weaknesses, with their lack of talent. Do we really need to? George Burns's presence in this movie invalidates Simon's maudlin view. Burns is living proof of the transcendence that Simon can't believe in.

[November 17, 1975]

Becoming an American

*L*ike Czech movies of the mid-sixties (*Loves of a Blonde, Intimate Lighting*), the independently produced American film *Hester Street* is essentially an anecdote—a small, ironic story told without much attempt at depth of characterization. Adapted from a story by Abraham Cahan, the movie is about the assimilation process among a group of Russian Jewish immigrants living on the Lower East Side in 1896. When Jake (Steven Keats), who works at a sewing machine in a sweatshop, has been in New York for three years, his wan little wife, Gitl (Carol Kane), comes to join him with their tiny, bird-faced son, who looks just like her—a silent, watchful child with a promising gleam. But Jake wears his saloon sport's derby with his prayer shawl; he has fallen for Mamie (Dorrie Kavanaugh),

79

a flashy dresser, who works at a dancing academy that is a social center for the greenhorn Jews trying to become more "American." Jake doesn't want anything to do with Gitl; a pious waif in drab clothes and an Orthodox wig, speaking only Yiddish, she reminds him of everything he's trying to break away from. The film begins lamely; most of the performers—Steven Keats especially—have a terrible time with their accents, and he and Dorrie Kavanaugh are awkward in their shallow roles. It takes a little while for the picture to get under way and to win one over.

Carol Kane's shy, tentative Gitl gives the film an unusually quiet center; perhaps she is too slow in her responses at first, a shade too expressionless, but she has a lovely pale-eyelashed bewilderment. And as Bernstein, the scholarly boarder who sleeps in Jake's and Gitl's kitchen, Mel Howard manages to make stillness rather sexy. The writer-director Joan Micklin Silver handles the anecdote form very well: she has an instinct for how long a scene should run, and though she filters folk-tale material through current attitudes too pointedly, the scenes are under-dramatized in a likable way. The narrative simplicity is defenselessly appealing. Joan Silver may not have a very large talent (at least, in this first feature there's no evidence of shattering vitality), but she *is* gifted. The black-and-white cinematography and the simple characterizations recall Hollywood's early talkies in which the city bad girl lured the hero away from the ingenuous country girl, and bumptious Irish immigrants got into brawls at wakes. But *Hester Street* is without the melodramatic elements of those films; it's less practiced, more pure.

The slightness of the film comes out of its condescension to Jake; he has been made to stand for vulgar American materialism, and he speaks such lines as "I don't care for nobody. I'm an American fella." The audience can laugh knowingly. Jake's best scene—his animal high spirits at a picnic, playing ball with his son—suggests what is missing from his character elsewhere. It's what the freedom to enjoy sports, to enjoy oneself physically, to play at *anything,* must have meant to a semi-literate Jewish peasant who grew up in a tradition that valued learning above all. A rawboned, long-jawed worker like Jake was escaping not only from persecution by the Russians but also from that oppressive messianic Jewish tradition, with its stress on worthwhile activities. Mamie, in her coarseness, would represent freedom and gaiety to him; Gitl, passive, superstitious, impressed to have Bernstein mumbling over his book at their table, would recall him to a world in which he would never be respected. The film—nostalgic for what the immigrants lost—never shows us that there are grounds for Jake's wanting to be Americanized. Instead, he's a fool, abandoning a jewel for a flashy pastework imitation of "class." Mamie is done up as if she were a woman of the world—practically a madam. A young shyster lawyer hired by Jake to offer Gitl a cash settlement if she'll agree to a divorce is an amateurishly acted cartoon. The aggressive characters don't have enough sensitivity—or juice—to come to life; the problem appears to be in the casting, in the director's not knowing how to bring more out of the performers, and in her own feelings.

Joan Silver's modest, restrained directing style is in tune with Gitl and Bernstein. The movie is on their side; that's probably part of the secret of its commercial success. (Blue-collar people might react to this film very differently from the audiences who are seeing it now, because there is an element of class put-down in it.) Gitl's peasant docility may seem pensive and sweet to us, and refined, but that's because Joan Silver presents her as we might see her, not as Jake experiences her. Gitl's slender body and her Pre-Raphaelite face are beautiful in modern counterculture terms, while Mamie's buxom, hourglass-figure flirtatiousness went out a long time ago. And while Jake is a bullying, dumb jock, Mel Howard's gentle, bearded Bernstein is the classic Jewish type that has come back into fashion in recent years—a Talmudic flower child. Gitl, who learns English practically in front of our eyes, has our good will, and her accented speech is soft and doesn't sound coarse. Mel Howard, who speaks Yiddish with ease, is even more fortunate. Bernstein's sarcasm and defeatism, which might have been considered reactionary a few decades ago—the mark of an embittered man who couldn't adapt—sound hip now. Howard underplays quietly, with enough authority to get by with the lines that cue the audience to the derisive view of the immigrant experience that is expected of them. He curses Columbus and complains, "When you get on the boat, you should say, 'Goodbye, O Lord. I'm going to America.'"

It is to the director's credit that she manages to hold down Doris Roberts' performance as the *yente*; Joan Silver allows herself such audience-pleasers as the *yente's* lacing Gitl into a merry-widow corset with the words "If you want to be an American, you gotta hurt," but at least she doesn't linger—she gets the ironic laugh without squeezing for it. At the end, the go-getters are left to a graceless, yokels' future; we see that Mamie has accumulated her capital by penny-pinching, and that life with her won't be the good times Jake had expected. The timid Gitl, who has been betrayed and humiliated, comes out with everything—even with the better man, Bernstein. Has ever woman won so much by doing so little? Gitl even gets Mamie's money, and without having to raise her voice.

As a commentary on the American experience—the materialist loses the real prizes, etc.—the film has the pedagogic folk humor and the appreciation of the "old ways" which had me wriggling in discomfort at school whenever a story was presented as a fable. I feel measly-minded when I'm put in the position of identifying with Bernstein's view—his traditionalist's suspiciousness about the New World, which blends all too neatly with late-sixties counterculture cynicism. But within the limited terms that Joan Silver has set she's brought the movie off—and, by the end, with a flourish. When Gitl slowly flowers, we don't get the sense that she has been transformed; rather, we see that she was so uprooted, and was so hurt by Jake's rejection of her, that she was almost paralyzed—her character is only now being revealed. And Bernstein's rueful wisdom—the eyes on the ready for lamentation, the praying head that nods in recognition of thousands of years of folly—is a fragrant conceit.

□ □ □

Sometimes you can tell from the very first shot that a movie is going wrong. Louis Malle's *Black Moon* opens with a badger snuffling along a road; the image is ominous, as a speeding car approaches and you wait for the animal to be smashed. There isn't anywhere for a movie to go after a deadpan zinger like this, and *Black Moon* is a collection of such wayward effects, set in a future war between men and women, which is also no more than a whammy. Louis Malle is a director in search of new stimulation; his projects are often so different from each other that, seeing a new Malle film, one can't quite tell how he got to that. (It's as if he were trying to astonish himself.) With *Black Moon,* he appears to be travelling with the sixties zeitgeist, trying to loosen up and become an American underground man. This is a post-apocalypse film, in which the few characters in the scarred landscape speak mainly by body language and gibberish—a Warholian view of the future that's reminiscent of Jim McBride's *Glen and Randa* and Jodorowsky's druggy *El Topo.*

But Malle is a sane man trying to make a crazy man's film. He's temperamentally unsuited to the disordered, meandering vision he's aiming for, and his meticulously planned chaos has no visionary compulsion. You can feel that this is a cultivated, rational artist striving for perverse, enigmatic innocence. Talented directors often have bad ideas— Altman with *Brewster McCloud* and *Images,* Coppola with *The Rain People,* Truffaut trying to be Hitchcock—but there's generally an obsessive quality in the films, a sign of something the director is trying to work out. That isn't the case with *Black Moon.* The surreal effects Malle uses don't connect with anything in his imagination, so there's no instinctive wit in them, no ambivalence, no friction. It's deadly. Fifteen-year-old Cathryn Harrison plays Alice in this bombed-out Wonderland; as brother and sister, Joe Dallesandro and Alexandra Stewart have a handsome, blank twinship; the late Therese Giehse is a bedridden old woman who bawls out her whimpering, apologetic rat companion. This rat and a talking unicorn—a mangy, plump old Shetland pony wearing a horn—are the two liveliest characters. You get the feeling that the animals *want* to talk, which is more than you get from the people. A pussycat who plays the piano and two kids who sing *Tristan and Isolde* are happy surprises; the flowers who squeal when they're stepped on are, however, of a whimsey that may haunt Malle. He's carried eclecticism too far with this apocalyptic *Francis, the*

Talking Unicorn. Not everyone has it in him to be a fantasist, and when a civilized director like Malle tries, the results may, as in *Black Moon,* be colder, less inspired, less *fantastic* than in any other movie he's ever made.

□ □ □

*T*he British studio workmen employed on Ken Russell's *Lisztomania* must have had some debonair conversations when they got home. A carpenter's wife asks, "What did you do today?" and he explains, "Well, Mum, we built this phallus twelve feet long, so it would come out of this actor, Roger Daltrey, who's playing Liszt. It had to be a cannon strong enough to support five dancing girls, who get to kick and strut on it." Or he describes building a giant-size model of the crotch and legs of Princess Carolyne Sayn-Wittgenstein (Sara Kestelman), so that Liszt can disappear in her voracious vagina. These adolescent demonic high jinks are the two funniest sequences in *Lisztomania*—they erupt with a wholehearted, controlled comic-strip craziness that the picture in general lacks. Russell was in better control in *Tommy,* which was enjoyable at a dumb pop level; the pre-recorded score gave the picture drive, and the director found a showy crudeness that worked for him. Russell didn't even begin to get at the Dionysian-Wagnerian possibilities of the rock-opera form that the three-image footage of the songs from *Tommy* in *Woodstock* had had, but he did have Tina Turner, and there was one great shot of her, from her vibrating ankles on up. Tina Turner is what Ken Russell has always needed in a performer: she starts at climax and keeps going. In *Tommy,* her Acid Queen was like pure, concentrated acid sex—the high may have even got too high for some viewers, and scared them. In *Lisztomania,* Russell tries to use Sara Kestelman for some of the same wild, ecstatic Cobra Woman effect, but she doesn't have it in her. And he doesn't have a rock-opera score—only a mash of rocked-up Liszt and Wagner themes, plus some new songs that are so forgettable you barely register them.

Does Russell's love-hate relationship with composers have any connection with his lack of a musical sense (his editing is chopsticks) and his tin ear for language? The dialogue he wrote for *The Devils* was dumbfoundingly flat; in the middle of porno orgies, people talked like pedants. The dull schoolboy slang (with puns) of *Lisztomania* sounds so remote and disembodied that you feel you're looking at *Captain Marvel* while somebody translates the captions from Russian or German. For all his lashing himself into a slapstick fury, Russell can't seem to pull the elements of filmmaking together, and it's probably inconceivable that he'd let a writer become a full collaborator. Since he doesn't use actors as creators, either (the last *performance* in a Russell movie was probably Dorothy Tutin's in *Savage Messiah*), we're getting nothing but Russell's own hangups, in the form of sacrilegious-mischief comics. Why is he making a movie about Liszt, whom he has contempt for, and Richard and Cosima Wagner (Paul Nicholas and Veronica Quilligan), whom he despises? Giggly hate of one's betters is not promising motivation for an artist. *Lisztomania* is more entertaining than *Black Moon,* but then Malle is out of his element. Russell is *in* his—so far in that who wants to follow him? He's disappearing in a giant crotch, too.

[November 24, 1975]

The Bull Goose Loony

*O*ne Flew Over the Cuckoo's Nest is a powerful, smashingly effective movie—not a great movie but one that will probably stir audiences' emotions and join the ranks of such pop-mythology films as *The Wild One, Rebel Without a Cause,* and *Easy Rider.* Ken Kesey's novel about a gargantuan rebel-outcast, McMurphy, locked up in a hospital for the insane, was a lyric jag, and the book became a nonconformists' bible. Written in 1960 and 1961, and published early in 1962, the novel preceded the university turmoil, Vietnam, drugs, the counterculture. Yet it contained the prophetic essence of that whole period of revolutionary politics going psychedelic, and much of what it said (and it really *said* it; the book intentionally laid out its meaning like a comic strip) has entered the consciousness of many—possibly most—Americans. For young dissidents, the book was the first—the original—hallucinatory trip. Chief Broom, the schizophrenic who narrates the story, has had two hundred rounds of electroshock; his white mother emasculated his Indian-chief father—made him "too little to fight"—and since from childhood people have treated him as if he were deaf and dumb, he's so depressed he acts the part. In his account of life in the ward of an Oregon hospital for the insane, Big Nurse—Nurse Ratched—runs the place for the Combine, the secret power center that controls society. The Combine sends society's nonconformists to the hospital, and Big Nurse forces them into submission—if necessary, by turning them into vegetables. Chief Broom's view is a psychotic metaphor for a society awaiting revelation, and the revelation comes in the person of the red-headed gambler-logger McMurphy. He is presented in the rhapsodic mode that Steinbeck, in *The Grapes of Wrath,* reserved for the poor. McMurphy, who hasn't "let the Combine mill him into fitting where they wanted him to fit," McMurphy, with his "free and loud" laugh, his "broad white devilish grin," and "the man-smell of dust and dirt from the open fields, and sweat, and work," is a jock Christ. By standing up to Big Nurse, he proves that the soul-crushing machine can be beaten; he enables the men in his ward to liberate themselves from their fears, and to understand that they're sane. They are freed, but he is trapped.

Miloš Forman, who directed the movie version, with Jack Nicholson as McMurphy, has understood how crude the poetic-paranoid system of the book would look on the screen now that the sixties' paranoia has lost its nightmarish buoyancy, and he and the scenarists Lawrence Hauben and Bo Goldman have done a very intelligent job of loosening Kesey's schematism. It had to be done. As a postgraduate student in the writing program at Stanford, Kesey was in on some early LSD experiments at a veterans' hospital, and Chief Broom's subjective vision is full of dislocations and transformations, but Kesey is systematic in fusing Christian mythology with the American myth of the white man and the noble red man fighting against the encroachment of civilization, represented by women. Though in modern society women are as much subject to the processes of mechanized conformity as men (some say *more*), the inmates of this symbolic hospital are all male, and McMurphy calls them "victims of a matriarchy." There's a long literary tradition behind this man's-man view of women as the castrater-lobotomizers; Kesey updated it, on the theory that comic-strip heroes are the true American mythic heroes, and in terms of public response to the book and to the stage productions of it he proved his point. The novel is comic-book Freud: the man who achieves his manhood (keeping women under him, happy whores in bed) is the free man—he's the buckaroo with the power of laughter. Leslie Fiedler described Kesey's novel as "the dream once dreamed in the woods, and now redreamed on pot and acid." Kesey's concept of male and female is not so very remote from that in Mailer's writing, though Kesey celebrates keeping the relationships at a mythic comic-strip level, while Mailer, in his foolhardy greatness, delves into his own comic-strip macho.

The movie (set in 1963) retains most of Kesey's ideas but doesn't diagram them; we're not cued at every step, and the end isn't so predictable. (On the shock table, McMurphy doesn't ask, "Do I get a crown of thorns?"—as he did in the book.) Miloš Forman appears to have recognized the strong realistic material within Kesey's conception. We all fear being locked up among the insane, helpless to prove our sanity, perhaps being driven mad; this fear is almost as basic as that of being buried alive. And we can't formulate a clear-cut difference between sane and insane. So Forman replaces the novel's trippy subjectivity with a more realistic view of the patients which leaves their mental condition ambiguous. They seem not much more insane than the nurses, the doctors, the attendants. They're cowards, terrified of Big Nurse (Louise Fletcher), but then the staff is intimidated by her, too.

What has disappeared from the film version is the Combine (to be known a little while after the book came out as the Establishment). Forman could have exploited the Watergate hangover and retained the paranoid simplicities that helped make hits of *Easy Rider* and *Joe,* but instead he (with, it appears, the support of his producers, Saul Zaentz, of Fantasy Records, and Michael Douglas) has taken a less romantic, more suggestive approach. McMurphy's sanity isn't so clear-cut, and he doesn't give his buddies the courage to go back out into the world; the ward isn't emptied, as it is in the book. (Now only the Indian walks out.) Cut off from the concept of the Combine, the ward symbolizes the pressures and ambiguities of society as we know it, and the movie comes at a time when we're all prepared to accept a loony bin as the right metaphor for the human condition. But this leaves a problem that isn't completely solved: Big Nurse. Instead of the giant-breasted terror of the novel, Louise Fletcher's Nurse Ratched resembles Shirley Temple Black. She's the smiling, well-organized institutional type—the dean of women who was disappointed in you, the phone-company supervisor who tells you why she has to interrupt your service for nonpayment. Nurse Ratched's soft, controlled voice and girlishly antiseptic manner always put you in the wrong; you can't cut through the crap in her—it goes too deep. And she's too smart for you; she's got all the protocol in the world on her side. In *Thieves Like Us,* Louise Fletcher played Mattie, the strong, no-nonsense betrayer. Here, thinner and almost baby-faced, she's a middle-aged woman wearing her hair in a forties wartime style and still seeing herself as an ingenue. Louise Fletcher gives a masterly performance. Changes in her flesh tone tell us what Nurse Ratched feels. We can see the virginal expectancy—the purity—that has turned into puffy-eyed self-righteousness. She thinks she's doing good for people, and she's hurt—she feels abused—if her authority is questioned; her mouth gives way and the lower part of her face sags. She's not the big white mother that she is in the book; that part of the symbolism has been stripped away. She's the company woman incarnate; the only way to reach her is to go for her throat—though neither the novel nor the film perceives that women, too, would want to strangle her. Forman isn't a manhood-and-size obsessive like Kesey, but the film's plot structure derives from Kesey's male-female symbolism, and when that is somewhat demythified, the plot goes a little out of kilter, into melodrama. Those who know the book will probably feel that Nurse Ratched is now more human, but those who haven't read it may be appalled at her inhumanity. The melodramatics are flagrant in the episode involving Billy Bibbit (Brad Dourif), the stuttering, mother-fixated virgin of the ward. McMurphy fixes him up with his own hooker girlfriend Candy (Marya Small), and the next morning Billy is cured of his stutter—until Nurse Ratched tells him that she is going to inform his mother of what he's done. Then the stutter comes back. Brad Dourif gives the role a fey spark, but without Kesey's giddy pop view this crybaby-juvenile bit is a bummer—psychiatric dramaturgy circa Lon McCallister and, before him, Eric Linden.

McMurphy has been successfully modified, however. As Jack Nicholson plays him, he's no longer the Laingian Paul Bunyan of the ward, but he's still the charismatic misfit-guerrilla. Nicholson is an actor who knows how to play to an audience; he knows how to get us to share in a character. In *The Last Detail,* his sweet-sadistic alternating current kept us watching him, and we followed his lowlifer's spoor through *Chinatown.* Nicholson is no flower-child nice guy; he's got that half smile—the calculated insult that alerts audiences to how close to the surface his hostility is. He's the people's freak of the new stars. His specialty is divided characters—vulgarians, such as J. J. Gittes, with his *Racing Form,* his dumb jokes, and his flashy clothes, who are vulnerable. Nicholson shows the romanticism inside street shrewdness. As the frizzy-haired, half-bald clown, he provided the few funny moments in *The Fortune*; when this lecher for larceny gave himself over to the hysterical joy of confession to the cops, Nicholson demonstrated that he could get his own high going and lift himself single-handed into slapstick, like a demented Laurel & Hardy in one. But that isn't really what people go to see Jack Nicholson for. He stretched himself right out of the public's range of interest in *The Fortune*; and in *The Passenger* Antonioni, who seemed to have no idea what kind of actor Nicholson was, wiped him out.

Since Nicholson doesn't score when he plays unmagnetic characters—and he must know it by now—the danger in *Cuckoo's Nest* is that he'll take over: that he'll use his boyish shark's grin, the familiar preening, brutal one-upmanship. He's won the audience with his cocky freaks, and this is the big one—the bull goose loony. Nicholson can be too knowing about the audience, and the part he plays here is pure temptation. Before Kesey went to Stanford to study writing, he'd gone to Los Angeles in the hope of becoming an actor, and role-playing is built into McMurphy's character: he's swept up by the men's desire for him to be their savior. Except for the red-haired-giant externals, the authority-hating hero of the book is so much of a Nicholson role that the actor may not seem to be getting a chance to do much new in it. But Nicholson doesn't use the glinting, funny-malign eyes this time; he has a different look—McMurphy's eyes are farther away, muggy, veiled even from himself. You're not sure what's going on behind them. The role-playing is still there, in the grandstanding that McMurphy does when he returns to the ward after shock treatment; it has to be there, or there's no way of accounting for why he's sacrificed. But Nicholson tones it down. As McMurphy, he doesn't keep a piece of himself out of the character, guarding it and making the audience aware that he's got his control center and can turn on the juice. He actually looks relaxed at times, punchy, almost helpless—you can forget it's Nicholson. McMurphy is a tired, baffled man, and with his character more unresolved he gains depth. Forman hasn't let the McMurphy character run away with the picture, and it's Nicholson's best performance.

The movie is much less theatrical than the romantic, strong-arming book, yet it keeps you attentive, stimulated, up. Those who got a terrific charge from the book and the play may be disappointed by the more realistic approach, but even when there are clashes between Kesey's archetypes and Forman's efforts at realism there's still an emotional charge built into the material. It's not as programmed a mythic trip, yet Will Sampson, the towering full-blooded Creek who plays Chief Broom, brings so much charm, irony, and physical dignity to the role of the resurrected catatonic that this movie achieves Kesey's mythic goal. The film has its climactic Indian-white love-death, and at the end Kesey's reversal of the American legend (now the white man is sacrificed for the Indian) is satisfying on the deepest pop-myth level. When a movie has this much working for it, it doesn't have to be all of a piece to give an audience pleasure.

However, it has an element (which has nothing to do with Ken Kesey) that may go slightly against the grain of some people's enjoyment. In 1966, I wrote a review of Miloš Forman's Czech-made *Loves of a Blonde* and then backed away, filed the sheets in a drawer, and wrote about something else; it is the only occasion on which I've done such a thing. *Loves of a Blonde* seemed to me too painful for the intentionally comic scenes to function as comedy, and when the camera got in close to unattractive people I wasn't sure what for; we in the audience knew our advantages— not just economic but mental—over the desolate, hopelessly hopeful heroine, which hardly made her plight funny. There wasn't any of the stylization that makes it possible to laugh at pitiable people in Chaplin's comedies. Forman himself must have kind feelings for his characters— perhaps even love—and he must be trying to encompass a wider spectrum of ordinary people than most film directors do. His parents were sent to concentration camps (where they died) when he was a small child, and he could be said to be tough-minded and to have a dispassionate, unblinking eye. Neo-realism asked us to identify with ordinary people; he puts us in a neutral position, asking us to accept ordinary people as humorous without the melting gaze of identification. Yet in *Loves of a Blonde* what he must have thought he was doing was a considerable distance from what I experienced. (Diane Arbus's photographs affect me similarly.) He might feel at one with his losers; maybe that explained his refusing to spare them from exposure. But what of the audience? The audience laughter at what I found painfully embarrassing—was that the right response, was that what he wanted? Did it really mean humane acceptance?

Forman's effort in *One Flew Over the Cuckoo's Nest* is to make the situation "real"; he aims for individualized faces and gestures. Yet by American standards (at least by mine) there's a stolid, impassive element in his humor; I experience a streak of low, buffoonish peasant callousness running through his work. He locks people into their physical properties; he likes faces that don't take the light—thick features and muddled stares that bespeak a limited, closed-off emotional life. Forman may be drawn to the European myth that the real people are those close to the land. His characters often seem to be sleep-heavy, not yet emerged from clay. In this film, Cheswick (Sydney Lassick), the infantile, bleating middle-aged inmate, is the most glaring example, and perhaps Forman allows the character of the innocent Billy Bibbit to be overstated because he believes in that kind of innocence also. Maybe the reason the inmates remain unaffected when they see Billy lying in his blood—nobody flips out—is that in Forman's view it is the innocent and the messianically possessed (McMurphy) who *pay*. He wants us to react to Billy's body, but he assumes a peasant opacity in the other inmates—assumes that they'll go back to playing cards.

It's this opacity in Forman's own approach, particularly to humor, that keeps me from yielding to his work. In his first American film, *Taking Off,* he dropped his ambiguous neutrality in the slapstick centerpiece—the meeting of the Society for the Parents of Fugitive Children, where the parents try to get closer to their runaways by receiving instruction from a hairy pothead on how to smoke a joint. He drops it again here when McMurphy takes the inmates on a fishing trip and we are shown the men's stupefying comic clumsiness about baiting hooks. These inmates are Northwesterners, living in fishing country, and even if they've never fished before they're not ignorant men. But Forman gets laughs by pretending that mental disturbance is the same as ineptitude. The fishing trip, like that pot party, is Forman's own comic-strip side. (I think I prefer Kesey's, even with his view of women.) The borderline insensitivity is only a minor aspect of *One Flew Over the Cuckoo's Nest*, but it relates to questions about Forman as an artist.

When a director like Sam Peckinpah puts a group like his Wild Bunch on the screen, the men are so alive that the last thing that would ever come into your head is that some of them are plug-uglies. When Forman introduces his characters, that's the first thing you see, and in *One Flew Over the Cuckoo's Nest* it takes a while for you to get beyond that introductory shocked response (often a laugh) and begin to know the people and, in some cases, to enjoy them. I'm not sure that we ever get as far with them as we do right smack from the start with Peckinpah. It's doubtful if anyone else could have made as good a movie out of Kesey's book, but I miss the sureness, the energy, and the visual style that, say, a Scorsese might have brought to it. Forman gets his effects here through closeups and cutting, and through such staging as the boat scene, when the men desert their posts to peek at what McMurphy is doing below with his girl. An American director would have carried through on this scene, would have made it pay off. Forman is an intelligent, tentative director—which is another way of saying that his virtues are largely negative. *One Flew Over the Cuckoo's Nest* is one hell of a good film, but it works emotionally only because of its story and acting; it lacks the excitement of movie art.

[December 1, 1975]

Poses

*R*ancho Deluxe, from a jaunty, picaresque original script by the novelist Thomas McGuane, played around the country last spring and summer, but it is just now opening in New York. Shot against the regal Montana Big Sky country by the elegiac cinematographer William A. Fraker, it is a flip, absurdist modern Western. Jack (Jeff Bridges), a dropout from the upper middle class, and Cecil (Sam Waterston), a wryly bemused Indian, are rip-off artists—cattle rustlers. They rustle cattle because the facetious machismo of it appeals to them. They do it, Jack says, "to keep from falling asleep." McGuane's specialty is the comedy in the disparateness of American life, and he provides idiosyncratic dialogue and laconic juxtapositions. Jack and Cecil dismember steers with a chain saw and shoot up a shiny Continental Mark IV with a buffalo gun; the cow-country girls they date work in a factory tying flies for fishermen and chatter about the *I Ching*. Brown (Clifton James), the cattle baron that Jack and Cecil rustle from, calls a press conference to announce that he's declaring war on the rustlers; and his twitchy wife (Elizabeth Ashley) isn't getting the action she hoped for when they sold their beauty-parlor business in Schenectady and headed West. The only charge Brown is getting is from the tingles that the rustlers are giving him; as the movie sees it, they're doing him a favor. *Rancho Deluxe* is far from stupid, but it isn't very likable. In its view, the world is divided between the Browns—clowns who get piggishly worked up about their distractions—and the bored, lost-generation heroes for whom the West is a carnival wasteland and rustling is a trip.

McGuane updates the star-novelist romanticism of earlier eras. Hemingway appeals to the little boy in readers, that little boy who feels he must be tough and win the fight and prove himself a man; Fitzgerald appeals to the adolescent in readers, that adolescent who believes in the ideal girl and moonlit romance. McGuane seems to see himself as the inheritor of both attitudes—with a difference. Jack and Cecil kill animals cleanly and perfectly but with a wanton casualness; they don't feel more manly for it. And they're mock-courtly with their girls, Betty Fargo (Patti d'Arbanville) and her sister Mary (Maggie Wellman), because they don't feel connected to them. Jack and Cecil do what they do as a joke; that's what makes them McGuane heroes. McGuane's pose is romantic absurdism, and disconnectedness—maybe of necessity, since he's miserably lost when he tries to establish ordinary human relations (as in a scene where Jack goes home and has dinner with his parents and his estranged wife). Jack and Cecil—stoned aristocrats—consider themselves "the last of the plainsmen," and they have their own, existential noblesse oblige. *Rancho Deluxe* is rooted in Nick Carraway's naïve, snobbish "A sense of the fundamental decencies is parcelled out unequally at birth," but for McGuane hipness is included among the decencies. Fitzgerald, like his Gatsby, was defenselessly, blindly romantic. McGuane may be just as much of a victim, but his writing here is all jumpy defenses and elliptical throwaway jokes to smarten up the attractiveness of the doomed. (His Gatsby would have had a million frizzy retorts.)

The movie medium has a way of exposing snobbery right down to its puerile roots. One of the most offensive films I've ever seen—*The Sporting Club,* directed by Larry Peerce—was based on a small, trim McGuane novel. It dealt with a similar situation: a private deer park in northern Michigan where the grotesque affluent frolicked. When I saw it, the audience booed. *Rancho Deluxe* isn't as antipathetic as that was; it's sputteringly enjoyable. But I gather that it has had a negative response in some theatres, and I can see why. It isn't just because of Frank Perry's lusterless direction and unvarying pace. It's because when McGuane is stripped of the prose style of his novels, what's left is self-conscious, self-protective cleverness. As in *The Sporting Club,* the hero is a rich boy contemptuous of his own class and playing tricks on it. McGuane uses American self-mockery to glamorize the young who dig the crazy incongruities and turn alienation into sport. Jack's and Cecil's sly asides are too kicky, too pleased. Sitting in the audience, we're not as charmed as we're meant to be. If the Big Sky area has been defiled by being turned into a backdrop for the macho posturings of nouveau-riche yokels, McGuane's romanticized macho posturings aren't much of a step up. The film is too dandyish to be satirical about the desecration of the West which the pickup-truck-and-gun-rack culture represents; McGuane and Perry are busy showing off their world-weary distaste for the vulgarity of the pink-shirted slobs, though it's not the slobs who do the killing in this movie—it's the heroes. Cecil shoots a grazing steer just to try out a gun, and we're supposed to admire his grace, because he perceives the comedy in his own *acte gratuit*. We're supposed to believe that there's no alternative between joining the pompous, paunchy middle class and trashing yourself mad. I think that at least some of the people in the audience reject this film because of its spoiled-schoolboy bravura. Like Gatsby, the greatest arrested adolescent in our literature, the heroes of *Rancho Deluxe* have no possibility of growing up. Pranksters forever, they have no past and no future—just a stoned limbo. McGuane is saying that he finds the world boring, and that it's the world's fault.

If the picture had had a roller-coaster drive to it, it might have been a hit with young audiences, who could enjoy the parent-baiting. If it had had even a few big, combustible comic scenes, Perry might have got by with it, because McGuane sets up some funny situations—his situations are much wittier than his near-beer epigrams. But the deadpan distancing makes everything seem anti-climactic, and the stunt of leaving the audience off-balance—not knowing what's going on in some of the vignettes until they're almost over—backfires; the moviemakers appear to be staying ahead of us for their own amusement, and we feel left out. The whole movie happens too far away for us to react. It's an undramatic, literary conception, with emblematic heroes, and Jeff Bridges, the most "natural" of young actors, couldn't be more wrong for it. Except in the scene of Jack and Cecil bowing to their ladies, Bridges looks physically uncomfortable; he's pudgy—his chin flows softly into his neck—and you can see him glumly struggling to find a face for a character that is no more than an attitude. As the author's mouthpiece, Bridges has to demonstrate that some ways of keeping from being bored have more style than others, and this fakery isn't in his range. He's also trapped in a hateful scene: when the Fargo girls' father breaks in on the four of them in bed and denounces the girls, Jack, the virile cavalier, forces the father to kneel and beg his daughters' forgiveness. (McGuane and Perry ought to be the ones kneeling in penance—for tainting the picture with this ugly self-righteousness.) Sam Waterston, who gave such a fossilized, unresonant performance as Nick Carraway, is surprisingly appealing as the smily pothead Cecil. Waterston is generally detached and recessive when he shouldn't be; here everything he is fits. He's got the McGuane cool—Cecil seems to be the apple of his own eye—and this relaxed, flyblown performance gives the film a hum.

In an ideal world, Frank Perry would probably be a producer rather than a producer-director; he has the taste to go after real writers, but he doesn't know how to shape the material they give him, or what to discard.

This film has no emotional center; it wakes up when the minor characters are on the screen—particularly Slim Pickens as a detective specializing in livestock thefts, a tough old bird who pretends to be a folksy fool, and Harry Dean Stanton and Richard Bright as the Browns' clumsily companionable ranch hands. They don't have the theme-carrying burden that the heroes and the villains do; McGuane wrote woozily inventive scenes for them, and Perry's directing is more conventional but also warmer and livelier in this material—he seems on more secure comic ground. Stanton, who is one of the best character actors in American movies right now, gives the film its high spots—a conversation with Bridges in which they test each other while playing a game on a TV Ping-Pong machine, and some spaced-out-on-love routines with a smooth floozy (Charlene Dallas, who signals the audience too energetically).

Rancho Deluxe wouldn't be worth talking about if McGuane weren't so talented and so elegantly controlled, even here. The picture is an oddity, because he has turned in on himself, diddling his talent, and when you play games with yourself in a movie script it shows up on the screen on an enormous scale. The film is a genuine curiosity, which is the only genuine thing about it.

□ □ □

*J*oseph Losey directed *The Romantic Englishwoman,* so it naturally has very long pauses, time in which to ask yourself why Michael Caine, a pulp writer who is successful enough to live in high-swank style—a glass gazebo-greenhouse, a swimming pool, couches and chairs that crush down just right, a French au-pair (Beatrice Romand) for his little boy, and black chiffon trailing around his sexy, restive wife (Glenda Jackson)—has such awful, sticky hair. Is it because he's a self-made bourgeois, or is it to indicate that he hasn't settled into the bourgeoisie and never will, quite? Or is it something else altogether, such as the actor's negligence? This may not be a big issue, but it's as big (and as clearly motivated) as anything else that you run up against in *The Romantic Englishwoman,* another flaccid essay on infidelity with prissy-mouthed Helmut Berger as the gigolo-intruder. Caine, who's writing a film script about a discontented wife, pushes Glenda and Helmut together, and whammo! They take off for the Continent, leaving him to suffer the consequences of his blockheadedness. Losey persuaded Tom Stoppard to do the rewrite on Thomas Wiseman's adaptation of his own novel, and Stoppard has given the dialogue a few Noël Cowardish bitch-nifties, but not enough to keep the viewer's blood coursing. The movie is a twist on life imitating art and vice versa; here it's life imitating pulp and vice versa—which might be an entertaining premise for a light comedy. In Losey's brand of mystification melodrama with leftish overtones, it's a very parched conceit. There may be some giggly amusement in the Pinteresque, cerebral chic, but the floundering scenes aren't improved by pinning them on Caine's infertile imagination; besides, we recognize these screwed-up, smoldering connotations as Losey's. As usual, he empties everything definite out of the characters, as if that would make them richly suggestive. Themes such as women's liberation are tossed in as part of the décor. Losey is deep on the surface.

Glenda Jackson is a warped choice for the conventionally acquisitive wife, but that warping is the only distinction the attenuated movie has. With her slitted eyes showing malice and her teeth on edge for grating, she's certainly not a woman that a man need feel he has to be gentle with. That could be quite a come-on, and so you can almost believe her stodgy husband's jealous obsessiveness about her—or is it meant to be just rotten bourgeois possessiveness? She flashes a handsome rump when she strolls nude away from the camera. You watch Glenda Jackson, all right, though she and the role—which provides no excuse for her affectations—never mesh. Glenda Jackson is a coiled-tight actress, who articulates each shade of emotion with such exactness that she has no fluidity and no ease. She carries no-nonsense precision to the point of brutality; she doesn't just speak her lines—she flicks them out, disgustedly. And Joseph Losey casts her as a housewife who has nothing to do except complain about the rigors of shopping, a woman who's unaware of her own emotions and has never had a clear thought in her life. Glenda Jackson is a limited screen actress, because she doesn't transcend her own conscious technique—she doesn't let go and allow us to see into her character; she's so actively in control that her performances are choppy. Yet Losey uses her as a wife who drifts with the tides, like Jeanne Moreau in the wet of *The Lovers*. The casting is so deceptive that it takes a while before one realizes that Jackson's cold, macabre quality expresses Losey's inchoate hostility to the character she's playing. He has no sympathy at all for the wife (after all, she's bourgeois); he tries to score against both the clod novelist (who yells when angry) and his wife by romanticizing the sponging Berger with tender suggestions that he's a free man and a generous-hearted poet. Can Losey really be the director who made *Modesty Blaise*? What's happened to his camp sense of humor? The key passages of Berger's winning Jackson's flinty heart take place offscreen, for which one duly records one's gratitude. But what is Losey thinking of when he uses Helmut Berger, in his Yves Saint Laurent ensembles, to denounce bourgeois possessions? The title *The Romantic Englishwoman* is ironic; the film's oblique message is that the bourgeois wife consumes everything—even her lover. (But Berger is hard for the audience to swallow.) Losey's admirers interpret the nebulous politics, congealed nastiness, and languorous visual style of his movies as artistic intellectuality. I guess we don't need to ask why the sex couplings in *The Romantic Englishwoman* are always interrupted, but those who wonder why almost every sequence in the house and grounds of the bourgeois couple involves mirror reflections may be interested in Losey's explanation: "I wanted to convey that their reality was totally unreal." And if you can go for that, you're ready for a Joseph Losey retrospective, to include *Boom!, Secret Ceremony, Figures in a Landscape, The Go-Between,* and *The Assassination of Trotsky.*

Both *Rancho Deluxe* and *The Romantic Englishwoman* are gilded with dialogue about boredom and dialogue about movies. When Helmut asks Glenda "Why have you come to Baden-Baden?" she answers "I came for the waters." When Sam Waterston asks Jeff Bridges "Did you ever see *Cheyenne Autumn?*" Bridges mutters that he did, and Waterston says "Well, in a few years they're going to make *Aluminum Autumn.*" Did Tom Stoppard and Tom McGuane—the peacocks of English and American letters—actually write these spuddy exchanges? They've turned boredom and movies into the same subject—if God is good, for this week only.

[December 8, 1975]

Political Acts

When Costa-Gavras made his first film, *The Sleeping Car Murder,* practically all he needed to think about was how to give it verve and a high-strung pace. A few years later, when he made his political detective-story thriller *Z,* he had such fierce conviction about the urgency of its message, and he was still so young, that he tore right through it, using every trick he knew to get the ideas across. He heated up the material explosively, and the film's muckraking energy was almost impossible to resist. In those years, it was as if he were on a sensory binge, doing what his instincts told him. When he came down, he wasn't free anymore. He was too intelligent not to see the danger in using films for rabble-rousing, and he became more scrupulous in his methods of affecting the audience. *Z* had the simple point of view appropriate to melodrama. Costa-Gavras has never been so simpleminded or so sensationally successful since. Obviously, he could have used his percussive, bruising narrative techniques to make smash crime thrillers. (*The French Connection,* borrowing liberally, proved how profitable a cops-and-robbers jam session could be.) But Costa-Gavras has sought to make films that are political acts—films about power and justice. Like *Z,* his two subsequent pictures, *The Confession*

95

and *State of Siege,* and his new one, *Special Section,* all deal with different faces of the same horror: a legal government in the role of a crime ring plotting against its own citizen-victims.

A cross between an investigative journalist and a melodramatist, Costa-Gavras lays out a dossier, and as the data accumulate, the audience begins to perceive the implications. *Special Section* is set in the Second World War, in Occupied France. In 1941, after the Wehrmacht invaded the Soviet Union, French Communists organized acts of resistance against the Nazis in their midst, and a young German naval cadet was killed in the Paris Métro. As the film tells it, the French Secretary of the Interior (Michel Lonsdale) was a toady who decided that German reprisals would be forestalled if the French took reprisals themselves and sent six men to the guillotine for the one dead cadet. The six were to be selected from prisoners who had been convicted of minor political offenses. In order to provide a veneer of legality for this maneuver, the French government had to pass a new anti-terrorism law, to be applied retroactively and to be administered by a newly created court called the Special Section; the court was to hold quick trials and convict the prisoners, who had actually been condemned in advance. The question that the film raises is why highly placed officials (Cabinet ministers, judges, and prosecutors), who were in no immediate danger themselves, cooperated in this scheme, which flagrantly violated the system of justice they had been trained to uphold. It's an Augean subject—the same one that Americans were confronted with as the Watergate scandal unfolded—but the film hardly gets near it.

Costa-Gavras has dropped most of his techniques for hyping an audience but hasn't got rid of the melodramatic thinking that lay underneath. The prisoners brought to trial are touching and heroic figures—they shine with humanity—while the judges who condemn them are vain, ambitious, militaristic weaklings, easily soft-soaped. The collaborators are smaller than life, and we feel contemptuous of them from the first glance. The casting and the writing are so prejudicial that the film's purpose is undercut. In *State of Siege,* the cartooning of the representatives of the different forces was like a pamphleteer's shortcut; the demonstration that the repressive U.S.-supported government of Uruguay drove the Tupamaros to terrorism wasn't dependent on our understanding of the individuals involved. But in *Special Section* the whole point is an investigation of the character of collaborators, and if you cartoon them there's no point left. After we've seen *The Sorrow and the Pity,* with actual collaborators discussing what they did and why, and seen the fears, moral confusions, and stresses they succumbed to, how can we have any respect for this simplistic vulgarization of history?

Actually, Costa-Gavras and his co-scenarist, Jorge Semprun, blew the movie in the early stages, when they decided to shape the story to make it appear that the French were merely fantasizing the danger of large-scale reprisals. There's no possibility of examining the psychology of collaboration and resistance if the French officials are obviously fools, cowards, and climbers. With the situation that Costa-Gavras and Semprun set up, they'd have done better to make a satiric farce about the craven eagerness to collaborate, and among the officials the standout performance—that of stooped-over, old Louis Seigner as the doddering Minister of Justice, who imagines that the Nazis are going to make hostages of the most highly placed Frenchmen—is a farcical Chicken Little skit. But for a great many people in Europe at that time the sky did fall. Some historians say that the Germans did in fact want to take a hundred lives for the one, and gave orders for fifty hostages to be executed immediately, and that the French bargained the number down to six. Costa-Gavras claims a solid basis for his interpretation, but it's ruinous to the movie. In condescendingly shucking off the officials' moral dilemma, he and Semprun are left with no core for their seriousness, and the film's emotional weight shifts to the wrong places. We become unnecessarily involved in the trials and fates of the small-fry political offenders—Trzebrucki (Jacques Rispal) and Bastard (Yves Robert) particularly—and the flashbacks to their lives, which are the only sequences with any sense of personality, are detours. We don't need to have our sympathies aroused—we already understand that the prisoners are innocently caught in a net. The movie wastes its time and our emotions on what should be the given of the situation. (There are no lyrical flashbacks to the early lives of the judges.)

Costa-Gavras' specialty has been visceral journalistic immediacy—quasi-documentary techniques that were like newsprint leaping off the page. We wouldn't expect (or want) a Second World War film to jump at us that way, but we do expect a visual style that brings the collaborators close enough for us to get the scent of what breed of men they are; we need to feel them so vividly near that we can understand why others in positions of authority will do what they did, whenever there's an opportunity. That must be why he's made the film: to show us the terrifying possibilities in law-abiding people. Yet he's at his most prosaic and least involving when he's dealing with the judges, and he keeps sidetracking us: we follow a lawyer (Jacques Perrin), a pale offshoot of Trintignant in *Z*, as he dashes off to Vichy in the hope of getting Pétain to stop the parody of justice, and we listen to one of the prisoners—the fearless editor of *L'Humanité* (Bruno Cremer)—as he denounces the court and shakes up the judges. When this editor proclaims ringingly that there will be no more convictions, he seems to be speaking out of Costa-Gavras' knowledge, and he convinces us. But the drama and the politics don't climax together: after this stirring speech, the closing titles tell us that the prisoners not yet convicted at the film's end died in concentration camps or were executed, and that other Special Sections were formed.

After the earlier Costa-Gavras films, we remembered the forward drive rather than specific images. He sped us through, showing us just what was necessary to get the political situation into our heads; there was no waste. (He had to freeze a frame to catch his breath.) In *Special Section,* he packs in the information at the beginning, staccato, as if he were in a great hurry, and then he pauses and loiters, without framing the compositions well enough for us to know why. When he gives us time to look, there's nothing to see and nothing to reflect on. Without the graphic excitement of his streaking frames, Costa-Gavras has no temperament. This film is lifelessly worthy, like those André Cayatte pictures showing the injustices perpetrated in French courts. Pamphleteering about an ongoing crime, *State of Siege* had shocking vitality; it wasn't a great movie, but it had valuable repercussions—it *was* a political act. *Special Section* is ineffective politically, congratulating you on your virtuous indignation over the hypocrisy of officialdom, with its legalized cruelty to the warm, harmless Communist-Jewish-Anarchist victims. This movie doesn't put even one scummy person among them to test your sympathies. As in old Hollywood, victims of injustice are lovable little men or heroic big ones. Trying to avoid squeezing audiences' guts, Costa-Gavras winds up squeezing their hearts. He's going to turn into the European Stanley Kramer if he doesn't pull himself together.

[December 15, 1975]

Killing Yourself with Kindness

An inhuman amount of judgment is required of a comedy writer-director-star. In his first attempt at a tripleheader, *The Adventure of Sherlock Holmes' Smarter Brother,* Gene Wilder fails on the level of judgment, though he's got the talent. He might have brought the film off if only he'd thought out the script. The premise—Sherlock Holmes' bringing in his insanely jealous younger brother, Sigerson, to help on a case involving Queen Victoria's state secrets—is so lushly promising that Wilder must have somehow skipped over the fact that he needed to work it up into a story, and gone right on to dream up comic situations without any underpinnings. Or did he perhaps have a story and then panic, discarding the essentials and substituting a batch of lopsided ideas? Whichever way it happened, the plot never thickened. There's no mystery, and since you can't have a parody of a mystery without a mystery to solve, there's no comic suspense. We don't have the expectations that help laughter build and make it satisfying.

The idea has such mouth-watering possibilities that I imagined Wilder's Sigi would be a demented caricature of his suavely assured brother—more brilliant by far but so neurotically indecisive that he didn't follow through on his own deductions. I thought Sigi might be so pettish that he'd resent Watson's position as his brother's confidant, and I visualized competitive fraternal feats of outlandish deduction, and the brothers triumphing over England's enemies by the intuitive exchange of key information, with Sigerson becoming at last a master detective. But the film is a series of missed opportunities. As Sherlock, Douglas Wilmer, who has done the part on British TV, has that fearfully precious Basil Rathbone assurance, the camp polish of the actor whose role gives him all the smart answers, yet the relationship of the brothers isn't developed. Wilder seems scarcely aware of the comic potential in the contrast between his limply wavering expressions and Sherlock's cool fixity—an ideal situation for a satire of sibling rivalry. He just passed it over. He didn't even do anything to account for his American accent vis-à-vis Sherlock's impeccably British snootiness, though what American doesn't feel *that* sibling rivalry? Wilder forgot what he had seemed so conscious of in the script he and Mel Brooks wrote for *Young Frankenstein*: the necessity of building on the conventions of the genre and of playing the jokes off against those conventions. Abandoning the beautiful comic idea that's ready to hand, he goes spinning off at cross-purposes into swashbuckling fencing scenes and low-comedy excursions that are so unrelated to anything that in the middle of big showcase sequences you can't remember how you got to them or what they're supposed to lead to.

As Orville Sacker, Sigi's helper, who has a "photographic memory" for conversations, Marty Feldman bats himself on the head to get his instant-replay machine running; he's like one of The Three Stooges making himself his own victim. Feldman doesn't grab the camera as insistently as in *Young Frankenstein,* but he still uses his eyes too much. He doesn't pop them (like Giancarlo Giannini in the screechy *Swept Away*); they look fully popped by nature—those white marbles are so startling they seem almost a deformity, and he might be funnier if he deëmphasized them. But Feldman's awareness of his own cunning is converted into eccentricity here; Orville has a secret, locked-in self-satisfaction that just misses being hugely funny. As Jenny, the red-haired mystery-woman songstress, Madeline Kahn misses, too, though she looks sweetly upholstered, in her Gay Nineties costumes, and, with that ladylike control of hers that goes a little awry, she's a perfect comic cupcake—ready to parody Jeanette MacDonald in *The Merry Widow* if only she had the material. Wilder made the awful mistake of thinking that Feldman, Kahn, and he himself were already comic characters. He wrote the roles for the actors but didn't write characters for them to play. He provided lots of lovely, sideswiping bits of business but no conceptions that would allow the actors to surprise us with something new. One longs for their scenes to come off better, particularly Madeline Kahn's, because her comic element of sham seems on the verge of exploding into something marvellous. Too bad that there is no logic behind the villains' attempts to bump her off, so we don't even feel scared for her.

Wilder's direction in the carriage-top fight between Sigi and a minor heavy (Roy Kinnear) suggests that when he gets going he may have a directing style halfway between Mel Brooks' and Woody Allen's—not as free-form as Brooks' or with as much concentrated wild energy, yet more all-out, old-movie nutty than Allen's. That's one of the few sequences here that really work. The running gags—such as Orville's replays of conversations and Sigi's feeding lines of a song to Jenny—are dropped before they really pay off, and though Wilder uses flash cards for furtive communication between Sherlock and Watson, he fails to use them between Sherlock and Sigi. And there's real discomfort for the viewer when Sigi, Jenny, and Orville suddenly break into a vaudeville number, "The Kangaroo Hop"—because the format is too much like that of the "Puttin' on the Ritz" specialty in *Young Frankenstein*. Whether Wilder is taking from himself or from Brooks hardly matters: the device isn't fresh—it was probably a mistake to use a composer (John Morris) and a choreographer (Alan Johnson) who have done three of Brooks' films. It was probably also a mistake for Wilder to work in England and to attempt an expensive period picture his first time out as a director; the anxiety about the visually over-rich production (there are enough camera setups to have fatigued a veteran director) must have got to him. Sometimes it's better for comedy not to go first class: without the fanfare, the director is forced to keep his attention on what counts, and the performers don't get overpowered by the fruit and flowers. From the way this picture looks, the planning must have gone into the non-essentials.

Wilder is a deadbeat as Sigi. In the passages where he presses Jenny to tell him the truth about her identity, he doesn't have the seer's demented intensity that the scenes seem to require—Sigi's passion for the truth does not appear to be out of control. The characterization is so perfunctory that it's never clear whether he's smart or traumatically stupid. What Wilder seems to want to show is that he, Sigi, is brave, loyal, and good. And where's the humor in that? As the director, Wilder is fatally kind to himself as a performer. In the past, he has had a demonic tenseness in his blurry personality—something so strange we couldn't puzzle it out. Nor did we want to; we wanted to experience that inspired, moony hysteria that is the modern clown's lyricism. Wilder's facial glissandos between confused emotional states expressed the total uncertainty we all sometimes feel. But in *Holmes' Smarter Brother* we can see him sanely producing each effect—acting funny. As he directs himself, he's a second-rate clown playing the hero. Wilder must be trying to fulfill a dated aspiration to be glamorous; he doesn't seem to understand that the heroes we believe in now are the clowns. But, as Wilder demonstrated in the sheep-lover episode of Woody Allen's *Everything You Always Wanted to Know About Sex,* he's far from a second-rater. I can't think of any other clown, past or present, who could have done that routine so well. His shyly obsessed sheep-lover was the comedy variant of the mad killer who cries out, "Lock me up—I can't stop myself!" His ecstatic, smudgy face said, "You think that the way I *look* is crazy? If you only knew what I feel in my heart!"

Wilder loses his performing rhythm by keeping his director's eye on his responsibilities, but his inventiveness as a writer and a director is evident in the many nice, leafy touches—such as Madeline Kahn's lead-in to the first rendition of "The Kangaroo Hop," and the episode featuring an arch, doggerel version of *A Masked Ball,* with Kahn and Dom DeLuise. The words they sing suggest what opera sounds like to people who can't stand opera, and it might be a gem of a sequence if the sound hadn't got inexplicably garbled and the effect lost. As the mustachioed opera-singer crook Gambetti, Dom DeLuise doesn't need to be a character, and he's in his best form—like a highbrow Lou Costello—particularly in his scenes with Leo McKern, who plays a goopy, comic-strip Moriarty, gigglingly evil. Wilder's direction makes McKern more acceptable than he's ever been before. *Holmes' Smarter Brother* isn't the kind of failure you write an artist off for; it got out of hand in the way that ambitious projects by talented people sometimes do, but there's always something to watch in it. With luck, a simpler approach, and less self-romanticizing, Gene Wilder could make it next time.

[December 22, 1975]

Kubrick's Gilded Age

Stanley Kubrick's *Barry Lyndon,* from Thackeray's novel, is very deliberate, very smooth—cool pastel landscapes with small figures in the foreground, a stately tour of European high life in the mid-eighteenth century. The images are fastidiously delicate in the inexpressive, peculiarly chilly manner of the English painters of the period, and the film is breathtaking at first as we wait to see what will develop inside the pastoral loveliness. An early bit of sex play between Barry (Ryan O'Neal) and his teasing cousin Nora (Gay Hamilton) is weighted as if the fate of nations hung on it. While we're still in a puzzled, anticipatory mood, this hushed atmosphere is intriguing, but then we begin to wonder how long it will take for the film to get its motor going. Thackeray wrote a skittish, fast-moving parody of romantic, sentimental writing. It was about the adventures of an Irish knave who used British hypocrisy for leverage; unscrupulous, he was blessed and cursed with too lively an imagination. However, it must have been Barry's ruthless pursuit of wealth and social position rather than his spirit that attracted Kubrick. The director may also have been drawn to the novel because of its externalized approach; Orwell was describing Thackeray's gift for farce when he said that one of Thackeray's heroes was "as flat as an icon." Kubrick picks up on that flatness for his own purposes and tells the story very formally. After an hour or so, Barry has deserted the British Army, only to be impressed into the Prussian Army and then into service as a police spy in Berlin, and we have begun to long for a few characters as a diversion from the relentless procession of impeccable, museum-piece compositions. All we get is Patrick Magee, encased in the makeup of a noble in the time of George III and wearing an eye patch, as the gambling Irishman that Barry is sent to spy on. The two of them head for the Prussian border, to begin a cardsharp partnership that will keep them travelling, and, with Barry at last a free man, the mood *could* lighten. It doesn't. O'Neal looks slack-faced and phlegmatic—exhausted from the effort of not acting—and one gets the feeling that Kubrick is too good for a light mood. Instead, in Spa, Belgium, Barry sets his sights on the rich, walking-doormat countess he will marry, and the film's color fades ominously to a colder tone. This ice pack, coming at the end of the first half, warns us that in the second half there will be none of the gusto we haven't had anyway.

As it becomes apparent that we are to sit and admire the lingering tableaux, we feel trapped. It's not merely that Kubrick isn't releasing the actors' energies or the story's exuberance but that he's deliberately holding the energy level down. He sets up his shots peerlessly, and can't let go of them. There are scenes, such as the card-room argument between Barry and the gouty old Sir Charles Lyndon (Frank Middlemass), that just sit there on the screen, obsessively, embarrassingly. Kubrick has worked them out visually, but dramatically they're hopeless. He has written his own screenplay, and the film lacks the tensions and conflicting temperaments that energized some of his earlier work and gave it jazzy undercurrents. Has he been schooling himself in late Dreyer and Bresson and

Rossellini, and is he trying to turn Thackeray's picaresque entertainment into a religious exercise? His tone here is unexpectedly holy. The dialogue, taken from the book, is too light to support this, so, right from the start, there's a discrepancy between what the characters are saying and the film's air of consecration. If you were to cut the jokes and cheerfulness out of the film *Tom Jones* and run it in slow motion, you'd have something very close to *Barry Lyndon*. Kubrick has taken a quick-witted story, full of vaudeville turns (Thackeray wrote it as a serial, under the pseudonym George Fitz-Boodle), and he's controlled it so meticulously that he's drained the blood out of it. The movie isn't quite the rise and fall of a flamboyant rakehell, because Kubrick doesn't believe in funning around. We never actually see Barry have a frisky, high time, and even when he's still a love-smitten chump, trying to act the gallant and fighting a foolish duel, Kubrick doesn't want us to take a shine to him. Kubrick disapproves of his protagonist. But it's more than that. He won't let Barry come to life, because he's reaching for a truth that he thinks lies beyond dramatization. And he thinks he can get it by photographing externals.

The film says that all mankind is corrupt. By Kubrick's insistence that this is a piece of wisdom that must be treated with Jansenist austerity and by his consequent refusal to entertain us, or even to involve us, he has made one of the vainest of all movies. He suppresses most of the active elements that make movies pleasurable; he must believe that his perfectionism about the look and sound of *Barry Lyndon* is what will make it great. It's a coffee-table movie; we might as well be at a three-hour slide show for art-history majors.

Ryan O'Neal has worked on his Irish lilt, he knows his lines, he's all psyched up for the assignment, his face straining with the effort to be what the Master wants—and all that Kubrick wants is to use him as a puppet. As Lady Lyndon, Marisa Berenson is just a doll to hang the lavish costumes on; her hairdos change more often than her expressions. In Kubrick's *A Clockwork Orange,* Malcolm McDowell brought his own vitality and instinct to the bullying hero; here Kubrick manipulates the actors the way he did in *2001.* The men are country bumpkins or overbred and ugly (they're treated rather like the writer—Patrick Magee—in *Clockwork*); the women, long-necked and high-breasted, are lovely, but they're no more than the camera's passing fancies. Kubrick doesn't want characterizations from the actors. It's his picture, in the same sense that Fellini's pictures have become *his.* Where Fellini, the caricaturist, hypercharges his people, makes them part of his world by making them grotesque, superabundant, Kubrick, the photographer, turns actors into pieces of furniture.

Even the action sequences in *Barry Lyndon* aren't meant to be exciting; they're meant only to be *visually* exciting. But when we have no interest in who is fighting a battle, or what the outcome will mean, the action must make an appeal to the senses all by itself, by its graphic strength and visual-emotional movement. It won't do to have soldiers being moved in patterns just to see what original effects a director can get. When Barry, as a soldier, is in a military skirmish during the Seven Years' War, Kubrick proves that even a battle can be pastel—the British Army's red coats are blanched to a photogenic rosy pink. This aestheticizing touch is symbolic of Kubrick's folly; the soldiers are pink toys—they don't die, they merely fall over. And this isn't used for its satiric potential: there's no comedy in it. The opposing line of soldiers wears lavender-pink cuffs, and that seems to be the reason they're on the field—so we can see the ravishing pinks and greens. Yet there's nothing like the extravagant sensuousness of *The Leopard*. When Barry is wenching, with his arms around two half-naked bawds, the scene is so statically composed that it's pristine, and when Kubrick looks at the wanly bored Lady Lyndon, palest pink in her bath, and you notice abstractly how her flesh tones blend with the appointments of the bathing salon, all you can say is "Pretty."

War has its own graphic power; we can turn on the TV and be moved by a combat scene in an old movie even if we don't know anything about the issues. Obviously, Stanley Kubrick does not have a gift for sensual fury—he's interested in the contemplative spectacle of war. Yet he's indifferent to the possibilities in the interaction of images and doesn't build his sequences by editing—which is how memorable war sequences are made—so his beautiful images are inert. If they seem like slides (certainly the narrator, Michael Hordern, seems like one of those museum tour-guide machines), it's because they don't do anything for each other. The episode of Barry's entrapment by the sly, grinning Prussian officer (Hardy Krüger), which is hammily obvious anyway, is so laborious because Kubrick spells it out instead of making the point by editing. The sequences of the gambling partnership might have been entertaining if they'd been telescoped, like Welles' account of Charles Foster Kane's first marriage.

But Kubrick's mode in this film is oracular and doomy: the narrator tells you what's going to happen before you see it—you're even told long in advance that the end is going to be unhappy. The music, off-puttingly classical under the titles (an omen of a consequential film), gets to be enough to make one want to fight back. What with the marches, dirges, and adagios, there's so much foreboding and afterboding that the music might as well be embalming fluid. Kubrick is doing the opposite of what the revolutionary Russian directors of the late teens and early twenties were attempting: he's going back to the pageant—to using film as a procession of images. And he's going back to impressing people by the magnificence of what is photographed; he's taking pictures of art objects. That antiques-filled room at the end of *2001* must have been where he wanted his own time machine to land. Kubrick seems overwhelmed by the cool splendor of the great manor houses, with their rich interiors and sweeping vistas. The people are repulsively corrupt, but the style in which they live is treated with reverential longing. He simply thinks they're the wrong people to be living there. The star of the picture is the aristocratic domicile.

The misanthropy is right on the surface. Kubrick makes no attempt to hide it; he thinks too highly of it. The few amiable characters—Captain Grogan (Godfrey Quigley) and the compliant German girl (Diana Koerner)—are dispatched quickly. Kubrick is on a hanging-judge trip. When he lets Barry's son, Brian, have sparkling, gamin eyes, you can guess that he's going to kill the kid off and make us suffer. He takes forever over the boy's dying, though at last, in the deathbed scene, Ryan O'Neal, telling the child a terminal tale, gets his one chance to do a Ryan O'Neal specialty: he smiles through tears marvellously. If Irving Thalberg had hired Antonioni to direct *Marie Antoinette,* it might have come out like this film—grayish powdered wigs and curdled faces. Some people may go along with it, because it *is* beautiful—if you like chilly fragility. And, since it's essentially a bloodless, elongated version of a thirties costume picture, it could have a camp appeal. One's response will probably depend on one's tolerance for the Kubrick message that people are disgusting but things are lovely. The trend in Kubrick's work has been toward dehumanization, and when Barry and Lady Lyndon have their dry-as-dust courtship and then a wedding that is so lifeless it could be a frozen image, Kubrick seems to have reached his goal: the marriage of robots.

This film is a masterpiece in every insignificant detail. Kubrick isn't taking pictures in order to make movies, he's making movies in order to take pictures. *Barry Lyndon* indicates that Kubrick is thinking through his camera, and that's not really how good movies get made—though it's what gives them their dynamism, if a director puts the images together vivifyingly, for an emotional impact. I wish Stanley Kubrick would come home to this country to make movies again, working fast on modern subjects—maybe even doing something tacky, for the hell of it. There was more *film* art in his early *The Killing* than there is in *Barry Lyndon*, and you didn't feel older when you came out of it. Orwell also said of Thackeray that his characteristic flavor is "the flavor of burlesque, of a world where no one is good and nothing is serious." For Kubrick, everything has become serious. The way he's been working, in self-willed isolation, with each film consuming years of anxiety, there's no ground between masterpiece and failure. And the pressure shows. There must be some reason that, in a film dealing with a licentious man in a licentious time, the only carnality—indeed, the only strong emotion—is in Barry's brutally caning his stepson. When a director gets to the point where the one emotion he shows is morally and physically ugly, maybe he ought to knock off on the big, inviolable endeavors.

□ □ □

Barry Lyndon is a mistake, but it's not disreputable. It's not a mangy insult, like *Lucky Lady,* which is an agents' picture—everybody's rip-off. The only drama involved was in the deal. It started with a script financed by an agent and manufactured by Willard Huyck and his wife, Gloria Katz. They'd worked on the script of the money-making *American Graffiti,* and that meant that their new script would be read as if it were a target map to the mother lode. Probably it hardly mattered that this script has no basis in experience and owes nothing to imagination, either. It's an example of a new cottage industry—the handwrought computerization of movie hits. 1930 . . . rum-running between Mexico and Southern California . . . a blond floozy-singer with two rival lovers—one canny-eyed and knowing, the other a well-meaning stupe . . . a fast boat . . . a darling orphaned "native" boy for a deckhand . . . action . . . little guys against the mob . . . high society . . . "native" boy killed by the dirty mob . . . vengeance . . . action climax . . . big. The idea was so aggressively charming that Twentieth Century-Fox was persuaded that the film would be another *The Sting,* and put up $450,000, which, in perfect justice, considering the picture, went to the agent, with the writers receiving a sixth of it. And the agent, Michael Gruskoff, now became the producer. It's too bad that we don't have access to the dialogues of all the agents involved, because they must have been inspired.

By the time Stanley Donen was hired as director and Liza Minnelli was slinging her body around in sleazy glitter and a blond wig, and Gene Hackman and Burt Reynolds were playing her competing lovers, something between $13,000,000 and $15,000,000 had got pyramided onto the shifty base. The mother lode is what this picture cost. When sneak previews revealed some dissatisfaction, the company tried to protect its huge investment by arranging to have a new ending shot. That new ending is like the desperation finishes on comedies of the forties, but it's no worse than the original finish (as described in the novelization of the screenplay). And it's not much worse than the beginning or the middle. A new new ending is now being pieced together out of the older footage; it can't make any aesthetic difference—there's no good way to end a picture that should never have been begun. However, the film has some handsomely shot, reassuringly fancy destruction scenes—boats exploding, burning, sinking, people shot up, blown to bits—and maybe audiences will go for that. Maybe, with a big enough campaign, *Lucky Lady* can combine the audience for *The Sting* with the audience for *The Towering Inferno.*

It's a movie for people who don't mind being treated like hicks: the audience is expected to shudder with delight every time it hears an obscenity or sees a big movie-star grin. Gene Hackman keeps a low profile and comes off better than the others, but it's not much of a contest.

Reynolds does the same simp act he did in *At Long Last Love*, letting you know he's miscast. He's willing to play a twit, but he plays it a little cute, so you'll know Burt Reynolds could never be convincing as a twit. There's nothing to be done with the role anyway, and he isn't obstreperously offensive; he and Hackman are both forgettable. What isn't is the deformation of Liza Minnelli's personality and appearance. To take a woman whose only sin is her naked overeagerness to make contact with an audience, and to turn her into a strident, selfish bitch, and then to sentimentalize *that*, as if her viciousness and rasping out at everyone were really adorable—that's tying Liza Minnelli to a block of cement. I know she consented to do this role, but I was offended for her. She has not earned *Lucky Lady*, and she does not deserve to be made so crude. She plays a scene of comic feminine incompetence—she's unable to light a match—that would be a low point in the annals of women on the screen if one could for a moment believe that the characters in this movie were men or women. The plastic is so thick that when Liza Minnelli puts on a record of Bessie Smith singing "Young Woman's Blues" you can barely register that it's really Bessie Smith's voice. This mercenaries' film is so coarsely conceived it obliterates any emotion, any art.

[December 29, 1975]

Brotherhood Is Powerful

John Huston's *The Man Who Would Be King,* based on the Rudyard Kipling short story, is an exhilaratingly farfetched adventure fantasy about two roughneck con men, Danny and Peachy (Sean Connery and Michael Caine), in Victoria's India, who decide to conquer a barbarous land for themselves, and set out for Kafiristan, a region which was once ruled by Alexander the Great, to make themselves kings. With twenty rifles, their British Army training, unprincipled rashness, cunning, and a few wild strokes of luck, they succeed, for a time. As a movie, this Empire gothic has elements of *Gunga Din* and of a cynical *Lost Horizon,* along with something that hasn't been a heroic attribute in other Empire-gothic movies: the desire to become the highest-ranking person that one can envision. The heroes are able to achieve their goal only because of the primitiveness of the people they conquer, and this is very likely the stumbling block that kept the movie from being financed for the twenty-odd years that Huston wanted to do it. Maybe he was able to, finally, on the assumption that enough time has passed for the heroes' attitude toward the native populations of India and Kafiristan—the benighted heathen—to seem quaint rather than racist. Huston's narrative is both an ironic parable about the motives and methods of imperialism and a series of gags about civilization and barbarism. When savages in war masks are hit by bullets, the image is a sick-joke history of colonialism, and when the vulgarian heroes try to civilize the tribes they conquer, they obviously have not much more than their own military conditioning to draw upon. Danny and Peachy are British primitives who seek to turn the savages into Englishmen by drilling them in discipline and respect for authority. Danny becomes as sanctimonious about that mission as Victoria herself, and is baffled when the natives show ingratitude.

The script, by Huston and Gladys Hill, is a fine piece of craftsmanship, with every detail in place, and with some of Kipling's devices carried further, so that the whole mad, jinxed adventure is tied together. But *The Man Who Would Be King* isn't rousing, and it isn't a comedy, either. It's a genre movie made with full awareness of the campy pit into which it will sink if the laconic distancing ever lapses. Huston has to hold down the very emotions that most spectacles aim for; if he treated the material stirringly, it would take the audience back to the era when we were supposed to feel pride in the imperial British gallantry, as we did at some level, despite our more knowledgeable, disgusted selves, at movies like the 1935 *Lives of a Bengal Lancer*. This film doesn't dare give us the empathic identification with what's going on inside the heroes which we had with Gary Cooper and Franchot Tone in *Bengal Lancer*. And Huston, who has never been interested in spectacle for its own luxurious sake, doesn't make a big event of the adventure, the way Capra did with the arrival at Shangri-la—when he practically unveiled the city. Shot in Morocco, with Oswald Morris as cinematographer and Alexander Trauner as production designer, *The Man Who Would Be King* is in subdued reds and browns, and the persistent dusty earth tones underscore the transiency of the heroes' victory. There are no soaring emotions. Huston tells his whopper in a matter-of-fact tone, and he doesn't play up the cast of thousands or the possibilities of portentous spectacle in the bizarre stone "sacred city" of Alexander the Great, built on a mountain.

The director's love of the material is palpable; it makes one smile. Yet the most audacious parts of the film don't reach for that special clarity which makes action memorably poetic. There are lovely, foolish poetic bits—a panoramic view of warring armies pausing to genuflect when holy men walk through the battlefield, and the brave last flourish of Billy Fish (Saeed Jaffrey), the interpreter for the heroes, who dies charging their enemies, pointlessly, in the name of British military ideals—but these episodes are offhand and brief. Huston's is a perverse form of noblesse oblige—he doesn't want to push anything. He won't punch up the moments that are right there waiting, even though we might have enjoyed basking in them, and getting a lift from them. He sets up the most elaborate, berserk fairy-tale scenes and then just sits back; he seems to be watching the events happen instead of shaping them. Huston has said that Danny and Peachy are destroyed because of *folie de grandeur,* and that's what he risks, too. I admire his pride; he treats the audience with a sophisticated respect that's rare in genre films, and this movie is the best sustained work he's done in years. Even Edith Head's costume designs and Maurice Jarre's musical score rise to the occasion, and the animal noises (they sound like cows lowing through giant megaphones) that accompany the primitive rites are terrifyingly creepy. But Huston's courtliness has its weakness. No doubt he believes in telling the story as simply as possible, but what that means in practice is that he shoots the script. It's exemplary, and he's a good storyteller. But he's not such a great *movie* storyteller here. I don't think Huston any longer plans scenes for the startling sprung rhythms of his early work. The camera now seems to be passively recording—intelligently, beautifully, but without the sudden, detonating effects of participation. Huston has become more of an illustrator. And so the ironies in *The Man Who Would Be King* go by fast—when we want them to vibrate a little.

Huston's even-tempered narrative approach doesn't quite release all that we suspect he feels about the material. It may be that he's so far into the kind of thinking that this story represents that he doesn't take us in far enough. If he had regressed to an earlier stage of movie history and presented Kipling's jingoism with emotional force, the film might have been a controversial, inflammatory epic. If he had rekindled the magical appeal of that jingoism and made us understand our tragic vulnerability to it, it might have been a true modern epic. The way he's done it, the story works only on the level of a yarn. But it's a wonderful yarn. Huston shares with Kipling a revelling in the unexpected twists of behavior of other cultures, and he doesn't convert the story into something humanistic. The ignorant natives are cruel and barbaric; if they're given a chance, they don't choose fair play. And Huston leaves it at that—he doesn't pussyfoot around, trying to make them lovable. Huston has a fondness for the idiosyncrasies of the natives, and he doesn't hate the heroes who go out to exploit them. Huston is cynical without a shade of contempt—that's why the film is likable. Yet when you play fascinated anthropologist, equally amused by the British and the natives, you may have licked the problem of how to do Kipling now without an outcry, but you're being false to why you wanted to film the story in the first place. Despite the film's ironic view of them, Danny and Peachy, who can sing in the face of death, represent courage and gallantry. Huston may spoof this when he has Peachy bawl out

Danny for rushing in to attack an enemy army, and Danny, who has won the battle single-handed, apologize that his "blood was up," but the love of this crazed courage is built into the genre, and even if you leave out the surging emotion of the arrival of the British relief column, it's the Britishers here—and their devoted Billy Fishes—who represent civilization. Their ways of killing are cleaner—they don't kill for pleasure. Huston's irony can't remove all this—it merely keeps it from being offensive.

The theme of *The Man Who Would Be King* gets at the essence of the attitudes underlying John Huston's work. Huston might be the man without illusions on a quest. Here, as in *The Maltese Falcon, The Asphalt Jungle, The Treasure of Sierra Madre,* his characters are after money. But when Danny and Peachy are battling mountain snowstorms, risking blindness and death to get to the backward country they mean to pillage, one knows that it isn't just for gold—it's because conquering and looting a country are the highest score they can imagine. And when they view Alexander the Great's treasure, the jewels and gold pieces seem a little ridiculous; the treasure will be scattered, like the gold dust in *The Treasure of Sierra Madre.* What matters in Huston films is the existential quest: man testing himself. It's a great pity that Huston didn't get to film Mailer's *An American Dream*, which is also about a man who would be king. (All Mailer's writing is.) Mailer's book, being in contemporary terms, might have challenged Huston right to the bone. The Kipling story, with its links to old adventure-genre movies, and its links to the childhood tastes we have disowned, doesn't quite.

Huston finds a grisly humor in the self-deceptions of ruthless people chasing rainbows; that might almost be his comic notion of man's life on earth. He earns esteem by not sentimentalizing that quest. (Yet his inability to show affection for characters who live on different terms shows how much the rogues mean to him.) Huston isn't too comfortable about any direct show of emotion; he's in his element (and peerlessly) with men who are boyishly brusque, putting down their own tender feelings shamefacedly. When he first prepared this script, Gable was to be in the Connery role and Bogart in the Caine role. Connery is, I think, a far better Danny than Gable would ever have been. Gable never had this warmth, and never gave himself over to a role the way Connery does. With the glorious exceptions of Brando and Olivier, there's no screen actor I'd rather watch than Sean Connery. His vitality may make him the most richly masculine of all English-speaking actors; that thick, rumbling Scotsman's voice of his actually transforms English—muffles the clipped edges and humanizes the language. Connery's Danny has a beatific, innocent joy in his crazy goal even when he's half frozen en route; few actors are as unself-consciously silly as Connery is willing to be—as he *enjoys* being. Danny's fatuity is sumptuous as he throws himself into his first, half-embarrassed lofty gestures. Connery plays this role without his usual hairpieces, and, undisguised—bare-domed—he seems larger, more free; if baldness ever needed redeeming, he's done it for all time. Caine has the Bogart role, which means he's Huston's protagonist; Peachy is the smarter of the two, the wise-guy realist, loyal to Danny even when he's depressed by Danny's childishness. We see through Peachy's sane, saddened eyes the danger in Danny's believing himself a man of destiny, and Caine manages this with the modesty of a first-rate actor. He stays in character so convincingly that he's able to bring off the difficult last scene, rounding out the story conception, when it becomes apparent that Peachy has "gone native."

The central human relationship is between these two uneducated working-class blokes, who at first share a fantasy, and who remain friends—brothers, really, since they're Masons—even when their fantasies diverge. The entire plot hinges on Freemasonry—not however, used philosophically, as it was in *The Magic Flute,* though Kipling himself was deeply involved in the brotherhood, and Christopher Plummer, who plays him here, wears a Masonic watch fob. Plummer, hidden by a thick brush mustache, gives a blessedly restrained performance as the straitlaced young editor in India. In terms of historical accuracy, however, he's not young enough for the part. Brother Kipling—an "infant monster," Henry James called him—was only twenty-two when he published the story. In the movie, it seems appropriate that the watch fob should set the whole adventure in motion; the brotherhood that links the two rowdy crooks, the nearsighted journalist, and the shaven-headed monks in the temple of Kafiristan is like a schoolboys' secret society that has swept the world. In the story, Kipling was able to satirize his own gnomic vision of fraternity, and at times Huston and Gladys Hill, ringing changes on the mystic-fraternity theme—"rejuvenating" it—might almost be borrowing from Edgar Rice Burroughs. Huston seems to be enjoying himself in this film in the way he hasn't for a long time. It communicates the feeling of a consummated dream.

One of the incidental benefits of movies based on classics is that filmgoers are often eager to read the book; Allied Artists, which produced this film, and Bantam Books have just struck a low note by putting out a gold-covered paperback *novelization* of Kipling's story. This makeshift Kipling, written by Michael Hardwick, combines the story and the screenplay, unnecessary descriptions, and bits from Kipling's life to fill a hundred and thirty-seven pages. The whole new practice of film novelizations is a disgrace. It sickens the screenwriters who have written original screenplays to see their dialogue debased into a prose stew, but at least they are alive and in a position to fight against it. If they're suckered, it's partly their own damned greedy fault. But here is a movie inspired by love of Kipling—apparently, Huston first read the story when he was twelve or thirteen, and it meant enough to him to nag at him many years later—and this love has had the effect of temporarily displacing the story and putting drivel in its stead.

Hunger cannot be the excuse: Allied Artists and Bantam Books are not poor and desperate, and the profit to be made from this venture is not likely to be vast. What is the rationale for this garbagizing of literature? I don't think "The Man Who Would Be King" is a great story, but it's a good one—good enough to have turned people into Kipling readers, maybe, if it had been made readily available in an edition with one or two other Kipling stories, and with the movie-photo tie-ins that will attract readers to this gold beauty. Since Kipling's work isn't in screenplay form but in a highly readable form, the motive for this mass-marketed paperback seems almost like giggly mischief—a *folie* of debasement. That could be another term for business as usual. Allied Artists and Bantam Books, why are you doing this?

[January 5, 1976]

Notes on the Nihilist Poetry of Sam Peckinpah

Sam Peckinpah is a great "personal" filmmaker; he's an artist who can work as an artist only on his own terms. When he does a job for hire, he must transform the script and make it his own or it turns into convictionless self-parody (like *The Getaway*). Peckinpah likes to say that he's a good whore who goes where he's kicked. The truth is he's a very bad whore: he can't turn out a routine piece of craftsmanship—he can't use his skills to improve somebody else's conception. That's why he has always had trouble. And trouble, plus that most difficult to define of all gifts—a film sense—is the basis of his legend.

Most movie directors have short wings; few of them are driven to realize their own vision. But Peckinpah's vision has become so scabrous, theatrical, and obsessive that it is now controlling him. His new film, *The Killer Elite,* is set so far inside his fantasy-morality world that it goes beyond personal filmmaking into private filmmaking. The story, which is

112

about killers employed by a company with C.I.A. connections, is used as a mere framework for a compressed, almost abstract fantasy on the subject of selling yourself yet trying to hang on to a piece of yourself. Peckinpah turned fifty while he was preparing this picture, and, what with booze, illness, and a mean, self-destructive streak, in recent years he has looked as if his body were giving out. This picture is about survival.

*T*here are so many elisions in *The Killer Elite* that it hardly exists on a narrative level, but its poetic vision is all of a piece. Unlike Peckinpah's earlier, spacious movies, with Lucien Ballard's light-blue, open-air vistas, this film is intensely, claustrophobically exciting, with combat scenes of martial-arts teams photographed in slow motion and then edited in such brief cuts that the fighting is nightmarishly concentrated—almost subliminal. Shot by Phil Lathrop in cold, five-o'clock-shadow green-blue tones, the film is airless—an involuted, corkscrew vision of a tight, modern world. In its obsessiveness, with the links between sequences a matter of irrational, poetic connections, *The Killer Elite* is closer to *The Blood of a Poet* than it is to a conventional thriller made on the C.I.A.-assassins subject, such as *Three Days of the Condor*. And, despite the script by Marc Norman and Stirling Silliphant that United Artists paid for, the film isn't about C.I.A.-sponsored assassinations—it's about the blood of a poet.

*W*ith his long history of butchered films and films released without publicity, of being fired and blacklisted for insubordination, of getting ornerier and ornerier, Peckinpah has lost a lot of blood. Even *The Wild Bunch*, a great imagist epic in which Peckinpah, by a supreme burst of filmmaking energy, was able to convert chaotic romanticism into exaltation—a film comparable in scale and sheer poetic force to Kurosawa's *The Seven Samurai*—was cut in its American release, and has not yet been restored. And Peckinpah was forced to trim *The Killer Elite* to change its R rating to a PG. Why would anybody want a PG-rated Peckinpah film? The answer is that United Artists, having no confidence in the picture, grabbed the chance to place it in four hundred and thirty-five theatres for the Christmas trade; many of those theatres wouldn't have taken it if it had an R and the kids couldn't go by themselves. The film was flung into those neighborhood houses for a quick profit, without benefit of advance press screenings or the ad campaign that goes with a first-run showing. Peckinpah's career is becoming a dirty, bitter game of I-dump-on-you-because-you-dump-on-me. Increasingly, his films have reflected his war with the producers and distributors, and in *The Killer Elite* this war takes its most single-minded form.

*P*eckinpah's roots are in the theatre as much as they're in the West; he loves the theatricality of Tennessee Williams (early on, he directed three

113

different stage productions of *The Glass Menagerie*), and, personally, he has the soft-spoken grandness of a Southerner in a string tie—when he talks of the way California used to be, it is in the reverent tone that Southerners use for the Old South. The hokum runs thick in him, and his years of television work—writing dozens of "Gunsmoke" episodes, "creating" the two series "The Rifleman" and "The Westerner"—pushed his thinking into good-guys-versus-bad-guys formats. The tenderness he felt for Tennessee Williams' emotional poetry he could also feel for a line of dialogue that defined a Westerner's plain principles. He loves actors, and he enjoyed the TV-Western make-believe, but that moment when the routine Western script gave way to a memorably "honest" emotion became for him what it was all about. When Peckinpah reminisces about "a great Western," it sometimes comes down to one flourish that for him "said everything." And Peckinpah lives by and for heroic flourishes; they're his idea of the real thing, and in his movies he has invested them with such nostalgic passion that a viewer can be torn between emotional assent and utter confusion as to what, exactly, he's assenting to.

As the losing battles with the moneymen have gone on, year after year, Peckinpah has—only partly sardonically, I think—begun to see the world in terms of the bad guys (the studio executives who have betrayed him or chickened out on him) and the people he likes (generally actors), who are the ones smart enough to see what the process is all about, the ones who haven't betrayed him yet. Hatred of the bad guys—the total mercenaries—has become practically the only sustaining emotion in his work, and his movies have become fables about striking back.

Many of the things that Peckinpah says in conversation began to seep into his last film, *Bring Me the Head of Alfredo Garcia* (1974), turning it into a time-machine foul-up, with modern, airborne killers functioning in the romanticized Mexico of an earlier movie era. Essentially the same assassins dominate the stylized, darkened San Francisco of *The Killer Elite*. In a *Playboy* interview with William Murray in 1972, Peckinpah was referring to movie producers when he said, "The woods are full of killers, all sizes, all colors. . . . A director has to deal with a whole world absolutely teeming with mediocrities, jackals, hangers-on, and just plain killers. The attrition is terrific. It can kill you. The saying is that they can kill you but not eat you. That's nonsense. I've had them eating on me while I was still walking around." Sam Peckinpah looks and behaves as if he were never free of their gnawing. He carries it with him, fantasizes it, provokes it, makes it true again and again. He romanticizes himself as one of the walking wounded, which is no doubt among the reasons he wanted to direct *Play It As It Lays*. (He was rejected by the businessmen as being strictly an action director.) In that Murray interview, he was referring to the making of movies when he said, "When you're dealing in millions, you're dealing with people at their meanest. Christ, a showdown in the old West is nothing compared with the infighting that goes on over money."

Peckinpah swallowed Robert Ardrey whole; it suited his emotional needs—he *wants* to believe that all men are whores and killers. He was talking to Murray about what the bosses had done to him and to his films when he said, "There are people all over the place, dozens of them, I'd like to kill, quite literally kill." He's dramatizing, but I've known Sam Peckinpah for over ten years (and, for all his ceremonial exhibitionism, his power plays, and his baloney, or maybe because of them, there is a total, physical elation in his work and in his own relation to it that makes me feel closer to him than I do to any other director except Jean Renoir) and I'm convinced that he actually feels that demonic hatred. I think Sam Peckinpah feels everything that he dramatizes—he allows himself to. He's a ham: he doesn't feel what he doesn't dramatize.

Peckinpah has been simplifying and falsifying his own terrors as an artist by putting them into melodramatic formulas. He's a major artist who has worked so long in penny-dreadful forms that when he is finally in a position where he's famous enough to fight for his freedom—and maybe win—he can't free himself from the fear of working outside those forms, or from the festering desire for revenge. He is the killer-élite hero played by James Caan in this hallucinatory thriller, in which the hirelings turn against their employers. James Caan's Mike, a No. 1 professional, is mutilated by his closest friend, George Hansen (Robert Duvall), at the order of Cap Collis (Arthur Hill), a defector within the company—Communications Integrity Associates—that they all work for. Mike rehabilitates himself, however, by a long, painful struggle, regaining the use of his body so that he can revenge himself. He comes back more determined than ever, and his enemies—Hansen and Cap Collis—are both shot. But when the wearily cynical top man in the company (Gig Young) offers Mike a regional directorship—Cap Collis's newly vacated position—he rejects it. Instead, he sails—literally—into unknown seas with his loyal friend the gunman-mechanic Mac (Burt Young).

There's no way to make sense of what has been going on in Peckinpah's recent films if one looks only at their surface stories. Whether consciously or, as I think, part unconsciously, he's been destroying the surface content. In this new film, there aren't any of the ordinary kinds of introductions to the characters, and the events aren't prepared for. The political purposes of the double-crosses are shrouded in a dark fog, and the company itself makes no economic sense. There are remnants of a plot involving a political leader from Taiwan (he sounds off about democratic principles in the manner of Paul Henreid's Victor Laszlo in *Casablanca*), but that fog covers all the specific plot points. Peckinpah can explain this disintegration to himself in terms of how contemptible the material actually is—the fragmented story indicates how he feels about what the bosses buy and what they degrade him with. He agrees to do these properties, to be "a good whore," and then he can't help turning them into revenge fantasies. His whole way of making movies has become a revenge fantasy: he screws the bosses, he screws the picture, he screws himself.

*T*he physical rehabilitation of the hero in *The Killer Elite* (his refusal to accept the company's decision that he's finished) is an almost childishly transparent disguise for Peckinpah's own determination to show Hollywood that he's not dead yet—that, despite the tabloid views of him, frail and falling-down drunk, he's got the will to make great movies. He's trying to pick up the pieces of his career. Amazingly, Peckinpah does rehabilitate himself; his technique here is dazzling. In the moments just before violence explodes, Peckinpah's work is at its most subtly theatrical: he savors the feeling of power as he ticks off the seconds before the suppressed rage will take form. When it does, it's often voluptuously horrifying (and that is what has given Peckinpah a dubious reputation—what has made him Bloody Sam), but this time it isn't gory and yet it's more daring than ever. He has never before made the violence itself so surreally, fluidly abstract; several sequences are edited with a magical speed—a new refinement. In *Alfredo Garcia,* the director seemed to have run out of energy after a virtuoso opening, and there was a scene, when the two leads (Warren Oates and Isela Vega) were sitting by the side of a road, that was so scrappily patched together, with closeups that didn't match, that Peckinpah appeared to have run out of zest for filmmaking. Maybe it was just that in *Alfredo Garcia* his old obsessions had lost their urgency and his new one—his metaphoric view of modern corporate business, represented by the dapper, errand-boy killers (Gig Young and Robert Webber as mirror-image lovers)—had thrown him off balance. He didn't seem to know why he was making the movie, and Warren Oates, who has fine shadings in character roles, was colorless in the central role (as he was also in the title role of John Milius's *Dillinger*). Oates is a man who's used to not being noticed, and his body shows it. When he tried to be a star by taking over Peckinpah's glasses and mustache and manner, he was imitating the outside of a dangerous person—the inside was still meek. And, of course, Peckinpah, with his feelers (he's a man who gives the impression of never missing anything going on in a room), knew the truth: that the actor in *Alfredo Garcia* who was like him, without trying at all, was Gig Young, with his weary pale eyes. In *The Killer Elite,* James Caan is the hero who acts out Peckinpah's dream of salvation, but it's Gig Young's face that

116

haunts the film. Gig Young represents Peckinpah's idea of what he will become if he doesn't screw them all and sail away.

*P*eckinpah is surely one of the most histrionic men who have ever lived: his movies (and his life, by now) are all gesture. He thinks like an actor, in terms of the effect, and the special bits he responds to in Westerns are actors' gestures—corniness transcended by the hint of nobility in the actors themselves. Like Gig Young, he has the face of a ravaged juvenile, a face that magnetizes because of the suggestion that the person understands more than he wants to. It's a fake, this look, but Peckinpah cultivates the whore-of-whores pose. He plays with the idea of being the best of men and, when inevitably betrayed, the worst of men. (He's got to be both the best and the worst.) Gig Young has the same air of gentleness that Peckinpah has, and the dissolute quality of an actor whose talents have been wasted. Gig Young's face seems large for his body now, in a way that suggests that it has carried a lot of makeup in its time; he looks rubbery-faced, like an old song-and-dance man. Joel McCrea, with his humane strength, may have been Peckinpah's idealized hero in *Ride the High Country,* and William Holden may have represented a real man to him in *The Wild Bunch,* but Gig Young, who represents what taking orders from the bosses—being used—does to *a man of feeling,* is the one Peckinpah shows the most affection for now. Gig Young can play the top whore in *The Killer Elite* because his sad eyes suggest that he has no expectations and no illusions left about anything. And Peckinpah can identify with this character because of the element of pain in Gig Young, who seems to be the most naked of actors—an actor with nowhere to hide. (Peckinpah's own eyes are saintly-sly, and he's actually the most devious of men.) Peckinpah could never for an instant identify with the faceless corporate killer played by Arthur Hill. When you see Arthur Hill as Cap Collis, the sellout, you know that it didn't cost Collis anything to sell out. He's a gutless wonder, something that crawled out of the woodwork. Arthur Hill's unremarkable, company-man face and lean, tall body are already abstractions; he's a corporate entity in himself. In Peckinpah's iconography, he's a walking cipher, a man who wasn't born of woman but was cast in a mold—a man whose existence is a defeat for men of feeling.

*J*ames Caan goes through the athletic motions of heroism and acts intelligently, but he doesn't bring the right presence to the role. His stoicism lacks homicidal undercurrents, and he doesn't have the raw-nerved awareness that seems needed. The face that suggests some of what Peckinpah is trying to express—the residual humanity in killers—is that of Burt Young, as the devoted Mac. The swarthy, solid, yet sensitive face of Burt Young (he played the man looking at pictures of his faithless wife at

117

the beginning of *Chinatown*) shows the weight of feelings. Mac's warm, gravelly croak and his almost grotesque simpleness link him to the members of the Wild Bunch. His is a face with substance, capable of dread on a friend's account. In *The Killer Elite,* his is the face that shows the feelings that have been burnt out of Gig Young's.

*P*eckinpah has become wryly sentimental about his own cynicism. When the Taiwanese leader's young daughter pompously tells the hero that she's a virgin, and he does a variation on Rhett Butler, saying, "To tell you the truth, I really don't give a shit," the director's contempt for innocence is too self-conscious, and it sticks out. Peckinpah wants to be honored for the punishment he's taken, as if it were battle scars. The doctor who patches up the hero says, "The scar looks beautiful"—which, in context, is a sleek joke. But when the hero's braced leg fails him and he falls helplessly on his face on a restaurant floor, Sam Peckinpah may be pushing for sympathy for his own travail. From the outside, it's clear that even his battle scars aren't all honorable—that a lot of the time he wasn't fighting to protect his vision, he was fighting for tortuous reasons. He doesn't start a picture with a vision; he starts a picture as a job and then perversely—in spite of his deal to sell out—he turns into an artist.

*M*uch of what Peckinpah is trying to express in *The Killer Elite* is probably inaccessible to audiences, his moral judgments being based less on what his characters do than on what they wouldn't stoop to do. (In Hollywood, people take more pride in what they've said no to than in what they've done.) Yet by going so far into his own hostile, edgily funny myth—in being the maimed victim who rises to smite his enemies—he found a ferocious unity, an Old Testament righteousness that connects with the audience in ways his last few pictures didn't. At the beginning of *The Killer Elite,* the lack of sunlight is repellent; the lividness looks cheap and pulpy—were those four hundred and thirty-five prints processed in a sewer? But by the end a viewer stares fixedly, not quite believing he's seeing what he's seeing: a nightmare ballet. In the free-form murderous finale, with guns, Samurai swords, and lethal skills one has never heard of before, there are troops of Oriental assassins scurrying over the phantom fleet of Second World War ships maintained in Suisun Bay, north of San Francisco. Wrapped up in their cult garb so we can't tell one from another, the darting killers, seen in those slow-motion fast cuts, are exactly like Peckinpah's descriptions of the teeming mediocrities, jackals, hangers-on, and just plain killers that Hollywood is full of.

*T*he film is so cleanly made that Peckinpah may have wrapped up this obsession. When James Caan and Burt Young sail away at the end, it's Sam Peckinpah turning his back on Hollywood. He has gone to Europe, with commitments that will keep him there for at least two years. It would be too simple to say that he has been driven out of the American movie industry, but it's more than half true. No one is Peckinpah's master as a director of individual sequences; no one else gets such beauty out of movement and hard grain and silence. He doesn't do the expected, and so, scene by scene, he creates his own actor-director's suspense. The images in *The Killer Elite* are charged, and you have the feeling that not one is wasted. What they all add up to is something else—but one could say the same of *The Pisan Cantos*. Peckinpah has become so nihilistic that filmmaking itself seems to be the only thing he believes in. He's crowing in *The Killer Elite*, saying, "No matter what you do to me, look at the way I can make a movie." The bedevilled bastard's got a right to crow.

[January 12, 1976]

Kaputt

U niversal has gone back to one of the most primitive forms of movie advertising for *The Hindenburg*—TWO YEARS IN THE MAKING . . . PRESENTED AT A COST OF $15,000,000. And that's what it's selling: a hefty enterprise. Everything's been done to produce the illusion of a giant zeppelin sailing along, but the film doesn't have the flotation it needs—we don't experience the beatific sensations of lighter-than-air travel. In the late twenties and early thirties, before transatlantic plane service, people with enough money could make the crossing by dirigible; smoothly and noiselessly, they were wafted across the ocean in two and a half days. This form of vibrationless travel, perfected by the Germans, got a black eye when the Hindenburg—filled with explosive hydrogen, because the United States wouldn't sell Nazi Germany nonexplosive helium—blew up while coming down for a landing at Lakehurst, New Jersey, on May 6, 1937, with ninety-seven people on board. Thirteen passengers and twenty-two members of the crew were killed. Since there were newsreel cameramen waiting there to photograph the arrival, they recorded the disaster, and millions of people saw it in theatres. In thirty-four seconds, this great luxury airship, longer than two football fields, became a mass of flames, and its aluminum-alloy skeleton was exposed as it crashed. The movie is a fictional version of what happened on its last flight.

Zeppelins have an inflated-toy, sci-fi humor. Compared to the structure of planes, the fat-cigar shape seems amorphous, loony—a blob. Yet travel in them, with windows open to the fresh air, must have been intoxicating. There are so many easy ways that *The Hindenburg* could have suggested the giddiness—couldn't one of the passengers have at least picked up the hundred-and-twelve-pound aluminum grand piano in the lounge? But Robert Wise directed with tame, impersonal good taste; there's none of the blissful trippiness of being carried in the belly of a zeppelin, and none of the carnival vulgarity of the recent disaster thrillers. How can you agree to do one of these disaster epics and then con yourself into thinking that you can do it like a gent? There's a time-honored Hollywood device that enables those who compromise on all the important things to convince themselves that they're engaged in something of real importance: they give it social content. Robert Wise turned his disaster picture into an anti-Nazi disaster picture. The plot is an elaboration of the speculative thesis that the Hindenburg was destroyed by a saboteur's bomb, as an act of resistance to Hitler. But the elaboration of this plausible idea is so pompous that one might think Hollywood was taking credit for the explosion. The film builds up every kind of sympathy for the saboteur, who, being anti-Nazi, didn't intend for anyone to get hurt; he's infinitely courageous, and he even loves dogs. Wise brings all his flatulent seriousness to this endeavor. One gasbag meets another.

The introduction of the cast of characters is the most routinized part of the movies of this genre; it's like the animals going up the ramp to the Ark, and moviegoers have become connoisseurs of this assembling process. Robert Wise's convocation doesn't measure up. He was the director of such Academy Award–winning hits as *West Side Story* and *The Sound of Music,* and even a few pretty good pictures, but he'd never make it as Noah. He dawdles over the gathering of the clan, and the transatlantic swingers in *The Hindenburg* must be the frowziest bunch ever put together outside an ABC "Movie of the Week." Anne Bancroft plays the blasé doper Ursula, a sneering German countess whose hair has been coiffed to be so authentically thirties that it looks like black potato chips stuck to her head. (If Bancroft takes this *Ship of Fools*–Signoret spinoff role, what can the roles she rejects be like?) As soon as she speaks with that familiar New York intonation, her hauteur crumbles, though her eyebrows remain elevated. She's such a likable actress you want her to come off the great-lady pose. When she uses her classy allure on George C. Scott—a disillusioned Luftwaffe colonel—those eyebrows waggle like Groucho's. This cast really ought to get the troupers' award; perfectly good actors like William Atherton, Burgess Meredith, and Charles Durning all hang in there while Wise and his scenarist, Nelson Gidding, shuffle the subplots in order to create the impression of action. Wise tries to force conviction into the hollow characters; and dialogue that might pass if it were casually overlapped is delivered with such stick-to-itiveness that the actors could be bulldogs playing charades.

It's obvious that the logistics of this production were a real killer, and Albert Whitlock's matte effects are very fine trompe-l'oeil. Authenticity has been the keynote of this production—right down to the copying of the pattern of the Hindenburg's crockery and silverware. When moviemakers don't have strong feelings about what they're doing, solid research is the only kind of integrity left. This is a technically complicated primitive film that has been made in such a spirit of self-deception that it fails to work on the primitive level. It's so dry you begin to feel dehydrated and your mind goes on the fritz. Still, with the promotion it's got going for it (which may be included in that suspiciously high fifteen-million-dollar figure), chances are that it will do all right at box offices anyway—it can be *The Great Gatsby* of disaster movies.

The Hindenburg has, however, been the cause of a new complaint: some viewers (and members of the press, too) say that they've been gypped—that the disaster footage is *real* rather than *faked*. They don't like the ten-minute climax, which is the famous newsreel footage extended and intercut with newly shot scenes showing the actors—some perishing, some fleeing the wreckage. If the movie had begun with the newsreel material, followed by a large-scale detective story trying to account for the crash, probably no one would feel let down, but it's likely that Universal wanted to retain the formula of the recent fantasy-disaster money-makers, which have big, showcase climaxes. What Wise may not be able to accept is that, despite his efforts at authenticity, the movie is essentially every bit as fakey as *Earthquake* or *The Towering Inferno*, and the audience sits waiting for the final thrills. So when people complain, they're not necessarily being stupes: they could be expressing the feeling that the movie hasn't earned the right to bring in actual suffering; they may want the gaudy finish that would be more appropriate to the twerpy story. If it's possible to violate the disaster genre, *The Hindenburg* has done it. Blending documentary-catastrophe footage with simulated-catastrophe footage is fundamentally insensitive: how can a viewer look at true horrors and be a jaded connoisseur of movie thrills in practically the same instant? The mixture is like a visual *Ragtime* without satire. The original newsreel material is blown up, padded, interrupted, frozen, though when flames are shown in still shots you don't see more—all you get is the feeling that people are playing around and turning a newsreel into graphics. I had a very strong desire to see the newsreel as it was before all these graphics wizards got to work on it: I wanted the integrity of that famous thirty-four-second catastrophe respected. After the climax, the moviemakers appear to be clowning around when they give a report on which of the fictional characters have survived; when they provide the upbeat news that the pet Dalmatian on board, released from its cage by the saboteur, came through, they seem to be playing the audience for ninnies. At the close, Wise has tacked on to the sound track the words delivered to the 1937 radio listeners by a reporter at the scene: "Oh my, this is terrible. . . . This is one of the worst catastrophes in the world. . . . It's a terrific crash, ladies and gentlemen. . . . It's smoke and it's flames. . . . I don't believe it. . . . I'm going to have to stop for a minute. . . . This is the worst thing I have ever witnessed." Is Robert Wise, recent president of the Directors Guild of America, nostalgic for the relatively innocent days of radio reporting? Probably he is. But this ending may be less naïve than it seems. In the film, Scott, who is endowed with wry hindsight, calls the Hindenburg a flying dinosaur. Since the passengers who died in the actual explosion were the only passenger fatalities in nearly three decades of commercial dirigible service, what purpose does the film's contempt serve but to reinforce the impression given to the world by the newsreel and radio accounts? In order to make the disaster seem retribution for the Nazis and large enough to rival the fantasy horrors of recent hit films, this movie omits the most remarkable aspect of the Hindenburg story—that the media coverage of the crash resulted in the end of a mode of air travel which was superior to the airplane, and far safer. The crockery may be authentic all right, but the picture is a crock.

□ □ □

*I*f ever a movie needed to be made on location and in a loose, hand-held-camera style, it's *The Black Bird*—an attempted takeoff on *The Maltese Falcon*—because the only base for its humor is the contrast between the lives of Humphrey Bogart's Sam Spade and George Segal's Sam Spade, Jr. In the 1941 John Huston film, the crooked fantasists trying to get hold of the jewelled falcon invaded Spade's orderly life in the sophisticated metropolis of San Francisco. Spade Junior's San Francisco is the zonked city of fantasists, and he's scrounging around for a living in an inherited trade that makes no sense to him. Something could have been done with the idea of a renewed search for the falcon in these changed circumstances if this new film, written and directed (more or less) by David Giler, had been able to roll along, moving among the street people and their throwaway conversations, and parodying modern filmmaking techniques as against the controlled, studio style of the Huston film. There are bits of this attempted, and there's potential humor in seeing Effie (Lee Patrick), who was Bogart's proper, adoring secretary, arrive at Segal's office in a hostessy caftan and make no bones about her loathing of her boss. But the movie was shot in L.A., with only a few days of actual location work in San Francisco, and Giler, a writer making his début as a director, is too inexperienced to achieve anything like the slouchy, wacked-out style that might have released the humor in some of his gag ideas. Instead, *The Black Bird* is a dumb comedy, with an insecure tone and some good jokes mixed with some terrible ones.

The picture uses a lot of faces from the past—performers such as Lionel Stander (dressed in a frogman's suit, he's grotesque to the point of adorability), and the enigmatic John Abbott, and Elisha Cook, Jr., as Wilmer the Gunsel again—but Giler didn't manage to write roles for the actors which would satirize the roles they used to play, and no character in the movie gets a chance to develop. However, as a red-haired scholar trying to translate an Aramaic fragment for Spade, Signe Hasso is as trim as ever and speaks with a precision that recalls the gilt-edged intonations of the forties. And George Segal salvages scene after static scene. He's got his comic transparency back, after looking ill and exhausted in *Russian Roulette* (and letting Richard Romanus, as one of the villains, take the film clean away from him), and though he can't make *The Black Bird* go, his peppiness is so engaging that you keep rooting for the picture to pull itself together. Stéphane Audran makes her American début in the old Mary Astor mystery-woman role, and she's right on the edge of being charming, though her deadpan makes it apparent that nobody let her in on the mystery, either.

David Giler didn't initiate the idea of a comedy sequel to *The Maltese Falcon*; the producer Ray Stark bought the sequel rights over a decade ago, and Giler is just one of many people who worked on the project—not even the last, apparently, since he refused to direct the *Jaws*-joke ending. If this picture seems dumb, it's because so little of the humor (or the attempted humor) is organic to the subject: people went to work to try to give the producer what he wanted, and the raft of names in the credits suggest that he had fluctuating desires. (It seems an act of kindness that these overflowing credits don't mention Dashiell Hammett.) *The Black Bird* has the same look that some other Ray Stark productions have had: the look of interference. There are movies that go off the track but at least you know you're on a train. With *The Black Bird*, someone in a gym suit comes in and blows the whistle and calls out, "All right, everyone out of the pool! This is now a Ping-Pong pavilion."

[January 19, 1976]

123

Dirty Harry with Weltschmerz

Hustle opens with the discovery of the body of a young girl on the beach at Malibu, but about midway in the picture the two Los Angeles police-officer heroes (Burt Reynolds and Paul Winfield) who have been investigating her death are assigned to go to the airport to meet a plane carrying a suspected terrorist. And in terms of dramatic plotting a very odd thing happens. The plane is delayed, and the heroes go into an airport bar, where they have a philosophical chat and look at an Oriental B-girl's sexy rear end, which the director, Robert Aldrich, frames invitingly, in closeups. We never do see the arrival of the plane, and the episode has nothing to do with the case of the dead girl. *Hustle*, which was written by Steve Shagan, is essentially set up like that scene—as an excuse for philosophy sweetened with sex. The mystery of the dead girl isn't solved; in fact, it turns out that there is no mystery. Her case is merely Shagan's pretext for a movie about his own sentimental pessimism. As Lieutenant Phil Gaines, Burt Reynolds despairs over the American loss of innocence, and over the corruption that he can neither adjust to nor escape. Like the earlier Shagan hero played by Jack Lemmon in *Save the Tiger,* Phil Gaines reveres the baseball players and swing musicians of the thirties, and plays big-band cassettes in his car. Once again, the hero's failure to pull his life together is blamed on America's collective guilt—on a pervasive moral poison.

Burt Reynolds wanted to make this script; he brought it to Aldrich and they co-produced it, and one may assume that Phil, who knows that "everyone has a hustle" but is sorrowful, looking back to a time when there were rules and people listened to "Begin the Beguine" and were happier, strikes a nerve in Reynolds. But he has miscast himself. Reynolds attempts to drop his TV persona—the amoral realist, the man who believes in whatever he can get by with. Purging himself of his rakish complicity with the audience, Reynolds tries to do a solid job of non-cartoon acting, but his mouth doesn't look comfortable when he yearns for the past or tells his girl (Catherine Deneuve) about his dreams of escape to Rome. Steve Shagan's weltschmerz—the sorrow one feels and accepts as one's necessary portion in life—isn't becoming to Burt Reynolds. Liberal piousness isn't his style—it doesn't go with the way he moves. When Phil talks of his father's death in the Spanish Civil War, or, in a metaphor of corruption that is too reminiscent of the title metaphor of *Chinatown*, refers to L.A. as "Guatemala with color TV," it's apparent that Shagan's jeremiads make Reynolds self-conscious. And they don't trigger much remorse in the director. Aldrich lets the creamy pain-of-it-all scenes meander—and there are a lot of them. He dutifully sends Reynolds and Deneuve to undergo the bittersweet pangs of Lelouch's *A Man and a Woman,* or shows them aching to the sound of Aznavour's "Yesterday When I Was Young," but he snaps to attention only for the violent action, or when he gets a minute with a character like Herbie—Jack Carter as a grungy night-club m.c. who stopped dreaming a long time ago.

What Shagan has done that may—along with Burt Reynolds' popularity—help to explain the box-office success of this film, which opened at Christmas, is to create a romantic-liberal basis for taking the law into one's own hands. According to this movie, the whole system is rigged on the side of the rich—the somebodies, they're called here—and one can right the balance only by chivalrous outlaw acts. In order to protect society against the vermin, Clint Eastwood's cop hero, the tough saint Dirty Harry, had to ignore the laws, made by liberals, that sheltered the criminals. Reynolds' Phil Gaines also violates the laws, but it's because the economic corruption is total and the poor—the nobodies—don't stand a chance. The police protect the big guys, and the high-priced lawyers make a mockery of the courts; the chief villain (Eddie Albert) is an immaculately self-possessed counsellor for the mobsters in the unions and is also a vice lord. So when the dead girl's father (Ben Johnson), who hasn't been right in the head since Korea (Shagan must keep checklists), kills the smooth counsellor, Phil Gaines tries to "turn the wheel around" by making the murder look like self-defense. It doesn't matter that the counsellor had nothing directly to do with the girl's death; Phil knows that he's had plenty to do with other deaths. At another point in the film, this liberal Dirty Harry behaves just like the fascistic Dirty Harry: Phil Gaines pumps lead into a wounded psychopathic murderer, doing the dirty work of execution-er for a society that doesn't know how to protect itself.

Phil Gaines is a strong man who believes in the old-fashioned virtues, but, unlike the Clint Eastwood character, he knows pain. (Or, rather, he says he does; Reynolds' physical assurance tells a different story.) Everything in the movie is laid out to educate us in the economic basis of the general depravity. The film is ideological and moralistic in a hyped-up, pulp-profound style, like a Harlan Ellison rewrite of Dore Schary, and when Phil reprimands his colleagues in the police department for their brutal mistreatment of a suspect who's an albino, the audience is treated to a little lecture on the misery of those who are different which takes one right back to Schary's *The Boy with Green Hair.* Expressing opposite political views, *Hustle* and *Dirty Harry* nevertheless have the same simplistic self-righteousness toward the hero's violent actions. *Dirty Harry*, however, was able to endow Eastwood's actions with a charge that sent many people home feeling triumphantly satisfied. That's not the spirit of *Hustle*. Phil Gaines is the good guy who loses because "you can't win." It's no accident that his girl is played by Catherine Deneuve. The film is soaked through with the defeatism of such pre-Second World War French films as *Port of Shadows* and, especially, *Pépé le Moko*—films that said that no one is free. Phil Gaines is an American Pépé le Moko, longing for the lovers' paradise of Rome, or even Sausalito, as Pépé, trapped in the Casbah, had dreamed of Paris; and Deneuve embodies that dream, as Mireille Balin's glorious tart did for Jean Gabin in the 1937 French film, and as Hedy Lamarr did for Charles Boyer in the 1938 American remake, *Algiers*. *Hustle* is caught between Steve Shagan's Francophile soulfulness—that sloshy softheartedness he mistakes for poetry—and Robert Aldrich's tawdry indifference to it. Aldrich is a brutally harsh director. He has made insensitivity a style—sometimes a ruthless, slamming style, as in the hit film *The Dirty Dozen*. He brought caricaturing energy to *The Longest Yard,* which also pitted Reynolds against Eddie Albert. But when he tries for tenderness, it turns to sleaze.

If Catherine Deneuve had made only this film, one might consider her hopelessly pallid. Deneuve, with her icy yet mysterious perfection, is the French Grace Kelly, but something is hidden—a suggestion of humor and of depth. She was a marvellously witty choice for the closet hooker of *Belle de Jour*; she acted out the male fantasy of the secret life of frozen-faced beauties, and her perfection seemed the bourgeois hypocrite's mask concealing dirty impulses. But when she's cast as a full-time L.A. hooker, who consorts with gangsters yet never loses her blandly sweet sadness, she has no personality at all—far less than in her Chanel ads, which allow one to project a personality onto her dream-princess cool. (She doesn't look as good, either; her cheek muscles are slack, as if she were nervously unsure of herself.) The most embarrassingly unrealistic aspect of *Hustle* is its misty-eyed glorification of this hooker—Nicole, she's called—who is wistfully ladylike, without a trace of coarseness. When Nicole talks about being good at her profession, her tone suggests a vocation—curing cancer, at the very least. She's such a highfalutin whore that when she echoes the sentiments of her thirties prototypes and says that she will give up her profession as soon as Phil can support her, you think, Well, why should he· have to take care of her? This woman hasn't been trapped by life; she could easily turn to something else. Shagan was thinking in terms of poetic tragedy, but a woman who'd rather be a whore than lower her luxurious standard of living isn't a victim, and the thirties French fatalism isn't at home in this L.A. setting. When Pépé le Moko, unable to break out of his exile, died as the siren sounded for the boat leaving for France with his girl on deck, the scene had a flamboyant, brilliantly kitschy inevitability. But when Nicole, waiting for Phil at the airport, learns that he is dead just as the flight for Rome is called, the movie is making a pass at an emotion that Steve Shagan once felt and wants to feel again.

Hustle is the right title for this attack on materialism, which is full of plugs for products (the hero, for example, drinks only Old Bushmills) and was financed on a tax-shelter basis. Shagan would probably say that that was just what he was writing about—that it was further evidence of the rot in the system. But it may be that his garish writing seems deep and truthful to people in the movie industry precisely because it justifies corruption by saying that it is total. If "everyone has a hustle," the big Hollywood hustlers can feel that they are merely doing what everyone else would do if they were smart enough. The film removes any individual guilt by locating honesty in the romantic past of one's impressionable youth—ah, those big bands. Burt Reynolds has selected a script that is a covert justification for his sure-I'm-a-bum-but-I-don't-hide-it clowning on the talk shows. He doesn't work well with Catherine Deneuve—there's no tension between them—but when has he ever had an emotional connection with the women in his pictures, or with the men, either? It could be that he's too complete a thing to need a co-star. And that may help to explain his immense popularity. No matter what he appears in, as far as the public is concerned, he seems unable to do wrong. The premise of this picture—everyone has a hustle—is actually the same as that of the talk shows that made him a star.

[January 26, 1976]

The Artist as a Young Comedian

*I*n the fifties, when improvisational acts were booked into night clubs and coffeehouses, and the entertainers satirized middle-class interpersonal relations, young actors had a hip edge to their conversation. Freud had got into everything, and acting was now thought of in terms of awareness. Acting coaches who had been political activists turned into psychiatric philosophers. This is the atmosphere of Paul Mazursky's new, autobiographical comedy, *Next Stop, Greenwich Village*. The hero, a twenty-two-year-old Brooklyn College graduate, Larry Lapinsky (Lenny Baker), who has never wanted to be anything but an actor, moves out of the Brownsville apartment of his parents (Shelley Winters and Mike Kellin) into an apartment of his own in the Village. The film is about Larry's acting classes and his relations with his girl, Sarah (Ellen Greene), and his friends. Mazursky knows this scene so well that every word, every hangup, every awkward, flip hesitation rings a bell. *Next Stop, Greenwich Village* gives the best portrait of Village life ever put on the screen; the casualness, the camaraderie, and the sexual freedom are balanced by glimpses of the lives of those who are in the Village because they don't fit in anywhere else. Yet there's more to the movie than that. Like Alexander Portnoy, Larry is the son in the Jewish joke, but, unlike Portnoy, he isn't crippled by it. In both *Portnoy's Complaint* and *Next Stop, Greenwich Village,* guilt is funny; but the Philip Roth book is satire from within a fixation, and Portnoy is screaming with rage. Larry Lapinsky is rather like what the young Alex Portnoy might have been if he had recovered from his complaint. He learns to live with his guilt; that's the comedy of growing up which is celebrated in *Next Stop, Greenwich Village.*

As Larry's Mom, Shelley Winters is a hysteric on the loose, barging into his apartment in the middle of a party, embarrassing him so much he wants to crawl under the furniture. It is high-mania acting, like Winters' ever-hopeful Charlotte Haze in *Lolita.* Mrs. Lapinsky pours so much brute emotion into every small detail of her life that she has lost all sense of proportion; everything to do with her becomes of world-shaking importance. Her unused brains have turned her into a howling freak, but you can recognize in her the sources of her son's talent and wit. And, even seeing her through her son's agonized-with-shame eyes, you don't get too much of her—or, rather, you can't get enough of Shelley Winters' performance. With her twinkly goo-goo eyes and flirty grin, Shelley Winters is a mother hippo charging—not at her son's enemies but at him. Fat, morose, irrepressible, she's a force that would strike terror to anyone's heart, yet in some abominable way she's likable. She's Mrs. Portnoy seen without hatred. When Larry visits his parents, she hands him a bag of apple strudel to eat on the plane taking him, first class, to a job in Hollywood. Her husband says to her, "I told you he'd get angry," but Larry says, "I'm not angry. I'm crazy, but I'm not angry." When he has said goodbye and is on his way to the subway, he stands on the Brownsville street listening to a fiddler and he eats the strudel.

Larry is crazy in a sane way: as a comedian, he puts his craziness to work for him. And that's Paul Mazursky's own greatest gift. What made his earlier films (*Bob & Carol & Ted & Alice, Alex in Wonderland, Blume in Love,* and *Harry & Tonto*) so distinctive was the acceptance of bugginess as part of the normal—maybe even the best part of it. In his films, craziness gives life its savor. When Mazursky makes fun of characters, it's not to put them down; quite the reverse—the scattier they are, the more happily he embraces them. (His quarrel is with the too controlled.) The star of *Next Stop, Greenwich Village*, the relatively unknown Lenny Baker, looks like a gangly young boy but has had almost a decade of professional experience, and he gives the central character the manic generosity that holds the film together. Starting as a runny-nosed, funny-looking kid, Larry becomes stronger and handsomer. Having survived his mother's aggression, he's got the craziness and the strength to make it as an artist.

On his own road from Brownsville through the Village and on to becoming a writer-director, Mazursky performed in improvisational cabaret theatre, wrote skits for "The Danny Kaye Show," and taught acting. Like Larry, who gets his break when he's cast as a tough punk, Mazursky got a role as one of the delinquents in *Blackboard Jungle* (1955), though he had gone West earlier, in 1951, to play a leading role as a psychopath who assaults a captive girl, in Stanley Kubrick's first feature, *Fear and Desire*. Mazursky has appeared in several of his own pictures (he was funniest as the itchy, voracious producer in *Alex in Wonderland*), and his directing style is based on the actors' intuitively taking off from each other, as they did in the coffeehouses. He does something that no other American movie director does: he writes, shapes, and edits the sequences to express the performing rhythm—to keep the actors' pulse. As a result, the audience feels unusually close to the characters—feels protective toward them. Mazursky brings you into a love relationship with his people, and it's all aboveboard.

This picture suggests that for Paul Mazursky (as for many theatre people) acting is at the basis of all judgment. Not all of Larry's friends are studying to be actors, yet one can interpret almost everything that happens to them in terms of acting. Ellen Greene's Sarah is intelligent and quick-witted, but she's already a little hard in the places where Larry is still sensitive—where you feel he'll always stay sensitive. (That's what will keep him an artist.) Sarah violates the rule that Larry's patriarchal acting teacher, Herbert (Michael Egan), says may be important "for the rest of your life": "The worst kind of joking you can do is to keep life out." According to Herbert, you shouldn't use your brain "to keep the stuff out," but "to take it in." Mazursky satirizes Herbert's litany, but very gently. (The famous acting teacher Herbert Berghof appeared in *Harry & Tonto* as Harry's New York friend the aged radical.) And Larry lives by Herbert's rule. He humors his parents, but he's really on his own; he has made the plunge—he's taking life in. Sarah, however, is still at home, and playing the lying-to-your-folks game along with the Greenwich Village game. She's a compromiser, and so elastic she doesn't know where she'll snap. Ellen Greene gives a beautiful, prickly, sensual performance; she has a big, avid mouth, which she uses for comic tics, taking us by surprise each time. The proof of her talent is that it's Sarah's hardness that makes her seem poignant. Being independent-minded has got mixed with something sharp and self-destructive; Sarah cuts herself off from people by acting sure just when she's least sure. This role is written with a respect for the ways in which savvy people with everything going for them can screw up. Mazursky keeps it all light and blowsy, yet the characters have depth, and a lot of damaging things are happening to them while they're frisking along. Sarah is attracted to Robert (Christopher Walken), a narcissistic, affectlessly calm poet-playwright. He's the sort of person who destroys a party—the one who says "Let's play the truth game." Robert is a passive sadist, who draws women to him and shrugs off any responsibility for what happens. And it's true that they've hurt themselves, but it's his passivity that has invited them to do it. Walken uses his light, high voice for an ambiguous effect, and he gives Robert an air of physical isolation that makes him seem always withdrawn from the rest of the group. When Larry, who has suffered because of him, accuses him of having nothing under his pose but more pose, it's as if Larry were using the old slang term and saying "You're a bad actor," meaning that he's untrustworthy, a crook—someone not in touch with himself. Robert might almost be the Nazi villain—he's every son of a bitch whose only interest in sex is for power. He's the only character without spontaneity, and the only one that Mazursky can't resolve his feelings about.

As a homosexual who is sick of role-playing but too frightened to stop, Antonio Fargas keeps just enough reserve to be affecting without pushing it; Lois Smith finds the archetypal Lois Smith role as the sodden Anita, a depressive who plays at suicide; Dori Brenner's Connie plays at being everybody's favorite good sport. And on the fringes of this group there's Barney (John Ford Noonan), a bearded, soft giant with a striking resemblance to Mazursky's old writing partner Larry Tucker. (Larry Lapinsky's first name may also be a nod to Tucker.) Most of these actors have been in movies before, but they didn't have Mazursky's lines to speak, or the hip timing he gets. The subsidiary characters help to form just the sort of human zoo that many of us live in. Jeff Goldblum plays a big, handsome young actor named Clyde Baxter—a goofed-up Victor Mature type. Lou Jacobi is the proprietor of a health-food lunch counter, whooping as if his whole life were vindicated when a customer comes in feeling rotten from having eaten a corned beef on rye. And Rochelle Oliver as Dr. Marsha and John C. Becher as Sid Weinberg, a casting director, contribute to making this picture Off Broadway's finest hour.

In refining his comic style, Mazursky has suffered a few losses. I miss the messy romanticism of *Blume*; there Mazursky was "too close" to the subject—he was gummed up in it, and the chaos felt good. This movie is set in his past, and the blood has cooled. But Mazursky's earlier scripts were splotchy; *Next Stop, Greenwich Village* has the intertwining of a classic American play. And if the mechanics seem a little too theatrical when

Larry's Mom waddles into his apartment without knocking and pounces on him, still, in 1953 Village doors weren't always bolted. (Bolted doors wouldn't stop Shelley Winters anyway.) As in some other films shot by Arthur Ornitz, there doesn't appear to be a light source, and the color is muddy. You can't tell the blacks and browns and blues apart; Ornitz seems to get the shots to match by making them all dark. Luckily, this movie has so much else going for it that it can get along without visual beauty. Mazursky was so smitten by Fellini that his early films sometimes seemed to be commuting between cultures. But *Next Stop, Greenwich Village* isn't an imitation of *Amarcord,* it's Mazursky's own Amarcord. And I like it better than Fellini's. It isn't showy—Mazursky works on a small scale. Yet this satirist without bitterness and without extravagance looks to be a comic poet. His subject is the comedy of wisdom—how to become a good actor.

[February 2, 1976]

Underground Man

*T*axi *Driver* is the fevered story of an outsider in New York—a man who can't find any point of entry into human society. Travis Bickle (Robert De Niro), the protagonist of Martin Scorsese's new film, from a script by Paul Schrader, can't find a life. He's an ex-Marine from the Midwest who takes a job driving a cab nights, because he can't sleep anyway, and he is surrounded by the night world of the uprooted—whores, pimps, transients. Schrader, who grew up in Michigan, in the Christian Reformed Church, a zealous Calvinist splinter (he didn't see a movie until he was seventeen), has created a protagonist who is an ascetic not by choice but out of fear. And Scorsese with his sultry moodiness and his appetite for the pulp sensationalism of forties movies, is just the director to define an American underground man's resentment. Travis wants to conform, but he can't find a group pattern to conform to. So he sits and drives in the stupefied languor of anomie. He hates New York with a Biblical fury; it gives off the stench of Hell, and its filth and smut obsess him. He manages to get a date with Betsy (Cybill Shepherd), a political campaigner whose blondness and white clothes represent purity to him, but he is so out of touch that he inadvertently offends her and she won't

131

have anything more to do with him. When he fumblingly asks advice from Wizard (Peter Boyle), an older cabdriver, and indicates the pressure building up in him, Wizard doesn't know what he's talking about. Travis becomes sick with loneliness and frustration; and then, like a commando preparing for a raid, he purifies his body and goes into training to kill. *Taxi Driver* is a movie in heat, a raw, tabloid version of *Notes from Underground*, and we stay with the protagonist's hatreds all the way.

This picture is more ferocious than Scorsese's volatile, allusive *Mean Streets*. *Taxi Driver* has a relentless movement: Travis has got to find relief. It's a two-character study—Travis versus New York. As Scorsese has designed the film, the city never lets you off the hook. There's no grace, no compassion in the artificially lighted atmosphere. The neon reds, the vapors that shoot up from the streets, the dilapidation all get to you the way they get to Travis. He is desperately sick, but he's the only one who tries to save a twelve-and-a-half-year-old hooker, Iris (Jodie Foster); the argument he invokes is that she belongs with her family and in school—the secure values from his own past that are of no help to him now. Some mechanism of adaptation is missing in Travis; the details aren't filled in—just the indications of a strict religious background, and a scar on his back, suggesting a combat wound. The city world presses in on him, yet it's also remote, because Travis is so disaffected that he isn't always quite there. We perceive the city as he does, and it's so scummy and malign we get the feel of his alienation.

Scorsese may just naturally be an Expressionist; his asthmatic bedridden childhood in a Sicilian-American home in Little Italy propelled him toward a fix on the violently exciting movies he saw. Physically and intellectually, he's a speed demon, a dervish. Even in *Alice Doesn't Live Here Anymore* he found a rationale for restless, whirlwind movement. But Scorsese is also the most carnal of directors—movement is ecstatic for him—and that side of him didn't come out in *Alice*. This new movie gives him a chance for the full Expressionist use of the city which he was denied in *Mean Streets,* because it was set in New York but was made on a minuscule budget in Southern California, with only seven shooting days in New York itself. Scorsese's Expressionism isn't anything like the exaggerated sets of the German directors; he uses documentary locations, but he pushes discordant elements to their limits, and the cinematographer, Michael Chapman, gives the street life a seamy, rich pulpiness. When Travis is taunted by a pimp, Sport (Harvey Keitel), the pimp is so eager for action that he can't stand still; the hipster, with his rhythmic jiggling, makes an eerily hostile contrast to the paralyzed, dumbfounded Travis. Scorsese gets the quality of trance in a scene like this; the whole movie has a sense of vertigo. Scorsese's New York is the big city of the thrillers he feasted his imagination on—but at a later stage of decay. This New York is a voluptuous enemy. The street vapors become ghostly; Sport the pimp romancing his baby whore leads her in a hypnotic dance; the porno theatres are like mortuaries; the congested traffic is macabre. And this Hell is always in movement.

No other film has ever dramatized urban indifference so powerfully; at first, here, it's horrifyingly funny, and then just horrifying. When Travis attempts to date Betsy, he's very seductive; we can see why she's tantalized. They're talking across a huge gap, and still they're connecting (though the wires are all crossed). It's a zinger of a scene: an educated, socially conscious woman dating a lumpen lost soul who uses one of the oldest pitches in the book—he tells her that he knows she is a lonely person. Travis means it; the gruesome comedy in the scene is how intensely he means it—because his own life is utterly empty. Throughout the movie, Travis talks to people on a different level from the level they take him on. He's so closed off he's otherworldly; he engages in so few conversations that slang words like "moonlighting" pass right over him—the spoken language is foreign to him. His responses are sometimes so blocked that he seems wiped out; at other times he's animal fast. This man is burning in misery, and his inflamed, brimming eyes are the focal point of the compositions. Robert De Niro is in almost every frame: thin-faced, as handsome as Robert Taylor one moment and cagey, ferrety, like Cagney, the next—and not just looking at the people he's talking to but spying on them. As Travis, De Niro has none of the peasant courtliness of his Vito Corleone in *The Godfather, Part II.* Vito held himself in proudly, in control of his violence; he was a leader. Travis is dangerous in a different, cumulative way. His tense face folds in a yokel's grin and he looks almost an idiot. Or he sits in his room vacantly watching the bright-eyed young faces on the TV and with his foot he slowly rocks the set back and then over. The exacerbation of his desire for vengeance shows in his numbness, yet part of the horror implicit in this movie is how easily he passes. The anonymity of the city soaks up one more invisible man; he could be legion.

Scorsese handles the cast immaculately. Harvey Keitel's pimp is slimy, all right, yet his malicious, mischievous eyes and his jumpiness are oddly winning. Jodie Foster, who was exactly Iris's age when she played the part, is an unusually physical child actress and seems to have felt out her line readings—her words are convincingly hers. Cybill Shepherd has never been better: you don't see her trying to act. She may actually be doing her least acting here, yet she doesn't have that schoolgirl model's blankness; her face is expressive and womanly. There's a suggestion that Betsy's life hasn't gone according to her expectations—a faint air of defeat. The comedian Albert Brooks brings a note of quibbling, plump pomposity to the role of her political co-worker, and Leonard Harris, formerly the WCBS-TV arts critic, has a professionally earnest manner as Palatine, their candidate. Peter Boyle's role is small, but he was right to want to be in this film, and he does slobby wonders with his scenes as the gently thick

Wizard, adjusted to the filth that Travis is coiled up to fight; Boyle gives the film a special New York–hack ambience, and, as the cabby Doughboy, Harry Northup has a bland face and Southern drawl that suggest another kind of rootlessness. Scorsese himself is sitting on the sidewalk when Travis first sees Betsy, and then he returns to play a glitteringly morbid role as one of Travis's fares—a man who wants Travis to share his rancid glee in what the Magnum he intends to shoot his faithless wife with will do to her. As an actor, he sizzles; he has such concentrated energy that this sequence burns a small hole in the screen.

As a director, Scorsese has the occasional arbitrariness and preening of a runaway talent; sometimes a shot calls attention to itself, because it serves no visible purpose. One can pass over a lingering closeup of a street musician, but when Travis is talking to Betsy on a pay phone in an office building and the camera moves away from him to the blank hallway, it's an Antonioni pirouette. The Bernard Herrmann score is a much bigger problem; the composer finished recording it on December 23rd, the day before he died, and so it's a double pity that it isn't better. It's clear why Scorsese wanted Herrmann: his specialty was expressing psychological disorder through dissonant, wrought-up music. But this movie, with its suppressed sex and suppressed violence, is already pitched so high that it doesn't need ominous percussion, snake rattles, and rippling scales. These musical nudges belong back with the rampaging thrillers that *Taxi Driver* transcends. Scorsese got something out of his asthma: he knows how to make us experience the terror of suffocation.

Some actors are said to be empty vessels who are filled by the roles they play, but that's not what appears to be happening here with De Niro. He's gone the other way. He's used his emptiness—he's reached down into his own anomie. Only Brando has done this kind of plunging, and De Niro's performance has something of the undistanced intensity that Brando's had in *Last Tango*. In its own way, this movie, too, has an erotic aura. There is practically no sex in it, but no sex can be as disturbing as sex. And that's what it's about: the absence of sex—bottled-up, impacted energy and emotion, with a blood-splattering release. The fact that we experience Travis's need for an explosion viscerally, and that the explosion itself has the quality of consummation, makes *Taxi Driver* one of the few truly modern horror films.

Anyone who goes to the movie houses that loners frequent knows that they identify with the perpetrators of crimes, even the most horrible crimes, and that they aren't satisfied unless there's a whopping climax. In his essay "The White Negro," Norman Mailer suggested that when a killer takes his revenge on the institutions that he feels are oppressing him his eruption of violence can have a positive effect on him. The most shocking aspect of *Taxi Driver* is that it takes this very element, which has generally been exploited for popular appeal, and puts it in the center of the viewer's consciousness. Violence is Travis's only means of expressing himself. He has not been able to hurdle the barriers to being seen and felt. When he blasts through, it's his only way of telling the city that he's there. And, given his ascetic loneliness, it's the only real orgasm he can have.

The violence in this movie is so threatening precisely because it's cathartic for Travis. I imagine that some people who are angered by the film will say that it advocates violence as a cure for frustration. But to acknowledge that when a psychopath's blood boils over he may cool down is not the same as justifying the eruption. This film doesn't operate on the level of moral judgment of what Travis does. Rather, by drawing us into its vortex it makes us understand the psychic discharge of the quiet boys who go berserk. And it's a real slap in the face for us when we see Travis at the end looking pacified. He's got the rage out of his system—for the moment, at least—and he's back at work, picking up passengers in front of the St. Regis. It's not that he's cured but that the city is crazier than he is.

[February 9, 1976]

Seven Fatties

In Lina Wertmüller's *Swept Away,* a Sicilian Communist deckhand working on a yacht and the rich blond shrew who chartered the ship for a pleasure cruise are marooned on an island. She gave him a bad time when she had the upper hand, so when he takes charge on the island and starts whacking her around maybe one can say that he isn't hitting a woman, he's hitting the capitalist class. However, when she kisses his feet and gathers flowers to garland his phallus she isn't the capitalist class, she's a woman who finds fulfillment in recognizing a man as her master. She not only experiences new sexual bliss, she wins the prize that has often been said to be woman's highest goal: because of her submissiveness, the man loves her and worships her as his goddess. Uncorrupted by social forces, the couple live the "true" relations of the sexes and find paradise. But he, fearful that he loves her more than she loves him, insists that they put their love to the test of society, and they go back. When they do, she can't resist returning to her life of privilege, and he is left heartbroken. Under the guise of a Socialist parable about the economic determinism of personal behavior (class interests determine sexual choice, etc.), Wertmüller has actually introduced a new version of the story of Eve, the spoiler. There is a noteworthy peculiarity: only the woman's behavior is economically determined. She's a self-centered materialist, but the man has deep feelings—he's a romantic prepared to sacrifice all for love. If there has been considerable confusion about how to interpret *Swept Away,* the reason may be simple: despite the clamor of politics in Wertmüller's movies, her basic pitch is to popular prejudice.

Wertmüller's films are very primitive in their appeal: Punch-and-Judy shows made with the cruelty that is available to the film medium, yet with an overlay of moralizing, and with a moist wistfulness. The quote from the *New York Times* in the ads for her newest movie says, "*Seven Beauties* is Miss Wertmüller's *King Kong,* her *Nashville,* her *8½,* her *Navigator,* her *City Lights.*" This isn't necessarily praise: if *Seven Beauties* is all these things, what is it? Does the quote mean merely that it's her big one? I liked Wertmüller's first film, *The Lizards,* when I saw it back in the early sixties; a woman's view of the vegetating small-town boys that Fellini had dealt with in *I Vitelloni,* it gave tentative promise of some new perceptions. Instead, she headed in a crustier, more overtly political direction. Still, in 1972, within the enamel-gloss bordello of *Love and Anarchy,* there would be quiet moments when the whores' faces were unusually pliant, or when the beauty of the dark, innocent Tripolina (Lina Polito) would recall the breathtakingly fresh-faced young stars of silent films. However, Wertmüller's recent work appears to be taking confident strides into the most obvious kinds of theatrical excess. She says she has a penchant for the grotesque, but that's not the same as having a talent for it. *Seven Beauties,* her twelfth feature, is a grotesque vaudeville show. It's one act after another, with political labels stuck on the participants so you'll know what you're watching. The players come on at a sprint; they're overly spirited—the juice of life oozes out all over the place in a chorus of "*Mamma mia*"s. Wertmüller dances around with a hand-held camera and hauls the acts offstage fast, swinging from pathos to burlesque so that audiences won't become restless. She heightens so many effects that the film is a barrage of squeals and screams, and the imagery is also too loud—too bright. Wertmüller is a playwright-director; her scripts are a succession of dialogue scenes in which characters give vent to ideological positions. These are piled on top of folk clichés, and the point of view being expressed isn't intelligible. The political speeches are given the this-is-profound treatment, but something contradictory comes winging along the next moment. The effect suggests an *opera-buffa* G. B. Shaw—a theatre of garbled ideas. Wertmüller keeps her films moving by hurling salamis at the audience.

Seven Beauties is a slapstick-tragedy investigation of an Italian common man's soul, set during the Second World War, with flashbacks to the thirties. Pasqualino, or, as he's called, Pasqualino Seven Beauties (Giancarlo Giannini), deserts the Italian Army in Germany, is captured by the Germans, and is sent to a concentration camp. In flashbacks, we see his pre-war life as a two-bit mafioso: a man of mildly lecherous leisure, he promenades the streets of Naples with a leering compliment for every woman he passes. His mother has taught him that all women want sugar. He dispenses it freely, and the women adore him. He struts while his fat sisters—the "seven beauties"—work in the family mattress-stuffing factory. Pasqualino first comes to grief from trying to protect his family honor: after killing the man who has turned his aggressively stupid oldest sister, Concettina (Elena Fiore), into a whore, he is sent to an insane asylum. He uses his sugary wiles on a woman doctor and gets preferential treatment, and so later, when he's starving in the concentration camp, he goes to work on the Bitch-of-Buchenwald commandant (Shirley Stoler).

The satirical "Oh Yeah" song that opens the film has a good cabaret pungency (though the political montage that accompanies it is mediocre), and there is an imaginative moment of gallows-humor cheekiness when the emaciated Pasqualino woos the commandant by humming a little love song. On the plus side, that's about it. Giancarlo Giannini appears to be a very limited actor, and except for his love hum his work here is a series of hand-me-downs from Pietro Germi films—particularly Mastroianni bits from *Divorce—Italian Style.* In the tradition of broad popular theatre, *Seven Beauties* is all punctuation, and the Neapolitan scenes reinforce the clichés of Italian noisiness. In the German scenes, Wertmüller achieves the effect of liveliness through one whammy after another. The starving prisoners in the camp are beaten and murdered to the tune of the Ride of the Valkyries; a Spanish anarchist (Fernando Rey) who recites the film's most noble messages about the need for creative disorder kills himself, in disgust at Pasqualino's toadying to the Nazis, by jumping into a vat of excrement. Past and present, Pasqualino's life is a comic strip of horrors: preparing to chop up the pimp's body, then carrying it in three grisly suitcases; raping a tied-down madwoman in the asylum; being given shock treatment; and the culminating buffoonery—his mounting of the two-hundred-and-fifty-pound commandant, scaling her like a fly settling on Mount Rushmore.

Pasqualino is everybody's dupe—a man who has swallowed all the lies that society hands out. He believes what the Mafia tells him, what Mussolini tells him, what anybody in authority tells him. As Giannini plays him, he's a Chaplinesque Fascist—the Italian Everyman as a pathetic worm. He's the man who never fights back—the one who wheedles and whimpers and crawls through. He's the contemptible survivor. In *Swept Away*, Wertmüller enthusiastically reactivated such audience-pleasers as the notion that a frigid rich woman gets her first sexual satisfaction when she has a working-class lover. In *Seven Beauties,* she reactivates the entire comic-opera view of Italians as cowards who will grovel to survive. The commandant is an intelligent, dedicated idealist-sadist—a master-race superwoman on the model of those Nazi supermen we used to get in Hollywood movies, like Walter Slezak in Hitchcock's *Lifeboat*. Actually, women in Nazi Germany couldn't rise to anything close to the post of commandant; Ilse Koch's power at Buchenwald derived from her being the commandant's wife. Literal truth isn't required of an artist, but we can ask, Why distort in this direction—what is the vision that requires giving the woman the whip hand? Wertmüller's grotesqueries, such as the gross commandant, as bored as a sphinx, sitting, yawning, with her thighs spread while the scrawny, enfeebled Pasqualino tries to penetrate her, and the incessant, shrill obnoxiousness of the shrew on the yacht in *Swept Away*, are appeals to the coarsest prejudices. In *All Screwed Up*, a pleasantly sprawling, undistinguished political comedy about life in a Milanese rooming-house commune (made early in 1974, just before *Swept Away*, but only now released here), the women are tightfisted and scheming, while the men are likable proletarians just trying to get along. Wertmüller is not at all averse to tapping the hostilities that float around in the popular consciousness. If it's easy to get laughs by sending the camera up fat women's thick legs and fleshy arms or by showing women as barnyard creatures—or as petit-bourgeois manipulators, like the women in the commune, or as rich teases, like Mariangela Melato's role in *Swept Away*—Wertmüller runs with the pack.

There is hardly any point in discussing the stated ideas in a Wertmüller film, because they can't be sorted out. In an interview in the *Voice* with Molly Haskell (one of the few critics who haven't acclaimed Wertmüller), the director explained that the woman in *Swept Away* wasn't really a woman at all. She was "a symbol of bourgeois enlightenment," Wertmüller said. "She represents bourgeois society, therefore she represents the man. That's what women didn't understand. The Mariangela Melato character was really a man." There's no arguing with this kind of thinking; obviously, the political ideas in Wertmüller's films are anything that suits her convenience. If one asks "Why are the working-class women in *All Screwed Up* such avaricious petit-bourgeois climbers?" she'll say "That wasn't a woman, that was the Shah of Iran." Wertmüller must know perfectly well that the success of *Swept Away* is due largely to its element of erotic fantasy. It is like a modern version of Valentino's *The Sheik*—blissful rape for the trendy, dissatisfied liberated woman. And solid reassurance for the men in the audience that women only want to be mastered, yet are sly little beasts, never to be trusted.

Maybe because Wertmüller changes her act so fast, her films have a very high energy level. The last three also stay on the same high energy level throughout. That was why I found *Swept Away* tiresome (as well as generally offensive). The characters never shut up, and since the post-synchronization is so careless that their voices are several beats off from their lip movements, the effect is as irritating as if the movie were dubbed, even though it's subtitled. *Seven Beauties* goes beyond annoyance, however: it's extremely ambitious, and I think it's a gloppy mess. After seeing the film, one can't visualize it: the staging and the compositions haven't taken hold in the mind. That quote from the *New York Times* isn't wrong, exactly; *Seven Beauties* can be compared to just about anything. The way Lina Wertmüller makes movies, she *has* to believe that disorder is creative. She plunks in whatever comes to mind, and rips through the scenes. It's all bravura highs and bravura lows, without any tonal variation. She almost makes one long for Ken Russell: at least his trashiness has a gutter spunk, and he doesn't think he's raising the consciousness of the masses.

Seven Beauties might have had some comic shape if it had been structured so that Pasqualino's sugaring the commandant stirred a romantic response in her. But Wertmüller betrays her own comic premise, pushing for something big, and so we get prescient speeches by the commandant about how Nazism is doomed by its idealism and vision of order, and how worms like this little Italian will survive. And Pasqualino must go on to shoot his best friend (in a brackish, drawn-out scene) and select fellow-prisoners for the firing squad. The terrible thing about the movie is the absence of weight in these passages. The humiliations, the punishments, the horrors don't develop out of the characters or situations. They're just injected into the clowning-around atmosphere. They're hypes for us—kicky effects to give us a charge. But with that pious moralizing on top of them. So when the anarchist sinks in the muck, we're supposed to grin and shudder at the effect and, at the same time, think, Yes, he's doing that because life for him has become drowning in excrement. You don't feel a thing. You wait for the next shock, the next lesson. Wertmüller turns suffering into vaudeville not as part of a Brechtian technique but, rather, as an expression of a roller-coaster temperament. The suffering is reduced to fun-house games. Wertmüller says she's a Socialist and/or an Anarchist, but the ugliness of the human material she shows us cannot all be blamed on economic oppression; the habitual closeups are merciless because the faces have no depth. She also says she's a feminist, but the struggling woman patient whom Pasqualino rapes is made ridiculous, and his dumb-cow sisters are well content to become whores. Wertmüller's Everyman jamboree puts everything down.

For all the political babbling of her characters, the meaning of *Seven Beauties* is deeply reactionary and misogynous. It gets an audience response by confirming what people, in their most superstitious recesses, already believe: that "human nature" stinks and nothing can be done about it. The characters are squealing pigs and worms or else they're martyrs—a perfect dichotomy for the guilt-ridden in the audience who know damned well they don't want to be martyrs. Pasqualino the worm is also the most human of the characters. And, look, he isn't entirely soft and wormy: he can get an erection. All that's left at the end of the movie is his ability to procreate and bring more larvae into the world, which is a teeming bordello. Wertmüller presents all this in a goofy, ebullient mood. The box-office success of the picture represents a triumph of insensitivity.

Libel

*I*f a pretty face and hard work were what made a man a movie star, Richard Chamberlain would certainly be one. But he doesn't have an actor's face; he has a ballet dancer's face—the blank, masklike beauty of a face that isn't expressive—and there's nothing going on when he's on the screen. Not that maybe he wouldn't be a boring dancer, but at least he'd look right. Subtle, almost ineffable factors determine star magnetism, or the lack of it. Keir Dullea's spaced-out vagueness—the very quality that made it so right for him to become an astral angel-child at the end of *2001*—keeps him from connecting with the audience. Stacy Keach is unable to project on the screen; he's withdrawn, and the audience gets a sour feeling. A whoriness settles into the manner of TV veterans like James Franciscus and David Janssen; something essential to movie stardom decays. And although actresses such as Lee Remick, Susan Clark, and Karen Black are touted as stars, you can feel that they're not. The test is playing a star. It's just about impossible to get by with it unless you are one and have the incandescence that Streisand had as Fanny Brice and Diana Ross as Billie Holiday. Franco Nero, who played Valentino on TV recently, sank in the role without a trace, just as Anthony Dexter did in the 1951 *Valentino*. By conventional standards of symmetry, James Brolin, who appears as Clark Gable in the new film *Gable and Lombard,* is much more handsome than Gable, though he manages to look quite a bit like him and does a pretty fair imitation of Gable's voice besides. But Brolin's manner is keyed to moderate involvement; he's primarily a TV actor—you can watch him with only half an eye and ear and not miss a thing. As Gable, Brolin doesn't totally disappear; he has his own TV actor's engaging, lightweight presence. But he doesn't have a dominant personality, and the more he tries to fill the big screen the more callow he seems. He lacks what was the essence of Gable's appeal: his cocksure masculinity. (Gable was one of the few actors never thought to be—even a little

140

bit—homosexual.) There was also something tough and slightly shady about Gable that redeemed his virility act. There was the gleam of a bad boy in him; he looked as if he'd been around. When Brolin uses Gable's vocal rhythms, the faintly derisive, unrespectable overtones are missing; the character has a hollow ring. He's wooden—unmagical.

As Carole Lombard, Jill Clayburgh is in much worse trouble. Having admired Jill Clayburgh on the stage and in small parts in movies (she was Ryan O'Neal's ex-wife in *The Thief Who Came to Dinner*) and on TV in *Hustling,* I think that she might be distinctive enough to play a star, but who could play the walking disaster area that the screenwriter, Barry Sandler, dreamed up? The actual Carole Lombard probably wasn't a more skillful comedienne than Jean Arthur or Claudette Colbert, but she had a special luminous, Art Deco look that really went with the décor in those black-and-silver-and-white movies. She wore clothes superbly, in high-fashion style, with her slim hips thrust out; yet, unlike high-fashion models, she seemed more alive than other women. Her vibrancy was linked to her extreme whiteness—the blond hair, the pale skin, and the slinky, skin-tight white satins. In visual terms, she was the sexiest of the comediennes, and her daring décolletage and her free, loose, wiggly body were part of her manic charm in such movies as *Twentieth Century* (1934), *My Man Godfrey* (1936), *Nothing Sacred* (1937), and *True Confession* (1937). She threw herself into her scenes in a much more physical sense than the other women did, and her all-outness seemed spontaneously giddy. It was easy to believe that a woman who moved like that and screamed and hollered with such abandon was a natural, uninhibited cutup—naturally high-spirited. Taking their cue from this, Sandler and the director, Sidney J. Furie, have turned their heroine into a howling hysteric.

In the Depression comedy *My Man Godfrey,* Lombard was a rich, gorgeous nit who went to the city dump to find a "forgotten man." The man she found was played by William Powell. When she told him she needed to take him back to her party in order to win the scavenger hunt, he asked what that was, and sighing, she said, "A scavenger hunt is just like a treasure hunt, except in a treasure hunt you find something you want and in a scavenger hunt you find things you don't want and the one who wins gets a prize, only there really isn't any prize, it's just the honor of winning, because all the money goes to charity if there's any money left over, but then there never is." There was a delirious, breathless plaintiveness in Lombard at a moment like this—recognition dawning in her. Jill Clayburgh has a comic urgency, and if Sandler had written a speech like that for her, she might have emerged as a star; instead, this talented actress has been turned into a whirring machine—dithering frantically. She's kept spinning around the way Lombard was in the punching scene of *Nothing Sacred,* when Fredric March was working her out so that her heartbeat and temperature would convince people she was sick. Clayburgh doesn't look anything like Lombard; if she resembles anyone, it's Jean Arthur. And, like Jean Arthur, she has a voice that flutters between a purr and a seductive gargle, but the lines she's required to speak might be Archie Bunker's idea of how Lenny Bruce talked—a fool's idea of salaciousness. The problem isn't her not resembling Carole Lombard—it's that she's not allowed to resemble a human being.

Sandler belongs to that new batch of screenwriters who have a fan-magazine sensibility: they believe that movies are everything. Their feet have never touched the ground, and their scripts come out of this mid-air sensibility, which is probably the shallowest form of alienation imaginable. It's a daydream view with no breath of realism, and no understanding of the actual company-town Hollywood. Sandler doesn't distinguish between the offscreen Gable and his primal-man roles; rehashed, misconstrued episodes from old movies (such as that scavenger hunt) become the stars' life stories. Inexplicably, Furie has contrived to transfer this drivelling state of mind to the screen.

This is the most limply raunchy, meaningless movie about Hollywood yet. *Gable and Lombard* has nothing to say about the movies, about love, or about stardom. It has no point of view whatever. The movie represents upwardly mobile nostalgia—nostalgia used for its safeness, its uncontroversial, Ford-era nothingness. The only romance in *Gable and Lombard* is Hollywood's love for itself. And that's for a fake self. The very first scene, in 1942, shows Gable in Army Air Forces uniform, learning that the plane Lombard was in has crashed; but Gable wasn't in the service at the time of her death. Then the action cuts back to his memory of meeting her in the early thirties, when she was a big star and he was an unknown; but, as it happens, Lombard didn't become a really big draw until 1934, and in 1931 Clark Gable slugged Norma Shearer in *A Free Soul,* made love to Garbo in *Susan Lenox, Her Fall and Rise,* and wound up as one of the top four male box-office stars. Scene by scene, this film is a silly fraud. It cooks up a fake tension about Gable and Lombard in love and unable to be seen together because Gable was married to a woman who wouldn't give him a divorce. But in the three years—from 1936 to 1939—that Gable and Lombard were together before they were married, they were just about the most public pair in America. In *Life,* in newspapers, in fan magazines, there was the handsome couple at the races, the fights, the tennis matches, at Harlow's funeral, in 1937, and at just about every movie première. The climax of the film is a courtroom scene, when a woman accuses Gable of being the father of her unborn child and Lombard risks her career by testifying that he couldn't be, because he's been with her every night and she has "a sore back to prove it." A woman did in fact try to get money out of M-G-M by threatening to expose Gable as the father of her thirteen-year-old. She claimed that the affair had taken place in England, and Gable had no difficulty proving that he wasn't there at the time. The woman was sentenced to a year in prison—Lombard was nowhere near the courtroom.

The ludicrous pathos of this $4,200,000 production (roughly double the cost of *Nashville* or *Taxi Driver*) is that the moviemakers couldn't come up with any subject but the sex drive of its hero and heroine, who keep hopping on each other like deranged rabbits. One of the most famous quotes in Hollywood history is Lombard's "My God, you know I love Pa, but I can't say he's a hell of a lay." Their love affair must have had a great many things going for it besides sex, but this movie can't imagine what they might be. Since there's no current between Brolin and Clayburgh, and Furie can't work up any sensuality, the dry-run sex gets depressing—we're treated like tourists looking for something gamy. The ad campaign says, "They had more than love—they had *fun*." This turns out to mean that they played practical jokes on each other. When movie stars were satirically glorified in the Pop Art of the sixties, the famous faces seemed set forever—congealed smiles in the sunshine, blazing emblems of fantasy. Who would have guessed that in the next turn of the wheel Hollywood would trivialize and degrade its own legends, and not even out of malice—just out of movie-besotted, eager-beaver ignorance.

[February 23, 1976]

Lion-Hearted Women

*I*n the early sixties, Jeanne Moreau was the love-hungry-bored-wife goddess of the international cinema. The Moreau heroines kept their thoughts to themselves, but her famished mouth and the puffy shadows under her gentle, swollen eyes revealed a sulky dissatisfaction. Moreau had started in movies in 1948, at the age of twenty, and was thirty when she appeared in *The Lovers* and became that charismatic, intuitive, sensual heroine with so many undercurrents that her supple silences would often take over a movie. She's tantalizingly older in *French Provincial,* which had its première at the last New York Film Festival but is just now opening. Age has made her seem like a battle-scarred sex veteran; the drooping, pouty face appears to have been ravaged by sensuality itself— she's love-punchy. Moreau has changed over the years more than most actresses do, and her resemblance to Bette Davis has become almost cartoonish; in her late forties, Moreau looks like the Davis of *Beyond the Forest,* but with a lot of Lillian Gish in her, too, when the mouth pulls down and the softness in the cheeks goes mesmerically wrong. Moreau having been what she was to us, we simply cannot look at her performances now as if she were a new actress; seeing her is a richer, more ambiguous experience. At the start of *French Provincial,* we may juggle our memories, uncomfortably trying to accept this older Moreau—whose face says that she's been through everything—as a young woman. Then we realize that we don't need to. This movie is, among other things, a chronicle of changing film styles, and Moreau is used for her associations, even when she deliberately plays against them. Her age is flexible, especially since her character, Berthe, is a seamstress who comes from the wrong side of the tracks and has had a rough-and-tumble early life. Walking with a determined, jerky little step, wearing plaids or prints and worrying about whether her makeup is too heavy to be respectable, Berthe is the sort of no-nonsense person you think of as stout even though she isn't. Moreau clearly enjoys Berthe's doughty peasant vitality. The outgoing, pragmatic Berthe doesn't know what boredom is.

French Provincial (no way could be found to translate the original, punning title, *Souvenirs d'en France*) presents an overview of French life and politics through the changes within one family in southwestern France. A flashback to the beginning of the century shows the arrival of Pedret, a Spanish immigrant, who becomes a blacksmith, and his marriage to Augustine, the daughter of the village baker. The movie proper takes up the life of this family in 1936, when Pedret's forge has become a foundry where his three sons are the managers, and carries it through the war and labor troubles into the seventies, when the business gets an influx of American capital. Homage is paid to the classic, tragicomic French-family movies by the casting of Orane Demazis, the heroine of *Harvest* and the Fanny of Pagnol's trilogy, as the bourgeois matriarch Augustine, but *French Provincial* has a very different impetus. When Augustine realizes that her son Hector (Michel Auclair) is having an affair with the seamstress, she tries to ruin Berthe's business and drive her out of town. But old Pedret, who knows that his sons have had their spirits broken, can see that Berthe has the blunt good sense they lack, and he arranges for Berthe and Hector to be married. While the bourgeois wives of the two other sons mope and become peevish, Berthe makes herself useful. In the war, she is a heroine of the Resistance; when the business is imperilled by a strike, she settles it by acceding to the workers' demands. She takes over the dominant role in management, and becomes the new matriarch as well.

On this level, *French Provincial* is an unabashed, playful, and politicized version of the kind of films that Irene Dunne and Barbara Stanwyck used to appear in, often based on Edna Ferber novels. It's *Stella*

Dallas mixed in with *Cimarron* and *So Big* and *Mildred Pierce* and *Imitation of Life* and all the others; it's the American-dynasty stories and the "women's" pictures of the thirties come back to us transformed, and though *French Provincial* is by no means as startlingly innovative as Godard's transformations of the American gangster film, the cross-fertilization brings some juice to the traditional French saga of provincial life. The young director, André Téchiné (he's thirty-two), and his co-writer, Marilyn Goldin, an American in her early thirties, try to cram in too much; you practically need a road map to find your way through the movie—at the outset you feel stupid because you can't sort out who is married to whom. Téchiné's dashing style also presents a problem: he and Goldin prepare wonderful, humor-filled scenes, teasingly evocative of whole batches of earlier films, and then he skims over them so lightly that they often don't quite sink in and the story just seems sketchy. But this movie isn't very realistic anyway; it's an ironic romantic fantasy on women's-picture themes. And it has a tickling personality—consciously, sloppily casual here and there (the characters age inconsistently), and bumping around in time, yet always with the jittery, airy understanding that its own situations and characters are fair game. There's not a labored moment in it.

Earlier the team of Téchiné and Goldin collaborated on a French TV program about the Brontës, and they've written a new movie, *Barocco,* for Isabelle Adjani, which is being shot now. One can surmise that Téchiné provided much of the political background of *French Provincial,* but surely the women's fantasy structure must have come mostly from Marilyn Goldin, a former critic, who has also worked with Bertolucci. *French Provincial* is that rare picture in which the basic conflict is between two women: Berthe the frump, who gets rich but never learns how to dress, and the slick, dark beauty Régina (Marie-France Pisier), who is married to Prosper (Claude Mann), Pedret's youngest son and the only one with a college education. Régina and the handsome, refined Prosper seem a mismatch from the word go; Berthe, with her soft little pot, and the clumsy, crumpled Hector seem a perfect pair for a comfortable existence. Yet both marriages fail, because both women are too much for their husbands. Régina is a rapacious dreamer. Fed up with the dull austerity of provincial society, she runs off with an American soldier, and she comes back years later, more stunning than ever, with an American industrialist lover. Whatever her emotional susceptibilities are, Régina keeps them hidden, but we're clued in on her hatreds when she and her industrialist visit the family home and (in a scene lifted from Proust) have sex with a silent third partner—a photograph of Pedret looking on. Régina is the cold villainess of earlier movies seen in a hot new light.

Early on, there's a choreographed showpiece sequence that declares the movie's obsession. Godard frequently displayed movie posters and made allusions to films that had a special meaning for him; when Bertolucci, Scorsese, and others have adopted this practice the films they refer to are usually action pictures, with male-fantasy heroes. But when the family of *French Provincial* go to the local theatre, the lobby is decorated with posters of pairs of lovers, and the film they see is Garbo's *Camille*. Leaving the theatre and walking out into the rain, the members of the family are still in a trance, wiping their eyes and blowing their noses—all except the new bride Régina, who is laughing shrilly, in ostentatious contempt of the film's romanticism and the family's fatuousness. She whirls in the rain, defiant in her openness to the elements, exciting her half-admiring, half-embarrassed bridegroom. Régina's own romanticism is nose-thumbing effrontery—sneering and selfish, yet with a nasty grandeur. When she returns from America, brittle and swinger-chic, she is the exact opposite of Berthe. This is the story of two tough, fearless broads: one holds the family together; the other goes out looking for luxury and laughs.

French Provincial sees both women as heroines, yet it keeps a distance from them, too. We're not asked to admire them—that was what made the American prototypes gushy. We're merely invited to be alive to the women's portion of the human comedy. There are startling, original moments, like the one when Berthe, taking a bedpan to the ailing old Pedret, is taunted by her sister-in-law, who says that there's not much pleasure to be had from "wiping an old man's ass." "How do you know?" Berthe asks. And earlier, Moreau has a balletic routine all to herself. Raging over Augustine's maneuvers to force her to leave town, Berthe prepares herself a meal—an omelet and a salad. She sets them on the table, and then, angry and preoccupied, reaches for her hat and muffler, and goes out to confront Hector with what his mother is doing to her. There's a scrubby, zigzag humor in a woman's spurning her own cooking which is pure, irrational inspiration.

French Provincial is marvellous, even though in ordinary terms it isn't good. Téchiné's visual style is a passionate mingling of European and American masters—Godard, Bertolucci, Welles, William Wyler, Cocteau, Hitchcock, Jacques Tati, and God knows who. Scenes take you back through so many layers of film history that you can't sort out all the influences; you don't need to. You can see that this rich impasto is essentially new. Téchiné is a monstrously gifted romantic wit who has turned parody into something so emotionally charged that the meanings radiate every which way. The flashback sequence of Pedret's youth wings from *Wuthering Heights* and the flaming silhouettes of *Gone with the Wind* to *The Conformist* and *The Spider's Stratagem*, with the characters spinning toward the camera in formalized turns that are Gothic variants of a Godard device. It's gorgeous, heady stuff, and, throughout, Téchiné invests the images with so much dramatic beauty that you're busy just taking it in. In some way that I can't figure out, he charges even static compositions. But Téchiné's talent runs away with him. *French Provincial* is effective on the most sophisticated level but seems naïve and scatterbrained on some of the simplest levels. He and Marilyn Goldin have had the slyly poetic idea of treating the bourgeois home as the primal, mysterious movie set, but they don't seem to have thought it all through. When Berthe delivers an arch little Godardian lecture to the head of the strike committee, we have no idea how to read the scene. At other times, the movie stoops to the kind of leftist-historian résumé of political events that does nothing for an audience. It doesn't add up, quite, and Berthe's character isn't as satisfyingly conceived as Régina's. But from scene to scene this movie is a film festival all by itself. I particularly liked the way Michel Auclair, with his resonances from the forties (*Beauty and the Beast, Les Maudits*), was transformed into the burly, earthy figure of the humanitarian thirties. Téchiné and Goldin may not know anything except movies, but the way they know movies is enough for me.

□ □ □

*I*f there are gradations in the pits, *I Will, I Will . . . For Now* is even worse than *Gable and Lombard.* It combines the most simperingly forced elements of fifties mistaken-identity farces with a mushy, soft-core version of the sex-manual pornos. The director, Norman Panama, who used to be half of the writing team of Panama and (Melvin) Frank, has shamelessly modelled this film on Frank's *A Touch of Class,* even down to the hero's back going out—in this case, when he tries a new position from *The Joy of Sex.* Elliott Gould is the unfortunate back patient; a Manhattan business-man who has a womblike office that looks as if Saarinen had carved it out of ice cream, and who earns a quarter of a million dollars a year, he suffers from premature ejaculation. His ex-wife, who suffers from frigidity, passivity, and compulsive cleanliness, is played by Diane Keaton. The Santa Barbara sex clinic they repair to is run by Madge Sinclair and Robert Alda; he exudes affability, like Liberace, and makes smily speeches, the gist of which—"Nothing is unnatural"—is also emblazoned in neon in the patients' cottages. The message is false: swallowing this movie is an unnatural act for any person of average intelligence. As Gould's lawyer, Paul Sorvino is also involved in the infantile games that Panama and his co-writer Albert E. Lewin, devised; I'm not altogether sure that he deserves better. And if Elliott Gould, the best loose comedian we've got (when he's on his own frequency), doesn't know enough to keep his shirt on and stay out of Rock Hudson's tight shoes, he's going to lose the good will that he builds up whenever he works for Paul Mazursky or Robert

Altman. However, Diane Keaton, whether she's in bed with Sorvino or with Gould, manages to keep her head, and she acts with such plangent friendliness that she proves it's possible to lie down with dogs and not get covered with fleas.

[March 1, 1976]

A Bit of Archie Rice

John Osborne's play *The Entertainer,* set during the Suez crisis of 1956, was staged by Tony Richardson in 1957, starring Laurence Olivier as Archie Rice; it has been his greatest contemporary role, and he also appeared in the 1960 film version, again directed by Richardson. The play is a lewd, tragic vaudeville about the life of a bankrupt pursued by creditors, a crapulent song-and-dance man whose emotions break through onstage in stale blue jokes as he ogles the half-naked chorus girls, razzes the orchestra leader, and jeers at the audience. "Don't clap too hard—it's a very old building," he cautions the audience, which is sitting on its hands. And if there's mincing hatred in his tone, and the desperate self-disgust of a performer who can't get a response, there's also a trace of affection for the run-down theatre, which is dilapidated, crumbling England.

The action shifts between the music-hall stage and the rooms that Archie and his wife, Phoebe, share with his father, Billy Rice, who was a headliner in his day but now, in his seventies, is retired to a life of mildewed gentility. Old Billy—"Granddad" to Archie's three grownup children—wears ancient, carefully preserved smart clothes and conducts himself with the rakish dignity of an Edwardian gentleman. Osborne explained in his introductory note to the play, "The music hall is dying, and, with it, a significant part of England. Some of the heart of England has gone; something that once belonged to everyone, for this was truly a folk art." Billy was a great performer, part of a living tradition; Archie, still hanging on at fifty, has never had the purity that his father had—he refers to himself as "old Archie, dead behind the eyes." He's smart, self-analytical, obscenely angry as he lashes out at us, the audience, in frustration at his own mediocrity.

Osborne is a master of invective. He can't bring Archie's principled, observant daughter, Jean, to life, but when it comes to characters like

Archie Rice, or Jimmy Porter, in *Look Back in Anger,* or Bill Maitland, in *Inadmissible Evidence*—heroes who do so much to make you hate them that you can't—he gives them a Shakespearean fury. Their sour, profane declamatory rages have the sustained dramatic tension of Shakespearean soliloquies.

Language may be the only true glory that England has left, and so it seems just about the final insult to Americanize *The Entertainer.* That is what has been done in the new version, starring Jack Lemmon, which will be shown on television in this country (Wednesday, March 10th, over NBC, from nine to eleven) and in theatres in other countries. Osborne's name is very small in the credits; his work has been rewritten by Elliott Baker, and directed by Donald Wrye, under the aegis of Beryl Vertue and her co-producer, Marvin Hamlisch, who also wrote the music. The publicity material for this new version says that the setting has been "switched from a British seaside resort to an American counterpart." But, of course, there is no American counterpart of the long music-hall tradition. The new setting is an imaginary, unnamed oceanside town somewhere between San Francisco and Los Angeles, and the time has been backdated to 1944 and the Second World War, possibly to obscure just how peculiar and unrooted Archie's revue theatre is—a carnival-midway show that is doing Broadway tryouts. Osborne's rhetoric—which is his greatness—is terribly diminished not only by the extensive rewriting but also by being delivered in American rhythms. A California-set *Entertainer* is like *A Streetcar Named Desire* laid in Edinburgh, with a rugby-brute Stanley and a Blanche who talks like Miss Jean Brodie. Actually, it's even more of an act of cultural vandalism than that would be, because in Osborne's metaphor the decay of music hall stood for the decay of England, and though that entire range of associations has been neutered this Americanized *Entertainer* will go to England with big promotion and be seen, probably, by many more people than ever saw the Olivier stage or screen version. And so English audiences will lose out on Osborne's muddy, bitter romanticism. In the original, Archie contrasted the uptight-ness of the British who don't make "a fuss" with a fat black woman he once heard in America who sang "her heart out to the whole world." "If I'd done one thing as good as that in my whole life," Archie said, "I'd have been all right. . . . I wish to God I were that old bag. I'd stand up and shake my great bosom up and down, and lift my head and make the most beautiful fuss in the world." At the news that his nineteen-year-old son, Mick, had been killed in Suez, Olivier's Archie tried to break out of his Englishness; he sang the blues to release the pain. In this version, audiences won't get the blasphemous fifties disillusion that seemed to come sniggering up from the repression. When, at the climax of Archie's raucous, clairvoyant, scrubby revue, Britannia was exposed as a half-naked bimbo, the too easy cleverness—the very cheapness of the shot—worked

149

for it. Now, with the Second World War setting, and with Archie's pacifist daughter changed to a Navy nurse, his son Frank no longer a jailbird conscientious objector, and Mick no longer sacrificed at Suez but merely killed in an accident, the rancid atmosphere is puzzling, since the story is only about show business, and a mid-Atlantic form of it that we don't quite recognize.

The producer, Beryl Vertue, is an Englishwoman who has made a career out of transplants. She was one of the agents who handled the sale to Norman Lear of the concepts of the British series "Till Death Us Do Part" and "Steptoe and Son," which became "All in the Family" and "Sanford and Son." She also handled the conversion of "Upstairs, Downstairs" into "Beacon Hill," on which she was executive producer. Except for her involvement in the new weekly show "Almost Anything Goes," in television terms she's a very classy cultural force, and Mobil Oil is sponsoring this *Entertainer*. But it's not only the English who lose out. Archie still describes the black woman; the moment when he should sing is prepared for, but it never arrives. The film is full of bits of dialogue that have lost what they connected with, character relations that have become disjointed, scenes that dribble off. And theatrical devices, such as the family's waiting for Mick, who we know will never show up, stick out uncomfortably. Elliott Baker isn't a hack writer; he's a novelist (*A Fine Madness*) who comes from a theatre family, and some of the grungy details he adds are good, but the characters are no longer embodiments of the society that they live in, or comments on it, either. Yet since even the remnants of Osborne's plot and characters—and his poetry of anger—are far more compelling than most TV fare, this program is sure to be honored, and, in fact, one's apprehensions about Lemmon in the Olivier role dissolve midway. However, his performance doesn't cancel out this inexcusable case of cultural homogenization.

There has been an element in Jack Lemmon's screen personality of his not having grown up, quite, yet of his having grown tired, exhausted. Last year, in *The Front Page* and *The Prisoner of Second Avenue,* he seemed to be straining under a terrible lump of anxiety; he just about *was* Archie Rice—manic and empty. But here Lemmon has got his talent in control again. He begins uncertainly, but he hits some new notes and does some very sure line readings, without falling back on Jack Lemmonisms. There's no tender-heartedness, no asking for sympathy. He's particularly effective in his seduction of the beauty contestant Bambi, played by Annette O'Toole, the willowy, freckled redhead of *Smile.* She does the raw, innocent Bambi without any affectation, singing in a naïve, cotton-candy style reminiscent of the young Angela Lansbury. Annette O'Toole's simplicity brings out the pain in Archie's dirty boyishness. His relationship to this girl is better defined than in the Olivier film, and when they're in bed the scene has enough sensuous conviction to make it plausible that Archie would decide to get rid of his spongy-cheeked old-girl wife to marry her. Lemmon's cavalier kindliness toward his old Phoebe (Sada Thompson), whom he betrays, patronizes, and infantilizes, is well done—there's the stupor of habit in it—though if the stage actress Sada Thompson is ever to be fully effective on the screen (which seems doubtful), she'll have to have a director who knows where to put the camera. Wrye gives the actors more help than they need; he keeps ramming closeups at us whenever he wants the actors to "move" us. There's a particularly gross use of closeups when Archie, in full, smeary Pagliacci makeup, gets bad news on the telephone.

The Tony Richardson film erred in comparable ways, but it had a venomous excitement; Richardson didn't completely wreck what had made the play such a hit—the audience's ambiguous relationship to "the entertainer." In the stage numbers, Olivier's Archie was in combat with us, and we felt his contempt; the routines he did were his way of pissing on us. He was the entertainer as scapegoat—a hyena-clown. Without this, the new version falls apart. Lemmon's stage routines need to be viciously rotten and they're just bad—as if their sole purpose were to prove to us that Archie is a bum performer. They're frenetic rather than weary unto death, and Lemmon doesn't perform them with that decadent profession-alism which was electrifying in Olivier's performance (and in Joel Grey's m.c. in *Cabaret*). We can't ask Lemmon to do the role the way Olivier did—to have the soulless, button eyes, the predatory smile, or the queasy castrato-satyr overtones—but he isn't "working the house," and the routines, choreographed by Ron Field to Hamlisch's tunes, suggest that Field couldn't figure out what tradition they were supposed to derive from.

Considering the magnitude of Lemmon's attempt, it's a considerable achievement that he doesn't disgrace himself. He doesn't create a new Archie Rice: we're not drawn in all the way. And maybe because he isn't convincingly repellent as a song-and-dance man, and because we don't feel any true malice in this Archie's relation to the audience, we can't quite get a fix on the character. This Archie isn't shocking. But Archie Rice's pain gives Jack Lemmon a new dignity. He's best in his thoughtful, quiet moments offstage, and, considering how obstructive the direction is, and how overexplicit Elliott Baker has made the scenes, his reticence is an advantage. Even the star treatment he's given when he's at the piano and looking serious, like angel Harpo at his lousy harp, is restful, and it's lucky that the director does give Lemmon star treatment, because Lemmon provides the rhythm for most of his scenes, and they're the only scenes that *have* any rhythm. Tyne Daly's performance as Archie's daughter Jean is mangled by strident editing and camerawork. Jean, the only one in the film whom Archie levels with, is meant to be so clear-eyed that Archie can't put on an act with her; what this comes down to is that she's a boring outsider, passing judgment on him. But Lemmon has a fine moment when she is going away and he asks her to stay to see her granddad, old Billy Rice (Ray

Bolger), do his return engagement; Archie's sense of isolation here has terror in it. Lemmon's ability, however, can't obscure the fact that this scene (it's not in the play) is psychologically offensive. Jean's leaving the theatre at the most suspenseful moment in the action, just before her famous grandfather is about to give his first performance in twenty years, seems inhumanly self-denying, like turning your back on fireworks. Fortunately, we can stay.

It's a dizzyingly happy dance that Ray Bolger does, with a frightening element built in, because we know that something disastrous has to happen. Bolger, that great dancer-comic-mime, at seventy-two still a lithe high-stepper, turns the number into a celebration of the entertainer's art. Old Billy comes on with Archie, each one end of a horse, to do a father-and-son double. But Billy is so excited that he's uncontrollable, and he takes off into a beautiful eccentric single—a kicking, prancing pony dance that is perfectly in character and at the same time is pure, floppy Bolger. It's a triumphant sequence—old Billy going out in glory—and we want the pleasure of mulling it over, but the people in charge won't permit it: they won't let us feel anything for ourselves. The more the meanings are explained, the less this show means, and vice versa. The producers say that this isn't a television version, it's a film. That's what they think.

[March 8, 1976]

A Piece of Music

The Claude Sautet film *Vincent, François, Paul, and the Others* is infinitely preferable to such other recently opened films as *Salut l'Artiste*, directed by Yves Robert, and *The Slap*, directed by Claude Pinoteau, but they all have something in common: they seem to have been worked up out of nothing in particular, and they share the faint despondency of commercial projects. It used to be that American films looked machine-made compared to the more personal French imports; now it's the reverse. Jean-Loup Dabadie was co-writer on all three films and probably contributed to the creeping mediocrity—the shallow poetry of ordinary lives—that links them. I debated walking out on *The Slap*, with its generation-gap misunderstandings and its captivating teen-ager (even though Isabelle Adjani performed the part with smiling ease), and I would have been happy to give *Salut l'Artiste* four stars for sincerity and compassion and make my escape. It's about the life of a wilted, second-rate actor (Marcello Mastroianni) who's also a second-rate person; his mistress sums him up when she says that he doesn't have presence, he has absence. This is meant to be not a joke but a tragic perception. *Salut l'Artiste* is a hollow pop film, with a little gas from undigested Antonioni.

Claude Sautet is such a princely craftsman and the all-star cast of *Vincent, François, Paul, and the Others* is so physically attractive that I had no wish to leave, but I felt some resistance to the picture. I know this is unfair to Sautet, but it's the way I feel on those occasions (rare) when my attention is held by a story on the "family/style" pages of the *New York Times*. There's an element of the good host in Sautet's craft here: the lushly beautiful actresses, with their chromatically assembled dye jobs, seem to be at a party, and who wouldn't want to be there when the guest list includes Yves Montand (Vincent), Michel Piccoli (François), Serge Reggiani (Paul), Stéphane Audran (Catherine, Vincent's wife), Ludmilla Mikael (Marie, his mistress), Marie Dubois (Lucie, François's straying wife), Antonella Lualdi (Julia, Paul's wife), and Gérard Depardieu (Jean, a young boxer)? They're all playing average people, but that opulent cast list has more than its share of glamour; it's the menu for a fat-cat banquet.

Sautet doesn't tell a story here; rather, he orchestrates a slice of middle-class life. (On one level, that's what "family/style" does, too.) Vincent, the owner of a machine shop, François, a physician, and Paul, a writer, are old friends who are hitting fifty, and on Sundays they and their families get together. The picture, which shows us the three men's lives during a crisis when their friendship appears to be falling apart, is about aging and survival—about people trying to adapt to what they have become and to everything that happens that they can't control. It's all conceived musically; the dialogue might be lyrics, and the whole studio-made film moves rhythmically, as if it were a melancholy, romantic tune. Sautet shoots in controlled, studio-lot conditions for the unified, pulsating effect. Jean Boffety's whizzing camerawork suggests that Max Ophuls is looking over Sautet's shoulder; the frequent car sequences (as when Vincent rushes from one place to another trying to raise money to save his business) are little scherzos. This is Sautet's sixth feature film, and before making his own films he was an assistant to several directors, and was a well-known screenwriter besides, but he was for a period a distinguished music critic, and possibly he works so well with Montand, who also appeared in his last film, *César and Rosalie,* because Montand is a singer. Reggiani sings, too. (Many of his recordings have lyrics by Dabadie.) Piccoli, the son of two musicians, who has been married to the singer Juliette Gréco since 1966, has worked with Sautet often, and, like

Montand, he expands in Sautet's films. Here he plays against his usual stylized, elegant cool, exposing it as tightness. The film is a French-Italian co-production, and that may explain why the three French friends of the title are played by actors of Italian background (Piccoli was born in Paris of Italian parents, and the two others in Italy), but probably these three also have the more physically expressive temperaments that the film's conception requires. They're Sautet's solo instruments.

Although *Vincent, François, Paul, and the Others* is adapted from a novel (*La Grande Marade,* by Claude Neron, who also collaborated on the screenplay), it gives practically no sign of characterization, except for what the performers bring to their roles. Sautet's method is to reveal the characters' souls contrapuntally, through their everyday behavior, and we don't particularly register what is said. We're caught by the tone of voice—the loudness, the bellicosity—or by a twinge, or a catch in the throat. During the middle-age crisis—something like male menopause—that the film covers, the men are forced to look at what they've become, and we see what they see. We also see that they're still hesitating over choices made long ago—and stewing over lost possibilities. Sautet understands something that a lot of earlier moviemakers didn't: that as people get older their emotions may be as unresolved as ever. They may be giddy fifteen-year-olds under their sagging skins. In this post-Freudian tragicomedy of manners, the characters are still listening to old tunes in their heads, clinging to their obsessive desires even though they don't get what they hope for. They don't get what, on the basis of our moviegoing experience, we've come to expect, either. If the film "says" anything, it's that nobody knows what's right for anybody else, or can do anything about it if he does. The women, however, are so straight, illusionless, and determinedly honest that it's almost as though they were what the men would be if only the men were wiser and stronger. The film treats the women as so principled because it's primarily concerned with the men. And so the scenes between men and women are lifeless, or worse. When the doctor's errant wife, Lucie, tells him he's a cash register and leaves him, it would make enough sense if she indicated that his acquisitiveness and snobbery repelled her so much that she didn't want to go to bed with him. But the movie suggests that his moral defects wrecked him as a sexual partner. This is a little romantic fallacy that Hollywood, too, always loved—virtue and virility went together so neatly.

The stars, busily inventing humanizing details, provide the size and assurance that save the roles they play from being "little people." Depardieu, Europe's Robert De Niro, is hearty and pink-cheeked as the prizefighter-mechanic whom Vincent treats as a son; Depardieu plays a minor part, but, as with most of the others, you know you're seeing a star. And the more ordinary Montand acts, the larger and more Raimu-like he becomes. His upper lip is growing impressively long, and like Jeanne Moreau, he has developed his own way of changing the emotional color of a scene; he can do it by drawing down that lip, or with a blink or just a second's painful awkwardness. These are the movie actor's infinitesimally small variants of bravura stage technique, and when Montand takes them out here he's showing his portfolio. We may be impressed by what a fine actor he has turned into, yet our assessment is impersonal. As this film, deliberately transient in mood, speeds along, we are meant to see ourselves up there and to care about the characters' everyday pain and pleasure— even about the bitterness of Piccoli's status-hungry doctor. Yet I found myself perceiving the distress signals—the vacant expressions, the sickly grins, the clouded eyes—without feeling involved. The film's discreet, gutted sensitivity is self-sufficient; it softens and takes the edges off. Montand's tender-gruff decency is too professionally touching, Reggiani's simple goodness is too winning, Marie Dubois is too level-eyed; everybody is too understandable. This film wears its humanity like a badge of commerce. I could be projecting, but I think there's more inexplicable dirty terror in people than this gracefully calibrated conception allows for. Montand's Vincent has pendulum swings of emotion, but even those are held in comfortable check; failure isn't failure here—it's "life." Observing the doctor's telltale tensions (smoking, smoking), the writer's wife's full-bodied, maternal love for her weak husband, and so on, I feel as if we in the audience were being pressed into membership in the society of the noble failed. In the best sequence, the doctor quarrels with his friends at Sunday dinner, and previously concealed hostilities emerge. It's one of the rare screen arguments in which all sides are convincingly weighted, and it suggests that we'll get a closer look at the myths that bind people in friendship. But the film is more concerned with how the rupture is healed. The appurtenances of French middle-class existence protect us too much here; they pad the falls. The very thinginess of the contemporary city life the film shows—the fast cars, the unobtrusive chic, the small cafés—seems to deprive us of any illumination.

Probably audiences will take this film as a tribute to human resilience. It presents the middle-class version of the indomitability of man—patching up your life, behaving as well as you can, and taking refuge in friendship. One can't fault this, exactly, and it's certainly not a happy view, but it's a blandly, mathematically tragic, almost congratulatory view. Sautet is a wizard at juggling and balancing a large cast; he keeps the incredibly complex *Dinner at Eight* situation spinning in thin air, and the smoothness of his technique has its own beauty. Yet he's like a classical composer writing a jazz symphony. He's got all the control and refinement—all the externals—but he can't find the insides. He's put his craft on the screen and left himself out.

*T*here is no outside to *Inserts*—no world that any of the five characters belong to. The advertising campaign for this film is far more ingenious than the movie, which is like a kid's view of a Strindbergian conflict, crossed with a rip-off of Michael McClure's *The Beard*. The action takes place on one set; the characters come in and out, and they shout as if they were on a stage. The author-director, John Byrum, is trying to make a movie, but his script is a long one-act play. His fantasy-conceit is that the set is a house in Hollywood around 1930, where The Boy Wonder (Richard Dreyfuss), a once famous director, now shoots stag movies. Since Dreyfuss's acting isn't located in a recognizable world, as it was in *The Apprenticeship of Duddy Kravitz,* or in a framework of illusion that we can accept for the moment, as in *Jaws,* the claim that this blustering kid, waggling his head in imitation of John Barrymore, was a great man never takes hold. Dreyfuss struts about, as uncomfortable in his body as a high-school amateur; it's a booby-prize performance, by a major young actor. Byrum's notion is that The Boy Wonder's moviemaking genius burned out and that this is related to his present sexual impotence, which is cured in the course of the film by the earnest efforts of an aspiring actress, Miss Cathy Cake (Jessica Harper), who works on him lovingly because she thinks her exertions are being filmed. She has no reason for believing that the camera is turning by itself when they're in bed together, but then that's only one of many unconvincing plot devices—devices that don't add up to much, since the restoration of The Boy Wonder's virility doesn't, at the absurdist end, seem to mean anything in particular. The film finishes up by putting itself down.

This fantasy about a genius of the hand-held camera is like the ideas that a lot of students have for making movies. The picture should be more fun than it is, but Byrum hasn't worked out the motivation for the dialogue twists; he falls back on absurdism by necessity. And he falls down on his stunts. When The Boy Wonder shoots brief "inserts"—closeups—for his stag reels, you see the footage in black and white, but when he takes an "insert" closeup of Cathy Cake's genitals, the shot is discreetly omitted. You don't set up a device like this black-and-white switch-over and then drop it at the crucial moment—not if you know what you're doing. Byrum is only twenty-eight, and this film was made (in England) on a small budget (around a half million). Still, The Boy Wonder's callow paradoxes ("Nothing pure, old sport, is ever simple," followed by "Nothing simple is ever pure") and the pearls of condescending wisdom that he drops are mere juvenilia. And Byrum likes his own worst lines so much that they're the ones he repeats. The picture loses whatever energy it has when Harlene (Veronica Cartwright), the marcelled star of The Boy Wonder's stag film, ODs. Even hampered by the poor sound recording, which makes her shrill and partly unintelligible, Veronica Cartwright (who started as a child actress, and played Rod Taylor's kid sister in *The Birds*) goes way beyond the silly material. She flings herself into her role in the dissolute romantic manner of Jeanne Eagels—nervous, intense, vivacious, acting with her entire body. She's a grownup, quicksilver talent in a kid's show.

[March 15, 1976]

Suicide Is Painless

Robin and Marian, starring Sean Connery and Audrey Hepburn as the lovers in the forest, grown older, sounds like a dream movie. "When you are young, you are too bashful to play a hero; you debunk it." That's what Laurence Olivier said after he had hit the great stride of his middle years. And he added, "It isn't until you're older that you can understand the pictorial beauty of heroism." There's more to it than pictorial beauty, as Olivier, in his modest reluctance to spell it out, surely knew. For Connery in the last few years, as for Olivier earlier, it's a change of soul—an openhearted acceptance of the human potential for courage and bravery. As they grow older, these actors stop repressing their most glorious impulses; they let out the stops. Connery now—big, fleshy, graying—is the most natural-looking of heroic figures. He seems unrestrained, naked: a true hero. And a perfect counterpart to Audrey Hepburn. He's animal-man at its best; she's an innocent yet passionate sprite. Coming from different continents, the young Audrey and the young Katharine Hepburn, different as they were, shared more than the name: they were both girlish tomboys. Neither could play stupid or vulgar women or conventional maternal roles. Both magically transparent actresses, they were nevertheless limited by their feyness. Audrey, however, wasn't disliked by the public the way Katharine was for a time. Katharine Hepburn never quite represented an ideal for American girls, but Audrey Hepburn did. She was the *jeune fille* that American teen-agers (and older women, too) aspired to be: she revived daintiness and the wistful look, and made childish stick arms seem seductive. From her first starring role, in *Roman Holiday,* in 1953, when the director William Wyler brought out her elfin heartbreaker's charm, she was too dominatingly radiant ever to play a minor part. From that time on, until her temporary retirement in 1967, she was perhaps the most disarming of stars.

157

The years have been generous to her—not that she's very old (she was born in Belgium in 1929) but that they have added depth to her delicacy. Richard Lester, the director of *Robin and Marian,* and David Watkin, the head of the camera crew, have photographed her and Connery (who was born in Edinburgh in 1930) superbly. The two of them are so wittily matched, and their dark-brown eyes are so full of life, that they achieve an elemental splendor. Hepburn was always a woodland creature, and when you see her and Connery together in Sherwood Forest, their eyes shining, you want so badly for the emotion in their faces to break through into the story that what does in fact happen in the James Goldman script seems like a betrayal of them, and of us.

The advertising suggests that this film is a love story. It isn't, except maybe for those who thought *The Lion in Winter,* also by Goldman, a love story. The author has a revisionist approach to legends. We are not to be allowed our idealistic pleasure in the prankish rebel-outlaw figure of Robin Hood, the high-spirited rogue who fought the wicked and aided the poor and mistreated. Goldman's Robin is a brave simpleton, an illiterate, thoughtless man who never could do anything about the barbarous injustices of the world. All he could do was steal from the rich to dole out pennies to the poor. Wearying of that nonsense, he and Little John (Nicol Williamson) joined Richard the Lion-Hearted (Richard Harris) and went off to fight in the Crusades. After serving Richard faithfully for twenty years (and thus taking part in the massacres and greed-motivated atrocities committed in the Holy Land), Robin and John finally say no when Richard orders them to slaughter the undefended women and children at Châluz, in France. That's where the movie begins. Wounded by a mad old man at Châluz, Richard delivers some of Goldman's pursed-lips verse, written in the manner of Robert Bolt. Goldman's lines are succinct; the slush is the thought underneath. "It's cold. I never liked the dark," Richard announces importantly. And, breathing his last, "Clever fellow, Death is." The camera has nowhere to go during these constipated flourishes, so it's a relief when Richard conks out and Robin and John head home to England. Unfortunately, Goldman, in all his pomp, goes along.

Returning to Sherwood Forest, Robin meets up with some of his old band (no longer merry, of course) and idly asks what happened to Marian, remarking, "I haven't thought of her in years." It's a kick in the face—to us. This trivializing put-down is as clever as Death. Marian, it turns out, slashed her wrist when Robin left her, and was taken to Kirkly Abbey, where she is now the Abbess. Since rotten King John (Ian Holm) has ordered the higher clergy out of England, the Sheriff of Nottingham (Robert Shaw) is coming to arrest her. But Robin defies him and takes her to the forest, and there is a moment in this brief idyll, after she has shed her wimple, when her large eyes and drawn little face recall Olivia De Havilland's valentine-Marian in the 1938 Errol Flynn version, *The*

Adventures of Robin Hood, which is the progenitor of this film. But these few love scenes are the only ones that deliver on the promise of the film's title, and they are marred by such cryptic chic as Marian's pre-coital address: "Robin. Hurt me. Make me cry." Hepburn, most of whose longer speeches seem to have come from a spiritualist claiming Elizabeth Barrett Browning as a familiar, has no possibility of giving a good performance. Her fragile strength is perhaps even more touching than before, and those who saw her in her most demanding dramatic role, in *The Nun's Story,* know that she can act. But all you can do here is look at her, and, when she's sententious, feel sorry about the waste. Most of the movie is taken up by the plots against Robin and by the fighting he engages in. A whole new army of ragged farmers joins him in the woods, but the film avoids building up any spirit of fellowship among the oppressed. The contest isn't between oppressors and oppressed; it's between Robin and Robert Shaw's Sheriff of Nottingham, who, not unexpectedly, turns out to be realistic-minded and a fair, if wily, adversary. He curls a thin-lipped smile as he sets a trap for Robin. "I know him," the Sheriff says. "He's a little bit in love with death. . . . He flirts, he teases. I can wait."

Connery and Hepburn are a love match. James Goldman and Richard Lester aren't. I don't think that the emotion we feel about Connery and Hepburn would break through so urgently if the director didn't feel it. Lester must be trying for something simpler and more human than what he's been up to in recent years. He seems to be working on equal terms with the actors; this picture isn't just his show. He lets Richard Harris carry a scene or two, and Nicol Williamson, who isn't saddled with too many oratorical passages, carries several. Williamson uses his twanginess for a light, bemused effect that is very appealing in the early part of the film, when we accept Little John's loyalty to Robin as a comic-sidekick relationship. But once John actually defines himself as nothing more than Robin's friend, a masochistic whine wrecks the fun. Still he and Connery don't fare badly. Connery's wide-eyed, blunt Robin has its own heroic-warrior force—that of a Ulysses or a Macbeth. The film wants to expose heroism as a sick fraud, yet it also wants this grizzled-giant hero in all his pictorial beauty. As in *The Lion in Winter,* there's no comprehending the characters' self-definitions, or their switches of mood, aim, strategy. They strike poses—whimsical modern attitudes that Goldman gives them for the sake of paradox. And how can a director achieve plain glorious feeling when the script is trying to attain grandeur of sentiment by such flossy means as having the Sheriff of Nottingham calculate on Robin Hood's death fixation?

Somehow—it must be a matter of temperament, although, of course, it's also related to his continuing success in TV commercials—Lester has never developed into a master of long sequences. He doesn't appear to have the patience or the sound equipment for Goldman's formal lines,

159

which demand to be heard right down to the dead letdown, and the higher rhetoric mixes so oddly with his usual airy overheards that his technique seems indifferent, convictionless. In most of Lester's films, bit players abound; often they are well-known actors who turn up for a gag or two, and they help to populate the screen—to give it a gibbering vitality. But Goldman's text makes such a rigid distinction between the principals and the bit players that for the first time in a Lester film the bit players are faceless. Even Denholm Elliott, who plays Will Scarlett, stays cramped in his tiny role. Visually, Lester is no slouch; except for the salon-photography look of the beginning and the end, he keeps the images active. Yet nothing seems to come of this activity—no suspense, no spirit of adventure.

The most emotionally upsetting element is that Lester doesn't adapt his Keatonesque, almost abstract use of the film frame or his editing style to the brutal combat. The editing touch is so deft and clipped that the line between tragic horror and joking make-believe has got smudged. We don't know when the film is fooling and when it isn't, or whether to be tickled or appalled—and so we sit in discomfort, listening to the fake warmth of John Barry's picture-postcard score. Goldman's speeches about the inevitability of cruelty don't make much sense in a movie that treats men mangling each other as a medieval version of The Three Stooges. The Sheriff's first words as he looks at his soldiers are "They never learn." And the film's contempt for those who fight—they are viewed as bloodthirsty clowns—goes so far that at the end, when Robin Hood's ill-equipped farmers battle against the King's armored legions, the movie veers off in a different direction and doesn't bother to tell us the outcome.

Lester and Goldman must have wanted to out-Kubrick Kubrick. The lack of sympathy for the farmers and the soldiers turns the film into an impersonal essay in carnage, and I began to get a knot in my stomach when I realized there was nothing to look forward to but more brutality. When Robin—who has survived body-smashing combat with the Sheriff—is poisoned by Marian, who has also poisoned herself, I was disgusted and angry. Though Marian makes the decision for the two of them, love—Goldman gives us to understand—transcends death, and the suicide scene is treated triumphantly, as pure romantic exaltation. The film says that life on this earth is so horrible that death is preferable. Robin was packed off to the Crusades to prove that even the best of men is corrupt and a butcher. He was made ignorant so he could not possibly lead his army of farmers into anything but death and misery. Robin is a fool who lives to fight, and it doesn't matter who wins the war in Sherwood Forest—nothing good will come of anything. This ironic curtsy to chaos is the Easter attraction at the Radio City Music Hall.

[March 22, 1976]

PART THREE

Creamed

Did you get caught up in the "Mairzy Doats" rage? How about "Hi-Lili, Hi-Lo"? Have you ever bought a statue of a pissing cupid? Attended a church-sponsored Tom Thumb wedding? Do you tie ribbons in your dog's hair? Or smarten him up with a rhinestone collar? If the answer to any of the above is yes, then chances are you'll dote on *Bugsy Malone,* a first feature by an English writer-director, Alan Parker, made with a cast of children, average age twelve. *Bugsy Malone* isn't actually about children, and it doesn't use children to make a satirical comment on the adult world, either. Laid in New York in 1929, this picture functions in a borderland of its own. Little boys with their hair slicked down impersonate the Hollywood-movie racketeers of the Prohibition era. In their fedoras and double-breasted suits, these hoods look like midgets, and the speakeasies, molls, automobiles are all slightly miniaturized. Operated by pedal power, the tin lizzies are a cross between a Model T and a Kiddie Kar. This is a kiddie-gangster musical, with slapstick gang wars. One side is armed with cream cakes, the other with "splurge" guns that shoot thick patties of white goo. The setting is a meticulously detailed doll-house world for the audience to coo over.

Many of the boys seem to have been selected for their resemblance to the Warners goons of the thirties: stubby bodies, Struwwelpeter naughty-boy faces. And, except for the knowledgeable performances of Jodie Foster as the vamp Tallulah and Martin Lev as the suave villain Dandy Dan, most of the acting has the limpness of non-professionals. When the children deliver their lines, it takes a half-second's concentration to grasp what they've said, because their untrained speaking voices are a little furry. For the ingenue, Blousey (Florrie Dugger), klutzy amateurishness works as impishly as it does for Vicki Lawrence on "The Carol Burnett Show." Blousey's flickering expressions of complacent inanity are close to perfect bits of parody. When Blousey and Tallulah—the good girl and the bad girl—spot each other, there's a teasing depravity in the contest of Lolita-sirens who don't yet have cheekbones, but nothing comes of their rivalry for the nice-guy underworld hanger-on Bugsy, played by Scott

Baio, a trim boy with precise features and an easy, pretty smile. Alan Parker has a very perfunctory sense of drama; the plot never gathers momentum, and many of the situations that he sets up (such as Bugsy's taking on a fighter to manage, or a mobster's importing a torpedo from Chicago, or the speakeasy janitor's waiting for his chance to show the boss, Fat Sam, that he can dance) don't pay off. The boys—much duller and more innocuous than the girls—go through their gangster charades like puppets. We're not watching actors in a story, we're watching kids doing a stunt, and so we're primed to ooh and aah, the way the audience does for a chimp on the Carson show. This film operates on darlingness—on reactivating the clichés of gangster films and musicals by using children in place of the Hollywood performers of the past.

At thirty-two, Parker is already a veteran of British television, where he often made commercials that spoofed old movies; he knows the mechanisms of Hollywood musicals, and he can glide from a dialogue scene right into a musical number. The Paul Williams score must have been pre-recorded: adults do the singing (Williams' own voice issues from a character called Razamataz), though the kids mime their songs dexterously. Several of these songs go on for much longer than they're worth, and give away the confused nostalgic yearnings of the show. When the small black Cinderella boy Fizzy (Albin Jenkins) sings forlornly about his dreams for tomorrow while mopping floors in the speakeasy, a black girl joins him and dances silently to his song; it's sweet, all right—it's the Carol Burnett char routine, such a guaranteed touching crowd-pleaser that Burnett has almost totally abandoned it. But with kids in the roles, Parker can milk the audience with turns that are too shameful for a self-respecting TV artist. When Blousey thinks she's been stood up by Bugsy, she mouths an interminable number about being "an ordinary fool with an ordinary dream" which is meant to soften us to a jelly. And at the finale, after the rival gangs have splattered each other in a slapstick battle, everybody joins in an inspirational chorus: "You could be anything that you wanted to be. . . . You give a little love and it all comes back to you."

Bugsy Malone apparently originated in the stories Alan Parker made up for his children during car trips. Movies, along with magazines, books, TV, comics, and newspapers, go into the pop storehouse of our minds; addicted to the characters and situations of old American movies, Parker used them as folklore, which, by now, they are. (E. L. Doctorow's *Ragtime* is about the joke that mass culture plays on us, taking over everything in our lives and dreams, our past and present, and turning it all into pop folklore. The capper to the novel is that the character Tateh, having risen from the melting pot to become a Hollywood producer, goes on to make pictures about "a bunch of children who were pals, white black, fat thin, rich poor, all kinds, mischievous little urchins who would have funny adventures"—the *Our Gang* comedies.) Who would have thought that anybody would have the freak obsessive nostalgia to do what Alan Parker has done? He has made an elaborate version of an *Our Gang* comedy, stuffed with stale whipped cream. Without irony.

Even an aberrant conception like Parker's might be forgivable if he had been able to provide the streamlining of a fast-paced gangster film or the irrational, light-headed lift of a happy musical. But, as it is, *Bugsy Malone* is nothing but its godawful idea, so if the picture, already successful in England, becomes a hit, that won't be in spite of the idea but because of it. There's a special kitsch of innocence—sugary, lewd, Germanic. Disney tapped it; so did Shirley Temple, shaking her blond ringlets.

An actress friend told me that once when she was a young girl in vaudeville she came out of her hotel room one morning, still groggy, to find the hall full of little people. She thought she'd lost her mind, until she discovered that the Singer Midgets, en masse, had checked in during the night. That kind of almost pornographic dislocation—which is the source of this film's possible appeal as a novelty—is never acknowledged. The camera lingers on a gangster's pudgy, infantile fingers or a femme fatale's soft little belly pushing out of her tight satin dress, and it roves over the pubescent figures on the chorus line. But the movie stays on the level of refined, wholesome grotesqueness—like Disney without the energy—and never takes up the underlying suggestiveness and creepiness of its own material.

□ □ □

Sparkle, the story of the three daughters of a domestic servant who become a singing group, in the style of the Supremes, opened in April and closed a few weeks later. Now, partly because of the success of the Aretha Franklin album of the Curtis Mayfield score, the picture is being reissued in some cities. This means that moviegoers have another chance to see Lonette McKee, a young singer-actress so sexy that she lays waste to the movie, which makes the mistake of killing her off in the first half. But in that first part she and Dorian Harewood show a sixth sense for being alive. The fact that nobody has picked up on these two and starred them together is just one more proof that the new studio heads don't go to the movies.

Sparkle is the first film to be directed by Sam O'Steen, the well-known editor (*The Graduate, Rosemary's Baby, Chinatown*), who also directed *Queen of the Stardust Ballroom* for TV. He must have got carried away with the black cast and the smoky theatrical milieu, because the images are sometimes irritatingly dark, but he keeps them full of atmospheric detail, and the tawdry black-vaudeville scenes have the teeming, bodies-spilling-out-the-edges quality of Toulouse-Lautrec. The crowded look of the film helps to compensate for the Joel Schumacher script, which appears to be no more than a skeleton.

The outline for *Sparkle* follows the moral scheme of the old Production Code days: the "bad" characters (Lonette McKee as Sister, the hell-bent lead singer of the trio; Harewood as the teen-age boy who nonchalantly steals a car to take her out; Tony King as the dope pusher who hooks her) die or are punished, and the "good" characters (Irene Cara as the meek Sparkle who goes on as a single, and dimply Philip M. Thomas as her hardworking young manager) are rewarded. As often happened in the old movie days, the "bad" performers are terrific and the "good" are insufferable.

Sister is a hot number, talented, smart, impudent—an inflammatory, exhibitionistic singer who wants to turn the whole world on. And as Lonette McKee plays her, Sister has the visceral beauty, the voice, and the sexual energy to do it. Sister puts the dirty fun of sex into her songs, with the raw charge of a rebellious, nose-thumbing girl making her way. She has barely had a taste of singing in public when she falls for the sadistic pusher who beats her up and degrades her; she goes downhill unbelievably fast—and the picture with her—and then she ODs. What isn't explained is the why of this relationship; instead, we move on to the way the dewy-eyed Sparkle achieves the fame Sister might have had. And in order to keep the story going the action shifts to the almost canine devotion of Sparkle's young manager; his true-hearted courage defeats the attempts of gangsters to muscle in on her career.

The subject that's passed over—why the thug wants to possess and destroy Sister, who so obviously has everything it takes to become a star, and why she's drawn to him—is a true modern subject, and not just for the rock world. Lonette McKee is the actress to drive this theme into one's consciousness, because she has the sexual brazenness that screen stars such as Susan Hayward and Ava Gardner had in their youth. You look at the sheer taunting sexual avidity of these women and you think "What man would dare?" And the answer may be: only a man with the strength to meet the challenge or a man so threatened by it that he's got to wipe the floor with the girl, and there are more of the latter. If the women who are "too much" for men fall for sharpies and rough guys who brutalize them, it probably has a lot to do with the scarcity of the other men, and something to do, too, with the women's insecurity about being too much. The stronger a woman's need to use her energy, her brains, and her talent, the more confusedly she may feel that she has a beating coming. Besides, having had to make her own way, and having—at some levels—been coarsened doing it, she may feel some rapport with the tough operators who are used to knocking people around. Whatever else these men are, they're self-made, and they instinctively know what she's gone through and how to handle her.

Movies now seem to be almost begging for this theme to come out. It's highly unlikely that a woman can become a major screen star at this time unless she has a strong personality, yet if she does—like Jane Fonda, or Barbra Streisand, or Liza Minnelli—she's likely to be experienced as threatening by some of the audience (and by women who play by the standard rules as well as by men). These stars raise the problem in their relation to the audience which is implicit in their screen roles: resentment of their dominating presence. Yet at the movies audiences are far more interested in the "bad girls" than in the ingenues, and not just because wickedness gives an actress more of a chance; these roles give an actress a better chance because there's something recognizably there in those bad girls, even when it's frustrated, soured, and self-destructive. The "bad girl" is the cheapest, easiest way for the movies to deal with the women with guts.

In *Sparkle,* we can believe in Sister but not in the rise to rock stardom of the docile, unassertive Sparkle, because, given the social and biological circumstances of women's lives, a woman who isn't called a hard-driving bitch along the way is not likely to reach any top. A movie can show us the good girls winning the fellas, mothering the kids, succoring those who have met with adversity, but a good-girl artist is a contradiction in terms.

[September 27, 1976]

Charmed Lives

Before seeing Truffaut's *Small Change,* I was afraid it was going to be one of those simple, natural films about childhood which I generally try to avoid—I'm just not good enough to go to them. But this series of sketches on the general theme of the resilience of children turns out to be that rarity—a poetic comedy that's really funny. Truffaut demonstrates the fickle, unexpected toughness of children; he endows them with the slyness of Sacha Guitry's boulevardiers and with M. Hulot's eager, short attention span. Early on, we're told that children are in a "state of grace . . . they bounce back," and the boys he shows us do seem to lead charmed lives. Their faces are perfect illustrations of the transparency that adults lose. Set in a pleasantly moldering village, *Small Change* is a fair-weather movie, brightened by the primary colors the children wear and their splotchy pink cheeks. The humor has the spontaneity of children's play—which is recognizable as the distinctive Truffaut humor in its purest form. The kids

167

seem to be photographed in the act of inventing slapstick: they take improbable falls, turn ordinary food items into comic props, leer with confident innocence as they tell their first off-color jokes. Truffaut has reabsorbed slapstick into the everyday life from which it sprang, so that the picture celebrates both childhood and the beginnings of movie comedy, which is re-created before our eyes. When he stylizes the kids' behavior and points up their wit, his deadpan, disjointed style is quicker and more sure than ever before, and if he had been content to treat the material as a collection of skits—a fairy-tale comic strip—*Small Change* might have been a lovely, flawless trifle. It *is* lovely: some of the gags are timed with such sneaky rightness that they pop, like party surprises. But it's far from flawless.

We accept the town as a world viewed in a particular light—a sunshine land with well-meaning, child-loving, generally understanding people. It is a world without villains (only a pair of witchlike crazies), and the children can seem funny to us partly because they are so magically safe. Truffaut, however, appears to believe that his land of the good is the actual world. That's sentimentality, and it's why, despite his unaffected, light touch, he seems here, as in some of his other films, the blinkered, generous poet of the middle class.

Stepping outside comedy, Truffaut tries to convert his wonder at children's resourcefulness into a thesis. The stories of two boys run through his scenes of village life. Patrick (Geory Desmouceaux), shy, blond, eleven or twelve, lives with his disabled father and, in the confusion of needing a mother and wanting a girl, develops a crush on the mother of his best friend. Patrick's story—far from inspired—works reasonably well. But the other story—that of the mistreated Julien (Philippe Goldmann), whose suffering isn't noticed by the townspeople—is planted much too deliberately. It's obvious from the way the camera follows the dark, lonely Julien that the film is working up to a melodramatic revelation, and this long preparation violates the casual springiness of the comedy scenes. When the thesis is finally declared, it comes in a schoolroom lecture about children's rights that kills the rhythm and stops the movie cold. The schoolteacher Richet (Jean-François Stevenin) explains to Julien's classmates that there is a law of compensation, and that children such as Julien, who have had a tough time, may actually be stronger for what they've undergone. Throughout, Richet has been sympathetic and unauthoritarian—the children's ally, like a beatifically kind older brother—and now, in this speech, he tells us that he, too, had a bad childhood. Since we know from Truffaut's semi-autobiographical first feature, *The 400 Blows,* of his own neglect and suffering, we realize, of course, that Richet is speaking for Truffaut. Yet, as often happens when a director uses a mouthpiece, we're made uncomfortable; we don't know how we're meant to react. And, worse, here the words seem to falsify the experience of the film. We've been enjoying the shaggy illustrations of children's buoyancy without taking them too seriously. Now, having concentrated the miseries of childhood in the one abused boy, Truffaut asks us to believe that children really are as resilient as his jokes have been saying, and that the battered Julien will spring back, like a hardy weed that's been trampled.

Once the film has lectured us, we start examining its thesis. Children, as each of us knows, don't have to be mistreated by adults to experience misery. Truffaut has left out of his charmed world many forms of childhood suffering, such as terrors, guilts, the cruelty of other children. Despite Truffaut's affinity with children, the happy-go-lucky world of the kids in *Small Change* is an adult's fantasy of normalcy, and never more so than at the end, when the Everyboy hero Patrick, at summer camp, gets his first kiss and the story is complete, with this symbolic end to childhood and the information that in the fall the village school is going coed. Patrick doesn't fall in love, exactly; he's selected by a girl to be her first love. (She writes to a friend, "His name is Patrick"—probably a nod to Godard, who, two years before his first feature, *Breathless,* made a warm-up for it, a short, from a script by Eric Rohmer, called *All the Boys Are Named Patrick.*) This end-of-innocence view of adolescence is so archly conventional that it makes us aware of how remote and precious Truffaut's view of that earlier "state of grace" is. Is childhood really a different country, from which we emerge unscathed? Only for the purposes of comedy.

Truffaut's unassuming manner here enables us to share his delight in the shifty gestures that he has caught, and in the improvised performances of a hellion toddler and of a little boy who is overcome by the dirty joke he's telling, and of many others. Unlike the run of trained actors, who tend to predetermine a few emotions and communicate them, children permit us to read their faces and movements, and to perceive the infinite shadings. This is what some of the most prodigious screen actors do, too, using their training and instinct to expand a character and achieve the openness of a child; actors such as Brando, De Niro, Gérard Depardieu, Blythe Danner in the TV presentation of Tennessee Williams' *The Eccentricities of a Nightingale,* and Geneviève Bujold, at moments, sometimes in very bad pictures, make this leap beyond self-protection. What one gets from children who try to *act* is, however, likely to be the opposite: the awkward self-consciousness that Truffaut is stuck with from a few of the older boys who play structured parts and also from some of the adults. He takes the curse off it by the dry offhandedness of his tone, which obviates the necessity of expressiveness. This serves him, too, with the girls in the cast; he hasn't the subconscious rapport with them that he has with the boys, and he keeps their roles to a minimum. But he badly needed more than the one-mood performance he gets from his Julien. The delinquent in *The 400 Blows* felt isolated and was in pain, but we knew he hadn't been destroyed—his face was practically iridescent. Julien is numb and closed in; he lacks precisely the transparency that the whole film is about. Clearly, Truffaut was after more than a comedy, but the jokes in *Small Change* are what make it worth seeing.

□ □ □

Martin Ritt, the director, and Walter Bernstein, the screenwriter, old friends who had worked together before and after they were blacklisted during the McCarthy era, wanted to make a movie about the ugly injustice done to Communists and Communist sympathizers in the entertainment industry during those years, without getting into too much politics. Bernstein finally hit on what seems like a nifty idea. Since he himself had been able to sell scripts to TV during the early fifties by means of "fronts"—nonpolitical people who allowed him to use their names—he would center his story on just such an innocent.

The result is *The Front,* a morality comedy starring Woody Allen as Howie, a restaurant cashier and penny-ante bookie, always in debt, who, for a percentage, lends his name to a pinkish friend from high-school days, a well-known TV writer (Michael Murphy). But damned if the subject didn't get the better of Bernstein. He didn't develop the comic potential of his idea; instead, almost as if by reflex, he has written one of those scripts about how the common man must become involved, must learn what he stands for. Like the heroes of the forties wartime movies written by those who were later blacklisted, Howie must face up to the choice between right (refusing to inform on his friends, and thus accepting the collapse of his career and maybe a jail term) and wrong (naming names in front of the House Un-American Activities Committee and living prosperously with the shame). *The Front* is slightly archaic, not because it's set in the early fifties but because of its problem-play dramaturgy—craftsmanlike, careful, skimpy. There is little suggestion of the pervasive fear of Communism, and no attempt to get into the psychology of the Communist sympathizers or to indicate why they defended Stalin's totalitarian policies when he was wiping out dissent in the Soviet Union. Bernstein avoids a political context so thoroughly that the film is nondenominational—just the good guys versus the bad guys. Martin Ritt had an emotional commitment to the project, which was probably financed on his record, yet the director of such films as *Hud, The Long, Hot Summer, The Spy Who Came in from the Cold, The Molly Maguires,* and, more recently, *Pete 'n' Tillie, Sounder,* and the too-little-seen *Conrack* has, to put it gently, done better work. Whatever the causes (has he perhaps so much bitterness still bottled up that the subject paralyzed him?), his pacing is off, the sequences don't flow, the film seems sterile and unpopulated, and passionless. It has, however, got a theme one can't be against. At its most appealing, this movie says that people shouldn't be pressured to inform on their friends, that people shouldn't be humiliated in order to earn a living. Humbly, this film asks for fairness.

The Front also has a character—Woody Allen's Howie. Making his début as a "straight actor," Woody Allen is able to fill out Howie with "Woody," and that gives him a great advantage over the rest of the cast. Howie is a smart bum and harmless chiseller who begins to like the idea of himself as a gifted writer. In the most original scenes, Bernstein provides lines that show the stirrings of literary vanity within this non-writer, and Allen's timing and Stan Laurel–Alec Guinness smiles bring everything possible out of the material. When you see Woody Allen in one of his own films, in a peculiar way you take him for granted; here you appreciate his skill, because you miss him so much when he's offscreen. Allen manages to give something close to conviction even to his romantic scenes with Andrea Marcovicci, a deadening partner. Playing an assistant TV producer, she has a dark, solemnly woebegone face, like Joan Hackett doing a takeoff on a Greek tragedienne, and her spirits never run much higher than a big, wan smile. As this heroine comes across, she's a woman of deep political commitment who falls in love with Howie, the front, because she thinks he's a writing genius. Could this have been intended seriously? Played for laughs, it might have done for Rogers and Astaire. The humorless heroine lets us know that the man she gives herself to has to be of impeccable moral fiber; at one point, when she thinks Howie is too cynical an artist to do the right thing, she actually says, "I've made that mistake before—confusing the artist with the man." Inexplicably, Howie is so impressed by her classy dedication to high principles that he rises to the challenge and proves worthy of her. It was ever so in the Hollywood anti-Nazi movies, of which this is a seventies offshoot.

Apart from Howie, there are few tonal changes in the characters. We don't get the feeling of any life going on in or around a character such as Hecky Brown (Zero Mostel), a broken man—a blacklisted TV comic who agrees to spy on Howie in order to clear himself. We don't see the elements in Hecky's personality which would have led to his involvement in Communist causes, so when he tries to wheedle his way out of trouble by claiming he was just chasing a girl and didn't know she was a Red, we don't understand how to read the scene. Mostel is always a problem on the screen, but with more of a context his profoundly antipathetic vibes might have been right for the self-hating Hecky. As it is, the only moment in the movie that conveys the obscenity of those days is a shot of a Red baiters' spy snapping pictures of the mourners at Hecky's funeral.

The Front is set in a period that was a Byzantine tragicomedy—a period in which the Communists were under attack and had nowhere to turn because they themselves had taken over the largest liberal organizations and had denounced the anti-Communist left as Fascist. The heads of the networks and Hollywood studios, because of the publicity about those Jewish Communists who worked for them, were terrified by Catholic pressure groups, a few women's clubs, and the American Legion. There was no way to conceal the high proportion of Jews among the blacklisted. The ominous words "international conspiracy" hovered in the air, and the entertainment industry was afraid of bringing down the wrath of the gentiles. All this was going on, and *The Front* gives us a mistaken-identity plot—just as TV's only treatment of blacklisting, *Fear on Trial,* dealt with the mistaken-identity case of John Henry Faulk. Even at this late date, blacklisting gets by as a subject only if the victim is totally apolitical—as in those movies that exposed the evil of lynch mobs by showing them killing the wrong person. Is this because it's assumed that TV-watching has made us so lazy and ignorant that we couldn't comprehend the moral and political confusion of that day? Or wouldn't be interested? There's also the possibility that reducing everything to the good guys versus the bad guys may serve a mythologizing function for the once blacklisted who worked on this movie and for those others who will see it: by turning them into simple victims, it protects them from the recognition that their plight, horrible though it was, was also ludicrous. They'd gone to bat for Communist oppression; they'd blown their talents defending an illusion. Naïveté is still being protected. *The Front* is hiding behind another front.

[October 4, 1976]

Running into Trouble

*M*arathon Man starts with the amplified sound of breathing. What is it? Some rough, snuffling beast? With embarrassment, one recognizes the nasal-clogged exertions of Dustin Hoffman running around the Central Park reservoir. Has a parodist taken over the sound controls? No, it's just that *Marathon Man,* a project that seemed a lead-pipe cinch to be the kind of visceral thriller that makes audiences almost sick with excitement, has fouled up right from the word go, and nothing in it works quite the way it was meant to.

Hoffman isn't an ideal choice for the runner, Babe Levy—a poor but brilliant Jewish graduate student at Columbia, the younger son of a famous historian driven to suicide by charges made against him during the McCarthy era. This script takes Hoffman back to the age range of *The Graduate,* and someone like the tall, skinny Lenny Baker (the hero of *Next Stop, Greenwich Village*), who exactly fits the description William Goldman gave in the novel, might have been fresher, more convincingly naïve. Yet Hoffman acts young, has never before looked so fit, and there isn't a bum note in his performance. It doesn't come to anything, though. The way the Goldman book is constructed, we watch a giant trap being set: on three continents, various agents, couriers, and big-time hoods are engaged in a vast criminal action converging on the defenseless student. Babe is unaware of the impending horrors, but the suspense operates at all levels for us, since we see the malignancy closing in on this joking patsy. The book was a best-seller because Goldman is an unconscionable master at squeezing the reader; he involves us in the hero and turns the heat higher and higher, making the forces arrayed against Babe so hideously ruthless that anything Babe can do in retaliation will seem justified. The chase story is infused with righteousness, since the head conspirator, Szell (played here by Laurence Olivier), is a surviving Nazi war criminal, obscenely rich and arrogant, with a fortune derived from robbing the Jews in the death camps, and the student is a symbol of intelligence, moral strength, and endurance. Babe is punched around, tortured, and deceived, and then, when he's on the run and doesn't seem to have a chance, he shows what's in him. It's *Death Wish* with a lone Jewish boy getting his own back from the Nazis. It's a Jewish revenge fantasy. But in the movie our curiosity is never stimulated. Instead of setting up the situation and showing Babe's encirclement, the director, John Schlesinger, opts for so much frazzled crosscutting that there's no suspense. There isn't the clarity for suspense.

It's understandable that Schlesinger might be too proud to reproduce Goldman's sweatbox techniques, but those techniques are integral to the story. If you're hoping for elegance, don't begin with William Goldman. Probably a director like William Friedkin (*The French Connection, The Exorcist*) could have believed in the material and engineered an equivalent of the book—a movie that would have pounded audiences to a helpless pulp. And if a gullible talented director wasn't available, a crude hack could have done the dirty deed. But Schlesinger is a Faust who just couldn't live up to the pact he made. His fantasies may or may not be more sophisticated than William Goldman's, but they're certainly different. For Goldman, competitive fraternal badinage spells love, and the relationship between Babe and his older brother, Doc (Roy Scheider), is like the male gamesmanship in *Butch Cassidy and the Sundance Kid* and most of his other scripts. Schlesinger is probably too aware to play these games, but when the central brotherly-love relationship is cut to a minimum, there's nothing much left except Babe's victimization, suffering, and revenge. And even that doesn't hold together. Like Schlesinger's *The Day of the Locust*, *Marathon Man* seems to have lapses of attention, as if the director had lost track of the action.

Schlesinger keeps the cast under control, and his work is professional, yet he never gets a grip on how the scenes should play. We don't have the fun and excitement of being tantalized by terror. Babe's meeting with Elsa (Marthe Keller) and their love idyll lack the frightening undertones that are needed, and the film shows the two being mugged by Nazi henchmen without ever explaining why. Babe's neighbors—Puerto Rican kids who rib him—are directed with the same heavy spirit and unvarying rhythm as the rest of the action. When the movie retains Goldman's zingers, such as the revelation of Doc's relationship with the government agent Janeway (William Devane), Schlesinger seems to back away from them, and with the cheap kick gone there's nothing to take its place.

The advance stories on *Marathon Man* have been about the lavish care taken by its perfectionist producer, Robert Evans, yet seven million dollars and two years of planning haven't bought even a very good-looking movie. A producer's care may be greatest after the irredeemable mistakes have been made. In preparing the film script, Goldman apparently wasn't warned off some of the most troublesome aspects of his book, and since Schelsinger doesn't get the viewer's insides knotted, the holes in the plot are big and gaping. Why is Doc in an unholy alliance with the Nazi villain, Szell? Szell's fear that Doc means to rob and kill him sets the whole plot in motion, yet there's no indication that Doc does intend to, so Doc's character is left an utter cipher. And though the best sequence in the movie is Szell's stroll through New York's West Forty-seventh Street diamond market (it was the best passage in the book, also), what the devil is he doing there? The explanation we're given—that he needs to ascertain the price of a carat—is so tacky it's a howler: he's been living off the sale of diamonds for thirty years. Even worse is the false expectation set up by the mysterious political crimes of which Babe's father was accused. Apparently, this is just a moral flourish meant to provide a background for the brothers, but such a point is made of the McCarthy persecution that we keep expecting it to have some connection to Szell's ring of thieves. There's more background than foreground in Babe's character, and the actors have so little time for characterization that the people in walk-through roles (such as Marc Lawrence and Richard Bright, as Szell's gunmen) actually come off best.

Goldman's imagination must have been fed by movies like *Lives of a Bengal Lancer,* in which sticks were driven under Gary Cooper's fingernails and set on fire but he never betrayed his comrades-in-arms. *Marathon Man* has to have been conceived in this same boys'-book rites-of-manhood universe. (The hero of *The Great Waldo Pepper,* which Goldman also wrote, dreamed of fighting an air battle with the No. 1

German ace; there's considerable consistency in the writer's fantasies.) Babe is no more than Destry Riding Again as a Jewish pain freak. His heroism is proved by the amount of punishment he can take, and Szell has been made a dentist so that he can torture Babe by cutting live nerves. Dentistry has never been very photogenic, and, because of one's indifference to the outcome of this scene and of the other, more gruesome bloodlettings, the only emotion one is likely to feel is revulsion at the general unpleasantness. There are enough Schlesinger films by now to provide ample evidence that he has no talent for violence. (Jon Voight's assault with a telephone was the most grotesque piece of staging in *Midnight Cowboy*.) A director doesn't have to be able to do everything, but he should have some idea of what he can't do. Still, it's not hard to guess why Schlesinger attempts material that lesser directors can do better. Directors working on action films they don't believe in haven't necessarily "sold out." This may be the only work they could get, or their best chance for a box-office hit that would put them in the winner's circle and buy them a little freedom to operate in. You don't work for Robert Evans these days unless you work on a thriller. That's fine for some directors, but not for Schlesinger, and when he stages a chase, with Hoffman on foot being pursued by a car full of killers, his heart, understandably, isn't in it. *Marathon Man* is his worst film ever. To cap it all, running around with cut nerves gives Hoffman more of an excuse for that gasping sound. Can you imagine what he'd do if he played in *Humoresque* or *Golden Boy*? With a violin to breathe to, he'd be the Paganini of snufflers.

□ □ □

Marcel Ophuls is one of the few directors who work on projects they do believe in, and after years of difficulties he has managed, finally, to obtain control of his four-hour-and-thirty-eight-minute *The Memory of Justice* and release it. Much has already been written in praise of this mammoth documentary on the Nuremberg Trials, and no doubt much more will be; I wish I could join in. I feel a pang of guilt, because I think it's a very bad film—chaotic and plodding, and with an excess of self-consciousness which at times Ophuls seems to mistake for art.

In *The Memory of Justice,* the definitions of war crimes formulated by the Allies at Nuremberg are examined in terms of the atrocities committed in Dresden, Hiroshima, the Soviet Union, Algeria, Wounded Knee, Latin America, and, especially, Vietnam—which, in a sense, the whole thing is about. The film raises the question: Were the Americans who deserted in Vietnam treated as criminals because they refused to carry out orders that, according to the principles set down at Nuremberg, it would be a crime to carry out? The film attempts nothing less than an investigation of the nature of war guilt and of guilt in general, with an ironic look at the tendency of nations to judge their enemies differently from the way they judge themselves. Striving for complexity, Ophuls extended his inquiry in so many directions that he lost his subject. It's obvious that an investigation of any issue can reach out to include the whole world, but the demonstration of that extension is better left to parable. When Ophuls is searching for a woman doctor he wants to interview—a woman who was tried at Nuremberg—he meets people along the road who tell him that she no longer lives in the village where he thought she did, and he proceeds to interview them. Now, it's true that what they say has *some* connection with the subject, but so would the conversation of almost anyone he chose to talk to; indeed, in the course of the film he brings in his film students from Princeton, Robert Jay Lifton discussing the shame felt by the surviving victims at Hiroshima, Yehudi Menuhin (because he was the first Jewish artist to perform in Germany after the war), and dozens of others with a tangential relation to the issues, as well as Albert Speer, Telford Taylor, Lord Shawcross, and many others actually involved in the Nuremberg Trials.

The atrocities that are described or shown are often devastating. As was apparent from Peter Davis's *Hearts and Minds* (which I also thought a poor film, though for its hammerlock on simplicity), an American soldier beating a helpless Vietnamese boy is even more distressing on the giant movie screen than on the TV screen. We're affected in a different way: we feel it closer, bigger—it achieves a mythic, classical, inescapable horror. But when a film uses such footage in the course of an inquiry into moral issues, the argument is likely to be swamped by this emotional and kinesthetic response. That didn't happen in Ophuls' *The Sorrow and the Pity,* but here the director never finds a rationale for the probing, and the painful identification we make with the victims seems to be the only answer to all the moral dilemmas. After a few hours, we develop a numb impatience with the new issues Ophuls introduces, as he brings in more and more data and keeps cutting back to people he interviewed earlier. The case that Ophuls develops—that it's by no means as easy to determine what war crimes are as the prosecutors at Nuremberg thought, and that the Americans, the French, and many others have committed crimes indistinguishable in horror from those of the Nazis—is not as complicated as the crosscutting makes it appear. It could be set out in an essay of a few thousand words, along with the alternative conclusions expressed here by Daniel Ellsberg and Telford Taylor: Ellsberg says that the Americans in Vietnam were no different from the Nazis, while Taylor makes a distinction between premeditated murderous policies and rash, rancorous actions. At *The Memory of Justice,* we wait hour upon hour while the obvious is pointed out to us, and finally the issues, instead of being made clearer, are muddied, as if this rendered them more subtle.

Ophuls took on much more than he knew how to handle, and then he kept taking on more, and at the same time he tried to be autobiographical and open—an effect he sought to achieve by pinning his German wife in closeup so that we see her insecure expression while she answers questions about her days in the Hitler Youth. At one point, he asks his family what kind of films they would like him to make. His wife answers, "A Lubitsch film, or *My Fair Lady* all over again," and then we hear "New Sun in the Sky" and "I Guess I'll Have to Change My Plan" from the soundtrack of *The Band Wagon.* Ophuls here presents himself to us as a driven man who must do the unpopular, and so—unwittingly, perhaps—*The Memory of Justice* becomes a put-down of frivolous escapist films, and of his wife besides.

Collecting atrocity footage could easily have an overpowering effect on a filmmaker's judgment. Ophuls tries to combine his newsreel and archive film with such material as a clip from an old happy-go-lucky Hans Albers movie, photographs of his own father and of Max Reinhardt and Richard Tauber, an interview with the widow of the refugee actor Fritz Kortner, scenes from a stage production of *The Devil's General,* and such oddities as a sequence involving Germans of both sexes nude in a sauna discussing anti-Semitism, Joan Baez singing "Where Have All the Flowers Gone?" in German, a discussion of Nixon's tapes at Kent State, and a scene of German girls at a swimming pool while the song "Bel Ami" is heard on the soundtrack. I doubt if the greatest editors around could fit all this footage together and give it rhythm and shape. And Ophuls isn't even a good editor. That was evident in his last film, *A Sense of Loss,* about Northern Ireland, where he kept piling on data after we were so exhausted that we waited for the end as for a liberation. Yet *A Sense of Loss* had an emotional core. We could actually see that the long history of injustice went on festering in the souls of the people. And the subject of Ireland brought out Ophuls' compassion. The subject of *The Memory of Justice* brings out his unresolved feelings, and they take the form of clumsiness and a certain stiffness of attitude. He presses down too hard, and sometimes—as with Edgar Faure, the president of the French National Assembly, who was a prosecutor at Nuremberg—he's reproving, and pedantically opaque. There are some remarkable interviews—one with the widow of a German judge who doled out death sentences to anti-Nazis— and there are hair-raising stories. But there are also sudden cuts to a close shot of a person's hands to show you nervous stress, and other forms of banal visual editorializing. This is more than four and a half hours of collage without the transformation that an artist's technique should have brought to it. It is ambitious, it is earnest, yet so are films by Stanley Kramer and Joseph Strick, who also aim high and wide.

□ □ □

*A*merica at the Movies, a compilation film shaped in terms of some amorphous idea about the American people and the American spirit as they have been shown on the screen, was put together by the American Film Institute for the American Revolution Bicentennial Administration. The picture reeks of sycophancy, as if the head of the Institute, George Stevens, Jr., had thought that he was finished if he didn't come up with a giant World's Fair movie, certified by Charlton Heston, properly disembodied, intoning the message that America began as "a dream—a candle burning in the mind." Usually, this kind of official film wants something from you: you're to stand up straighter and develop a firmer resolve to serve your country's ideals, or, at least, determine to do better on your next report card. But you can't tell why *America at the Movies* has been made. It has some of the clean patriotism of the propaganda films for overseas consumption which Stevens used to produce when he was with the United States Information Agency, and you can feel the latent wish to be upbeat. Yet the assemblers weren't sure what response to aim for; the film is anxiously inspirational.

There is no sense to the transitions: James Stewart in distress in *It's a Wonderful Life* giving way to Marlon Brando contorted with agony in *A Streetcar Named Desire,* thirty seconds from one film, a minute from another, scenes from *Plymouth Adventure, Drums Along the Mohawk, A Raisin in the Sun*—bits of eighty-three films in all. Technically, the assemblers knew what they were doing. The sound level and the visual dimensions of the original prints are respected; the film isn't a cacophonous mess, like the recent *That's Entertainment, Part 2* (the Gene Kelly Memorial Service, conducted by Gene Kelly). *America at the Movies* is smoothly put together but impersonal. The Institute's preferences in movies are much like Mussolini's taste in architecture—grand, public, inflated, a series of gestures toward an idealized past. Static cloud formations imply the source of Heston's voice, and in the clip from *The Treasure of Sierra Madre* Heston's redundancy competes with Max Steiner's. The only meaning I can extract from *America at the Movies* is that cultural bureaucrats develop imperial tastes—or is it that people who love pomp become bureaucrats? The few glimpses of spitball comedy— Fields disgustedly pushing his overaffectionate daughter away from him, the child actress Jane Withers playing mother by beating her doll—seem the last traces of sanity.

You can't just enjoy the clips as reminders of the movies they're from, because the whole enterprise is so prestige-laden. I did notice that a tiny piece of *Life with Father* looks as bad as the whole film did, that a bit of *The Godfather, Part II* had me wanting to see the whole again, that Jennifer Jones makes you feel her physical need of her lover in her romantic scene in *Since You Went Away,* and that Elizabeth Taylor acts much better in *A Place in the Sun* than she does in *Who's Afraid of Virginia Woolf?* But the films aren't even identified for those who won't recognize them; the clips are presented seamlessly, as if what they said about America were far more important than the contexts from which they're torn. Stevens may have a U.S.I.A. hangover; he may think it's the function of the American Film Institute to sell America. The Institute people ought to stop lighting candles in their skulls; they're burning their brains out.

The big thought that Heston delivers is that the America of the movies is "a country existing only in the imagination, but that, after all, is where America began." (The Indians might disagree.) If you're going to talk about the America of the movies as a country of the imagination, shouldn't you ask whose imagination? The story of the movies is the story of how, by the grandeur of its aspirations and the lowness of its taste, a small, stunted community—intermarried, interacting, full of crown princes, and run by favoritism—affected the whole world. That community was dominated by a group of tyrant dreamers who imposed their wills on producers, directors, and writers. They were pirates, ransackers of other people's ideas, talents, and inventions, and they were merchants. They imposed their own unexamined cultural and sexual wish-fulfillments on us all and had a marvellous time doing it. The pieces of film in *America at the Movies* have lost their narrative charge; they've lost body—they're dried, pressed flowers. Without weeds. This compilation leaves out the juice, the vulgarity, the energy, the adoration of conformity, and the morbid infatuation with royalty, wealth, and high birth. *America at the Movies* represents the potentates' scrubbed-up side and the establishment status they aspired to. They were tough men; they lived a long time, and their strength is reflected in their movies—which still have money in them, because they still have life in them. What those men did will literally influence mankind forever. It's a worldwide culture (virus?) that can't be destroyed—perhaps the first.

[October 11, 1976]

A Cuckoo Clock That Laughs

*J*onah Who Will Be 25 in the Year 2000 stays suspended in the air, spinning—a marvellous toy, weightless, yet precise and controlled. Who would have expected the Swiss director Alain Tanner and his co-writer, John Berger, to turn out a bubbleheaded political comedy? Their last collaboration, *The Middle of the World,* ended with the words "There is no hope for rebirth," yet *Jonah* leaps about like an Easter bunny. This film is drunk and lit up on the possibilities of rebirth. At the same time, it has a fully developed sense of irony—the laconic kind that informed Renoir's *Boudu Saved from Drowning* and Buñuel's *The Discreet Charm of the Bourgeoisie.*

Jonah is set in Geneva, and the statue of Jean Jacques Rousseau (he was born there in 1712, the son of a watchmaker) presides over the film. *Jonah*'s spirit—romantic, Socialist, mystical—suggests that people were changed by the political upheavals of 1968 and that the new ways of thinking go beyond Marx, back to utopians such as Rousseau. That poetic social thinker, with his love of nature and man, didn't believe in original sin; he believed that the roots of evil were in the very existence of society, and that education should save children from contamination. There are eight key characters in *Jonah,* all in their twenties or thirties, and all seeking solutions to the problems brought to general consciousness by the events of 1968. Not one of them is a comfortable bourgeois; they're the sort of fantasists and obsessives who were considered marginal before 1968. They were fewer in number in those days and were likely to be called crackpots. Now that bourgeois norms have begun to look disreputable, these eight buggy dreamers aren't social outsiders. They're insiders, though in a precarious, existential way. In the course of the film, the eight become friends and accept each other's oddities without so much as a lifted eyebrow; they band together communally as the metaphorical parents of Jonah, and then disperse.

They're not a band of disciples; there's no faith they share. But each, in a small, self-contained way, is a prophet, or, at least, a prophetic crazy. They're all in this world, but each is also somewhere else, listening to his own different drummer. Snub-nosed, rounded Mathilde (Myriam Boyer), the most physical and the most innocent of them, finds fulfillment in pregnancy and massages people's tiredness away. Her husband, long-jawed Matthieu (played by an actor known as Rufus), a typesetter and union leader laid off in a cutback, goes to work for a produce gardener and sets up a Rousseauist school in a greenhouse. Marcel, the gardener (Roger Jendly), a withdrawn primitive artist, is engrossed in the life of animals, where he finds his answers to human problems. Marguerite, the gardener's rough-spoken wife (Dominique Labourier), a no-frills woman in witches' black, is fastened on organic farming. Big, worldly Max (Jean-Luc Bideau) has given up on organized political activity and works as a proofreader; roulette has become his game. Yet, though he doesn't believe in the revolution, he doesn't not believe, either; he's an agnostic about revolution—he's waiting. Meanwhile, he learns that a bank land swindle is under way and goes to warn the potential victims (and thus meets the farm couple, Marcel and Marguerite). Red-haired Madeleine (Myriam Mezière), a secretary in the dirty-dealing bank, gets Max copies of the documents he needs, though she has her mind fixed on the Tantras. Warm, tubby, intelligent Marco (Jacques Denis), a neighbor of the farm couple, is a high-school history teacher; his unorthodox methods and cloud-built theories please the students but not the administrators, and after he's fired he finds a new vocation working in a home for the aged. He falls in love with Marie (Miou-Miou), a cashier in a supermarket, who doesn't charge him for his liquor and wine. Marie is a French citizen, who must go back across the border each night. She's a border person in other ways, too: she filches food for elderly people on pensions. There may be some simple reason for all these prophets to have names starting with "Ma," or maybe there's no reason at all. (I hope the latter.)

Each of the eight Ma characters is a utopian of some sort, except for the disillusioned former activist, Max. By conventional standards, they are people who will never "amount to anything," and that's the originality of the film—it sees hope and renewal in all their methods, and honors Max, the Marxist turned gambler, as their spiritual ancestor, the man whose activities culminated in the events of 1968, and thus changed their world. The film honors precisely that "lunatic fringe" that the Marxists have always derided. Each of these people is autonomous, looks for his own answers, and acts upon them, and together, the film suggests, they can give birth to a Jonah who will have the acumen to connect their visions.

Tanner juggles all these extraterrestrial travellers, each of them into his own thing—a lunar colony interacting. *Jonah* moves so fast that one's mind races to keep up with what the characters are saying and doing; regarded with Tanner's appreciative detachment, their activities become a form of vaudeville. In movies, nobody has attempted anything quite like this whirling play of ideas. It may draw a little from Renoir's *Rules of the Game* and *The Lower Depths* and some from *La Chinoise* and other Godard films, but it's essentially a poetic original, simple and unstressed from shot to shot, with a visual luster. The colors are softer than in Godard; Tanner is more interested in the erotic qualities that go with different attitudes toward society, and each of the people has very distinctive flesh tones, suggesting sensuous contrasts. The ideas they expound are often woozy, and the history teacher's lecture on time, which is a key to the mechanism of the film, is the wooziest of all—it's impenetrable. I assume that the history teacher as seer is being satirized, and that this is also Tanner's and Berger's self-satire. I can't swear to that; what I take for droll, dry Swiss humor may be intended straight. But this slight perplexity may also be intentional: the film is willing to entertain possibilities for rebirth even if they're cracked or pickled. It doesn't ask us to believe anything. But we do believe that the *idées fixes* belong to the characters we see—at least, I did, for all except the earth mother,

181

Mathilde. The phoniness of her lines ("I hate empty spaces. . . . Give me a child") seemed the authors' mistake rather than the character's self-view. Apart from this lapse, there's not a word I felt was wasted; I had confidence that Tanner and Berger wanted it just so. The whole film seems to have been conceived in a greenhouse.

Jonah doesn't operate on identification with a hero or on suspense. Yet it provides the kind of pleasure that one can generally get only from movies that involve us by those primal means. I hesitate to invoke the word "Brechtian," because, except for a few sixties films by Godard, that has generally meant a didactic pain. But before this nobody has had a Miou-Miou to sing a Brechtian cabaret song. She's the most purely enjoyable person in the movie. This tumble-dried blonde, the Brigitte Bardot the cat dragged in, doesn't look as if she could be an actress, but she certainly is. When this placid creature, with her broad-mouthed fey smile, breaks into a song, she turns on the charm like a scroungy Cinderella, creating instant empathy; yet she distances her character and kids the empathy. That naughty, plummy smile of hers makes her the director's confederate. In *Going Places,* a mean, funny film with sequences that had a Henry Miller–like erotic-fantasy quality, Miou-Miou was the abused girl who was so overjoyed when she had her first orgasm that she ran out to tell the news to the men who had called her frigid. It doesn't occur to the women Miou-Miou plays to hide anything; they're spacey right on the surface. In *Jonah,* she brings the missing magic to the Brechtian method; her Marie, a bewildered, feathery Pierrette, is as defiantly, forlornly romantic as Cyrano's plume dipped in horse manure. Marie has a friend in France, Old Charles, a retired railroad worker, to whom she brings stolen groceries; he is played by the veteran French character actor Raymond Bussières, familiar from *Casque d'Or* and films by Clouzot and René Clair. Together, Miou-Miou and Bussières act out fantasies in brief set pieces that do what Brechtian numbers are supposed to do, and without didactic jostling.

The whole film is designed as a collection of little routines—the red-haired Tantrist bringing the Marxist gambler to her exotic lair and spinning theories about the loss of semen which might have come right out of *Dr. Strangelove,* the history teacher meeting Old Charles and talking of railroads, and so on. They all add up to a vision of changes much like the ones that have taken place in this country, with many of the students who became politicized in the late sixties not retreating to bourgeois values but dispersing into various mystical movements. *Jonah* is so ingeniously constructed that one can enjoy it the way one enjoyed Renoir's egalitarian films of the thirties, relating to each character in turn. Yet the people are cultists and are conceived in Brechtian terms: we see their wheels going round. Tanner's inspiration was in allowing these metaphorical creations to be silly. They're silly, yet they're no sillier than the people I know in

Berkeley, who are probably the brightest people I know. In life, bright people can bore one senseless with their talk of crafts and ecology and children who are free to grow, and so it's a giddy surprise to discover how charming they are here on the screen, greening Switzerland with the same lunar poetry they've been using on America. When this genuinely eccentric movie gets its group of eight linked up, the themes of time, history, capital and labor, and education tie together, and Jonah the savior is born out of the whale of the old society. This is an Easter fable, all right, but with a dialectical bunny.

□ □ □

Alex & the Gypsy is off the beaten track, too, but that's just about the only thing you can give it points for. Whoever had the idea of turning Stanley Elkin's short novel *The Bailbondsman* into a romantic comedy by giving Alex, the bailbondsman (Jack Lemmon), a love affair with a gypsy (Geneviève Bujold) doesn't seem to have thought out how this love affair would *play*. Alex is still mostly Elkin's creation. He's one of those revelling-in-their-own-exacerbated-cynicism characters whom authors show off with; he's barely tolerable on the printed page and outright offensive on the screen, where he expresses himself in torrents of cleverness. (Jack Lemmon shouts the words.) Acccording to the plot that the movie adds, Alex and the gypsy used to live together but he didn't know how to be in love; he was so afraid of losing her that he made her miserable, and she left him. Now she's in jail and he risks thirty thousand dollars to bail her out for the four days before her sentencing. Afraid she'll skip, he keeps her locked up with him, and during these four days he is supposed to learn the meaning of love by accepting the gypsy's need of freedom. If Lemmon trusted himself as an actor, and relaxed and did less, we might be able to see the necessary contrasts in Alex's character; in the flashbacks we might even glimpse the happiness that he wrecked, and so there could be some core to the movie—a hint of the paradise lost that he's trying to regain. But Lemmon is always up, and working desperately hard. And so Bujold, who's meant to be the vibrant, tempestuous one, has to fight him for every bit of audience attention, and what should be a love story is a shouting match—ersatz D. H. Lawrence and ersatz Billy Wilder.

Where was the director, John Korty, on this picture? He allowed James Woods, who plays Alex's neurasthenic clerk, to use his face muscles like a telegrapher's code; and he didn't control Lemmon, who has become a glib actor, sentimental about the characters he plays. Frenzied melancholic mannerisms come so easy to Alex that we don't participate in the suffering. Lemmon needs a director who will unearth his talent by challenging him—forcing him to explain and justify each specific thing he does. Korty used to be his own cinematographer, and his early films *The*

Crazy Quilt and *Funnyman* had a nice soft-edge quality, and the characters had air to breathe. Has he picked up such bad habits from working in TV that he thinks making movies means cutting to a close shot each time a person has a line of dialogue? In the cramped, ugly-looking *Alex & the Gypsy,* Korty does the things that he seemed promising for not doing. He was never a forceful director but had a plain, uncoercive approach that suggested a principled reticence, and this was the distinguishing mark even of his television films, such as *The Autobiography of Miss Jane Pittman.* So it's puzzling to see this slam-the-camera-in-for-a-closeup way of working; the movie gives you the feeling that it was shot in rooms so small the cameraman could never back away.

Geneviève Bujold has such intensity that she might have carried the picture if Korty had just cleared some space around her, but the whole production lacks rhythm as well as visual grace. Somebody should have persuaded the screenwriter, Lawrence B. Marcus, to simplify the structure; the flashbacks come and go so fast that you have to keep track of what the two principals are wearing to know whether you're in the past or the present. There's another clue: Bujold handles her soft gypsy accent easily, but the thick vulgate she's required to speak in the flashbacks sounds like pidgin Greek Creole. So you locate yourself in time by whether she's talking funny. Her role not only is vocally booby-trapped but forces her to demonstrate her heritage by doing a sensual gypsy dance. There isn't an actress on the American screen who could get by with this number. Bujold's strongest scenes come at the beginning, when she's in jail and Lemmon, on the other side of the bars, can't get in her way. All through the film, one wants her to get a chance to show what she can do, as in that great hysterical scene that momentarily brought *Obsession* to life—her turning into a screaming nine-year-old right before one's eyes. But *Alex & the Gypsy* never does set her free.

[October 18, 1976]

No Id

*E*ric Rohmer's *The Marquise of O . . .* is a word-for-word, gesture-for-gesture transcription of the Heinrich von Kleist novella, published in 1808, when the author was thirty-one. (He committed suicide at thirty-four.) The story—which I love—is a bold, funny variation on many tales of mysterious pregnancies, and is perfectly straightforward; Kleist doesn't indicate the characters' thoughts but only their actions and speech. After her husband's death, the young Marquise (played by Edith Clever) and her children return to the home of her parents. Her father is the commandant of a citadel, and when Russian troops attack, the Marquise is carried off screaming by a gang of soldiers. A Russian officer, a count (played by Bruno Ganz), appears, like an "angel from Heaven," and drives off the brutes; he takes her to safety, and she faints dead away. The next day, the handsome Count leaves with the troops, and the Marquise and her parents, who now idolize him, are grieved to hear that he has been killed in a skirmish. But he recovers from his wounds, returns, and, presenting himself to the startled family, asks the Marquise to marry him at once, for his soul's peace. When her father points out that she doesn't even know him, the Count impetuously risks his military career to stay to court her, but he is persuaded to go on about his duties and press his suit when he can return. During his absence, the Marquise discovers that she is pregnant, and her parents, angry at her protestations of total innocence, drive her out of the house. In despair, she risks public ridicule by taking out an ad in the local press asking the unknown man who is responsible for her pregnancy to come forward, so that they may be married.

What's obvious to the reader is that in the excitement and disorder of the siege, with people running in panic and buildings on fire, the dashing Count was so keyed up by fighting off the would-be rapists that when the Marquise swooned gratefully in his arms he raped her himself. The irony in the story is that the Marquise, educated to believe in noble conduct, is so much in love with the Count—the angelic hero of her dreams—that, despite his fevered, precipitate pleas that she marry him, it's impossible for her to imagine that he could be the one who got her pregnant.

In an explanatory title, Rohmer informs viewers that he has taken only a single liberty with the story: in the film, instead of raping the Marquise during the fighting at the citadel, the Russian Count rapes her afterward, when she has been given a sleeping potion. Rohmer has written that this alteration makes the story more believable for moviegoers. But it can't be an accident that he's taken out the central mad, impulsive action. And in Bruno Ganz he has given us a Count without the hot-blooded, ecstatic spontaneity that the violation was part of. In the story, each time the Count appears to plead his suit the shock waves from his single-minded fervor confuse and excite everyone; in the movie, the Count is gloomy and guilt-ridden, and the family is politely bewildered. What's lost is not only the sense of the narrow experience of the virgin-hearted Marquise but Kleist's spirit, what made him an avant-gardist and a modern—his acceptance of the id released by the chaos of war. In the movie, since the rape takes place through furtive calculation, the Count isn't Kleist's wild, natural man—he's a Rohmer character, slyly slipping his hand over Claire's knee.

Kleist wrote in German, and the film is acted in German, by German stage actors, who accord each line full stage weight. Attempting to achieve an objective version of Kleist's style, Rohmer gives us the surface—a quaintly amusing account of a woman whose idealism is betrayed. We sit and wait until the Marquise realizes what her symptoms mean, and then we wait for her to discover, to her outrage, who is responsible. And it isn't until toward the end, when, at last, she does know, that the movie picks up interest and becomes gently witty. The director missed the larger story, which was in the undercurrents (and, maddeningly, those who read the novella after seeing the movie are likely to get from it only what's in the movie). Kleist made the Count a Russian for a reason that doesn't come across when he's played by a German. In the movie, we fail to recognize that the Count, the foreigner, carrying the threat of what isn't understood, is a whole man; impetuousness hasn't been bred out of him, and if the widowed Marquise would just wake from her civilized trance she could begin to live. He's Prince Charming with a rape for a kiss, and she's too repressed to know it.

Rohmer isn't the director to bring us Kleist's hero—a precursor of Dostoevski's and Lawrence's. Rohmer's even-toned method precludes animal passion. The movies that Rohmer has written himself are generally compared to novels, but his *The Marquise of O . . .* is like a documentary film of a play. His method is murderously arch. He's taken a highly filmable story and treated it as if it were an official nineteenth-century stage classic, to be given a wooden, measured reading. Deathly pauses precede the cadenced lines of dialogue, and the actors are so meticulous you can hear the quotation marks. Rohmer uses few of the storytelling shortcuts available to film. Why prepare us for a lapse of time with the title "Not long after" when the Marquise's belly does the job? The movements of the performers are so deliberate they look preordained—the actors never miss their chalk marks. How can the Count's arrival or his plea for a hasty marriage have any vibrations? These actors were all expecting him. The film is so formal it's like a historical work re-created for educational television; the costumes wear the actors.

Bruno Ganz, a brooding, introspective type, has about as much dash to him as Anthony Hopkins, whom he resembles. These actors have angst to spare. They droop; they're hanged men. And Ganz's Count has the same metronomic control as the rest of the cast—which kills the point. Rohmer has treated the Count's first appearance, when he bounds from a parapet during the group assault on the Marquise, as his only moment of glory. It's treated as a vision—almost an illusion—and we never glimpse that hero again. From then on—even before his proposal—the Count is so abject that he seems to be less a remorseful Dionysiac man than a man with a sickly, kinky nature; in his big, flat-brimmed brown hat, he looks a suffering Puritan prig.

Edith Clever's Marquise is more solid physically than one expects, but this actress is skilled and likable in her moments of comic pathos. The Marquise has affectionate domestic scenes with her mother (Edda Seippel), the liveliest, least inhibited member of the family, and is very funny when she tosses holy water on her parents to save them from the Count, who, now that his act is revealed, seems to her a devil. Though Rohmer supplies the midwife who examines the Marquise with one good joke not in the original, he seems reluctant to add anything more, and so, since the Marquise's children don't have any actual dialogue in the story, they don't make a sound here. It's a little unnerving—they're like Kabuki ghost-children. Rohmer gives a very faithful version of the father-daughter reconciliation scene, when, as Kleist describes it, the father "pressed long, warm and avid kisses on her mouth: just as if he were her lover!" Yet this doesn't have the full subtext it has in the story, either, where it represents a celebration of forbidden impulses coming forth and freeing the people. In the story, it can make even a Freudian gasp; in the film, it has no great impact. Rohmer, with the help of his cinematographer, Nestor Almendros, keeps everything serenely pictorial. But without Kleist's demon sitting inside all that calm and mocking it, asking when the sleeping beauty is going to come to life, there's no urgency to this film. It's tame and archaic.

□ □ □

Car Wash, which played on the West Coast before opening in New York, is already a hit, and no wonder—it's the movie equivalent of junk food. The jokes date back to one's childhood and have come through the sit-com mill, so they supply the comfort of familiarity. The picture goes down so fast you don't know you're eating, and yet it supplies the illusion of energy. The Norman Whitfield rock songs that come blaring out over the car wash's loudspeaker system aren't much in the way of music; they're more like crunchiness. And there's no denying that the grossness of *Car Wash* provides some kind of gratification. Many people resist quality; they're afraid of being outclassed. They're safe with *Car Wash*: it has no more class than a Hostess Twinkie, though it, too, may make you gag a little.

The action is centered on one workday in an L.A. car wash that is white-owned but staffed mostly by blacks. The material, however, has almost nothing to do with car washes, and we never get an impression of what the car wash charges or how the tips run or how many cars come in. The movie isn't *Car Wash*, it's Car M*A*S*H, made in imitation of the Altman film and using Altman's loudspeaker device to bind skits and characters that have no organic connection with the subject.

A large cast of black and white actors and comedians appear in blackout sketches, cut fast to the rhythm of the rock score, and the audience laughed at so many stale bad jokes that it sounded like a laugh track. This is the second "black" script (*Sparkle* was the first) by Joel Schumacher, the talented costume designer of *Sleeper,* who appears to have convinced somebody again that he's a writer. Schumacher has a pop memory-box mind, and he throws in rotting fragments to be delivered with right-on intonations. The picture is hyperactive; it has to be—it's so empty.

As T.C., one of the attendants, Franklyn Ajaye has a gleam of jivey good nature; when he squinches up his urchin's face under his towering Afro, he's a little like Shelley Duvall, and when he pushes his arms straight out to the side to indicate that everything's fine, the film momentarily seems ingenuous. I also laughed once when Garrett Morris (of "Saturday Night Live") did a routine with an invisible man in a huge body cast. That's about it; the rest of the jokes are damp firecrackers. George Carlin plays a cabdriver in a hopeless running gag, Richard Pryor is spectacularly unfunny as a preacher in a gold Rolls-Royce, the Pointer Sisters are wasted as his retinue, and Professor Irwin Corey has nothing but a wheezer of a skit about a urine sample in a Coke bottle. Does the bathroom humor get such hysterical laughs because it's more graphic and explicit than the bathroom humor on TV? When I saw *Murder by Death,* the white audience seemed absolutely overjoyed at Peter Falk's toilet joke. At *Car Wash,* the audience was almost all black, and it, too, knew what it liked.

The director, Michael Schultz, has a considerable background in the New York theatre; he directed for the Negro Ensemble Company, and his stage credits include *Kongi's Harvest, Does a Tiger Wear a Necktie?,* Douglas Turner Ward's *The Reckoning,* and Sam Shepard's *Operation Sidewinder.* He also did the TV versions of *To Be Young, Gifted and Black* and *Ceremonies in Dark Old Men.* And there are traces of sensitivity in *Car Wash*: Michael Fennell, a thirteen-year-old who skateboards around the car wash, has a euphoric moment when he's completely absorbed in the sensation of floating; Ivan Dixon is forceful and reserved in the musty role of a hardworking ex-con who isn't making enough on the job to feed his family; and something is being attempted in the wavering, understated scenes with Lauren Jones as a forlorn whore who hangs around the car wash. But what are these things doing here? How can Schultz and Schumacher try to throw poetry and black anger in with the bathroom humor, the worn-to-the-stump faggot jokes, the tediousness about the boss's son turning revolutionary and reciting from Chairman Mao's Little Red Book, and an attempted robbery? I guess that Schultz is trying to make life rise up out of these schlock ingredients, that he's trying to show that soul food can come out of junk food, but don't all purveyors of junk food claim that it's nourishing?

Schultz's earlier film, *Cooley High,* was about a group of black teen-agers who attended Cooley Vocational High School in Chicago in 1964—the film's title being also a pun on the black kids who were trained there to be coolies. *Cooley High* was about kids discovering themselves, and about their hopes for a different life. It was young, amateurish, and sentimental, and I sneaked out before it was over. But I was there long enough to hear the tremendous empathic response of the black audience when the kids were joyriding in a stolen car with the cops in pursuit. In *Car Wash,* Schultz seems to be trying to sustain the kind of high-spirited empathy that he got during that car chase: he keeps the car-wash attendants joyriding all over the place—jiggling, joking, always in motion, having the time of their lives. It may be worth pointing out that there's a world of difference between the young poet-hero of *Cooley High,* with his aspirations to get out of the ghetto, and T.C., who celebrates being yourself and knowing that that's all you are. "I am your prince," T.C. tells the pretty black waitress (Tracy Reed) who doesn't want to date him and the audience applauds. T.C. accepts being a coolie, and since it's the film's point of view that the waitress could only be holding out for a man with more money, when she gives in it's a victory for romance. In *Car Wash,* there is no different life—only better jobs and upward mobility, represented by comic-strip phonies: Pryor's preacher, and a Beverly Hills hysteric (Lorraine Gary) who's so ghastly that the audience screams with laughter when her child throws up all over her.

In quality, *Car Wash* isn't very different from Ossie Davis's 1970 film *Cotton Comes to Harlem,* but it's less innocent, more processed, and its specialty is yanking laughs by having adult blacks do dirtier versions of the standard pranks that naughty kids used to do in comedies. Sometimes not even dirtier: one attendant actually puts Tabasco in another attendant's sandwich, and this most primitive of *Our Gang* jokes gets a laugh, too. I can't help feeling that the audience is being insulted, even though the audience doesn't think so.

[October 25, 1976]

The Hundred-Per-Cent Solution

*T**he Seven-Per-Cent Solution*** starts from two pieces of common knowledge—that Sherlock Holmes used cocaine, and that Sigmund Freud took the drug for a period—and puts the two together. The fictional Holmes "lived" at the same time as the historical Freud; they're both myths by now, and by crossing these mythologies the film, adapted by Nicholas Meyer from his 1974 best-seller, gives us a luxuriant straight-faced parody. In this hybrid, Holmes (Nicol Williamson), pathologically obsessed with the criminal mastermind Prof. Moriarty (Laurence Olivier), is in such terrible shape that Dr. Watson (Robert Duvall) tricks him into going to Vienna to be cured of his cocaine addiction by Freud (Alan Arkin). It is but a few more steps to have the two great detectives pooling their deductive skills—the circumstantial and the psychological—to solve the mysterious kidnapping of one of Freud's patients (Vanessa Redgrave).

The film is a civilized light entertainment—somewhere between the genial "little" English comedies of the fifties, with their nifty plots and overqualified performers, and the splashy, stylized James Bond pictures. The director, Herbert Ross, works fluidly, serving the actors and the script unassumingly, and the designer, Ken Adam (who also did the Bonds), has done the plush sets, stuffed to their Victorian gills. Movies don't often splurge on such a clever idea, and it's very pleasurable to see the casting and the details brought off without stinting. Shot by Oswald Morris on European locations and at Pinewood Studios, in London, the production covers a lot of ground (five million dollars' worth). The cast—which contributes to the deluxe quality—includes Joel Grey (in too small a role, as usual), Samantha Eggar, Georgia Brown, Jeremy Kemp, Anna Quayle, Charles Gray, Régine, as a brothel keeper (she sings Stephen Sondheim's "The Madame's Song"), and a bloodhound (called Toby) who might be an emblem of Holmesian parody. (The 1956 film *Goodbye, My Lady* got my family hooked on basenjis; this wise, tolerant bloodhound is the only movie dog I've seen since then who has tested my loyalty.)

The actors seem to be having an actors' holiday, performing in roles that allow them to playact, to be somebody different. Their roles are really impersonations: they do their own variations on what previous actors have done with the characters. The fun of watching Robert Duvall as Dr. Watson is in his contrast to Nigel Bruce's bumbler and, of course, in his new British accent. And Olivier, who couldn't rise above the material in *Marathon Man,* is in tremendous high form. His Moriarty, a prissy, complaining old pedagogue who feels persecuted by Holmes, is performed with the covert wit that is his specialty. It's not a big part, but this Moriarty—his face expressing injury to the verge of tears—is amusingly dislikable, a Dickensian monster.

Is it right to use a figure drawn from recent history as a character in a detective comedy? The film treats Freud with scrupulous tact, and as Alan Arkin plays him the humor is in his almost coy diffidence. There's true comic intelligence in the way Arkin can suggest the workings of a character's mind by minimal movements and the driest of small inflections. His Freud is ingratiating, deeply kind, and never to be taken seriously. He's the hero of the piece—the greatest detective of all. And without an authoritarian bone in his body—which may upset those who want Freud to be treated less worshipfully. But this is not an imitation of life; it's a honeyed platonic cartoon of a mythic figure. It's Freud without libido.

Movies have been mixing fact and fantasy for a long time—in the De Mille epics, in *Lloyds of London,* in *Beau Brummell,* in the biographies of Edison, Cole Porter, Fanny Brice, Billie Holiday, and Gable and Lombard, in the swashbucklers, where a king reprieved the hero and gave him a title, or played cupid to the hero and heroine. However, the earlier movies didn't utilize the comedy potential in the mixture; it wasn't yet a fact-and-fantasy game. The new form of celebrity fiction uses ready-made characters for a shortcut to comic effects, which are dependent on our awareness of the put-on. It's a shared conceit—mutually acknowledged prestidigitation—and so the method runs the risk of preciousness, and of being too literary a stunt for the mass movie audience. But I think *The Seven-Per-Cent Solution* stays free of these traps, and maybe even bright kids—at least, those over twelve—would be delighted by the way the pieces fall into place. Coherence like this is a form of cleverness that kids appreciate, and they don't often get it from movies. *The Seven-Per-Cent Solution* is no more than an ingeniously contrived spree. It never rises to any heights of style, and it limps in places, but it doesn't make the mistake of taking itself seriously.

Nicol Williamson has the borderline role. Holmes the loner, the social outsider, who, according to Conan Doyle, "loathed every form of society" and "never spoke of the softer passions, save with a gibe and a sneer," is the essential mystery in *The Seven-Per-Cent Solution.* For the film's interlocking puzzles to release their wit, Holmes must be the detective genius, yet Freud, who solves the riddle of why Holmes is an addict, and why he is a detective, is the greater genius. The movie is effective because it respects both these mythic characters and enjoys the idea that they'd get along. But Williamson's role is by far the more difficult, since he has to have the equilibrium to writhe in suffering and still be funny. He does it, by turning his customary speed-freak ranting into self-satire. Williamson's Holmes is so hopped up on cocaine that his deductions are as accurate as ever, instantaneous, and he rattles them off with berserk velocity. His hyper-excitement keeps the first part of the picture hopped up, too. I became a bit uneasy during his withdrawal period in the Freud household, because while he was lying there hallucinating, everything seemed to come to a halt, and I was afraid the picture would go dead, the way *Murder on the Orient Express* did when the train stopped. The director tries to make our flesh creep in the hallucination sequence, and he doesn't seem quite sure of his satirical edge. The pace does slacken, but even though the detoxified Nicol Williamson is something of a zombie, Alan Arkin, Vanessa Redgrave's come-hither smiles, the supporting cast, and the narrative itself carry us along. There's a long action sequence on a train that involves a duel as well as the dismantling of a railway car in order to fuel the engine, and it's a few shades too farcical; it's a reworking of a Marx Brothers routine in *Go West,* and it doesn't have the first-generation humor of this film's premise. But even with these semi-lapses, and the missed opportunities—the kidnapping plot could use more flair, and not much is made of the brothel staffed with red-haired whores (a parody spinoff of Conan Doyle's "The Red-Headed League"?)—the film stays on course.

Those who have read the novel will have a pleasurable shock at the finish. After the book had gone to press, the author got the perfect Freudian answer to the mystery of Holmes' fixation on the arch-villain Moriarty; he was able to change only the foreign editions. But he uses this ending here, and it is one of the wittiest wrap-ups of any mystery movie. (The primal-flashback sequence that unravels the secret is also eloquently staged, with the child Holmes psychically bloodied forever, and Moriarty a criminal bug scuttling away.) The movie has a bum title, though: the reference to Holmes' seven-per-cent cocaine solution, with its punning allusion to mysteries, hasn't much allure. And with Meyer's new Freudian-joke ending, this movie is so ingeniously worked out that it has a hundred-per-cent solution.

□ □ □

Vincente Minnelli's *A Matter of Time* has been grossly tampered with; it was taken away from the director before he could supervise the dubbing and the musical scoring, and the film was recut. From what is being shown to the public, it is almost impossible to judge what the tone of his film was, or whether it would have worked at any level, though what's left of *A*

Matter of Time has some of the same convictionless musky romanticism that did in Minnelli's last picture, *On a Clear Day You Can See Forever.* But even if his own version was less than a triumph, that was the film I wanted to see—not this chopped-up shambles, with footage from his epilogue put at the beginning, scenes removed, and two hideous travelogue montages (from stock footage) inserted. The excuse that the businessmen always give for taking a picture away from a director is "to save it," but has anyone ever heard of a movie taken over to be saved that wasn't a disaster financially? This particular project is based on a Maurice Druon novel called *Film of Memory,* and its complicated time-and-fantasy structure required the most delicate transitions. The mangled film exposes the performers—in particular, Liza Minnelli—to ridicule, and I can only assume that it is a cause of sorrow and shame to Minnelli, as a director and as a father.

The film is set in 1949, in Rome. Liza Minnelli plays a peasant girl from the provinces who gets a job as a maid in a Roman hotel, where a contessa (Ingrid Bergman), who was a great demimondaine at the turn of the century, languishes, drifting in and out of the present. As the Contessa tells the maid about her early life, when she was the model for great painters and the mistress of kings and poets, the maid visualizes herself living through those scenes. It's a pity that this perfectly acceptable ironic conceit is fused with an uplifting plot about how the chambermaid, heeding the Contessa's words that one must never imitate others but must be "an original," proceeds to become an international movie queen.

The ideas don't mesh, and even allowing for the evisceration by the producers, the John Gay script shifts between old-fogey bull about women as the inspirers of genius and new-fogey speechifying about the plight of women. And there doesn't appear to be any recognition that the chambermaid should be funny when she fantasizes herself on the Contessa's femme-fatale road to glory. Back in 1928, in *Day Dreams,* a twenty-three-minute comedy written by H. G. Wells, Elsa Lanchester appeared as a servant girl who dreamed of herself as a clotheshorse, a passionate aristocrat, a scandalously famous actress, and so on; Wells slyly worked out the slapstick potential in each incarnation. Here the chambermaid, in fantasy, appears in Belle Époque finery, embracing the Contessa's celebrated lovers, and we're meant to swoon and wish we were there. At times, as the country-girl heroine, Liza Minnelli suggests a young Anna Magnani. With her hooded look, her heavy eyelids, and her sturdy frame, she has the mystery of a Corot, and one can see that her father was aiming to bring out a sensual ripeness. But at one awful moment, just when the Contessa has made her up and she should be transformed from a peasant into a ravishing original, we see her in a closeup that emphasizes her broad nose and libidinous underlip; her features look gargantuan. In that shot, the cameraman and the editor murder the star. She has a few songs, and in one of them, Gershwin's "Do It Again," she's in supple low voice, but the technicians betray her by the synching and the metallic sound. And Liza Minnelli doesn't do very well for herself. When she falls back on her strident gamine mannerisms—all fizzy, bright-eyed eagerness—she's too chummy with us; she reaches out to grab us, and, without proper editing to prepare us to receive her, we recoil.

Ingrid Bergman, however, looks eight feet tall and every inch a star. When she was young, she had a slightly stodgy quality along with her radiant freshness (as Liv Ullmann does also), and as the missionary in *Murder on the Orient Express* Bergman seemed to be parodying those dumpy nice-girl roles. When one sees her here, with her kohl-blackened eyelids and her leopard-trimmed cape, it's hard to remember that she was the actress publicized for her natural, no-makeup look—the actress who used to charm audiences a little too easily with her cherubic, clean-young-student smile. She has a glamour in this role beyond anything she's had before onscreen; the Contessa has the ruined look of a woman steeped in her narcissism—a woman who has cared about nothing but being attractive to men, and now, in her seventies, has nothing left but memories of her conquests, and bitterness.

Bergman, who began studying acting in her teens, has been in movies since 1934, and even though she was often dull in that healthy *fräulein* way, she kept working, whether on the screen or on the stage, and by now when she makes a gesture it has all that experience behind it. At sixty-one, she could emerge as the foremost practitioner of the grand manner. (Had she played in *Travels with My Aunt,* it might have been a dazzling exhibition.) Her daughter Isabella Rossellini appears here in the small role of a nun (Sister Pia—a family in-joke), and is a soft, ethereal version of Bergman herself in *The Bells of St. Mary's,* but with an Italian accent. It must be a relief to Bergman to pass her nun's habit on to her daughter and bask in the Contessa's fancy duds and Circean melancholy. Her always thrilling voice is deeper than ever, and her strength goes way beyond that of younger actresses—even beyond that of Vanessa Redgrave, though Bergman doesn't approach Redgrave's artistic inventiveness. One of the Contessa's old lovers appears to be modelled on D'Annunzio (who was Eleonora Duse's lover), and so it's probably not an accident that Bergman has brought into her acting a little of the stillness that one responds to in Duse's work on film. Bergman is aware of the line of her body, she's assured enough to do much of the role in statuesque repose, and when she lifts one of those huge hands the gesture is poetically complete. You feel she could waft those hands and blow you right out of the theatre. Charles Boyer turns up in one sequence, and he's trim and distinguished, in his beautifully polished way, but he seems a little too limited—too mortal—to have been one of the Contessa's lovers. Bergman's role has been reduced to shreds, so one cannot judge whether her performance had any rhythm; scene after scene has been cut. Still, there's something going on when she's on the screen, and with her gowns hanging straight down from her shoulders she's as tall as a legend.

[November 1, 1976]

Notes on Evolving Heroes, Morals, Audiences

In *Jaws*, which may be the most cheerfully perverse scare movie ever made, the disasters don't come on schedule the way they do in most disaster pictures, and your guts never settle down to a timetable. Even while you're convulsed with laughter, you're still apprehensive, because the editing rhythms are very tricky, and the shock images loom up huge, right on top of you. There are parts of *Jaws* that suggest what Eisenstein might have done if he hadn't intellectualized himself out of reach—if he'd given in to the bourgeois child in himself. While having a drink with an older Hollywood director, I said that I'd been amazed by the assurance with which Steven Spielberg, the young director of *Jaws*, had toyed with the film frame. The older director said, "He must never have seen a play; he's the first one of us who doesn't think in terms of the proscenium arch. With him, there's nothing but the camera lens."

It's not only the visual technique of *Jaws* that's different. The other big disaster movies are essentially the same as the pre-Vietnam films, but *Jaws* isn't. It belongs to the pulpiest sci-fi monster-movie tradition, yet it stands some of the old conventions on their head. Though *Jaws* has more zest than a Woody Allen picture, and a lot more electricity, it's funny in a Woody Allen way. When the three protagonists are in their tiny boat, you feel that Robert Shaw, the malevolent old shark hunter, is so manly that he wants to get them all killed; he's so manly he's homicidal. It's not sharks who are his enemies; it's other men. When he begins showing off his wounds, the bookish ichthyologist, Richard Dreyfuss, strings along with him at first, and matches him scar for scar. But when the ichthyologist is outclassed in the number of scars he can exhibit, he opens his shirt, looks down at his hairy chest, and with a put-on artist's grin says, "You see that? Right there? That was Mary Ellen Moffit—she broke my heart." When Shaw squeezes an empty beer can flat, Dreyfuss satirizes him by crumpling a Styrofoam cup. The director, identifying with the Dreyfuss character,

195

sets up bare-chested heroism as a joke and scores off it all through the movie. The third protagonist, acted by Roy Scheider, is a former New York City policeman who has just escaped the city dangers and found a haven as chief of police in a resort community on an island. There, feeling totally inadequate in his new situation, he confronts primal terror. But the fool on board the little boat isn't the chief of police who doesn't know one end of a boat from the other, or the bookman, either. It's Shaw, the obsessively masculine fisherman, who thinks he's got to prove himself by fighting the shark practically single-handed. Shaw personalizes the shark, turns him into a fourth character—his enemy. This fisherman is such a macho pain that it's harrowingly funny when he's gobbled up; a flamboyant actor like Robert Shaw, who wears a proscenium arch around him, has to be kidded.

The high point of the film's humor is in our seeing Shaw get it; this nut Ahab, with his hyper-masculine basso-profundo speeches, stands in for all the men who have to show they're tougher than anybody. The shark's cavernous jaws demonstrate how little his toughness finally adds up to. If one imagines George C. Scott or Anthony Quinn in the Robert Shaw role, these anti-macho jokes expand into a satire of movie heroism.

*T*he actor who has put our new, ambivalent feelings about the warrior male to account is Jack Nicholson. Despite his excessive dynamism (and maybe partly because of it), this satirical actor has probably gone further into the tragicomedy of hardhat macho than any other actor. He exposes cracks in barroom-character armor and makes those cracks funny, in a low-down, grungy way. With his horny leers and his little-boy cockiness and one-upmanship, he illuminates the sources of male bravado. His whole acting style is based on the little guy coming on strong, because being a tough guy is the only ideal he's ever aspired to. This little guy doesn't make it, of course; Nicholson is the macho loser-hero. (In an earlier era, Nicholson would probably have played big guys.)

When you see the celebration of adolescent male fantasies in the film *The Yakuza,* directed by Sydney Pollack, or in a John Milius picture—*Dillinger* or *The Wind and the Lion*—you may wonder of the filmmakers, "Are these boys being naughty just because they're old enough not to be scolded by their mothers?" That's the kind of naughtiness Jack Nicholson keeps us aware of; he includes it in his performances. He's the kind of actor who gives you a character and then lets you follow him around the corner and watch as he reacts to what he just pulled off back there.

*T*he most ambiguous bumper sticker I've ever seen was "Thank God for John Wayne," though it wasn't ambiguous for the people who had put it on—they had also plastered two decals for the Patrolmen's Benevolent Association on their car windows. Yet even their assertive clinging to the old Wayne image—the very one that he can't cling to anymore himself—speaks of the changes they must feel around them. They want something that can't come back.

In recent years, John Wayne has been looking for a new image, and that great bulk has been falling flat. You can see now that, though Wayne was never much of an actor, there was a ham underneath just the same; he'd rather turn his mythic Western hero into a clown than quit. Wayne is so transparent an actor that he's foolishly likable, and so when he tries to play a Clint Eastwood city-cop role (as in *McQ*), you may feel embarrassed for him. (You don't get embarrassed by anything Clint Eastwood does; he's so hollow you don't have to feel a thing.)

In *The Shootist*, Wayne attempts to go back and complete his Western legend, but it's always dangerous when a movie sets out to be a classic, and the director, Don Siegel, who has an enjoyably trashy talent, has been so paralyzed by his high intentions that he's made a piece of solemn, unenjoyable trash. *The Shootist* has no emotional movement, despite Wayne, who has the dignity here that he'd lost in *Rooster Cogburn*. As an aged gunfighter dying of cancer, he's a noble figure; he knows the movie is trucking him out to exhibit that nobility, and he's got the farewell-tour catch in the throat. He's like an old dancer who can only do a few steps yet does them with great pride and style. The film, however, is a rigged setup. There's no conflict, no tension in his encounters with the small-minded townspeople; the old man, with his Westerner's code, is always morally superior. The bad operators in town want to get him, but he's such a nice guy you can't figure out what they've got against him, and in the climax he arbitrarily selects the three men in town who need killing without our ever understanding what they've done. In 1976, after the Western hero is dead, how can movies go on bringing us the message that he's dying? *The Shootist* digs him up to rebury him, and then has the gall to tell the story of how other people want to exploit him. Siegel has no real interest in the code; he's in his element when he stages the final shoot-out, but there's no rationale for it—no greed, no anger, and no moral drive.

*T*he stirring, emotionally satisfying early Westerns had a narrative push forward, a belief in the future of a people. That epic spirit has—understandably—been missing from recent Westerns. It comes back in a new form in the surprising *The Return of a Man Called Horse*; in this Western, the surge of elation comes from the spiritual rebirth of an Indian tribe. The hero is John Morgan, an English lord, played by Richard Harris. In the earlier *A Man Called Horse*, Morgan was captured by the Yellow Hand, a tribe of the Sioux nation; he was accepted as a brother, and, free, returned to his own country. The new picture, directed by Irvin Kershner, is about how, once having known that brotherhood and accepted its magical religion, he is lost as a white man. We see Morgan in his English mansion, and his face shows that he's split off from the life around him; his soul has become Indian. The early part of the film, which cuts from an attack on the Yellow Hand to a foxhunt in England, has an emotional power that is almost comparable to that of the early scenes of *The Godfather, Part II,* and the sequence that replaces the usual cattle drive is of supernal landscapes—the dark shapes of buffalo running over blinding pale-green meadows. Despite a pulpy script and the sometimes awkward acting, *The Return of a Man Called Horse* may be the first Hollywood epic in which the rituals of the Indians make sense. Driven off their land, their braves killed, their young women enslaved, the Yellow Hand have become so weak that they have even lost the will to hunt buffalo. Morgan and some of the children take on themselves the burden of suffering. When, through this sacrifice, the Yellow Hand satisfy their gods, they are able to triumph over their enemies and regain their homeland, and the English lord is content to be one of the tribe. This Western, with its Old Testament mysticism, which appears to be authentically Indian as well, is a startlingly affirmative vision.

A few decades ago, if a character in a novel did something irrational— that is, out of character—the other people in the book would say, "It's so unlike John to have done that," and we'd read on for chapters to find out why he had behaved so uncharacteristically. The characters in movies also used to operate from a fixed position: if they were proper, they were supposed to look proper, and behave within certain patterns. What we call spontaneity now would have been called irrationality then. But since there are no set codes of behavior today, we accept the irrational. We like the diversion of surprising behavior in movies; we don't respond to those Charlton Heston heroes who lack irrational impulses. And we don't want over-elaborated motivation—we want just enough for us to get the sense of what a person is about.

In *Dog Day Afternoon,* we don't want any explanation of how it is that Sonny (Al Pacino) lives in both heterosexual and homosexual marriages. We accept the idea because we don't really believe in patterns of behavior anymore—only in behavior. Sonny, who is trapped in the middle of robbing a bank, with a crowd gathering in the street outside, is a working-class man who got into this mess by trying to raise money for Leon (Chris Sarandon) to have a sex-change operation, yet the audience doesn't laugh. The most touching element in the film is Sonny's inability to handle all the responsibilities he has assumed. Though he is half-crazed by his situation, he is trying to do the right thing by everybody—his wife and children, the suicidal Leon, the hostages in the bank. In the sequence in which Sonny dictates his will, we can see that inside this ludicrous bungling robber there's a complicatedly unhappy man, operating out of a sense of noblesse oblige.

The structure of *Dog Day Afternoon* loosens in the last three-quarters of an hour, but that was the part I particularly cared for. This picture is one of the most satisfying of all the movies starring New York City because the director, Sidney Lumet, and the screenwriter, Frank Pierson, having established that Sonny's grandstanding gets the street crowd on his side against the cops, and that even the tellers are on his side, let us move into the dark, confused areas of Sonny's frustrations and don't explain everything to us. They trust us to feel without our being told how to feel. They prepare us for a confrontation scene between Sonny and Leon, and it never comes, but even that is all right, because of the way that Pacino and Sarandon handle their contact by telephone; Sonny's anxiety and Leon's distress are so pure that there's no appeal for sympathy—no star kitsch to separate us from the nakedness of the feelings on the screen.

This kind of male acting is becoming much more common in movies. In the past, the corruption of stardom has often meant that the actor was afraid of carrying a role through and exposing the insides of a character; a star began to have so large a stake in his own image that he was afraid of what the audience might think of the revelation. But new stars such as Pacino and Nicholson and Gene Hackman and Robert De Niro go as far into their characters as they can psychologically allow themselves to go; that's how they work. Robert Redford *could* do that, but he has been holding back—he doesn't want you not to like the people he plays.

Yet if Redford is the closest thing we've got to the self-congratulatory American Protestant Eagle who flourished in the Second World War movies, that eagle has had his wings clipped. Redford, with his glamorous remoteness and passivity, combines the romantic appeal of the inverts and the matinée idols of those days with a new, uneasy consciousness that is supposed to account for his passivity. The new heroes don't soar; they can barely see straight. The myopically spacey Timothy Bottoms plays such characters as the gentlest and least harmful of the representative Americans in *The White Dawn*; he's frazzled, out of it, ineffective. One of the reasons that there are so few women's roles is that men have coöpted them. In earlier decades, if a hero wanted something he went out and got it. Uncertainty was the basis of many of the women stars' roles; the women asked, "Do I dare?" and sat at home, wheedling and plotting. Now that the men are so uncertain, what could a woman wheedle out of them?

In primitive societies, and in this country until quite recently, a man proved his courage by exposing himself to a dangerous test. If there's any equivalent to that now, it's exposing himself to the danger of going crazy—so crazy that he loses the capacity to feel. (And women do it too.)

Historically, people have recognized strong individuals as heroes or heroines by their willingness to accept the responsibility for their acts. And in the past if a movie hero broke the law because he felt he had to, we could respect him for it, because we knew—as he did—that there would be consequences, and not only legal and social consequences but moral ones, too. Now we're in a period when we know that most wrongdoing—the worst wrongdoing especially—isn't socially punished. And it's terribly apparent that the wrongdoers face no moral consequences. So it's not surprising that the standard action-movie heroes today aren't men who, after searching their consciences, violate the law; the heroes now are lawbreakers at heart. What appears to separate them from the villains is that they're lawbreakers trying to confirm that they're courageous men. Whether they seek this confirmation of their masculinity on the police force or in crime or, like the rebel McMurphy, in an insane asylum, they're all lawless. On TV, when cops like Baretta (who's all heart) or the slimy-smart Starsky and Hutch club someone on the head, they explain that there was no other way. The law doesn't apply to them, and reading a prisoner his Miranda rights is just a joke, since they know their prisoners are guilty. And lawbreakers like the Burt Reynolds heroes know that if they're arrested the cops will kick the hell out of them, so the Miranda rights are a joke to them, too. The bond between the lawless cops and the lawbreakers is contempt for the law.

When there doesn't appear to be any alternative to Clint Eastwood's relentless law-givers and Burt Reynolds' self-satisfied lawbreakers, it's easy to see why we get Ken Russell and *Tommy,* who isn't a man, but a numb child. It's as if the tough-guy movies said, "Either you feel our way or you feel nothing." Androgynous catatonia is the answer to repulsive macho. The alternative to *Macon County Line* and *Walking Tall* and *White Line Fever* sure as hell isn't Fred Astaire anymore; it's closer to David Bowie.

Nicolas Roeg's *The Man Who Fell to Earth,* which stars David Bowie, is *The Little Prince* for young adults; the hero, a stranger on earth, is purity made erotic. He doesn't have a human sex drive; he isn't even equipped for it—naked, he's as devoid of sex differentiation as a child in sleepers. (He seems to be the first movie hero to have had his crotch airbrushed.) Yet there's true insolence in Bowie's lesbian-Christ leering, and his forlorn, limp manner and chalky pallor are alluringly tainted. Lighted like the woman of mystery in thirties movies, he's the most romantic figure in recent pictures—the modern version of the James Dean lost-boy myth. Nicolas Roeg has a talent for eerily easy, soft, ambiguous sex—for the sexiness of passivity. In his *Don't Look Now,* Donald Sutherland practically oozed passivity—which was the only interesting quality he had. And at the beginning of *The Man Who Fell to Earth* (which was shot in this country with an American cast except for Bowie), when the stranger splashes down in a lake in the Southwest and drinks water like a vampire gulping down his lifeblood, one is drawn in, fascinated by the obliqueness and by the promise of an erotic sci-fi story. It is and it isn't. The stranger, though non-human, has visions of the wife and kiddies he has left—an old-fashioned nuclear family on the planet Anthea. He has come to earth to obtain the water that will save his people, who are dying from drought, but he is corrupted, is distracted from his mission, and then is so damaged that he cannot return. Although Roeg and his screenwriter, Paul Mayersberg, pack layers of tragic political allegory into *The Man Who Fell to Earth,* none of the layers is very strong, or even very clear. The plot, about big-business machinations, is so uninvolving that one watches Bowie traipsing around—looking like Katharine Hepburn in her transvestite role in *Sylvia Scarlett*—and either tunes out or allows the film, with its perverse pathos, to become a sci-fi framework for a sex-role-confusion fantasy. The wilted solitary stranger who is better than we are and yet falls prey to our corrupt human estate can be said to represent everyone who feels misunderstood, everyone who feels sexually immature or "different," everyone who has lost his way, everyone who has failed his holy family, and so the film is a gigantic launching pad for anything that viewers want to drift to.

A former cinematographer, Roeg has more visual strategies than almost any director one can think of. He can charge a desolate landscape so that it seems ominously alive, familiar yet only half recognizable, and he photographs skyscrapers with such lyric glitter that the United States seems to be showing off for him (the better to be despoiled). The people pass through, floating, using the country without seeing its beauty. Roeg's cutting can create a magical feeling of waste and evil, but at other times his Marienbadish jumpiness is just trickery he can't resist. In *The Man Who Fell to Earth,* the unease and sense of disconnectedness between characters also disconnect us. Roeg teases us with a malaise that he then moralizes about. His effects stay on the surface; they become off-puttingly abstract, and his lyricism goes sentimental—as most other Christ movies do. In *Blow-Up* and *The Passenger,* Antonioni showed a talent (and a propensity) for mystification; it would be a present to audiences if just once he would use his talent frivolously—if, instead of his usual opaque metaphysical mystery, he'd make a simple trashy mystery, preferably in those *Réalités* travel spots he's drawn to. And it would be a blessing if Nicolas Roeg—perhaps the most visually seductive of directors, a man who can make impotence sexy—turned himself loose on the romance of waste.

*B*owie's self-mocking androgyny is not a quality that one associates with the heroes of imperial nations. Imperial movie heroes are just about gone, and even much of what comes out on the American screen as sexism isn't necessarily the result of conviction; it may be the sexist result of simple convenience. In the movies or on television, the two cops in the police car don't have to think about each other. When a cop-hero's partner is shot, it's supposed to be worse than anything, but the reason it's worse than anything is always explained *after* he's been shot. Then the survivor—let's call him Frank—explains that Jim took the bullet for him, that Jim was the one Frank spent more time with than anyone else. And Frank's wife can say, "Frank and Jim were more married than we are"—and she says it sympathetically. She understands. The theme of mateship is such a clean, visible bond. It doesn't have the hidden traps of the relationship between men and women, or between lovers of the same sex. In a number of movies, the actors playing the two cops seem palpably embarrassed by the notion that women are those creatures who come into the story for a minute and you jump them. Some are embarrassed that that's all you do with them; others are relieved that that's all you have to do—because if there's anything more it may involve the problem of what men are supposed to be in relation to women.

Two human beings who are sexually and emotionally involved cause pain to each other, and it takes more skill than most writers and directors have to deal with that pain. Besides, with the Supreme Court decision leaving the determination of what is pornography to the communities, almost any treatment of the psychology of sex may get a film into serious legal problems. The porno filmmakers, whose investment may be thirty-five thousand dollars a picture, are closed in one city, hop to another, and come back with a few cuts or a different title. Porno films are all over the place, so it looks as if the screen is wide-open, but actually the studios aren't taking chances on sexual themes.

*T*he changes in movies, responding to the changes in the national psychology, have come about mostly unconsciously. The comedies now are almost all made by Jewish directors—directors who are themselves anarchic comics. Comedies are no longer about how to win or how to be a success, but about trying to function in the general craziness. Some of the veteran directors may face insoluble problems—a director's craft isn't enough to see him through when that craft is itself an expression of the old, fixed patterns. In a country where the Protestant ethic doesn't seem to have worked out too well, it makes sense that directors of Catholic background—Francis Ford Coppola and Brian De Palma, of Italian-Catholic parents; Martin Scorsese, of Sicilian origins; Robert Altman, from a German-Catholic family in Kansas City, Missouri—speak to the way Americans feel now. These men have grown up with a sense of sin and a deep-seated feeling that things aren't going to get much better in this life. They're not uplifters or reformers, like some of the Protestant directors of an earlier era, or muckraking idealists, like some of the earlier Jewish directors. Pictures such as *Mean Streets* and *Taxi Driver, California Split* and *Nashville, The Godfather, Part II,* and the new *Carrie* combine elements of ritual and of poetry in their heightened realism. The Catholic directors examine American experience in emotional terms, without much illusion—in fact, with macabre humor. The Western heroes faced choices between right and wrong; these directors didn't grow up on right-and-wrong but on good-and-evil—and then they lost the good.

*I*f *Jaws* represents a new affability about the tough American male, it also contains a token of a new ruthlessness. There's a lull in the action, a becalmed interlude, which is filled by a long monologue delivered by Robert Shaw. He tells the ultimate shark horror story—it's worse, even, than anything that we see in the movie. The story he tells concerns the men of the Indianapolis, a heavy cruiser that was torpedoed after delivering key elements of the atomic bombs to be dropped on Japan. As Shaw, in drunken, sepulchral tones, describes the events, the survivors were attacked by sharks, which returned day after day, using the ever-smaller group of survivors as a feeding ground. Actually, it is not known how many of the Indianapolis crew died because of sharks, or how many died from exposure, or from injuries sustained when the ship was hit. The monologue, conceived by Howard Sackler, embellished to a length of nine pages by John Milius, and then trimmed by Spielberg and Shaw to a feasible length, could easily have dealt with a fictitious ship, but using the correct name gave it an extra plausibility. In the rest of *Jaws,* we're worked over right in the open, but in this Indianapolis episode we're fooled by a hidden confusion of historical fact and sadistic fantasy. The writers probably didn't consider—or were simply indifferent to—the nightmarish pain that their gothic embroidery would give to the relatives of the men who died in those waters.

*T*he only morality that many of the best young filmmakers appear to have is an aesthetic morality. They may show us geysers of blood that tear us apart, but they're true to what they think is good filmmaking. In their movies, the human logic is secondary to the aesthetic logic. A movie is like a musical composition to them: they'll put in a bloody climax because they need it at a certain point. They're not afraid of the manipulative possibilities of the medium; they revel in those possibilities and play with them. Catholic imagery has a kind of ruthlessness anyway—the bleeding Jesus, the pierced, suffering saints. But even without a Catholic background, Spielberg is as ruthlessly manipulative as Scorsese or De Palma (though he doesn't rely on instinct as much as they do—he plans, like Eisenstein). Film is their common religion. For some people in the audience, their films may be too shocking; they overwhelm us emotionally in a way that more crudely manipulative directors don't, and so people tend to become much more outraged by a *Taxi Driver* than by a *Towering Inferno*.

New action films often seem to be trying so hard to beat the tube that they reach right out to grab us—not with the technique of a Steven

Spielberg but by crowding out any aesthetic distance. There has always been an element of dread in the pleasure of suspense movies, but it was tangled up with childish, fairy-tale excitement and the knowledge that the characters we cared about would come out safe; the dread was part of the fun. But in many current movies the suspense is nothing more than dread. The only thing that keeps us watching some films is the fear of what the moviemakers are going to throw at us next. We don't anticipate the climactic scenes pleasurably; we await them anxiously, and after the usual two hours of assault the punishment stops, and we go home relieved, yet helplessly angry.

On the basis that they can't say they were bored, large numbers of people seem willing to accept heavily advertised shock-and-dread pictures (such as *Marathon Man*) as entertainment. But in a neat cultural switch, a sizable number of educated people who used to complain of Hollywood's innocuous pampering, and who went to foreign films for adult entertainment, now escape to bland French romances, such as the Lelouch pictures or *Cousin, Cousine*, to find the same innocent reassurance that the mass audience used to obtain. They've become afraid of American movies, and not just of the junk but of *The Godfather, Part II, Nashville*, and the best this country has to offer. They're turning to Europe for cuddly sentiments—for make-out movies. The success of *Cousin, Cousine*, a rhythmless, mediocre piece of moviemaking, may be in part attributable to its winsome heroine (Marie-Christine Barrault), who is sexy in a fleshy smiling-nun way, and in part to its silliness. With its wholesome carnality, *Cousin, Cousine* is so pro-life that it treats sex like breakfast cereal. It features adultery without dirt—adultery as carefree nonconformity—and the way the chorus of understanding kids applauds the parents' displays of innocent happy sensuality this could be the first Disney True Life Adventure about people.

[November 8, 1976]

Travesties

To think that we were spared Ken Russell's Sarah Bernhardt only to get Richard Fleischer's. *The Incredible Sarah*, a Reader's Digest film, opens to the strains of Elmer Bernstein's schlocked Johann Strauss, and on the screen are the famous Mucha posters, fudged up with Glenda Jackson's face. If one were to make a game of selecting the least suitable person to play that frizzy-haired, passionate Jewish Catholic girl, with her yielding body and sultry voice, who became the supreme French actress of her age, maybe it wouldn't be Glenda Jackson. Maybe it would be Tammy Grimes or Stockard Channing, but wouldn't Glenda Jackson come close? Someone was needed who could suggest what feminine genius meant in that period and how it expressed itself; Glenda Jackson is as much like Sarah Bernhardt as she is like Virginia Woolf. Arthur Symons wrote of Bernhardt, "One's pulses beat feverishly before the curtain had risen; there was almost a kind of obscure sensation of peril." Critics described her suppleness, her "admirable limpidity of diction," her melodious flow of moods. Glenda Jackson simply does not have the physical softness or the voice to play a tragedienne of that era; her body does not sing. Glenda Jackson can no more play the lyrical, incandescent Sarah Bernhardt than Sarah Bernhardt could have played the staccato, wrenchingly modern Glenda Jackson, the least lyrical major actress of our day. (Who could have played Bernhardt? I'd like to have seen Geraldine Chaplin have a shot at it.)

The Incredible Sarah is an aberration. Stiffer and more anachronistic than the Warner bios of the thirties, it's in the stupefying tradition of *Song of Norway*. Glenda Jackson flounces in for her first try at acting, an audition at the Comédie-Française, primped up in bright ruffles and as rude as a duchess. Those interested in theatre history may recall that Bernhardt, born in 1844, was fifteen at the time she auditioned for the Conservatoire, the government-sponsored school of acting, where she appeared dressed in oppressive black silk, with a burn in the bodice covered by lace. The garbling isn't accidental: the movie Sarah is starched and confident in order to make her desire to act seem simply the whim of an arrogant girl. It is the fashion now for American movies to extend self-derision into the past, leaving no heroes and heroines standing, and I suppose that the scenarist, Ruth Wolff (late of *The Abdication*), the producer, Helen M. Strauss, and Fleischer took pride in their modern, unsympathetic approach: their young Sarah is an incomprehensible bitch, an obnoxious smartass whose only interest in the theatre is her glinting-eyed desire for curtain calls. From the way they treat Bernhardt, you'd think she'd been part of the Plumbers' Unit. They omit any indications of the loneliness and privation of her early years, when her mother gave her to a peasant wet nurse and indifferently lost track of her; locked up in a concierge's apartment in Paris, the abandoned, scrawny four-year-old flung herself out a window, and among her injuries was a smashed kneecap. (Many years later, the leg, which had been injured again in a fall on stage, had to be amputated.) The movie shows her sleeping in a coffin, and it seems a spoiled girl's affectation; what isn't explained is that, frail and consumptive, she had been told she was going to die, and was so frightened by the prospect that she wanted to get used to being in a coffin. Nor is there any clue to her tenderness and generosity: at twenty she was taking care not only of herself and her child but of a tubercular half sister, also cast off by their whorey mother, and a few years later she took in her Orthodox Jewish grandmother, newly arrived from Holland. This movie features a well-heeled cutup who cares about nothing but herself. She's ferociously self-sufficient and likes to smash things so much that the movie gives her two complete destruction orgies.

A glorified mechanic, Richard Fleischer pleases movie executives because he has no particular interests and no discernible style. *The New Centurions, Mandingo, The Incredible Sarah* are all the same to him. I wonder if he ever thought about what drove the young Bernhardt, so ill that she bled from the mouth, to her fanatical study of acting, and what kept her going out on the stage night after night, even on one leg, until she died, in 1923. Ellen Terry wrote, "She was as transparent as an azalea only more so; like a cloud only not so thick; smoke from a burning paper describes her more nearly." Yet there is not one moment in the movie when one feels that this woman has become an actress out of a spiritual need for expression. Glenda Jackson shows Sarah's pleasure in the ovations she got by a twinkling self-satisfaction that degrades Bernhardt to a rank lower than her own. It was bad enough to have Louis Pasteur as Paul Muni, Émile Zola as Paul Muni, Benito Juárez as Paul Muni; now we're stuck with Sarah Bernhardt as Glenda Jackson.

□ □ □

*B*eware of producers who speak with pride about creating roles for women. Before the titles of *The Next Man* there's a briefing on a war between oil cartels, and then a string of grisly assassinations. We don't have any idea who's on which side; these slaughters are for the camera's sake—a teaser, an apéritif. The central figure in the story is indeed a woman—a killer female—and the title refers to her next victim. As I reconstruct the genesis of this glamour-and-gore picture, the producer, Martin Bregman, wanted a starring vehicle for his protégée Cornelia Sharpe, who had appeared as the blond dancer in *Serpico,* which he also produced. He and a team of writers came up with the idea of an international professional assassin—Nicole Scott, the bored playgirl daughter of the former Ambassador to the Court of St. James's, who makes love to her targets and kills for kicks. That has to tell us something.

With sequences staged in the Bahamas, Bavaria, Ireland, Morocco, Nice, the United Kingdom, and New York, the picture looks like the record of a producer's vacation. Cornelia Sharpe is photographed in exotic locations shampooing herself, waterskiing, riding, dancing (excruciatingly) at a West Indian carnival; she wears feathers, furs, and a lot of nothing at all. The movie is a series of picture postcards of her long thighs and tidy bottom, and the cast of Arabs, Iraqis, and various Mideastern spies and potentates, plus New York police and federal agents, seems handpicked so that their rough skins and bulbous noses will set off her porcelain smoothness. She's the only young woman in the crowded cast, and wherever she is and whatever she's doing—shooting intruders or kissing a man before suffocating him in a plastic bag—her skin is taut and creamy, and her pouty lower lip is moist. There's no role here, but then she's no actress, either; a lynx-faced former model, she speaks tonelessly and slits her eyes to express emotion. There are chansons on the sound track for class, and behind each scene is the fervent yet unwarranted hope of turning Cornelia Sharpe into the hot-ice blond princess of Hollywood—the new Faye Dunaway.

The hero, played by Sean Connery, is a visionary Saudi Arabian diplomat who's trying to bring about world peace and whose first step is to form a partnership with Israel. (Bregman himself plays the Israeli leader who makes the pact.) The Arab is a gourmet cook, a sportsman, a connoisseur of art objects, and a wizard at backgammon; he's Christ and James Bond, too, and he and the killer shiksa display their competitive gamesmanship and romantic prowess. Connery, in the unenviable role of the best of men, walks through the picture dutifully, reciting gaseous speeches; he's such an image of perfection that a likable young actor named Marco St. John, who plays a federal agent, swipes the picture from him by the simple strategy of chewing gum. *The Next Man* teeters on the edge of parody without giving itself the relief of falling over. It's a four-million-dollar Grade B movie, with anti-terrorist sentiments tossed in between the bombs, bullets, and knives, and the bodies being hurled out windows. When the director, Richard C. Sarafian, can get the cheesecake and the high-flown dialogue out of the way, he and his crew show their skill by the urgency and speed of the brutal suspense scenes—so violence is the only thing *The Next Man* has going for it.

This movie is about a love object who, the movie tells us, has no love in her. That's not such a bad theme; it certainly worked in *Double Indemnity*. But *The Next Man* doesn't seem to know that that's its theme, and so it doesn't know that it needs some playful sadomasochistic chemistry between the lofty hero and the cold-hearted woman; it needs the suggestion that he couldn't love a woman who loved him. *The Next Man* doesn't seem to get the point that its hero has hangups; it just wears its subconscious on its sleeve.

[November 15, 1976]

The Curse

*C*arrie is a terrifyingly lyrical thriller. The director, Brian De Palma, has mastered a teasing style—a perverse mixture of comedy and horror and tension, like that of Hitchcock or Polanski, but with a lulling sensuousness. He builds our apprehensions languorously, softening us for the kill. You know you're being manipulated, but he works in such a literal way and with so much candor that you have the pleasure of observing how he affects your susceptibilities even while you're going into shock. Scary-and-funny must be the greatest combination for popular entertainment; anything-and-funny is, of course, great—even funny-and-funny. But we come out of a movie like *Carrie,* as we did out of *Jaws,* laughing at our own childishness. It's like watching our team win a ballgame—we're almost embarrassed at how bracing it is.

This little gothic in a high-school setting has a script by Lawrence D. Cohen taken from Stephen King's unassuming potboiler about a miserable, repressed high-school senior—the daughter of a fanatically religious woman—who has never been accepted by other kids. Carrie (Sissy Spacek) is so withdrawn that she's a slug; her energy is released only telekinetically, in small ways that people don't recognize. (Objects have a habit of crashing when she's around.) At the beginning of the movie, she has her first period—at sixteen—in the gym shower, and doesn't know what's happened. She panics—she thinks she's bleeding to death. Her ignorance makes her a scapegoat for the other girls in the gym; their ugly feelings about their own periods erupt, and, like junior versions of Russ Meyer's Supervixens, they laugh hysterically and pelt her with tampons and sanitary napkins. The gym teacher penalizes them for their cruelty, and a few of them scheme to get even with Carrie. Their plan is to have her elected prom queen and then humiliate her publicly. What we see that they don't see is the depth of Carrie's desire to be accepted by them. Her joy at having Tommy, the most popular boy in the class, ask her to the prom and at becoming prom queen transforms her; her home life is so horrible that this is her first taste of feeling beautiful, and she's a radiant Cinderella. De Palma, a master sadist, prolongs her moments of happiness; he slows the action down to a trance while we wait for the trap to be sprung, knowing that it will unloose her bottled-up telekinetic anger. It's a beautiful plot—a teen-age Cinderella's revenge. *Carrie* becomes a new trash archetype, and De Palma, who has the wickedest baroque sensibility at large in American movies, points up its archetypal aspects by parodying the movies that have formed it—and outclassing them.

De Palma was born in 1940 and started moviemaking when he was a sophomore at Columbia, in 1959. *Carrie* is his tenth feature. His eighth, *Phantom of the Paradise,* a rock-horror satire, was, I thought, an underground-movie explosion—a slapstick Guignol mad ball—but it got a substantially bad press and is just now going into general release. His ninth, *Obsession,* though no more than an exercise in style, with the camera swirling around nothingness, was great on-the-job training for *Carrie.* Here, the layered gags that have always been his specialty are joined to his new sweeping, circling camera movements. In the Joyce Carol Oates story "Where Are You Going, Where Have You Been?" a teen-age girl's desire for romance also turns into a teen-age nightmare, but the story has the ineluctable *National Enquirer* horror that often makes one recoil from Oates, wanting to go on reading yet not sure if one can bear what's coming. De Palma's humor—his delight in trashiness—saves us from that kind of distress. *Carrie* is a menstrual joke—a *film noir* in red. This picture has some of the psychic grip of *Taxi Driver,* yet isn't frightening in the same way, because it's essentially a pretty piece of paste jewelry. *Carrie* looks like a piece of candy: when De Palma is most distinctive, his work calls up so many junky memories it's pure candied exploitation—a funny archetypal nightmare. De Palma uses tawdriness as a tuning fork. No one else has ever caught the thrill that teen-agers get from a dirty joke and sustained it for a whole picture.

There are no characters in *Carrie*; there are only schlock artifacts. The performers enlarge their roles with tinny mythic echoes; each is playing a whole cluster of remembered pop figures. Sissy Spacek's Carrie goes to Bates High—Norman Bates ran the motel in *Psycho*—and her gym-shower scene is a variation on the famous *Psycho* shower. At home, Carrie is the unloved Patty Duke in the early scenes of *The Goddess,* but when, having made herself a dress, she goes to the prom, she's also Katharine Hepburn in *Alice Adams,* and when she's with her yellow-haired escort, the sensitive jock Tommy (William Katt), they're a puppy-love version of Streisand and Redford in *The Way We Were.* ("Love Among the Stars" is the theme the students have selected for their prom.) After Carrie's fall from grace, she's a teen-ager gone bad, an avenging angel with a fiery sword. At her command, fire hoses stand up like hissing serpents and attack her schoolmates, and she moves through the pandemonium with psychedelic grace, as remote as the queen in *She.*

De Palma has a background in theatre as well as in film; he's very canny about young performers (in his first, shoestring feature, *The Wedding Party,* he used Jill Clayburgh and Robert De Niro), and he appears to have had a freedom in casting which wasn't evident in *Obsession.* William Katt doesn't just look like Redford but acts like a fantasy of Redford at seventeen. The dark girl with the frizzies who persuades Tommy to take Carrie to the prom is played by Amy Irving; this girl's involvement in trapping Carrie is left too ambiguous, but Amy Irving is affectingly troubled in every scene she has, right up to the film's last shocker, when De Palma does a triumphant reprise of a poorly staged bit in *Deliverance.* (The shocker here is as startling as Finlay Currie's appearance in the graveyard in *Great Expectations.*) The older "normal" characters don't have much life; there's no ricochet effect from the movies they're drawn from, and they're just puppets. But the high-school students—each with a whopper crop of hair—bounce off the beach-party movies and *Peyton Place* and *Splendor in the Grass* and *American Graffiti.* The villains, the exuberant, beer-guzzling Billy (John Travolta, who might be Warren Beatty's lowlife younger brother) and his bitchy girlfriend Chris (Nancy Allen), with her lewd dimples and puffed ringlets, have the best dialogue— their language is so stunted that every second word is profane. When these two make out in a car, Andy Hardy is brought up to date: besieged by a voracious female, he's the Neanderthal stud in a porno. Later, when Billy and Chris are enjoying their viciousness to Carrie, they have a bile-green tinge like Margaret Hamilton in *The Wizard of Oz.*

Though few actresses have distinguished themselves in gothics, Sissy Spacek, who is onscreen almost continuously, gives a classic chameleon performance. She shifts back and forth and sideways: a nasal, whining child pleading for her mother's love, each word scratching her throat as it comes out; a chaste young beauty at the prom; and then a second transformation when her destructive impulses burst out and age her. Sissy Spacek uses her freckled pallor and whitish eyelashes to suggest a squashed, froggy girl who could go in any direction; at times, she seems unborn—a fetus. I don't see how this performance could be any better; she's touching, like Elizabeth Hartman in one of her victim roles, but she's also unearthly—a changeling. Though her showiest scenes are the luminous moments with her fresh-faced, lion-maned young Redford, her acting range is demonstrated in the scenes with her loony mother—played by Piper Laurie, in a spectacular return to the screen. (Her last film was *The Hustler,* in 1961.) They're marvellously matched, and they perform duets on themes heard earlier from Tuesday Weld and Lola Albright in *Lord Love a Duck.* The skinny, croaking Carrie, with her long, straight reddish-gold hair, and the ripe woman, with her mass of curly red hair and deep, pipe-organ voice (the chest tones of an evangelist or of a woman giving testimony in church), are beautiful in such different Pre-Raphaelite ways that their scenes go beyond the simple mother-daughter conflicts of the rather crude script. Piper Laurie's face is soft—she's like a rosy Elizabeth Taylor—and you feel that the daughter is bound to her by ties of love and pain. This fundamentalist mother is powerful and sexy, yet she sees herself as a virgin damaged by sex. When the wounded daughter retaliates against her mother's assault, and the kitchen utensils fly into Mama, pinning her like St. Sebastian, Piper Laurie's face is relaxed and at peace—she's a radiant martyr in a chromo. Like Buñuel, De Palma has a sacrilegious sense of humor; he plays with a sense of sin.

The director James Whale worked sophisticated parody into some of his horror films, such as *The Old Dark House,* in 1932, and *The Bride of Frankenstein,* in 1935, but I don't think that before *Carrie* anyone had ever done a satiric homage to exploitation films. Who but De Palma would think of using old-movie trash, and even soft-core pornos, to provide "heart" for a thriller? The banal teen-age-movie meanness that the kids show toward Carrie gets the audience rooting for her, and it becomes the basis for her supernatural vengeance. This is the first time a De Palma picture has had heart—which may explain why De Palma, despite his originality, has never made it into the big winners' circle before. I liked the surreal sophomoric humor of his 1968 X-rated *Greetings,* with its draft-dodger hero; the style was deliberately offhand. In those days, De Palma didn't move the camera much; he used a lot of single-camera setups that went on for several minutes—he let the actors play out their scenes. When he did move the camera, sometimes the movement was itself a gag—a parody of film "magic." His early films were cheaply made and badly distributed, but even so they didn't score with young audiences as they should have scored. Maybe this was the audiences' fault as much as his. Like some others of us, he probably assumed that counterculture movie-lovers had much hipper tastes than they turned out to have; they didn't go for the old patriotic, pro-war sentimentality, but they wanted more emotion and romance than De Palma, with his sense of the ridiculous, provided. However, he was always primarily a creator of comedy, an entertainer, so if the audience wouldn't change, he had to.

By the time of *Obsession,* De Palma had dropped his theatrical play-out-the-scene style; rock had unified the wild *Phantom of the Paradise,* but the camera itself did it for *Obsession.* He made a romantic movie without, as far as I can judge, a single romantic impulse; he was proving that he could tell a fluid, rhythmed story—that he could master camera magic. It was all calculation—camera movements designed to make an audience swoon. If the De Palma spirit was barely in evidence in *Obsession,* that was because the romantic conception operated on only one level; it lacked humor—this is where Paul Schrader, its scenarist, is weak (a weakness compensated for by the director and actors in Schrader's *Taxi Driver*). And *Obsession* lacked good, cheap dirt. In *Greetings,* Allen Garfield had hawked stag films; De Niro was a voyeur making Peep Art films in both *Greetings* and De Palma's *Hi, Mom!* After the rarefied phoniness of *Obsession*, De Palma has come back to his own exploitation themes in *Carrie*; the voyeur has got into the girls' locker room this time, bringing that romanticizing, hypnotic camera with him. De Palma was always a sexual wit; now he's a voluptuary wit, with the camera coming very close to Sissy Spacek's body, and with closeups of her wraithlike, hair-veiled face. We know her skin better than we know our own.

The technique is so absorbing that I don't think I blinked during *Carrie*. I assume that a virtuoso combination of the spiky editing of Paul Hirsch and the special effects by Gregory M. Auer is what gives us images such as Carrie's eye exploding a car. Mario Tosi's slithering cinematography seemed especially effective in Carrie's California-gothic home, and I assume that the art directors, William Kenny and Jack Fisk, made that possible. The music for *Obsession* was so emotive that the picture drowned in its score; the Pino Donaggio music for *Carrie* is modest and inoffensive, though more derivative than one might like. There are only a few places where the film seems to err in technique. The speeded-up sound when the high-school boys are trying on tuxedos is a dumb, toy effect. And at the prom, when Carrie sees red, the split-screen footage is really bad: the red tint darkens the image, and there's so much messy action going on in the split sections that the confusion cools us out. But the film is built like a little engine, and it gets to us.

For a sophisticated, absurdist intelligence like De Palma's, there's no way to use camera magic except as foolery. He's uncommitted to anything except successful manipulation; when his camera conveys the motion of dreams, it's a lovely trick. He can't treat a subject straight, but that's all right; neither could Hitchcock. If De Palma were an artist in another medium—say, fiction or poetry—he might be a satirist with a high reputation and a small following. Everything in his films is distanced by his persistent adolescent kinkiness; he's gleefully impersonal. Yet, working in movies, he's found his own route to a mass audience: his new trash heart is the ultimate De Palma joke.

[November 22, 1976]

Stallone and Stahr

Chunky, muscle-bound Sylvester Stallone looks repulsive one moment, noble the next, and sometimes both at once. In *Rocky*, which he wrote and stars in, he's a thirty-year-old club fighter who works as a strong-arm man, collecting money for a loan shark. Rocky never got anywhere, and he has nothing; he lives in a Philadelphia tenement, and even the name he fights under—the Italian Stallion—has become a joke. But the world heavyweight champion, Apollo Creed (Carl Weathers), who's a smart black jester, like Muhammad Ali, announces that for his Bicentennial New Year's fight he'll give an unknown a shot at the title, and he picks the Italian Stallion for the racial-sexual overtones of the contest. This small romantic fable is about a palooka gaining his manhood; it's Terry Malloy finally getting his chance to be somebody. *Rocky* is a threadbare patchwork of old-movie bits (*On the Waterfront, Marty, Somebody Up There Likes Me,* Capra's *Meet John Doe,* and maybe even a little of Preston Sturges' *Hail the Conquering Hero*), yet it's engaging, and the naïve elements are emotionally effective. John G. Avildsen's directing is his usual strictly-from-hunger approach; he slams through a picture like a poor man's Sidney Lumet. But a more painstaking director would have been too proud to shoot the mildewed ideas and would have tried to throw out as many as possible and to conceal the others—and would probably have wrecked the movie. *Rocky* is shameless, and that's why—on a certain level—it works. What holds it together is innocence.

In his offscreen bravado, Stallone (in Italian *stallone* means stallion) has claimed that he wrote the script in three and a half days, and some professional screenwriters, seeing what a ragtag of a script it is, may think that they could have done it in two and a half. But they wouldn't have been able to believe in what they did, and it wouldn't have got the audience cheering, the way *Rocky* does. The innocence that makes this picture so winning emanates from Sylvester Stallone. It's a street-wise, flowers-blooming-in-the-garbage innocence. Stallone plays a waif, a strong-arm man who doesn't want to hurt anybody, a loner with only his pet turtles to talk to. Yet the character doesn't come across as maudlin. Stallone looks

213

like a big, battered Paul McCartney. There's bullnecked energy in him, smoldering; he has a field of force, like Brando's. And he knows how to use his overripe, cartoon sensuality—the eyelids at half-mast, the sad brown eyes and twisted, hurt mouth. Victor Mature also had this thick sensuality, but the movies used him as if it were simple plushy handsomeness, and so he became ridiculous, until he learned—too late—to act. Stallone is aware that we see him as a hulk, and he plays against this comically and tenderly. In his deep, caveman's voice, he gives the most surprising, sharp, fresh shadings to his lines. He's at his funniest trying to explain to his boss why he didn't break somebody's thumbs, as he'd been told to; he's even funny talking to his turtles. He pulls the whiskers off the film's cliché situations, so that we're constantly charmed by him, waiting for what he'll say next. He's like a child who never ceases to amaze us.

Stallone has the gift of direct communication with the audience. Rocky's naïve observations come from so deep inside him that they have a Lewis Carroll enchantment. His unworldliness makes him seem dumb, but we know better; we understand what he feels at every moment. Rocky is the embodiment of the out-of-fashion pure-at-heart. His macho strut belongs with the ducktails of the fifties—he's a sagging peacock. I'm not sure how much of his archaism is thought out, how much is the accidental result of Stallone's overdeveloped, weight lifter's muscles combined with his simplistic beliefs, but Rocky represents the redemption of an earlier ideal—the man as rock for woman to cleave to. Talia Shire plays Adrian, a shy girl with glasses who works in a pet store; she's the Betsy Blair to Stallone's Marty. It's unspeakably musty, but they put it over; her delicacy (that of a button-faced Audrey Hepburn) is the right counterpoint to his primitivism. It's clear that he's drawn to her because she isn't fast or rough and doesn't make fun of him; she doesn't make hostile wisecracks, like the other woman in the pet store, or talk dirty, like the kids in the street. We don't groan at this, because he's such a *tortured* macho nice-guy—he has failed his own high ideals. And who doesn't have a soft spot for the teen-age aspirations congealed inside this thirty-year-old bum?

Stallone is the picture, but the performers who revolve around him are talented. Carl Weathers, a former Oakland Raiders linebacker, is a real find. His Apollo Creed has the flash and ebullience to put the fairy-tale plot in motion; when the champ arrives at the ring dressed as Uncle Sam, no one could enjoy the racial joke as much as he does. Adrian's heavyset brother Paulie is played by Burt Young, who has been turning up in movies more and more frequently in the past three years and still gives the impression that his abilities haven't begun to be tapped. Young, who actually was a professional fighter, has the cracked, mottled voice of someone who's taken a lot of punishment in the sinuses; the resonance is gone. As Mickey, the ancient pug who runs a fighters' gym, Burgess Meredith uses the harsh, racking sound of a man who's been punched too often in the vocal cords. The director overemphasizes Meredith's performance (much as John Schlesinger did in *The Day of the Locust*); Meredith would look better if we were left to discover how good he is for ourselves. I found *Marty* dreary, because the people in it were sapped of energy. But Stallone and Talia Shire and the others here have a restrained force; you feel that they're being pressed down, that they're under a lid. The only one who gets a chance to explode is Paulie, when, in a rage, he wields a baseball bat, and it's a poor scene, out of tune. Yet the actors themselves have so much more to them than they're using that what comes across in their performances is what's under the lid. The actors—and this includes Joe Spinell as Gazzo, Rocky's gangster boss—enable us to feel their reserves of intelligence; they provide tact and taste, which aren't in long supply in an Avildsen film.

Rocky is the kind of movie in which the shots are underlighted, because the characters are poor and it's wintertime. I was almost never convinced that the camera was in the right place. The shots don't match well, and they're put together jerkily, with cheap romantic music thrown in like cement blocks of lyricism, and sheer noise used to build up excitement at the climactic prizefight, where the camera is so close to the fighters that you can't feel the rhythm of the encounter. And the film doesn't follow through on what it prepares. Early on, we see Rocky with the street-corner kids in his skid-row neighborhood, but we never get to see how these kids react to his training or to the fight itself. Even the bull mastiff who keeps Rocky company on his early-morning runs is lost track of. I get the feeling that Avildsen is so impatient to finish a film on schedule (or before, as if it were a race) that he hardly bothers to think it out. I hate the way *Rocky* is made, yet better might be worse in this case. Unless a director could take this material and transform it into sentimental urban poetry—a modern equivalent of what Frank Borzage used to do in pictures such as *Man's Castle,* with Spencer Tracy and Loretta Young—we're probably better off with Avildsen's sloppiness than with careful planning; a craftsmanlike *Rocky* would be obsolete, like a TV play of the fifties.

Stallone can certainly write; that is, he can write scenes and dialogue. But as a writer he stays inside the character; we never get a clear outside view of Rocky. For that, Stallone falls back on clichés, on an urban-primitive myth: at the end, Rocky has everything a man needs—his manhood, his woman, maybe even his dog. (If it were rural-primitive, he'd have some land, too.) In a sense, *Rocky* is a piece of innocent art, but its innocence doesn't sit too well. The bad side of *Rocky* is its resemblance to *Marty*—its folklorish, grubby littleness. Unpretentiousness shouldn't be used as a virtue. This warmed-over bum-into-man myth is unworthy of the freak macho force of its star; talking to turtles is too endearing. What separates Stallone from a Brando is that everything Stallone does has one purpose: to make you like him. He may not know how good he could be if he'd stop snuggling into your heart. If not—well, he may be to acting what Mario Lanza was to singing, and that's a form of bumminess.

□ □ □

Monroe Stahr, the young hero of Scott Fitzgerald's *The Last Tycoon,* is meant to represent the last of a breed; he's an individualistic artist-businessman who runs his movie studio like a small grocery store. Polite and paternalistic, he's beloved by the studio technicians, but he's not necessarily a princely figure to the directors, writers, and actors. Stahr hires teams of writers to work—unbeknownst to each other—on the same project. He is the inventor of the factory system of movie production, and he treats the artists as irresponsible children. *He* provides the unity, he says: he is the moviemaker. And, as Fitzgerald sees him, Stahr has the heart and soul of an artist without the crazy weaknesses of artists.

The Last Tycoon is possibly the only Hollywood novel that takes a producer for its hero. Fitzgerald's view of Stahr, who was based on the boy wonder Irving Thalberg, the head of production at M-G-M in the twenties and early thirties, is one that few besides studio heads, and possibly Sam Spiegel, who produced the new film *The Last Tycoon,* are likely to share. But Fitzgerald wasn't merely being sycophantic about power; the aloof Thalberg had represented "quality" films, and his battle with Louis B. Mayer for control of M-G-M was central to the Hollywood of the thirties. The novel, which was no more than a rough draft of the early sections, plus notes, when Fitzgerald died, in 1940, was envisioned as a large-scale portrait of an artist-businessman corrupted by corporate pressures. A number of movies could be made from the fragmentary material. One of them might be a story about Monroe Stahr as a fallen angel, but the most promising story would probably be that of a man whose whole conscious, creative life is the movie business. He has more class and more imagination than his business associates have, and more of an instinct for what audiences want from movies. But the barracudas who care only about profits hate him for his artist's sensibility and his rabbinical righteousness. And so when he falls in love and, temporarily distracted, fails to protect his flank, they take the business away from him. Or, to put it vulgarly, he blows it for a broad. Vulgar or not, that's essentially what Fitzgerald's rough draft is about, though it comes through only feebly in the Spiegel production, directed by Elia Kazan, from a Harold Pinter script.

While we're still in an anticipatory frame of mind, wondering why the inside views of big-studio moviemaking in the thirties and our first glimpses of Robert De Niro as Stahr are so dispirited, the story shifts to Stahr's affair with Kathleen (Ingrid Boulting), the Anglo-Irish girl he's attracted to because she resembles his dead movie-star wife. And every time Ingrid Boulting appears onscreen the picture comes to a full stop. There's lovely goo in most of Fitzgerald's fiction; it's the most fragrant essence of adolescent romanticism in American literature—and who else, except maybe Salinger, could turn snobbishness into a form of sensitivity? But though the dreamy crushes of Fitzgerald's doomed heroes are very appealing on the page, they don't come across on the screen. And, of all his implausible heroines, Kathleen (presumably based on Sheilah Graham) is the most vaporous. She wrecks the book: her conversation has no trace of life. I can't imagine how Fitzgerald's conception of her could be redeemed and I don't understand why the movie didn't just dump her and come up with a woman who could excite a man like Stahr yet leave him feeling so uncertain that he'd fail to grab her when he had the chance. The point is, Stahr loses the broad as well as the business; I put it in this offensively basic way because the movie has no sense of basics. It heads for fanciness every time, and its attempt at exact re-creation of the dim Kathleen—the runaway mistress of a European king—is fatal.

De Niro's Stahr may be the most authentic interpretation yet of a New York–Jewish Hollywood intellectual giant of the thirties. At first, De Niro's voice takes a little getting used to, it's so quiet, flat, uninflected. Then everything seems right: the formal manner, the double-breasted dark suits and thick, wavy, carefully brushed-back hair, the controlled exercise of power. De Niro's handsome profile belongs in the California-Spanish Art Deco settings; it was the era of profile-consciousness, and he has the sleek thirties look one sees in photographs of George Gershwin. De Niro catches the seriousness of a young genius who acts much older than he is; when Stahr grins, he looks furtively silly. When he explains to Boxley (Donald Pleasence), the illustrious British writer he has hired, how a movie should get an audience involved in a story, he enjoys acting out his demonstration; it's Stahr the pedant giving a lesson and having his little joke. De Niro's young-old man performance is finely modulated, yet there's no charge in it. He might be acting under a blanket, which he can never shake off. He stands there waiting while Ingrid Boulting—a pretty young girl with a big, round head, like those face lollipops we used to have as kids—loiters over inane remarks, breaking up her sentences with pauses and looking off to the side. Trying to be mysterious, she seems dazed, yet aware of her darlingness. This performance has to be at least partly the director's fault; she's so shallow that De Niro obviously can't get anything from her to react to. Besides, he doesn't have the lines.

Harold Pinter is said to have spent a year and a half working on the script—presumably in reverent noodling, since he has rearranged the book's dialogue and hasn't added much. Kazan has been quoted as saying, "I didn't change any of Pinter's words." This is reverence piled upon reverence. If the movie is, as I think, a tragedy—a series of disastrous mistakes by intelligent, gifted, well-meaning people—probably the first mistake was to approach the book cap in hand, and the next was to hire

217

Pinter. The film needed a writer who would fill in the characters and clarify the conflict between the creative Stahr and the crass Louis B. Mayer figure—Brady (Robert Mitchum), who's out to shaft him. Stahr can't just be reticent; we have to see the fighter in him. But Pinter doesn't supply what's missing; Pinter's art is the art of taking away. And less can be less. Though Pinter's specialty is threat and tension, the movie doesn't make us aware of the danger that Stahr is in. Inexplicably, Pinter has left in practically every damned letter and telegram that the characters in the book sent each other, and there are pointless, dangling scenes, such as Brady's daughter Cecilia (Theresa Russell) discovering a naked woman in her father's office. But there's so little time given to the fight for control within the studio that those who haven't read the book will think that Stahr is dumped from power just because he got drunk and took a swing at a union organizer (Jack Nicholson).

The film is bewilderingly mute and inexpressive. Kazan's work seems to be a reaction against the shrill energy he has sometimes used to keep a picture going. He's trying for something quiet and revelatory, but he seems to have disowned too much of his temperament. Though the picture certainly has promising characters, they remain potential, tentative. There's no impetus, so you question everything you see; you're aware of the lame discomfort of the performers—the closeups of Theresa Russell's traumatic, overcosmetized face, the absence of dialogue which strands Ray Milland (as the studio lawyer), Dana Andrews (as a director whom Stahr fires), and many others. The scenes remain scenes; they don't flow together. When Stahr orders a sequence in a glamorous melodrama to be reshot because of the high-toned falseness of the dialogue that the Britisher Boxley wrote, we don't know how to react, because the dialogue isn't the only thing wrong with the footage. The faces don't have the thirties sheen, the lights and shadows don't jump out at you the way they should, there's no buoyancy in the action, and even the rejuvenating makeup job on the aging woman star (Jeanne Moreau), for which Stahr congratulates the makeup woman, is singularly ineffective. Early in the film, most of the characters are gathered at a writers' ball, which probably has more of the old Hollywood aura than anything else we see; when Stahr, pursuing Kathleen, leaves, we resent her for taking him—and us—away from the party. We want to be back inside, where there might be some action.

You can't really believe that Stahr is running a factory that's churning out pictures. The movie world that Kazan shows us has no hustle. The characters are so enervated that *The Last Tycoon* is a vampire movie after the vampires have left. There's only one performance with true vitality: Tony Curtis as Rodriguez, the boudoir-swordsman star who has become impotent and, ashamed to face his public, rushes to Stahr, the father figure, for help. Rodriguez's eyes are so busily alive as he describes his plight that you can see the eager young actor he once was inside the tanned, upholstered-in-muscles star. (Rodriguez is avid, like Curtis's Sidney Falco in *Sweet Smell of Success*.) However, the moviemakers don't seem to have paid any more attention to the lesson in moviemaking which Monroe Stahr gave Boxley than Boxley did; they feel so little respect for the plain fun of storytelling that they have Stahr cure Rodriguez's impotence without our ever finding out how he did it. Worse, Spiegel and Kazan let Pinter get away with a Pinteresque dribbling-away finish: we don't learn what happens to Monroe Stahr—instead, we see him demonstrating once *again* how to tell a story in the movies. They must not have respected Stahr's crude, honest point: he was explaining how you hook an audience, not what you send it home with. The film's ending is the real confession of impotence.

[November 29, 1976]

Hot Air

In *Network,* Paddy Chayefsky blitzes you with one idea after another. The ideas don't go together, but who knows which of them he believes, anyway? He's like a Village crazy bellowing at you: blacks are taking over, revolutionaries are taking over, women are taking over. He's got the New York City hatreds, and ranting makes him feel alive. There *is* something funny in this kind of rant—it was funny in Fred Wiseman's *Welfare,* too; with the number of things that are going wrong in the city, it's a bottomless comedy to see people pinning their rage on some one object, person, or group, or a pet collection of them. Cabdrivers used to get it off on Mayor Lindsay, liberals on the moon landings, and now Chayefsky's getting it off on television. Television, he says, is turning us into morons and humanoids; people have lost the ability to love. Who—him? Oh, no, the blacks, the revolutionaries, and a power-hungry executive at the UBS network named Diana Christensen (Faye Dunaway). In Chayefsky's 1958 movie *The Goddess,* the Marilyn Monroe–type heroine (Kim Stanley) sought movie stardom, fame, and adulation in order to compensate for her inability to love. This empty girl was supposed to symbolize our dreams; moviegoers were his morons then. Chayefsky said in 1958 that his heroine "represents an entire generation that came through the Depression with nothing left but a hope for comfort and security. Their tragedy lies in that they never learned to love, either their fellow humans or whatever god they have." God and love came together in his 1959 play *The Tenth Man*, which ended with an old man saying of the hero, whose demon (of lovelessness) had been exorcised, "He still doesn't believe in God—he simply wants to love—and when you stop and think about it, gentlemen, is there any difference?" This mushy amalgam of God and love is Chayefsky's faith, and if you don't share it you're tragic. The new goddess, the unprincipled career girl Diana Christensen, is explained in *Network* in these terms: "She's television generation. She learned life from Bugs Bunny. The only reality she knows comes to her over the TV set." What Chayefsky is really complaining about is what barroom philosophers have always complained about: the soulless worshippers at false shrines—the younger generation.

In Chayefsky's last film, *The Hospital* (1971), the fiftyish Jewish chief of medicine (George C. Scott) has lost his potency, fails at suicide, and is disappointed in his children; he blows off steam about what's wrong with the society but ridicules the Puerto Rican community-action groups who march on the hospital. After an affair with a young Wasp (Diana Rigg), who urges him to leave with her, he decides that *somebody* has to be decent and responsible, and so, with his potency restored, he stays to make his stand for sanity. Youth-baiting played a strong part in *The Hospital*, but Chayefsky's slapstick exaggeration of the chaos in a big-city institution had so much silly, likable crackpot verve that the diatribes against the disrespectful younger generation could be shrugged aside. *Network*, however, is all baiting—youth, TV, the culture, the universe. The UBS network has been taken over by a conglomerate, and Howard Beale (Peter Finch), a veteran anchorman whose ratings have slipped, is given two weeks' notice by executives who want to jazz up the news to make it more entertaining. Angry at being dumped, Beale goes out of control, and his blasts on the air about "this demented slaughterhouse of a world we live in"—blasts sprinkled with cusswords—accomplish what his restrained behavior didn't: his ratings go up. His best friend, the head of the news division—the fiftyish hero, Max Schumacher (William Holden), who is Paddy Chayefsky in the guise of the unimpeachable Ed Murrow—loses his fight to keep the news independent. The chief of operations (Robert Duvall) fires him and turns the news division over to Diana Christensen, the vice-president in charge of programming. So when Beale begins to have visions (either he's having a breakdown or he's in a state of religious exaltation) and is advertised as "the Mad Prophet of the airwaves," Schumacher is on the sidelines, and has nothing to do but hang around Diana Christensen, with whom he has an affair, and denounce her, television, and us soulless masses. The Mad Prophet and the sane prophet both deliver broadsides—enough to break a viewer's back. The screen seems to be plastered with bumper stickers.

The central gag in *Network*—Howard Beale becomes the first man killed because of lousy ratings—sounds like a good premise for a farce about TV, which has certainly earned farce status. (And, even if it hadn't, satire doesn't have to be fair to be funny.) But in the *Network* script Chayefsky isn't writing a farce: he's telling us a thing or two. And he writes directly to the audience—he soapboxes. He hardly bothers with the characters; the movie is a ventriloquial harangue. He thrashes around in messianic God-love booziness, driving each scene to an emotional peak. When Schumacher tells his wife (Beatrice Straight) that he's in love with Diana, his wife launches into a high-powered speech about "all the senseless pain that we've inflicted on each other," referring to his affair as "your last roar of passion before you settle into your menopausal years." It's a short, self-contained soap opera; she hits her peak—then she's invisible again. The director, Sidney Lumet, keeps the soliloquies going at a machine-gun pace. The movie might have been modelled on that earlier talk binge, Billy Wilder's *One, Two, Three*; Lumet is right—it's best not to let the words sink in. With Schumacher experiencing a "winter passion" and discussing his "primal doubts," you have to hurtle through to the next crisis. Lumet does Chayefsky straight, just as Chayefsky no doubt wanted. The film looks negligently made; the lighting bleaches the actors' faces, like color TV that needs tuning, and the New York views outside the office and apartment windows feel like blown-up photographs. The timing in most of the scenes is so careless that you may be aware of the laugh lines you're not responding to, and there's a confusing cut from Diana and Schumacher planning to go to bed together to Howard Beale in bed by himself. *Network* even fails to show the executives at meetings getting carried away by the infectiousness of Diana Christensen's ideas—getting high on power. But Lumet keeps it all moving.

Chayefsky is such a manic bard that I'm not sure if he ever decided whether Howard Beale's epiphanies were the result of a nervous breakdown or were actually inspired by God. Yet Beale's story has a fanciful, Frank Capra nuttiness that could be appealing. Peter Finch's sleepy-lion head suggests the bland, prosperous decay of an anchorman whose boredom is swathed in punditry. His gray aureole is perfect: the curly, thick hair, cropped short, is the only vigorous thing about him. (Does Finch, who is British-Australian, seem American? Not really, but then does Eric Sevareid, who comes from North Dakota?) If Chayefsky meant Beale to represent his idealized vision of the crusading mandarin journalists of an earlier day who are now being replaced by show-biz anchorpersons, Finch is miscast, but his fuzzy mildness is likable, and in a picture in which everybody seems to take turns at screaming (Robert Duvall screams the loudest) Finch's ability to seem reserved even when he's raving has its own satirical charm. Unfortunately, when Beale's wild-eyed ramblings are supposed to make his ratings zoom up, you can't believe it; he doesn't give off enough heat.

Beale the Prophet's big moment comes when he tells TV viewers to open their windows, stick out their heads, and yell, "I'm mad as hell and I'm not going to take this anymore!" But is the viewers' obedience proof of their sheeplike response to TV or is it evidence that the Prophet has struck a nerve—that the public is as fed up as he is? Considering that the entire picture is Chayefsky sticking his head out the window and yelling (in Chayefsky's world, that's how you prove that you're capable of love), it must be that Beale's message is supposed to be salutary. Yet there's no follow-through on this scene, and that's where the movie goes completely on the fritz. Chayefsky whirrs off in other directions—Max's winter passion for Diana, and the Saudi Arabians taking over the conglomerate.

Early on, Howard Beale is awakened at night by the voice of the Lord or some Heavenly Messenger, who affectionately calls him "Dummy" and tells him what he must do on the air. The voice may be simply Beale's delusion, but how are we to interpret the turn of events when Beale is summoned to a meeting with the piggy-eyed master salesman Arthur Jensen (Ned Beatty), the head of the conglomerate, and Jensen addresses him as "Dummy"? Jensen, a corn-pone Grand Inquisitor, tells Beale that the multinational corporate state is the natural order of things now, and that he should embrace this one-business world, in which all men will be taken care of as humanoids. Converted, Beale asks the TV audience, "Is dehumanization such a bad word?" He preaches his new corporate faith—"The world is a business . . . one vast, ecumenical holding company." But people don't want to hear that their individual lives are valueless; he loses his ratings and is killed for it. Chayefsky, it seems, can be indignant about people becoming humanoids, and then turn a somersault and say it's inevitable and only a fool wouldn't recognize that. And he's wrong on both counts. There are a lot of changes in the society which can be laid at television's door, but soullessness isn't one of them. TV may have altered family life and social intercourse; it may have turned children at school into entertainment seekers. But it hasn't taken our souls, any more than movies did, or the theatre and novels before them. I don't know what's worse—Beale's denunciations of the illiterate public (Chayefsky apparently thinks that not reading is proof of soullessness) or Schumacher's pitying tone. When Schumacher tells Diana Christensen that she can feel nothing, while he's O.K. because he can feel pleasure and pain and love, you want to kick him. Doesn't Chayefsky realize that everybody can feel—even a kittycat?

The screw-up inside Chayefsky's message of kindness shows in the delight he takes in snide reactionary thrusts. Diana Christensen has no difficulty coöpting an Angela Davis–like activist (Marlene Warfield), the Communist central committee, and an extremist group that's a parody of the Symbionese Liberation Army and the Black Panthers. (Chayefsky can't even resist a sideswipe at Patty Hearst.) Christensen propositions them to perform terrorist crimes—kidnappings, robberies, hijackings—on a weekly basis, in front of a camera crew, and their only quarrel is over money. Whatever one's disagreements with Angela Davis, she's hardly a sellout. Yet Chayefsky's venom is such an exuberant part of him that the best scene in the movie is the slapstick negotiating session in which the black revolutionaries, their agents, and the network attorneys haggle over residuals and syndication rights, and a revolutionary who wants to be heard fires his pistol to get some order. This is in the paranoid-comic-strip style of Norman Wexler, the scriptwriter for *Joe, Serpico,* and *Mandingo.* Chayefsky's speeches may be about humanism, but baiting gets the old adrenalin going.

And what of Diana Christensen, the hopped-up *Cosmopolitan* doll with power on the brain? Look at her name: the goddess of the hunt, and some sort of essence of Christianity? In bed, on top of Schumacher, she talks ratings until orgasm. Chayefsky, in interviews, actually claims that he has created one of the few movie roles in which a woman is treated as an equal; this can be interpreted to mean that he thinks women who want equality are ditsey little twitches—ruthless, no-souled monsters who take men's jobs away from them. Diana Christensen is, Schumacher says, "television incarnate"—that is, she is symptomatic of what's spoiling our society. And, in case we don't get Chayefsky's drift, he presents us with that contrasting image of a loving woman who has the capacity for suffering—Max's wife, to whom he returns after he leaves rotten Diana.

As Schumacher, Holden is in good form, and now that he has stopped trying to conceal the aging process his sunken-cheeked, lined, craggy face takes the camera marvellously—he has a real face, like Gabin or Montand. He does a lot for the movie—he's an actor with authority and the gift of never being boring—but he can't energize the phoniness of a man who claims to be superior to his society. This hero is trampling out the vintage where the sour grapes of wrath are stored. Dunaway chatters as Kim Stanley did in *The Goddess* (Chayefsky must believe that women talk because of their tinny empty-headedness), and even when she's supposed to be reduced to a pitiful shell by Holden's exposing her "shrieking nothingness" she's ticky and amusingly greedy. She snarls at underlings and walks with a bounce and a wiggle. In the past, Dunaway hasn't had much humor or variety; her performances have usually been proficient yet uneventful—there's a certain heaviness, almost of depression, about them. It's that heaviness, probably, that has made some people think her Garboesque. A beautiful woman who's as self-conscious as Faye Dunaway has a special neurotic magnetism. (The far less proficient Kim Novak had it also.) In this stunt role, her usual self-consciousness is turned into comic rapport with the audience; she's not the remote, neurotic beauty—she's more of a clown. And though her Diana isn't remotely convincing—she's not a woman with a drive to power, she's just a dirty Mary Tyler Moore—it's a relief to see Dunaway being light. She puts us on the side of the humanoids.

The watered-down Freudianism that Chayefsky goes in for—i.e., people want fame or power because they're sick—seems to get by almost everywhere these days. It became popular with those analysts who, taking Hitler's crimes as evidence, deduced that he was sexually crippled; they really seemed to think they were explaining something. And it spread in TV drama and in movies as a form of vindictive, moralizing condescension. The trick in *Network,* as in *The Goddess,* is to use a woman's drive toward fame or success as the embodiment of the sickness in the society. What's implicit is that if she could love she wouldn't need anything more. You couldn't get by with this bulling if a man were television incarnate. *Network* starts in high gear and is so confidently brash that maybe people can really take it for muckraking. But it's no more than the kind of inside story that a lot of TV executives probably would secretly like to write. Chayefsky comes on like a patriarchal Jackie Susann, and he likes to frolic with the folksy occult. What happened to his once much-vaunted gift for the vernacular? Nothing exposes his claims to be defending the older values as much as the way he uses four-letter words for chortles. It's so cheap you may never want to say **** again. Chayefsky doesn't come right out and tell us why he thinks TV is *goyish,* but it must have something to do with his notion that all feeling is Jewish.

[December 6, 1976]

Affirmation

*B*ound for Glory, based on Woody Guthrie's autobiography, is superbly lighted and shot, and has the visual beauty of a great movie. It opens in 1936. The young Guthrie (David Carradine), having fled from the poverty of his native Oklahoma, is living in the Texas dust bowl. He has been trying to feed his wife, Mary (Melinda Dillon), and their two daughters by his varied talents—he paints signs, he plays at local square dances—and by his wits. He earns a buck by analyzing a man's character—which is mistaken for fortune-telling—and then two women, hoping that he's also a faith healer, ask him to try to cure a grieving mother. Her little girl died of "the dust pneumonia," and she sits speechless, unable to swallow water. Guthrie talks to her, and his sympathy and good sense reach her, and when he pours water into her mouth she drinks it down. The two women, grateful and relieved, hand him a coin—fifty cents, or perhaps a silver dollar. *Bound for Glory* would be a better movie if he had taken the pay, knowing he had earned it; part of the charm of folk artists is their practicality, and the logic of this scene requires that Guthrie accept what is his due. When he refuses it, he turns into holy Tom Joad, the lover of pore folks. I know that in his autobiography Woody says he refused the money, but it's too self-serving a story for a man to tell about himself. That's part of the problem of making a movie about Woody Guthrie: How can you stay clear of the embalming fluid of saintliness when Guthrie injected it into his own veins?

The man who called his autobiography *Bound for Glory* mythicized himself, and it wasn't just the innocent brag of a four-flusher, it was the deep-seated conviction of a man who saw himself as the voice of the downtrodden—as the embodiment of the masses moving into a bright future, on a train bound for glory. Guthrie published this autobiography in 1943, when he was only thirty; Steinbeck's *The Grapes of Wrath*—both the 1939 book and the 1940 John Ford movie—must have had a huge influence on him. The first half of Guthrie's book, which deals with his happy childhood and then with the family misfortunes that resulted from his mother's illness and pyromania, is a near-classic, and it gains additional poignancy because we know what he didn't when he was writing it—that the undiagnosed illness that destroyed her would claim him also. (He was hospitalized in 1954 with Huntington's chorea, and deteriorated until his death, in 1967.) But when he gets beyond the account of his growing up and into his moving on—which is the part of his life that the film deals with—he seems to swap his own identity for that of Tom Joad. (He later wrote a song about him, and also named one of his sons Joady.) Just past the middle of the book, he writes, "And there on the Texas plains . . . I got a little braver and made up songs telling what I thought was wrong and how to make it right, songs that said what everybody in that country was thinking. And this has held me ever since." But when he starts telling readers "how to make it right," his cocky prose turns folksy. He's no longer a person (he even leaves out his wife and daughters), he's a living rhetorical device. His anecdotes begin to make points about brotherhood, and his characters' talk is rendered in a people-of-the-earth dialect that is as patronizing as Steinbeck's. I think that maybe the moviemakers—particularly the director, Hal Ashby—got seduced by Guthrie's Whitmanesque role-playing. Any movie about the Depression is likely to call up memories of the flatulent Biblical-folk John Ford film, but there's more than a resemblance here. The poor people in this movie seem to be at a rhetorical remove; they made a stop in Steinbeck–John Ford country on the way to us.

Woody Guthrie had a storyteller's gift, the gift of a true folk artist, but he violated it with the rhetoric of a politician. He became a pitchman-troubadour. His best-known song, "This Land Is Your Land," which originally served as an inspirational anthem for the left, is an expression of professional Americanism, with the demagogic uplift of most other anthems. His songs were often calls to action set to music, exhortations—commercials for Popular Front causes, professionally affirmative. His authentic folk poetry and his inauthenticity, too, have come down to us—complexly merged—in the music of his inheritors: Bob Dylan, Phil Ochs, Tom Paxton, Jack Elliott, his son Arlo Guthrie, and many others.

The movie is aware that he was an ornery, contradictory man, who loved "the people" but was too restless to hold on to those who loved him and depended on him, yet it sets him up as a hero by making it appear that he couldn't keep his family without compromising his ideals. The movie contrives a conflict for Guthrie, who has just been given his own show on a Los Angeles radio station. He is put in the position of having to sell out to the radio bosses, who want him to sing innocuous pop-folk music, or abandon his family in order to remain true to the poor people, to whom his songs bring spiritual comfort and encouragement in the fight against injustice. As Carradine plays Guthrie—and he plays him very well—a stubborn integrity seems to be what keeps him, instinctively, an artist, and you can believe in his commitment to singing his own songs. You can believe in his instinctive dedication to the poor. But when Randy Quaid is on hand as a migrant farm worker, Johnson, helping Guthrie make the right choice by telling him that the poor folks out in the fields need those songs of his and would feel betrayed if he stopped singing them, the picture is pouring on the same brand of sanctifying horse manure that Guthrie did. You stop believing, and start wondering if the poor people wouldn't prefer nonpolitical folk music, or even frivolous pop, rather than the songs of the dispossessed which the radicals think are good for them.

The movie sees Woody Guthrie as a man who wasn't corrupted, because he never sold out to the bosses. The more complex story—which it passes over—is whether his identification with the people wasn't self-deceiving. (It could have been another form of corruption.) In the movie, he is seen at a union-organizing meeting where the speakers have failed to convince the workers that they should join up. The workers are fearful of retaliation, and they don't trust the speakers. Woody ends the discussion: he sets doggerel lyrics to an old tune, arouses the workers' spirit, gets their pulses pounding, and convinces them. What was needed, maybe, to do

226

justice to the period was some insight into the possible consequences. Suppose we saw that Communist and quasi-Communist organizers sometimes had such big goals in mind that they were very careless of the immediate consequences for the people they were dedicated to helping, so that in the name of ending suffering they caused additional suffering. Suppose we saw that, because of their political ends, these organizers were often rightly feared and distrusted by the poor. Wouldn't this make Guthrie a more complicatedly involving (and less saintly) figure? Didn't he have to blot out his own doubts about using the emotional power of folk music to organize these homesick migrants? By assuming that Guthrie knew what was best for them, the movie makes the past seem a simple matter of right versus wrong; it sentimentalizes his commitment, and his compulsive drifter's existence. If it had shown that he was perhaps an even bigger hit with the upper-middle-class liberals and leftists at fund-raisers than he was among the poor, the movie might have begun to get at some of the ambiguities of our actual past. This movie is a mythological reworking of Guthrie's spinoff of Depression mythology—which may help to explain why it seems to be pulled back a few years. (It seems to be set in the early thirties rather than in the late thirties.)

David Carradine is one of the seemingly endless supply of talented sons of John Carradine. (They don't all have the same mother.) The father—his gaunt, elongated face like an African mask and his voice like molasses dripping—played the mystical unfrocked preacher Casy in *The Grapes of Wrath*. David, who has a masklike quality of his own, made his name as the Inca king in the Broadway production of *The Royal Hunt of the Sun*, then lost it playing the catatonic sage-hero of the catatonic TV series "Kung Fu." He has given confident star performances in low-budget pictures, such as the ingratiatingly tacky *Death Race 2000*, but this is his first starring role in a major film. He brings *Bound for Glory* a mulish, bastardly intransigence that gives the movie a core. Even when it isn't clear what the picture is getting at, his leathery, lined neck and sensual arrogance are convincingly proletarian, and convincingly special. He might be a little more intense and more varied; he could use a little more spring and be a shade faster with his lines. At times, he seems to be acting in a reverie of the past as a quieter time, and to be slowed down for truth and beauty, like James Stewart in *Mr. Smith Goes to Washington*. But the main thing is that he's got the hardheaded, closed-off quality that is essential to Guthrie, the mixture of the devious and the rhapsodic, and the satyr's sexiness. His singing voice, deeper and fuller than Woody Guthrie's, and with more emotion in it, has a similar conversational quality. His voice is drier, more laconic and impersonal than the voice of his brother Keith. In *Nashville*, Keith Carradine's voice insinuates itself; that tremolo makes it seem as if he were singing just to you. David Carradine sings like a kid who grew up holding things in. At times, he has his father's gaunt-angel Casy look, but even though the movie makes him a political innocent and rather too sweet, Carradine's own hellion's unreachableness saves him. This is not a man looking for love; this is one tough customer. He's a very sculptural actor—the neat, close-cropped head, somnolent yet alert, the lower lip debating possible pleasure, the body lean but with the gut poking out a bit. He may not have much range, but he's a wonderful image—wiry and self-contained.

It's right for the role Carradine is playing here that he doesn't fully interact with the other performers, though the picture doesn't go far enough with the rootless qualities he brings to it. While Woody is still living in Texas, a fat man (Lee McLaughlin) who announces that he's insane and has newsreels going in his head comes for help, and the scene is so entertainingly baroque that one can pass over Woody's generosity and his intuitive understanding of the therapeutic power of art. But once Woody lights out for California and starts riding the rails this movie lets us know it's bound for glory. On his very first hitch, he pals up with Snedeger (Ji-Tu Cumbuka), who is full of folk comradeship and talks like a black Edgar Guest. That's the first hint of the tin-ear trouble that afflicts the movie. You begin to understand that uplift is actually its theme, and that the movie is supposed to do for an audience what singing "This Land Is Your Land" often does for a crowd. The tautness of Carradine's voice is betrayed by the Leonard Rosenman score, which uses conventional instrumentation on Woody Guthrie themes. This is the kind of picture that Hollywood gives awards to, with great pride. Coming out now, it can seem the first movie of the Carter era.

The film has a feeling for detail—the matching profiles of two young Baez-like sisters in a squatters' camp, the landscapes with lonely figures walking along the roads, Carradine's lived-in, seat-sprung pants. Every shot is a softly lighted stunner, and there's always something going on in the background or something coming into frame. The cinematographer, Haskell Wexler, has startling graphic vitality in his images, yet they're toned and sensitive. From shot to shot he achieves a consistency of light and texture—a documentary lyricism. The rolling dust cloud and the other special effects have unusual power, because of the unifying romanticism—the film's colors seem alloyed with dust. Hal Ashby is about as far from a hack as a director can be. There's real love in his staging of the incidents and in the way he controls the physical movement of the extras and bit players. Ashby was a famous editor—he won an Academy Award for his work on *In the Heat of the Night,* which was also shot by Wexler. The directors he worked with included William Wyler and George Stevens, and his care here reflects some of their perfectionism, and perhaps their respectful distancing also. This is the kind of filmmaking which is possible only when a director is backed up by his studio. (United Artists, with the participation of a tax-shelter syndicate, put close to seven and a half million dollars into *Bound for Glory*.) Ashby deployed thousands of extras—nine hundred were used in the migrants' camp—and I didn't see any who looked anachronistic. Yet two of the principals stuck out every time they turned up. As Johnson, who stands for the learning power of the masses, Randy Quaid overplays his hand—he's like a road-company peasant. And as the singer-organizer Ozark Bule, who recruits Guthrie to work for the union, Ronny Cox is like the host of a TV children's show; he talks in a semi-falsetto and beams with Scoutmaster fervor—he's so phony I wanted him to be exposed as a labor-faker. Ashby and the scenarist, Robert Getchell (he wrote *Alice Doesn't Live Here Anymore*), didn't provide much substance for Melinda Dillon's role as Mary Guthrie. (Melinda Dillon also plays a second role, as Guthrie's singing partner, Memphis Sue.) Since Mary—Guthrie's first wife—takes her children and leaves him, preferring to make a life on her own rather than wait around for a man she can't depend on, she must be fighting for her own version of integrity. Yet we never get a glimpse of the woman who's capable of making that decision; the woman we see just worries and nags.

This movie is scaled to be an epic, yet it has only one character, and it's straggly. When Guthrie auditions for the radio station, he lets out his voice on "Way down yonder in the Indian nation . . . In the Oklahoma hills where I was born," and there's strength and excitement in the sound. He has more charge in this scene than anywhere else: when the station manager is sold on him and tells him he can stop, we feel the momentum that drives him on and his artist's fury at the station manager who doesn't understand that he's not just singing for an audition. A film this large needs the kind of assertion that this scene represents; it's an audience awakener—we see the humor in the situation, we feel Guthrie's dogged need to consummate the song, and we respect him completely. If the film had gone forward from this point, so that we could see more of the tension locked in this man, I think it might have been a great picture. But it doesn't build dramatically; it seems to be a movie in search of itself and never finding itself. It bogs down in backward and forward movement: Guthrie sings to squatters and is attacked by goons; he sings at an organizing meeting, and goons break it up; he rides the rails, sings to workers in the fields, is chased off, rides the rails, sings to workers in a fruit-packing plant, is beaten up, rides the rails some more. We weary of his itinerary, and so the visual beauty turns self-conscious. *Bound for Glory* isn't quite an epic; it's a hole-in-shoe pastoral, and we can't help being aware that this is the most expensive-looking Depression we've ever seen.

Clearly, Ashby didn't want to force a dramatic pattern on his rambling-loner hero. For some directors this would mean trying to find the natural flow and rhythm of the material while shooting it, but for Ashby it probably meant trying to find the rhythm after completing the shooting. Ashby's last film, *Shampoo,* was tightly structured by its script, but this time he has used the script as a taking-off point. Ashby's approach is indicated by these words in an interview: "From my being an editor . . . I don't camera cut; I leave everything as open as I can, because that provides more alternatives . . . It gives you choices." I think that probably what happened was that he and his crew kept getting so much marvellous material and seeing so many possibilities in it that he lost any clear sense of how to put it together. He may have thought by then that the material was so rich that the film worked just as the portrait of a folk artist and his time; he probably believed he had found what the material was really about—but what that meant was that his own feelings had become the subject. He didn't go all soft on Woody Guthrie the man but on his own warm, spacey sentiments about what Guthrie stood for and about the period itself. This movie is about what a lot of people want to think their roots are. It's filled out with woozy generalities about Woody Guthrie as a man who fought the good fight against greed, and about his radicalization's being the same thing as his finding himself as an artist. It's about being in touch with the people—not just people but the people. Ashby's open approach led him to imbue the movie with the sort of mythologized idealism that stirs people when they listen to political folk and rock music—the generalized piousness and good will of youth. This is nothing terrible, but since it's the glue that holds the picture together, *Bound for Glory* is like a dreamy, druggy young kid's view of hard times. It's so beautiful you can get a high from the dust.

[December 13, 1976]

This Is My Beloved

*E*very time Jeanne Moreau opens her mouth in *Lumière,* a *pensée* drops out. As the international screen star Sarah Dedieu, she is so solicitous of everyone's welfare that when she isn't reciting bits of Gallic wisdom of the heart or quoting weighty lines from Ingmar Bergman she picks up a book that's handily close by and reads us an enriching passage. It's no wonder, then, that lovers swarm all over Sarah and that her friends adore her—she gives fully of herself to each, and the lowliest worker on the set of the movie she's starring in may expect her loving consideration.

This appears to be how Moreau sees herself, and how she wants us to see her—as an impulsive, Colette-like woman eagerly sniffing a visiting friend's new perfume, or putting nasturtiums into a salad and serving it charmingly with her fingertips. The film, which marks her début as a director and also as a scenarist, is made up of treasured scraps; the script suggests a process of accretion rather than writing. Even the name Sarah Dedieu has the highest associations: not only Bernhardt but "Rachel when from the Lord," the actress about whom Proust speculated on "the power of the human imagination, the illusion on which were based the pains of love"; and, like Rachel, Sarah has had a lover named Saint-Loup. For a first film, the title *Lumière* is superbly confident, a dazzling pun, calling up not only the Creation, and Louis Lumière, the pioneer filmmaker who photographed actual events, but also the bright lights that theatrical people live in, the glow that stars give off, and the cry that is traditionally heard on movie sets—"Lights, camera, action!" The meaning is essentially the same as Chaplin's *Limelight,* and *Lumière* is perhaps the most elevated daydream of an actor's life since Chaplin's Calvero performed at a gala benefit, demonstrating to those who thought him a has-been that he was still the greatest performer of them all, and then died in the wings as the applause faded.

Watching the movie is rather like attending a queen's levee. Sarah awakes, sits up in her pomegranate-red nightie, her hair freshly done, as her servant brings in her fan mail. Admitted into her world of friends, we can see that she has no fears about her work, no pangs of anxiety about aging, no paranoia about the new actresses coming up. In the course of a week, she discards one lover firmly, honestly and takes on another— predestined for her, she feels. She visits the laboratory of Grégoire (François Simon), a cadaverous biologist, an ascetic so devoted to her that he is a husband in all but sex, and she listens to his scientific discourse with an absorption that makes us feel like bums: she does not merely understand science, she understands it with her whole soul. They walk together in white corridors that are like the inside of a machine; truly they are in a different world. At the end of the week, she wins something like the Academy Award, except it's at a ceremony where she is the only one being honored, and her girl friends and boy friends are all there, gathered round, to be happy for her. This bliss-out is the movie every actress must at some point have dreamed of making. Inadvertently, *Lumière* becomes a film about an actress's narcissism.

When word is brought to Sarah that her platonic husband was dying of a disease contracted because of his dedication to his work, and has killed himself, the camera moves in for a closeup. But she cannot react. We are invited to admire the virtuosity of her shocked impassivity. "That light," she complains. "*Le soleil m'enmerde.*" Ah, yes, her star's ambience has blinded her to his suffering. Her grief must be terrible to be so bottled up.

Then she goes to her movie set, takes off her flaming pomegranate cape, and, dressed appropriately in a Hamlet black tuxedo, breaks down. You feel you should applaud.

Jeanne Moreau has always made love to the camera—in effect, to the director. She has had her own way of changing her emotional coloring—surprising the director, entrancing him. The most dismaying aspect of *Lumière* is that she's making love to herself. In the sixties, Moreau used to say that she liked directors to decide for her what they wanted her to do, because "the ideas you can have about yourself are not very interesting." She said, "I think it is much better to see yourself through somebody's eyes." She was right. It's one thing to be seen as a goddess; it's quite another to see yourself as a goddess. And she was right when she discussed her "mystery" as "the director's mystery, for him to unravel." Of all the performers one can think of, she is probably the one who would naturally suffer the most from directing herself. The great thing about those sulky women she played in the early sixties was how little they said and how much they implied. Now that she's laying on the aphorisms, she isn't implying a thing. The flip-overs from mood to mood are visible, and there's nothing underneath to hold the tricks together.

Lumière suggests a refined, thin-blooded *All About Eve.* That American film is so telegraphic in style that the characters seem to be talking in headlines, but here the conversation is so gracefully marginal that you long for a headline or two. Sarah is offered to us as a chic, theatrical version of an earth mother, and as she drifts from appointment to appointment everything basic is left out. Moreau once said, "When I see something I want, I go *right* for it. I really won't let *anything* stand in my way. Shame, self-respect—nothing can stop me. I *always* get what I want." A decade later, she presents us with considerate, thoughtful Sarah Dedieu. But we never cared about whether Jeanne Moreau was nice; the point was, we couldn't take our eyes off her. We can, now that she's gone soft on herself; there is no strength of any kind in *Lumière*.

Rarely has there been so much camera movement to such static effect. The film is full of "artful touches": the camera plays peekaboo, or swirls whimsically, without dramatic impetus; a pair of women are photographed back to back, in a reversal of Bergman's face-to-face encounters; Sarah's shade of red turns up on her lovers—everybody in the movie is color-coördinated with her. In a prelude, shot in Moreau's house near Saint-Tropez, a quartet of holidaying actresses exchange confidences, and we are alerted that this is going to be a gentle, woman's view of women. The relaxed intimacy among the four is unlike the views of women's friendships which men directors have given, but it's a little too sun-sweetened; we seem to be in an idealized girls' dormitory, or an overage budding grove. The most animated moments in the movie involve Julienne (Francine Racette) and Caroline (Caroline Cartier), who probably represent Sarah at earlier stages in her life, just as Laura (Lucia Bose), who has married rich, retired from the theatre, and become a little dull, probably represents what might have happened to Sarah if she had quit. As a director, Moreau brings out the possibilities in the young actresses. Francine Racette, a tall brunette, indecently pretty and with a monkey grin, is like a showgirl Katharine Hepburn; she has the popping-out-of-her-skin sexiness of the glittering Parisiennes of thirties movies— Jacqueline Delubac in the Guitry films, or Mireille Balin in *Pépé le Moko*. While Moreau sees the comedy in the seduction scene that Racette plays with a visiting American (Keith Carradine), Sarah's passions are treated with the utmost earnestness, even though she appears to have excruciating taste in men. The lover she sends packing is a mewling infant, and her new predestined soul mate (Bruno Ganz), a German writer whose books she says have "invaded my mind," is clammy and passive. But no one in the film expresses any awareness of her predilection for weak, asexual men, and her romantic scenes with the somber Ganz, which are a killing mixture of *La Notte* and *Now, Voyager,* are played absolutely straight, even when she rests her head, pictorially, on his manly shoulder. When Sarah is with her women friends, the scenes are arranged so that she can embrace them and be infinitely supportive and generous. The picture is a valentine to a wonderful woman's life of art and love. It shares a weakness of many other high-flown junk movies: it is less interested in pace than in culture.

Lumière is delicately dissociated; it nibbles around the edges of its subject, and this can be taken as feminine sensibility. But this is also what has given feminine sensibility a bad name. The affectation of *Lumière* is that its heroine is closer to the earth than men are, and yet has higher, more spiritual feelings than men. Which is where many men, too, have wanted to place women—leaving them out of the middle range, where the action is. There is no middle range in Moreau's picture—nothing between innocent girlish sensuality and poetic conceits. Jeanne Moreau keeps herself in too good a light. The film never rings true: it's a wrong-note sonata.

[December 20, 1976]

Here's to the Big One

The greatest misfit in movie history makes a comeback in the new *King Kong*. Monster, pet, misunderstood kid, unrequited lover, all in one grotesquely oversized body, the innocent ape is martyred once again. I wanted a good time from this movie, and that's what I got. It's a romantic adventure fantasy—colossal, silly, touching, a marvellous Classics-comics movie.

Kong has become a pop deity in the years since the 1933 version came out, and the tone of the new film, directed by John Guillermin, from a script by Lorenzo Semple, Jr., is different from that of the first. It had to be, since we know what's coming. Semple turns our knowledge to advantage by giving the characters lines that are jokes on them. Yet, with this *Beat the Devil* edge to the dialogue, the romantic appeal of the material is, if anything, even stronger this time around. The film doesn't have the magical primeval imagery of the first version; it doesn't have the Gustave Doré fable atmosphere. It's big in a much simpler, clunkier way, but it's also a happier, livelier entertainment. The first *Kong* was a stunt film that was trying to awe you, and its lewd underlay had a carnival hucksterism that made you feel a little queasy. This new *King Kong* isn't a horror movie—it's an absurdist love story. Taking into account the feelings that have developed about Kong, the moviemakers have pared the theme down to that of the instinctive animal-man of the collegiate graffiti: "King Kong died for our sins." (The hair on the college kids is noble-savage hair, and Kong has more of it than anybody.) The film moves unhurriedly, in a clean, straightforward progression to the ritual love-death. When the forty-foot Kong stands bleeding and besieged at the top of the World Trade Center, and his blonde (Jessica Lange) pleads with him to pick her up, so that the helicopters won't shoot at him, even Wagner's dreams seem paltry. This is opera at its campiest, yet that doesn't mean our feelings don't soar. We might snicker at a human movie hero who felt such passion for a woman that he'd rather die than risk harming her, but who can jeer a martyr-ape?

The plot is a tale of two islands—Skull Island, where Kong is god, and

Manhattan, where he is a rampaging menace. In the first version, Robert Armstrong played an explorer-showman who made jungle pictures. Just before setting sail on a highly mysterious moviemaking expedition, he went looking for an actress to provide love interest for the film; he needed somebody desperate enough to sign on, no questions asked. After casing the women in the breadlines, he spotted a blonde (Fay Wray) stealing an apple in the Bowery; an orphan who had been working as an extra at the Astoria studios, she was unemployed, starving, and ready for anything. They sailed immediately, and on board, en route to the island, the tough showman tested her for her chores by photographing her screaming for her life. The hero was Jack (Bruce Cabot), the first mate, who rescued the girl after the savages on Skull Island abducted her to be the bride of Kong.

For the updating, this trio had to be reassembled in plausibly modern terms. Semple went a step beyond that, treating the updating as a comedy, and inviting us to peg the differences between old and new. The expedition to the island is now financed by Petrox, an oil company, and it's headed by Fred (Charles Grodin), who has convinced the Petrox executives that he'll make an oil strike. An "environmental rapist" with a flat haircut, trimmed long sideburns, and a dark mustache for twirling, Fred is a snarling villain out of an animated cartoon. Grodin roots around in the comedy of measliness: Fred is so money-hungry he's funny. And he's so fatuous he's the butt of all his own remarks—like the square-riggers Ralph Bellamy used to play. Jack (still called Jack) is now a Princeton paleontologist (Jeff Bridges) who specializes in primates; having heard where the ship is going, and having a suspicion of what's to be found on the island (he's the only one who does), he sneaks on board as a stowaway. Jack is more a hitchhiking hippie than an obsessed scientist, and there's a satiric point in casting the rough-hewn Bridges in this role: As the long-haired, shaggy-bearded friend of animals, Bridges is like man in his natural state in a Time-Life book on evolution; you can see him in one of those plates with a rock in his hand, except he's got a shirt on. His Jack is the human equivalent of Kong, and, like Kong, he falls for the blonde.

Semple has hold of an idea, all right: the big corporations *are* the show-business entrepreneurs now. But in using Petrox as an ecological target he gets awfully glib and topical, and remnants of the earlier conception still turn up, because the mythic structure requires them. Grodin's pomposity is ludicrously endearing when he's the company toady in the early sections. Coming ashore and putting his foot down on Skull Island, he attempts a historical pose, like General MacArthur returning to the Philippines, and can't make it; he doesn't have the conviction of a true fraud—he's a weasel, a cluck. However, the plot requires him to shift into the Robert Armstrong–showman role, and he loses his character in the process—his later scenes have no humor. Both the men's roles are pieced together out of scraps of old and new, but they're passable.

The movie is sparked mainly, I think, by the impudent new conception of the screaming-in-fear blonde, and Jessica Lange's fast yet dreamy comic style. Her Dwan has the high, wide forehead and clear-eyed transparency of Carole Lombard in *My Man Godfrey*. Dwan, an aspiring starlet, doesn't join the expedition; she's picked up along the way, unconscious, from a rubber raft in the ocean, the sole survivor of a yachting party. The yacht belonged to a movie mogul, and she'd been on board hoping to get a part that he'd promised her. Dwan (she changed it from Dawn) is one of the cloud-borne movie groupies who lead charmed lives. The way she's photographed, she seems to have stepped out of an expensive shampoo commercial; languorous and polymorphous, like a taller Tuesday Weld or a more slightly built Margaux Hemingway, she has the sensuousness of a kitten. Dwan is so innocently corrupt she's as childlike as Kong himself, and her infantilism gives the picture a sexual chemistry that the moviemakers couldn't have completely planned—some of it just has to be luck. She has one-liners so dumb that the audience laughs and moans at the same time, yet they're in character, and when Jessica Lange says them she holds the eye, and you like her, the way people liked Lombard.

The story is no longer an ape going for a blonde but the loneliest creature in the world—the only one of his species—finding the right playmate. Dwan is the smart nit American *femme fatale*—a daisy, impulsive, well-meaning, yet so giddy, unstable, and self-centered that you know exactly why Kong is driven to despair. The elusive Dwan is the kind of crackbrain who can delight and exasperate the most controlled of men; this poor big ape never knows what hit him. Lolita accepted Humbert Humbert's devotion with barely a flicker of interest in how desperate he was; that's how Dwan is with the Great Ape. She concentrates on what she's interested in: if you told her World War III had just started, she'd say, "Save it and tell me later, would you? I'm off to the hairdresser." Kong, brought to New York, is caged and exhibited to the public at Shea Stadium. (It was a theatre in the earlier version.) He thinks that the photographers are hurting Dwan with their flashbulbs, so he breaks his bonds, tears up the place, and chases after her. Sniffing her out, trailing her to Manhattan, the obsessed, faithful ape is like Blume in Love. When he carries her off and reaches his final destination at the top of the World Trade Center, his eyes keep saying, "Do you love me?" And Dwan can't give him a truthful answer, any more than she can give Jack a truthful answer. Neither of them holds it against her. She's forgotten the question.

The central enjoyment in the film is Dwan's relationship with Kong; she humanizes him, as Streisand humanized Redford in *The Way We Were*—she makes you love him. On the island, she talks to him the same way she might have talked to her movie mogul in a Beverly Hills bedroom. When he's got her in his paw and she screams "Put me down!" many of us women know we've played that scene, and many men will know they've played the ape. This verbal gag becomes a visual gag when Kong breaks down the gates of a high wall to get to her: it's as if a man and a woman had been having a fight and the woman had done about the most infuriating thing she could do—locked herself away from him. Dwan may seem out of contact with reality, but there's a craftiness in her—an instinct for the main chance. Even with the ape, she half believes he can do something for her, and he does—he makes her a star.

The eroticism of the earlier *Kong* was rather nightmarish, especially for women—though black women may have experienced it differently, as a slap. Whites have sometimes spoken of the movie as a racial slur, but the black men that I've known have always loved it. It was their own special urban gorilla-guerrilla fantasy: to be a king in your own country, to be brought here in chains, to be so strong that you could roar your defiance at the top of the big city and go down in a burst of glory. This time, Kong is less threatening, and the sexual references are out on top. After the Skull Island savages abduct Dwan and put her on the altar as a full-moon sacrifice to Kong, they scurry back to safety on their side of the high wall and slide a prodigiously long, slick black bolt across the gate. However, it's almost an invasion of the viewer's privacy when one of the men on the expedition (Ed Lauter) quizzes Jack about what the ape wants with Dwan. Since the conception of the movie is a phallic joke carried to the level of myth, why raise this lame, prosaic question of what Kong wants? Obviously he wants to consummate his passion, and just as obviously he can't. He's the misfit extraordinaire. Like the earlier Kong, this one has no visible genitals; he doesn't need them—Kong is a walking forty-foot genital. What makes him such a pop mythic hero is that he's also pre-phallic—the Teddy Bear Christ of the sixties flower children, Christ as a mistreated pet.

Modernizing a forty-three-year-old pop fantasy is a tricky business. One might assume that the very first thing the moviemakers would do would be to work out a more authentic view of the culture on Skull Island and get away from the African "savages" from Central Casting of the thirties version, but there isn't much way to do that without disrupting the basic story. The original *King Kong* wasn't made innocently: it was an ingeniously made exploitation picture, and camp elements are integral to it. This version accepts what the material is and treats it playfully. (Contrary to rumors, the original has not been legally withdrawn; it is still available in 16 mm. and for television, and it will be available again in 35 mm. for theatres after a discretionary period—probably a year.) Some of the new details fizzle because they haven't been changed enough, others because the changes involve dated, sophomoric counterculture attitudes. The big presentation of Kong to the public at Shea Stadium is clumsily staged, and when this Kong emulates the first and tears down an elevated train, he might be playing with an antique toy; the sequence lacks excitement—it feels half-hearted, as if Guillermin did it because it was expected of him. The direction isn't as assured in the New York footage as it is on Kong's island or on the ship, but this may be because the script is weakest here. The special effects are generally enjoyable, though the full-moon scenes on the island are dark and don't give the impression of moonlight, Kong's fight with a serpent is lackluster, and, at the end, Kong's actual fall from the World Trade Center—which cries out for a slight slowing down, for a Peckinpah poetic image—is skimped and is over before we've seen it.

There are earlier scenes that stay with one: Kong dipping Dwan in a waterfall and blowing her dry, his cheeks puffed out like a fairy-tale illustration of Zephyrus, the billowing wind god; Kong when he's trapped, his head and arm lifting out of the miasmal fumes and dropping back, then his hand rising again and falling in defeat. The original version skipped over Kong's trip to New York, but this time we see him imprisoned in the hold of a supertanker, and Kong, morose, enslaved, with the ship's crew throwing food down into his cell, is a spectacular image of a degraded king. When he roars and beats against his prison, it's like the sound of a gorilla battering the bars of his cage at the zoo, but magnified so that the whole ship is pounding. The reverberations prevent Dwan from going to bed with Jack; they're ominous—Kong is shaking the universe. There's a lovely, campy sequence with Dwan's scarf, caught in a gust of wind, drifting down to Kong in the hold, and also a visit, when Dwan falls into his prison and he catches her. This is his finest scene: knowing the pain of being a prisoner, he frees her, and is grief-stricken as she leaves.

Guillermin is rather too Spartan; he rations the use of imagination. But he has an uncluttered style; he knows what point a scene should make and why. He sets a visual tone by the clean bigness of his images and by his long takes; if the original *Kong* was nightmarish, this one has a monumental comic dreaminess. The ape is always slow; his movements as he climbs the World Trade Center have the Bruckner feeling of heavy orchestration. When Guillermin needed a little more poetry, he may have been locked into his overall style. Still, the unity of the film is impressive: it doesn't fall into the choppiness that often results from extensive use of special effects. Guillermin, who is British, directed his first feature in 1949, when he was twenty-four, and worked steadily in a variety of genres—including two Tarzan pictures (the rousing *Tarzan's Greatest Adventure,* in 1959, might have been a warmup for this *Kong*) and two with Peter Sellers (the demonic-gangster melodrama *Never Let Go* and the Anglicized, hacked-up-by-the-producer *Waltz of the Toreadors*)—before settling into big international co-productions and action films (*Guns at Batasi,* 1964; *The Blue Max,* 1966; *The Bridge at Remagen,* 1969; *Skyjacked,* 1972; and *The Towering Inferno,* 1974). This picture must have been a backbreaking series of problems, yet, with his action director's experience, he has streamlined the myth. The original *Kong* had long passages without dialogue—just Max Steiner's music heaving, shrieking, and portending doom, and Kong grunting and beating his chest in triumph. (Oscar Levant once said that the film "should have been advertised as a concert of Steiner's music with accompanying pictures on the screen.") The new score, by John Barry, doesn't heighten the imagery with quite so many premonitory rumblings; it's more of a love poem—a great big swatch of mood music sweeping you along. It gives the picture an amplitude that goes well with Guillermin's big, bright-colored storybook imagery.

In a movie of this scale, Fred's lickspittle villainy comes across as trivializing, and the virtuous scientist Jack, with his gibes about the oil company and the environment, might also seem undersized if Jeff Bridges didn't have such heroic reserves of good humor. Without his amiable slouchiness, his hand pushing his dirty-blond hair off his face, his quick, natural-sounding delivery, Jack might have been a stick. (Instead, the role may help to give Bridges the popularity that he's earned in the past few years.) There is an awkward lapse toward the end—an insert of Jack cheering as Kong rips off pieces of the World Trade Center and hurls them at his attackers. This cue to the audience to be on Kong's side cheapens everything—Kong, the picture, us. Yet the story is paced majestically, and no mistake or excess seems to matter much, since Kong himself is an emotionally consistent protagonist, whose flickering expressions—lechery, bewilderment, tenderness—amuse us at the same time that we're in thrall. The picture works because, despite what you know, you believe in Kong as a living creature. You feel bad that the ape is killed—but you also feel tickled that you feel bad.

Guillermin, his boss (the producer Dino De Laurentiis), and his associates started with a powerful, silly idea that gets to people in a special way, and some of these people may regard the remake as desecration. Others may be put off by the scale of the advertising campaign and the very concept of a twenty-four-million-dollar movie. There is an element of obscenity in this kind of moviemaking—a remake that costs more than thirty-five times what the original did, and is so plugged into merchandising idiot items that the script's ecological claims acquire an extra layer of embarrassment. Nevertheless, the moviemaking team has come up with a pop classic that can stand in our affections right next to the original version. The most meritoriously intentioned movies are often stinkers, and this epitome of commercialism turns out to be wonderful entertainment. I don't think I've ever before seen a movie that was a comic-strip great romance in the way this one is—it's a joke that can make you cry.

[January 3, 1977]

Contempt for the Audience

There's a trap built into the story of *A Star Is Born,* and though just about everybody who has worked on the various versions must have been aware of it, each picture, in turn, falls into it. The story is about the marriage of a fading, boozing male star to a woman who's rising, and while the man is glamorously, tragically self-destructive, the Cinderella heroine is so hardworking, loyal, and untemperamental that she's insufferable. For reasons that go beyond the bounds of criticism, this role attracted Judy Garland, as it has also attracted Barbra Streisand, who stars in the new version with Kris Kristofferson. The story originated with Adela Rogers St. John and was turned into an early talkie, *What Price Hollywood,* directed by George Cukor in 1932, in which the boozer, a director, played by Lowell Sherman, was the central character; Sherman patterned his performance after the self-mocking alcoholic style of his brother-in-law John Barrymore, and Gene Fowler, who worked on the script, later wrote the Barrymore biography *Good Night, Sweet Prince.* It was reshaped into a "woman's picture" in the 1937 *A Star Is Born,* with Janet Gaynor's Esther Blodgett passively ascending to stardom, and trying to conceal her heartache over the deterioration of her actor-husband, Norman Maine; she never stops loving him, even after he kills himself. And that was basically the story of the 1954 version, though Judy Garland looked far from fresh and rising. The men who played Norman Maine (Fredric March and then James Mason) gave the performances, though the overwrought Garland was galvanizing—like it or not, you couldn't take your eyes off her. Her turbulent behavior during the making of the film drove the budget so high that the costs weren't recouped, but the film presented her as the true-blue show-must-go-on heroine who never causes anybody any trouble. Garland's Esther Blodgett was prepared to give up her stardom to save her husband, and the emphasis was on her loyalty to him, rather than on his revulsion at having become a disgrace—a figure in a comedy. In the Streisand version, supposedly set in the rock world, the heroine, Esther Hoffman, isn't about to sacrifice her singing career. But this, too, is a "woman's picture"; that is, it's designed to make you weep not for the dead hero but for the noble heroine.

If Streisand hadn't gone on the noble wagon—if she'd played Esther Hoffman as a little bullet of talent who met a big star, used him and loved him at the same time, and pushed him to compromise his career for her ends—there might have been a movie with some tension to it. As John Norman Howard, the rock idol, Kris Kristofferson has the angry frustration of a man who's doing something he's sick of. He has the despair of an entertainer whose contempt for the audience is the only emotion he has left. John Norman no longer has anything to give his public: when he sings, he goes through the gyrations of a demonic performer, but his voice is shot—it's gravelly and raspy—and you can hardly hear him above the instruments. (Kristofferson doesn't sing in his usual sleepy manner; he's aggressive here, a shouter, and it's exciting, but—deliberately, I assume—empty.) John Norman is mean and boozing, because he can't handle the life that goes with being a rock star; the craziness has got inside him. His body is still young, but his eyes are clouded and frightened—the soul has moved out. If he were trying to pull himself together by hanging on to Esther's sanity, and she knew that and parlayed it, there would be some dynamics, and some edges. The vacuum in this movie is the purity of their relationship. John Norman catapults her to success without her knowing what his plans for her are; each is above using the other. The picture is a drippy love story about two people who love each other selflessly. And so the scenes between Barbra Streisand and Kris Kristofferson, which one would expect to have some sexual combustion, are exhaustingly, fraudulently romantic. When they have a physical fight, it's just an exhibition match. The picture is really a little insulting to us in assuming that we want to accompany them on their honeymoon in the desert, to share their kisses and admire her trousseau. A Star Is Born treats us as if we were gawkers at the gates of the stars' homes, and when it opens the gates—for an admission fee—it fobs us off with a carefully posed view.

The picture has had the worst advance press I can recall (with the possible exceptions of Cleopatra and the 1954 A Star Is Born). A press junket to the outdoor concert site in Arizona last spring resulted in a flood of negative publicity, and those who have written pieces exonerating themselves include John Gregory Dunne, who—along with his wife, Joan Didion, and the director, Frank Pierson—gets the screenplay credit. In November, Pierson published his apologia before the fact—an article in which he wrote that the picture he turned over to Streisand and her co-producer, Jon Peters, was, according to the "unanimous" view of the Warners people, "a huge hit." He rigged things both ways for himself: if the picture we got to see was anything less than great, it would be because Streisand and Peters had wrecked it in the final cut, while if it *was* great, we had him to congratulate. Pierson did not mention that he had previously directed only one movie, the 1970 spy thriller *The Looking Glass War*; it was a failure, largely because there was no controlling dramatic intelligence at work—it didn't involve the audience. Neither does *A Star Is Born,* and its faults can't all be laid to Streisand's interference or to her and Peters' editing.

When John Norman Howard enters the joint where he first meets Esther, she's singing between two black women, in a group called The Oreos; the camera centers on her before he's even inside—it has selected her before he gets a chance to. Why doesn't he first hear her voice—a voice with the eagerness and drive he used to have—and be turned on by it? (That's something we could identify with.) And wouldn't he then look to see whom it belonged to? Instead, Esther comes over and bawls him out for being noisy; he admires her sass and "cute" face and figure, and then he listens. And does she know who he is when she bawls him out? If she does, wouldn't this affect how she speaks to him? And if she doesn't, when is the moment when she finds out? According to this picture, Esther is so indifferent to his fame that she doesn't take cognizance of it at any point; she's a little princess from another planet. There are two smart, intuitive, supporting performers—Gary Busey, as John Norman's fast-talking road manager, and Paul Mazursky, as his unsentimental record producer— but their roles are at subsistence level. The movie concentrates on the love between Esther and John Norman, yet in that abomination *For Pete's Sake* Streisand looked at Michael Sarrazin with more affection than she shows for Kristofferson. This man has a burly physical beauty, like Sean Connery's, and she rakes him with her fingernails as if he were a dead fish.

Thinner, and in a soft, curly Harpo hairdo, Streisand doesn't have the unhappy look she had in *Funny Lady,* but she acts a virtuous person by not using much energy. She seems at half-mast, out of it, and you don't get engrossed in reading her face, because she's reading it for you. She wants to make sure we get what's going on all the time. That kills any illusion—that and the camera, which is always on her a second too soon, and seconds too long, emphasizing how admirable she is, how strong yet loving. How gracious, too. When she blows a commercial that The Oreos are doing, the two black vocalists don't even get sore at her; they have no personalities, and practically no lines or singing sound, either—they're there for her to hug. Streisand comes on all soft and sincere. Why? Is it for Esther's image or her own? Esther doesn't have to be done up in big hats and desert ensembles out of *The Sheik*; she doesn't need to be glamorously noble. She just needs to be *sane.* Surely that has to be her attraction for John Norman, who's been high too long and needs to come down—he would respond to a woman who was grounded. And Streisand is, but tries to cover it up with an ethereal haze, as if the important thing for him (and for us) were to find her adorable. The movie loses its last chance to make a character of Esther when it shows that she's guiltless of John Norman's death. Has there ever been a husband or a wife of a suicide who could feel as guiltless as Esther does? In the Garland version, we could see from James Mason's performance that what was killing the husband was his wife's pity for him; the last shred of dignity he had left was to design his own death. Here Esther is as innocent of her husband's death as she is innocent of her own success. She's not as humble as Janet Gaynor, but she's just as pure.

Streisand has got herself into too many false positions: her singing isn't rock, as it's meant to be, but show-biz pop, and we're acutely aware of the Broadway–Las Vegas intonations. The director and the writers, those credited and those uncredited, must be partly responsible, but the sinking feeling one gets from the picture relates largely to her. One is never really comfortable with her, because even when she's singing she isn't fully involved in the music; she's trying to manage our responses. Streisand loses that managerial eye in only one number—"The Woman in the Moon," when she faces down the people at a benefit who wanted John Norman to sing and resent his foisting her on them. It's not much of a song, but she gives herself over to singing it, and her voice—rougher than usual—is joyously confident. This is the moment when the "star is born," and it's the only time in the movie when she has the force to match Kristofferson's. The picture, which still has some drive up to this point, goes completely to hell afterward. The romping honeymooners' bliss as they build their own house in the desert is enough to do the movie in, without Streisand's image dissolving into a sunset. There doesn't seem to be any script, and the film wobbles around, from montages of Esther's success to convictionless adaptations of bits from the earlier versions, such as John Norman at home taking phone messages for Esther. There is even a replay of the old Academy Awards scene; in the last version, as Garland accepted her Best Actress award the drunken, broken-down Mason climbed on the stage, told the élite assembled there that he needed a job, and then, flinging out his arm in an expansive gesture, inadvertently walloped her in the face. Now the sequence takes place at the Grammys, and John Norman breaks into Esther's receiving the award for best performance to ask for the award for worst performance. If you're going to do this sort of maudlin scene, you ought to make it count for something. In the earlier version, this extravaganza of self-humiliation prepared for the husband's suicide; here it serves no particular purpose, except as an occasion for Esther to show her fighting spirit. And whoever adapted the scene doesn't seem to have noticed that times have changed: John Norman's drunken display wouldn't produce the shocked response it does in the movie—he'd be the media hero of the week.

Kristofferson is actually the star who's born in this picture, and because of the physicality of his performance, the hidden, weak eyes, and the suggestions of depth, we're ready to feel a lot more for John Norman than the film encourages us to. When John Norman crashes his Ferrari and lies dead, the emphasis is on Esther's reaction. The weeping Streisand does a star turn, asking for something to cover him with, and the scene is so underdirected she seems to want a sack to shove him into so she can get on with the grieving. Later, at home, Esther hears a tape of him singing; apparently unfamiliar with the technology of voice reproduction, she thinks he's alive, and runs through the many, many rooms looking for him. Time is wasted on these drivelling, just about unplayable scenes while the picture fails to raise the issue that seems at the very heart of the rock-fame subject. We see the conditions in which John Norman worked—the noise and amplification and orgiastic crowds—which turned him into a sadomasochistic wreck, but we don't see Esther contending with the same problems. Is Esther invulnerable, or does she, too, become infected with the craziness, and the hatred of the audience? Streisand herself can't summon up the love of performing to make Esther's rise to stardom convincing. There's contempt implicit in Streisand's awareness of how she wants us to react to her. She wants more from us than she's giving out; even her singing is tightly controlled—she's singing for effect.

The songs (by Paul Williams and a batch of other people, including Leon Russell and Streisand) are often terribly slow and slurpy, with flight-of-fancy lyrics; they're disappointing throughout, with orchestrations that are fake gospel, fake soul, fake disco, or fake something else. At the end, there's some sort of commemoration service for John Norman, and Esther is introduced to sing. Here is the spot for Janet Gaynor's and Judy Garland's great mawkish moment: "This is Mrs. Norman Maine." Streisand does a compromise update on it: she's introduced as Esther Hoffman Howard—which is worse, but let it pass. What doesn't pass is her song, a double number that goes on for more than seven minutes, in a single take, with changing light cues. When she did her virtuoso finale in her first movie, she had a great song—"My Man"—and her strange, disturbing face was mesmerically involved in reaching us; the song was an act of assertion that carried all before it. Here the song dramatizes the widow's restoration to life, and she sheds tears, she smiles through her tears, she has an orgasmic interlude, she gets tougher and faster. But the song itself is endlessly uninteresting, and when, at the last, she flings her head up and the frame is frozen, her self-dramatization has got out of hand. It's one thing to act your songs, it's another to overact your songs. Streisand has more talent than she knows what to do with, and the heart of a lion. But she's made a movie about the unassuming, unaffected person she wants us to think she is, and the image is so truthless she can't play it.

[January 10, 1977]

244

Processing Sludge

How can you enjoy a movie if every joke is told twice, and the audience only laughs the second time? There are funny things in *The Pink Panther Strikes Again,* but after a while I was gripping the arms of my chair to stay awake. I can't believe people don't get the joke the first time: it must be that they're so eager to laugh that they're softened and give in on the repeat. Peter Sellers, the star of this picture, once said, "Write any character you have in mind and I'll shape myself to what you have written. But don't write a part for me." Yet that's what the director, Blake Edwards, and his co-writer, Frank Waldman, have done. They've written a part derived from Sellers' last Police Inspector Clouseau—in *The Return of the Pink Panther,* of 1975, his third tour of duty—so he is required to imitate himself, and his fish-eyed deadpan is joyless as he flogs the same old plummy-vowel sounds. Clouseau's clenched-jaws politesse is a joke that has run its course.

The first time around, early in 1964, in *The Pink Panther,* Clouseau was so unbearably frustrated, both sexually and professionally, that he kept falling all over himself. He couldn't catch the jewel thief he was tracking, because the thief's accomplice—and mistress—was his own wife (Capucine). *The Pink Panther* was a bedroom farce, an amusingly engineered slapstick chaos with the deceived Clouseau trying to preserve his brave jauntiness. At the end, when the thieves pinned the robberies on him, he even tried to make the best of being the patsy. That first film was a sophisticated comedy that also worked at a slaphappy cartoon level; the new one operates only at a cartoon level, and animated cartoons are usually seven minutes long. By now, Clouseau is simply a man who is oblivious of the fact that he cannot do anything right. Sellers has mastered the stiffness of officialdom; he has the rigidity of a cartoon bureaucrat as he walks into a gym, hoists himself manfully on the parallel bars, jumps off down an unnoticed stairwell, and then, scrambling to his feet, affects suave control. But he has already almost exhausted the possibilities in Clouseau. When Peter Sellers has a character to create, the precision of his satiric intonations is a weirdo's poetry, as in such films as *I'm All Right Jack, Only*

Two Can Play, Lolita, and *The Naked Truth* (also known as *Your Past Is Showing!*). And in a film such as the commercially unsuccessful *The Bobo* he has a relaxed, pleasant melancholy about him that he doesn't push too far.

Everything here is pushed. Was the production schedule too fast for the routines to find their rhythm? Edwards sets up promising situations and then the payoffs are out of step, so after the first half hour or so the film loses momentum. Dreyfus (Herbert Lom), Clouseau's former boss—the Chief Inspector of the Sûreté, whom he drove to nervous collapse in both *A Shot in the Dark* (mid-1964) and *The Return of the Pink Panther,* and has now replaced—turns into a Bondian villain. He's a criminal mastermind who threatens to destroy the world if the major powers don't turn Clouseau over to him. This plot could be used to provide suspense, but Edwards seems to be flipping through the pages of the script. He skims over the kidnapping of a scientist who has a Doomsday Machine, and the centerpiece sequence, in which twelve nations send their top assassins to dispatch Clouseau at the Munich Oktoberfest, is so offhand it's a fizzle. And the wide-screen images look crowded and gummy. When a film draws upon some of the broadest, earliest movie gags, such as Clouseau's opening a washing machine that floods over, or sitting on a pneumatic cushion, or exiting into a closet, it desperately needs a visual style. A picture that aims for Tom-and-Jerry effects has to be graphically clean; the jokes require sharper detail. I'm not wild about these slipping-on-banana-skins Keystone Cops routines even when the Keystone Cops do them (have the people who like to describe them as balletic ever really looked at them?), yet they sometimes work for Edwards, because, tossed together with spoofs and verbal gags, they seem to be quotations from the movie past. I like the *idea* of his throwing these comic styles together, yet Edwards loses the parody edge that makes his addiction to frantic buffoonery funny. In his best films, he loses it only momentarily; in *The Pink Panther Strikes Again* he loses it for so long that the film is tone deaf.

Omar Sharif turns up for a gag—playing an assassin, whom a competing woman assassin (Lesley-Anne Down) mistakes for Clouseau—and there are times when the aura of a guest appearance does something for a star. Burt Reynolds was the comic high point of *Silent Movie,* and here Sharif, looking spectacularly leonine, with his great bloodshot eyes shining, has a touch of fierceness. One could take him for a wild, fiery actor.

□ □ □

When Richard Pryor appears on a TV talk show and he's asked questions, sometimes you can see that his squirming isn't simple contempt for the host, it's more like boredom and frustration—creative impatience. He knows he is trapped and isn't using the best part of himself: he's being forced to speak in his own voice, and he needs to take off into a character in order to be funny. We're not after the real Richard Pryor (whoever that might be), any more than we were ever eager for the real Peter Sellers to stand up. Pryor's demons are what make people laugh. If he had played the sheriff in *Blazing Saddles,* he'd have made him *crazy*—threatening and funny, both. Pryor shouldn't be cast at all—he should be realized. He has desperate, mad characters coming out his pores, and we want to see how far he can go with them.

Pryor's comedy isn't based on suspiciousness about whites, or on anger, either; he's gone way past that. Whites are *unbelievable* to him. Playing a thief in the new mystery comedy *Silver Streak,* he's stupefied at the ignorance of the hero (Gene Wilder), and he can't believe the way this white man moves. For about fifteen minutes, Pryor gives the picture some of his craziness. Not much of it, but some—enough to make you realize how lethargic it was without him. This movie not only casts him, though—it casts him as a friend to good-guy whites. We're supposed to be touched when he returns Wilder's wallet to him and affectionately advises him to "stay loose." But when he's soft-hearted about his buddy Gene Wilder, he's a bad actor. These moments come at the tag ends of scenes and could easily have been cut. Are they the moviemakers' unconscious revenge on Pryor's craziness? He saves their picture for a few minutes—he gives it some potency and turns it into the comedy they hoped for—and they emasculate him, turn him into a lovable black man whose craziness is only a put-on. Interracial brotherly love is probably the one thing that Richard Pryor should never be required to express. It violates his demonic, frazzled blackness. The suspense built into watching him is that we don't know what's coming out of him next, or where it's coming from. Those deep-set, somewhere-else eyes and that private giggle don't tell us much, but they do tell us this: his comedy doesn't come from love-thy-white-neighbor.

Most of *Silver Streak* is set on board a train from Los Angeles to Chicago, and the picture is so apologetic that it starts with a mess of exposition, explaining why each of the principal characters didn't take a plane. Wilder plays a Los Angeles publisher of how-to-do-it books, with a specialty in gardening, and the heroine, Jill Clayburgh, is the secretary of an art historian. After much badinage about the publisher's how-to-do-it expertise in the tending of flowers (i.e., sex), they go to bed, he lies back with his arms under his head, and she proceeds to do everything. This discrepancy isn't meant to be funny. The scriptwriter, Colin Higgins, and the director, Arthur Hiller, are merely showing us how liberated she is—liberation here meaning eagerness to perform oral sex. Besides, they need to have the man lying back and the secretary bent down over him, so that he can get a clear view of what happens outside the window: a murdered man falls from the top of the train and is caught on a hook, hanging upside down for a few seconds before dropping from sight. The next morning, the hero sees the new book the secretary's boss has written, and from the jacket photograph recognizes that the art historian is the dead man. *Silver Streak* is so helplessly unslick that it doesn't even have the wit to show Wilder looking at the book upside down.

□ □ □

Nickelodeon, a slapstick homage to early fly-by-night moviemaking, begins in 1910 and ends in 1915, when the director hero (Ryan O'Neal) attends the Los Angeles première of *The Birth of a Nation,* discovers what movies can be, and realizes the inadequacy of the pictures he's been churning out. But Peter Bogdanovich has known *The Birth of a Nation* from the start of his career, yet has made *Nickelodeon.* Bogdanovich has once again—and catastrophically—misunderstood his talent, and attempted an exercise in style instead of trusting to his gift for telling popular stories with feeling. The result is sustained clutter: *Once in a Lifetime* played at the wrong speed—a movie with a large cast, and everyone on his own. Bogdanovich seemed to know just what to do with Tatum O'Neal in *Paper Moon,* but here he tries the stunt of having this little girl play a role that requires her to age from girlhood to young womanhood. The miscasting is worse than in the Michael Ritchie film *The Bad News Bears*; there nothing could conceal the fact that she didn't have the lean, muscular body of a girl athlete, but, at least, she gave a performance. Here she's lost in her deadpan, and as ageless at the end as at the beginning. And seeing her paired with her father adds to the viewer's discomfiture. Ryan O'Neal does a flustered variation of the bespectacled priss he played in *What's Up, Doc?* His face shows the honest desperation of a performer who isn't sure what he should be registering, and his voice becomes high and light out of sheer nervousness. Playing a young Southern roustabout turned movie hero, Burt Reynolds looks a little mature for boyish fighting and strutting. He works professionally hard, trying to stay in character even though there is no character. His teammate, the very pretty new ingenue Jane Hitchcock (she resembles Stella Stevens, who's also in the picture), is so carefully made up, lighted, and posed to be romantic that the first shot of her gives you everything you ever get. No one comes out of *Nickelodeon* with his reputation enhanced. The Laszlo Kovacs cinematography is handsome but off-putting; the characters are outlined against the backgrounds, like cardboard cutouts. The whole movie suggests process shots. (Was Kovacs thinking of possible ways to shoot *Ragtime*?) The effect is totally without sensuousness, and the various couples match up by rote. This picture makes you feel terrible, because you realize how deeply involved the director must have been to go so blindly wrong.

[January 17, 1977]

Harlan County

Barbara Kopple isn't a great documentarian, but she has a great subject in *Harlan County, U.S.A.*, and she has the taste and sensitivity not to betray it. She may not have the vision of an artist, but artists with vision didn't go to live among the coal miners of Kentucky and didn't scrounge up the money to put together a feature about them. She did. And the directness and simplicity of her approach give us something we wouldn't necessarily get from an artist. No matter what their subject, the great documentarians give us films that express them; their vision transforms the material. This film is humbler—it conveys the material without imposing its own way of seeing. When you hear the director's voice asking questions, she doesn't seem at a distance from those who answer; she's another character in the film rather than the artist conceiving it.

Harlan County, U.S.A., was made between 1972 and 1976, with money raised from foundations, the United Church of Christ, the United Methodist Church, and individual donors, and through loans. Committed to making films for social change, Miss Kopple began by filming the fight against the old guard within the United Mine Workers, and then, when the miners in Brookside, Harlan County, went on strike in July of 1973, seeking recognition of the U.M.W. as their union, she went there and stayed for the thirteen months of the strike, living among people with a legendary history of bloody labor strife—a heritage of bitterness that goes back so far it is ingrained. The people's rawboned gestures and harsh, sad twangs ("thing" is pronounced "thang") are signs of community; they share a hatred of the company and a practiced distrust of the union leaders. The resentment that has been passed down for generations may be the only thing the miners of Harlan County have to pass on to their children, yet they're tenacious, resilient people. Injustice has developed in them a fierce belief in justice. They looked to a union that was itself in turmoil. Joseph A. Yablonski, who had contested W. A. (Tony) Boyle's power in the U.M.W. and offered some hope of democratization, had been murdered, along with his wife and daughter. Boyle was charged with murder, tried, and convicted, and, with his power at last broken, Arnold R. Miller took over; but by the time Miller came to give encouragement to the people of Harlan County, their strike was in its sixth month. The film has a clear, well-paced narrative line; when the violence comes and there's gunfire at night, we've been well prepared for it. The fear that stiffens the faces of the miners and their wives as they go out together to face armed strikebreakers gives their defiance weight and solemnity. The movie tells the story of their strike, but it isn't just about people fighting for safer working conditions and decent pay; it's about an underdog group with its own folk culture, based on the unending struggle with "the owners."

Early on, there's a soft, lovely shot of a woman in big pink plastic curlers as she washes her children. Having none of the satirical condescension that Hollywood movies often show toward working-class people, the director (and the cameraman, Hart Perry) can perceive a beauty that includes five-and-dime plastic. This is not the sort of film in which one would expect the sex of the director to make much difference, but Barbara Kopple has unusual rapport with the women, and throughout—in groups, at meetings, talking—they're observed in a relaxed, friendly way. It's apparent that they've had to be tough when they wanted to be pretty and tender. They try to keep themselves up, no matter what hell is breaking loose. Bouffant hairdos frame wrinkled, big faces—they're never beyond caring how they look, except maybe in the presence of death. A gaunt, long-jawed woman—Sudie is her name—resembles Lily Tomlin, and has similar speech patterns, but looks stronger; her voice is low, with an emotional crack. The sensitivity in Sudie's face is concentrated; she has the trace of melancholy that converts plainness to beauty. She's lived for a long time with deprivation and knows that what's been lost is irretrievable. When she talks of her life, lets go of her emotions, and tears come to her eyes, we still see a bobby pin holding a pin curl in place above her ear, and the moment has an authenticity beyond the power of fiction films. Straight and scrawny in her white dress with its little puffed sleeves, Sudie has the classic sadness of the poor. By contrast, the curly-haired heavyweight Lois Scott, the dominating force among the women, seems to belong to the lower middle class, and, resourceful and quick-witted though she is, we don't stand in awe of her. (She's a miner's wife, all right, but from a neighboring town; she has come in sympathy, and she always sticks out a little.)

The director doesn't appear to have been in a position to achieve comparable glimpses of the men; only the old-timers, raspy-voiced but proud of what they've lived through, take the camera in the special way that we associate with Depression photojournalism—worn faces confronting us like truth capsules. A handsome, square-headed old man speaks directly to us, and then, in a blown-up detail of a Lewis W. Hine photograph of children working in the mines in 1911, we see him among the pinched, accusatory faces that stare out at us, and we realize the moral and physical strength this man had to have to emerge unscathed, speaking civilly, as a survivor, not a victim. The older men are willing to pose for conversational portraits; the younger ones are involved in action, so we don't see them as they see themselves.

The camera is respectful, like a longtime friend. The miners and their families are not aestheticized by being seen in stasis as tragic figures, and they're not emotionalized as "the simple, good people." The camera doesn't move in close for poignancy—it doesn't emphasize the missing teeth, the collapsed jaws, the shapeless print dresses. You never get the feeling that the subjects would be shamed by anything in the film. They're not just the subjects, they're participants, and they are not pushed to make phony revelations. The women are fairly ferocious when they bicker over picket duty; there's plenty of hatred under their solidarity. But the camera doesn't try to score off them. It does score off the spokesmen for the company—Eastover Mining, which is a subsidiary of Duke Power, one of the largest utility companies in the country—but they present an almost irresistible target. A filmmaker wouldn't be human if he or she didn't move into closeup for the executive who creates an imaginary antagonist and asserts, as if embattled, that "it is not true that inhalation of coal dust *necessarily* results in any impairment of pulmonary functions." And when Norman Yarborough, the head of Eastover, deplores the picketing and activism of the wives, saying he would hate to see *his* wife "reverting to this type of behavior," the cinematographer has every reason to feel that the camera is a microscope, and that only by prying into the speaker's pores can one discover the nature of the beast. This sort of obviousness is rare, however. When the picketing women, the striking men, and the strike-breakers are lined up on a turn in a road, with state troopers looking on, the sheriff comes over and gives orders to the women, and the bulldozing Lois Scott, who has obviously known him all her life, bawls him out. She tells him he doesn't have the guts to do his job fairly. The camera stays on him as he walks back across the road to confer with the company foreman, and his self-conscious walk tells you he's trying to look strong and in command while feeling crummy and unsure of himself. That's real filmmaking—catching the moment, having the judgment to keep it intact, and having an editing scheme that allows it to fall into place, right where it belongs. Barbara Kopple has worked as an editor, a camerawoman, and a sound woman, and she was involved in *Hearts and Minds, Winter Soldier, Gimme Shelter,* and other films and TV projects, but this is her début as a director. For a novice filmmaker, she has some impressive intuitions, though she doesn't always rise above her mentors.

It's dramatically right that we should see the faces of the people after the violent confrontations are over—hear the miners singing and see that the tenseness is gone and that their eyes have lost that pale stare of fear. One of the strikers—Lawrence Jones—has been killed, leaving a sixteen-year-old wife and five-month-old daughter; at his funeral a group of men sing and people weep, giving vent to their relief and their grief, mixed together. But I wish we didn't hear Mrs. Scott talking to the miners about the *meaning* of Jones's death, explaining it in terms of their victory. She says that it's when you're ready to die for something that you get it. There's a professional public speaker's glibness about her that is really a turn-off. The film itself is not glib: it shows that, though the men get their union contract, subsequent events make this a dubious triumph. However, at the end it rings in an organizer and a young miner to tell us the meaning of what we've been looking at. The young miner tells us that the strike was won from below. Since that seemed to be obvious, the effect is to make us doubt it. Why are we getting these union speeches now, by people we haven't seen before? Were there outsiders—beyond the camera—directing this strike? Were there pros working out the strategy with the men while we were off with the women? Have we been conned? Maybe a little. Maybe somewhat inadvertently.

The photojournalist documentary is essentially a mixed form, a compromise. In *Harlan County, U.S.A.,* the director is exploring a folk society that draws her in, as good ethnographic filmmakers have almost always been drawn in, to admire, and even to revere. But this is not a remote village thousands of miles away; it's right among us, and the filmmaker is also a muckraker, a sympathetic propagandist, who wants to serve the people she reveres. (Sometimes, fairness is sacrificed for a satirical point. The film might have indicated that Yarborough's "reverting" remark didn't refer just to the women's picketing; the women, who had been whopping strikebreakers, got carried away by their new activism and beat up a state trooper.) Barbara Kopple keeps a fairly steady balance, but in a documentary film, no matter what one's intentions, there is always a certain amount of shaping, in terms of what footage the crew was able to get and what is worth using. Events that are badly shot get thrown out, as if they had never happened, and sometimes, in assembling the footage, the director discovers that there is nothing to link up certain events. Not having used any voice-over narration, Miss Kopple must have worried that she hadn't clarified the issues of the strike or shown some of its leaders, and so at the end—plop—they've been put in.

The angry, inflammatory grief of a woman wailing "Oh, Death" at Yablonski's funeral is so strong it's purifying. But not when we first hear her—only when we see her (it's Phyllis Boyens, singing with her father, Nimrod Workman) and perceive the unity of the haggard face and the lacerating voice. When Florence Reese, a grandmotherly woman in a checked dress, sings her 1930s composition "Which Side Are You On?" in a quavering voice, there's unity, too, and, because the camera is very objective, there's no bathos—the Southern-mountain-people faces validate even the most messagey ballads. But we have to see who is singing. When

Hazel Dickens' songs—"Cold-Blooded Murder," "They'll Never Keep Us Down," and "Black Lung"—and an updated version of "Which Side Are You On?" are used on the track to supply sound for the passages without dialogue, the contrasts of images and lyrics are too shallow; the people's faces speak of more than the lyrics encompass. At the graves after a mine explosion, the ballad on the track (Hazel Dickens' "Mannington," sung by David Morris) diminishes the power of the images; we need the dignity of quiet, or, at least, music without the intrusive irony of editorializing lyrics. The director doesn't leave us to our own resources enough; she doesn't allow us a chance to fill in from our own feelings.

It's an understandable fault—an effort to reach us by a director who doesn't know that she's already done the job. (She doesn't need the dig of "U.S.A." in the title.) Elsewhere, she avoids sentimentality, though there are bound to be some who will think the whole film sentimental, because the people of Harlan County come off as heroic. Most of us don't live in such clear-cut terms of right and wrong. We're probably more like that poor sheriff shuttling back and forth between opposing forces, trying to be fair to everybody and feeling small and stinky. But coal miners, working below ground, with the threat of sudden death by cave-ins and explosions, and the slow debilitation of black-lung disease, are a different breed. And if we recognize that they've never had rightful legal protection—that they are, in fact, permanent victims of injustice—we ought to be able to accept the idea that their clinging to the idea of justice, and shoving it into the faces of "the owners," and often sticking it to the union, too, makes them strong and likable. People who are willing to risk their bodies take the camera gracefully, dauntingly. Fiction films have never been able to fake this.

□ □ □

Dirty Harry, starring Clint Eastwood as Harry Callahan, the San Francisco police inspector who embodies a higher law, was a wizardly piece of vicious, brutal filmmaking; its sequel, Magnum Force, was poorly made but did have some cheap nastiness; the third in the series, the new The Enforcer, doesn't have the savvy to be sadistic. It's just limp. Yet each film has done bigger business than its predecessor. Have people become so accustomed to the series idea from television viewing that they go to another Dirty Harry movie because it's a known quantity? It may be that moviegoing is so expensive and people have been stung so often that they want to know what they're going to get. And maybe after a couple of Dirty Harry movies they're conditioned: they no longer need Eastwood plus violence plus fantasy—all they need is to see a picture of him.

In the first of the series, if Eastwood had thought out Dirty Harry we'd have had to hate that brutally self-righteous cop. But Eastwood played

Harry as a comic-book saint. By now, he appears to be taking Harry's saintliness so seriously that he's tense with indignation; Harry can't relax, because of his sense of higher duty. Eastwood has lost the ominous sensuality he had in the spaghetti Westerns. The machinery has tightened up. He looks stricken—he hisses his lines angrily, his mouth pulled thin by righteousness. Is it time for Eastwood to turn villain? This drawn, creased face could have a George Macready sinister charm. Or has he gone past that already? At the climax of *The Enforcer,* when he yells "You ******* fruit!" as he kills his enemy, he looks ready to drool and climb the walls.

The Enforcer, produced by Eastwood's own company, with a hand-picked director, James Fargo, who was the assistant director on several Eastwood pictures, uses the same basic plot strategy as the Western *The Outlaw Josey Wales,* Eastwood's previous film. It sets up a collection of villains so disgustingly cruel and inhuman that Eastwood can spend the rest of the movie killing them with a perfect conscience. The Dirty Harry movies adapt to the latest in exploitative topicality; this time Harry is up against a terrorist group, the Revolutionary Strike Force. The members of this group are not really revolutionaries, though. They're just what Archie Bunker could have told Harry they'd be: pimps and hookers, who are in it for the money. And they've been directed to sneer and leer, like a gay landlord foreclosing the mortgage on the old homestead. There's also a black militant group with a panicky guru who serves as a police informer, and, of course, the usual contingent of liberal twits running the city government. When Harry, single-handed, goes in and rescues a batch of hostages from some robbers—an act that would make him the hero of every cop in town—he's reprimanded, and suspended from duty. They wouldn't try to get by with that on "Kojak."

Though the script, by Stirling Silliphant and Dean Riesner, is just scaffolding, and there isn't one well-written line, a fast, lurid action film could have been made out of this garbage (as was done in *Dirty Harry*) if Eastwood and Fargo had got some velocity into their chases, and if they had created the atmosphere of corruption and lurking fear that would make us accept the idea of a city imperilled by thrill-seeking mercenaries. People get killed in this movie, but the violence has no rot or meanness in it. The staging is lackadaisical; the jowly revolutionaries shoot with one eye on the time clock. Does Eastwood's production company purposely choose bad actors to surround him with—to make him look better? Probably not—probably it's the director's fault that the actors look sedated. The movie comes to an amateurish full stop while the mayor's representative on the police board—a woman—shows her lack of comprehension of police problems; the acting is so archaic you expect her to pull out a lorgnette. The one smart move the filmmakers made was to cast Tyne Daly (she played Jack Lemmon's daughter in *The Entertainer*) as the heroine—a policewoman who is assigned to work with Callahan. Deliberately unglamorous in a clumsy work suit, Tyne Daly manages to show some believably human expressions of confusion and discomfort; she has worried eyes, and she isn't afraid to let her mouth go slack. It's such a warm performance that Eastwood's holy cool seems more aberrant than ever.

Harry is the source of the only venom we see; he's the one who's rancorous and strung out. And what is he snarling about? It's not that the villains are kidnappers and murderers—their real crime is that they're homosexual. In *The Eiger Sanction,* Eastwood sneered at the decadent killer (Jack Cassidy), whose dog was named Faggot; in *Magnum Force,* he mowed down a homosexual Nazi group inside the police department; in *The Enforcer,* he's got his "fruit." Is this the last outpost for the Western hero—killing homosexuals to purify the cities?

[January 24, 1977]

Werewolf, Mon Amour

The first hour of Alain Resnais' *Providence* is so dark it might have been shot by Samuel Beckett's Watt. In the gloom, patrols hunt down an old man; wounded, suffering, and turning into a werewolf, he begs to be killed. This part of the movie is set inside the mind of a dying novelist (John Gielgud); alone at night, in pain, he drunkenly plots a novel about the members of his family, and we see his barrister son, Claude (Dirk Bogarde), his daughter-in-law, Sonia (Ellen Burstyn), his illegitimate son, Kevin (David Warner), and his dead wife (Elaine Stritch) in the guises of his fictional distortions of them. As his characters, they drink chilled white wine while sitting in icy décor, in a nameless, forbidding old city with tall houses like ornate glaciers. Their brittle epigrams reveal—naturally—dank lust, moral rot, and ennui. The novelist sees his son Claude as a pasty-faced, frostbitten prosecutor, Sonia as restless and unfulfilled, and Kevin as a saint in the wrong period. He tries them out in different dramatic postures—always at odds with each other, spiteful and disconnected—while old buildings are being toppled and in the outskirts of the doomed city insurrectionists keep up their shelling and bombing. Then, in the last part, the picture moves into the sunlight. It is the novelist's seventy-eighth birthday, and the children come to lunch in his garden, and we see that his night thoughts were delusions and unfounded self-accusations. Claude and Sonia are devoted to each other; Kevin isn't an alienated wanderer; and they are all fond of the old man.

The problem with the structure is that if the sunlit "reality" section is supposed to be the truth, the sooty stuff we've been watching has come out of nowhere—except the Freudian stockpile available to all. If the novelist has whipped up this family fantasy in order to stimulate "the creative process," shouldn't the movie be about *why* he imagines what he does? If this movie is about anything, it's about a dying man who has nothing but contempt for everyone, and the guilt that goes with that contempt. He sees Claude as a spiteful prig who hates him, and imagines scenes with his dead wife as Claude's mistress. The motor of this movie idles, it is true, but the only motor it has is the father's loathing of Claude. This loathing gives the scriptwriter, the playwright David Mercer, a chance to show off his talent for bitchy invective, and Gielgud, master ranter that he is, savors every mean syllable. The apparent indecision on the part of the filmmakers about whether the night and day sides of the film are to match up and reveal what's missing from the half views or whether the novelist is a genial old man—carnal and bilious in imagination only—is a considerable flaw. It stands out, because the script is so intricately planned and overarticulate that every line seems crystallized. That is a bigger flaw.

The movies, which learned to talk late, and often speak casually and colloquially, are too frequently praised for talking the language of the theatre. I don't mean to suggest that David Mercer's script would be a good play—it would be an awful play. But it's worse as a movie that sounds like a play. For a full hour, we sit listening to impossibly elocutionary lines: Gielgud, in bed in red silk pajamas, delivers himself of observations like "How darkness creeps into the blood—darkness, the chill obsidian fingers." Mercer writes like Maxwell Anderson imagining himself as John Osborne; it's corrugated-brow writing. Listening to this class trash, are we supposed to think that the old literary lion whose skull we're inside is a very bad writer? He chortles at his own cleverness while composing lines such as "Do I have to oppose you to reassure myself that I exist?" and "In my own curious fashion I think I've always loved you." Yet can we be meant to laugh at his satisfaction with his own virulence after we've seen Florence Malraux's name on the credits as assistant to the director, and remembered that Resnais is the son-in-law of André Malraux, who died a few months ago after a long illness?

No doubt Mercer intended an edge of florid fatuity through much of the first hour; we must be intended to smile at the archness when the barrister's mistress asks him how he and his wife live, and he answers, "In a state of unacknowledged mutual exhaustion, behind which we scream silently." But who can distinguish between Dirk Bogarde acting arch and just acting as usual? And when the old novelist tells us that "style is feeling," surely Mercer means it, though in an Alain Resnais movie that's the funniest line of all. If the formal elegance of his *Last Year at Marienbad* proved anything, it was that for Resnais style goes it alone.

When you go to an Alain Resnais film, you take it for granted that the only instinct that will come into play is his film instinct—his grasp of technique. Alone among major-name directors, Resnais has little grasp of character or subject; he's an innovator who hasn't got a use for his innovations. Most of the giants of film haven't been able to find the form for everything they've got in their heads; Resnais seems to have nothing but form in his. He does some artful editing in *Providence*: four people will be in a room and then suddenly the same four people will be in the same room but with a party going on around them, or an empty stadium will be magically filled with people—as if it had happened when your head was turned. What he doesn't seem able to do is to imbue his situations with enough feeling for these tricks to mean something to us—they're just beautiful diddles. And when form takes over and becomes an obsession, it is not just that everything else is absent—everything else is being denied.

Resnais' movies come out of an intolerable mixture of technique and culture. His tastes run to abstract concepts (time, memory) and to musical, literary language enunciated to the nines. (Gielgud's legato is the apotheosis of the Resnais sound track—it's probably as close as one can come in English to the style of French classic tragedy.) In *Providence,* Resnais' technique and culture are right out on top for you to admire, and there's nothing else—no spilling over, no earth or blood or uncontrollable terror. Resnais is in such immaculate, distanced control that when Gielgud screams at the pain in his bowels, he could be doing vocal exercises—it's part of a construct. How can the novelist have pain in his bowels when *Providence* has no bowels? Even the werewolf bits—quick views of men growing hairy moss on their hands and cheeks—lose their murky mystery; the novelist's seeing himself as a werewolf, for his sons to slaughter, one out of pity, one out of repugnance, is just tidy psychological games-manship. The effect of the pearl-gray tones, the swift, smooth cutting, and the fearful literacy is peculiarly fastidious and static, as if Resnais had amused himself by chopping up a bad novel or a bad play. You feel as if the movie were going to dry up and blow away. I don't know whether it's more difficult for a director working in a foreign language (Renais is working in English, for the first time) to make a hallucinatory film or a naturalistic one, but the night and day sections are just about equally stilted. The day perhaps more so: the Miklós Rósza music provides horns and woodwinds for happy thoughts—Disney-Debussy.

With John Gielgud and Dirk Bogarde playing father and son, *Providence has* to be a comedy. They pair up superlatively—that's what's funny. But it works at cross-purposes with the film's ritzy morbidity—the slashed-open cadaver of a desiccated old man, elderly people being herded together in a stadium, and the anguish of aged werewolves. You can't take two of the most familiar, most stylized actors who have ever lived, put them inside all this darkling imagery, and expect the audience to have a profound experience—a sort of *Wild Strawberries* revisited.

Gielgud has a longer death scene than Camille's; it's the whole movie. Every line in his fat role is an overwrought blooper, and he can't create a character out of what he's been given, yet he whoops it up with a marvellous zest. His polished effrontery makes him a sight to behold, just as it did a few weeks ago on Broadway, in *No Man's Land*. These days, he seems to delight in impersonations. He did a takeoff of W. H. Auden in the Pinter play, and here, in the garden scenes, in his rattan chair, wearing an off-white suit, a pale-pink shirt, and a broad straw hat, he does a neat Cecil Beaton. God, how this old knight loves to act, loves the sound of his great singsong. There's lip-smacking joy in his dirty-old-man rant. He's lean and wiry, turkey-faced, a tough old bird—so alive to the kinetic pleasures of playacting that he bounces through the role, savoring its pipsqueak grandeur. It hardly seems to bother him that the picture is an ice bag; he's entertaining himself acting. Bogarde has certainly proved that he knows how to give bad lines a twist, but in this film, which seems to offer him a license to be as warped and disdainful and masochistic as he could desire, he is unaccountably dim. Is he bored to sogginess with playing rotters? Even when his vagrant eyebrow takes off on its own trip, he doesn't have the old gleeful peevishness. As Elaine Stritch's lover, he looks small and bewildered—if this is the point, nothing is made of it. And Stritch acts like a soap-opera tired wife; her baritone could be from housecleaning fatigue.

When you see the list of who is in *Providence,* you think, What could link those actors? Nothing does. David Warner had his biggest film success in *Morgan!,* which Mercer also wrote, but here, shrouded in a heavy knit turtleneck, he gives a dejected performance. His role is probably based on Resnais himself—a man who carries equanimity to the edge of dissociation, and beyond, into a sci-fi cool. The Hesse-like sanctity obliterates Warner; except for a moment or two of lofty discourse about the poetry of space travel, he's a passive, blobby spot on the screen. Resnais frequently uses women for the high-couture pretty pictures they make gliding in long skirts, trailing scarves and capes; he likes them to be inexpressive, and Ellen Burstyn, traipsing around in Yves Saint Laurent gowns and a modified Marienbad haircut, appears to be trying to oblige. But his scenic use of her picks up a dullness of spirit under the winsome smiles and fake radiance; attempting to be soft and ladylike, she's custardy. This actress is in the wrong place, and at some level it must have got to her. When she's being blithe and loving in the garden at the end, you can feel the anger underneath—the anger that worked for her in *Alice Doesn't Live Here Anymore.* In *Providence,* the track and the images operate in two different realms, leaving a dead space between. Ellen Burstyn's performance seems to be locked in that space. It's not only that her voice seems slightly out of synch but that her acting is a few frames behind—as if someone had slugged her before each take. She could be growing moss, too, in the time it takes her to register a thought.

Everything that doesn't feel right could be explained as intentional. And since Mercer appears to have put together a script modelled on the themes and obsessions of Resnais' earlier films, there is so much tucked in about the intermingling of the characters' pasts and present, and there are so many Freudian reversals, that one could perform miracles of exegesis and think that one was explicating a masterwork. But what you come away with is the pain of a "clever" English play—Borges with chilblains.

[January 31, 1977]

The Late Show

*I*n repose, Lily Tomlin looks like a wistful pony; when she grins, her equine gums and long, drawn face suggest a friendly, goofy horse. Either way, she takes the camera and holds it for as long as she wants to, with the assurance of a star. On TV, when she does one of her characters—such as the squinchy-eyed five-and-a-half-year-old Edith Ann, sitting sly and lonely in a big chair—you feel that she is creating this character out of the possibilities in herself. She can make you respond the same way in a movie role conceived by others. In *Nashville*, she played a sane woman who knew what mattered to her, and each time that she had a scene she brought calm into the movie. As Margo in the new detective film *The Late Show*, written and directed by Robert Benton, everything she does is a little off center. Margo is a nervous talker; her perceptions are faster than her ability to process them, and her conversation is a humming sound that she barely hears. Margo came to L.A. to be an actress, and she still has ties to show business—she's trying to manage some performers. She's also trying to start a dress-designing business, while hanging on by dealing a little grass and transporting stolen goods. That's how she gets into the trouble that the movie is about: she keeps five hundred dollars that doesn't belong to her, and the hoods she's working for take her cat, threatening to strangle it unless she pays up. At first, Margo doesn't seem very smart, or particularly likable. But then she's so exhilarated by her prowess at driving a van away from a pursuing car that she cackles in triumph and begins to fantasize a whole new life for herself, and we see the gleam as she realizes that Ira Wells (Art Carney), the old private investigator who has been trying to find her cat, may be overweight and out of condition but he's different from the other men she knows. An instant later, she suggests that they could become a team like Nick and Nora Charles. Without any encouragement from the embarrassed yet pleased senior citizen, she dreams on, higher and higher, and her euphoria is openhearted. Lily Tomlin has the magical timing to do this dizzy, difficult scene in character and make it seem totally unrehearsed. If anyone else were playing Margo, she might be a mere kook; Tomlin makes her a genuine eccentric—she isn't just the heroine, she's the picture's comic muse.

In *The Late Show*, Robert Benton has followed the rules of the detective-movie genre, but he's also added something. The movie starts with Harry (Howard Duff), another detective trying to locate Margo's cat, showing up at Ira Wells' rooming house with a bullet hole in his stomach. Ira talks to Harry, watching, in a rage of helplessness, as his old friend dies. The film prepares us for Ira's determination to find out who murdered Harry. Ira doesn't unravel the mystery for us. We discover what's going on as he does; we react with him to the frightening things that happen when you break into a motel room at night and follow a trail of blood. Ira isn't cool, or fast on the draw, or able to outwit the scummy new-style operators; he's the hero because he is none of these things and is still determined to do the job. The something that's been added to the genre is that Ira Wells is scared. He's old and he's sick, with a perforated ulcer. He's humiliated by his physical weakness, and he can't take being roughed up anymore. Yet finding Harry's killers is his only way to prove to himself that he's not over the hill. In the standard detective movie, you have to accept the detective's integrity as a given; here you really believe in Ira's integrity, because that's all that old age has left him.

Spiritually, Ira Wells might be wearing a string tie, like the old Westerner Joel McCrea played in Peckinpah's *Ride the High Country*. There's an air of Sunday-suit formality about him. He's a dignified, big man, using a hearing aid and shifting his weight painfully from one foot to the other; you think his shoes must be pinching until you discover he's been carrying lead in one leg for over twenty years. He is what a private eye of the forties movies might have come to—living alone in a furnished room, without a car, retired because any two-bit chiseller can shove him around. Unprotected, Ira lumbers into a gangster's mansion, hoping to bluff his way through, only to have his bluff called. You feel his desperation—Art Carney seems to be working inside a nightmare that he's known for a long time. He gives Ira a human gravity, which contrasts with the inconsequentiality of the sharpie killers; they're comic heavies, lightly satirized, and this makes them even more of an insult to the old man. Eugene Roche plays Birdwell, a jolly fat-man fence, who treats Ira as harmless—calls him Pop, and gives him a handout. As the cheating Mrs. Birdwell, who lies as unconsciously as she draws breath, Joanna Cassidy has some of the luscious sluttiness that Rita Hayworth had in the late thirties. Mrs. Birdwell might be wearing sweaty satin; she's all curves, and she has a jive come-on, like James M. Cain's dirty charmers who can persuade a man to do anything.

This is only Robert Benton's second film, but he has become a much stronger director than he was on his first, *Bad Company*, in 1972. (*The Late Show* is the first script that he has written alone; he did *Bonnie and Clyde* in collaboration with his usual writing partner, David Newman.) Benton has learned the smartest thing anybody could learn from Robert Altman, who produced this picture—to pick actors with the ability to bring the characters up out of themselves, and then to encourage them to trust themselves and each other. Each character is an original. Lily Tomlin's Margo, who wanders off in her head and loses track of what's going on around her, needs a keeper, and she finds one in Art Carney's steady, close-lipped Ira. Eugene Roche makes the despicable Birdwell one of the loosest villains ever seen. Birdwell doesn't plan his swinishness—it comes so naturally to him he just plays it by ear. Birdwell the fence is a living ode to materialism; he loves his stolen goodies—his cajoling speeches about the joys of freeloading are delivered like comic arias. And Bill Macy, who plays Margo's scrounging bartender friend Charlie, is practically reborn. Macy drops the middle-class intonations and gestures familiar from his dutiful Walter Findlay in the "Maude" series; with his hair combed back and a pencil-thin mustache, Charlie is a dude lizard. He's a failed talent agent, a cruddy, marginal man—not guilty and not innocent. The jokes involving Ruth Nelson as Ira's straitlaced landlady are a little coy; the director seems to want laughs without having enough conviction to go after them. And though as Birdwell's natty bodyguard John Considine has one plum scene—he's forced to jump into a swimming pool and tries to protect his cashmere jacket—his role isn't much more than a comic variant of the darkly handsome lowlife sheiks that Jack La Rue used to play. Considine had the springiness of a perfect fool in the role of Annie Oakley's philandering husband in *Buffalo Bill and the Indians*, but here we're primed to find him funny, and the movie is too subtly toned for this kind of comic relief. The performers are so good that we want more of the characters than we get—it's slightly frustrating that the script holds them in check.

The Late Show never lets up; the editing is by Lou Lombardo (who has often worked with Altman) and Peter Appleton, and I can't think of a thriller from the forties that is as tight as this, or has such sustained tension. Chuck Rosher's cinematography does what's needed without making you feel you should applaud each shot, and the music, by Ken Wannberg, with saxophone themes that shift to strings for the sultry Mrs. Birdwell's con jobs, doesn't overdo the "haunting" bit. There may be a shortcoming. We expect the clichés of the genre to crack open and they don't. Benton knew he had the writing to fall back on, and he stuck to it too closely; his balanced approach to writing and directing evens things out so that the point of the picture is muted. If Benton hadn't written the script, he might have pushed some of the situations further, so that the cutthroat nastiness would give us shivers, as in *Double Indemnity*. Perhaps if Ira were the kind of man who had to fight his own susceptibility to Mrs. Birdwell, we might be drawn in deeper. From the bullet in his leg and the framed photo of Martha Vickers (the sweet psychopath of *The Big Sleep*) in his room, we get the idea that he's been played for a fool in the past. This is his "late show," and the whole conception requires that he be beyond temptation, but the cooling of his blood distances the crime plot. The events he uncovers don't mean enough to prickle in our imaginations, especially since, except for Howard Duff's Harry, we never see any of the murder victims alive. And the solution doesn't provide enough coherence—it's a paperwork solution. *The Late Show* doesn't quite pay off in the way a thriller is expected to—in thrills. It pays off in atmosphere, spooking us by the flip, greedy ordinariness of the evil. Benton's nostalgia for the genre works imaginatively in every detail of the film. What he lacks is low cunning. Working in the thriller genre, he's a sensitive craftsman infatuated with a painted whore. *The Late Show* is fast and exciting, but it isn't a thriller, exactly. It's a one-of-a-kind movie—a love-hate poem to sleaziness.

[February 7, 1977]

Boss Ladies

Glenda Jackson's claws always show. In her performance as Alexandra, the patrician nun of *Nasty Habits*, those claws and her hard, amused eyes reveal the wolf disguised as Red Riding Hood's grandmother. Since *Nasty Habits* is the film version of Muriel Spark's 1974 novel *The Abbess of Crewe*, the Watergate travesty set in a convent, and Alexandra represents Nixon, this flash of the wolf inside the nun's clothing gives her imperiousness a mythic edge. Alexandra, a woman with the *idée fixe* that she must be elected abbess—that it was for this that she was born—is never a mere villainess. She's a sacred monster, a romantic authoritarian, rather like Mrs. Spark's Miss Jean Brodie, but far more intelligent and regal. Alexandra moves, the author tells us, "like a Maharajah aloft on his elephant."

With Glenda Jackson's normal biting delivery—her almost vengeful enunciation—softened by unctuousness, and her pared-down, abrupt manner smoothed by the needs of campaigning for office, Alexandra is the compleat hypocrite, her malice and intensity kept in check. Addressing the assembled nuns or the television public, she has a connoisseur's ear for her own gift of language: she regards her articulateness as a mark of natural superiority. She believes in nothing but herself and appreciates her own refinement and aplomb. In Alexandra, snobbery achieves perfection.

Except for the title, there is little that is gross about *Nasty Habits*, directed by Michael Lindsay-Hogg from a screenplay by the producer Robert Enders, who retains much of Mrs. Spark's dialogue. The film is set in Philadelphia (though most of the footage was shot in England, using an actual convent near the Elstree studios). At the start, the old abbess (Edith Evans) dies, and in a few weeks the nuns are to elect her successor. The arch-conservative Alexandra tells her minions Walburga and Mildred (Geraldine Page and Anne Jackson) that they must discredit Felicity (Susan Penhaligon), the liberal challenger. They arrange with Jesuits from a nearby seminary to send a couple of novices to break in and steal Felicity's love letters, which are kept in her sewing box. The first night that the novices break in, they are frightened off before they obtain the letters, but they take a thimble to prove to their superiors that they made the entry. Felicity discovers its loss, and when they return the next night, she locks them in and calls the police. Alexandra manages to keep the lid down and is elected by a landslide, but she's blackmailed by the burglars, and Felicity takes her case to the public and creates a scandal.

Having bugged the convent, and even the poplars on the grounds, Alexandra and her Haldeman and Ehrlichman—Walburga and Mildred— try to clear themselves by putting the blame on their patsy, Winifred, their own John Dean (Sandy Dennis). The conception does not require that the actresses impersonate the Watergate troupe. It's a comic bonus that Sandy Dennis, wearing big, round specs and grinning like a rabbit, isn't just a cartoon of John Dean smiling—she's John Dean crossed with Amy Carter. In the book, Winifred is described as speaking "in her whine of bewilderment, that voice of the very stupid, the mind where no dawn breaks," and Sandy Dennis turns blurting into woozy slapstick. Her Winifred has never learned how to modulate—she is always louder than anyone else, and her tactless remarks come crashing through the air, dislocating Alexandra's sensibilities. How can Alexandra maintain her aloofness from the coverup when Winifred forgets to be covert and belts out details, while calling her Alexandria to boot? When Sandy Dennis appeared in *The Out-of-Towners*, she rang so many sad-sack variations on "Oh, my God" that it was apparent that the movies had been wasting her in snivelling, suffering roles. This is her first real crack at screen farce, and she parodies her own mannerisms. It's bliss watching her—the same kind of bliss one feels each time Jack Gilford or Bob Dishy comes onstage in *Sly Fox*. Winifred the sneak, pulling down her upper lip in order to think, is a transsexual Uriah Heep. She doesn't walk, she teeters. When she dresses up in her idea of civvies—platform soles, short skirts, and shocking-pink pantyhose—in order to make a payoff to the blackmailing Jesuit novices in the ladies' lavatory at Wanamaker's, or disguises herself as a man in order to make a payoff in the men's lavatory at Independence Square, she's such a drip she's creepy. As Sandy Dennis plays her, she's a feminine version of a Shakespearean fool—her stupidity is a form of enchantment. This movie has a great batch of braying fools and clowns, and with Rip Torn turning up for a bit as a Jesuit it even has a satyr. At its best—high wit and inspired silliness—*Nasty Habits* suggests a Midsummer Night's Dream of Watergate.

The nuns group together, forming pretty patterns; with each one framed by her coif and habit, their comings and goings have a Book of Hours ceremoniousness. They circle around Alexandra, her willfulness magnetizing them. The Watergate plot could be set in almost any bureaucratic institution, but putting it in a convent has the burlesque advantage of the sex transposition: not only do we have women playing power games but we get to see nuns, in their austere draperies—enclosed in sanctity—reveal their crass thoughts. Alexandra and Walburga and Mildred look serene among the other nuns; when they talk among themselves, their words are toads jumping out of their lovely mouths. Venting their hatred of Felicity and her supporters, or making jokes about their own flunky, Winifred, they're a coiffed little wolf pack. Anne Jackson's Mildred sails into a room, smiling beatifically—the Madonna as contented matron—and then speaks out of the corner of her mouth like a ward heeler chewing on a cold cigar.

Most movies that lift stylized dialogue straight from a novel become arch and awful, but this cracked-crystal surface comes close to matching the tart chastity of Mrs. Spark's prose. Contemptuous of Felicity's bourgeois sewing box, Alexandra speaks of the stolen thimble with withering arrogance. When she speculates, "If the thimble was a symbol," there's a bit of the hypercivilized impishness of Bea Lillie's "You will find the dinghy by the jetty" in *On Approval*—a movie that *Nasty Habits*, in its heraldic camp, somewhat resembles. There is just one episode taken from the book that doesn't play. Alexandra recites a tediously long list of words that Felicity has used in her bill of particulars against the tyranny in the convent; the scene is too writery—it's an author's equivalent of an actress's demonstrating her powers by reading the telephone directory aloud. Except for this, the movie wobbles only when it employs more naturalistic speech, and it loses its visual tone then, too.

The novel itself is cryptic and very slight, even though it is padded with a running series of long-distance phone conversations between Alexandra and the Abbey's plenipotentiary missionary nun, the Kissinger figure (played by Melina Mercouri, who apparently qualifies by the timbre of her voice and the thickness of her accent—it can't be for her acting). The book doesn't give the film quite enough to draw upon, and though the scenarist has added a Gerald Ford figure—Geraldine, played by Anne Meara—he leaves her on the sidelines. Even without much in the way of dialogue, Anne Meara combines the brassy, gum-chewing delivery of the wisecracking gold diggers of the thirties with the expressive gestures of a top banana. Everything she does is funny. The other additions are mostly dramatic filler, and Enders' interpolated lines don't have the sureness of Mrs. Spark's cadences. A couple of added scenes featuring Eli Wallach as a monsignor in Rome are transparently designed to placate Catholics by suggesting that the Abbey, which is "quasi-Benedictine" and "quasi-Jesuit," isn't under the control of the Vatican. And there are some street scenes of Felicity handing out leaflets and soliciting public support that lack the finesse of Douglas Slocombe's cinematography in the soft-lighted convent, with its formal walks and ornamental enclosures.

Right at the center of the material there's a quirk. Somewhere between Muriel Spark's conceiving this satire of Watergate and completing it, she developed a crush on her prime creation, and Alexandra became a living work of art, who "stands like the masthead of an ancient ship." Alexandra began to represent Muriel Spark herself—an ascetic romantic, drawn to the preservation of forms. And since the author shares Alexandra's contempt for Felicity's innocence—for her attacks on materialism and her campaign for a "love abbey"—she saw no need for a paranoid flaw in Alexandra's character. Nixon may have been Mrs. Spark's starting point, and Watergate the device for her plot, but Alexandra eventually becomes the culmination of centuries of very grand breeding, her monarchical values enshrined even while her clique is being satirized for its bungling.

Alexandra loathes Felicity's do-goodism; she sees Felicity as a weakling, a worm for squishing. But Alexandra isn't maniacal enough, or even insecure enough, to feel threatened by Felicity's revolutionary followers. She is above fear. Alexandra is so lofty that the forces are never joined in battle, and Susan Penhaligon's Felicity doesn't come across as a character. One could say the same thing of McGovern, but Felicity doesn't come across even as a nebulous character. She's just a smudged-face flower child, so ordinary she's hardly worthy of Alexandra's gibes at her commonness. We expect a final clarity, some whopping irony—Felicity's triumph and the recognition that Alexandra's wolfishness brought it about—and we don't get it, partly because the author couldn't bear to degrade Alexandra by making fun of her. So toward the close, when the film uses lines derived from Nixon himself, it seems to be falling back on Watergate. Ideally, the movie should have the structure to stand as a travesty of convent life, independent of the Watergate burlesque. It doesn't, quite—it tapers off toward topicality and obviousness, and the end seems premature. This movie goes by all too quickly. The actresses seem to be warming up—and the show is over.

Despite his name, the thirty-six-year-old director, Michael Lindsay-Hogg, is American (though he also has Irish citizenship, via his mother, Geraldine Fitzgerald). He began in the theatre as an actor, then ran a small-town stock company (with Peter Bogdanovich) in upstate New York in 1961, and from there went to Ireland to work in TV and the theatre, and then to England, where he did promotional films for the Beatles and the Rolling Stones, and directed TV plays by Simon Gray and Trevor Griffiths. This is only his second feature; his first was the 1970 Beatles documentary, *Let It Be*. This film might be low comedy burdened with rarefied dialogue if it weren't for the balmy gracefulness of his comic tableaux and the measured flow of clipped language, which at times calls up Evelyn Waugh. Other satires of Nixon have hustled their own political pieties, and they've pointed up his lower-middle-class tone for the derision of counterculture audiences. The serious *All the President's Men* was poisonously mediocre and, finally, a celebration of the journalistic benefits of having an informer tucked away in a garage. But even those who voted for Nixon may be able to laugh at *Nasty Habits*, because it has a midsummer madness about it. Simpleminded satires usually make the points they set out to make; the satires that are truly funny often don't. Their authors' feelings come through and gum things up. That isn't a problem, it's a paradox. And, as we're told in *Nasty Habits*, "a paradox you live with." In this case, happily.

[February 21, 1977]

Where We Are Now

With *Roots*, TV found a way to keep the audience away from movies for eight nights in a row. Even though the first two hours, which should have been shot in Africa with Africans, were glaringly fake, the film accumulated raw strength; it had a theme and a narrative sweep that caught you up emotionally and flung you around the room. Great filmmakers have been called grandiose dreamers for attempting considerably less than a twelve-hour black epic. (Without commercials, ten and a half hours.) Nights now, I still wake up and go over incidents in my head; it's been a while since I did that with a movie—*The Godfather, Part II* and *Nashville* were the last ones. The black actors in *Roots*—Louis Gossett, Jr., John Amos, Madge Sinclair, Ben Vereen, Olivia Cole, Georg Stanford Brown, and others—delivered performances that made most of the movie acting of the past year look spindly, practically disembodied. Partly because a handful of talented directors have been away working on big projects, this has been a terrible year for movies. I resented having to go out to a movie on the second night of the two-part TV film *Sybil*, because Sally Field's performance went way beyond anything I was likely to see. These longer narrative forms on TV enable actors to get into their characters and take hold of a viewer's imagination.

The movie studios aren't putting up a fight. The lassitude of the studio heads—in for a year or two, or just a half year, and then moving around in the conglomerate chess game—is a sign of their powerlessness. Suddenly, there are no strong men at the top. Heads of production come and go without having had a chance to build a reputation. They're not concerned with developing talent; they won't be in their jobs long enough to reap the benefits. For the first time in movie history, even the names of the studio heads are a blur.

The structure of the movie industry has broken down to the degree that there is no industry. Good films get made and don't get promoted, because there's nobody to promote them—no hucksters, no field representatives, no distributing apparatus to guarantee a picture a claim on the public's attention. New releases join the pantheon of dumped movies; prints never reach outlying areas, sometimes never even reach New York.

Pictures open with so little advance preparation that now and then the companies neglect to invite the press to review them. They're tossed into theatres and close before anybody finds out what they are; they may never reappear. The major companies don't know how to sell pictures anymore. They don't know how to create audience anticipation. Have there even been any good trailers in recent years? Most of them are so full of gory climaxes that audiences laugh at them, or groan. Though frequent moviegoers, who buy half the admission tickets, are a very small percentage of the total population (probably smaller than five per cent), the only way that the majors know to promote a movie is on TV. Since a national media blitz costs from three to eight million dollars, the companies go all out for just a few of their pictures. They ignore the frequent moviegoers (whom they don't understand) and use the bulk of their advertising budgets trying to attract the people who will leave their TV sets and go out to a movie only two or three times a year. So the companies lose money on the majority of their movies. It's a failure of energy and ingenuity. The only thing the nervous executives can think to do is to cheat everybody extra hard. Their staffs are engaged in a holding action; people try to hold on to their jobs by being as close to invisible as possible, and, except for a few pictures with big campaigns, they let everything slide by. And even the big ones they often mishandle, making them seem so violent and exploitative that many people are frightened off.

Millions of those who watch the Academy Awards show on TV probably haven't seen any of the movies nominated; the *idea* of movies still has an appeal, but once you've lost the habit you have to make decisions. If you consider going out to a movie and open your newspaper to the movie pages, that mess you see is a sign of the societal changes that are making going-to-the-movies obsolete. There are ads for pictures you've never heard of, ads for foreign films that could be porn or could be earnest pictures disguised as porn, and perhaps one for a movie that you've read a good review of and thought you'd like to see but decide not to go to, because the ad makes it look bloody. There are now pictures playing in first-run theatres that are Z pictures—zilch that *nobody* has heard of.

The executives at the top have to decide what you'll go to see or what they can persuade you to go to see. But they aren't showmen with instincts, who worked their way up; they're agents plunked down in the jobs—deal-makers, not picture-makers. There is no longer any vital connection between the people who finance the movies and the people who go to them (or stay at home). There's a morass between. And there are no safe subjects. Except for the overseas market for Clint Eastwood or Charles Bronson, it's all hit or miss, and if the audience doesn't respond to a big new picture, the producers say, "What do the goddam people want?" Lacking the conviction that they know what the public wants, and fearing to trust what they themselves might want, most of them stall for as long as they can. Since one mistake can wreck their power position, they make fewer and fewer pictures. When the word gets out that a studio head is about to move or be moved, the studio becomes a production graveyard for months. The major companies have scheduled only ten movies to go into production in the first quarter of this year, and some of these may be cancelled.

Among the "independents," the selling of movies has gone back to the nickelodeon days: the pushiest pitchmen are drawing the public. Wilderness con jobs and "scientific" scams, such as *In Search of Noah's Ark*, are sold via regional saturation ads on TV. The kids who drag their parents to these snake-oil salesmen's operations don't realize that the TV commercial is the film; what's playing in the theatre is virtually outtakes. These con-men producers know that they don't need good pictures. What little word-of-mouth there is doesn't hurt them; by the time it catches up with them, they're into another area. Salesmen who go out to high-pressure an individual picture can peddle almost anything; having left Paramount, Frank Yablans, the top salesman in the business, has flogged his own first production, *Silver Streak*, so effectively that I'm beginning to get letters from people who are indignant that I panned it. In the new zilch-movie world, these salesmen-entrepreneurs function as parodies of the moguls of the past. But they could be all that will be left.

The vibes sent out by the major studios are that they don't want to make movies—they want to get out of the business. The fate of American movies as a great popular art form is in the hands of a very small group of artists. It's only the expectation of such films as *3 Women, New York, New York, Close Encounters of the Third Kind,* and *Apocalypse Now* and the hope of a few surprises which keep some excitement up for moviegoers.

□ □ □

*R*oots shows how TV could finish off movies, and *Fun with Dick and Jane* makes it seem like a good idea. Jane Fonda looks radiant in it, but what does it say about an actress's judgment to look so relaxed and happy in this picture—a leftover from the Nixon era, another movie telling us we're all crooked and looking for a bigger piece of the pie? She and George Segal play Dick and Jane of the children's primers grown up, married, and living beyond their means in a materialistic heaven. He's a Los Angeles aerospace executive, and they've become accustomed to credit-card affluence; when he loses his job, they turn to armed robbery in order to maintain their suburban-palatial dream house. The central idea is a variant of *Save the Tiger*: it offers the same sort of irrational solutions to basic economic problems, except that here the criminal behavior is played for farce, and instead of pitying the characters for being corrupt we're meant to find them enchanting. Robbing and being chased provide the sexual stimulus that the lackadaisical marriage needed; the resourcefulness required of Jane liberates her, and—final triumph—the couple's larcenous methods result in Dick's becoming head of the aerospace company that canned him. So they live on happily in their jerry-built mansion—American-dream winners. Since this sour message represents the point at which the cynical right and the idiot left meet, the film—for all its political stabs—means precisely nothing. It starts by saying that America makes everybody corrupt, and then, having rationalized crookedness, makes the biggest crooks the heroes. We're asked to cheer the trashy values it set out to attack. This is a nitwit comedy on the order of *For Pete's Sake*, though it's much worse made.

The director, Ted Kotcheff, shoves the camera too close to his actors; the lighting looks like early Elaine May; and his idea of rhythm is to alternate high-angle and low-angle shots. The editor tries to hide how badly directed the scenes are by piecing them together out of shots that don't seem to last more than seven seconds. In his previous film, *The Apprenticeship of Duddy Kravitz*, Kotcheff got by with this jerkiness, because Mordecai Richler's Dickensian energy was under it. *Fun with Dick and Jane* is based on Gerald Gaiser's screenplay for a serious film, which was turned into a lampoon by David Giler, then reworked by Jerry Belson, and, finally, sent to Richler for a fast (three-week) shuffle. You can perceive the comic effects that the scriptwriters intended (for example, in the sequence at the aerospace company when Dick comes out of the inner sanctum after being fired and everyone in the outer offices already knows), but the gags don't make you laugh; they make you flinch.

Kotcheff is the kind of director who thinks ugliness is funny. He really should be locked up for what he does to the performers. Many of the minor actors are playing "ethnic" roles, and the camera violates their features and strips them of dignity. These actors misread their lines so consistently that one has to assume they were directed to do so. The lines involve ethnic and homosexual jokes and some sick jokes (such as a real stinker about a man without vocal cords), which on paper may have appeared to be satiric; as Kotcheff handles them, they're so coarse they've gone back to being the material satirized. What kind of political comedy can you have with a director who makes practically every employee of every institution—every janitor or clerk—look stupid? When Kotcheff puts the Bach Magnificat on the sound track while a street crowd scrambles for money that's been tossed out of a car, we're supposed to see the contrast between man's possibilities and what men have become. The director doesn't even have the grace to indicate that some of these people may need the money. They're just swine heading for slops.

Fun with Dick and Jane was moderately costly (over four million dollars), but everything about it feels cheap—the watery pastels of the inept children's-book titles, the rattling rock ballad at the start, and the background music, which sounds like a car radio when the stations are jammed together. The mixture of counterculture politics, madcap comedy, and toilet humor is given the illusion of class by the presence of Jane Fonda and George Segal, and the tinge of smugness they confer on the material. The smile lines around Jane Fonda's mouth are ingratiating, and her long chestnut hair makes her seem warm and friendly; that's the extent of her performance. She plays one scene on the commode—probably because that's the only way anybody could figure out to keep the audience watching the scene. As for the constantly genial Segal, his insipid crinkly grin has become such a protective reflex that you want to wipe it off his face. For an actor with the talent he showed a few years back, that grin is like a death announcement; he looks ready for a TV series. The attraction of this piece of junk for the stars, and for the producers, Peter Bart and Max Palevsky, must have been the idea that it would be popular and also "say something." The more financially secure Hollywood people are, the more they seem to feel the need to teach us the perils of American materialism. Millionaires illustrate greed for us by showing people on the streets grabbing and crawling for a few dollars. The film demonstrates Dick's and Jane's sham values by placing them in a tract mansion that offends the moviemakers' tastes, though it probably does look like a dream house to most of the movie audiences throughout the world. But then those audiences are the same people who are represented here as swine. Moviemakers who turn out a film that looks like *Fun with Dick and Jane* shouldn't give anybody lessons in taste.

□ □ □

Thieves is a turkey that falls over without being shot. The Herb Gardner who wrote it must be a man of ninety-five who has been lying to himself all his life. *Thieves* is the story of a New York City marriage. The husband (Charles Grodin) has lost the wild, free spirit and the civil-rights convictions of his youth; he is the principal of a private school and has become the slave of propriety and possessions. But his pregnant wife (the inimitable Marlo Thomas) has kept her faith in people; she is dedicated to her job in a ghetto school and writes what she calls "children's poems." She lectures him on the glories of a mad, carefree existence—with full dedication to the underprivileged—and he is restored to being "the craziest kid in the neighborhood." Gardner is a proponent of the urban poetry of craziness—the phoniest rapture of William Saroyan stuck inside the staginess of Sidney Kingsley's *Dead End*. The husband and wife are followed around by mute ghosts of the city—an emblematic ragpicker (Mercedes McCambridge) and a token skid-row bum (Gary Merrill). The wife's cab-driver father (Irwin Corey) is a prejudiced but wise seventy-

271

eight-year-old leprechaun who chases "tootsies," because tootsies are "hopefulness itself," and there are dozens of clever, despairing, lonely people.

Considering that nobody talks—they make speeches, every one of them profound—Charles Grodin (who directed the stage version) gives a highly creditable performance. But even if everybody on the screen were as polished as he is, and even if the camera weren't always on Marlo Thomas's tight, anxious face, there still would not be a believable minute. John Berry is listed as director but was actually fired and replaced by Gardner; surely no one else would have retained the scene of the husband's breaking into the Loew's Delancey he had attended as a boy to climb onstage and deliver a paean to the vanished heroes of the screen. ("And Bogart is dead.") With just the tiniest shift of inflections, this script could be played as a Nichols-and-May routine. "Oh, Pop, what's it all for?" Marlo asks, and Pop, furious that she's planning an abortion, cocks his head lyrically and says, "It's for staying alive."

□ □ □

I was all primed for *Fellini's Casanova*. I'd given the *Memoirs* a squeeze—enough to perceive that the episodes were tempting screen material; I'd reread Edmund Wilson's essay in *The Wound and the Bow*; and I'd gone through some of the recent articles about Fellini. But the picture never got started, and after an hour I staggered out. Fellini has done something no one else in screen history has done: he has made an epic about his own alienation. And perhaps this can't be done successfully—not with all this pageantry, anyway. When an artist moves inward yet deals with his own spiritual crises on a spectacular and lavish scale, there is a conflict in form. Something goes rotten.

Fellini gives great interviews; he has turned into the Italian Orson Welles. He talks such a remarkable movie that maybe he doesn't need to make it. He has become the work of art.

[February 28, 1977]

Hill's Pâté

Nothing in movies is surefire anymore, yet George Roy Hill, who directed *Butch Cassidy and the Sundance Kid* and *The Sting*, two of the ten biggest money-makers of all time, will probably have a third with his new *Slap Shot.** The picture is set in the world of minor-league ice hockey, and the theme is that the public no longer cares about the sport—it wants goonish vaudeville and mayhem. Hill's last picture, *The Great Waldo Pepper*—a box-office failure—was bright and clear; it had the coolness of a schoolboy reverie. This time, he's heated up his technique. *Slap Shot* is darker-colored and grainier; it's faster, noisier, more profane, and more brutal than previous Hill productions. Dede Allen's hot-foot editing moves it along from zinger to zinger, and the Maxine Nightingale record "Right Back Where We Started From" punches up the pacing, and is even played on top of some of the dialogue scenes, competing with the talk. The beat gives the film a relentlessness; *Slap Shot* never slows down. You're aware of the seams and joins, but you can admire their proficiency; Hill directs with dispatch. Nancy Dowd's script—her first to be produced—resembles other scripts that have been turned out by film-school writers (she took her master's at U.C.L.A.) but has a more ruthlessly clever blend of old devices, standard sentiment, and new kinks.

Hill's attitudes are elusive; he's making a comic hymn to violence, and yet you can sense his own reserve, his qualms. *Slap Shot* might be the work of a coldly sensitive man who has seen Scorsese's films and can't decide if their heat is great or just cheap and nasty; he simulates it ambivalently. The simulation works, but it's also unsettling; it's rough on the surface but slick underneath—like machine-made graffiti. The flag is defaced at the start by running the credits on it; a hockey player is nudged by another during the playing of "The Star-Spangled Banner" and says, "I'm listening to the ******* song"; a busload of players and another busload of their boosters arrive in a town, are greeted by hecklers, and make moons out the bus windows. Hill is shooting the works. You feel as if he were telling

*He didn't, though; the movie wasn't the hit I expected it to be.

himself what the picture says about ice hockey: that there's no longer any way to play the game except as a dirty, violent joke. Expletives are sprinkled around like manure to give the film a funky seasoning—the stink of reality. But they're plastic turds—you're conscious of every dirty word. The director has thrown up his hands; he's like the character Ned Braden (Michael Ontkean), the one college-educated member of the Charlestown Chiefs, who at first refuses to play the thug's game of his teammates but finally gives up—he goes out on the ice and does a striptease, to the delight of the fans. Much of the script dates back to the movie era in which a college education made a man an intellectual and imbued him with principles; Braden broods and looks dissatisfied—a gentleman-jock Hamlet. When he strips, he retains his jockstrap. The meaning of his act is left in doubt: Has Braden degraded himself or has he joined the human race? It may be that the director isn't convinced there's a difference. Hill has technique, but he lacks the conviction or the temperament to hold *Slap Shot* together. What holds it together is the warmth supplied by Paul Newman. As Reggie, the player-coach of the Chiefs, he gives the performance of his life—to date.

Newman is an actor-star in the way that Bogart was. His range isn't enormous; he can't do classics, any more than Bogart could. But when a role is right for him, he's peerless. Newman imparts a simplicity and boyish eagerness to his characters. We like them but we don't look up to them. When he's rebellious, it's animal energy and high spirits, or stubbornness. Newman is most comfortable in a role when it isn't scaled heroically; even when he plays a bastard, he's not a big bastard—only a callow, selfish one, like Hud. He can play what he's not—a dumb lout. But you don't believe it when he plays someone perverse or vicious, and the older he gets and the better you know him, the less you believe it. His likableness is infectious; nobody should ever be asked not to like Paul Newman.

He's one of the few stars we've got in a normal emotional range. The Actors Studio may have contributed to the situation of many of our leading actors (such as Al Pacino): they can do desperately troubled psychological states—gloom, defeat, manic joy—but they're so inward you can't see them getting through a competently managed average day. Newman's range has become more normal with the years; in this he's rather like Mastroianni—he has grown by going deeper into the emotions of ordinary men. He's too modest and too straight inside for the strutting blowhard Buffalo Bill of *Buffalo Bill and the Indians*; Warren Beatty, who's not nearly as skilled an actor, could have done the role better. Newman is one of the least vain of stars; he used to smirk sometimes, but it wasn't vanity—it was nervous self-mockery, a shamefaced recognition of the effect that his handsomeness was having on other people. Now he has no need to be self-conscious; he's earned the right to be proud of how he looks. No other star in screen history has gone into middle age the way

Newman has. At fifty-two, he doesn't have an ounce of flab on him; he shows no sign of deterioration—even his gray hair is curly and thick.

What Newman does here is casual American star-acting at its peak; he's as perfectly assured a comedian as Bogart in *The African Queen*, even though the role isn't particularly well written and the picture itself isn't in the same class. In *The Sting*, he was smooth and charming, but there was no hardness in him; he wasn't a con man for a minute. He's gone beyond that sweetie-pie succulence here. What he does as Reggie isn't very different from what he's done before: it's that the control, the awareness, the power all seem to have become clarified. He has the confidence now to value his own gifts as an entertainer. In a picture such as *Winning*, he was impressive but a little somber; there was nothing to crack open—he couldn't use his resourcefulness. Here his technique seems to have become instinct. You can feel his love of acting; he's not fighting it or trying to hide it.

The essence of his performance as Reggie is that Reggie has never grown up; he's beautiful because he is still a child. Reggie is scarred and bruised, and there are gold rims on his chipped teeth; you don't see much of his eyes. But with Newman leaner, and his bone structure more prominent, the childlike quality is inner, and the warmth comes from deeper down. He makes boyishness seem magically attractive. Whizzing around on the ice, Reggie is a raucous American innocent. He's thin-skinned but a little thick-headed—a good-natured macho clown who can't conceal his vulnerability. Newman gives Reggie a desperate, forlorn quality. He suggests an over-age jock's pain from accumulated injuries—and the despair under Reggie's manic behavior. It's Newman's being a star who makes himself smaller that contributes to the funniest scene in the movie—which is also the only lusty, sensual scene. He's in bed with Melinda Dillon, who plays the runaway wife of an opposition-team player; she talks in a good-humored twang about her recent discovery of lesbian fun while he nuzzles her and looks up at her big breasts. There's a luscious infantile carnality about the scene—they're like kids playing doctor in a tree house.

How and why Newman broke through in *this* picture, I don't know; maybe his attempted stretch—and failure—as Buffalo Bill shook him up. But this is the kind of breakthrough that doesn't often happen with movie stars. And when a star grows as an actor, there's an extra pleasure in it for us. We know Newman so well in his star roles—he is so much a part of us—that we experience his development as if it were our triumph. Newman proves that stardom isn't necessarily corrupting, and we need that proof as often as possible.

The story premise is that the steel mill in the mythical town of Charlestown (most of the film was actually shot in Johnstown, Pennsylvania) is closing, and the Chiefs, a third-rate team, dependent on the support of the local workers, are going to fold at the end of the season. Reggie, who has nowhere else to turn and nothing else he knows how to do, convinces himself that if the team has a winning streak a buyer may be found, and in order to improve morale he bluffs the men into believing that a Florida syndicate is interested. They begin to play dirty and to draw crowds, and Reggie deliberately provokes fights with their opponents to raise the bloodshed level. Shabby as the team is, it would mean a lot to the decaying town, but we don't get to see this or feel it. The director skims the material, as if he were directing from a low-flying helicopter. (Actually, the shutdown of a mill might be expected to improve hockey attendance; laid-off workers have to get out and do something—and a minor-league-hockey ticket isn't that expensive, even if you're on union benefits, or welfare. People kept going to the movies during the Depression.)

Nancy Dowd's connection with ice hockey is through her brother Ned Dowd, a Johnstown Jet, who served as technical adviser on the film and plays the giant terror Ogilthorpe (though Ned Braden is probably based on Dowd). But the plot hasn't come out of her knowledge of ice hockey, it has come out of her knowledge of old movies, and her recognition that what used to be discreetly left out can now be larded on. Nancy Dowd has proved that a woman can write a script as profane and manipulative as a man's—but did anybody doubt it? The plot of *Slap Shot* and its asserted theme never get together. The purpose of the plot is simply to provide for bone-crunch humor, like that in Robert Aldrich's farce *The Longest Yard*, where the brawling convict footballers went at each other like mastodons. We're told that the fans only want blood and gore. Yet toward the end, when Reggie inspires his men to go out and play "old-time hockey," they don't get the chance to play, and we never find out whether the fans would actually reject a good fast game. The film is too buffoonish to care about its own theme. *Slap Shot* is *The Longest Yard* on ice, but with much sharper timing. The bruisers bash each other more dexterously—you laugh without groaning—and the locker-room scenes, and the glimpses of the Chiefs on the road or in their home city, are comicked up with throwaway humor, in the manner of *M*A*S*H* and *California Split*. Hill, however, uses this manner for archaic running gags, such as one teammate's grinning lecherousness and a pompous sportscaster with a toupee that's more of a doormat than a rug—you wait for it to be knocked off.

When a movie is manufactured out of old parts, like this one, the characters are forced into situations for the laugh payoffs. Newman provides his own emotional truth, and two of the actors playing members of his team—Allan Nicholls (the Bill of the Bill, Mary, and Tom trio in *Nashville*) and a French-Canadian, Yvon Barrette, as a bearded little goalie—have the timing to make their bits seem spontaneous. Most of the others are just shoved along tracks from joke to joke. The parallel love stories are treated almost ritualistically: Reggie's marriage to Francine

(Jennifer Warren) has collapsed, and Ned's marriage to Lily (Lindsay Crouse) is in trouble. We get the idea that Francine, a beauty operator, has left Reggie because he'll always be a kid. This is a cheat: Newman deserved the chance to take a bigger bite out of the character—Reggie shouldn't have had to be the bouncing boychick even in his dealings with his wife. And as Jennifer Warren plays her she's so self-contained she doesn't look as if she'd ever given him the time of day, much less a moment's tenderness. What's gone wrong with the younger couple is utterly opaque. Michael Ontkean has an expressive deadpan—his dark angel face magnetizes the camera. But Ned's Hamlet act includes the surly rejection of his devoted wife, for no apparent cause; we can only assume that the reasons for it weren't written or were cut. We get the reconciliation scene, though. Reggie takes Lily to Francine's beauty parlor; a few hours later, Lily emerges with heavy makeup and an upswept mass of baby-doll curls—and is her husband really supposed to be dazzled? The film lavishes condescension on the players' wives; they wear their cheapness like a costume. Hill isn't strong on male-female attachments—the ones here are so kitschy that they're still part of the old movies they came out of.

The modernizing element is the Hill-Dowd ribaldry—the constant derisiveness about homosexual practices and the outright baiting. In the ugliest scene in the picture, Reggie goes to see the owner of the team and discovers that the owner is a woman—a young widow. When she tells Reggie that she *could* sell the team but is going to fold it instead, for a tax write-off, he's defeated—but not quite. He has the laugh: he tells her that her little son is going to be a faggot if she doesn't get herself a man and loosen up. That's the worst fate he can promise her. This scene could have been directed so that it exposed Reggie's narrowness—and certainly Newman understands Reggie's narrowness and is capable of playing it that way. But we're goaded to laugh; it's not only Reggie who's telling her off—*we're* telling her off. It's obvious that the owner has been made a woman just for this thrust; she's been set up, like the man with the toupee, the busloads of mooners, and the rest of the incidents. (If Newman had refused to play the scene this way, what could the moviemakers have done? You can't blackball Paul Newman.)

There's a lot of ugliness in this movie, yet Hill sanitizes things even when he tries to be tough. That's probably why this film will be a huge hit. The profanity is dirty but meaningless—Broadway blue. The use of hockey as a metaphor for what has been going on in movies—the greater intensity of effects—is self-serving. Hill is a technician, not an artist. Yet he's not just putting down the bums who use shock effects—he's putting down the artists who use violence organically. Scorsese gets in there and digs around and makes you feel it; the relentlessness of *Taxi Driver* isn't just rhythm and pacing. Hill is like a big-money Broadway-blue playwright complaining of the crude tastes of the avant-garde while ripping them off. His crudeness here is livelier than anything he's done before, but I don't know that I've ever seen a picture so completely geared to giving the public "what it wants" with such an antagonistic feeling behind it. Hill gets you laughing, all right, but he's so grimly determined to ram entertainment down your throat that you feel like a Strasbourg goose.

[March 7, 1977]

Stag Show

There may be a time for a Hemingway revival, but this isn't it. His themes don't link with our preoccupations, and *Islands in the Stream*, the movie version of his posthumous novel, seems to belong to another age. The director, Franklin J. Schaffner, distances it further by his magisterial realism. The beach, the boats, the water and sky of the Bahamian village where the artist hero, Thomas Hudson (George C. Scott), lives have the incredible clarity and solidity of a David Lean encampment. The world is laundered every day for directors like these; they scan spotless horizons and impose their epic scale. In a typical shot, Scott, with his back to us, is in the foreground looking into the distance, with every detail bright and sharp, as if the hero had superhuman vision. The jumbo images confer antique heroic power on Thomas Hudson.

At times, the film takes you back into an elephantine-movie ambience that you've already almost forgotten. Schaffner ignores what has been going on in movies for the past decades; he ignores even what he was doing in the sixties, when Haskell Wexler shot *The Best Man* for him in a flashing, semidocumentary technique. Schaffner seems to have found his natural monotone. He's in love with hard edges and space, without emotional coloring—ceremoniously. He always directs our eyes to the farthest possible point in the image; the actors are sculptural objects in the way of the view. They pace about and deliver their lines as they would on a stage; it's almost as if we were in a theatre looking up over their heads toward the ceiling. Natural expanses have become so much more important to Schaffner than the expressiveness of the actors that he might be making earthworks, not movies. But *Islands in the Stream* has a mood; its implacable stodginess is stupefying yet impressive. Schaffner's *Nicholas and Alexandra* was a mausoleum, with every slab of marble nudged into place; his *Papillon* was endless—a Devil's Island version of the myth of Sisyphus. *Islands* is a monument to something people don't believe in any longer, but it's fascinating to see Hemingway's themes placed in this huge glass jar for our inspection.

Set at the outbreak of the Second World War, the novel wasn't published until 1970; it had been worked on from the late forties into the early fifties and was put aside long before Hemingway's suicide, in 1961. "If I could be something else," Hemingway told a friend in the fifties, "I'd like to be a painter." Thomas Hudson is the only artist hero in any of Hemingway's published novels, and represents the author's most straight-forward attempt to deal with his own mistakes and failures. Twice married, twice divorced, Hudson in his island home is a natural king in a self-imposed exile. The film's story is minimal. His sons, whom he hasn't seen in four years, come to spend the summer with him, and his love for them is mixed with guilt and regret. After they have gone, he decides to return to the mainland to be more of a father; en route, he is accidentally pulled into the war. In the film, as in the book, there is a personal grandiloquence about Hudson that is not questioned; it is simply assumed that everyone loves and admires him—his adoring retinue, two of his three sons.

The testing of the third son—the middle boy, Davy (Michael-James Wixted)—is a major episode: he hooks a giant marlin and in the battle with the fish wins his self-respect and is also freed from his resentment against his father for mistreating his mother. There's hokey melodrama in Hemingway's masculine rites: you see the test being set up and you know how you're supposed to judge the person, and how he judges himself. Davy's rite of passage—his proving himself by showing the stamina to fight a big fish and in that ordeal learning to respect, even to love, the fish—doesn't have much more immediacy than the code of the Westerner. If an Eskimo were killing an animal because that was necessary to his survival, we could believe in his respect for his adversary. But when a little preppie like Davy has to prove himself by an artificial primitive test—when he hunts game to increase his own self-respect—how can we be told that he respects his prey? Or that he changes from a screwed-up kid into a fine lad? In the old Hollywood action films, the suspense about whether the hero would be able to stand up to danger was exciting, and we could go along with the courage-cowardice formulations for the sake of the action. And even in the earlier films based on Hemingway material, in which the moral dimensions of this tension were enlarged and universalized, the action was still central. But here, with everything slowed down and writ large, there's nothing except the Hemingway code, with its boys'-world snobbery and cruelty about physical cowardice. There appears to be only one way to be a winner in Hemingway's world—through red-blooded courage, manifested in sports, in killing game, in bullfighting, in war. And though the hero is meant to be an artist—we see Hudson at work on welded-iron, David Smith–like sculpture—art seems to be his hobby, fishing his life. In terms of what happens in this movie, Hudson doesn't need to be an artist—he only needs to be rich and famous. His art is an excrescence. When Hudson decides to leave the island, we expect to see him pack his iron pieces aboard his boat, but nothing of the kind—he is unencumbered. This is probably just an oversight, but it's perfectly faithful to the spirit of the book.

In the early fifties, a double-page spread appeared in large-circulation magazines. On the left page, a picture of Hemingway outdoors, seated, wearing shorts, holding a book on his lap. The caption read, "Ernest Hemingway, who has been called the greatest living American writer, is also internationally famous as a deep-sea fisherman. Since publication of *The Sun Also Rises* in 1926, his novels and short stories have enriched the literature of the English language consistently, year after year. His latest best seller is *Across the River and Into the Trees*." And on the facing page was a letter from Hemingway, on the stationery of his plantation in Cuba, endorsing Ballantine's Ale. This spread was repeated a little later with the *Across the River and Into the Trees* tag changed to "His newest book is *The Old Man and the Sea*." Those pages bothered me; I tore them out of *Life* and stuck them in a pile of papers, and when I looked for them the other day, I found that they had somehow travelled with me. They still bother me. Hemingway shamed us, and I wish that something of that world-famous-celebrity four-flusher—the big-game hunter and official greatest living American writer—had been brought into this movie. It's the missing underside of Hudson's lordly standing with his friends, yacht crew, and servants—who are hard to separate, since all pay him obeisance. What does it do to an artist to live as if he were a sportsman seigneur? (The movie directors who begin to keep stables finally seem to have as little interest in the arts as the equestrian queens of England do.) In the Cuban film *Memories of Underdevelopment*, when a guide takes visitors through Hemingway's house, pointing out the heads and tusks and guns, and the stuffed gazelle, it might be the hunting lodge of a deposed czar.

The issues implicit in Hemingway's portrait of the artist as a hard-drinking fisherman aren't raised in this movie—yet our sensing them provides a compelling subtext. Morley Callaghan wrote of Hemingway, "His imaginative work had such a literal touch that a whole generation came to believe he was only telling what he, himself, had seen happen, or what had actually happened to him. His readers made him his own hero." Yes, and it was far more than that: Hemingway was the virile great writer that the age of photojournalism needed; he and *Life* were made for each other, and they both knew it. He played literary lion; he lived his fantasy life in public, and became a celebrity-clown before it was fashionable. The

Hemingway-Hudson of the movie is the legend, but he's never the man who fed that legend. Except for an early drinking binge, *Islands* gives us only the dignified side of Hemingway's life, without the contradictions and pressures that led him to the desolation that Scott, however, makes us feel.

As a portrait of one side of Hemingway—the controlled, proud-minded man of feeling, a Karsh portrait—Scott's performance is admirable. Scott's features are totally unlike Hemingway's, but with a crewcut, a grizzled gray-white beard, neatly clipped, the chestiness, and the familiar Hemingway shirts and shorts and bush jackets, Scott suggests Hemingway as he looked on the *Time* cover in 1954, when he won the Nobel Prize—reflective, slightly withdrawn. Scott's Hudson, a titan with slate-blue eyes, a crumbled nose, and a booze-busted, I've-been-through-hell voice, is terribly grand, but the grandeur is underplayed. The performance is different from the kind of acting Scott has so often done: fixing his stare on the other performers and magnetizing the audience—half with fear. Scott has, at times, overdone force, with his overweening, diabolic presence and the way he would go chugging into his locomotive act. (In the Broadway play *Sly Fox*, he even tries to force his scenes to be funny; he substitutes command of the stage for comic acting. There may be no other way, however, to get laughs from his role.) Scott has to be dominating or he's nothing, but as Thomas Hudson he has found a more subdued form of domination. His Hudson is a scrupulous performance that runs deep, without much surface excitement. It's a little too studied, too stern and august. He doesn't try to go beyond the text; there are no revelations, no insights. Yet he does something very difficult: he supplies the consciousness to this film. He's a sensitive statue, and his observant face keeps us involved. The weakness of the material—the reason that there's no drama in it—is that his is the only consciousness; everyone else in the movie is a child compared with him. He is Papa, the big man—though that's a weakness in Hemingway, not in Scott.

The screenplay, by Denne Bart Petitclerc, is so carefully thought out that we become overly aware that the episodes have graceful contours. Hemingway has too many fantasies sloshing around in the book; Petitclerc has cleaned out what used to be put into Hemingway movies. (Remember *The Snows of Kilimanjaro*, with the twenty-five-page story padded with such additions as Ava Gardner's being injured in the Spanish Civil War and dying in Gregory Peck's arms, a bullfight in Madrid, and the decadent rich on the Riviera?) Petitclerc has de-Hollywoodized *Islands*, except for the climax, with Hudson trying to help a Cuban skipper (Gilbert Roland, in his seventies but not showing it) who has a boatload of refugees from Hitler. At this point, the picture shifts into the Bogart-Hemingway *To Have and Have Not*, with a sidelong glance at *The African Queen*. Schaffner doesn't revitalize these action episodes: the final, expensive shoot-out is dishevelled. The only element in it that has meaning for us is Hudson's fatalistic shrug. (Scott is becoming a whiz at rue.) In general, the liberties that Petitclerc takes with the novel make good sense—such as changing Hudson's first wife (who comes to visit him) from a Dietrich-like star to the tense, pale, dark-eyed woman played by Claire Bloom. The modelling of Claire Bloom's face resembles that of Martha Gellhorn, Hemingway's third wife, as well as that of his widow, Mary. She looks right, and she brings such an air of formality and strain to her scenes that you can feel the edginess between her and her ex-husband yet believe that he means it when he says she is the only woman he's ever loved. Despite the quality of the acting—her wiredrawn imperiousness and his superb line readings—the sequences with the two of them are so flossy and so pompously directed that they turn into rich, melodious camp. As a director, Schaffner has no unconscious; his style is based on rendering each nuance with complete precision. But since the discords that split Hudson and his first wife are buried in history (Hemingway failed to clarify them in the book), Schaffner is at a loss, and the two walk with their arms around each other uncomfortably, posed like a mystery man and woman.

The scenes involving Hudson's sons, and those with "the rummy," played by David Hemmings, a younger version of the Walter Brennan character in *To Have and Have Not*, are on an archaic, sentimental level. The marlin's leaps out of the water are edited like travelogue footage, and the music—Jerry Goldsmith's reject Delibes—seems to be trying to evoke movie classics. Despite the long vistas (the Bahamian village was constructed in Hawaii), *Islands* has no visual flow; closeups come in like blips. Schaffner keeps cutting to the face of the person delivering a line or the person whose emotions he wants you to register. Though David Hemmings is a likable actor, he's made to look a fool—always wearing his heart on his sleeve for his beloved master Hudson, and grinning, cherry-lipped and short of tooth, like Elizabeth Taylor. Hudson's sons get closeups almost every time they speak, plus Disneyesque reaction shots for the youngest (plump, freckled Brad Savage) when he's particularly squeezable. It's an abuse of the actors, who are not allowed to interrelate or to develop a characterization. Hart Bochner, who plays the oldest boy, Tom, is shown in so many radiant closeups that he might be the star of an Army recruiting film, and Wixted, a tousled, juvenile Jimmy Carter, who is well cast as Davy, and looks as if he could do a good job on his own, is force-fed us. Julius Harris is the intelligent black mate on Hudson's boat; it's frustrating to see him used emblematically—to represent loyalty.

In a way, the whole stiff movie is emblematic. When Hudson's quest is cut short, we see his final vision and hear the universal truths he has learned. That's the trouble with quests: the puny payoff that has to be bathed in white light—wisdom swathed in gauze. By being so respectful and dedicated, and so incompetent at action, *Islands* brings out the worst in Hemingway—his mystique. It's a devastating essay on Hemingway the thinker.

[March 14, 1977]

Oh, Anomie, I Love You

Welcome to L.A. was written around a suite of nine rock songs by Richard Baskin called "City of the One Night Stands," and its mood is whimsical, laid-back alienation. The ten characters tell us that L.A. is "daydreams in traffic" and that "people deceive themselves here"; they sing about "the stale taste of decay" and exhibit the very latest in quirks and nervous disorders. The central figure is a young composer (Keith Carradine) with an endless supply of flask-size bottles of Southern Comfort in his pocket, in his car, in his bed; he drinks without its having any effect on him. That makes him the hero right there. He has come home after three years in London, because a rock star is recording an album of his songs—"City of the One Night Stands," naturally—and he effortlessly attracts a collection of lost women. Lauren Hutton, his father's smiley, fey mistress, is a photographer who shoots corners, and sits in them, too. Geraldine Chaplin, also a corner freak, is a businessman's lonely, movie-struck wife; she pretends she's Camille and takes Valium for her cough. Sally Kellerman, the realtor who finds him his house, is a desperate vamp, stifling from lack of love. Sissy Spacek, his housemaid, has starry dead eyes—she vacuums topless, and hustles a little on the side. Viveca Lindfors is his cynical, fiftyish agent—she laughs and cries at the same time, flashes her eyes tempestuously, and goes through the vocal histrionics of a seedy Carmen, all to show us the plight of the unwanted older woman. Denver Pyle plays Carradine's Colonel Sanders–like yogurt-millionaire father. Harvey Keitel is the father's hardworking assistant; he's Chaplin's husband and Spacek's customer. John Considine is Kellerman's furniture-dealer husband—a muscular stud who looks like an overused department-store mannequin. The idea is that they all screw around but they're really looking for—what? Values? Love? Religion? Set, shamelessly, at Christmas, *Welcome to L.A.* is a tale of beautiful sad people who have everything and nothing.

Alan Rudolph, who wrote and directed the film (it's his first time as director), is literary in a sub-literate way. He overvalues mournful poetic thoughts: his characters say a line and then stare at the camera, so that the words will have enough dead space around them to impress us. The words are like feathers drifting to earth—the picture seems drugged. Partly this is because of Baskin's sick-soul-of-Los Angeles songs. You can't tell one from another, and, as the tenth major character—the rock star doing the album—Baskin sings most of them himself. He sings like someone trying to play the double bass who doesn't know how; the quavering anal growl on the sound track might be Kissinger serenading NBC. Baskin is so serious he won't even grant us the relief of a few inflections. With his Versailles-fop hairdo and his stone-age frown, he leans toward the mike, heavy with creativity.

Alan Rudolph was Robert Altman's assistant on *Nashville*, and Baskin, who played Frog, did the musical arrangements. Altman enabled them to make *Welcome to L.A.* by functioning as its producer. It's quite possible that Rudolph, who seems to have tried to make a *Nashville* about Los Angeles, wasn't fully conscious that in several sequences he was coming mortifyingly close to plagiarism. (Carradine once again phones a married woman when her husband is at home; Geraldine Chaplin, who used a tape recorder in *Nashville*, talks while writing in a notebook.) The spirit of the film is, however, altogether different: it's stagnant—an American version of a European "art film" with the characters in their solitude wandering around Capri in winter. Rudolph is trying for a tone poem, but, like Baskin, he's got only one tone. *Welcome to L.A.* is an Altman film with all the juice squeezed out.

The actors (many of them from the Altman stock company) perform attentively, but they're undirected, and you can sense their unease. The singer that Carradine played in *Nashville* was petulant and narcissistic; he was a sexy little boy grown tall, and you could feel how his dissatisfaction drew women to him. Here, with a hunk of hair on his chin, a squashed little Irish hat, and a big bow tie, Carradine looks like a goat at a village fair. The author-director uses Carradine as a deliberate blank at the center of the film and at the same time oversells us on his quizzical-leprechaun beauty. Even Carradine's singing lacks the sexual plangency it had in *Nashville*, since he's singing only to himself, and Baskin's guru-wisdom lyrics—Leonard Cohen turned into Edgar Guest—are no aphrodisiac. Carradine's fixation on the wiggy, coy wife played by Geraldine Chaplin seems to be based on charity: she's the neediest case. And this actress, who in *Buffalo Bill and the Indians* registered a whole battery of emotions in the second's panic before she got a word out, can't find a clue to what she should express. The mixture of impishness and terror in her eyes is glazed before the film is over. As her husband, a middle-class man with fluffy tinted hair, Harvey Keitel looks half asleep. Keitel needs his usual intensity—he needs his meanness and blowups; miscast here, he's bland and wooden. There's a good script idea behind this businessman's getting turned on by a promotion and wanting a new affair, but the director is so high on tangents that this scene, like the others, has no core. In offscreen life, people generally manage to have some fun at the beginning of affairs—things don't go sour until later. Here, the affairs start at such a low energy level that when Diahann Abbott, in a small part as the millionaire's receptionist, goes to bed with Carradine, her lush, tropical sexiness seems to belong to another movie—where people enjoy themselves. The other characters get hot only when they look in the mirror. Rudolph has emptied his L.A.: there are a few minor roles but there are no extras in the film, and there's no sense of anyone living in the city except in this prosperous, shell-shocked, love-hungry way. (At one point, the Screen Extras Guild picketed the production, thinking it must be using nonunion extras.)

Rudolph's conception called for a totally designed look; in the homes and offices, the performers move around in their jewelled frames. Nothing is casual, to be perceived or ignored at will; the paintings and furnishings and art objects are marked out for us, like the words. Rudolph is totally explicit yet completely vague—there are no underpinnings for what the people do. He worked on the script of *Buffalo Bill and the Indians*, which suffered from a similar floating explicitness. With Rudolph, you're told everything, and it's all generalizations. This film takes place—spiritually— at sunset, and the cinematographer, Dave Myers, sustains an amber calendar-art quality, naturally lighted yet so clear it has a glitter: L.A. becomes a supernal city. The film is a considerable technical achievement for a first-time director, and it was made for $1,200,000 at a time when the average Hollywood picture costs $4,000,000. But for the viewer this accomplishment doesn't count for much.

There's an irritating quality about the film's sophomoric homilies and pronouncements. It wears its existential despair like a black turtleneck sweater, for effect. Rudolph's blank hero drives around the way Antonioni's characters used to walk—aimlessly, to express disconnected- ness. The director appears to be so innocent of the past that he's reinvented the clichés of the sixties; it may be that Altman's are the only movies he knows. Tuesday Weld already did this anomic driving in *Play It As It Lays*, and, whatever the metaphoric purposes, ten characters suffering from anomie is too much—it's a goddam epidemic.

□ □ □

Gérard Depardieu has huge features—a long, thick nose and a lantern jaw. He moves with the sturdiness of a robust peasant, and acts with everything—his beer-barrel chest, his lank, dirty-blond hair, his simian arms. Depardieu redeems physical coarseness; he's both earth and spirit, like the peasants in a Piero della Francesca. In the Swiss writer-director Claude Goretta's *The Wonderful Crook* (*Pas Si Méchant Que Ça*), Depardieu plays Pierre, a contented married man, a workman employed in his father's furniture factory. When his glum, embittered father (Jacques Debary) has a stroke, Pierre is in charge. He discovers then what was gnawing at his father: the world has moved into the age of plastics, and nobody is buying the expensive, handcrafted wood furniture that the factory turns out. Faced with the responsibility of meeting the payroll, the only thing Pierre can think to do is to rob a bank. And to meet the next payroll, another bank, or perhaps a supermarket. It's like a child's game that he takes up; in his heart Pierre is never a robber, and he's innocently considerate of his victims. He's a petit-bourgeois Robin Hood with a bad stomach. His direct solution to the problem of how to handle the burden his father passed over to him is simply consistent with his generosity, his limited outlook, and his essential caged animality.

The film is based on an actual case; Goretta (his last film was *The Invitation*) has given it a provincial setting and developed it like a subdued piano concerto, with Depardieu as his piano. Pierre loves his wife, Marthe (Dominique Labourier), but in the course of a robbery he meets Nelly (Marlène Jobert). She becomes his mistress and confederate, and he loves her, too. As in the Alec Guinness comedy *The Captain's Paradise*, each woman is unhappy because she's deprived of the half of the man's life that he shares with the other. But this isn't played for farce; rather, we feel the wife's sense of loss and Pierre's misery at having shut part of himself off from her.

Yet Goretta doesn't seem to have had enough to go out and make a movie about; *The Wonderful Crook* starves the viewer's mind. Goretta develops the small stresses and breaks of feeling, but his wheels grind so fine that when a subsidiary character (Philippe Léotard, as Nelly's former lover) turns up, we glom on to him gratefully, expectantly. And when there's a textural bit of business (a bar scene, with an Italian worker drunkenly dancing with a vase of flowers, which is sure to be smashed) we immediately register it as a motif. In other films, Depardieu has demonstrated an outlaw side, similar to Brando's, but Goretta doesn't want that side; there's only one scene in which Pierre reveals anything uncontrollable—when he's swirling around, swinging his little son in the air, and he experiences the same exciting vertigo as the child. Goretta's conception requires that Pierre's criminal activity frighten him and isolate him from everyone but his confederate, and while we wait for the situation to be resolved Depardieu's quietly despairing face is all we've got to look at. The pacing is determinedly sensitive, academic; we become impatient with Pierre—his arrest is our reprieve. The cinematographer, Renato Berta, uses natural light for a lustrous, even-tempered effect. You know you're seeing a film made by artists—in fact, there is never a moment when you're not conscious that this is a film made by artists. When a bad film is as cleanly made as this one, there are no cheap thrills to sustain you, no rotten acting to giggle at. No mistakes. You have to sit there and appreciate.

[March 21, 1977]

PART FOUR

Contrasts

The loudness, the smash-and-grab editing, the relentless pacing drive every idea from your head; for young audiences *Star Wars* is like getting a box of Cracker Jack which is all prizes. This is the writer-director George Lucas's own film, subject to no business interference, yet it's a film that's totally uninterested in anything that doesn't connect with the mass audience. There's no breather in the picture, no lyricism; the only attempt at beauty is in the double sunset. It's enjoyable on its own terms, but it's exhausting, too: like taking a pack of kids to the circus. An hour into it, children say that they're ready to see it all over again; that's because it's an assemblage of spare parts—it has no emotional grip. *Star Wars* may be the only movie in which the first time around the surprises are reassuring. (Going a second time would be like trying to read *Catch-22* twice.) Even if you've been entertained, you may feel cheated of some dimension—a sense of wonder, perhaps. It's an epic without a dream. But it's probably the absence of wonder that accounts for the film's special, huge success. The excitement of those who call it the film of the year goes way past nostalgia to the feeling that now is the time to return to childhood.

Maybe the only real inspiration involved in *Star Wars* was to set its sci-fi galaxy in the pop-culture past, and to turn old-movie ineptness into conscious Pop Art. And maybe there's a touch of genius in keeping it so consistently what it is, even if this is the genius of the plodding. Lucas has got the tone of bad movies down pat: you never catch the actors deliberately acting badly, they just seem to be bad actors, on contract to Monogram or Republic, their klunky enthusiasm polished at the Ricky Nelson school of acting. In a gesture toward equality of the sexes, the high-school-cheerleader princess-in-distress talks tomboy-tough—Terry Moore with spunk. Is it because the picture is synthesized from the mythology of serials and old comic books that it didn't occur to anybody that *she* could get The Force?

Most of the well-known writers who have tried to direct movies have gone at it briefly and given up in frustration. Cocteau was an exception;

Marguerite Duras is another. She has been writing scripts since 1959 (*Hiroshima, Mon Amour*) and directing her own scripts since 1966, and the control in her new film, *Le Camion—The Truck*—suggests that she has become a master. But there's a joker in her mastery: though her moods and cadences, her rhythmic phrasing, with its emotional undertow, might seem ideally suited to the medium, they don't fulfill moviegoers' expectations. Conditioned from childhood, people go to the movies wanting the basic gratification of a story acted out. Many directors have tried to alter this conditioning, breaking away from the simplest narrative traditions, and they've failed to take the largest audience with them. Duras doesn't even get near the mass of moviegoers, though somehow—God knows how—she manages to make her own pictures, her own way. Hers is possibly the most sadomasochistic of all director relationships with the audience: she drives people out of the theatre, while, no doubt, scorning them for their childish obtuseness. At the same time, she must be suffering from her lack of popularity. Her battle with the audience reaches a new stage in *The Truck*, in which the split between her artistry and what the public wants is pointed up and turned against the audience. She brings it off, but she's doing herself in, too. And so it isn't a simple prank.

There are only two people in *The Truck*: Marguerite Duras and Gérard Depardieu. They sit at a round table in a room in her home, and never leave it. Small and bundled up, her throat covered, her unlined moon face serene, half-smiling, Duras reads aloud the script of a film in which Depardieu would act the role of a truck driver who picks up a woman hitchhiker. He would drive and ask a question or two; the woman would talk. Depardieu doesn't actually play the truck driver: this actor, whose physical and emotional weight can fill up the screen, is used as a nonprofessional. He merely listens trustingly, a friend, a student, as Duras reads. Hers is the only performance, and there has never been anything like it: controlling the whole movie visibly, from her position on the screen as creator-star, she is so assured that there is no skittish need for makeup, no nerves, quick gestures, tics. The self-image she presents is that of a woman past deception; she has the grandly simple manner of a sage. Unhurriedly, with the trained patience of authority, she tells the story of her movie-to-be about the woman hitchhiker—a woman of shifting identities, who drops clues about her life which are fragments and echoes of Duras' earlier works. This woman, a composite Duras heroine, strews a trail of opaque references to Duras' youth in Indo-China (the daughter of two French teachers, Marguerite Duras spent her first seventeen years there), and when the hitchhiker talks to the truck driver about her disillusion with the politics of revolution, and says that she has lost faith in the proletariat, that she believes in nothing anymore—"Let the world go to rack and ruin"—she speaks, unmistakably, for Duras herself. *The Truck* is a spiritual autobiography, a life's-journey, end-of-the-world road movie;

it's a summing up, an endgame. The hitchhiker travels in a winter desert; she's from anywhere and going nowhere, in motion to stay alive. Reading the script, Duras speaks in the perfect conditional tense, beginning "It would have been a film—therefore, it is a film." And this tense carries a note of regret: it suggests that the script is to be realized only by our listening and imagining.

Her seductive voice prepares us for the unfolding of the action, and when there is a cut from the two figures at the table to a big blue truck moving silently through cold and drizzle in the working-class flatlands west of Paris, we're eager to see the man and woman inside. But we don't get close enough to see anyone. The truck crawls along in the exurbanite slum, where housing developments and supermarkets loom up in the void, Pop ruins. Its movement is noiseless, ominously so; the only sound is that of Beethoven's "Diabelli" Variations, and the images and music never quite come together rhythmically. With nothing synchronized, the effect is of doomsday loneliness. Quiet is Duras' weapon. The Beethoven is played softly, so that we reach toward it. The stillness provides resonance for her lingering words—those drifting thoughts that sound elegant, fated—and for the music, and for the cinematographer Bruno Nuytten's love-hate vistas of bareness and waste, like the New Jersey Turnpike in pastels. The foreboding melancholy soaks so deep into our consciousness that when the director yanks us back to the room, you may hear yourself gasp at the effrontery of this stoic, contained little woman with her mild, Chairman Mao deadpan. When we were with the truck, even without seeing anyone in it we felt that "the movie"—our primitive sense of a movie—was about to begin. And it's an emotional wrench, a classic rude awakening, to be sent back to Square One, the room. The film alternates between sequences in the room and sequences of the rolling truck, always at a distance. Each time she cuts to the outdoors, you're drawn into the hypnotic flow of the road imagery, and though you know perfectly well there will be nothing but the truck in the landscape, you half dream your way into a "real" movie. And each time you find yourself back with Duras, you're aware of being treated like a chump, your childishness exposed.

Buñuel played a similar narrative game in parts of *The Discreet Charm of the Bourgeoisie*, parodying the audience's gullibility by involving us in scary ghost stories and then casually interrupting them. But that was only one of his games and he wasn't onscreen himself pulling the rug out from under us, the way Duras is, returning to her narration, all dulcet modulations, as if she thought we'd be delighted to listen. The audience reacts at first with highly vocal disbelief and then with outbursts of anger, and walkouts. Even those of us who are charmed by her harmonious, lulling use of the film medium and in awe of her composure as a performer are conscious that we have, buried under a few layers, the rebellious instincts that others are giving loud voice to. They're furious in a way they never are at a merely bad, boring movie, and this anger is perfectly understandable. But it's high comedy, too: their feelings have been violated by purely aesthetic means—an affront to their conditioning.

When *The Truck* opens at the New York Film Festival this week, there's likely to be a repetition of the scene in May at Cannes. After the showing, Marguerite Duras stood at the head of the stairs in the Palais des Festivals facing the crowd in evening clothes, which was yelling insults up at her. People who had walked out were milling around; they'd waited to bait her. It might have been a horrifying exhibition, except that the jeering was an inverted tribute—conceivably, a fulfillment. She was shaken: one could see it in the muscles of her face. But Robespierre himself couldn't have looked them straighter in the eye. There can't be much doubt that she enjoys antagonizing the audience, and there is a chicness in earning the public's hatred. *The Truck* is a class-act monkeyshine made with absolutely confident artistry. She knows how easy it would be to give people the simple pleasures that they want. Her pride in not making concessions is heroic; it shows in that gleam of placid perversity which makes her such a commanding camera presence.

She can take the insults without flinching because she's completely serious in the story of the despairing hitchhiker. In her method in *The Truck*, she's a minimalist, like Beckett, stripping her drama down to the bones of monodrama, and her subject is the same as his: going through the last meaningless rites. ("I can't go on. I'll go on.") What *The Truck* doesn't have is Beckett's bleak, funny commonness. Beckett sticks to lowlifers, and his plays are the smelly vaudeville of the living dead, the grindingly familiar slow music of moronic humanity. Duras is bleakly fancy, with a glaze of culture. She's all music, too, the music of diffuseness, absence, loss, but her spoken text is attitudinizing—desultory self-preoccupation, mystification. Not pinning anything down, she leaves everything floating allusively in midair. This is, God help us, a vice women artists have been particularly prone to. Who is this hitchhiker on the road of life? Ah, we are not to know. Indefiniteness is offered as superiority to the mundane, as a form of sensuousness. It's a very old feminine lure—presenting oneself as many women, as a creature of mystery, and, of course, as passive and empty, disillusioned and weary. Dietrich used to do it in sequins, feathers, and chiffon. Duras clothes it in Marxist ideology, and puts forth her disaffection as a terminal, apocalyptic vision: Nothingness ahead. Some of her remarks ("Karl Marx is dead," and so on) have a tinny, oracular ring. (You wouldn't catch out Beckett making personal announcements.) The hitchhiker's declaration that she no longer believes in the possibility of political salvation is meant to have shock value; the world—i.e., Paris—is being told what Marguerite Duras' latest stand is.

There are some people who are too French for their own good. True film artist though she is, Marguerite Duras has a sensibility that's infected with the literary culture of a *précieuse*, and partly because of the development of movies out of the common forms of entertainment, this sensibility exposes itself on the screen much more than it does on paper. Faced with the audience's impatience, Duras fights back by going further, defiant, single-minded. There's something of the punitive disciplinarian in her conception of film art; *The Truck* is a position paper made into a movie. It's accessible, but it's accessible to a piece of yourself that you never think to take to the movies. Let's put it this way: if you were studying for a college exam and knocked off to go see *The Truck*, you wouldn't feel you were playing hooky. Duras makes us aware of our own mechanisms of response, and it's tonic and funny to feel the tensions she provokes. Her picture has been thought out with such supple discrimination between the values of sound and image that one could almost say it's *perfectly* made: an ornery, glimmering achievement. At the opposite extreme from popcorn filmmaking, it's a demonstration of creative force—which doesn't always cut as clean as that laser sword in Alec Guinness's hand.

□ □ □

*R*ight from the beginning of the film *Short Eyes*, directed by Robert M. Young from Miguel Piñero's adaptation of his play about life in a men's house of detention, you hear the play coming through the documentary surface. The film was shot entirely in the Tombs, and the details of cells and showers and of trays being emptied are completely convincing, yet the illusion that this is "life" never takes hold. Each time someone has a line, there's a cut to him; it's as if the director had pointed to the actor and said, "It's your turn now, *go*." Many of the actors (an overlapping group of ex-convicts, ex-addicts, and professionals) appeared in the stage versions, and you recognize the rhythm of well-practiced stage readings. And some of these actors love their lines too much; they've been revving up, stiffening their faces, holding their breath. Piñero dances through his own role—the hairy little hipster Go Go, a ratfink wearing a cross and a yarmulke. Piñero knows how to breathe as if he weren't acting, and his lines have a pulse—watching him, we can tell how the script was meant to sound. But the scenes involving him are brief, and rushed; we barely grasp that he has planted a weapon in the bunk of another prisoner (played by Curtis Mayfield) before the men take their reprisals, and he's gone from the movie. Still, *Short Eyes*, hung up somewhere between photographed play and prison documentary, has an obsessive interest, and when the child-molester, Clark Davis (Bruce Davison), one of the few men in the cellblock who aren't Hispanic or black, delivers a confessional monologue about how he got started when he was fifteen with one of his little sister's friends and how he has gone on, with acquiescent eight-year-olds who will do anything for a quarter, the film gets us by the throat, choking off petty reservations.

Born in Puerto Rico, Piñero was brought to New York at the age of four; within a few years his father deserted the family, and by the time Piñero was eight he was stealing milk and bread to help feed the younger children. The police started to pick him up when he was eleven; he had been a shoplifter, mugger, burglar, addict, and drug pusher and was serving a five-year sentence for armed robbery when he joined a theatre workshop in Sing Sing, where he began to work on this play. Paroled, he was twenty-seven when it was first performed publicly, by a group of former convicts and addicts, in 1974 at Riverside Church; it went on to win two Obies and a Drama Critics Circle award.

Short Eyes is an insider's view of prison life. Piñero doesn't sentimentalize the men as victims. His is a reverse sentimentality, a cocky insistence that they got caught doing what they wanted to do. This insider's "realism," a neo-Cagney bravado, is much more entertaining than the usual liberal-humanitarian version of prison life; the prisoners flaunt their vices and never ask for sympathy. Their tough talk is the prison equivalent of locker-room boasting, and perfectly believable; what other form of cool could they have? Piñero, however, pushes bravado as truth: he has one of the men deliver an applause-jerking speech about being a dope fiend not because he's black or suffering from a "personality disorder" but because he likes the stuff, and there are other speeches about how the men are "responsible" for themselves. This comes from a playwright who at the completion of shooting on the film was picked up, with another member of the cast, driving the wrong way on a Lower East Side street in a stolen taxi, and was indicted for grand and petit larceny, robbery, and possession of marijuana and a dangerous weapon. A more self-destructive hellion's gesture would be hard to find; if he's convicted, he could be sent up for twenty-five years. Of course, people are responsible for what they do, no matter what they've been through. But what does that actually mean in terms of those who have been damaged from childhood—in some cases, from infancy? What's underneath Piñero's defensive, macho oratory is what gives the film its strength: the pain that is the bedrock of the prisoners' lives.

The plot centers on the revulsion that men in prison feel toward child-molesters—"short eyes." (Child-molesting is said to be the one crime for which a man in prison is ostracized. It's at the bottom of the scale; armed robbery is at the top.) Dostoevski grappled with the horror of sexual passion for children; the Fritz Lang film *M* touched on it; *The Mark* flirted with it. The intensity of *Short Eyes* derives mainly from its getting close enough for us to feel some heat. But we're not flung into the furnace. The men's revulsion is taken for granted, without our seeing that they react to child-molesters with such profound, murderous hatred because of their fear that they're capable of this sexual debasement. We need to see that Clark Davis, the child-molester, has given in to something the other prisoners haven't sunk to and that this may be the last barrier for some of them—the only proof of their self-control. If he were rash or crazed, if he had dark, thick blood in him—if he were a man like the others—then maybe we'd see that their sexual conflicts and miseries belong to the same world as his. But Clark Davis is a miserable whiner. A cartoon of white-collar cowardice, he's everything Piñero feels superior to; he's no more than a trivial whitey to be squished.

Bruce Davison's previous screen work (he was the student hero of *The Strawberry Statement*, had the title role in *Willard*, and was the nephew in *Mame*) doesn't prepare one for his subtly objective performance as the molester; he's playing a conventional weasel, but he gets inside that weasel. His facial movements are so small and tense that he suggests the tininess of Clark's petty-clerk soul—so small that you even begin to think he couldn't have done any physical damage to the little girls. Clark brings a pale chill into the prison. This is his first arrest, and his fear is like a shiver he can't let out. His antennae give him all the wrong signals, and he doesn't even know how to plead for his own life: he asks to be spared for the sake of his wife and child. Davison's guardedness, his constricted voice, the suggestions of calculations that can't help failing are all prissily exact. Even in his confessional speech—the only lines he's got that haven't been written from the outside, that have been felt, imagined—he doesn't leap out of the character (though it must certainly have been a temptation).

Yet by making Clark Davis repugnant for reasons other than his crime Piñero diverts the script from its great subject and, at the end, is left flailing about, looking for ironies and meanings to tie the movie together, so that it will "say" something. The ideas haven't been worked out, and the film even has a stock figure of goodness and decency—the prisoner Juan, called Poet (José Perez), who appears to be the author's fantasy of himself. Juan, Clark's father-confessor, is a hip version of the kindly wardens and loving priests in old movies. But with sensational material like this, disorganization is preferable to a slick, false structure. And parts of this movie seem as good as they could possibly be. When Longshoe Murphy (Joe Carberry), a white prisoner, taunts Clark, referring to his "nice cheap summer suit," the condescension in the word "cheap" is worthy of Tennessee Williams at his peak. When Murphy gets stoned, he looks uncannily like the last photographs of Hart Crane and he has a passage of dialogue in which the language has broken down. Nothing in it is quite literal or rational, and yet the meaning is eerily clear to us. Whether Joe Carberry is acting stoned or this is stoned acting, it has a beatific quality, and the movie just eases into it. Piñero's humor, which spurts up freely, is often surprisingly gentle in this feral atmosphere. An older man, Paco (Shawn Elliott), corners a slender, boyish prisoner (Tito Goya) and propositions him, forcefully. But the scene turns around: what looked as if it would lead to violence is actually a love idyll. Paco is really a petitioner; he wants the boy to want him—it's just that he doesn't know how to express love except with threats. And the boy, known as Cupcakes, is a dish; only semi-reluctant, he has the whole cellblock turned on by his Bianca Jagger androgyny.

Young, the director, isn't overbearing, he doesn't lean on the finest bits. (It's in the least inspired material that the actors seem to be yelling "Bingo!") The director's one big attempt at ensemble playing—a musical number—recalls the inevitable spirituals sung in the early "big-house" movies; we know too well what we're supposed to feel. But the violent moments are handled with a restraint that intensifies our terror; sometimes a few quick cuts show us all we need to see. During the attack on Go Go near the beginning, the suffering has just the right immediacy, and at the climax of the film the timing of the cut to Murphy's face—a vengeful God at his instant of decision—couldn't be improved on; the effect is so economical it's pure. These are the scenes that really count, because if the danger, the pain, the cruelty weren't convincing, the movie would seem a fraud. It's far from a fraud; it may even be the most emotionally accurate—and so most frightening—movie about American prisons ever made. Yet *Short Eyes* doesn't stay in the mind. Its potency is in its words. They're live, raw, profane. But a movie that is primarily words tends to evaporate.

[September 26, 1977]

The Sacred Oak

The Taviani brothers have learned to fuse political commitment and artistic commitment into stylized passion. Their film *Padre Padrone* has the beauty of anger that is channelled and disciplined without losing intensity. When it appeared in competition at Cannes this year, there was no question among members of the jury but that it had to win the grand prize, the Golden Palm. It also won the independently awarded International Critics' Prize. No movie has ever won both before, and *Padre Padrone* wasn't even made as a theatrical feature—it was shot in 16 mm. for Italian television. Yet there has been very little talk about the film, which opened at the New York Film Festival on September 25th. Its subject—and, even more, the sudden flare-up of its scenes—may intimidate people. Paolo and Vittorio Taviani, who wrote and directed this adaptation of Gavino Ledda's 1974 autobiography, are not new film-makers; Paolo was born in 1931, Vittorio in 1929, and they've been working in movies—starting with documentaries—since 1954. They've developed a dissonant technique that is remote from the terms of most moviemaking. *Padre Padrone* is a high-strung, intransigent work—deliberately primitive and barbaric. It's constructed as a series of epiphanies; each sequence has its own painterly design and is set off from the one before, as if a new slide were held up. The images are simplified down to their dynamic components, like the diagrams of great artists' compositions in painting texts, and this, plus the faintly psychedelic Romanesque color, creates a pungent, viselike atmosphere.

Gavino Ledda himself appears on the screen to introduce the story; a man in his mid-thirties, he stands in the village of Siligo, in northern Sardinia, at the school he attended for only a few days, and hands the actor (Omero Antonutti) who plays his father an indispensable prop—a large stick. Then Ledda disappears, and is replaced by the six-year-old Gavino (Fabrizio Forte) on the fateful day when his father comes to the school to take him away. Terrified, the boy urinates in the aisle. When the father and child are out of the room, the boys laugh at the puddle, and the father storms back in and shouts at them, "Your turn will come!" From their stricken faces it's clear that there is a terror they all live with.

Gavino says goodbye to his mother (Marcella Michelangeli), is taken to a sheepfold several miles from his family's home, and is left to live there alone. This is not the sylvan myth of the shepherd with his pipes; families here enslave their first children, so that the younger ones won't die of hunger. Gavino's father lashes him if he shows fear or tries to run away or talks with other boys in neighboring fields. Imprisoned in their sheepfolds and beaten into submission, Gavino and the others sink into apathy, with no outlet for their rancor except their unlucky animals. The oppression is systematized—a Gulag Archipelago that's been built into the mores of society for thousands of years. Forced to be a "wild child," Gavino lives in silence and illiteracy until he's twenty. The movie deals with his rebellion: his struggle for words.

The spirit of *Padre Padrone* isn't naturalistic; rather, it's animistic. This sets it apart from de Seta's classically structured, neo-realist *Bandits of Orgosolo* (1961), also a primal Sardinian story. Except for Disney-style films, *Padre Padrone* may be the only fully consciously animistic movie ever made. Without people to talk with, trained to listen for bandits, Gavino lives by sounds, and as he learns to listen to the rustling sacred oak tree we hear it, too, and we hear the dawn, the animals' thoughts, the cries of far-off people, the heavy breathing of a shepherd as he prepares for a sexual assault on his burro: breathing that gathers force as younger shepherds mount their sheep, still smaller boys attack their chickens, Gavino's father rushes home to his wife, and then men and women—the whole village—are heard panting. It's a gale, a squall that sweeps over the countryside. Sound is the Expressionist element in this movie. The heightened whispers of nature, the percussive clangings of Gavino's rage—these are uncontrollable sounds that come up out of the silence. But when Gavino, sullen-faced, spaced out in the stupor of loneliness, hears a distant accordion playing the waltz from *Fledermaus*, it's fiercely pleasurable. It's more than an accordion, it's a whole band. It's the world outside his field coming to him. Gavino slaughters two lambs and trades them for the accordion, and it's his first, furtive defiance of his father-master—an attempt to gain a piece of the human inheritance.

When the family fortunes improve, with the acquisition of an olive grove, the now fully grown Gavino (Saverio Marconi) is put to work there, and his father keeps him obedient by humiliating him, taunting him for his ignorance. And others humiliate him when he's called away for his military service: it's not just that he can't read but that he can't speak Italian—only his local dialect, which is forbidden. He begins to study—incessantly, voraciously—stays on as a volunteer so he can continue studying, and, finally, has a breakthrough. It's in radio class: the soldiers have had to build their own sets, and on test day an officer tries them out. If Gavino's radio works, he tells himself, he'll try for a scholarship, he'll study Latin and Greek, he'll go to college. The officer turns on the set and there is a second of silence and then, soaring up, the *Fledermaus* waltz of the accordion and band. The music has never sounded more joyous. This movie is not, however, naïvely triumphant in tone. There is a memorable sequence of Gavino in a tank during maneuvers calling out Latin words over his walkie-talkie to a soldier friend in another tank, and reciting lines from the Aeneid like a student prince, and he goes on to take a degree in linguistics. But Ledda himself, replacing the actor, comes on at the end to indicate that he can never be like those who haven't experienced a childhood of solitary confinement. The adult Gavino is left rocking his body back and forth, as we had seen the child Gavino rock in the sheepfold—a motion like the rocking of the blind or of caged primates. (Ledda's thesis at the University of Sassari was on Sardinian dialects—the language of the shepherds.)

The film has the air of a performance, each set piece bare yet carnal. Trying to find out what actually happened to the two missing lambs, the father eavesdrops on Gavino's night thoughts as if the boy were speaking aloud. When the members of Gavino's family lay out a well-to-do neighbor's corpse, each of them thinks of what he wants from among the dead man's possessions, and their voices fill the room. The shepherds bearing a statue aloft in a religious procession chatter about whores' not being satisfactory, because they don't have tails. And all through the film the oak tree, seen against the blackness of night, is a malevolent presence. The Tavianis' vision is on the nightmare side of primitivism, where the elements themselves are your enemies, and mindless cruelty seems grotesquely natural. The peasants' ignorance and greed are Boschian, mythological. As in Kosinski's *The Painted Bird*—the boy there loses his voice, loses the will to speak—the cruelty is almost rhapsodic. (This is the sensibility that Roman Polanski tries for.)

Though the acting is conceived to be slightly stolid—taciturn, distanced—the performances in the minor parts, such as Gavino's sisters and brothers, are often merely wooden; that, however, isn't distracting, like the carryings-on of Gavino's mother, a road-company Anna Magnani in an Italian version of *Sons and Lovers*. A small budget ($300,000) may explain the absence of sheep in the field where Gavino's father trains him but doesn't account for some imperfections: The sounds of the violent thrashings Gavino receives are a fraction of a second off synch—possibly for an intentional stylized effect; however, the viewer is uncertain whether this is deliberate or just sloppy. When the father opens his mouth as if to cry out and a chant comes from far away, from ancient time, the viewer is aware of the ambitiousness of the effect; it's like watching a dress rehearsal. Yet none of these blemishes is disturbing for long. What's disturbing is the tone: the Tavianis are barbaric in a very assured way.

When Ledda himself is on the screen, his plainness is emotionally overwhelming. A man not molded by society to be lettered who yet becomes so uses language differently from those who take their education for granted; he may make out of language something that no one thought of before. There is a mystery in Ledda's plainness: he is a "wild child" trying to tell us what life without us was about. He had to fight his father—a man built like an oak—and physically defeat him before winning the right to study, and when your slavemaster is your father and he wants to kill you for your defiance, that defiance must destroy all you've ever known. Ledda's isolation now that he has won that fight may be deeper than before. There is a moment in the film when the olive crop has been ruined by frost, and the father, suddenly puny, sits on his bed in his underwear, eating a dish of frozen milk—a child finding solace. And the grown-up Gavino, looking on, knows that his own hatred is pitiful. His progenitor, the tyrant, is smaller than the hatred, which will always be within him.

One's tenuous reservations about the picture come down to this: Ledda experienced the terror of being alone; the Tavianis didn't—they're interpreting it. They've learned from Brecht, they've learned from Godard. And their style is possibly—well, too stylish for Gavino Ledda's suffering and his struggle. They've put all their layers of modernism to work, and their method may be just a shade too intelligently dramatic;

their perception insulates them. This could be the danger in being two—in talking everything out. A little plainness can be redeeming: Renoir knows that; De Sica did, too. Eisenstein didn't. The Tavianis know all about the uses of visual and aural austerity, but there's never a moment in this near-great movie when you hear the beat of a simple heart.

□ □ □

*I*f Al Pacino had sent forth his agent to search the world for the role that would call attention to all his weaknesses, the agent could not have come up with an unholier grail than *Bobby Deerfield*. Pacino plays a Newark-born Grand Prix racing-car driver who falls in love with a dying girl called Lillian (Marthe Keller), but if you think that means he'll be a spirited tough guy who's fun to be around but so adolescent he doesn't fear death until he begins to care for the girl, you've reckoned without the director, Sydney Pollack, the screenwriter, Alvin Sargent, and their source material—*Heaven Has No Favorites*, an Erich Maria Remarque novel. *Bobby Deerfield* is about a life-hating racer who's incapable of human relationships—a careful man who has turned himself into a precision instrument—and a woman whose closeness to death has made her the custodian of wisdom and psychological acuity. Now, whether the hero is life-loving or life-hating, this kind of movie is trashily sentimental or it's nothing. But Sydney Pollack recoils from his own deals—he signs up for a *Love Story* and then munches on it as if he were Antonioni. He and Sargent must have had a real *folie à deux* going on this one—Sargent presenting Pollack with literary blossoms, and Pollack basking in the fine aroma.

In the first shot of Lillian, in a Swiss sanatorium where Bobby has gone to see an injured driver, she's reading Saint-Exupéry. She's a questioning spirit, and she starts almost at once. A magician is performing for the patients after dinner. "Do you believe in it? Magic?" she asks Bobby. "No," he says. "Destiny?" she queries. The dialogue of this metaphysical kook—a dying Mame—comes out of the blue. It appears to be Lillian's destiny to liberate Bobby. "There is no plan," she says, "unless, of course, you believe in God. Do you believe in God?" The meddlesome Lillian does have one endearing trait. "When do you wace next?" she asks Bobby. Dissatisfied with his spiritual progress, she can be quite severe: "You are not weady to spend a weekend in the countwy with me." Marthe Keller, a tall, toothy, Swiss-born actress who looks like a more lyrical Diana Rigg, showed some professional skill in her last American picture, the dim *Black Sunday*; but she's been thinned down to a death's-head boniness—surely one look at her and Bobby would be terrified of infection? And when she talks to Bobby about "wabbits"— which she does fwequently—she falls into a wabbit hole. Then Anny

Duperey, a statuesque French actress making her American début, who plays Bobby's stone-faced secretary-mistress, has her only big scene and buggers *her* "r," and you begin to dweam of Barbara Walters conducting an interview with the two of them. For reasons in no way apparent, Bobby is deeply affected by Lillian's abrupt, inquisitorial style. (Does he have happy memories of Elmer Fudd's pwissy thweat to Bugs Bunny: "I'll get you, you twicky wabbit"?) And though there isn't much change in Bobby's slack-jawed moroseness, we are given to understand that his soul is reborn. In a sloth, or a slug?

Bobby Deerfield is an actor's dream of himself—high-cheekboned (actually sunken-cheeked), thin and tanned, a celeb driving fancy cars, being chased by girls and idolized by crowds. Bored, he acknowledges their wild cheers with a small gesture of condescension—the bullfighter of *Blood and Sand* has gone through est. Bobby buzzes around Leukerbad, proceeds to Bellagio and other towns on Lake Como, to Florence, the Boboli Gardens, San Gimignano, Paris, and Le Mans; it's a journey through great villas and epicurean hotels. (There's no trouble signing on a cast and crew for this type of rich-meets-rich picture.) Lillian is a well-heeled free spirit, and Pacino wears a twenty-thousand-dollar wardrobe, with forty-seven changes. I make that out to be $425.50 an ensemble, which should brighten an actor's cheeks. But torpor is Pacino's idea of acting romantic. Dressed up in his super-casual clothes, he's like a Polo Lounge pimp playing Hamlet. In *Dog Day Afternoon*, Pacino was pure energy; he could be *on* in that role, making the character's tensions felt. However, Pacino has a tendency to monotonous, passive reactions; in a role that allows him to sit around, overcoiffed, and let us observe the "inner" man, he falls into a kiss-me catatonia. He loses even the simplest forms of competence: referring to parts of his car, he might be reading from a TelePrompTer. And in the climax, comforting his dying love, he still looks sleazy and debauched; he has the sallow smile of a wine steward trying to seem trustworthy. Or of an actor lying to himself: the camera is on his face as Lillian dies, and we know it isn't the director's tact, it's because Pacino is the one whose name is on the marquee.

As with *Three Days of the Condor* and *The Yakuza*, Pollack hasn't figured out in advance where the drama is in the scenes, and he doesn't find out during the shooting, either. There seem to be about eleven thousand cuts in the first three minutes of this movie—enough for a four-hour picture. Pollack is like a photographer who, asked for a portrait, thrusts dozens of contact sheets at you; it takes a while to discover that he never got the one picture that was needed. Bobby and Lillian drive amid scenic splendors, with no emotional development of their relationship. And during the big car-race sequences we're not briefed on who the chief competitors are; we're supposed to be above caring who wins. Pollack isn't even drunk on images: he stages a hot-air-balloon regatta, and almost the only use he makes of it is to have Lillian in a gondola advising Bobby, "Come with the wind." With the cinematographer Henri Decae in charge, the film has a golden, burnished look, like parts of *To Catch a Thief* and *Claire's Knee*. But Pollack needs a Decae to turn out a film that looks half as expensive as it actually is. He's been coasting for so long that if by now he's afraid to trust any shot to hold our attention for more than six seconds he's right to be scared. The shots he does hold—the uninhibited Lillian in a tunnel letting out a primal scream, Bobby doing the imitation of Mae West he did as a child and then showing Lillian his childhood photographs—are so solemnly meaningful you long for the mercy of a cut. Pollack was in control of his overelaborate *They Shoot Horses, Don't They?* and he showed some ability with actors in *The Way We Were*, but, trying for a Lelouch effect, he's reduced to buying atmosphere that is only the glitter of cash outlay, and to falling back on Dave Grusin's score—fraudulent romantic exoticism that gushes forth from Bobby's car radio. It has no period or culture—just a pervasive datedness. For those involved, this six-million-dollar movie is an example of handsomely reimbursed self-deception. If Sydney Pollack had directed *The Other Side of Midnight*— which is on the same level as *Bobby Deerfield*—no one would have got laid. They'd all have been engrossed in Saint-Exupéry.

[October 3, 1977]

A Woman for All Seasons?

To say that *Julia* is well lighted doesn't do Douglas Slocombe's cinematography exact justice. It's *perfectly* lighted, which is to say, the color is lustrous, the images so completely composed they're almost static—picture postcards of its heroine Lillian Hellman (Jane Fonda) as a national monument. This is conservative—classical humanist—movie-making, where every detail of meaning is worked out, right down to each flicker of light in the bit players' eyes. The director, Fred Zinnemann, does all the work for you, the way George Stevens did in *A Place in the Sun*. He does it beautifully—and there are very few directors left who know how to do it at all; the younger directors who aspire to this style, such as Alan Pakula or Dick Richards, don't achieve anything like the smoothness of Zinnemann's control, the glide of one sequence to the next.

304

The man who made *From Here to Eternity* and *The Nun's Story* and *The Sundowners* hasn't forgotten his trade. Yet there's a cautiousness and reserve in his control now. Though Zinnemann takes a very romantic view of his two heroines—Lillian and Julia (Vanessa Redgrave)—the film is impersonal, its manner objective. Zinnemann's imagery isn't as inflated as David Lean's; he doesn't hold the frames too long; *Julia* is never ponderous. But this is important-motion-picture land, where every shot is the most beautiful still of the month. *Julia* is romantic in such a studied way that it turns romanticism into a moral lesson.

"Julia," one of the stories in *Pentimento, A Book of Portraits* (1973), Lillian Hellman's second volume of memoirs, is an account of how her childhood friend Julia involved her in smuggling fifty thousand dollars into Nazi Germany ("to bribe out many in prison and many who soon will be"). Of the stories in the book, it comes closest to Hellman's plays and scenarios; it's the one most like a movie—specifically, the anti-Nazi adventure movies made in Hollywood in the forties. The author uses the smuggling operation as a suspense mechanism, and as a framework for her recollections about Julia. Zinnemann lets this suspense element slip between his fingers, indifferently, as if it would be vulgar to grip the audience's emotions. The Georges Delerue score is lovely, in Delerue's special, under-orchestrated way, and gives the imagery a reminiscent edge, but *it* doesn't provide suspense, either. Trying to be faithful to Lillian Hellman's recollections, Zinnemann and Alvin Sargent, the screenwriter, construct an ornate superstructure of narration, dissolves, flashbacks spanning decades, and telepathic visions. Yet without suspense this superstructure has no engine inside. The film is all mildly anticipatory; it never reaches a point where you feel "This is it." Sargent has demonstrated his craftsmanship in the past (the most gifted writers sometimes regress to the poetic follies of adolescence, and that probably explains his other Lillian, in *Bobby Deerfield*), and he's really trying this time. There's some shrewd, taut writing, but you can see that he's harnessed. The script fails to draw you in, and the invented scenes of the heroines as young girls are flaccid—a literary form of calendar art, and photographed like *September Morn*. The constraint and inertness must go back to the decision to treat the story as literary history, as a drama of conscience, a parallel to Zinnemann's *A Man for All Seasons*, with Lillian Hellman herself as a legendary figure, and the relationships she has written about—with Dashiell Hammett (Jason Robards), Dorothy Parker (Rosemary Murphy), Alan Campbell (Hal Holbrook), and others—assumed to be common knowledge. Pity the screenwriter impaled on the life of a living person. And Sargent is bound by that person's short account, to which a high degree of art has already been applied. He might have been liberated if he could have changed the names and fictionalized the story; that way, he could have plugged the holes in the material and supplied what's missing in the characters, and some skepticism. But then the film would have lost its air of importance, history, lesson. And, of course, its selling point. What other movie has had its trailer built into an Academy Awards presentation, the way *Julia* did last March, when Jane Fonda made a speech introducing Lillian Hellman, who, head erect, acknowledged a standing ovation?

The film opens with Jane Fonda's recitation of the epigraph to *Pentimento*, a passage about old paint on canvas aging and revealing what was underneath, what was obscured "because the painter 'repented,' changed his mind." Speaking as the elderly Lillian Hellman, she says, "I wanted to see what was there for me once, what is there for me now." The flashback structure, too, suggests that there will be shifting perspectives, and throughout the movie we wait for the revelation of something lost from sight, displaced, hidden. Yet the narrator also tells us, "I think I have always known about my memory: I know when it is to be trusted . . . I trust absolutely what I remember about Julia." And actually there are no shadings that change, nothing brought up that was painted over, no hint of "repentance." Except for some needed exposition and some filler scenes, the movie limits itself to what the author provides, and her terse style locks her view of the past in place; there's no space for us to enter into it—not even any junk rattling around for us to free-associate with. What, then, is the point of the first quotation? This sort of fidelity—presumably for the sake of a polished, literate tone—fuzzes up whatever chances the film has for clarity in its first, complicated half hour. Lillian's memories of the years shared with Hammett and her efforts to write are interspersed with her memories of Julia, the opening night of *The Children's Hour*, the play that made her famous, and scenes on the train when she's carrying the bribe money across Germany to Berlin. You need to stare at the wigs to locate yourself in time. After a while, it becomes apparent that the filmmakers are trafficking in quotations and too many flashbacks because they can't find the core of the material.

They trust the author's memory, but can *we*? Who can believe in the Julia she describes—the ideal friend of her early youth, the beautiful, unimaginably rich Julia who never fails to represent the highest moon-struck ideals? If ever there was a character preserved in the amber of a girlhood crush, she's it. The gallant, adventurous Julia opens the worlds of art and conscience to the worshipful Lillian. She recites poetry and is incensed at the ugliness of the social injustices perpetrated by her own family; she goes off to study at Oxford, then to medical school in Vienna, intending to work with Freud; she plunges into the dangerous opposition to Hitler, writes letters to Lillian explaining the holocaust to come, and in the middle of it all has a baby. This saintly Freudian Marxist queen, on easy terms with Darwin, Engels, Hegel, and Einstein, might have been a joke with almost anyone but Vanessa Redgrave in the role. Redgrave's height and full figure have an ethereal, storybook wonder, and she uses some of the physical spaciousness that she had on the stage in *The Lady from the Sea*; she can be majestic more fluidly than anyone else (and there's more of her to uncoil). She has a scene all bandaged up in a hospital bed; unable to speak, she points with maybe the most expressive huge hand the screen has ever known. She handles the American accent unnoticeably—it's not that awful flat twang she used for Isadora. In closeups, Vanessa Redgrave has the look of glory, like the young Garbo in Arnold Genthe's portraits; her vibrancy justifies Lillian's saying that she had "the most beautiful face I'd ever seen." Redgrave is so well endowed by nature to play queens that she can act simply in the role (which doesn't occupy much screen time) and casually, yet lyrically, embody Lillian Hellman's dream friend. Zinnemann has very astutely cast as the teen-age Julia a young girl (Lisa Pelikan) who's like a distorted Vanessa Redgrave—a fascinating, dislikable, rather creepy look-alike, who suggests that the intellectual goddess didn't appear out of a white cloud.

It's the dark cloud—Jane Fonda's stubborn strength, in glimpses of her sitting at the typewriter, belting down straight whiskey and puffing out smoke while whacking away at the keys, hard-faced, dissatisfied—that saves the film from being completely pictorial. It's a cloud-of-smoke performance; Bette Davis in all her movies put together couldn't have smoked this much—and Fonda gets away with it. It's in character. She creates a driven, embattled woman—a woman overprepared to fight back. This woman doesn't have much flexibility. You can see that in the stiff-necked carriage, the unyielding waist, even in the tense, muscular wrists, and in her nervous starts when anything unexpected happens. Her clothes are part of her characterization: Anthea Sylbert, who designed them, must have taken her cue from photographs of the author. These are the clothes of a woman who didn't choose them to be flattering—she chose them with a sense of her position in the world. They're expensive, selected with an eye to drama and to fashion—also not to get in her way. Outfitted in a style that combines elegance and impatience, Jane Fonda catches the essence of the Irving Penn portrait of Lillian Hellman reproduced in her first book of memoirs, *An Unfinished Woman* (1969). When she's alone on the screen, Fonda gives the movie an atmosphere of dissension, and she sustains this discordant aloneness in her scenes with everyone except Julia, with whom she's soft, eager, pliant. Her deliberately humorless Lillian is a formidable, uningratiating woman—her hair sculpted out of the same stone as her face. If you like her, you have to like her on her own implacable terms. How does a viewer separate Jane Fonda's Lillian Hellman from the actual Lillian Hellman? It's impossible to make clear distinctions between the live woman that Jane Fonda draws from (the performance could be called an inspired impersonation), the self-portrait in the story, and the semi-fictionalized activities on the screen. Almost anything one thinks or feels about this character seems an intrusion on a life, yet an intrusion that has been contracted for by Lillian Hellman herself—perhaps somewhat unwittingly.

The story itself has a *submerged* core: all of Hellman's attitudes, everything that goes into her woman's variant of Hemingway-Hammett stripped-down, hardboiled writing. Her prose is strong and clear, and also guarded, reluctant, pried out of a clenched hand. In the kind of situation-centered play Hellman writes, she doesn't give much of herself away. Her memoirs are dramatized, too, yet they're more exciting as drama than her plays are, since you can feel the tension between what she's giving you and what she's withholding. One expects a writer to trust his unconscious, to let go sometimes—not always to be so selective. Lillian Hellman carries thrift and plain American speech to a form of self-denial. The clue to some of the tension in the story "Julia" comes elsewhere in *Pentimento*—in "Turtle," the most compact Hemingway-Hammett story in the book, yet the one that reveals the cost of being hardboiled. In "Turtle," there are only two important characters—Hellman and Hammett, with whom she lived off and on for almost thirty years—and it's evident that for him strong and clear and definite meant masculine, while doubts and unresolved feelings were weak nonsense: feminine. Lillian Hellman tried to write (and to live) in a way that Hammett would approve of; he rejected much of what she actually felt, and she accepted his standards. (The question of why a woman of such strength and, in many ways, of such ruthless honesty should have deferred to the judgment of a man of lesser gifts than her own—that's the sexual mystery that would make a drama.)

The movie is about Hellman's career and doesn't really exist independently of one's knowledge of that career. The friendship between Julia and Lillian is obviously the emotional basis—the original material—for *The Children's Hour*. In that play, scandalmongers spread a sexual rumor about the relationship of two young women teachers, destroying their friendship and their hopes. Here, in *Julia*, Lillian is out drinking in a restaurant with Sammy (John Glover, who shows a nasty vitality, like an American Edward Fox), the brother of a former schoolmate. He says that "the whole world knows about you and Julia," and she slugs him, knocking him back in his chair and then slamming the table over on top of him as she leaves. (People in the theatre applauded.) In the melodramatic Victorian code that is integral to hardboiled writing, the suggestion of homosexuality is a slur—it sullies the purity of the two women's relationship. Only contemptible people—curs like Sammy—think like that. They don't know how to behave; they lack standards. (This was the theme that came out all too nakedly in Hellman's third book of memoirs, the 1976 *Scoundrel Time*.) The failure to look beyond "right" and "wrong" has limited Hellman as a dramatist, and in "Julia" (though not in other stories in *Pentimento*) she thinks in the same terms—judgmentally. "Julia" is an expression of outraged idealism—sexual, political, and in all areas of personal conduct. It is in this story that she shows the beginnings of her own political conscience, started and nurtured, according to her account, by Julia. And it is Julia's dedication to fighting Fascism and her subsequent mutilation and murder that serve as the concrete justification—the personal experience—behind Lillian Hellman's embittered attitude toward those she regards as cowardly or dishonorable. The motive force of the story is that those who have not lived up to her conception of honor stand morally condemned for eternity.

In the film, at the last meeting of Lillian and Julia, in a café near the railroad station in Berlin, Lillian turns over the money she has smuggled in, and Julia says to her, "Are you still as angry as you used to be? I like your anger. . . . Don't you let anyone talk you out of it." There's no way for viewers to understand what Julia is referring to: in their scenes together, Lillian has never demonstrated any anger. Julia has been the daring leader, railing at injustice, going off and doing something about it. Lillian has been the docile follower, the naïf. In the movie version of *A Man for All Seasons*, a respectable job of monument-making, Zinnemann enshrined the martyred Sir Thomas More as a man of conscience; audiences weren't forcibly reminded that what More got himself beheaded for was the belief that the Pope represented divine law. What people could take away from the film was that More stood by his principles and died for them. In *Julia*, it isn't nearly as clear why Lillian is a monumental figure. In the episode of carrying the money to Berlin, she's more of a hazard than anything else; the operation is so efficiently organized and she is supported by such resourceful anti-Nazi underground aides that she hardly seems to be needed at all.

And so it has to be from Lillian's mentors that we get her measure. As Hammett, Robards, who is gruff and funny at the beginning, has nothing to do once the film gets under way—he's just the all-wise, all-knowing Dash standing by, with love. But Dash is there for a reason: he's a judge of writing of such supreme authority—a Sainte-Beuve at the very least—that when he tells Lillian that *The Children's Hour*, which she has just finished, is "the best play anyone's written in a long time," there can be no question about it. Julia is the saintly political activist who certifies Lillian's anger as instinctive morality, and Dash is the stamp of approval that certifies her greatness.

The most difficult thing for an actor to suggest is what goes into making a person an artist—the tensions, the richness. And this is particularly difficult in the case of Lillian Hellman, who doesn't have that richness, and who in her own account makes herself so innocent of intellectual drives that anger seems to be her creative fount. If Julia's last advice to Lillian actually was to hang on to her anger, it was bad advice. Anger blinds Lillian Hellman as a writer. But anger is what holds the story

"Julia" together, and the movie doesn't have it. At moments, Jane Fonda supplies something better, because she understands how to embody the explosive Hellman resentment. She gets at what anger does to you. It won't let you relax. It boxes you in: you're on your own. When—as Lillian—she walks into Sardi's on the opening night of her hit, twitching slightly from drunken nervousness, revelling in the attention she's getting while stiffly living up to her own image of herself as the distinguished playwright, you want more of her. You feel that Fonda has the power and invention to go on in this character—that she could crack this smooth, contemplative surface and take us places we've never been to. The film's constraint—its not seizing the moments when she's ready to *go*—is frustrating. Perfectionism has become its own, self-defeating end.

[October 10, 1977]

Heart/Soul

Women's-lib sensitivity may be the worst blow to drama since fifties-TV Freud. *A Special Day* is like processed Tennessee Williams: a woman's sexual hunger and a man's sexual deviation are treated as a refined problem play. The two-character confrontation takes place in an apartment block in Rome, on May 8, 1938, during Hitler's visit with Mussolini to reaffirm the glory of the Rome-Berlin Axis—a day of celebration. Sophia Loren is an oppressed working-class housewife, the mother of six children, and Marcello Mastroianni is an announcer for government-controlled radio, a suspected homosexual who has just been dismissed from his job and is about to be interned in Sardinia. She idolizes Mussolini but has so much housework to do that she packs her Fascist husband (John Vernon) and the kids off to the parade, and then, guess what? Her mynah bird flies out of its cage and across the courtyard to the window of Mastroianni, who has also stayed at home—waiting for its arrival? No, preparing to commit suicide, because in addition to his other miseries he's lost his lover (which we learn in a telephone monologue that deftly miniaturizes Cocteau's *The Human Voice*).

The slavey mother of six is not used to the courtesies of the well-bred announcer and falls madly, urgently in love. She learns that he is homosexual, and softly, meekly, almost ritually seduces him. She experi-

310

ences sexual joy for the first time, and thinks she's proving him heterosexual; she doesn't realize that there's more than simple physical capability involved in one's choice of love objects. That is all that happens. She has learned something about passion, however, and has had a moment's doubt about the grandeur of Mussolini's policies. And the announcer, though still forlorn when he's hustled away by the police, is at least alive. It's so neat, so wimpy neat. The colors are desaturated—brown tones and gray tones—and then, suddenly, after Loren's awakening there's a splash of red roses in the courtyard as she looks out and sees him for the last time. Passion commemorated. Gratitude forever.

Loren wears a drab housedress that is meant to remind you of her unglamorous dishevelment in *Two Women*, for which she won an Academy Award, and you're supposed to applaud her for not being made up. With your husband as the producer and Pasqualino De Santis as the lighting cameraman, who needs makeup? Loren has never looked more richly beautiful or given such a completely controlled great-lady performance. This movie is perfectly calibrated for its teeny bit of courage: the big stars playing uncharacteristic roles—two social inferiors in this totalitarian-minded society having their brief encounter. Born in 1931, the director, Ettore Scola (*The Pizza Triangle, We All Loved Each Other So Much*), was a screenwriter for the great clown Totò and worked on the scripts of some seventy movies altogether (including many famous ones) before he turned director, in 1964; he and a couple of colleagues shaped this script with Loren and Mastroianni in mind. The early scenes of Loren getting her children up and into their uniforms have a little vaudeville bounce, but the further Scola goes from farce the more he's forced back on "sensitivity." This movie gets to be a strenuous exercise in sensitivity. He handles the schematic romance with all the grace he can muster, in a style that might be called genteel shamelessness—the turf so well tended by Noël Coward when he was being "real."

In the latest fashion in sympathy, when two unhappy people meet, one of them is an outcast because she's a woman, the other because he's a homosexual. Their humiliation draws them together for a few hours, and we see that society has wronged them, cruelly. There's fifties-TV irony and contrast here: the noise of the radio carrying the strident exultation outside is the counterpoint to the loneliness of the two left behind in the emptied building—the wallflowers left out of the party. Essentially, Loren and Mastroianni are both playing *Marty*—she's Marty as a passive, despised woman, he's Marty as a passive, despised homosexual. "When you're ignorant, there's no respect," she says, echoing Chayefsky's "little people," who have already dulled our sensibilities past compassion. The poetry of banality is a great big fraud: no matter how gracefully you pour it on, it's still condescension.

When the housewife tenderly begins to make love to the homosexual and puts his hand on her magnificent melon breast, it's embarrassingly tasteful. Your first thought may be *Pizza and Sympathy*, but it's your next that's fatal. The man lies there politely, joylessly; his face is drawn, tense, utterly still. How can you have any feeling for a man who doesn't enjoy being in bed with Sophia Loren? You lose any interest in the radio announcer afterward. He just fades away, and you barely remember the fine, subtle work Mastroianni did earlier in the film—a closely observed portrait of a diffident, cultivated, self-aware man, a little loose in the seat when he rumbas. If this man is a shade too wistful, too repressed even at the start to make us care very much about him, that may be in the writing. This kind of movie doesn't mean to get us angry or worked up; any big emotional response would destroy it. We're supposed to see the small hurts, the lilts of feeling, the fine-tuning of despair. It's neo-realism in a gold frame.

Loren is a star because of her beauty combined with the teasing good humor in her vitality—her great gift for seeming to be having the best time in the world up there on the screen. Here she shows that spontaneity in only one scene: when she describes her excitement the time she quite by chance got close to Mussolini and felt his sexual magnetism. There's nothing the matter with her careworn-Italian-woman-finds-love number (a reprise of Florinda Bolkan's role in De Sica's *A Brief Vacation*), except that this "mature," "eloquent" acting is self-conscious acting. If Loren would just get out of that dumb dress and stop bucking for prizes, she could drop her soulful, resigned expression and get some spirit back. The deprived-woman role starves her personality. Her self-consciousness—and Mastroianni's, too—is integral to the big-stars-playing-little-people conception. This movie is all heart. Calculatedly all heart. And so, although it's about sex, both stars become as sexless as possible. They try to purify themselves so they'll be properly little.

□ □ □

Angst-dark primary colors—reds and blues so intense they're near-psychedelic, yet grimy, rotting in the thick, muggy atmosphere. Cities that blur into each other. Characters as figures in cityscapes or as exiles in rooms that are insistently not home. And, under it all, morbid, premonitory music. This is the festering mood of the young German writer-director Wim Wenders' *The American Friend*, adapted from Patricia Highsmith's crime thriller *Ripley's Game*.

An American demi-crook, Tom Ripley (Dennis Hopper), operating out of Hamburg, suffers a small discourtesy: a Swiss picture restorer and framer, Jonathan (Bruno Ganz), who suspects Ripley of being involved in art forgery, declines to shake his hand. Minot (Gérard Blain), a gangster associate of Ripley's, needs the services of an assassin, and out of pique—it's no more than a perverse whim—Ripley suggests that Jonathan might be his man. Minot tricks Jonathan, who has a blood disease, into believing that his death is imminent, and proposes that he kill for hire—the target is someone he's never met—so that he'll have money to leave to his wife and child. Jonathan's moral values collapse once he thinks he's dying; suddenly something in him gives way—as (we fear) it might in any of us. He yields to the momentary temptation, and the trap closes; he's a criminal. There's a true thriller moment when this honorable, decent craftsman-shopkeeper carries out his mission. Feverishly, only half consciously, he shoots the victim on an escalator in the Paris Métro and then comes up into the daylight, and it's like waking from a nightmare—except that we know that now his whole life will be a nightmare.

Highsmith's thrillers—the sources of Hitchcock's *Strangers on a Train* and René Clément's *Purple Noon*—aren't concerned with bringing criminals to justice, and there's no moral principle or any other standard to separate the normal and the criminal. The symmetrical twist in the plot here is that Ripley develops an affection for Jonathan and tries to extricate him from Minot's clutches. (Does the title mean that an American friend is one who tries to help you after he's destroyed you?) Jonathan, who wanted to protect his family's future, is so changed that he leads a new, dislocated life in which he feels himself a stranger—a tourist who hasn't got his bearings. His wife barely knows him anymore; Ripley, who understands what is happening to him, replaces his wife as his mate.

Bruno Ganz's performance as Jonathan is one of the rare ordinary-decent-fellow portrayals that actually succeed (for a while, at least) in involving the viewer. Quiet, a man of inner strength, with watchful, anxious eyes and swansdown diction, Jonathan gives the film its only depth (except for the poignancy of the settings). Ganz doesn't talk, he croons—and you almost catch yourself leaning toward the screen. You feel you're reading Jonathan's soul each time you look at him; you soak into his face the way you soak into the rooms, the streets. If Wenders had written the role so that this patsy had some aggressive impulses that came out in the killing, or if he lost his inner dignity—if he were unpredictable—you could go on soaking into him. But there's not a lot of variety in Jonathan's soul. Ganz's character modulations are in too narrow a range; he's so inward that you begin to feel he's looking soulfully out of his deep brown eyes right down at his saintly tradesman's limp mustache. Jonathan is such a humble, anxious man that the picture needs a counter-force. A stronger Ripley might provide it. But as Dennis Hopper plays him Ripley is nothing but a cowboy hat and a fatigued face and aberrant buoyant flings into the air: Hopper bounds up, arms raised high—the arms that are generally held close in to his slightly rigid body, as if he were chilled.

The psychological union that develops between Ripley and Jonathan—which should be the heart of the movie—is indicated by nothing more than Ripley's picking up a little kinetic novelty item in Jonathan's picture-framing shop and Jonathan's telling him to keep it (a gesture that could signify contempt as easily as generosity). Ripley gives Jonathan a kinetic gadget in return and fastens glassy, sweet-Jesus stares on him, which, by extrapolation, can be interpreted to mean that Ripley is moved by Jonathan's dedication to his craft. These scenes are particularly awkward because the film's sound is hollow. The performers speak German or English or French, whichever is appropriate to their characters and the moment, but the sound is poorly recorded and some scenes are inexpertly looped. This technical defect underlines the eccentricity of Hopper's decaying-juvenile blandness. It takes him an eternity of concentration to perform a minor action, such as pouring coffee into a thermos, and you could drive a truck between the syllables each time he speaks a line of dialogue. Ganz's accented English is far more fluent than his American friend's: it's as if Hopper had just mastered the beginnings of human speech and expected us to share his joy that words come out of his mouth, slowly, but . . . yes . . . they . . . do . . . come . . . out. Even an existential epigram comes out: "I know . . . less and less . . . about who . . . I . . . am . . . and . . . about . . . who . . . anybody . . . else . . . is." He mutters that into a tape recorder. For posterity. You can't risk losing thoughts like that. Has the tape been stored in a safe place?

Though Wenders overdoses on mood, he creates the right apprehensiveness for a Highsmith story. But he's trying to do eighteen other things, too; he "enriches" the plot with incidental speculative themes relating to the oppressiveness of modern society—losing more in clarity than he gains in depth. (It could be argued that he loses more in depth, too.) Jonathan is rootless—an expatriate from Zurich—and the American Ripley, the infant philosopher who talks like the computer in *Alphaville*, doesn't really live anywhere; he hops continents (via jump cuts) and camps out in his big house in Hamburg. It features a jukebox and looks like an American Colonial museum of Pop Art, so at first you don't even realize he lives on the same continent as Jonathan. The internationalization of modern cities is another theme: Wenders moves the action from New York to Hamburg, Paris, and Munich, and in each city he shoots the high-rise anonymity that could be anywhere. He finds new New Yorks all over Europe, and this certainly makes a point, but in order to make it he deliberately confuses the viewer about where the action is taking place.

All we know about most of the characters in the movie is that they are played by directors. Ripley and Minot are represented by actor-directors (Hopper and Blain), and Nicholas Ray, who directed the young Hopper in *Rebel Without a Cause*, is cast as a famous painter who has pretended to be dead. He and Hopper have scenes together which, when they become penetrable, seem to relate to the painter's "forging" new paintings in his old style so they can be sold—a plot embellishment that has nothing whatever to do with Minot and the gangsters Jonathan has got involved with, who belong to porno-filmmaking rings. Other directors who turn up are Samuel Fuller as a Mafia chieftain, Jean Eustache, in a restaurant scene, Daniel Schmid as the man on the escalator, Peter Lilienthal as a hood, and Wenders himself, in an ambulance. This slyboots casting of directors as crooks has a deadening effect; except for Fuller, their acting is perfunctory (and, in the case of Ray, worse, since he tries for a mythic effect). In addition, Jonathan's shop and flat contain a magic lantern showing a speeding train, a zoetrope, a stereopticon, a praxinoscope; Jonathan's dedicated craftsmanship is thus linked to moviemaking. Yet none of this film-toy paraphernalia helps to create suspense or to move the action forward; rather, it suggests that though Wenders is attracted to the idea of telling a story he can't quite keep his mind on it. What about his own pride in craft? The simplest plot points are bobbled, and when there's mayhem, it isn't clear who the participants are or what the outcome is. We're never informed about Ripley's connection with Minot, which got the whole thing started. There's a gaping difference between moral ambiguity and this obscurity—which actually impedes the perception of moral ambiguities.

It's possible for a director to combine suspense narrative and essay, as Godard demonstrated in 1959 in *Breathless* and in several films in the sixties, doing it quickly, dartingly, in a visual style that could be read at a glance. But Wenders uses densely detailed imagery, his pacing is weighted, and there are no insights that relate to the characters—the film drags along on secondhand alienation. *The American Friend* doesn't have the nasty, pleasurable cleverness of a good thriller. Wenders has a moviemaker's visual imagination, and his unsettling compositions are neurotically beautiful visions of a disordered yet functioning world. Dramatically, though, the entire film is stagnant—inverted Wagnerianism. The unease of the generalized moral degradation overpowers Jonathan's individual story. Wenders has the style of someone who's aware of what he's doing, but that's not enough—look at Joseph Losey. Wenders is like a more garish, grainier Losey—Losey under mud. Is that why the film is being called a masterpiece? A great many new German films are being called masterpieces. After Vietnam and Watergate, it's understandable that Americans should begin to wonder if morally we are any different from the Germans, and experience a psychological rapprochement—a new closeness to directors who dredge around in guilt. With nihilism in the air here, the extreme moralism of the Germans may be appealingly exotic. (Moralism could be part of the new attraction of science fiction, too.) American directors may have lost the primitive-visionary qualities that make the new German films so mysterious, but they have an understanding of narrative that the young Germans don't have. *The American Friend* is a masterpiece for people who think a movie can't be worthwhile unless it makes you suffer. Emotionally, the drip drip of Wenders' poetic urban masochism—which is intended to be anti-bourgeois filmmaking—is indistinguishable from the heavy-going German films of the Emil Jannings period. Actually, Jannings was a more robust masochist than Bruno Ganz. And Wenders isn't satisfied by Ganz's anguish; he also gives Hopper a crackup and a lonely finish. Wenders is not only turgid, he's exhibitionistically turgid. There's too much imprecise, darkly lighted desperation in *The American Friend*. By the time it grinds to a halt, you feel your mind is clouded.

[October 17, 1977]

Goodbar, or How Nice Girls Go Wrong

The talented young actresses in *I Never Promised You a Rose Garden* and *Outrageous!* are made to suffer from lyrical schizophrenia (which is the very worst kind). Diane Keaton has been much luckier. In her Woody Allen comedies, her specialty has been lyrical neurosis—which can be deliriously reassuring to the nervous wrecks in the audience. As Annie Hall, Diane Keaton redeemed the flustered confusion of urban misfits—who *fits* in this city?—and made it romantic. In her more conventional roles in *Lovers and Other Strangers* and *I Will, I Will . . . For Now*, she seemed a graceful, highly competent comedienne, in a fresh, very American manner. In Woody Allen pictures, this competence is replaced by something more distinctive: she seems helplessly aware of the ineffability of her feelings. She's the mildest form of crazy lady, not threatening to anybody, just bewildered about herself. When the hero loses her in *Annie Hall*, it isn't really a loss, because she isn't quite there; she's disconnected from the start. The amateurish, self-conscious looseness that Diane Keaton has with Allen works for her. She seems not an actress but a girl trying to act, and this wavering, unsure quality gives her a Marilyn Monroe–like appeal. She turns apologetic self-doubt into a style. When she sings, she lacks a rhythmic sense, but she flirts her way through a song, rolling her clear eyes and acting out the suggestiveness of the lyrics. She becomes a consciously naughty little girl. And all the time she emanates warmth—

316

miraculously, naturally. It's in her long-legged softness, in her coloring, her flesh tones, her sunny, broad smile.

Diane Keaton draws so much empathy you don't worry too much about her skill. It's there, though. An actress who could retain her grace in the crude muck of *I Will, I Will . . . For Now* must have reserves of training. In her only dramatic performances in the past—in the two *Godfather* movies—she didn't look comfortable with what she was doing, but that could be pinned on a busy director who hadn't given enough thought to the character and didn't know how to use her warmth. This warmth could have been her greatest advantage in *Looking for Mr. Goodbar*. It could have made us care for the loner she plays—Theresa "Terry" Dunn—so that we'd feel the awfulness of what happens to her. However, about half a minute into *Looking for Mr. Goodbar*, in her very first blissful murmurs with her very first lover, Terry sounds just like Annie Hall. Diane Keaton doesn't play Terry like the dazed, iridescent Annie. She doesn't do any bad acting (which is remarkable when so much bad acting is going on around her); she stays on pitch. Still, this actress, who has been in only a few films, doesn't do anything as Terry Dunn that she hasn't done before. As Annie Hall, Diane Keaton isn't a character, exactly; she's a fuzzy sweet neurosis—which, for the purposes of comedy, is even better. But she isn't a character in *Goodbar*, either, though she needs to be. Diane Keaton hasn't a powerful enough personality to bull her way through the huffing and puffing of Richard Brooks, who wrote the screenplay and directed. It's a blurred performance; her warmth is meaningless.

Judith Rossner's novel *Looking for Mr. Goodbar*, which is a fictionalized version of the life of Roseann Quinn, a twenty-eight-year-old teacher killed by a man she'd picked up and taken home with her, rose to the top of the best-seller lists for an obvious reason: it's about something that most women have probably done at some time—or, at least, have wanted to do. Written in realistic detail, it's a woman's lurid sex-and-horror fantasy, with some of the pulpy morbidity of Joyce Carol Oates. It begins with the killer's confession, and you search out the victim's story: What sort of woman was Terry Dunn? Why was she killed? The story has an erotic, modern-Gothic compulsiveness; the reader is kept in a state of suspenseful dread of what is coming—wishing Terry Dunn could wriggle out. Terry cruises singles bars the way male homosexuals cruise gay bars and s-m hangouts; she'd rather have sex without love than love without sex. Her sex drive is so strong that all other considerations in life seem pallid evasions of the real thing, the only thing. The weakness of this thriller is its moralizing psychology; the author believes Terry's drive to be abnormal and explains that she is unable to have a "relationship"—unable to accept sex and love together. Terry has been maimed: her parents neglected her and didn't notice that polio had affected her spine; as a result of not having been loved enough, she is left with a scar on her back and a faint limp. It's as if a woman wouldn't want sex unsanctified by tenderness unless she was crippled, psychologically flawed, self-hating.

Richard Brooks has taken Terry's flaw even further: her spinal condition is hereditary, so that she dare not risk having children (i.e., becoming a full woman). And, beyond that, her fate is the consequence of living in a permissive society. Right in the first shots, when you see Terry on the subway, the man next to her is reading *Hustler*. Brooks might as well have put a balloon at the top of the frame: "Sexual freedom leads to death." He sets up signposts—the television news reporting the fifth-anniversary celebration of women's liberation, Terry watching dirty movies at a party and in a hotel room, Terry taking pills, trying cocaine. And after a couple of hours the movie spells it out. "I don't understand your crazy world—free to go to hell!" Terry's father (Richard Kiley) cries. Then he shouts, "Freedom! Tell me, girl, how do you get free of the terrible truth?" Whatever his subject, Brooks talks truths; he works up the head of steam of the professionally indignant. In *Goodbar*, he gets so involved in his truths that he loses the story he started with. Something similar happened, though to a lesser degree, in Brooks' film of *In Cold Blood*. The most promising element in the material was the contrast between the hardworking, planning-for-the-future victims and the grungy, living-from-day-to-day killers. But Brooks set the story in a bleakly ominous America that made the lives of the victims and the killers seem the same; watching it was like staring into a dark closet, and the film was edited so confusingly that at critical moments the viewer couldn't tell what was going on. His *In Cold Blood* wound up as a tract against capital punishment. *Goodbar* is an illustrated lecture on how nice girls go wrong. And the man in charge of the slides has the jitters, and bouts of insecurity—when he slams the pictures on at different angles.

It used to be said that when a director dies he becomes a photographer—meaning that he takes pretty pictures that don't move, that he's lost the feeling for action, narrative, drama. Now when a director dies he becomes an editor—he tries to force movement and excitement into inert footage by chopping it up. *Goodbar* has been edited into shorthand; the scenes are fragmented, with many flashbacks, and Terry's fantasies cut right into the action. The film begins at a jump, and you never have a chance to get into Terry's character, or to *like* her, even though you're already softened to like Diane Keaton. You're flung into Terry's first affair, with Martin, the self-centered professor (Alan Feinstein), which represents her only emotional commitment to a lover. Feinstein knows what he's doing as an actor, but his scenes are so hyped up and jagged he always seems to be dashing out of the frame.

There's nothing to bind the fragments of *Goodbar*—certainly not sensuality. The teasing near-subliminal bedroom flashes are "artistic," not sensual: photographed by William Fraker, spinning parts of bodies and bare bottoms are pinky-creamy, dry, clean, posed. The film's visual style is soft dark tones, jellied, slipping out of focus, with the backgrounds mushy; Brooks doesn't trust us to keep our minds on the principal players, so the nightlife in the bars is covered in ground fog. As Terry's older sister, an airline stewardess, Tuesday Weld matches up well with Diane Keaton, and she's charmingly confident weeping about her abortion in her first, shallow-pleasure-seeker speech. Later on, she has to be a terrible example of waste: she delivers dispatches from the front lines of the sexual revolution, periodically summarizing what she's been doing in terms of alienated self-destructiveness, prattling about "happy dust" and how her life is "going down the drain." The movie is designed to keep telling you that the punishment for impersonal sex is death—spiritually for the sister, physically for Terry.

The only times Brooks slows down the splintered pacing and holds a scene is in Terry's classroom, with the deaf children she teaches. Maybe he doesn't understand that we could empathize with Terry's sex drive; he feels he's got to balance that side of her with a good, sympathetic side. He keeps cutting to the deaf children, romanticizing the relationship of teacher and pupils, lingering on her smiling radiance with them to show us what a wonderful, loving teacher she is, so we'll see that she's a dual personality, and understand what a good mother she'd have been if only she weren't flawed. The film could be a half hour shorter if he didn't keep returning to the classroom. It's like a senile person saying, "Did I ever tell you what a loving teacher this swinger was?" and then, six seconds later, "Did I remember to tell you what a loving teacher this swinger was?" and four seconds later . . .

As Tony, the stud who roughs Terry up, Richard Gere looks like Robert De Niro without the mole on his cheek, but there's more than that missing. He does a soap-opera actor's impersonation of De Niro, with some feints and scowls from Brando, and he imitates Warren Beatty's self-love without having it. Gere shows off his weight-lifter's thick neck and powerful wrists, jumps around to suggest dangerous volatility, and tries to act orgasmic. But there's no animal grace in his movement, and when he flashes his eyes they don't say anything. Terry's final pickup, the punk who kills her, is a second Richard Gere. His name is Tom Berenger, and he has even thicker bodybuilder's muscles and an Arnold Schwarzenegger neck. These juveniles need to swell out their chests before they can register an emotion. Like Gere, Berenger is a modular acting unit; he holds his lips slack and takes more from the young Brando than from De Niro, but it's the same kind of programmed working-class lowlife, even less convincing. (Sylvester Stallone takes from everybody else, too, but he adds something of his own that fuses it all. These two don't.)

When Terry first meets Tony, she's sitting at a bar with a hardcover edition of *The Godfather* in front of her; he comes over and says he has seen the movie. What was the director thinking of? With a star who appeared in that movie, and with the two young actors imitating De Niro and Brando, couldn't the director give her a different book to use as a come-on? Does Brooks think *The Godfather* is an indispensable symbol of freedom gone mad, like *Hustler*, the pills, the poppers? Asked what the cocaine he's snorting does for him, Tony replies, "It makes America beautiful." Another balloon goes up: "Irony." In *The Wild One*, when Brando was asked what he was rebelling against he replied, "What have you got?" A pickup asks Terry Dunn what she's hooked on, and she answers, "Anything I can get." This is social climbing, seeking mythic resonance by association. Every sequence goes shopping for a tone. Terry and her sexually incompetent social-worker boyfriend (William Atherton) are always laughing ripples of false wild laughter. And at one point, after Tony has injured Terry, her sister, coming to her aid, reaches for a cloth to use as a compress and finds it full of cockroaches; the two girls' hysteria is almost as fraudulent as the cockroaches—which look more like black jelly beans.

Why does Terry's boyfriend bring her a gift of a strobe light? Why do we see a drawing of a face contorted in screaming agony on the wall near Terry's bed, when we can't make out anything else clearly? When Terry is being murdered, her contorted face and the drawing appear in the same strobe-bright frame, and she becomes it. After contorting in agony, she cries, "Do it! Do it!" to the murderer stabbing her—and dies peacefully, released from the torment of her sexual drive. In this florid conception, death is the ultimate orgasm she has been seeking.

Some of the anticipatory excitement about this film can be easily explained: the book was erotic. But, more than that, moviegoers want to see how other people are making out—in sex, at work, in the city. This was part of the direct response people had to *Annie Hall*; even if it was, finally, somewhat disappointing, it was still about living now—even the falling apart of the "relationship" was appealing. The good will built up by *Annie Hall* carries over to *Goodbar*. A lot of moviegoers are taking chances the way Terry Dunn did; it's what nice people do when they're not feeling so nice, or when they can't stand the complications of relationships like the one in *Annie Hall*. They're going to go to *Goodbar* to see their story, and what they're going to get is a windy jeremiad laid on top of fractured film syntax.

□ □ □

*H*andle with Care is exactly the kind of high-spirited light comedy that would have become a hit a few years ago. Today a picture is penalized if it isn't big enough, if it has no stars and no obvious selling point; hardly anybody hears about it. *Handle with Care* had, at least, some identity when it was called *Citizens Band*—its title when it was given regional playdates. Citizens Band is what it's about, literally and metaphorically. Now that it has lost that bit of identity, and is being advertised as if it were soft-core porno, it will probably have to wait, as *Smile* did, to be discovered by the public on Home Box Office and then—broken up and bowdlerized—on regular commercial channels. To expedite the bowdlerizing process, Paramount opened the picture in New York with its entire last sequence lopped off. This movie has one of the few fully rounded comic scripts of recent years, and in that sequence all the elements came together in a final fling; the amputation is the executives' way of punishing the film for their own ineptitude.

Paul Brickman, who wrote the screenplay, had an idea worthy of Preston Sturges: that the psychology of those who operate CB radio units might be like the psychology of crank phone callers, and breathers and obscene phone callers, too—that as disembodied voices, with identities borrowed from pop fantasies, and signal names to confirm their new self-image, people could live another life on the public airwaves. In the film, the CB users are secret celebrities, eloquent on the air, or, more often, aimlessly loquacious. Their voices have a tale-spinning seductiveness. But they dry up when they actually meet. Companionship comes easier to them across the airwaves; they feel safe then. CB functions as an authorized madness; it allows the characters to release their inhibitions while keeping one foot on the ground. The setting is a small Southwestern town where the people think they know each other; the story is about the collision of their free-floating ids.

The breathy carnal enticements of a young woman who calls herself Electra overheat a bespectacled young man, Warlock (Will Seltzer); a listening trucker, Chrome Angel (Charles Napier), gets carried away and piles up his rig. A bratty little kid calls himself The Hustler and boasts of his sexual conquests; lonely old Grandma Breaker pours out reminiscences of her childhood. The hero, Spider (Paul Le Mat), lives in a shack with his father and runs a CB repair shop and, at his own expense, an emergency-rescue station. He's a Samaritan, dashing to the aid of truckers in trouble, and he becomes so incensed when the channels are tied up by chatterers who violate F.C.C. regulations that he turns vigilante and goes out to bust up their equipment. And so he invades the obsessions of a collection of harmless nuts, among them The Red Baron (Harry Northup), The Priest (Ed Begley, Jr.), and a gym teacher (Candy Clark) who used to be his girl but now dates his virulently competitive brother (Bruce McGill), the high-school gym coach. No heroism has ever been more transparent than Spider's. Paul Le Mat has some of the James Dean–Beau Bridges timid-dangerous-animal sensitivity; it's naïve, easily wounded, unconnected to thought, and that's why it's so attractive. Le Mat uses this disarming quality comically, so that it's tinged with American idiosyncrasy. The loose screws rattle around in Spider's head rather gently. His father, an alcoholic retired truck driver (Roberts Blossom), is morose and ornery with his son; on his CB he comes to life—his voice leaps to a youthful register, he's convivial, hopeful, practically a raconteur. When he won't answer his son, who's standing next to him, Spider has to get on the CB in order to get a response. Spider's vocal rhythms are totally unactorish; they're easygoing. But when he pleads with his father, there's a tightness in his throat and a faint childish whine. Spider is the small-town Boy Scout who has never grown up—he's still collecting medals from local civic organizations, beaming with embarrassment at the honor. He's a technology nut—a half-cocked hero—and he's been given as a sidekick a hugely fat adolescent friend (Michael Rothman), who helps him operate his emergency service and trudges after him.

Directed by the young Jonathan Demme, who has graduated from cheaply made exploitation films (*Caged Heat, Crazy Mama, Fighting Mad*), *Handle with Care* is a palmy, elegantly deadpan comedy; the jokes aren't pushed, so it takes viewers a few minutes to settle into the comic style, which has the mellow, light touch of thirties Renoir—who would have thought that there could be such a thing as redneck grace? The format is almost as complicated as that of *Nashville*: about fifteen characters (plus their alter egos) interact. The lunacies aren't frenzied; they just function as part of a normally wigged-out mode of existence. And the director's unstressed lyricism—the subdued colors, the unhurried flow, the dissolves—ties everyone together visually. There's nothing harsh in this comedy, not even its funniest, most hard-bitten character, Marcia Rodd as Portland Angel. Her timing—with a gulp or a hesitancy functioning as a gigantic double-take—is comparable to Lily Tomlin's work in *The Late Show*. Portland Angel is obdurate and smart; she stares incredulously when she listens to Ann Wedgeworth, who plays the bedraggled passion-flower Dallas Angel. They are the two wives of the bigamous Chrome Angel, who happen to meet on a bus, and they're the best comedy team in years. The soft-headed Wedgeworth can convince herself of anything. Rodd, tough as they come, chews on Wedgeworth's gaga ideas as if they were jawbreakers; she can't swallow them, and she's too polite to spit them out. Charles Napier's Chrome Angel is a huge man with a great, jutting jaw; he looks like a Brian Keith made of granite, a thick-witted Steve Canyon. He's also lucky enough to have one of the friendliest mistresses in all movies—Alix Elias as Hot Coffee, a plump, motherly hooker. The impulsive, generous Chrome Angel helps her buy a motor home, so she can bring her service to her trucker-customers. Hot Coffee has a soothing, giggly disposition, and her nasal baby talk is blessed with a tiny speech impediment that's like a vocal dimple. When Chrome Angel's wives make their terrible discovery of each other and two happy homes are about to be torn asunder, Hot Coffee persuades the two tearstained women to settle down with their husband in a ménage à trois; it's a triumph of giddy sweet reason. These three women give the film its eccentric peaks. Candy Clark, as the heroine, doesn't blend into the atmosphere the way they do. Her line readings are too deliberate, she slows things—almost imperceptibly, but there's a down. But hers are the only scenes that go on an instant too long.

There are perhaps twenty-five million CB sets in the United States, and at least one person in every twenty holds a CB license. If the film's satiric explanation of what this phenomenon is about isn't all-inclusive, it still must be an element in the CB appeal. In a sprawling country with people constantly on the move—literally spaced out—CB must be a new form of connecting. And the film has caught the language of this subculture, in which technology and Yankee know-how are all mixed up with dreams of the past. This isn't a corn-pone special; it doesn't have a climactic car chase or a big fight. That's probably why Paramount failed to sell it in the small towns, where the Burt Reynolds comedy-melodramas succeed. It could be that *Handle with Care* is almost too likable a movie. Maybe it's too evenly directed; maybe it needed to be brought up to a higher pitch at certain points. It might not seem so small a picture if it had been. But its antic charm is in its even, unsurprised tone—in the absence of anger, the reasonableness toward creeps and crazies. There are a few times when you're afraid that the tone is becoming threatening and the action is about to descend into melodrama. But the film sideswipes your fears and stays on course. There is no obsession—even the crackpot Red Baron's Nazi-racist harangues—that it does not de-fang. *Handle with Care* has the consistent vision of a classic comedy; it undercuts all the characters' illusions without a breath of ill will.

[October 24, 1977]

Hail, Folly!

At a certain point in their careers—generally right after an enormous popular success—most great movie directors go mad on the potentialities of movies. They leap over their previous work into a dimension beyond the well-crafted dramatic narrative; they make a huge, visionary epic in which they attempt to alter the perceptions of people around the world. Generally, they shoot this epic in what they believe is a state of super-enlightenment. They believe that with this film they're literally going to bring mankind the word, and this euphoria conceals even their own artistic exhaustion. Afterward, in the editing rooms, when they look at the thousands upon thousands of feet of film they've shot, searching for ways to put it together, while the interest on the borrowed money rises and swells, and the businessmen or government representatives try to wrest control from them, their energy may flag and their confidence falter. Their euphoria had glossed over the initial compromises that now plague them—an unresolved, unfinished script, perhaps, or an international cast with no common language—and there is always the problem of excessive length. Griffith with *Intolerance*, von Stroheim with his ten-hour *Greed*, Abel Gance with his three-screen *Napoléon*, Eisenstein with his unfinished *Ivan the Terrible* trilogy, Bertolucci with *1900*, perhaps Coppola with his *Apocalypse Now* still to come—no one has ever brought off one of these visionary epics so that it was a hit like the director's preceding films that made it possible. Yet these legendary follies that break the artists' backs are also among the great works of film history, transforming the medium, discarding dead forms, and carrying on an inspired, lunatic tradition that is quite probably integral to the nature of movies.

Artists of an expansionist temperament are drawn to work in this medium, because movies are capable of being the closest thing there is to a total art. If success and personal acclaim win these artists their freedom, their love of the unexplored possibilities can't be contained; it spills over into dream epics. In movies, sanity is too neat, too limiting. Huston, Riefenstahl, Pudovkin, Welles, Dreyer, Fritz Lang, Visconti, Dovzhenko, Pabst, Max Ophuls, Francesco Rosi, Fellini, Peckinpah, Bondarchuk, John Ford, Altman, Scorsese, Kurosawa, Pontecorvo—does anyone doubt the self-destructive fulfillments that these artists would have reached out to if they'd had the chance? And isn't it a tragedy for us all—and for those who come after us—that they haven't? The calamity of movie history is not the follies that get made but the follies that don't get made.

Everybody knows that it is essential for there to be low-budget movies; how else can new young artists get their chance? And directors who work big carry the burden of guilt for the many smaller films that could have been made on the money they're spending. Not that they would have been anyway—though generous-minded directors sometimes manage to use the power derived from their own success to help other filmmakers along. But even for the directors who profess belief in economy production, the contradictory aesthetic drive toward the big plunge is like a fever that passes from one great talent to the next. It may be that anyone with a large enough imagination who works in movies will catch it, unless, like an Ingmar Bergman, he reaches inward, downward, or, like Lubitsch, toward elegant condensation. The impulse is essentially the same as the one that led Tolstoy to write *War and Peace*; but in movies, no matter how great the director's talent and imagination are, he becomes swamped in the physical details of the production. He has to give so much of himself just to hold the production together that he can't sustain his creative energy. Writing a nineteenth-century novel on film—which is what this epic usually comes to be—means that you have to be a great con man, a great general, and a great artist, and if you weaken in any of those functions your golden bowl is cracked, perhaps shattered.

This form of gigantism is not to be confused with the producer-initiated or studio-initiated big-budget pictures (*Cleopatra*, *Doctor Dolittle*, *The Towering Inferno*, the forthcoming *The Swarm*, and so on). The artist-initiated epic is an obsessive testing of possibilities, and often it comes out of an overwhelming desire to express what the artist thinks are the unconscious needs of the public. It comes, too, from a conviction, or a hope, that if you give popular audiences the greatest you have in you they will respond. The moviemaker has an idealistic belief that no matter how corrupted mass taste is, people still retain the capacity to receive a vision. These epics try to vault over the film industry and go directly to the public.

The crazed utopian romanticism of Bernardo Bertolucci's *1900* reaches a new high pitch in movie idealism. A director *dies* on a picture of this magnitude with this degree of personal commitment; he has to be brought back to life so that he can move on. In the history of movies, *1900* represents a triumph, because after losing control of his movie the director regained it. After years of dissension and litigation (and that's par for the course), *1900* was finally shown at the New York Film Festival, and will open in a theatre on November 4th. The producer, Alberto Grimaldi, acknowledges that the film has been doing reasonably well overseas and will not lose money, and Bertolucci, treating the over-five-hour European version as a rough cut, has been able to refine it and release it here in his own four-hour-and-five-minute cut—so we don't have to try to piece out his intentions from a mangled version. This film is his; it represents almost five years of elation and anguish in the life of one of the three or four greatest young talents working in the movies.

1900 is about two boys born in the North Italian region of Emilia-Romagna on the same day in 1901. Alfredo (Robert De Niro) is the heir to the vast landholdings of his grandfather (Burt Lancaster), and Olmo (Gérard Depardieu) is the bastard grandson of the patriarch (Sterling Hayden) of the peasant clan that lives on those holdings and labors for a share of the crop. *1900* opens on Liberation Day, April 25, 1945, then goes back to the birth of the boys and follows the course of their ambivalent friendship. Accepting the romantic convention that there is a lifelong bond between people who swam naked in a stream together as children, the film uses that bond as a dialectical opposition.

Alfredo inherits the estate after the death of his father (Romolo Valli) and marries a French girl, the neurasthenic sylph Ada (Dominique Sanda). But she is aesthetically repelled by his passive acquiescence in the Fascist takeover and leaves him. Olmo, "the elm tree," becomes a Socialist and lives with a comrade—a teacher, Anita (Stefania Sandrelli)—who is a militant peasant leader; she dies in childbirth, leaving him a daughter. The film includes the upheavals of a peasant uprising in 1908, the end of the First World War and the rise of the Fascists, who came to power in 1922, and the Fascist era. Then it returns to that pivotal day in 1945 when in fact the conquering Allies were "liberating" Italy from Fascism but when in Bertolucci's utopian fancy an agrarian revolution takes place. The peasants seem to be under the delusion that the liberation from Fascism means that they now own the land—they might be playacting a revolutionary spring festival (of the future). They stage a mock trial of Alfredo, the padrone, pronouncing him dead. Then, at the end of the day, the soldiers of the provisional government come and take away the peasants' guns, and Alfredo goes on as before. In an epilogue, he and Olmo are doddering old cronies, wrestling, quarrelling, hugging each other in love and in anger—in bafflement at the emotions and the social forces that have thrown them together and thrown them apart.

Bertolucci is trying to transcend the audience appeal of his lyrical, psychological films. He is trying to make a people's film by drawing on the mythology of movies, as if it were a collective memory. *1900* is a romantic moviegoer's vision of the class struggle—a love poem for the movies as well as for the life of those who live communally on the land. (It may be that Bertolucci believes that he loves movies so much *because* they are the people's art.) Though in form *1900* is an opera-novel, and its homage is to Verdi, the great Emilian who died on the day (January 27, 1901) of the two boys' birth, the characters of the two grandfathers (Lancaster and Hayden)—giants of an earlier era—are drawn from American Westerns and adventure films. *1900* represents an attempt to fuse the American movies that fed Bertolucci's imagination and the visionary agrarian paean *Earth*, made by Dovzhenko, the most lyrical of all Russian directors. Bertolucci attempts to do this while taking another look at the Fascist material that he dealt with in his 1970 films, *The Conformist* and *The Spider's Stratagem*. The latter was also shot in Emilia, in a town near Parma, and was about the need for myth. It dealt with a man, born in 1900, who was killed during a performance of Verdi's *Rigoletto* and became an anti-Fascist martyr-hero. In that film, set in a town that Bertolucci called Tara, he used the town itself as an opera stage, and in a memorable sequence *Rigoletto* was heard pouring forth from loudspeakers in the ghostly, floodlit streets. The staging of *1900* is often similarly theatrical: This movie never goes farther from the estate than a city in Emilia, and the courtyard of the landowner's manor house is used, like Tara, as a giant set.

Opera is in Bertolucci's blood and bones. When he stages scenes of peasants eating, the hearty bacchanalian imagery is out of Brueghel, but you wait for them to swallow their fake food and start singing. Bertolucci uses his peasants—actual Emilian peasants—as if they were a chorus, and as the film progresses they upstage the stars. (There is even a hunchback among them dressed as a jester and called Rigoletto.) He apparently believes that he can make the peasants larger than life by using the romantic conventions of opera, movies, and painting. He's trying for a "naïveté" like that of Verdi, who stayed within a tradition, adapting conventional forms, and he adapts the characters and devices of such movies as *Anthony Adverse* and *Gone with the Wind*. He knowingly risks grandiloquence, believing that this is the path to a people's art—that moviegoers want romance, myth, and their own struggles turned into poetry and fantasy.

There are sequences in *1900* as great as any ever filmed. The childhood scenes are steeped in memory—honeyed. Once again Vittorio Storaro is Bertolucci's cinematographer, and the lighting suggests that moment in art history when the Barbizon school gave way to the summer sun of Impressionism—when color burst open and became diffused, as if nature, like a film director, could no longer control its own exuberance. The little hellion Olmo, skinny-faced and barefoot, collecting frogs to sell to the manor house and wearing them tied together, still alive and wriggling, around his hat, is like Huck Finn in a surreal pastoral calendar. His freedom is balanced against the image of the plump-faced, spoiled, rich Alfredo, forced to eat those frogs' legs at dinner, and throwing up. The camera moves constantly, even in the interiors, which suggest a 1930s idea of *fin de siècle*; they have the tawny light of the Italian Impressionist Fattori—or a tilted, fuzzy Maxfield Parrish. In the most prodigious sequence, which appears to be one continuous shot, Bertolucci presents the peasant uprising of 1908 as a panoramic mural: poplars in the mist; the landowning hunters shooting ducks, which fall in the river; peasants who have been evicted from their land leaving on loaded wagons while, of those remaining, the men prepare to resist and the women stretch out on the road to block the oncoming cavalry, who ride up to their bodies, turn around, and leave. The camera executes almost a figure eight in this lyrical panning, tracking crane shot; it sweeps over the Po Valley, showing you the different, conflicting elements in the landscape. You're given the components of a novel at a glance, and every one of them is shown in relation to the others. Bertolucci has perhaps the greatest spatial-temporal sense of all film directors. The simultaneous actions that other directors have achieved only by cutting he puts in the same shot. The effect of this hunters-peasants-cavalry sequence is of a passage of visual music. Bertolucci is satisfied by its visual completeness, and he moves on to the next thing that interests him.

But for us in the audience his great sequences don't achieve their full power, because there's no follow-through. Years pass between sequences, when we want what happens next. Did the cavalry return? (Has there ever been a film that dealt successfully with so long a span of time? Maybe the *Godfather* films, jointly.) It's true that one remembers the great scenes from the nineteenth-century Russian novels, not the passages in between; but the greatness of those scenes derives from their meaning in the narrative, from the way they reverberate through what we have already read and what follows. There's a consistency of vision in Turgenev or Dostoevski or Tolstoy; we're told what we want to know. Bertolucci's great sequences don't make us think back or anticipate. He's attempting to achieve that Verdian naïveté, but, like many other directors now, he reproduces only the poetic form of the great moments from old movies (the cavalry sequence is an expansion on John Ford). There is a scene of a peasant celebration along the riverbanks which has a nostalgic yearning for simplicity; Bertolucci wants to make us feel the *goodness* of simplicity, the way John Ford did when he shot the frontier dance on the foundation for the church in *My Darling Clementine*, with Wyatt Earp (Henry Fonda), his hair pressed flat for propriety's sake, innocently hopping up and down with his lady. But there are too many divided emotions in *1900* for the riverbank scene to have its effect; Bertolucci does not have the gift of simplicity. After the Liberation Day opening, the childhood section—the first hour—flows seamlessly, until the sequence in which the boys go into town to a workers' Punch-and-Judy show that is broken up by mounted police. At this point, the continuity weakens. Yet even when the movie is flowing along there's an unease inside the virtuosity.

There is something off in the tone of *1900* right from the start. Partly it's the sound. In order to get the film financed (it cost eight million dollars), it had to be made with an international cast; there is no "original-language" version. The Italian version was all dubbed, but so many Italian directors employ visual effects they can achieve only by shooting silent and adding the sound later that Italians (and many other Europeans) ignore dead sound. We don't. In the English version that Bertolucci has prepared, Lancaster's performance has particular force, and that may be because his dialogue seems live. The track is a mixture of synch sound, post-synch sound, and dubbing, so within a scene there will be a shift in ambience—different hollows and bouncebacks, which weaken the emotion. Depardieu and Stefania Sandrelli are the only major performers whose voices are dubbed; De Niro, Dominique Sanda, Hayden, Donald Sutherland (who plays the Fascist Attila), and Laura Betti (who plays his paramour, Regina) all speak their own lines, but the post-synching has a slightly removed sound—and, of course, the minor players and the peasants who fill out the cast are dubbed. Visually and thematically, the film is conceived with so many contrasts, clashes, allusions, and symmetrical variations that one can see where the years of preparation went. The actual dialogue seems almost an afterthought, and the actors speak their lines without much confidence that they're worth saying. And so we're aware of the actors as actors, and of their different cultures. They're not all sure what they're meant to be conveying. And we're not, either.

The principal actors are characters but they're also puppets in this gigantic class-struggle puppet show, and so if we ask why it is that Alfredo, a decent, friendly fellow with an amused, wry glint in his intelligent eyes, is so weak that he allows his overseer Attila to tyrannize the peasant workers, the explanation can only be that at this point in history the landowning class had lost its strength, and had become passive collaborators in evil. Bertolucci doesn't show that Alfredo *needs* Attila—psychologically or economically. Alfredo's decision to keep the Fascist monsters Attila and Regina under his roof seems some sort of historical fatalism—as if he had the director's game plan in mind and behaved accordingly. And De Niro, acting the historical role assigned him—the withered seed of a once proud line—looks small, shrunken. As a child, Alfredo even has trouble with his penis: his foreskin is tight, while that of the peasant Olmo is loose and flexible. Alfredo is ineffectual—it's the Ashley Wilkes role—and De Niro, who might have tried to summon up some hamminess to see him through, didn't. He gives an ineffectual performance. There's an interior continuity in it, but there isn't any excitement—how could there be?

As a spokesman for the Socialist dream, Depardieu has the advantage of heroic physical presence; he has his wary jugface—he stares out at us like the rough-sensitive Botticelli in his self-portrait in *The Adoration of the Magi*. But he seems emblematic—without any clear personality—and his role is fragmented over the years. Some of his screen time is wasted in dangling scenes involving the theft of a gun—scenes we expect will connect with a later event. A larger disappointment is that the child Olmo, the fearless, unmanageable gamin who is the despair of his mother, doesn't grow up to be the firebrand one expects. When he returns from the First World War, he's a clear-eyed solid-peasant citizen, firm in the ways of courage and virtue. Bertolucci has set up the childhood sequences so that the boys seem destined to become the heroes of his epic—the carriers of history. We wait to see their lives become focussed, but then he pulls a dialectical switch. He deëmphasizes them, to indicate that they are not vital to the historical events of their time—they are merely figures borne along by the flood of history. Olmo may be a peasant leader, but it is those he leads who are the heroes. How many different games can a director play in a movie? Using two young stars known for their volatile, "dangerous" presence and turning them into supporting players—denying us individual heroes—Bertolucci betrays the romantic epic form.

Because of the switch from the two men to the peasants, the only characters who register fully are those who are allowed their movie-derived mythological roles—the grandfathers, Lancaster and Hayden, and, surprisingly, at moments Dominique Sanda. There is, mercifully, no capitalist class in this movie—only the remnants of feudalism. And as the feudal lord who still likes to sink his toes in earth and cow dung Lancaster expresses declining physical vigor with all the command of his thirty-odd years of movie heroics. He isn't the polished lord he played in *The Leopard*; he's a peasant at heart, a crude, honest man who despises Alfredo's father—his greedy hypocrite son who cheats the peasants and squeezes them dry. There's love in Bertolucci's portrait of the profane, raging old bull; even though he hangs himself in the stables, in disgust at his own impotence and the collapse of his world, there's no contempt for his act. And, though this isn't intentional, his death has more conviction than that of the man he respects and would like to consider a friend—the leader of the peasant clan, Hayden. This old peasant sits down to rest under an oak tree and slips away. Visually this is fine, but it's priggishly programmatic. Still, they're both old oaks, and if Hayden's performance isn't as strong as Lancaster's, he has his noble, weather-beaten presence. His hair is worn short, cut way up high on his head, and his neck is long and straight, with cords like organ pipes; he resembles the famous photograph of Dovzhenko that is reproduced in *Agee on Film*.

Except for her work with Bertolucci, and in De Sica's *The Garden of the Finzi-Continis*, Dominique Sanda's performances have been stilted, amateurish. With Bertolucci, she is all visual: the image, the essence, of movie glamour, Garbo without depth—a trifling Garbo. As Ada, she has a weird, boneless seductiveness, like the young Lauren Bacall become a wraith. She's all curves, her body a crescent and her crushed upper lip conveying ironic secret promises. It may be that Bertolucci doesn't know what to do with his "thinking woman"—the militant Anita, whose exhortations to the peasants have no conviction. But when this gauzy vamp Ada slithers across the screen, with her gowns floating half off, or with a soft big-brimmed hat framing her come-hither smiles, she's the past recalled, all right, and you don't want to let it go. Ada, a virgin Futurist bohemian who smokes furiously and drives a Bugatti, is all affectation—self-dramatizing spoofery. She composes free verse, but if she has an art it's the art of the moue, and she has been given the funniest lines in the picture. She and Alfredo's homosexual uncle Ottavio (Werner Bruhns) represent charming, frivolous decadence, and the film doesn't try to turn them into villains.

Fascism here is demonological—so lewdly melodramatic that it makes Visconti's excesses in *The Damned* seem courtly. In the second half of *1900*, when Attila and Regina—the Fascist Macbeth and Lady Macbeth—come to power, the imagery changes to the dark mists of autumn and winter. Their posturings are like a hurdy-gurdy variation on the strident,

Expressionist horror of Eisenstein's mad Ivan the Terrible. It's Fascism as a strain of diseased, perverted sexuality, and it explodes in a couple of scenes of shocking, Kabuki-wild violence. Attila and Regina are everything dirty, and we can almost hear the hiss of electric sparks shooting out of their heads. (Is it relevant that Bertolucci's father's name was Attilio?) These two are meant to embody the aggressive forces of the bourgeoisie; Alfredo and Ada's white wedding is followed by Attila and Regina's vile rites—they sodomize and murder a child. (The sequence would mean more to an audience if Bertolucci had indicated that the wedding aroused in Attila and Regina a need to defile it. When they go off to their debauchery, it's as if they did this every afternoon before tea.) Dressed all in black, at six feet four and with pale-blue eyes, Sutherland is already somewhat hyperbolic, and with a grotesque false high forehead he's a black-shirted vampire. All this curling of lips, baring of jagged teeth, and flashing of demented eyes must be what the director wanted, but only a very dedicated liberal would play a Fascist in this manner. Bertolucci wove a Hammer-Films gothic thread into his tapestry. What Attila and his guttural, leering accomplice Regina represent is what Fascism and Nazism became for those who made lampshades out of human skin, but it doesn't account for the attraction of Fascism and Nazism as political movements. The nightmare sadism gives *1900* a spaghetti-Western view of class struggle. This, too, must be partly intended: Bertolucci, who worked on the story of Sergio Leone's *Once Upon a Time in the West*, has used Leone's composer, Ennio Morricone; his creamy elegiac score heightens the emotion in the first half but suddenly, in the second, takes a dive into Peyton Place schlock–Chopin piano music.

The framing device—that pivotal Liberation Day—is the allegorical aspect of *1900*, and its worst stumbling block. Alfredo, held prisoner, is detached in his attitude; shuffling along in a cardigan, with a slack, dumb grin and a mustache two inches wide, he's no more than a nose-picking clerk. His trial, with the complaints of his accusers, who hold him to account for their rotting teeth and missing fingers, is coyly didactic, telling you that you should live right—under a playful veneer that makes you squirm. There are echoes of Chairman Mao's Little Red Book. It's a Maoist-Brechtian Judgment Day. Bertolucci's utopian future, with Olmo's daughter skipping among the haystacks, doesn't improve on the shots of little girls playing in the sun which were used by Griffith to demonstrate how beautiful life would be once people stopped being intolerant.

A solemn protest march ends the first half of the film: a funeral march displaying the charred bodies of four old men, who were in a *casa del popolo*—a workers' meeting hall—that the Fascists set on fire. The march signifies the unity of the workers, and it is magnificently staged, with a uniformed brass band playing the "Internationale"; it is set off from ordinary events by being photographed in a simplified palette—but it's

Communist-color-coördinated! The caskets are lined in red, and every mourning marcher, every horse wears a patch of exactly the same shade. Ribbons, bows, scarves, furbelows—they're all one ravishing, sumptuous red. This is visual Verdi; it's splendid—a Communist fantasy march. But a viewer doesn't know whether to exult in the beauty or to laugh. Is Bertolucci a Communist for the sake of color? Are we rooting for a team? Red banners fly from the train that bears the young Olmo and the other striking workers' children off to where they can be fed; a huge patchwork canopy—a rainbow of reds—is unfurled on Liberation Day. Isn't this aesthetic Communism as flighty as Ada's aesthetic anti-Fascism?

Bertolucci has somehow resolved his own political contradictions in a dream of a happy agrarian future that hasn't budged beyond the turn of the century. The belief that permeates this movie is that Communism will preserve the folk culture of the peasants. Still nostalgic for life "before the revolution," Bertolucci now thinks that that life can be preserved only after the revolution. His is an anthropologist's Communism: he doesn't want the peasants corrupted into selling native artifacts to tourists; he doesn't want them exposed to credit cards and 100% virgin acrylic. It may be that in Emilia (the birthplace of Italian Socialism as well as of Verdi and Bertolucci), a prosperous region that has been partly administered by Communists since the end of the Second World War, the peasant culture has in fact flourished. But this film is addressed to the world outside Emilia, where the sumptuous innocence of Bertolucci's vision suggests Marie Antoinette playing shepherdess. *1900* represents the thinking of someone who grew up at the movies and accepted the myth that all problems can be brought to a happy resolution. Communism is going to usher in a folk utopia, and an artist who loves style above all else can make a people's film by drawing upon the standard metaphors of American and Soviet movies.

Bertolucci has said that all his films are "desperately autobiographical," and in this one the desperation shows. He has cast De Niro, an actor whose responsiveness to the camera derives from his reserves of passion, and, having cast this man as himself, has not allowed him *any* passion. Bertolucci, locking himself away, locked out De Niro as an actor—gutted him. His Alfredo is an unfinished man: a man who hasn't tested himself. He's too emasculated even to suffer. Alfredo is the pampered, bourgeois liberal that Bertolucci guiltily fears himself to be, while Olmo is his proletarian dream self, and at the end it's as if the class struggle were just two boys trying to out-macho each other, still checking to see who has the bigger penis. Under the class struggle, that's the theme all the way through. Most directors are at their best when they deal with what's closest to them. In this film, Bertolucci is at his feeblest every time he gets near the adult Alfredo. He stays as far away as possible. This director has gone so much further than most movie directors that he's run up against what novelists and dramatists run up against: the desire to escape oneself. He has fled to the lives of the peasants and put an optimist's bland smile on top of the despair of his *Last Tango in Paris*. His utopia rests on the belief that peasants live in a pre-Freudian state; they have no conflict except with their oppressors. They're not plagued with the problems of bourgeois artists— they have loose foreskins. There is a connection between the film's blissed-out politics and the way Bertolucci treats the Fascist plunderers. He's not afraid to show violence, but he doesn't allow himself to identify with the person doing the violence. It is Dostoevski's identifying more with the characters who go out of control than with the others that makes reading him deeply terrifying. Bertolucci rejects the vile, violent possibilities in himself. That's why he lets Donald Sutherland go so far in his performance that human iniquity is turned into a cartoon. Bertolucci wants to believe in his peasants—who are so firm in their goodness, so split off from the Fascist criminality that they're less than human.

This film is about Bernardo Bertolucci's need for myth, and his self-denial. For those who are infatuated with what they loathe, the battle with themselves never stops. *1900* has all of Bertolucci's themes and motifs; one could call it the Portable Bertolucci, though it isn't portable. It's like a course to be enrolled in, with a guaranteed horror every hour. *1900* is a gigantic system of defenses—human fallibility immortalized. The film is appalling, yet it has the grandeur of a classic visionary folly. Next to it, all the other new movies are like something you hold up at the end of a toothpick.

[October 31, 1977]

The Lower Trash/
The Higher Trash

K en Russell uses Rudolf Nureyev in *Valentino* the way he used Twiggy in *The Boy Friend*; he gets the publicity value out of Nureyev's screen-acting début and doesn't worry about providing plausible material for him, giving him partners who will set him off, or protecting him. Twiggy was cast as a Cinderella, but with Russell as her godmother she remained a waif. Nureyev, however, despite his inexperience in speaking lines, is not a novice performer—and he knows how to laugh at himself. This is a movie

333

about a legendary silent-screen idol whose voice isn't known (Rudolph Valentino died in 1926), played by a legendary dancer whose voice isn't known, either. Hearing Nureyev is something of an unveiling, and his effort to adapt his facial movements (the movements of someone who grew up speaking Russian) to an Italian accent gives his performance an extra, *cinéma vérité* hazardousness. Nureyev doesn't have the bloom of Valentino, who was only thirty-one when he died. However, the disparity in age hardly matters; in a Ken Russell picture, the yowling characters aren't even recognizable as members of the human race. *Valentino* was shot in England and Spain, and there has been little attempt to match the sleekness of the remembered Valentino—the beautifully dressed, almond-eyed Latin in his California Spanish, Art Nouveau streamlined décor. Nureyev's high cheekbones, his imperious sniff, and the set of his full mouth are more reminiscent of Yul Brynner when he first played in *The King and I*. Nureyev doesn't evoke Valentino, but from time to time he has a captivating, very funny temperament of his own.

Seen up close, Nureyev has a camp devil loose in him; he has the seductive, moody insolence of an older, more cosmopolitan James Dean, without the self-consciousness. His eagerness to please would be just right for frivolous, lyrical comedy, and he could play cruel charmers—he has the kinky-angel grin. With the right director—Bob Fosse to release his athleticism, or someone like Michael Ritchie, perhaps, to catch the fickle, contradictory shades of feeling and register his easiest movements—he could be a supremely entertaining screen performer. He's a showman through and through. He has the deep-set eyes of a Zen archer: the public is the target. At the ballet, one may be too aware of him as a personality, yet what can be faintly distasteful there—his being a star before he's a dancer—is what makes him a full presence on the screen. He has to be photographed carefully: his nose (ski run, pointed, with flaring nostrils) is problematic, and when he's tense or the lighting is bad, he gets that jaded-gigolo look of Alain Delon. But he doesn't have the mime's masklike expressions that wreck most dancers as screen actors, and his justly celebrated "Blakean torso" is never rigid. He moves with the élan that dancers are supposed to have but usually don't, and when his face is relaxed, he suggests what Sabu should have grown up to be—a smiling, primitive-sophisticated rajah. His narcissistic menace is more complexly amusing than Valentino's famous smoldering menace. It's this narcissism that makes him (like James Dean) seem untamable—a "natural" rebel.

The surprise of Nureyev onscreen (although one should have guessed it from his work on the ballet stage) is how generous this narcissism is. He wants to give out; that has to be why he sets himself such a sweatshop schedule of performances with one dance company after another. Now thirty-nine, he must have considered that the movies could provide him with a new outlet. There's choreography, or directing a dance company, of course; but could a man who loves to perform as much as Nureyev does function successfully behind the scenes? He's old for a *premier danseur* but not for a movie actor. (Burt Lancaster, for example, made his first movie when he was about thirty-four; Pacino was thirty-one when he caught public attention in *The Panic in Needle Park*; Bogart didn't hit his full stride until he was in his forties.) Nureyev's generosity extends even toward the dancing required of him here, which, despite Russell's own dance background, is staged insultingly. The initial number—a tango, with Valentino, as a dance instructor, teaching Nijinsky (Anthony Dowell)—is photographed from much too far away, and others are so cheaply conceived that Nureyev is featured tapping or whizzing around to show off his speed, as if he were the José Iturbi of dance.

There is no artistry left in Ken Russell's work. By now, his sensationalist reputation is based merely on his "going further" than anybody else. And he doesn't even hold that record anymore: much better filmmakers have surpassed him in naughtiness. His films have become schoolboy Black Masses—a mixture of offensiveness and crude dumbness—and that is about the only attraction they may have. Russell takes people we're already interested in and makes them homosexual, grossly perverse, and rotten. Attaching the names of actual people to his sadomasochistic fantasies makes those fantasies easier to finance—gives them a publicity value that is highly exploitable, and a nasty inside-joke, turn-on appeal: flaming anti-faggotry. *Valentino* is a five-million-dollar graffito that will circulate around the world. What Senator Joseph McCarthy did to people's reputations is nothing compared with what Ken Russell does, and if his victims aren't around to lose their livelihoods, neither are they around to defend themselves. Whatever his legal rights, what gives Ken Russell the moral right to turn Alla Nazimova, the Stanislavski student who became the closest equivalent that the American theatre has ever had to Eleonora Duse, into nothing more than a cheap, vengeful, blackmailing bitch? As Mrs. Alving in *Ghosts* in 1936, Nazimova gave the greatest performance I have ever seen on the stage, and my parents, who had seen her thirty years earlier, said that even then she was the finest actress they had ever seen. Although Nazimova's full qualities didn't come across in movies, my mother—in 1936—could still describe details of Nazimova's work in her 1916 début film, *War Brides*. This transplanted woman brought a new purity and realism into American acting; she took away the clutter and made it more spiritual. There is corruption to be satirized in any period of the past, but there are also elements that represent a continuity worth preserving—it's all we've got to respect. If on the basis of an experiment that failed—Nazimova's production of *Salome,* which Natacha Rambova (who was married to Valentino at the time) designed in the manner of Aubrey Beardsley—a great actress is to be turned into a vain, shallow fool, then what is there to protect Laurence Olivier, say, or Martha Graham, or Jean Renoir? Leslie Caron, who plays Nazimova, is made up to look so much like her that the impersonation amounts to cannibalization of her reputation. And though Russell's own wife is the costume designer on this film (as on most of his other films), he has no feeling for Natacha Rambova (played by Michelle Phillips), who was a superb Art Nouveau designer, influenced by Léon Bakst and Erté. In the film, when Natacha is with Valentino, she doesn't look him in the eye; she's always looking away—to telegraph us that she's a lesbian. Russell uses the possibility of a liaison between her and Nazimova as if that meant they were both coldhearted skunks.

The "recklessness" that McCarthy was accused of is too mild a term for Russell. Spitefulness is almost the sole emotion in *Valentino*. The film exempts the figure of Valentino himself; in Russell's thinking, artists are egotist monsters, so in order to be sympathetic this Valentino has to be a farmer at heart—a young man who wants only to grow oranges. (If anything can be stated with certainty in this life, it is that *nobody* becomes a movie star who wants only to grow oranges.) Russell, the chief defiler of celebrities of the past and present, has the incomparable gall to attack Hollywood and the American public for their callous exploitation of this orange-lover. Everybody is out to defame Valentino's manhood; there seems to be a national vendetta against him. Jesse Lasky and Fatty Arbuckle and many others (a preponderance of them Jewish) are shown using and abusing Valentino, and people waltz around a prize ring, gloating, as he is punched to a pulp and hemorrhages while trying to defend himself against the charge of effeminacy. Then, when he dies as a result of this (apocryphal) fight, they smash through the glass windows of the funeral parlor to get at his flesh. Yet these sadomasochistic rampages, and a jail scene with Valentino smeared in vomit and forced to soil himself, aren't as essentially ugly as a prolonged sequence having to do with the shooting of Valentino's role in *Monsieur Beaucaire*, in which Nureyev is kept in a powdered wig, pasty white makeup, dark lipstick, and a beauty mark. This sequence is a textbook example of a director's sadism toward his own star: Nureyev looks wizened, prematurely aged—a gruesome parody of effeteness. A movie director who casts Rudolf Nureyev as a simple farmer and then shoots an extended sequence with the star nude, seen from the rear with his buttocks spread, as he grapples with the teasing Natacha, is doing things just for the obsessive hell of it. What's destroying Russell as a director is that his spitefulness includes the people he works with; he's turning the camera *against* them. There isn't even any fantasy logic left.

□ □ □

*T*he only honest sound I heard during the two hours and eighteen minutes of *Equus* was the snoring of the man in the row behind me. In this film version of Peter Shaffer's play, there are eight long soliloquies in which Richard Burton, as the psychiatrist, Dr. Dysart, does his elocutionary thing, sitting at his desk and talking right to us. Burton can't be accused of slacking off; he's intense as all getout. He gives an acting exhibition—a demonstration of how a laundry list can be turned into Shakespeare. He turns his lines into tongue twisters to rush us to the big ironies, squinching his eyes in pain. It's like Charles Laughton reading from the Bible and counting the house. Burton must be telepathic—his voice seems to rise in volume during every walkout; by the end of the movie, he sounds hysterical. The case that has shattered Dr. Dysart's defenses and made him long for an escape from his provincial existence—a loveless, barren marriage with a dentist—is that of a local teen-ager, Alan Strang (Peter Firth), a part-time stablehand who has blinded six horses. Investigating the crime, the Doctor discovers that Alan comes from a repressive, overprotective background in which religion is a pressure point between the boy's anti-religious father (Colin Blakely) and his devout mother (Joan Plowright). Alan has transformed her Christ worship into equine worship. He has been praying to a picture of a horse above his bed, a picture that replaced the Christ image his father tore down, and his worship of Equus is passionate and sexual. The night he blinded the horses, he had been in the stables trying—for the first time—to make love to a girl. In short, he is Oedipus, who, having disobeyed his horse gods, has blinded them instead of himself.

Dr. Dysart assembles all this Oedipal data at a slow crawl. The anxious, self-protective parents reveal self-incriminating details reluctantly. The owner of the stable (Harry Andrews) is upset and angry; his answers to the Doctor's questions are slowed down by much clenching of the jaw. Hesther, the magistrate (Eileen Atkins) who brought Dysart into the case, sees how it torments him ("You're going through a rotten patch at the moment. I'm sorry . . .") and persuades him to stick with it. Their scenes together have the measured, clipped archness of wartime British movies. Dysart: "You're really quite splendid." Hesther (leaving): "Famous for it. Good night." There's all this *acting*—these immaculate, orotund performances; each character has to reveal his sore spots, his tensions, and his basic decency. It takes so long for them to reach their little climactic revelations that they've been given busywork domestic chores to do while they talk about themselves—leaves to rake, objects to carry from one room to another. And when we finally move on, it's back to Dysart at his lectern, linking Alan's case to ancient Greece and to

Dionysian mysteries. (When a movie character starts invoking mythological deities, the movie is in trouble.) The dramatic conflict in the movie is meant to be in Dysart, who can cure Alan of his horse obsession only by taking away the boy's worship and his ecstasy—the passions that the sterile unbeliever Dysart envies and dreams of experiencing. In *Equus,* psychosis is passion and creativity, and the cure, which it is Dysart's professional duty to bring about, is cold conformity.

With most analysts having adjusted to the slowness of the puny changes they are able to effect—or in states of depression because of doubts about whether even those changes will last for long—Shaffer expects us to believe in psychiatrists as castrating soul surgeons. Dysart says that he cuts from children "parts of individuality repugnant to this God [of the normal] . . . parts sacred to rarer and more wonderful Gods." Much of the film is of this order of very classy gibberish about dualities. *Equus* was a stylized theatre piece, and there is not a detail that does not make a point. Yet underneath the Oedipal and homosexual aspects of Alan's case there is another—unacknowledged—layer in the material. When Dysart first meets Alan, the boy, refusing to speak, sings the jingle "Double your pleasure / Double your fun / With Doublemint, Doublemint / Doublemint gum." Dysart, the shrewdie, asks, "By the way, which parent is it who won't allow you to watch television?" And so we're set in a Freudian frame of reference. But Dysart never asks why *Doublemint,* and when Alan's mother says that the boy was "fascinated" by the word "equus" because "he'd never come across one with two 'u's together before," that isn't explained, nor is Alan's assertion that his God, Equus, tells him that "two shall be one." What this doubling wordplay and the talk of horse and rider as two male halves have to do with Alan, the stableboy, isn't at all clear. Peter Shaffer, who is the twin brother of Anthony Shaffer, the author of *Sleuth,* has got a twinship fantasy mixed in with the horse-blinding case. "Make us one person," Alan cries to his horse God. (This confusion—widely discussed in articles on the play—remains unchanged in the movie.) With all Dysart's self-flagellating pomp about the terrible thing he's doing in cutting away part of Alan so he won't be able to "gallop anymore," he never gets out of his mythological fanciness. It's always the boy's God he's killing. But a boy wouldn't have to be cut apart from his God. Shaffer has the Doctor preventing two from being one—separating them forever. Why else would he see the analyst as a knife wielder? The script spectacularly overestimates Freudianism and is terrified of it.

Sidney Lumet has directed the film with extreme care, and the cinematographer, Oswald Morris, has shot the orgasmic boy-and-horse night gallops very elegantly. But Lumet has made a mistake in working up to a big semi-realistic climax; as Alan, confessing everything to the Doctor, purges himself by recalling his blinding of the horses, we are shown it. And who knows whether this has been faked well or badly—who wants to look at it? By then, you're numbed anyway, from counting out the rhythms of the actors' words and pauses. The sensitive-important-picture pacing is like a black armband; the refined classical score, by Richard Rodney Bennett, is all too appropriate. Alan's face has the curly-lipped, flaccid sensuality of the young Dylan Thomas's, which leads one to expect wild, slovenly, dithyrambic emotion; but Peter Firth's performance has long since been worked out on the stage—his schizophrenic is almost as starched as the rest of the characters. The film sets Shaffer's worst ideas on a pedestal, and Burton, looking appropriately ravaged by the intellectual agony of thinking so many ornate thoughts, keeps spewing them out. *Equus* suffers from literacy—the movie sickens and dies from it.

[November 7, 1977]

Scrambled Eggs

*O*ne Sings, the Other Doesn't is as straightforward as its title. Agnès Varda, who wrote the script, and directed, also serves as narrator—in accented English, with gusto—telling us just what the film is about. It begins in 1962, with the efforts of the seventeen-year-old apple-dumpling schoolgirl Pauline (Valérie Mairesse) to raise money for an abortion for her twenty-two-year-old friend Suzanne (Thérèse Liotard), who already has two children by her photographer lover. The photographer takes pictures of nude women—deserted women, unwed mothers, women as victims—and Suzanne, a dark, slender girl, is one of his most dolorous subjects. But Pauline, a bouncy, orange-haired aspiring singer from the middle class, stares at his camera truculently. Suzanne, who comes from a peasant background, is left penniless when this guilt-ridden lover hangs himself; she's forced to take her children and go back to her parents' farm. The two heroines meet again at an abortion rally in 1972. Pauline—now known as Pomme (Apple)—sings with a popular feminist street-theatre combo. She tells Suzanne that she, too, has had an abortion, and Suzanne explains that she works in a family planning clinic. In flashbacks we see how each of them has got where she is—Pomme by her "energy and cleverness," Suzanne by determined studying (inspired by her memories of Pomme's boldness, she has taught herself to type in the winter, blowing on

339

her little blue fingers and pecking away at the typewriter while wedged up against a cow in her parents' barn). Then we pick up their lives in the seventies. Pomme goes to Iran with an Iranian (she had met him while she was in Amsterdam for her abortion), becomes blissfully pregnant, and marries him. But when her husband expects her to prepare dinner—an activity that would conflict with her creative thinking about a new song—she sees that being back in Iran has released the male chauvinist in him, and she leaves. Her husband joins her in France for the birth of their son, and he wants the baby. Rather than go back to Iran, she makes a deal with him: he can take the five-month-old infant if he'll impregnate her before he leaves. That way, they'll each have one. At the end, Pomme is content with her new child and her singing, and Suzanne is married to a pediatrician whom her teen-age children love and respect. The narrator concludes, "They were alike—they had fought to gain the happiness of being a woman."

The lives of Pomme and Suzanne between 1962 and 1976 are supposed to indicate the evolution of modern women's consciousness. Their own mothers are horrors—narrow, unloving housewives out of Balzac, or Zola—while these two represent the transition to a bright future, which is symbolized in the last sequence, a riverbank picnic. Suzanne's family and Pomme's extended family—a communal group of singers, actors, and protesters—are gathered in celebration of women's rise from victimization to new independence, and Suzanne's teen-age daughter (played by Varda's own daughter) faces the world of tomorrow confidently. *One Sings* is all up front. It's a cheery, educational feminism-can-be-fun movie. Pomme and her combo tour provincial towns, performing songs with lyrics (by Varda) such as "I'm neither a tough cookie nor a busy beaver nor a utopian dreamer—I'm a woman, I am me." Decked out in harlequin colors that suggest a French child's dream of what Haight-Ashbury was like, they chant "My Body Is Mine." Singing about the joys of pregnancy when it's "your choice and your pleasure," they wear pillows stuffed inside their long dresses—"It's beautiful to be a balloon." When these bubble dollies send actual balloons into the sky or sing about their "ovules," Varda brings a Disney touch to women's liberation. The sunshiny, masscult-hip simplicity of the feminist movement celebrated here is so laughable you can't hate the picture. You just feel that some of your brain cells have been knocked out.

Visually, the film has the glamorous real-unreal quality of the new feminine-hygiene ads—muted realism. Happiness here is a flower-print dress on a summer day in the country. The appeal of the film is of life seen as sensuous banality, in a pretty pastoral flow. Pomme has the look of an Auguste Renoir model with a bad dye job: a cherub with the frizzies. There's unforced charm in her complacent impudence. But she belts out her songs in a brass-lunged style, and she has a brute quality: her mind, like her lyrics, is a grab bag of feminist slogans. She swings ideas around like a baton twirler, and it's difficult to appreciate a struggle for self-expression which results in songs of the quality of hers. Pomme's middle-class hippie rebelliousness is contrasted with Suzanne's slow, hard-won self-education. Suzanne—reserved to the point of inexpressiveness—is a dimly performed, wan, Madonna-like character whose life seems to fit a traditional pattern. Circumstances force her to push beyond her youthful, Little Match Girl submissiveness, and she rises into the middle class, brings up her children with scrupulous devotion, and achieves the Sheila Levine goal: a doctor husband who loves her; i.e., what used to be called happiness and is now fulfillment.

The only real difference between Suzanne's life and the lives of countless poor, put-upon heroines of fiction who rose by their bootstraps is how colorless and humorless her fine doctor is. That's true of Pomme's Iranian, too; when you hear that he's an economist, you think there's been a mistake—he seems too vague to have acquired any skills. The men in the movie are shaded out. Varda doesn't appear to be antagonistic toward men; she just has no particular interest in them. The purpose of sex in this movie seems to be to have an abortion. That's the real high. Abortion is the new rite of passage, to be reported to one's friends with sad pride. Men are welcome in this balloons-and-sunshine land of the future. They're still needed to provide the plump, gurgling, freely chosen babies. Choice is what's important; the same women who choose abortion then choose pregnancy. There's no psychology in this movie—only sociology. The feminism here is a new form of asexual lyricism.

One Sings isn't sentimental in the manipulative manner of commercial movies. On the contrary, there's a whimsical randomness in Varda's approach. At times, as in the early sequence of Pomme's posing for Suzanne's photographer lover, the effect is so fresh it almost seems like luck. A photographer herself before she made her first feature, *La Pointe Courte,* in 1954, Agnès Varda has often said that she started making movies before she'd actually seen any. She has always written her own scripts, and she seems to express herself in film almost effortlessly. Years of sweat may go into raising the money for a production, but filmmaking itself comes easy to her—partly because she doesn't dramatize her material. She has a loose, simplified narrative method: in *One Sings,* people talk to each other, and she narrates the transitions and moves on. But the skin-deep characters don't involve us in their predicaments. They don't seem to have any consciousness—they're just part of the traffic she's directing. Though we're told that this movie is about how these two women grow, that's exactly what we don't see. There are no perceptible connections between the two heroines, or between them and their parents or their lovers or their children. The way Varda skims over their lives, they could be butterflies or duckies. In Varda's earlier films (*Le Bonheur* especially), the shallowness was sometimes redeemed by physicality; she gave a special tactile feeling to bodies, fabrics, landscapes. It was possible to believe that the characters in *Le Bonheur,* as in her *Cleo from 5 to 7,* were made deliberately vapid, and so a viewer could get the impression that something complex and elusive was being suggested, even if one couldn't locate it. This time, there's nothing enigmatic about Varda's tone. When Pomme, who treats children as toys for adults, comes up with her solution—to trade off one baby and keep the next—we're meant to think she's sensible. In the terms of this movie, she *is*: her idyll works. (The narrator reports that the child in Iran is doing fine and that the Iranian has a new wife and another baby.) Agnès Varda is perfectly candid; everything is as practical and simple as Pomme's approach to maternity. Varda is proud of Pomme's and Suzanne's accomplishments in becoming women. (In this film, being a woman isn't a fact, it's a profession.) Yet experience has no weight in *One Sings*; there are no women in it—only girls. Its vision of the future is of a frolicsome adolescent matriarchy. One cannot accuse Varda of jumping on a bandwagon: her films have always had a sympathetic responsiveness to the women characters, and a polymorphous affection for them. This seems to have become drippier, though, now that she's officially expressing the new awareness, and commenting on the heroines with "Then she had time to cry" or "She went on singing, changing."

Varda's lyricism is trivializing. If there were twenty seconds of footage of an actual abortion in the movie, Pomme's chirrupy songs would be chilling. It seems never to have occurred to Varda that her characters have no depth—that they're amoebic in the way they react to stimuli. She's a lively, sophisticated film technician who thinks that this ode to superficiality is poetic truth. If a big American advertising agency had been given the job of devising a feminist film to offend the smallest number of people, this mindless, cosmetic movie is exactly what it would have come up with. Charming young girls setting their belligerent jaws and singing about their ovules.

[November 14, 1977]

Shouldn't Old Acquaintance *Be Forgot?*

*I*n 1943, when John van Druten's comedy-drama *Old Acquaintance* was transferred to the screen, Bette Davis played the distinguished unmarried writer living in New York who arrived in her old college town and was carried through the streets by the enthusiastic students, right to the door of her bosom buddy from girlhood days—Miriam Hopkins—who had married and was now pregnant but had never got over her catty envy of the adulation her chum received, and was busy scribbling a novel. Eventually, Davis helped Hopkins' daughter, Deedee, at a critical time in the girl's life, and the picture reached its climax when Davis slapped Hopkins and, grabbing her by the shoulders, shook the crazy, jealous suspiciousness out of her; after a lifetime of rivalry, the two women drank a toast to their friendship. For many years, a fair number of people have been longing for more of those Bette Davis–Miriam Hopkins movies, and now there is a new one, *The Turning Point,* with Anne Bancroft as Emma, the celebrated, lonely, aging ballerina with "American Ballet Company" (modelled on American Ballet Theatre), which arrives for an engagement in Oklahoma City, where her old friend and rival, Deedee—Shirley MacLaine—lives. Deedee quit her own dancing career, married, had three children—and never stopped thinking about what she had lost out on. Emilia (Leslie Browne), the oldest of her children and a promising teen-age dancer, is Emma's godchild, and when Emma begins to mother the girl—to guide her and coach her—Deedee gets riled up. The two women have a big slapfest, whamming each other until they both get the rage out of their systems, start laughing, and wind up hugging. At the end, their arms are around each other's shoulders—friends forever.

Will anybody long for more Anne Bancroft–Shirley MacLaine movies? It's doubtful. The screenplay, by Arthur Laurents, centers on the turning point in Emma's and Deedee's lives, when they made the choices—dancing for Emma, marriage for Deedee—that settled their destinies. As a device, the turning point (like that synthetic summer when adolescent heroes grow into men) is so mechanical it's an exposed construction; Laurents' girders are showing. The two women's scenes are designed to reveal what each of them gave up and what each gained—it's one little lesson after another. *Old Acquaintance* was hair-pulling high camp: it had the verve of bitchery to keep one somewhat amused. Laurents, though, writes sodden, expository dialogue in which people are forever revealing truths to each other and then explaining those truths— *The Turning Point* comes with its own footnotes. Anne Bancroft overdoes her sacrificial-artist laceration. Trying for glamour and bravura, she holds her haggard head up gallantly, with her neck drawn so taut that it pulls her mouth down. She has a gnarled, ascetic look, and the worst case of nobility in the eyebrows since Greer Garson. Garbo's suicidally exhausted ballerina in *Grand Hotel* was a ball of fluff compared with Bancroft; suffering, not dance, seems to be Bancroft's art. Shirley MacLaine plays in a snappier spirit; she gives a shrewd performance, with her own version of Miriam Hopkins' narrow-eyed avidity—the sly greediness for attention which is so transparent it's comic. And she looks great: in fighting trim. But since the movie has been placed inside a backstage ballet atmosphere, with subsidiary roles played by a dozen or more famous dancers, and with the possibility of seeing them dance, Emma and Deedee would have to be larger personalities to hold our attention. We get a glimpse of something great in this movie, and Emma and Deedee—two harpies out of the soaps—block the view.

Earlier backstage ballet films had their mad-genius Diaghilev figures, such as the ruthlessly dedicated impresario played by Anton Walbrook in *The Red Shoes*—he smoldered, trailing noxious fumes of culture. (The foreign country they all came from was really hell.) But the whole effort here is to domesticate ballet—to remove the taint of European decadence. The ballet company was founded by the tactless, blundering Adelaide (Martha Scott—you can't get any more all-American than that), and her obsession is raising money. Most of the characters are so heartland ordinary—they're shaped to be so much like the filmmakers' idea of you and me—that they disinfect one's imagination. As soon as the dancing starts, dancers who stop our breathing become the stars of the movie: Mikhail Baryshnikov and, in a brief glimpse, Suzanne Farrell, who flies onstage—a dream on legs—during the company's annual fund-raising gala. The movie is Baryshnikov's. He plays Yuri, the Russian dancer whom the budding ballerina Emilia falls in love with, and his acting is lightly understated. Baryshnikov is so amazingly unaffected as a dancer that it is not surprising that he should also be matter-of-fact in his line readings. There are no wasted gestures, not a whisper of excess. His performance is exceedingly likable, and it gives us a chance for a semi-private look at a whirlwind in repose. He doesn't have the classically proportioned body or the stylized face of most male dance stars; his muscles are gently rounded, and his head is massive. When he's merely acting and his body is still, his huge blue-gray eyes could be gazing at another planet. He's like one of the cherubim grown up—a little puzzled about where he is but accepting it. The film never sets up the greatness of Baryshnikov: there's no fanfare. This blond-haired Russian with thick hands is simply there among the men in the company that Emma belongs to and that Emilia joins; except for the paleness of his face and those unearthly eyes, he could be a robust peasant. And with no visible preparation he's leaping into space—he's just up there, and *turning*. When he finishes his *Corsaire* solo, you want the director, Herbert Ross, to stop all the nonsense—the cheesy pairing, balancing, and squabbling—and just repeat the piece of film. It's like seeing a meteor streak by. There's a trace of regret mixed with your surprise and exhilaration—you haven't been able to take it all in.

The story element that will probably make *The Turning Point* a box-office hit is the romance between Yuri and Emilia. Leslie Browne is a new version of every big-dark-eyed sensitive-sprite ballerina; she has the traditional ballet baby face—a lemming in a tutu. The movie gives her showcase treatment: she is lighted to be the *jeune fille*, like Audrey Hepburn in *Roman Holiday*, tremblingly learning the meaning of love. Emilia is dancing with another partner when her eyes meet Yuri's; they dance together—a love-awakening from MacMillan's *Romeo and Juliet* (which serves the same purpose as the Jeanette MacDonald–Nelson Eddy duets)—and then they are in a bedroom together. It's tasteful, pretty, sweetly romantic, and utterly lacking in ingenuity—in the wit of romance. This stuffed, airless lyricism is just a facsimile of romantic fantasy, an appeal to teen-age swooniness.

The dancing is photographed with respect for the dancers' whole bodies, and against clear, bright backgrounds. The big screen gives it a boldness and immediacy greater, in some ways, than it might have on the stage. When Baryshnikov is in motion, Ross and the cinematographer, Robert Surtees, certainly know they've captured pure joy up there on the screen. But the script—and Ross, who initiated the project, must be a partial collaborator—exploits Baryshnikov's boyish, mysteriously simple heterosexual appeal to prop up the gratuitous thesis that though the men in ballet *used* to be sexually ambiguous the ballet world is now as wholesome as football and Mom's apple pie. The film's approach to ballet is like a recruiting poster: join up for clean living. In the last few years, the grace and idealism incarnated in ballet, and maybe, too, its freedom from "issues," have made it almost as popular an escape from the national mess as sports. Ballet is already a mainstream art form. Would movie audiences care whether the male dancers were actually homosexual, as long as they moved with precision and refinement, and could soar when necessary? Maybe some still would; maybe there is a sound commercial instinct behind this picture's attempt to ingratiate itself by showing ballet as "normal." But it bends over backward, like gays getting short haircuts and wearing crewneck sweaters—their straight drag. (It would be more honorable to take a chance on the audience.)

The only acting with any depth is by Tom Skerritt, as Deedee's husband, Wayne, who used to be a dancer, too, and now runs a dance school with her in Oklahoma City. Skerritt (he was the Southerner who bunked with Elliot Gould and Donald Sutherland in *M*A*S*H*) has an easiness as an actor that translates to the screen as relaxed, unthreatened masculinity. Wayne is so emotionally alert to what's going on in his family that you're conscious of his awareness even when he's off camera. His simple gratefulness for what he's got makes you understand how good Deedee's life really is—and how her envy of Emma has kept her from fully committing herself to him. Everything about Wayne is convincing except the scene in which he, too, must reveal his turning point—his unsureness early in life about whether he was homosexual or heterosexual, which was resolved when Deedee and he got together. Who would dream of accusing Wayne of being anything other than what he seems? There's not a suggestion of any repressed area in him—nor, one suspects, is there meant to be. The homosexual issue is raised so it can be dismissed as a bugaboo.

The script is practically a tree of life, with dozens of characters reaching their turning points and branching off. Wayne and Deedee's youngest child, a boy torn between baseball and ballet, has his junior edition of the decisive moment. (He picks dance.) Emma's and Deedee's former suitors are part of this tree, and there are also ballerinas of several generations so we can see where Emilia will be in a few years, and where Emma will end up. And in order to dramatize the price of fame (versus Deedee's cozy family future) the film makes stupid pathos of Emma's aging—as if the possibilities open to retired dancers (teaching, coaching, choreography, management) were rackingly degrading. As the horrible example of what's ahead for the lonely Emma, there is Alexandra Danilova in the role of the ancient coach Dahkarova, but Danilova looks as vital and engaged as when she danced with the Ballet Russe de Monte Carlo in the late thirties. She's living evidence that what she gave to me and hundreds of thousands of others when she was at her height as a dancer she's still giving out, in a different form. (She shows more strength and vivacity than the young heroine's dancing does.)

Herbert Ross was himself a dancer and then a ballet choreographer, before becoming a Broadway director; after directing the musical sequences in the film *Funny Girl,* he became a movie director. *The Turning Point,* his ninth picture, is also a bow to his wife (since 1959)—the celebrated ballerina Nora Kaye, who achieved fame for her dramatic eloquence in the ballet *Pillar of Fire* in 1942, quit dancing when she was forty-one, and devoted herself to her marriage. In a sense, Nora Kaye, who served as executive producer of this film (and works with Ross on his other movies, too), has been both Emma and Deedee, in succession. She was a charter member of Ballet Theatre (now American Ballet Theatre), and Leslie Browne, the daughter of two dancers, is, in fact, Nora Kaye's godchild. Ross is not a particularly resourceful director, but his unassertive approach saves *The Turning Point*—keeps it painless; if the picture had been directed with a rigidity to match that of the script, with its gothic fix on ballet geriatrics, it would be a clanger. Ross, though, doesn't give one the excitement that a confident director can. The film has no visual sweep; the camera doesn't track with the music, it has no lift. There are too many grays and dusty pinks and faded salmon tones; the picture looks like those men who always wear dark ties with gray suits because they're afraid of going wrong. Before a scene is over—sometimes even in the middle of a *word*—there's a cut to another scene. At times you feel that Ross keeps shifting the scenes so you won't notice them; he half erases them. After a bit of dance, he cuts to reaction shots—to Bancroft's face, or MacLaine's—for safety. Even in the way it's made, this movie is like TV—it's the Partridge Family in Ballet Land. On this project, which he's deeply committed to, Ross is so concerned not to betray or vulgarize backstage ballet life that he hides around corners from it. People seem to rattle about in the frame, and one could get the impression that the *sets* were dubbed: they have a hollow ring, as if the furnishings of a suburban home were jammed into a section of an airplane hangar.

When we go to see a ballet picture starring Bancroft and MacLaine, we don't expect a unified dance conception like *The Red Shoes*, but we do assume that the script will provide opportunities for dance which are integral to the story. Yet except for the love duet the dancing—such as that at the big gala, where we get a chance to watch snippets of dances with Peter Martins, Antoinette Sibley, Marcia Haydée, Richard Cragun, Lucette Aldous, Fernando Bujones, and others—has no dramatic function. Ross seems caught somewhere between the script's philistinism and his own love of dance. In the name of modern realism, Ross and Laurents have taken the personality and temperament out of the ballet world along with any whiffs of exotic, fetid culture. The moviemakers appear to confuse realism with banality (and heterosexuality). Ross's biggest weakness is that he doesn't trust the camera enough. If he did, it would take him right to Baryshnikov, whose attentiveness to his partners and whose contradictory image—an extrovert with spiritual eyes—overpower the script's musty calculations about career decisions. One leap and he knocks this house of cards down. Ballet is romance formalized; the script uses it just as romance. The lyricism of Emilia's affair with Yuri and the mythic speed with which she becomes a star suggest the way that some fourteen-year-olds fantasize ballet—as if it were a means of arresting development between pre-puberty and puberty. That's the place where Peter Pan lived.

[November 21, 1977]

The Greening of the
Solar System

C lose Encounters of the Third Kind is the most innocent of all technological-marvel movies, and one of the most satisfying. This film has retained some of the wonder and bafflement we feel when we first go into a planetarium: we ooh and aah at the vastness, and at the beauty of the mystery. The film doesn't overawe us, though, because it has a child's playfulness and love of surprises. There is a moment that is startlingly funny in its obviousness when a whole landscape of people in India who are ecstatically chanting a five-note theme are asked where these sounds came from, and a mass of arms are raised straight up, forefingers pointing. In routine science-fiction films, any bodies from space are alien invaders; they come from *out there,* and we start running or shooting. But in *Close Encounters* they come from *up there*—they're sunburst Gods arriving through Blakean Old Testament clouds. This isn't nuts-and-bolts, *Popular Mechanics* S.F.; it's beatific technology—machines from outer space deified. And to cap it all, the intelligent creatures in these machines are benevolent. They want to get to know us. This vision would be *too* warm and soul-satisfying if it weren't for the writer-director Steven Spielberg's skeptical, let's-try-it-on spirit. He's an entertainer—a magician in the age of movies. Is Spielberg an artist? Not exactly—or not yet. He's a prodigy—a flimflam wizard-technician. The immense charm of *Close Encounters* comes from the fact that, for all its scale and expense (nineteen million dollars), this is a young man's movie—Spielberg is still under thirty—and there's not a sour thought in it. (The title is from a book by the astronomer Dr. J. Allen Hynek—close encounters of the first kind are sightings, the second kind are physical evidence, and the third involve actual contact. Sightings aren't necessarily close and they're not encounters, and physical evidence isn't an encounter, either, but the title sounds good, anyway.)

The basic story is scanty: this unidentified-flying-objects movie is about those who are "looking for answers." In Muncie, Indiana, an electrical-power-company lineman named Roy (Richard Dreyfuss), a three-year-old boy named Barry (Cary Guffey), the boy's mother (Melinda

348

Dillon), and a collection of innocuous misfits, retired folks, and artists all catch sight of the flaring lights of spacecraft; some of them are sunburned, and a vision is implanted in them. They become obsessed with a shape they don't understand—a lumpy, sawed-off pyramid or mountain. At the same time, an international team of scientists, headed by a clearheaded Frenchman, Lacombe (François Truffaut), is dashing about the globe picking up word of other signals, which direct the team to a mountain in Wyoming. It is the spot the aliens have chosen for a rendezvous with us earthlings, and the dreamers—the invited guests—converge upon it. But military personnel who are working with the scientific team cut most of them off. It's a going-to-Bethlehem story. Only those with enough faith and luck make it.

Close Encounters is a vindication of village crazies. Those people always give you the feeling they know something you don't, and in this scientific fairy tale it turns out they do. God is up there in a crystal-chandelier spaceship, and He likes us. The stoned, the gullible, the half-mad, and just plain folks are His chosen people. To be more exact: *It* likes us. (The extraterrestrials appear to have evolved beyond sex.) The largest craft, the mother ship, is a great celestial body—a symmetrical, rounded Christmas-tree ornament as big as a city. When it descends from on high, looming over the mountain and hovering there, no storybook illustration can compete with it. This is something only movies can do: dazzle you by sheer scale—and in this case by lights and music as well. Spielberg is the son of an electrical-engineer, S.F.-addict father and a classical-pianist mother, and in the climax of the film he does justice to both. Under the French scientist's direction, the earthlings are ready with a console, and they greet the great craft with an oboe solo—variations on the five-note theme; the craft answers in deep, tuba tones. The dialogue becomes blissfully garrulous. And with light flooding out from the windows of this omniscient airship—it's like New York's skyscrapers all lighted up on a summer night—there is a conversational duet: the music of the spheres. This is one of the peerless moments in movie history—spiritually reassuring, magical, and funny at the same time. Very few movies have ever hit upon this combination of fantasy and amusement—*The Wizard of Oz,* perhaps, in a plainer, down-home way.

Close Encounters, too, is a kids' movie in the best sense. You can feel the pleasure the young director took in making it. With his gift for investing machines with personality, Spielberg is the right director for science fantasy. He made a malevolent character of a truck in *Duel,* his famous made-for-TV movie. In his first theatrical feature, *The Sugarland Express,* he had cars dancing, feuding, bonding. In his second film, *Jaws,* he turned a computer-operated shark into a personal enemy. And now he's got his biggest mechanical toys: the mother ship and the flying-saucer herald angels—whirring through the skies, flashing their lights. Some are intergalactic Pucks teasing earthlings and leading them on fools' chases; some are stately geometric forms spinning languorously. Each is like a musical divertimento, a delight unto itself. *Jaws* was a nightmare movie; this is a dream. In *Jaws,* the harrowing terror kept building; here the mystical good humor builds—the story envelops you. With Truffaut as Lacombe, the sympathies of the scientist don't have to be explained; he is essentially the educated man of good will that Truffaut played in his own *The Wild Child.* Truffaut suggests efficiency plus innate refinement; his forehead is noble, his features are modelled in a seraphic smile, and he's small. His Lacombe is a calm, wise child who responds to the vision of the dreamer-misfits—shares their instinctive trust of what is in space. (And when, at last, he communicates with a visitor from above, there is a fleeting suggestion of Jean Renoir's lopsided grin in the extraterrestrial's young-old face.)

There are, of course, limitations to science-fiction movies. People used to love to be frightened by ghost stories—those evil portents of a world beyond death, with their intimations of haunted, macabre sex. Those stories belonged to an age when people lived in fear of their own impulses, and in dread of punishment. And movies were able to bring out the stories' primitive-sophisticated power—their suggestiveness. Science fiction, the modern successor to tales of the supernatural, lacks those psychological dimensions, it doesn't have the whole nighttime apparatus of guilt and superstition clinging to it. The attraction of science fiction is that it's an escape into an almost abstract unknown. Those who are frightened of, despairing about, or bored with this world like to turn their hopes to other worlds in space, but they're not much interested in people. Imagination and idealism are expressed in simplified, allegorical terms. Generally speaking, when a speculative fantasy deals with human conflicts in any depth, it ceases to be called science fiction. The persistent fault of S.F. movies has been the split between the splendor of their special effects and the stilted mediocrity of their characters, situations, and dialogue. There has probably never been a first-rate characterization in an American science-fiction movie—how could there be, since the stories don't depend on character? (That's why science fiction used to be considered a pulp genre.) It's difficult to think of even one well-written role. Kubrick's *2001* was no exception: its only character who made any impression was Hal, the voice of the computer. In *Star Wars,* audiences fell in love with R2D2 and C3PO; people had the same reaction to Robby, the robot in *Forbidden Planet,* and to the drones in *Silent Running* (which was directed by Douglas Trumbull, who supervised the special photographic effects in *Close Encounters*). In S.F. movies, the robots have personalities; the actors usually don't. *2001* wasn't a pop escapist fantasy, like *Star Wars;* it was an attempt at a more serious view of the future, which was seen as an extension of now, a super-ordinary world. In Kubrick's conception, there was no richness, no texture—it was all blandness. He might as well have been saying, "I have seen the future and it put me to sleep." Spielberg's movie is set right now, and it has none of that ponderous seriousness—but it's the same bland now that S.F. enthusiasts seem to think we live in. The banality is really in *their* view of human life.

With a vast, clear sky full of stars, and a sense of imminence—much of the movie feels like being inside the dome of an enchanted cathedral waiting for the Arrival—terse, swift, heightened dialogue is called for. Instead, we hear casual, ordinary-man language, and, although it has an original, colloquial snap, Spielberg just doesn't have the feeling for words which he has for images. And he doesn't create the central characters (Barry's mother and Roy), or develop them, in a *writer's* way; he's thinking about how to get them into the positions he wants them in for his visual plan. Roy is supposed to be the Hitchcockian ordinary man in extraordinary circumstances; for Hitchcock that could be Cary Grant, but for Spielberg it means a sincere attempt to show how a lumpy average man living in pop-culture emptiness could get caught up in a quest. Richard Dreyfuss's Roy waddles in rear view, and becomes moist-eyed when he longs for knowledge. We seem to be asked to respond to Roy for being out of condition and, at times, out of control. There's a fine dinner scene in which Roy's children, who love him, are upset by the compulsiveness of his behavior; they can feel him growing away from them. But Spielberg doesn't follow through on the change in Roy; he jumps to a low-comedy marriage-breakup scene. And after we've had a few closeups of Roy's hectic fervor, as he attempts to share his U.F.O. experience with his pragmatic wife (Teri Garr), her dry philistinism has a hard-edged, comic-strip appeal. With her one-track mind, she's a frozen pizza in Roy's yearning-mystic eye. As one of the crackpots—a man who has seen Bigfoot as well as flying saucers—Roberts Blossom has the look of a true believer. That's what Dreyfuss lacks. Spielberg is far more successful with Barry, the three-year-old, whose pure lust for otherworldly entertainment is delicately funny. Barry, the toddling light-worshipper who sees the sky as a giant toy shop, is closer to the heart of Spielberg's vision than Roy, whose "looking for answers" Dreyfuss strains to represent.

Steven Spielberg is probably the most gifted American director who's dedicated to sheer entertainment. He may have different aims from the aims of people we call artists, but he has integrity: it centers on his means. His expressive drive is to tell a story in shots that are live and hopping, and his grasp of graphic dynamics may be as strong as that of anyone working in movies now. The spatial relationships inside the frame here owe little to the stage, or even to painting; Spielberg succeeds in making the compositions so startlingly immediate that they give off an electric charge. He puts us right in the middle of the action, yet there's enough aesthetic distance—he doesn't assault us. Though the perspectives don't appear forced or unnatural, they're often slightly tilted, with people moving rapidly in or out of the frame, rarely intersecting the center and never occupying it. By designing the images in advance, Spielberg is able to cut without any confusion. Nobody cuts faster on shots full of activity than he does, yet it's never just for the sake of variety: it's what the movie is about that generates the images and the cutting pattern, and there's a constant pickup in excitement from shot to shot—a ziggety forward motion. Even the weakly motivated sequences (which are needed for a later, visual payoff)—such as Roy's going batty, and tearing up his garden and throwing mud and plants in through his kitchen window, or the mountain scaling out of *North by Northwest,* which comes across as a delaying tactic—are partly saved by Spielberg's visual energy. *Close Encounters* is big and complex (in addition to Vilmos Zsigmond, who was the director of photography, other famous cinematographers—William A. Fraker, Douglas Slocombe, John Alonzo, and Laszlo Kovacs—worked on it), and there are sequences, such as the one in India, that are fine in themselves yet don't have Spielberg's distinctive graphics. But he never loses the emotional drive of his subject, and he gives audiences full opportunity to luxuriate in the sensuousness of the spectacle. It's too bad that John Williams, who did the score, thinks he's still working on *Jaws.* Movie music in general has reached the point where if it isn't meant to cheer you or to scare you, the composer doesn't know what to do. Except for the great duet here, Williams provides emotional noise, rising and shrilling in the Bernard Herrmann manner. The score fails to match the witty use of rapturousness in such images as that of Barry trotting out of his house at night—just a speck on the prairie under a blanket of stars and a huge roiling cloud.

Close Encounters shows an excess of kindness—an inability (or, perhaps, unwillingness) to perceive the streak of cowardice and ignorance and confusion in the actions of the authorities who balk the efforts of the visionaries to reach their goal. Having devised a plot in which the government systematically covers up information about U.F.O. sightings, Spielberg is much too casual about how this is done and imprecise about why. He has a paranoid plot, but he hasn't dramatized the enemy. The obstacles here are just Air Force and Army men doing their duty, and these authorities are shrugged off by the cranks, or humbly accepted. Roy and the others don't have the incapacitating hatred of smooth-talking authority which would make us respond to their frustrations—would make us feel what was unhinging them. Impersonality doesn't enrage Spielberg, because he hasn't got at the personality hidden in it. Stock villainy isn't what's needed—something deeper is. He had similar trouble with the corrupt local merchants and politicians in *Jaws*; their corruption was tired, ritualized—it was necessary for the plot, that was all. In *Close Encounters,* there is nothing behind what the military men do except bureaucratic indifference. But that means they don't know what they're doing—and to be so totally blind is tragic, crazy emptiness. Spielberg has a genuine affection for harmless aberrants, but he doesn't fathom the dangerous aberrance of authority—particularly an authority that in its own eyes is being completely reasonable. In terms of his plot, Spielberg needs some Terry Southern in his soul, or maybe even some Norman Wexler. He needs to show us how scared bureaucrats are of something they can't understand and don't know how to handle.

Steven Spielberg is commercial without really being commercial: that is, he's a popular entertainer who doesn't have a feeling for the profane, sneaky pleasures of tawdriness. *Close Encounters* is so generous in its feelings that it makes one feel maternal and protective; there's also another side of one, which says, "I could use a little dirty friction." Most directors who make sweet movies are unskilled, and you're supposed to forgive them their incompetence because of their niceness. Spielberg may be the only director with technical virtuosity ever to make a transcendently sweet movie. *Close Encounters* is almost the opposite of *Star Wars,* in which a whole planet was blown up and nobody batted an eye. It seems almost inconceivable, but nobody gets hurt in this movie, except the occupants of one police car, who are so delirious in their pursuit of a flying object that they hurtle off the highway into the air, and then bounce down to earth in a ditch—and they may be too surprised to be hurt. The film is like *Oklahoma!* in space, with jokes; it's spiritual cotton candy and it goes down easy. The summer-skies atmosphere is achieved by certain exclusions: the film is virtually sexless, and the aliens don't deliver any invitations to the Soviet bloc, so there's no political scrambling in the race to the rendezvous. Mercifully, there's no cosmological philosophizing, either: nobody stands around arguing about what the manifestations prove. As was the case with *2001,* though, the publicity is full of the usual announcements about the data in it not having been disproved. And statistics about how many millions of people claim to have seen flying saucers are used to give the film an almost official status, as if it were a daring inquiry into facts that the government is hiding from us. These publicity claims of credibility and usefulness only take away from what should be the film's enduring appeal as fantasy.

Close Encounters is a beautiful, big, enjoyable film that sends you out happy. It might be even better if there weren't so many people at the end looking upward with transfigured faces. *Star Wars* had its guru, Alec Guinness, in his neo-*Lost Horizon* trappings, and this film, too, has its gaseous naïveté. But it has the visionary magic to go with it. If Roy and Lacombe and the other dreamers do a lot of blinking and staring up with wet eyes, it's not like *The Miracle of Our Lady of Fatima*—here we at least get to see what they're staring at. And we watch Roy ascend the stairway to Heaven. Spielberg is busy, like that fine humbug Wizard of Oz, pressing buttons on his light panel. He puts on a great show.

[November 28, 1977]

The Unjoy of Sex

*F*rançois Truffaut's *The Man Who Loved Women* begins with the arrival of the mourners at Bertrand's funeral: all women, they arrive by ones, an army of attractive, sexy, young and not so young women. When, in flashback, we see Bertrand (Charles Denner), the dedicated skirt-chaser whose lovemaking these women are honoring by their presence, it's a letdown. He's dead even when he's supposed to be alive. An unsmiling man whose basic expression is morose, he has nothing in his existence but his work as an engineer in Montpellier (testing the effects of turbulence on planes and ships) and his compulsive mashing. Truffaut conceived the character Bertrand for Denner, which suggests a trace of his recurrent directorial masochism. Denner is a small man with a bright-eyed hawk face, rather like Jerzy Kosinski's, and in some roles (such as the dropout in Alain Jessua's *Life Upside Down*) he has had Kosinski's alert, hallucinatory quality—a willful, rapt solitariness. But in the eccentric character parts he has played in other Truffaut films (for example, the exterminator in *Such a Gorgeous Kid Like Me*) he has been somewhat obtrusive—not quite a movie actor, too deliberate about his effects—and when he attempts a cloud-borne comic style like that of Jean-Louis Barrault in *Bizarre, Bizarre* there's lead in his shoes. As Bertrand, he's playing a man about ten years younger than he actually is, and his face is tight; when he's thinking about how to track down a pair of legs he has spotted, he purses his lips or pinches them. For reflectiveness, for wryness—whatever—he just keeps working his mouth, twisting it around as if he were trying to hold his dentures in. Bertrand is like an elderly, dried-up pederast. There are, of course, joyless compulsive chasers, but Bertrand's chasing isn't intended to be joyless. Although his obsession may look to be about as exciting as building a two-foot replica of the Pentagon with toothpicks, he's meant to be irresistibly charming.

354

Bertrand's plight might have been a subject for one of Sacha Guitry's light farces—the absurd story of a roué who carries to extremes the proclivities that other men can keep in balance. And the movie has the structure of a boulevard farce. But it doesn't have a comic spirit. In its gross flippancy, it resembles *Such a Gorgeous Kid Like Me*—it may be even worse, because of the mixture of evasiveness and obviousness. The script Truffaut wrote (along with Michel Fermaud and Suzanne Schiffman) has plot turns—such as Bertrand's writing a book of confessions—that are feeble, time-wasting contrivances out of Hollywood-factory films of the forties. There's not much visual distinction, either, although the cinematography is by Nestor Almendros, who is a master and Truffaut's frequent collaborator. The comic high point is Bertrand's affair with Delphine (Nelly Borgeaud), a doctor's wife with a panther walk and a cuckoo-nympho gleam. Delphine revels in having sex in perilously public places—a department store, the garage of the apartment building she and her husband live in—and she tears off her clothes while crying out "Good Lord, the things you make me do!" Maybe this picaresque episode comes off with some humor just because it's an escape hatch—it has nothing to do with the film's theme. It's also creepily similar to an episode in Kurt Hoffmann's film *The Confessions of Felix Krull* (Mme. Houpfle tears off Felix's clothes while crying "Oh, how delightfully you debase me!"). And the sex-in-public mania has already been given satirical treatment in the Louise Lasser sketch in Woody Allen's *Everything You Always Wanted to Know About Sex*. Bertrand's chance encounter with Vera (Leslie Caron), whom he loved years before, and whose leaving him is supposed to indicate why he can't have an ongoing relationship, is so cryptically weighted with pauses, gulps, and shining eyes, and is so fundamentally uncommunicative, that it ranks with the flattest moments in all of Truffaut. In Bertrand's memories of his childhood with his promiscuous bitch of a mother, he recalls her use of the word *"insondable"*—"unfathomable." Is this meant to be the clue to the movie—that Bertrand wants each woman he sees because he couldn't fathom, couldn't get into, his mother? This, though, is Freud's clue to every man, and Bertrand's uncontrollable philandering suggests a special case. If a Freudian explanation is intended, wouldn't he be drawn to women who reminded him of his mother physically, or emotionally, by being bitchy and unloving to him, as she was? Psychologically, one of the least plausible aspects of this movie is that he's supposedly drawn to *all* women—he's an equal-opportunity fornicator.

If Bertrand were a highly respected, honored man—a man with children and friends, possibly a man with a deep commitment to his work (an artist, perhaps?)—and if he were split between other drives or goals and this, to him, shameful, somewhat incomprehensible compulsion, then there'd be a comic horror in his plight. Truffaut, however, doesn't set Bertrand's chasing in conflict with other aspects of his character; he isolates it. Bertrand is such a loner that he doesn't even hang out with men to talk about women. And what pleasure can he get? The women are so willing and compliant he can't get anything resembling the thrill of conquest. There isn't as much as a whiff of gunpowder from the sexual war. The film has a frosty, tony-swinger mentality: nobody's hurt, nobody pays. Can a man race from one affair to another the way Bertrand does without disrupting the women's lives, and without their interfering in his? Bertrand's existence is so smooth he seems programmed rather than sex-crazed; the film has the pacing of an industrial movie—one task after another.

Bertrand's book editor is played by Brigitte Fossey, who is one of the most beautiful young women in movies. At five, she was the lost child in *Forbidden Games*—blond, porcelain perfection; now her perfection is sensuous and she has a Carole Lombard antic funniness about her. In this movie, she is supposed to fall in love with this sterile dummy Bertrand—a cross between a Jesuit and a harlequin. The film's tone becomes slickly self-congratulatory when the editor suggests to Bertrand that he change the title of his confessions from *The Skirt-Chaser* to *The Man Who Loved Women.* Truffaut's having her make this switch is a way of reaching around the corner to pat himself on the back. The film begins with a halfhearted indictment of Bertrand—the suggestion that he's "sick"—and then the editor gives him a phony acquittal. We're actually asked to believe that he brought a little light into each woman's life.

□ □ □

*I*t is reported that when the James Ivory film *Roseland* was screened at the New York Film Festival it received a seven-minute standing ovation. Did those people stand up and cheer to get their circulation going again? Set in the famous, still functioning dance hall on Fifty-second Street off Broadway and using actual patrons in the crowd scenes, *Roseland* has three casts in three separate stories about the people who come to dance or to watch. As a form, the omnibus film has never worked out too well. For a viewer, having one's involvement shifted from one set of characters to the next is frustrating, and after watching three stories people may feel there hasn't been any story. The triple device requires style—a director who can start up the movie three times, vary the rhythms, and spin the tales daringly fast. *Roseland* never heard of anything so vulgar as pace. James Ivory has now made eight feature films without jeopardizing his amateur standing. In his early films, the absence of gloss suggested a fresh, noncommercial approach, but he's still taking beginning steps. In *Roseland,* he's a hesitant director, without much feeling for how to frame a shot, and the cinematographer Ernest Vincze's images aren't dark, exactly—they're just dim, lacking in contrasts. The writer Ruth Prawer Jhabvala has worked with Ivory several times before but never with any other director. Her script has a rounded-out finality that might read like a model of craftsmanship, but it's a writer's script, not a screenwriter's script; each story represents what high-school English teachers used to call fine imagination—there was dust on the pages before they were filmed.

Apparently, Roseland has survived—continuous music and all— because many of the people who were in the habit of going there when they were young have kept going, ritualistically, and it has become a haven for the middle-aged and the old. Not the sort of people benched on the traffic dividers on upper Broadway; that's the fifth ring of hell. The Roseland regulars don't let themselves go; they haven't given up. The men have their suits pressed and wear ties, and the women put on white gloves and ballroom chiffons with two or three petticoats underneath. This movie feels too much need for kindness, and refuses to see the schizzy comic aspects of this encampment for nostalgic aging people. Its hushed concern for their loneliness and its solicitude to protect their dignity are so respectful, washed-out, drab that the film denies them any spirit. The m.c., played by Don De Natale, an actual m.c. at Roseland, suggests a tawdry vivacity—a pleasure in the maudlin spectacle—that has more feeling for the customers than the film's faded genteel sensitivity.

Ivory keeps the camera on the actors, and they keep acting. In the first story, Teresa Wright, as a lonely sixtyish widow, never lets up; you can't relax when she's on the screen—she's reaching out, grabbing you, pelting you with her tender frailty. This fantasy episode is little-people occultism—an unholy union of Paddy Chayefsky and Rod Serling, but written as though the author had never heard of either. The triteness seems freshly minted. The best thing about the short-story structure is that as soon as the widow gets together with a new man (Lou Jacobi), she and her whimsey pass out of the movie. In the middle section, the writer got on to something, but, maybe because of being locked into the short form, she didn't develop it. Russel (Christopher Walken) is a dancer-gigolo, who is supported by an older woman (Joan Copeland) while he lets the pallid girl who loves him (Geraldine Chaplin) believe that he's going to break clean and go back to being a professional dancer. Russel has the dimpled, high-cheekboned look of movie idols from the past (Valentino, Phillips Holmes), but he also suggests emotional ties to the second-raters, the imitation movie stars who played rotters and handsome weaklings. Walken gives the character the polite veneer and the sullen self-sufficiency that would make Russel a successful lizard. This gigolo's courteous nastiness gives the film its only magnetic force—it's the only emotion in the movie (except for the m.c.'s) that isn't fully comprehended, chewed, and swallowed. There's another woman in Russel's life: his former dancing teacher and partner, Cleo (Helen Gallagher), who wants him to start training again, because she knows how good he could be—and how far they could go together. He doesn't care; Russel is content, even complacent, as the center of attention. Both the girl and Cleo are trying to force him to be more than he is. But because the emphasis is on his betrayal of the naïve girl, rather than on his betrayal of his talent (and of his partner), the episode never becomes dramatic. The final story—an extended anecdote, in which Lilia Skala and David Thomas play two aged habitués of the dance hall, and Skala acts right to the all too willing camera before twirling her life away—is a rather sad imitation of the man-dancing-himself-to-death sequence in Max Ophuls' *Le Plaisir*.

Roseland is a case of a movie made by people who have been educated out of their instincts. The picture is all decorum and no energy. It needs some sense of interaction between Roseland and the New York City that's outside. Roseland's waltzing colonials must be bushwhacked every time they leave their outpost—how do you keep your gloves white in the subway, or even in a taxi? Their world is treated with so much academic tact that we never make direct contact with them. *Roseland* has the defenseless, sentimental appeal that made hits of such pictures as *To Sir with Love* and *David and Lisa*. It has been put together without tough-mindedness and without showmanship. *Roseland* makes you feel that it was produced in 1936 but didn't reach the screen until now because nobody had the vitality to thread the projector. The movie has had a spinal tap.

[December 5, 1977]

Drip-Dry Comedy

The leering artwork in the ad for *Semi-Tough*, with Burt Reynolds and Kris Kristofferson, bare-chested, in backfield positions, reaching toward the rear ends of three crouching cuties, encourages people to believe that they're going to see a *Penthouse* version of Dan Jenkins' popular 1972 novel, an anecdotal burlesque about professional football players. The drawing, with its two famous men and the three anonymous women bending over for them, says that this is what big-time players do for entertainment. The three girls are lined up like utensils. (The extra girl provides the note of excess: orgy.) The implication is that they'd be delighted to do whatever these superstar football players wanted. It's a selling ad, all right; what it's selling isn't just tickets, though—it's also putting across the advertiser's view of us as porno-hungry slobs and, maybe, helping to make it true. It's a self-fulfilling insult. The book had an inoffensive, free-spirited raunchiness that this ad fouls—and that the movie doesn't come up to. As it turns out, the director, Michael Ritchie, and the screenwriter, Walter Bernstein, retained only Jenkins' title, some of his characters, and a few incidents, and the movie is a loose series of riffs on the human-potential, consciousness-raising movement.

Everybody except the hero, Billy Clyde Puckett (Reynolds), is into some quickie form of salvation or self-betterment. Shake Tiller (Kristofferson), Billy Clyde's close friend from childhood days in Texas, has just got the message from an organization called BEAT (a parody of est, it claims to have helped John Denver, Valerie Harper, and Joe Namath); the owner of the professional football team they play for practices Movagenics, which alleges that H. L. Hunt was a disciple, and requires giving part of each day to creeping and crawling on the floor like an infant; the captain of the opposing Super Bowl team believes in Pyramid Power; for others, there's Pelfing (a massage treatment, like Rolfing); and so on. Billy Clyde and Shake have been sharing a Miami apartment in a loving but nonsexual triangular union with Barbara Jane Bookman (Jill Clayburgh), the daughter of the owner. At the beginning of the movie, Barbara Jane, responding to the change in Shake wrought by BEAT—he radiates deep-dish confidence—begins to sleep with him, and they decide to get married. The romantic-comedy plot involves Shake's attempts to convert her to his new, ineffable contentment and Billy Clyde's sly, unobtrusive efforts to expose BEAT to her and keep her from getting married. What Barbara Jane is into is marriage. That's her cure-all, even though she's still a little shell-shocked from a couple of earlier matrimonial forays.

Semi-Tough is full of ideas—old and new—but it's so soft-pedal shaggy-cool it never draws us in. It assumes that we will find all the cults, fads, and systems a howl, and doesn't bother to point up what needs they fill. If the picture showed that the various self-realization organizations were geared to make people feel like winners and so, in some cases, become winners—even if that meant winning by being a bigger stinker or prig than anybody else—it might have a modern screwball-comedy breeziness to it. But we don't see anybody change; we never saw what Shake was like before he became convinced that he'd got his head together and started behaving as if he had superhuman powers. There's no comic contrast—no before and after. As the imperturbable Werner Erhard–like leader, the entrepreneurial show-biz singer Bert Convy might be Erhard's twin; Ritchie, though, seems to think that the physical and spiritual resemblance will suffice. And so there's no shock or hilarity in the two-day BEAT seminar that Shake enrolls Barbara Jane in. The moviemakers may feel that reproducing est's spiel is satire enough, but the film isn't crisp, like some of Ritchie's earlier work; there's no thematic drive to give tautness to his *cinéma vérité* doodles—the satiric aspects don't get anywhere. *Semi-Tough* ambles along in a sunshiny, woozy, hit-or-miss way. It's so loose it's visual Silly Putty, and the converts, salvation-seekers, and proselytizers like Shake are just amiably mush-minded.

It's not merely that *Semi-Tough* fails to dramatize its targets but that the alternative—Ritchie's and Bernstein's sportive conception of sanity—isn't nearly as scintillating as it's meant to be. Billy Clyde is the only person who isn't "taken in," and his sanity consists of jokiness, funny hats, and guessing the numbers on dollar bills. He's the madcap pragmatist who knows the value of frivolousness. Yet if he's not taken in, he doesn't give out, either. And there's a jeering, smart-ass quality to his put-on style which the film leaves suspended in the air—not judged, the way it judges everything else. (Reynolds already has the supreme confidence that Kristofferson's Shake is satirized for seeking.) Like thirties comedies, the movie believes in nonchalance. You mustn't express your feelings; they're true only if they're left unexpressed. Billy Clyde is secretly in love with Barbara Jane, but must win her without showing his cards.

Looking almost unbelievably fit, Reynolds wears boots, a giant silver belt buckle, a fine big ring, and a cowboy hat with a band of turquoise beads. He's neon-roadhouse macho perfection; what makes it possible for him to hold the picture in his open palm is that Billy Clyde, waiting on the sidelines for Barbara Jane to realize that it's not Shake she loves but him, has hurting eyes. So there's some depth of feeling below his banter, a poignance that helps to undercut the sleazy, cocky glibness. This isn't just another of Burt Reynolds' rakehell-bum roles: Billy Clyde is a good-ol'-boy Cary Grant. And Reynolds has the timing. He's swift and cagey—every gag line is super-casual, every inflection on the button. Probably no one could have been better than he was in that redneck fairy tale *W.W. and the Dixie Dancekings,* but it was crudely directed, and he was still being chased by a sheriff and using his beefy, childlike grin. In many ways, *Semi-Tough* is not as satisfying as the simpler *W.W.* was, but Michael Ritchie operates at a fairly high level of humor, and Reynolds gets a chance to show some class. He cuts down on his complicity with the audience—the tinny wink, the shrug. He knows that he can be less broad here and that we'll watch even more closely. Reynolds underplays so astutely that every line has a bevelled edge. He achieves a new grace and polish, but he's maybe less human than he was in *W.W.,* where you could see him working to keep the picture alive. He's got everything down so pat here—the trim muscularity, the velvety voice, the self-deprecating ease with which he projects his unspoken feelings about Barbara Jane—that the performance may fade from memory very quickly. There's not much juice in his Billy Clyde, though Reynolds is always fun to watch. He's convinced of his own charm; that's what carries his pictures. It's also the defect that limits him as an actor—it repels some people and may possibly frighten off directors.

But if he could ever strip off the rug—and the awareness of his public image that it represents—he might be great.

This whole film is set up to Reynolds' advantage—everybody else is a phony or a mark. There's never a moment when Kristofferson really seems to be in the movie. He doesn't suggest any connection with the world of pro football, and he and Reynolds are wrong for each other; it's a buddy marriage made in Hell. Kristofferson is still a novice actor, and, cast in the square, Ralph Bellamy role, he doesn't know how to use his pastoral, hairy-potato look to make us laugh when he's outwitted; he seems the stooge by inadvertence. You not only don't particularly like Kristofferson's chump-loser character—you can't find it. Jill Clayburgh comes considerably closer to holding her own with Reynolds. Barbara Jane seems to be convalescing from a nervous breakdown; she has that post-frazzled look. And she has an appealing soft and bewildered hyper quality, which plays off against Billy Clyde's shrewd calm. Barbara Jane is too bright and funny to succumb to the BEAT doubletalk; she's only a mark for men. Clayburgh doesn't have a very strong personality here; she doesn't have the precision of a Jean Arthur, yet she has some of that rueful, fluffy-in-the-head charm of someone whose brains are addled by her sexual impulses, and she adds the blur in the expression and those tremulous, zonky eyes. You can see why men with stewardesses and models available to them would still long for her: she's peering at them from a hazy distance, wistfully.

Football doesn't occupy much time in *Semi-Tough*—it's confined to a few montages of games and some locker-room pranks. The games are deliberate muddy chaos, like the ones in *The Bad News Bears,* which Ritchie also directed. But here he edits so fast that it's clear he doesn't want us to be involved in who wins, or even who's playing. That's understandable: once he decided to throw out Jenkins' book and go for consciousness-movement satire, that dictated his choices. The decision was probably a mistake, though: the material here is not as comically rich as Jenkins' novel, which Ritchie should have been just the right director for. Looking for a bigger subject, he found a smaller one. What's puzzling is that he clips most of the consciousness satire too short, too; frowzy, funny scenes flash by almost subliminally, as if he didn't want to give them enough time to pay off. They're so fast they become almost private jokes. And they don't develop out of the Miami settings, either. Location is part of the essence of American satire, and something like est doesn't take off from Florida, it takes off from California. Ritchie's beauty-pageant satire, *Smile,* had the advantage of a stable, West Coast–town location; the atmosphere felt right. Except for a scene at a Ramada Inn in Green Bay, *Semi-Tough* is highly confusing from moment to moment in terms of where the action is taking place, and that adds to the flighty, nothing-sinks-in style. The film has football characters in an undeveloped *Design for Living* situation jammed into a social satire they seem unrelated to, even by place.

There may be a further touch of perversity in the way the film lingers on its two worst scenes. In one, a prissy, sleek Ivy League publisher defends the role of the intellectual while Billy Clyde baits him; in the other, Billy Clyde accepts the bedroom services of a desperately aggressive heavyset woman who's so self-conscious she's pathetic. We can't tell what Ritchie and Walter Bernstein are going after in these scenes; here (and elsewhere) we can't always psych out what we're supposed to laugh with from what we're supposed to laugh at. And sometimes we don't know how to interpret Billy Clyde—for example, does he decide to write a book only to impress Barbara Jane? How are we to take his only partly facetious remark that "a writer can't be partying around like this—a writer has to be dedicated to his work"? Bernstein has an affectionate memory, stocked with romantic movie devices, but, from the sound of the dialogue, he could do with less work and some partying. Somehow, with Reynolds and about twenty minutes of bits that you catch out of the corner of your eye, the movie survives all its wrongheadedness.

Michael Ritchie has a true comedy gift: he's got a visual slapstick sense, and only a few directors have it—Blake Edwards, Robert Altman, Brian De Palma, Bertrand Blier, Marco Ferreri, Ettore Scola, maybe Jonathan Demme, not many more. Ritchie leaves people to get his humor on their own, though. This laid-back attitude gives his improvisational, camera-seized gags a special, tickling surprise, but on the written, fully staged gags—where the director and the actors need to be in there, with vaudeville timing—he's still laid back. And so when Big Ed Bookman, the Movagenics freak (Robert Preston), comes in for his morning crawl around his office, entering on all fours through what looks like a swinging door for a kitty, we know we should be laughing, but we aren't. The same thing happens when Lotte Lenya appears as Clara Pelf and demonstrates her muscle-moving Pelfing, and again when a girl at the BEAT seminar gets up with a glowing face to share with the others and announces, "I peed in my pants and it feels good." *Semi-Tough* keeps veering between offhand slapstick and these failed broad effects, and it doesn't settle right.

Ritchie's *The Candidate* was shallow, smugly cynical, yet his technique gave it a triumphant freshness; despite what it said politically, viscerally it was a real up. There's a liveness, a presentness, in all of Ritchie's films. Even when his material is as pasted together as it is here, he knows enough flip tricks to keep one interested. What he doesn't know is how to keep a sequence going, building, achieving something. *Semi-Tough* lacks the overriding spirit to carry an audience through to a really good time; Ritchie's comedy doesn't go deep enough—he uses a wedding brawl to fake a big-bang climax. At some level, this hip, detached manner becomes anti-comedic. Ritchie is so cooled down he's blowing Valium dust through the vents. Even the score—a series of Gene Autry songs—is stone tranquil. Big Ed Bookman is supposed to be a Gene Autry fan, and the three

362

buddies, parodying Big Ed, play Autry records and decorate their apartment with posters for his old films. *Semi-Tough* uses Autry's cowboy sentimentality—the warm-margarine voice and down-home lyrics—for camp. But this awareness seems Ritchie's, not the characters', and the atmosphere is so easy here anyway that the only humor wrung out of Autry is a tinhorn double-entendre on his "Back in the Saddle Again." The film is like a low-grade fever—you slip in and out of it painlessly.

[December 12, 1977]

Cutting Light

The great thing about Luis Buñuel's *That Obscure Object of Desire* is that it gives you the feeling that it was made by a happy man. The film was shot in Seville and Paris, and Buñuel's happiness shines especially in the luxuriance of Seville. This city is like an older, more southern, Mediterranean San Francisco; the surfaces shimmer, and the film is almost pink with happiness. The feeling that permeates *That Obscure Object of Desire* is that for Buñuel now life is more important than art. It is for everybody, maybe, but when artists are raging—straining to express themselves—they don't feel that way. Buñuel no longer has any trouble expressing himself: art has become simple for him, as it did for Matisse in his later years, with his cut-and-pasted papers. What Buñuel is expressing is his own pleasure in his command of the medium: he's at peace with himself, and art has become pure play for him. This has never happened in movies before: no one Buñuel's age (seventy-seven) has gone on making personal films, on material of his own choice.

"Cutting to the quick in color reminds me of the sculptor's direct carving," Matisse said. He had found a freedom he'd always wanted, and some of his late cutouts may be as good as anything he ever did: shallow great art. Though lighter, less palpable than the paintings, these cutouts have an energetic physical roughness, because of the scissors. They're airy—never static. Buñuel broke through with his buoyant late style in *The Discreet Charm of the Bourgeoisie* (1972). All the gloom, the cruelty, the outraged idealist's harshness seemed to have been transcended, and it was his humor that remained—that, and his moviemaking technique, which magically became almost weightless, yet with a storyteller's energy, uncomplicated, without fuss or pressure. Some men grow embittered as they age, but Buñuel got his bitterness out early on, and in old age he began to have a marvellous time, using what he'd learned. His films began to be set in his own period—a floating timelessness.

The Discreet Charm of the Bourgeoisie (made when he was seventy-two) had the surprise of relaxed virtuosity, as if he'd just discovered, at last, how to make movies, by a new, ironically matter-of-fact, thin-textured method—the visual equivalent of simple declarative sentences. His Surrealist vaudevillian's sense of parody had become more delicately precise, and his indifference to dramatic logic was total; the "sentences" might contradict and destroy each other. He showed this detached utter sureness of style again in 1974, in *Le Fantôme de la Liberté*, and he shows it now in *That Obscure Object*. But if age can give you a serenity that isn't available to youth, it also takes something away. There's a price you pay for serenity. *That Obscure Object* is far more pleasing than *Le Fantôme* was, but it's a little monotonous, and if the anti-bourgeois, anti-institutional jokes aren't exactly predictable, still one laughs not because they're funny but because one recognizes that they're distinctively Buñuelian—they have the cadence of Buñuel's wit.

The style of the film is peerlessly urbane; it moves along at a raconteur's pace as Mathieu (Fernando Rey), a rich, worldly French widower of perhaps fifty, boards the Seville-to-Paris train and makes the acquaintance of the other passengers in his first-class compartment. He seems a cultivated man, perfectly self-controlled, but before the train leaves Seville he dumps a bucket of water on a battered young woman who attempts to come on board, and seems rather pleased with himself. Observing that his travelling companions are nonplussed, he explains that she is "the worst of all women," and during the journey he entertains them with the story of why he drenched the terrible Conchita, whom he first met when she was hired as a maid in his home in Paris, and whom, over the years, he has supported, and even lived with, but never won. In *The Discreet Charm of the Bourgeoisie,* a group of people were never able to eat a meal; the film proceeded by interruptions. In *That Obscure Object,* Mathieu is never able to consummate sex with Conchita. She alternates between promises and postponements: she teases him, fleeces him, enrages him. She offers herself to him and then comes to bed armored in intricately laced heavy-canvas drawers; Conchita frustrates Mathieu to tears of exhaustion—and he loves her. The ambiguous element is that she also claims to love him, but says, "If I gave in, you wouldn't love me anymore." Is she really denying him because she loves him? This could be her gambit; it could be the truth.

That Obscure Object is the fifth movie version of Pierre Louÿs' short novel about a femme fatale, *La Femme et le Pantin,* published in 1898. It was filmed in 1920, starring Geraldine Farrar, again in 1929, with Conchita

Montenegro, and again in 1935, when Josef von Sternberg made the most famous version, *The Devil Is a Woman,* starring Marlene Dietrich. Buñuel wanted to do the story in the late fifties, but the producer and he disagreed about both the treatment and the star; the producer wanted Brigitte Bardot, who ultimately did the film—*A Woman Like Satan* (1958)—with Julien Duvivier directing. Buñuel got back to it when his style—and his outlook—had grown beyond it. The movie that Buñuel might have made in the late fifties would surely have been more provocatively irrational, more *animal* than the film he has made now. In the sixties, when he made *Belle de Jour,* he still had a dirty, sadistic, funny streak; if he had filmed the Louÿs story then, we might have felt a mean glee when Conchita taunts this rich, refined old goat who has everything in life he wants except her. But the runaround that Conchita gives Mathieu in *That Obscure Object* doesn't have much libidinal impact; repressed material doesn't poke up to startle us. The special quality of Buñuel's late, storyteller's style is that there are no layers, nothing hidden; that's what makes it so serene.

Buñuel has modernized the story; he has set it in a world askew, where the old forms and courtesies persist—appearances still count—and terrorist explosions are casual happenings. When Mathieu is out in his limousine, his discreet, correct valet (André Weber) sits up front next to the chauffeur; the class relationships are intact, though no one is surprised when a car in front of them is booby-trapped—revolutionary acts are just one of the inconveniences of city life. The film is randomly punctuated with muggings, bombings, hijackings, murders. The initials of the illegal organizations are sexual acronyms, and the blasts that these groups set off are the only orgasms poor Mathieu ever gets near. Yet these Surreal touches don't detonate the emotions in the Mathieu-Conchita tangle; they seem part of another game. Buñuel's deftness at amusing himself was just right for the social satire of *The Discreet Charm*—no passions were involved. Here the tone is satirical, though the subject is passion. The tone suggests that Conchita is simply taking this lordly boulevardier for a grand ride—that her putting him in bondage is the revenge of the poor on the rich, and of women on men. But the idea of the mysterious unknowability of women (it was hot stuff in silent pictures) still clings to the story.

The psychological weakness of the script (and this was a problem in the von Sternberg version, too) is that Conchita is seen totally from the man's point of view—there's no clue to what her actual feelings are. Since Conchita is a literary conceit—a deliberately unresolved character—the part requires an actress who can capture our imaginations and tease us, as she teases Mathieu. Buñuel had cast Maria Schneider in the role, but they severed relations after a few days of shooting and he decided to fill the part with two actresses—Carole Bouquet, a tall French girl, and Angela Molina, a Spanish girl, who's shorter, more rounded—plus a third woman to speak the French dialogue for both of them. (Fernando Rey is dubbed by Michel Piccoli.) The script, by Buñuel and his collaborator, Jean-Claude Carrière, shows no sign of having been rewritten to take advantage of the stunt of using the two women as one; perhaps there wasn't time. There's no interplay of qualities or gestures; they simply shift interchangeably, with their natural characteristics providing some contrast. Bouquet, who's like an angular, sly Ali MacGraw, is poker-faced, except for a squint of amusement and a foxy, crooked smear of a smile. She's the more tantalizing, modern Conchita, while Molina is physically impulsive, and sensual in a traditional heaving and weeping, heavy-eyed way. Using the two actresses doesn't add any meaning; perhaps there's less than if there were only one. We have to believe that Mathieu sees something extraordinarily erotic in Conchita (even if we don't); we have to believe in his passion, or else the basic love tragedy isn't funny. And with these two women ducking in and out as if they were playing charades, Mathieu's relationship to Conchita seems to depend on which actress will turn up in the next shot.

Fernando Rey is probably the most believable man of the world in contemporary movies; even the tilt of his hat here is a rotting signal of wealth and breeding. And so when Mathieu, in his finely tailored leisure clothes, is seen to pick up a burlap sack and carry it on his back like a hump, the audience laughs. But it's not because this sack has any resonance in the film—the resonance is in our memories of other enigmatic tricks, in other Buñuel films. Buñuel's Surreal tomfoolery—sprinkling his films with disconnected jokes—has become a trademark, and one could almost take this aspect of *That Obscure Object* as self-homage; it suggests a variant form of what turns up more heavily and blatantly in Hitchcock's late films. It isn't self-homage: it's simply that Buñuel has the same turn of mind he has always had, though without the violence underneath to make the connections for us. The gags seem reprises rather than originals because they're not shocking. He sets up the Louÿs story, then treats it glancingly—as a joke to hang other jokes on. All his films are cosmic comedies now; it's not expression that he seeks but play—the entertainment of the senses.

Here is a master, for whom every shot is a demonstration of joyous ease—like Matisse picking up his scissors and cutting light. Working without waste or calculation, Buñuel makes films more directly—from inside himself to up there on the screen—than perhaps anyone else ever has. His technique has become so direct that he seems freed from technique, and the effect is of supreme clarity. But now that he has sprung past all the technological hurdles, what themes can he find that will be at one with his new freedom? The projects that were once wickedly alluring are no longer worthy of him. The wholeness of spirit that informs *That Obscure Object of Desire* outshines the story; the artist delights us even as the film disappoints us.

There is a special affection that moviegoers have for Luis Buñuel—not just because of our familiarity with his films (that can work against him, as it does in places in *That Obscure Object*) but because in an industry that rewards sentimentality he's kept his no-slobbering, disenchanted attitude. And so when enchantment floods in on him it has a clean radiance. The light of Seville is very soft here.

[December 19, 1977]

Nirvana

There is a thick, raw sensuality that some adolescents have which seems almost preconscious. In *Saturday Night Fever*, John Travolta has this rawness to such a degree that he seems naturally exaggerated: an Expressionist painter's view of a young prole. As Tony, a nineteen-year-old Italian Catholic who works selling paint in a hardware store in Brooklyn's Bay Ridge, he wears his heavy black hair brushed up in a blower-dried pompadour. His large, wide mouth stretches across his narrow face, and his eyes—small slits, close together—are, unexpectedly, glintingly blue and panicky. Walking down the street in his blood-red shirt, skintight pants, and platform soles, Tony moves to the rhythm of the disco music in his head. It's his pent-up physicality—his needing to dance, his becoming himself only when he dances—that draws us into the pop rapture of this film. In his room in his parents' cramped house, he begins the ritual of Saturday night: shaving, deodorizing, putting on gold chains with a cross and amulets and charms, selecting immaculate flashy tight clothes. The rhythm is never lost—he's away in his dream until he's caught in a bickering scene at the family dinner table. He leaves his home; his friends pick him up on the street, and then they're off to the dream palace—2001 Odyssey—where Tony, who is recognized as the champion dancer, is king.

Inside the giant disco hall, the young working-class boys and girls, recent high-school graduates who plod through their jobs all week, saving up for this night, give themselves over to the music. Sharing an erotic and aesthetic fantasy, they dance the L.A. Hustle ceremonially, in patterned ranks—a mass of dancers unified by the beat, stepping together in trancelike discipline. Suggested by Nik Cohn's June 7, 1976, *New York* cover story, "Tribal Rites of the New Saturday Night," this movie has a new subject matter: how the financially pinched seventies generation that grew up on TV attempts to find its own forms of beauty and release. The Odyssey itself (the picture was shot in the actual Bay Ridge hall) has a plastic floor and suggests a TV-commercial version of Art Deco; the scenes there are vividly romantic, with the dancers in their brightest, showiest clothes, and the lights blinking in burning neon-rainbow colors, and the percolating music of the Bee Gees. The way *Saturday Night Fever* has been directed and shot, we feel the languorous pull of the discothèque, and the gaudiness is transformed. These are among the most hypnotically beautiful pop dance scenes ever filmed.

The director, John Badham, who is in his thirties, has made only one previous film, *The Bingo Long Traveling All-Stars and Motor Kings*, but he's well known for his work in television (*The Law* is probably his most impressive credit). The son of an English actress, Mary Hewitt, Badham grew up in Alabama, where his mother had her own TV talk show; his younger sister Mary played Gregory Peck's daughter in *To Kill a Mockingbird*. He went on to Yale, where he, the lyricist Richard Maltby, Jr., and the composer David Shire (who worked on the score of this picture) are reported to have been fervently devoted to putting on musicals, and he has staged *Saturday Night Fever* with a flowing movement that makes it far more of a sustained dance film than *The Turning Point*. When the patrons of the Odyssey clear the floor for Tony and he does a solo, he's a happy young rooster crowing in dance. And Badham, working with the choreographer Lester Wilson, the editor David Rawlins, and the cinematographer Ralf D. Bode, has designed this number so that it's as smoothly seductive to us as to the onlookers. There's no dead break between the rhythmed sequences at the Odyssey and the scenes when Tony is in hamburger joints with his friends, or at a dance studio with Stephanie (Karen Lynn Gorney), the girl who's "different" from the other dancers, or on trips to the Verrazano-Narrows Bridge or, later, to Manhattan. These, too, have their musical beat—and are scored to songs by the Bee Gees and other groups, or to Walter Murphy's variations on Beethoven's Fifth, or to Shire's "Salsation" or his Gershwin-like "Manhattan Skyline." The film's sustained disco beat keeps the audience in an empathic rhythm with the characters: we're physically attuned to their fear of being trapped—of losing the beat.

It's a straight heterosexual film, but with a feeling for the sexiness of young boys who are bursting their britches with energy and desire—who want to *go*—which recalls Kenneth Anger's short film *Scorpio Rising* (1963). Anger celebrated the youth and sexuality and love of speed of motorcycle gangs while mocking their fetishistic trappings—the swastikas and black leather and chains that they used to simulate fearlessness. Those boys lived in a homoerotic fantasy of toughness, and their idols were James Dean and Brando, as the motorcyclist in *The Wild One*. The boys in

Saturday Night Fever have more traditional desires, though in a new, pop form. Their saint is Al Pacino—the boy like them who became somebody without denying who he was. When Tony looks in the mirror, it's Pacino he wants to see, and he keeps Pacino's picture on his wall. (He also has posters of Bruce Lee, of Farrah Fawcett-Majors, and of Sylvester Stallone and Talia Shire in *Rocky*.) It's not just that Pacino is for the Bay Ridge boys what Brando was for their parents; Brando represented the rebellious antithesis of the conventional heroes of his time, while Pacino stands alone. These boys are part of the post-Watergate working-class generation with no heroes *except* in TV-show-biz land; they have a historical span of twenty-three weeks, with repeats at Christmas.

The script was written by Norman Wexler (*Joe, Serpico, Mandingo, Drum*), and it has his urban-crazy-common-man wit—the jokes that double back on the people who make them. And Badham's kinetic style, which shows the characters' wavering feelings and gives a lilt to their conversations (especially those between Tony and Stephanie), removes the ugliness from Wexler's cruder scenes; the comedy is often syncopated. But Norman Wexler can't seem to keep his mind on anything for long; you never wait more than four scenes for any issue to be resolved, and then he hops off to something else. The picture is like flash cards: it keeps announcing its themes and then replacing them. Trying for conventional family conflicts, it wanders into a deadening subplot about Tony's older brother—a priest who has lost his vocation—which is only a cut above "All in the Family." Trying for "action," it brings in a gang rumble, with unwelcome echoes of *West Side Story,* and when one of Tony's friends dies (for no more substantial reason than to strengthen Tony's moral fiber), the episode throws the whole last part of the picture off course. Yet the mood, the beat, and the trance rhythm are so purely entertaining and Travolta is such an original presence that a viewer spins past these weaknesses.

John Travolta doesn't appear to be a "natural" dancer: his dances look like worked-up Broadway routines, but he gives himself to them with a fullness and zest that make his being the teen-agers' king utterly convincing. He commands the dance space at the Odyssey, and when the other dancers fall back to watch him it's because he's joyous to watch. He *acts* like someone who loves to dance. And, more than that, he acts like someone who loves to act. It's getting to be a joke—another Italian-American star. *Saturday Night Fever* is only Travolta's second movie (he was the Neanderthal beer-guzzling Billy in *Carrie*); he has become a teen and pre-teen favorite as Vinnie Barbarino in the "Welcome Back, Kotter" TV series, though, and in his one previous starring appearance, in the TV movie *The Boy in the Plastic Bubble,* he gave the character an abject, humiliated sensitivity that made the boy seem emotionally naked. One can read Travolta's face and body; he has the gift of transparency. When he wants us to feel how lost and confused Tony is, we feel it. He expresses shades of emotion that aren't set down in scripts, and he knows how to show us the decency and intelligence under Tony's uncouthness. Tony's mouth may look uneducated—pulpy, swollen-lipped, slack—but this isn't stupidity, it's bewilderment. Travolta gets so far inside the role he seems incapable of a false note; even the Brooklyn accent sounds unerring. At twenty-three, he's done enough to make it apparent that there's a broad distance between him and Tony, and that it's an actor's imagination that closes the gap. There's dedication in his approach to Tony's character; he isn't just a good actor, he's a generous-hearted actor.

Playing opposite him, Karen Lynn Gorney, whose facial style is as tense and hard as his is fluid and open, has a rough time at first. The story, unfortunately, introduces Stephanie in *West Side Story* lyrical terms as the wonderful dancer Tony wants to meet, and Gorney isn't much of a dancer. She's proficient—she can go through the motions—but the body is holding back. So the film overworks soft-lighting effects. It takes a while before it's clear that Stephanie is a little climber and show-off—a Brooklyn girl who gives herself airs and talks about the important people she comes into contact with in her office job in Manhattan. Her pretensions to refinement are desperately nippy and high-pitched. (She's reminiscent of the girl Margaret Sullavan played in *The Shop Around the Corner*.) She's a phony (Tony spots that), but with a drive inside her that isn't phony (he spots that, too). As the role is written, this girl is split into so many pieces she doesn't come across as one person; you like her and you don't, and back and forth. You can't quite figure out whether it's the character or the actress that you're not sure about until Gorney wins you over by her small, harried, tight face and her line readings, which are sometimes miraculously edgy and ardent. The determined, troubled Stephanie, who's taking college courses to improve herself, is an updated version of those working girls that Ginger Rogers used to play (as in *Having Wonderful Time*). The surprising thing is that Stephanie's climbing isn't put down; in a sense, the picture is a celebration of individual climbing, as a way out of a futureless squalor.

You feel great watching this picture, even if it doesn't hold in the mind afterward, the way it would if the story had been defined. The script attempts to be faithful to the new, scrimping, dutiful teen-agers, who never knew the sixties affluence or what the counterculture was all about; for them maturity means what it traditionally meant—leaving home and trying to move ahead in the world. Once again in movies, Manhattan beckons as the magic isle of opportunity—not ironically but with the old Gershwin spirit. The awkwardness is in treating Tony as a character in passage from boyhood to maturity. The script drops the dancing, as if it were part of what Tony has to grow out of. But the dancing has functioned as a metaphor for what is driving him on to Manhattan, not what he's leaving behind. There is a happy going-to-the promised-land, boy-gets-girl ending, yet it misplaces Tony's soul, so it doesn't feel as up as it should. At its best, though, *Saturday Night Fever* gets at something deeply romantic: the need to move, to dance, and the need to be who you'd like to be. Nirvana is the dance; when the music stops, you return to being ordinary.

[December 26, 1977]

Fear of Heights

The congregating of the ravens and crows on the jungle gym in *The Birds* is ominously funny—it's a joke. When pigeons gather on a jungle gym in Mel Brooks' *High Anxiety,* it's just a rehash of Hitchcock's joke. Restaging some of Hitchcock's most famous thriller effects, Mel Brooks seems to be under the impression that he's adding a satirical point of view, but it's a child's idea of satire: imitation, with a funny hat and a leer. Hitchcock's suspense melodramas are sparked by his perverse wit; they're satirical to start with. Brooks replaces the wit with romping and yelling and yocks; now the birds spatter him, and one perches on his head. After Woody Allen used a movie-related theme in *Play It Again, Sam,* he moved on. Brooks went from burlesquing Westerns in *Blazing Saddles* to burlesquing mad-scientist / monster films in *Young Frankenstein.* That was a classic of crazy comedy, and he should have dropped genre parody then; for one thing, his disciples, Gene Wilder and Marty Feldman, were crowding into the same manhole. But he stayed in there for more Hollywood spoofery in *Silent Movie,* and now it's *High Anxiety* and Hitchcock. He's making a career out of travesties of old movies. At the rate he's going, with plans being discussed for *Bombs Away!,* a takeoff of Second World War movies, and for a Busby Berkeley or an Esther Williams send-up, the one after that will be *The Birth of a Nation.*

Mel Brooks grabs us by the lapels and screams into our faces, "Laugh! It's funny!" The open secret of his comedy is that his material isn't necessarily funny—it's being grabbed by the lapels that makes us laugh. (It's being grabbed by the lapels that makes us stop laughing, too.) Brooks has never been accused of being a director with a light touch; he has never needed one more than in *High Anxiety.* Brooks plays the central role of Dr. Richard H. Thorndyke, a Nobel Prize–winning psychiatrist, who arrives at the Los Angeles airport and is accosted by a homosexual exhibitionist and then greeted by a buffoon (Ron Carey) who announces, "I'm Brophy. I work at the institute. I came to pick you up. I'm going to be your driver and sidekick." Dr. Thorndyke is the new director of the Psycho-Neurotic Institute for the Very, *Very* Nervous—the previous one having died suddenly. The picture hasn't been on ten minutes but you've already had a sample of its kiddie-comics hyperbole, its cheesy casting, and the reflexive use of elderly jokes—all of which keep *High Anxiety* from making parodistic connections with Hitchcock's style, which is based on exaggerated situations but also on the performers' scrupulously controlled reactions.

As an actor, Brooks is proudest of his stunt of impersonating smoothies and swells—the sort of people who would consider Mel Brooks a manic vulgarian. You're conscious of the pleasure he takes in any dress-up sham. His Dr. Thorndyke is like a felon posing as a dapper college dean—the campus dandy. He wears a fedora with the brim turned down, and three-piece suits with a chain across the midriff and his Phi Beta Kappa key dangling right above the navel. With his chin tilted up, the better to acknowledge the obeisance of those he meets, he strolls in a modified lope that has just the faintest suggestion of Jack Benny's undulation. Brooks has prepared the accoutrements of a suavely comic character, but only the accoutrements, and Dr. Thorndyke quickly lapses into the standard Brooks character: a Jewish hobbit who behaves like a pickpocket. Despite the settings, and in a film full of psychiatrists, there's no satire of analytic attitudes. When Dr. Thorndyke leaves the *Spellbound* situation at the institute and goes up to San Francisco for a psychiatrists' convention, and into locations that recall *Vertigo,* Brophy accompanies him, delivering lines such as "Doc! Doc! Why did you do it? Why did you do it?" Brophy may be the single most unredeemed creation that Brooks has ever foisted on us: with his dialogue stamped out by a ditto machine, Brophy keeps boring us twice. And the way Ron Carey (of the "Barney Miller" TV series) acts the part, he and Brooks bring out the worst in each other. If a relentless slugger like Ron Carey were cast against a beautiful fighter, it might be an entertaining contest, but with Carey up against another slugger he has to keep punching harder, and you end up hating him.

The whole film suffers from the bad judgment that goes with cronyism. Dick Van Patten, who plays the round-cheeked simp Dr. Wentworth, a psychiatrist who's murdered in his car (in the ugliest, most misconceived sequence), overacts flaccidly—a type of overacting that produces a visceral rejection. (It's like seeing something and suddenly remembering that you have an upset stomach.) The film is full of the kind of performers who need to have a director say no to them, but Brooks likes them too much to restrain them. He doesn't seem to understand that they make us feel queasy. Most of the bad acting here isn't amateurish or unintentional, it's willfully overscaled. Brooks trusts his own excess completely and thinks that all kinds of excess are to be encouraged. That's his notion of stretching. He has cast his three writing associates—Rudy DeLuca, Ron Clark, and Barry Levinson (the team that also collaborated with him on *Silent Movie*)—in acting parts, and Levinson's shrill, clamorous performance as a bellboy wrecks the tone of the best-prepared gag in the movie, a twist on the shower scene in *Psycho*.

High Anxiety is dedicated to Hitchcock as "the master of suspense," and it doesn't have a whisper of suspense. It doesn't operate on any level except that of bumbling slapstick farce, where most of the custard pies miss their targets. The plot—a generous term for it—involves Madeline Kahn as Victoria Brisbane, whose father, an industrialist, has been imprisoned in the institute and is threatened with death. The villains are a masochistic doctor (Harvey Korman) and his sadistic paramour, the heel-clicking Nurse Diesel (Cloris Leachman), who's built like a menacing Nazi Barbie doll. Her breasts point up in a *"Sieg heil!"* salute, and she talks tough, through twisted lips, growling like Lionel Barrymore in *Duel in the Sun*. (It sounds as if she were rinsing her clenched teeth.) Nurse Diesel might be great in a blackout sketch, but she's too much like Leachman's Frau Blücher from *Young Frankenstein,* and once again the joke wears down. As the heroine, Madeline Kahn doesn't exist as a character; we never for a minute believe that Thorndyke and this girl in the long blond wig are meeting for the first time. Kahn seems to be in the movie because she's a friend of the family; she's taken for granted, like a regular in a TV series. How can *High Anxiety* be a parody of Hitchcock when nothing is at stake? The plot has no momentum, and we don't even see the endangered industrialist until the end. (He is called Arthur Brisbane, which was the name of Hearst's most famous columnist—an inside un-joke.)

Trying to stay within Hitchcock's frame of reference, Brooks loses his own anarchic way of thinking, and his imagination dries up. He drags in the phrase "north by northwest" and brings in a Mr. MacGuffin—as if just mentioning them were funny. He shoots a scene on the exact spot where part of *Vertigo* was filmed and assumes that our recognition of the spot constitutes a victory for him. He wants a laurel wreath for giving us a movie quiz. We sit there and tot up the score. This bit is from *Rebecca*. Oh, now he's going outside Hitchcock—this is *The Cobweb,* this is *Blow-Up*. The point of a satire of movies would be for the satirist to take something we've seen and show us that he had seen something more in it. All Brooks does is let us know he has seen some of the same movies we have. The most buoyant sequence in the picture has no connection with Hitchcock. Brooks is in a crowded piano bar with Madeline Kahn when the guests are invited to sing. He takes the microphone and delivers the title song; in a parody of Frank Sinatra's hyper-nonchalant tête-à-tête manner, he breaks up words into sizzling syllables, and moves about, tossing the mike cord from side to side and snapping it like a whip. This natty, sophisticated parodist Brooks steals his own movie, and afterward the gags about Hitchcock seem even worse.

If someone else sounded like Mel Brooks, you might think that rotgut liquor was what did it, or that his vocal cords had survived a rock slide; with Mel Brooks, you assume it's because he has been conducting a vocal reign of terror. Reading interviews with him is a prime comic experience, because you can hear the ecstatic hoarseness, the strangled shouts, the headiness of our greatest self-entertainer. Most people who enjoy their own jokes are a pain, but Brooks is so over-the-border effusive he's disarming. Off the screen, that is—on talk shows or in print. How can one resist his compulsive shamelessness—that demonic peppy kid in him who can't shut up? That kid would break up the Sermon on the Mount. In the movies, it's different. Brooks was half asleep in *Silent Movie*—"endearing" rather than funny. He wanted the public to take him onto its collective lap. In *High Anxiety,* the H. in Richard H. Thorndyke turns out to stand for Harpo, and when Brooks forgets about suavity and does openmouthed double takes he's so Harpo-lovable he seems ready to drag in a harp and favor us with a semiclassical interlude.

In a *Playboy* interview in February of 1975, Mel Brooks described the anxiety that sent him to an analyst when he was still in his twenties. He called it "fear of heights," but from his description it wasn't the kind of vertigo that Thorndyke suffers from; it was the fear in a boy who had grown up poor suddenly finding himself making $5,000 a week as a gagwriter on "Your Show of Shows" and terrified that his success was "unreal" and wouldn't last, that he would come down. Now that Brooks makes as much as $5,000,000 on a picture, is the fear even greater?

The timing in Mel Brooks' pictures has always been hit-'em-over-the-head obvious, and the cutting from one character to another is jabbing-at-the-audience cutting. His movies have a crude, mistimed, infantile feeling because they have no visual fluency; he doesn't edit for visual flow—he edits only to give emphasis to the words and gags. With this technique, he has never got subtle, off-center effects; for a joke to work, he really has to bowl us over. That rarely happens in *High Anxiety,* and so one may be very conscious of actors making faces and of a desperate pushiness in the editing. Some people, of course, having been television-trained, respond to the jabbing itself—to the technique that is a director's equivalent of lapel clutching. If something is tagged funny, there's a pretty fair chance they'll laugh. Maybe in advance: there's a built-in familiarity that makes it possible for the fans of a successful TV series to laugh before the gag happens—and in order to keep a series going the writers, producers, and directors learn how to feed this familiarity. That's what Brooks does. Movie audiences have begun to think that Mel Brooks is funny because he's Mel Brooks, and they can laugh at *High Anxiety* because if it weren't funny Mel Brooks wouldn't be in it. Brooks' directing manner says "I dare you not to laugh." And he does have a special knack (it may be unconscious): he manages to space the few good jokes so that some people get the idea that they've been laughing continuously.

The trained laughers are now Brooks' audience—the people in Des Moines who will, he claimed in a recent interview in the *Village Voice,* respond mightily to the bondage scene, with Harvey Korman in chains pleading with Cloris Leachman to spank him. When movie directors and performers start comparing the reactions of the audiences in what Brooks called "the smart houses on the East Side" with those of the real people out there in Des Moines who will love their picture, they've had it. Actually, the "smart" audiences watch TV, too, and are getting closer to "Des Moines" all the time. What "Des Moines" really stands for is people whose expectations have been scaled downward, and is making us one nation indivisible in the worst way. (How else explain the widespread success of *Blazing Saddles,* which is just dirty TV?) Brooks may be right about *High Anxiety*—it may well snowball at box offices. (Jerry Lewis snowballed for a while, too.) What it comes down to is that the snob audience exists now only in the minds of anxious directors who know they're not doing their best work—who are consciously aiming at the TV-conditioned audience.

Is Brooks actually much interested in Hitchcock? There's neither love nor malice in the imitations here. (If you're not going to get away with using someone else's material, you dedicate the movie to your source.) There was nostalgic affection for burlesque houses and B movies and early radio in Brooks' *The Twelve Chairs,* and there was an original, Brooksian finesse—a wild man's finesse—in the zest of the musical numbers in *The Producers* ("Springtime for Hitler") and *Blazing Saddles* ("I get no kick from champagne") and *Young Frankenstein* ("Puttin' on the Ritz"). The best scene in *Silent Movie*—Burt Reynolds narcissistically soaping his prime-cut body and turning into the god Siva—was also the most controlled scene. Brooks' high points are always rhythmed, stylized routines. When he jumps up in the piano bar here, you can feel that he's momentarily liberated from the master of suspense. He's entering his own frame of reference. When he and Madeline Kahn start to talk in vaudeville patter in a scene at the San Francisco airport and he does a ziggy little walk, he's in his element. The joyousness in his feeling for show business bursts forth in his "acts" and his musical numbers; his lyrics are genuine parodies, and the stylized routines have a grace that's missing from most of his work. Couldn't Brooks do something that would stand on its own feet—a modern satirical musical comedy? He might even manage to make it a *light* farce. If he needs a theme, there are dozens of possible variations on success and celebrity. How about a rich, unimaginably successful comic who's so afraid he'll lose the public if he tries something new that he loses it by doing the same thing over and over?

[January 9, 1978]

Regressions

Movie executives are eagerly ushering in "the era of good feeling," but the warmth doesn't go very deep—it feels like Eisenhower II. During the showing of *The Goodbye Girl,* a tearful comedy directed by Herbert Ross from Neil Simon's script, a friend and I sat in stony silence, listening to the weepers and the laughers in the audience. Afterward, I said, "I don't want to maul the same person over and over again, but Neil Simon is so damned prolific." My friend assured me that I didn't need to; he said that the people who went to see *The Goodbye Girl* would like it, and the ones who wouldn't would know enough not to go. But it hasn't worked out that way. The film has been around for a while now and is making some of the people who go to it angry.

It's not Neil Simon's one-liners that get you down in *The Goodbye Girl,* it's his two-liners. The snappiness of the exchanges is so forced it's almost macabre. Marsha Mason plays Paula McFadden, a thirtyish former chorus girl who has been deserted by an actor husband and then by an actor lover, and has become so defensive that she's hostile toward a new actor, Elliott Garfield (Richard Dreyfuss), who, through circumstances too contrived to be worth recounting, comes to share the apartment she and her ten-year-old daughter (Quinn Cummings) live in. Paula says gratuitously abrasive things to him; he won't let her get by with a thing; and they go back and forth. His position is the more reasonable, but as Dreyfuss plays him he's a smug pouter pigeon prissing his lips, and his ornate put-downs come rattling out like prescriptions. Of course, you have to say these Neil Simon lines very fast (unless you try saying them in Urdu). Pause for an instant, and there's a cavernous emptiness. This material was written directly for the screen (and shaped for Mason and Dreyfuss), yet when the actress who plays the building super takes an instant too long over an exclamation, it's like the agony in a live performance when an actor forgets his lines—a pause like the end of the world. Irritability provides the rhythm in Neil Simon's universe, and if you don't find this funny you may begin to feel a prickly resentment. Paula and Elliott are like woodpeckers clicking at each other's heads.

There's nothing to involve us until Elliott goes to his first rehearsal for the production of *Richard III* he is to star in; Dreyfuss drops his archness, calms down, talks at a normal rate, and begins to seem like a person. He's able to win us over in these Off Off Broadway sequences because the two-liner duelling rhythm is broken; Shakespeare's dialogue is a blessed sound. Dreyfuss never kids what he's doing: working within the homosexual interpretation of Richard III that the fool director (Paul Benedict) forces on him, he gives a game, intense performance. And so after the disastrous opening night you respect the small hell he's been through. Dreyfuss plays the morning-after hangover with considerable flourish, and echoes of John Barrymore's eccentric comedy style.

But what part of Neil Simon's material are we supposed to take as the springboard mechanism to set the romantic drama in motion, and what part is the drama? Just to set up some gags about health food, Simon humiliates the somewhat pudgy Dreyfuss by having him say in all seriousness that he considers his body a temple. And we can't see what Elliott is doing in a devoted, courting situation with Paula, who, when she isn't being abrasive, is soggy and whimpering. Neil Simon and Herbert Ross want us to feel Paula's need for love and her terror of being hurt again, but Simon doesn't develop her character—he simply stretches the material with gags. Practically everything to do with Paula seems to be a mere device—from her former lover's having sublet the apartment to Elliott, to her Broadway audition (out of *A Chorus Line*), to her redecorating the apartment. When she's mugged, it's supposed to be delightfully funny that she irrationally blames Elliott. When she gets a job at the auto show, it's assumed to be enchanting that she can't deliver a two-minute spiel without getting it balled up. And Simon's idea of depth is a tug at your heartstrings. Marsha Mason's chin keeps quivering. Her face is either squinched up to cry or crinkled up to laugh; this may be the bravest, teariest, most crumpled-face performance since the days of Janet Gaynor. No wonder those actors walked out on Paula: she's a domestic leech, with *House Beautiful* aspirations. She suffers and she decorates. And her precocious child—Cupid talking dirty for a laugh—is a baby harpy. Marsha Mason created a soft, giggly, compliant character in just a few scenes in her first picture, Paul Mazursky's *Blume in Love*: her Arlene, the woman who had an affair with the recently divorced Blume, was likably funny, because she couldn't understand her own messy feelings. But Mason hasn't found her footing in other movies; Herbert Ross overworks her teeth and eyes and charm and pathos, as Mark Rydell did in *Cinderella Liberty*. We're so obviously meant to find her "human" she becomes a charity case.

Paula, busy picking out white furniture, would be a menace to a serious young actor; this woman loves artists and wants them to function like suburban daddies. With a comic twist of emphasis, we would cheer when Elliott got the idea and joined the procession of deserters. Yet Simon not only provides Paula with an artist eager to take care of her and her child, he seems to think the man is lucky to get them. Can Neil Simon's commercial success be partly attributable to something as simple as his having the soul of a comic-strip Jewish mother? He fixes people up in his plays and movies. Dreyfuss is playing the good Jewish boy—a warmer version of Dustin Hoffman in the late sixties—who gives the shiksa the love and understanding she has always needed. His saintly steadiness cures Paula of her neurotic fears. We don't know why he loves her until after he wins her, when he says that he fell for her right from the start, as soon as he saw her little snub nose. Of course. That's the shiksa's secret weapon—she wins by a nose. The smartest thing the moviemakers did was to cast an actor who isn't a tall and muscular dream hero; the casting makes the film seem less regressive than it is. Dreyfuss brings *The Goodbye Girl* its only moments of substance, yet the role is demeaning. After Elliott's opening-night performance as Richard III, Paula visits him backstage, and his face is stricken with grief and humiliation; that should be Dreyfuss's face for what Neil Simon and Herbert Ross do to him—and what he does to himself—in most of this picture. He turns into a cuddly Teddy bear trying to be sexy, the Jewish boy next door.

□ □ □

*T*he Michael Cacoyannis film *Iphigenia* (from Euripides' *Iphigenia in Aulis*) isn't bad, and one can certainly sit through it gratefully, and with pleasure—at least until Iphigenia (Tatiana Papamoskou) makes her unconscionably extended farewells—but, oh, God, why isn't it better? Why isn't there the daring and the exaltation that our senses fairly cry out for? The sound of people speaking in the open spaces is well handled, and Costa Kazakos' robust, irresolute Agamemnon is very fine, and there's fervor and dedication here. It's the excitement of a new interpretation that's missing. This film is so literal-minded it's Sidney Lumet translated into Greek.

Magnificent as she is, Irene Papas seems too aware of the importance of the occasion. As Clytemnestra, mother of Iphigenia (who is to be sacrificed in order to propitiate the gods and bring favorable winds for Agamemnon's army), Papas visibly rises to the challenge. There may never have been an actress who combines as much might with as much beauty as the dark, olive-eyed Irene Papas does; her Clytemnestra certainly makes you believe in the vengeance she will take on Agamemnon. But the camera feasts too much on her seething magnificence, and this makes for a glaring contrast in style between Papas and the child-like, pre-nubile Papamoskou, who plays her role very simply and naturalistically, and doesn't have a trained voice to match up to Papas' deep alto tones. While other actresses take piddling roles and make themselves small, Papas becomes so titanic here that one recoils a little. Cacoyannis has her go a shade past greatness. (Others may need to turn to the classics, she perhaps needs to turn to the moderns.) The film is all rocks and scrub brush and Clytemnestra swelling with wrath and Menelaus (Costa Carras) expostulating. Performed this way, *Iphigenia* is like a wildlife film about rhinoceroses—everybody's snorting at each other.

Papas' performance suffers, too, because the role of Clytemnestra has what might be called a topical flaw. In raising questions about what her life has been while the king, her husband, has been chasing glory, and in venting her female rage, she sounds too much like what we've been hearing for the past five years. The times have caught up with Euripides, and Clytemnestra's angriest complaints have been stripped of their excitement, have staled. She has become a precursor, and less of a character. Other aspects of the play as it has come down to us—the anti-war ironies and almost everything to do with Iphigenia herself—are confusing. And in this version Artemis does not fly down at the end to scoop up Iphigenia (and leave a hind in her place on the altar), and so when the wind comes and the army runs toward the thousand ships and prepares to sail for Troy, it seems to mean that the gods did indeed want Iphigenia's death.

□ □ □

*I*n the thirties, Monogram and Republic made Westerns that had lackluster casts and no believability and no connection with art. There was just one thing to keep the predominantly male audience interested: the viewers could follow a moving object—a man on a horse in the great outdoors. *The Gauntlet,* directed by Clint Eastwood, is about a Phoenix cop, Ben Shockley (Eastwood), who is ordered to go to Las Vegas to bring back Gus Mally (Sondra Locke), a witness for a trial. He's a worthless souse; she's a hooker. The trip back, which is their redemption, is also a series of chases. They're pursued by the police and "the mob," so they're always in movement—on almost everything but a horse. They use a police car, a motorcycle, a train, a bus. The merest whisper of a plot (orders have been given to kill Gus to keep her from testifying) serves as a pretext for shoot-'em-ups with thousands of rounds of ammunition going into whatever buildings or vehicles the cop and the hooker are in or on. At times, the whole world seems to be firing at them; buildings and cars are turned to lace. And they keep moving. You look at the screen even though there's nothing to occupy your mind—the way you sometimes sit in front of the TV, numbly, because you can't rouse yourself for the effort it takes to go to bed. Afterward, leaving the theatre, a fair number of people were saying, "That's the worst movie I've ever seen"—in rather aggrieved, surprised tones, as if they were just coming out of a stupor.

Eastwood's face is more relaxed in this picture than in his last, *The Enforcer*, one of the *Dirty Harry* series; he probably enjoyed the part and thinks he's acting because he's playing somebody dumb—the slow-witted Ben has to be told the score by the smart hooker. At first, Sondra Locke plays Gus as a hysterical loudmouth subliterate, yowling four-letter words at Ben. Then, almost as if someone had written her dialogue as part of a heads-bodies-legs folded-page drawing game, Gus informs him that she's a Finch College graduate, and proceeds to lecture him in the cool tones of an intellectual sharpie, a leftist doctor of sociology. (Her slipping in and out of her education isn't explained.) Eastwood also gets beaten up and mutilated enough to satisfy his king-size masochistic fantasies. His companion—now purified by love of him and her new refined diction—suffers multiple rape in order to save his life. Can a script come up with anything more floridly primitive than that?

This movie may be distinctive on one count: the hideous villainy it deplores—the action the heroine witnessed that sets the chase in motion—is apparently masturbation. That seems to be the vilest crime imaginable, and the hooker heroine blanches when she refers to it. The only talent involved in this movie belongs to the agent who sold the script (by Michael Butler and Dennis Shryack); the sale price of $500,000 suggests genius.

[January 16, 1978]

The Duellists/The Battle of Chile

Set in Europe in the Napoleonic period, the English film *The Duellists*, from Joseph Conrad's sixty-odd-page story "The Duel," is about a cavalry officer's sudden flare up of rage over a trifling, imagined insult by another officer which grows into a private war. Lieutenant Feraud challenges Lieutenant D'Hubert to a duel and is injured, and the duel ends. But not in Feraud's mind. For the next fifteen years, whenever there are interludes of peace and Feraud isn't using his skills and tenacity on France's enemies, he seeks out D'Hubert and challenges him to further duels. These encounters—and the injuries that result—are a lifelong horror to the equable, rational D'Hubert. The origin of the quarrel becomes lost in legend, like the causes of the larger wars that they're both fighting in. Differences in class, in temperament, in regional background all enter into the enmity that the short, dark, powerfully built Feraud (Harvey Keitel) feels toward the lanky, fair-haired aristocrat D'Hubert (Keith Carradine). Everything fuels Feraud's bitterness; with the righteousness of the spiteful, he convinces himself that the quarrel represents a matter of political conscience. And when, a general, Feraud is involuntarily retired from the Army after Napoleon's defeat, and is broken by the emptiness of his existence as a pensioner, his learning where D'Hubert is to be found resurrects him. As Conrad put it, "A mere fighter all his life, a cavalry man, a *sabreur,* he conceived war with the utmost simplicity, as, in the main, a massed lot of personal contests, a sort of gregarious duelling. And here he had in hand a war of his own. He revived. The shadow of peace passed away from him like the shadow of death."

The film follows the Conrad story, without attempting to dramatize the events or to heighten their meaning. It doesn't even prepare the situations or introduce the subsidiary characters; they simply come and go, and at times we have a second's confusion as to who they are or whether we've met them before. The attitude toward the duels themselves (as toward the wars, in which the two men fight on the same side, and even, in Napoleon's army in Russia, side by side) is always factual and slightly ironic. The film is shot from the point of view of D'Hubert, a man with a graceful, satirical intelligence who becomes the prisoner of Feraud's obsession and can't quite believe it. Feraud is like a malignant God on his tail. Yet we're not asked to feel sympathy for D'Hubert, or to feel suspense when he's in jeopardy. *The Duellists* is an epic yarn: we sit back and observe it, and it's consistently entertaining—and eerily beautiful.

The special quality of the film is that the drama doesn't emerge from what the actors say and do—the drama is in the play of light and shadow against what the actors do. The grouping of the figures and their distance from the camera—whether they're close or at a short remove or mere specks in a landscape—are already inscribed in our memories. We've seen these people, these rivers and stone buildings and hussars' uniforms in Géricault, Gérard, Prud'hon, Gros; we've seen this strong light and the clear, deep shadows and the puritan, gray backgrounds in the paintings of the Le Nain brothers. Usually, a movie in which every composition suggests an Old Master is emptily pictorial—it doesn't move and its beauty is weak. What keeps the compositions here from palling is that they're more than imitative; they have a graphic power of their own, as if they'd been shot by a nineteenth-century Haskell Wexler, and they're coolly impassioned. You watch almost unblinking, because the imagery is so lustrous, yet a story of obsessive enmity is being told by way of these images. This light, which is so strong, isn't sunny. The vernal hills, the morning mists, the severe lowering skies—it's all ravishing yet ambiguous and unsettling.

This is the first feature film by the thirty-nine-year-old English director Ridley Scott, who attended the Royal College of Art, in London. While still at school, he made his first movie in 16-mm., and his interest in becoming a painter shifted to stage design and to film. Afterward, he worked at the BBC as a set designer and then as the director of a number of television series; eventually, he set up his own production company to make commercials. Some of the sense we get here of controlled turbulence, with the artist's feelings concentrated in the amber glow on the side of an old building, or in the fluting of a woman's bonnet, may be due to Scott's serving as his own camera operator. He's literally directing from behind the camera, and the imagery has an expressive tone, like the sentences of a writer whose flow of feelings is richer than any explicit statement he can make.

The film's flaws match up with those of the story—and in both cases seem not so much artistic as mechanical. Conrad, a Pole who didn't learn English until he was almost twenty, doesn't show a great ear in this tale (based on an actual compulsive French duellist), and the characters, who are all French, talk in an infelicitous English, salted with French phrases (" 'What an ass I was to think I could have missed him,' he muttered to himself. 'He was exposed *en plein*—the fool!—for quite a couple of seconds' "). The script that Gerald Vaughan-Hughes wrote for Scott is in straightforward language, with just enough formality (especially in D'Hubert's choice of words) to seem right for the Napoleonic period. The movie has its own linguistic oddities, though. Partly in order to get distribution, Scott used a mixed American and British cast. The American principals—Carradine, Keitel, and Cristina Raines, as the girl D'Hubert falls in love with—are surrounded by British performers, among them Albert Finney, Alan Webb, Edward Fox, Diana Quick, Jenny Runacre, Robert Stephens, John McEnery, Tom Conti, and Meg Wynn Owen, and with both groups pretending to be French there is an awkward disparity. These British, with their thumping stage voices, don't suggest Frenchness any more than the Americans do (perhaps even less), but we're so used to seeing English performers in period uniforms that their confident strutting may seem right to us, while the Americans may look somewhat ludicrous and appear to be underacting—lacking in tension, callow, unfinished. If the cast were all British, though, *The Duellists* would probably be far less engaging. The English actors are so up in their lines—so cadenced and glib—that they might be wearing BBC T-shirts. In terms of the camera, there are disadvantages to being the inheritors of an acting tradition; the Americans manage to speak without such a clatter of diction—without giving themselves theatrical airs.

It's a transatlantic innocence-versus-experience comedy to see Keith Carradine playing a scene with Albert Finney—as Fouché, the Minister of Police. Finney doesn't just make his presence felt; he fills the screen and then some—he comes on like British gangbusters. One thing about the British: when they get in a fancy-dress part, they let you know how much they love to act, and some of their hammy enjoyment is infectious. Finney's full-throated, rumbling Fouché is a big-time, scene-stealing impersonation (which would make more sense if Fouché had been an actor rather than a cop). Working very simply, on intuition, without that crust of "acting," Carradine draws us into D'Hubert's train of thought in the quietest possible way. His performance is short on presence; he needs to suggest greater resources in his character. He could use more tension, his speech is a little too American blurred-laconic, and there is one shot of him in which his idea of military bearing seems to be a stiff bounce. But his lightweight, colloquial performance gives this movie charm.

Carradine's freshness makes it possible for us to accept D'Hubert as the embodiment of honor, flexibility, reason. (Conrad wrote him as an incredibly—metaphorically—good man.) Walking in the country, Carradine blends into the pastoral vistas and the children's games. His D'Hubert thrives on peace just as Keitel's Feraud thrives on war. Feraud belongs with men in dark inns; his beady-eyed, secretive look is enough to cloud over Paradise. Yet Feraud could conceivably be more than he is here. Keitel doesn't give sides to his character; he plays only Feraud's central drive—the implacability. (Implacability may come a little too naturally to Keitel; it narrows him as an actor.) His performance has great concentration, but Feraud needs a few spangles, some looseness, or even wildness, with his comrades-in-arms and his followers, something from which to swing over into his monomania. In his own dogged way, Keitel is potent, though, and at the end his Feraud is a marvellous image, in his crow's black coat and black tricorne, with his thinking processes hidden and warped—a man devoured by bitterness.

The film is never totally convincing; there's a make-believe, costume-picture aspect to it, and a storytelling starchiness. And perhaps the conflicts and what they mean don't emerge sufficiently; the even-tempered, episodic approach suggests "Masterpiece Theatre" technique on a bigger screen. (On a modern subject, that could be deadly.) But it's a film with a love of light; it's infatuated with the continuity of dramatic techniques in painting and in movies. The emotional discord in the images affects one's susceptibilities like the pealing of bells. (No bell ever seems to be struck for the first time.) Carradine and Cristina Raines have a lamblike ease together, and in the scene when D'Hubert and his lady plight their troth and kiss, their white horses, standing just behind them, nuzzle each other. This is either the luckiest shot a beginner movie director ever caught or the most entranced bit of planning a beginner ever dared.

□ □ □

Great films rarely arrive as unheralded as *The Battle of Chile,* a two-part, three-hour-and-ten-minute documentary about the events leading to the fall of Allende. This film doesn't even present itself with fanfare, and it takes a while to get going. It opens in March of 1973 with inquiring reporters asking people how they're going to vote in the coming congressional election, which amounts to a plebiscite on the Allende government. The election is taking place after Allende has been in office for over two years and has been trying to reorganize the society and move it toward Socialism within the framework of democratic government. His Popular Unity coalition was put into office with only a third of the popular vote, so he has been on shaky ground. His efforts to nationalize certain industries have brought on a squeeze from the banking and industrial community and from foreign interests (especially the United States), and Chile is suffering economic deprivations.

The interviews show us the colliding points of view in the country and the self-assurance of each group, but we don't have enough background information to sort out the material and we tend to look at it in human-interest terms, enjoying the faces, being amazed at the unembarrassed articulateness of the Chileans. The mikes are shoved at them and they talk; this goes on for a long time, and we seem to be getting no more than a bystanders' view of history. Up through the election—in which Allende makes a small gain (to 43.4 per cent of the votes), though the opposition bloc also makes a gain (to 54.6 per cent), and the result is a continuing stalemate—we have a sense of the limitations of photographic journalism when it comes to analyzing what's going on. Besides the man-in-the-street interviews, the film seems to give us only the public actions—the speeches, the violent confrontations, the mobs and meetings, the parades with workers chanting funny, dirty rhymed slogans—and none of the inner workings. Those are supplied by an English narrator (a woman), who keeps interpreting for us. She is concise in exactly the wrong way. We need to have groups identified and their positions explained. When the miners in the nationalized copper mines strike, we want to know the issues; she tells us that the less politically sophisticated workers were deceived by the Fascists, while "the more politically knowledgeable stay on the job." There may be considerable truth here, but this kind of thing can drive one a little crazy. She gives us a strict ideological account—almost a parody of Marxism—in which everything that happens is the result of the imperialists' and the industrialists' strategy.

There is no suggestion of any form of regimentation under Allende, yet his supporters talk in terms of "worker consciousness" and other standard formulations which make us wonder where the indoctrination is coming from. When the miners' strike against the government ends (the

384

narrator tells us that it "falls apart"), Allende mobilizes the masses at a big rally and calls out, "Jump if you're not a Fascist!"—and a half-million people jump. It's a staggering image. But, oh, for a more open-minded narrator. We're told that the last strikers "have taken refuge at Catholic University." Who is it that they're taking refuge from—that benevolent papa pleading for a show of support? According to the film, any opposition to Allende is corrupt—as if there were no conceivable good reason to oppose him. Clearly, Allende, who isn't in control of most of the Army units, is hemmed in. The public transportation system is disintegrating: Chile can't get spare parts because of the American embargo. From that big rally on through the street violence that follows, Part I (*The Insurrection of the Bourgeoisie*) is terrifyingly well done. It concludes with newsreel footage from the camera of an Argentine who was photographing the skirmishes in the street. An Army man takes slow, careful aim right at us and kills the cameraman, and the image spins skyward. It's an intrusion for the narrator to say of that Army man, "This is the face of Fascism"; that's the voice of ideology, the diminisher.

Part II (*The Coup d'Etat*) begins with that summer's insurrectionary right-wing violence against the government; rebel Army troops seize control of downtown Santiago and fire at the Presidential palace, but this attempted coup is put down in a few hours. Now the film gets to its central question: Can a society dedicated to constitutional law make the transition to Socialism peaceably? The Marxist argument has always been that violence comes not from the revolution but from the counter-revolution, and that the workers have to be prepared to defend the revolution by violent means. And Chile serves as a demonstration. There appears to be no way that Allende's legally constituted revolutionary government can move toward Socialism within a legal, democratic framework. It can't defend itself against the industrialists' counter-revolutionary moves unless it suspends constitutional guarantees, forms a people's militia, and claps the opposition in jail. (Could Allende do that without precipitating an immediate right-wing putsch? Maybe not, but in the view here that was his only chance.) The film leaps from one group to another, from meetings of the Chilean Congress to bombings to street demonstrations to workers' discussions. It shows the different elements in the explosive situation with so much clarity that it's a Marxist tract in which the contradictions of capitalism have sprung to life. At a union meeting, the faces are intense and involved, but there are divided, competing strategies among the left-wing groups that support the government, and the workers have a tremendous concern for legality. Meanwhile, Allende is desperately wheeling and horse-trading to get the congressional support he needs, and failing. We actually see the country cracking open. The inner workings are now so public that they can be photographed. Allende asks Congress to declare martial law—which would give him the power to appoint military personnel. It's his only chance of preventing another attempt at a military coup. He is refused, and that same day troops go into the factories, searching for weapons. The violence escalates while Allende's supporters argue whether they should be armed or not, and, step by step, the legal government is overthrown.

This documentary cross-section view of a collapsing government is surely unprecedented. Everybody in the country seems to know that a coup d'etat is coming, and people talk about it freely and coherently. No one seems apathetic, not even the middle-class women, who speak vigorously about how much they hate Socialism. Has there ever been a more articulate culture? Now we understand why the picture laid all that inquiring-reporter groundwork: everybody knows that it's just a matter of time, yet the people who have the most to lose can't get together enough to do anything. Then Allende's naval aide-de-camp, Captain Araya, is killed, and at the funeral the camera moves around solemnly, in closeup, scanning the high-ranking officers gathered there—General Pinochet among them—as if they were a sculptural group. This is the military brass of Chile shown in all its formality, and at a time of utter stillness. We see these handsome, well-coiffed heads in their dress-uniform collars and hats, and this funeral is the funeral of a society. It's like a classic passage in Tolstoy. We know from this frieze, a monument to the past, that there's no hope for Socialism in Chile. In July, the truck owners, funded by the C.I.A., begin their long strike, which paralyzes the distribution of food, gasoline, and fuel, and there is a call for Allende to resign. Instead, he holds another rally, and eight hundred thousand people, give or take a few, arrive in the afternoon and stick around into the night. But those people have no weapons. On September 11th, the Navy (in touch with United States destroyers that are standing by) institutes the coup d'etat, and the Air Force bombs the state radio station. We hear Allende say he won't resign. The palace is bombarded from the air. And then we see the chiefs of the junta on television, presenting themselves as the new government. They announce that they'll return the country to order, after three years of Marxist cancer.

How could a team of five—some with no previous film experience—working with limited equipment (one Éclair camera, one Nagra sound recorder, two vehicles) and a package of black-and-white film stock sent to them by the French documentarian Chris Marker produce a work of this magnitude? The answer has to be partly, at least: through Marxist discipline. The young Chilean director, Patricio Guzmán, and his associates (all Chileans except for one Spaniard) had a sense of purpose. They considered themselves a collective, and they were making a work of political analysis. The twenty hours of footage they shot had to be smuggled out of the country; four of the filmmakers spent some time in custody, and the cameraman, Jorge Muller, hasn't been heard of since his imprisonment. The others fled separately, assembled in Cuba, and, together with a well-known Chilean film editor, Pedro Chaskel, and both Chilean and Cuban advisers, worked on the movie. (A planned Part III has yet to be completed.) There is still the sheer technical skill to account for—the quality of the sound, the camerawork that is discreet and mobile and live, and, above all, the editing, which is so smooth and unemphatic that it never calls attention to itself. Chaskel has an immensely subtle, fluid new technique; Part II has the effect of one long, continuous shot. He owes something to the Italian neo-realists, but his other influences aren't easy to place—maybe the early Russians, though he gets the emotion without the shock cuts, in legato.

Patricio Guzmán is, of course, the organizing force behind this production, and its controlling intelligence. He has said, in an interview with Julianne Burton (in the magazine *Socialist Revolution*), that during the street battles he could anticipate what was going to happen and, standing next to the cameraman, tell him when to pan or lower the camera or raise it. That is, he was so attuned to the possibilities in the situation that it was almost as if he were directing the action; he could use the fiction-film methods that he had studied at film school in Madrid in the late sixties. But if the imagination here is Guzmán's, so is the vise put on the material. The footage is so spectacular and so sensitively shot that one tends to laugh off the narrator's rigid, instructional approach, but it soaks in, because the whole film is structured to make the same analysis. When we listen to a fiery young leftist urging his comrades to arm in that summer of 1973, we can't help wondering if he's alive—or half alive—but Guzmán doesn't encourage elegiac speculations. His is a no-nonsense, revolutionary approach; he is recording the political process as Marx and Lenin described it. That was how he and his group selected what to film: they worked from an outline. In *The Battle of Chile,* the United States serves as the imperialist enemy that proves the necessity for revolutionaries to arm their supporters and lock up their potential enemies. Chile is set up as a model failure.

Guzmán and his associates have taken a relentlessly non-aesthetic approach, yet with their artistic sensibilities and superb taste *The Battle of Chile* is an elegy in spite of them. For us, it is an accusatory elegy. Aesthetically, this is a major film, and that gives force even to the patterning of its charges. We may have less faith than the moviemakers do in the masterminding powers of the C.I.A., but their dogmatic Marxist view of the role of the United States in Chile seems to coincide with all too many facts. Our own newspapers have given us corroborative evidence. But what else was going on? What was the United States counterpunching at, and why? And when the narrator tells us that the most powerful TV channel in Chile was funded by the Ford Foundation, what was involved in that? It's not enough for *The Battle of Chile* to run for a couple of weekends at the Film Forum. It needs to be seen on public television, with those government officials who formed our policy toward Allende explaining what interests they believed they were furthering. We're owed more discussion of what the United States was up to—even if we can get it only through the public service sponsorship of Mobil, Exxon, or I.T.T.

[January 23, 1978]

More Torment, or When They Broke the Silence

*I*n Ingmar Bergman's *The Serpent's Egg,* set in Berlin between November 3rd and November 11th in 1923, young Storm Troopers march into a cabaret, and the Jewish owner gets his head bashed against a table twelve (count 'em) times. The central character—Abel Rosenberg (David Carradine), an American trapeze artist—returns to his boarding house and goes upstairs to his room, and there is his circus-partner brother, a figure by Schiele, sitting on the bed, propped up against the wall; he has shot himself in the mouth, and the shattered top of his head is like a dozen red roses. Other people who live or work near Abel are turning up dead, and the grizzled old police inspector (Gert Fröbe) shows him a succession of cadavers with bruises and bloody heads. Abel bangs the head of a petty bureaucrat against the iron bars of a gate, and when he's assaulted by a guard, his assailant's head is squashed under an elevator, and the blood sprays Abel in the face. Abel keeps clutching his head in misery, and Manuela (Liv Ullmann), his dead brother's ex-wife, keeps holding it to comfort him. At *The Serpent's Egg,* it doesn't take long for us to get the idea: Ingmar Bergman's head hurts.

The actors are doing all this not for any reason that's apparent but because Bergman told them to. Because he's Bergman, they believed in him. Because he's Bergman, we want to believe, too. But we can't. Usually when we go to Bergman movies, we assume that he's "working out" something personal, and we respect that and accept the loose ends and the confusion. An artist can draw a lot of energy from obsessive material; we can practically feel Bergman climbing the walls. (Over the years, we've grown accustomed to giving him a leg up.) Here, though the material is almost explicitly obsessive, we don't feel the urgency or the pain that

388

would enable us to identify with what Abel and Manuela are going through. Liv Ullmann's devoted Manuela, a simple, religious whore who tries to save Abel, is out of Dostoevski; her passive suffering-animal quality is pure Sonia. Without his brother, Abel has no trapeze act, and he takes a job in a hospital archive that's out of Kafka. This archive is so mazelike that he has to be led through the corridors to the cranny where he works shifting files from gray folders to yellow ones; his superior describes these files as "full of reports of inconceivable human suffering." Everything in the movie seems out of somewhere (Pabst's *Joyless Street,* Bob Fosse's *Cabaret,* Bergman's own *The Silence,* etc.); everything is strained, insufficient, underfelt. There has never been another director who yielded to despair in his movies as often as Bergman does, but generally he has had enough theatricality to pull the audience along. When his inspiration flagged, he could swindle his way through, as in *The Hour of the Wolf,* and people in the audience might think the fault was in them. He stooped to a severed hand and a grisly eye in an inkwell in *The Magician,* but he did it with metaphysical flash. This time, his theatricality fails him, and his misery sits on the screen like a dull, dark ache.

The Serpent's Egg was made in English at the Bavaria Studios, in Munich, and though it was shot by Bergman's longtime cinematographer-collaborator, Sven Nykvist, it doesn't look like a Bergman film. The visual style isn't pared down to register the characters' emotions with maximum clarity, and Liv Ullmann's face doesn't have that radiant, supernal naturalness that one associates with Bergman. The cinematography is erratic: unusual, dreamy shots of the night city, interrupted by fitful camera movements and jarring zooms. Bergman's twenties Berlin is constructed on the basis of film memories, like the New York of *New York, New York*; this is a dilapidated, poisoned Berlin. The decadence here is of a special, liberal-moralist's variety: for De Mille, decadence was people boozing and dancing and watching drag shows; for Bergman, decadence is people doing all that and not enjoying it. Bergman and Nykvist use color in an anti-color manner, draining the light away. The rooms and buildings are muggy gray-green, and the streets feel enclosed. There's nothing beyond or above. No doubt much of this is intentional, but the heavy atmosphere tightens one's chest, and the brutality is literal and without suggestiveness—its only power is to offend.

In most of Bergman's films, what we experience as the intellectual, spiritual, and emotional background comes to us in terms of a very specific frame of reference. If he has his Scandinavians suffering from rootlessness, they suffer as rootless people within a deeply rooted society. We can feel that they are lost within a recognizable, traditional box. But Abel and Manuela are in an imprecise environment; they're rattling around in a set, waiting for their cues. Their vacancy of spirit—Manuela says that "people have no future, people have lost the future"—is intended to affect us, and if this were one of Bergman's Swedish films it would. Here Abel and Manuela seem to have come to Berlin just to experience the universal anguish and go vacant.

In plot terms, Bergman is back with his man of instinct (Abel) versus the icy, sadistic scientific intelligence, and once again—for unexplained reasons—the enemy is a pedantic Dr. Vergerus, played by Heinz Bennent. (Gunnar Björnstrand was Dr. Vergerus in *The Magician*; Erland Josephson was the architect Vergerus in *The Passion of Anna*; Max von Sydow was Dr. Vergerus in *The Touch*.) This new Vergerus, whom Abel knew when they were children, was a cat torturer then, and now conducts lethal torture experiments on human beings. He's the head of the hospital where Abel works in the archive and Manuela works in the laundry, and he provides them with an apartment attached to the hospital, which places them under his control. Vergerus is a variant of the bespectacled mad doctors in horror films, and is also the blond, blue-eyed Nazi prophet who in this November of 1923, when Hitler's first, abortive, putsch is taking place in Munich, dreams of what the Nazis will accomplish in the thirties. He says of his own period, "It's like a serpent's egg. Through the thin membranes you can clearly discern the already perfect reptile." Bergman has 20-20 hindsight. This movie, which fills the screen with images of fear and blood, of head-splitting pain and death, and then throws in gothic political theories, is a crackpot tragedy.

With Bergman's last movie, *Face to Face,* even if you gave up on the closed, orthodox Freudian script that was yet so blurry and unrealized, Liv Ullmann bailed Bergman out. Though one was held by the performance, afterward one couldn't remember the picture; its suspense had been in whether she could sustain her feat. And there's a penalty for this kind of solemn tour de force. Having acted out so much Bergman agony and depression and having redeemed so much banality in *Face to Face,* Liv Ullmann, with her transcendent sincerity, has begun to seem too clear in our minds. (That TV perennial *Scenes from a Marriage* has given her the aura of an evangelist with a nightly message.) She has been in a position that other screen actresses envy: who else has huge starring roles written for her by a great movie director, as stage actresses in the past had roles written for them by the leading dramatists? But the price of this advantage has been that in Bergman's pictures she is limited by his view of her. (On the screen, she is controlled far more than those stage actresses were.) And in recent years the roles he has written for her have brought out a shallowness, an overeagerness, a moo-cow anxiety. Do people look forward to a Liv Ullmann performance the way one looks forward to, say, a Jane Fonda or a Geneviève Bujold performance? It's doubtful; there's a never-resting luminous self-seriousness about her. She's a great boring actress. And, betrayed by her role in *The Serpent's Egg,* she's not great at all. She's always rushing about, walking in a nervous, crouched position—

like Groucho as a slavey—and she does so much staring and throat-quivering that she pushes naked vulnerability close to caricature. The tarty makeup—a smeary red mouth and thick false eyelashes—works against her, and her suffering is so bovine that, for the first time, Nykvist's camera seems embarrassed by her. Nykvist swings over to Carradine with almost audible gratitude.

As Abel, David Carradine is more of an object than a character, but he's also the only thing in the movie one wants to look at. Bergman seems to have conceived Abel Rosenberg out of abstractions: the Jewish outsider, the loner, the displaced person (like Bergman himself). All of Abel's scenes are fundamentally elliptical; the conception is so opaque we can't even tell what it is that's missing. (It may be that Bergman needs his usual artist-genius hero—or Liv Ullmann as a powerfully disturbed heroine—if the cosmic suffering that is his basic theme is to have any depth.) At times, Carradine is like an actor in an Antonioni film, looking over his shoulder for help. The tiny gold earring that he wears might be an emblem of his character: visual but inexplicable. Abel Rosenberg has only David Carradine's qualities: an elusive slowed-down intensity; palsied, broken-sentence rhythms; a finely modelled, worn, wary face with sunken cheeks and baggy eyes; a lithe, cat-burglar's grace. He says he's been drunk every night since he left the circus; we don't know why—except that the times are harsh.

The film is strewn with half-symbolic elements. No doubt something is intended by having an Abel involved with his brother's wife. The name Rosenberg (which was also the name of the married couple in *Shame*) is linked with Abel's ambivalence about being Jewish; at one point, when he sees the name on a shopwindow he smashes the glass with a cobblestone, and when the old shopkeeper and his wife come out to fight with him he kisses the old woman before shoving her away. In a tawdry, shrilly extended sequence, Abel pays a black American (Glynn Turman) to copulate with a whore—so he can watch. No doubt we're expected to feel that Abel is being sadomasochistic in goading someone from another minority to abase himself, but Bergman seems to have another idea going here, too, and it's an even worse bummer. The black man struggles humiliatingly, unable to perform. It's as crude as if Bergman had said, "Things were really bad in Berlin in '23," and, asked "How bad?," he had replied, "They were so bad even a black man couldn't get it up."

The Serpent's Egg has characters (such as Manuela's skulking landlady with a rancid-syrup voice) and passages of dialogue ("Can you guess what kind of experiments are performed under Vergerus? Very strange." "Strange?") that seem parodies of horror movies. Other bits—such as Abel's brother's indecipherable suicide note—seem parodies of Bergman, or a reworking (when Manuela goes to church to talk to a priest because God hasn't been paying attention lately, and "the fear is too much for me," the priest, a visiting American, played by James Whitmore, compounds her problems by explaining to her as gently as possible that there is no God). There are also oddities, such as the police inspector's mentioning another inspector, Lohmann, who's working on a case "that's insane"—an apparent allusion to Fritz Lang's 1931 film, *M,* in which Inspector Lohmann was trying to track down a compulsive murderer of little girls. Bergman doesn't seem fussy about time period; in 1923 Vergerus is a movie-camera hound who makes *talking* pictures of his victims breaking down.

We hear Bergman's cry of despair: the soul of man is an abyss. Now that he's got rid of God, he's pinning the Holocaust on the absence of God and laying the blame for everything bad that happens on the bottomless iniquity of man. How can the artist who made a film of *The Magic Flute* descend to this schlocky cry of hopelessness? He deals with major emotions only, and in failing to balance them with minor ones he tips the scale and everything falls off. This may be the only Bergman movie that one feels utterly dead to. He seems to have lost all sense of proportion in this fantasy, which he himself acknowledges to be related to his recent difficulties with the Swedish tax authorities. (What movies would he dream up for us if he experienced some real troubles?) He has split himself between the victim, Abel, unable to work without his old partners, and the sadistic moviemaker, Vergerus, who manipulates helpless people's lives. When we're told, at the close, that Abel "was never seen again," this might be Bergman's maudlin way of saying that as an exile he has lost his future. Vergerus, holding up a mirror to watch himself die in agony, is a film director's view of his own end which would be more seemly if played for comedy.

[January 30, 1978]

Soul-Snatching and Body-Snatching

Those who haven't seen a movie with an honest-to-God Greek chorus in a long time and have been pining for one will want to know about Lina Wertmüller's *The End of the World in Our Usual Bed in a Night Full of Rain.* The chorus here is the sort that talks directly to the camera, often in leering closeups, and it materializes whenever Paolo (Giancarlo Giannini) and Lizzy (Candice Bergen) need ideological prompting in their male-female warfare. One could say this picture was *Swept Away (by an Unusual Destiny in the Blue Sea of August)* without the water, except that there is all this rain. (And it's necessary: only the rain links the scenes.) Except for flashbacks, *Night Full of Rain* takes place during one very wet night after Paolo and Lizzy have been married ten years. He's a journalist and a bourgeois Italian Communist, and she's a photojournalist and a rich American feminist. They live in a lavish apartment that is gorged with objets d'art, family mementos going back hundreds of years, a photograph of Francis Coppola and Fidel Castro, a basset hound, a de Chirico; it represents Europe, or maybe history, or civilization. Anyway, it represents *something*. It seems that for ten years Lizzy and Paolo have been having sexual intercourse only in the missionary position, and on this night, when he's on top of her, she interrupts him—at the urging of the women members of the chorus, which is to say, of her own deepest feelings—and tells him it doesn't do anything for her anymore and she'd like to try something else. We don't hear what else, because she gets very close to his ear to tell him. (Maybe she doesn't want the chorus to overhear? Or is it assumed that we in the audience might go into deep shock?) From her sly, lewd expression, we get the idea that she might be suggesting that she get on top for a change. Whatever it is, he's outraged; he calls her a tramp, slaps at her, there's much dishevelment, hysteria, shrieking, and running out into the rain—and the marriage collapses. They love each other, but they must part.

Photographed by Giuseppe Rotunno, the entire film has a tutti-frutti romanticism; at times it has the glitter and swooniness of *Pandora and the Flying Dutchman*. But there's so much camerawork it's exhausting. This is Lina Wertmüller's first movie made in English, and probably also her first with live sound, which comes out dead. The dialogue reaches us in spasms—disconnected words that suggest brainstorms reduced to economy telegrams. In the first part—a flashback to Paolo's and Lizzy's meeting— Wertmüller attempts her own version of *Last Tango in Paris* (she has Candice Bergen intoning "I don't even know your name"), and these sequences, with Giannini and Bergen flopping against the angels and demons of a fourteenth-century Carthusian monastery, must take their place among the immortals, along with such classics of camp as *Youngblood Hawke* and *The Barefoot Contessa*. Doesn't Giannini ever freshen up? With his head and face covered with hair, and his gleaming eyes covered by horn-rimmed glasses, he looks like a beetle. When he tries to grab the big, blond Bergen you half expect her to shove that little bug away and stamp on him. At one point, Lizzy tells Paolo his eyes are the color of rain. Why didn't she think of some nifty like that to describe his voice? When Giannini, in his phonetically learned English, jabbers about "enchantment" or bats his eyelashes over such pronouncements as "All the poets are dying," he sounds like Akim Tamiroff in *Touch of Evil.* The film, which is symbolic beyond your wildest fears, and has a lot to say about the misery of the modern world, features a mechanical toy—a little monkey in a red hat, with cymbals in his paws. When he's wound up, he crashes his tiny cymbals, and then he winds down. That's life, folks. Wertmüller runs a fad factory for turning despair into kitsch.

□ □ □

*I*n *Coma,* Geneviève Bujold, with her piquant features, her waif's face and sharp jaw, is like a soft little furry animal—a mink—with a dirty mind. She plays Dr. Susan Wheeler, a surgical resident at Boston Memorial Hospital—an immense modern medical complex. After her closest woman friend (Lois Chiles) goes into an irreversible coma during an abortion, Dr. Wheeler begins to investigate, and discovers that large numbers of young, healthy patients undergoing minor surgery have been similarly brain-damaged—vegetablized—and then packed off to the Jefferson Institute, a government-sponsored facility that provides long-term life-support systems. When the action moves from the hospital to the grim, fortresslike Jefferson Institute (the exteriors are of the Xerox building in Lexington, Massachusetts), the story shades off from a factual, realistic view of current practices in a modern hospital to science-fiction fantasy, without any change in the film's tone.

Visually, *Coma* is like a prophylactic; it's so cleanly made, with such an impersonal, detached feeling, that it looks untouched by human hands. Even the actors seem vacuous and immaculate, disinfected of any traces of personality. But not Bujold. There's no way to sanitize this actress. With her slightly moldy Peter Pan pertness, she's irreducibly curious—that's her sexy-witch essence. This is the first Hollywood picture in which Bujold has had the central starring role, and she manages to sustain her performance by snuggling deep inside the shallow material. Dr. Wheeler's suspiciousness—the sneaky expressions she gets when she doesn't go along with what her superiors are telling her—is all we've got to hang on to in this sterile environment. There is not an instant when her closed-in face isn't intent; thin-skinned, touchy, she seems almost to sniff out fakery. When she crawls around in the dark places of the hospital, trying to track the tubes that feed anesthetic gases into the operating rooms, she's totally engaged in what she's doing, in the most sensory, little-beastie way. Climbing and wriggling around, high up, trying to get a foothold in a slippery place, she peels off her panty hose, and it would not seem surprising if the striptease continued. As she goes from one dangerous situation to the next, the narrative trap tightens: you fear for her safety, and the suspense gets you in the stomach, and maybe the chest, too. The director, Michael Crichton, did the adaptation of Robin Cook's book (they both have medical degrees). *Coma* is only the second movie that Crichton has directed (the first was *Westworld*), and though he doesn't yet show a sure enough control of tempo, there's a particular wryness in his style which suggests intelligence (even if we hadn't known it was there from his books). Crichton knows exactly what effects he's getting, but sometimes that can be a limitation. The picture is all plot; it glides along smoothly, as if computer-operated. Computers aren't very visual—just those tiny lights winking. And they may hum but they don't thunder.

The sequences at the Jefferson Institute have a chill, spectral beauty: the comatose bodies—handsome, muscular, youthful—aren't on beds, they're suspended horizontally from the ceiling, in a vast gallery; they're in tiers, floating on wires, like the marionettes of a lunatic puppet master, the women's long hair hanging. Yet the spookiness doesn't explode. We need a crescendo or two of real terror—a chance malfunctioning, perhaps, or a visitor's involuntary start of aversion at the tubes attached to the bodies which carry matter in and out, or at the wraithlike hanging hair. There's a big chase through the hospital anatomy lab, where cadavers are stretched on tables or hung vertically on racks, encased in plastic, like clothes at a dry cleaner's. These bodies—long dead—have the dignity of Leonardo's anatomical drawings; they are so far from life they're like noble phantoms, and when Dr. Wheeler is fighting off a killer and uses them as weapons, there ought to be a Halloween horror in the scene. Something needs to break loose; tossing cadavers around shouldn't be this hygienic. The story—about the body-snatching of the living—is essentially sleazy, yet the movie shies away from sleazy jokes. When Crichton shows us organs or sections of bodies, he makes them as clinically banal as possible, in order to demonstrate that for people in everyday contact with them they're just like a display on a butcher's counter. It could be that his cultivation and training are a hindrance on this kind of movie. He's too used to cadavers to be spooked by them; he doesn't identify with us (or with our superstitious dread) but with the doctors. He accepts impersonality as part of technological advance, so he's unable to satirize it.

In a formula exploitation thriller based on the rudimentary device of having the heroine pursue the killers single-handed (and never go to the police or the press for help), tastefulness can be a negative attribute. After we've cheered for the bionic Frankenstein monster-villain of *The Spy Who Loved Me,* who tears a van apart in a childish tantrum, it's a letdown to be asked to settle for the usual stalking gunman with a cruel, enigmatic smile (Lance Le Gault). This movie is underpopulated—even the hospital is much too empty. There's only the one story line, and the roles played by Michael Douglas, Elizabeth Ashley, Richard Widmark, and Rip Torn are just plot functions. As soon as Lois Chiles appears, we know she's going to be killed—she has the vibrant feverishness that actors get when they know they've got only one scene and have to make it count. That's the sort of human filigree *Coma* needs more of. The picture sticks so close to basics it doesn't give you a lift; all you get is a knot in the gut. We don't go to a film like *Coma* for realism; we want the director to push the big scenes over the edge, to give them a twist and dislocate them. We go hoping for the insane ingenuity and top-of-the-world, thinner-air excitement of the best thrillers. We want the fun of the illicit—what some people get only from doing illegal business. *Coma* is so cautious it pays its taxes ahead of time.

□ □ □

*T*he title *Mr. Klein* may sound like a Jewish detergent, but nothing gets washed away in this unsatisfying French quasi-thriller, set in Paris in 1942, during the Occupation. It's about an Aryan, a fashionable art dealer (Alain Delon), who buys up treasures from fleeing Jews, and then, through what may or may not be a bureaucratic mistake, becomes confused with another Mr. Klein, a non-Aryan. Written by Franco Solinas, this is the kind of parable-thriller that has to be tight to be effective, but the director, Joseph Losey, keeps it going for over two hours. Losey has only two modes of expression—the oblique and the obvious—and you never can be sure which is which. There isn't any kind of direct, emotional expressiveness in his movies, and that may be why people often pore over them—staying to see a film twice, trying to find out what he's saying. *Mr. Klein* is a classic example of his weighty emptiness. The atmosphere is heavily pregnant, with no delivery. Delon, his face widened with age, so that he has begun to resemble Tony Curtis, gives a serious, deliberately charmless performance. As Klein, he's stiff, almost military in bearing, with a dollar-signs-for-eyes look. We're not meant to have any sympathy for Klein (the German name is a pun—he's Mr. Little); we simply watch as this lackluster, repellent man, with a void where his soul should be, suffers the nervous, embarrassed anxiety of trying to prove that he's not Jewish. (The movie is a solemn, medicinal variant on *Gentleman's Agreement*.) The scenes are so pointed that they poke you in the eye, and as *Mr. Klein* stretches out, with Klein determined to find his doppelgänger, Delon doesn't have enough different things to do, and his trussed-up posture and ashen face become glumly monotonous. How long should it take an audience to get the idea of the identity of persecutors and victims? Does it require all this visual heavy breathing? The actors pose in the most unnatural, portentous attitudes, and at first this is a real teaser—we assume there must be some reason for them to be moving around so funny. Gradually, we realize that it's for the sake of the camera. Losey's visual style imposes its own sluggish determinism. And, outdoors and in, everything is in claustrophobic blue-green tones. Why does this kind of movie always get called cerebral?

[February 6, 1978]

The Calvary Gig

Suppose some people in their late teens or early twenties, imagining in their plain innocence that Bob Dylan is a famous composer-singer, no more, no less, go to see his film *Renaldo & Clara*—what can they make of it? During the opening titles, Dylan is heard singing "When I Paint My Masterpiece," and then we see a small man onstage performing; he wears a hat straight across his forehead, like Billy Jack, and a clear-plastic mask with a twisted big mouth and a stretched-out nose. Eventually, he pulls off the disguise and we see Dylan's scowling, impassive face, but during the three hours and fifty-two minutes of the movie Dylan puts on other masks, or paints his cheeks and nose white and then shows us the sweat pouring through the paint. The film was shot mostly in the course of a Bicentennial (1975–76) tour (the show was called the Rolling Thunder Revue), and the performance footage, with the singers and musicians lighted in strong, bright, near-psychedelic color against black or deep-blue backgrounds, is handsomely photographed and has good sound quality. But we never get the buildup of excitement that one can feel at a live performance (and sometimes at a performance film, too), because *Renaldo & Clara* keeps cutting away from the stage to *cinéma vérité* fantasies of Dylan's life, which occupy more than two-thirds of the movie. In this material, Dylan tries some role-playing, camouflage, going incognito, and he's joined by Joan Baez, Sara Dylan, Ronee Blakley, Allen Ginsberg, Arlo Guthrie, Sam Shepard, Ramblin' Jack Elliott, Harry Dean Stanton, and a large cast of other friends and musicians, who halfheartedly assume make-believe identities. Everything circles around Dylan, who, despite his many guises, is always the same surly, mystic tease.

Although the film was made by Bob Dylan, he didn't direct it (nobody did). The cameramen are following a floating crap game—panning, zooming, frantically trying to catch whatever looks promising. And he didn't write it: the participants seem to be saying whatever comes into their heads. (Only David Blue, working a pinball machine and telling us how he first met Bob Dylan, shows an instinctive feeling for the camera, and some

397

wit.) But Dylan must certainly have been in control of the editing. He has given himself more tight closeups than any actor can have had in the whole history of movies. They are so close you don't see the whole face—only from under the brims of his hats down to midway across the chin. His eyes are heavily lined in black, for a haunting, androgynous effect, and you get the skin blemishes, the face hair, the sweat and bad capillaries, and, when he sings, the upper lip pulling back in a snarl and the yellow teeth like a crumbling mountain range. He is overpoweringly present, yet he is never in direct contact with us—not even when he performs. We are invited to stare at the permutations of his masked and unmasked face in closeup to perceive the mystery of his elusiveness—his distance.

This is a shocking miscalculation, because, of course, Bob Dylan is no longer the oracle, perhaps not even to his entourage and his troupe of associates. In the sixties, his songs were said to have defined a generation, but what he does on the screen here is painfully out of key with the times. Where is the audience that will see him as he sees himself? He and Allen Ginsberg visit a Catholic grotto in Lowell, Massachusetts, and as they examine the glassed-in sculptures, Ginsberg, in the role of The Father, explains the Stations of the Cross to him. Dylan's songs include his own "What Will You Do When Jesus Comes?" and "Knockin' on Heaven's Door." A street philosopher holding forth in a diner says, "The people still love Dylan and they'll still follow Dylan." And wherever Dylan goes—visiting Kerouac's grave and observing, "I want to be in an unmarked grave," or tramping in the Vermont snow in his Chassidic-pathfinder costume—there is an aura about him. The camera keeps saying: This is no ordinary man who walks among you. In one sequence, he pays a visit to the Tuscarora Indians, and receives homage with a humility unrivalled by Jeffrey Hunter in *King of Kings*. It's not just people previously unexposed to Dylan who are likely to be repelled by his arrogant passivity; even those who idolized him in the sixties may gag a little.

The Bob Dylan they responded to was a put-on artist. He was derisive, and even sneering, but in the sixties that was felt to be a way of freaking out those who weren't worthy of being talked to straight. Implicit in the put-on was the idea that the Establishment was so fundamentally dishonest that dialogue with any of its representatives (roughly, anyone who wore a tie) was debased from the start. And Dylan was a counterculture hero partly because of the speed and humor of his repartee. (*Playboy:* "Did you ever have the standard boyhood dream of growing up to be President?" Dylan: "No. When I was a boy, Harry Truman was President. Who'd want to be Harry Truman?") In *Renaldo & Clara,* his mocking spirit is just bad news: he's a sour messiah. After you've watched him for a few hours, in his medicine-man paint, his superannuated hippie clothes, and the big hats that sprout feathers and flowers and plumes, you may begin to wonder if his visionary doubletalk isn't just another form of the usual show-biz patter of people who keep looking back. The chief duty of David Blue's monologues at the pinball machine is to give us the legend of how things used to be in the sixties—to place Dylan in history for those who never knew or have forgotten. When Blue explains how Dylan came to write "Blowin' in the Wind," it's not very different from Comden and Green onstage reminiscing about their great days, the fifties.

In recent years, in Hollywood, industry executives have been dumbfounded to discover that awesomely rich singers and TV stars will take a financial loss for a shot at the movies. Even for people whose faces and voices are known to many more millions than ever went out to the pictures, working in the movies still represents the real glamour and the real challenge. And artists whose reputations might suggest that they are above such dreams may also want to be movie stars. At the extreme, for Bob Dylan, as for Norman Mailer, stardom isn't enough. Though these artists don't—can't—give to moviemaking the struggle to find their way which went into their primary art, they take on the burden of the filmmaker as well as of the star. Except for a streak of messianism, Mailer's writing and Dylan's songs could hardly be more different, but when these men turn to film the results are startlingly similar. For all Mailer's theoretical bullslinging about how movies should be made, and for all Dylan's forlorn holiness, they both set themselves in the center of a group of friends, admirers, old flames, and flunkies, and, while *cinéma vérité* camera crews keep shooting, they playact identity games. It's what Louis and Marie Antoinette might have done at Versailles if only they'd had the cameras.

Like Mailer, Dylan is an artist who intended to do something in advance of conventional movies—more poetic, more "true"—yet *Renaldo & Clara,* like Mailer's *Wild 90, Beyond the Law,* and *Maidstone,* is marked by an *absence* of artistic intelligence. The picture hasn't been thought out in terms of movement or a visual plan. Dylan merely gives his actor friends some clues as to what he'd like them to do, and they improvise, without reference to what has gone before or what will follow. Thousands upon thousands of feet of film are exposed, and then editors, with "the filmmaker" supervising, try to cut it all into some sort of shape. It's a lazy, profligate way to make a movie; the technicians are forced to try to compensate for the fact that nobody has done the thinking. There were four camera crews working simultaneously on *Renaldo & Clara,* and, with the compositions left to the cameramen, there's no overall clarity of style.

Dylan has been involved with movies at least since the mid-sixties; *Don't Look Back,* in which he starred (and which his manager helped produce), was about his 1965 tour of Britain, and showed him as a sensitive artist harassed by people who didn't understand his art. He put them on mercilessly, and squelched them with satisfaction. *Renaldo & Clara* has the same ridicule of outsiders (in one sequence, the elderly women at a poetry reading are rattled by a hipster's deadpan remarks introducing Allen

Ginsberg); the same self-protective way of tossing out thoughts (one can never be sure whether Dylan means what he says); and the same sweet-Jesus liberalism (in *Don't Look Back,* the footage of the British tour was interrupted by a sequence of Dylan playing for Mississippi sharecroppers, while in *Renaldo & Clara* the footage of the Rolling Thunder tour is interrupted by man-on-the-street interviews with black people about the Rubin Carter case, which seem included to show us that Bob Dylan cares more about black people than they do themselves). *Renaldo & Clara* is a continuation of *Don't Look Back*; it hasn't solved any of that film's problems, it just extends them over almost three times the length. In movies, you can force connections in the cutting room and think you're using associational editing, but the result may still affect viewers as random footage spliced together. The variable color values in *Renaldo & Clara* and the frequent returns to situations that one thought were finished (for example, to the philosopher and the other men in the diner talking about God's work and what truth is and how "if you follow Bob long enough, maybe you can translate these things," or to scenes with several of the women dressed up as hooker señoritas and talking over life's problems) add to the feeling of randomness. *Renaldo & Clara* doesn't take form in the mind, like a movie, even though one can discern the thematic links. They're not hard to spot, so many of them are Biblical.

No matter how skillfully the footage is cut, there's still a basic discrepancy in using hand-held or shoulder-mounted lightweight *cinéma vérité* equipment on acted scenes, and this is particularly apparent when they take place in small rooms. The falseness of the amateur-theatricals acting here is compounded by the fact that the cameramen are bouncing around as if they were shooting a news event. In most Hollywood films, the danger is of setups so patterned that the film is static; the danger in this kind of film is that, with the camera necessarily active, the movement will be jumpy. In a backstage scene in which Ronee Blakley and Steven Soles act out a quarrel, the camera is a jackrabbit leaping from wall to wall, chasing the action. This sequence is so glaringly bad both as improvisation and in terms of film technique that one wonders why Dylan put it in. But it's followed by Ronee Blakley onstage singing her own song "Need a New Sun Rising," and then one can guess why. Singing in a rougher, more passionately all-out style than in *Nashville,* she gives the film a fresh, reckless energy that makes the other performers and Dylan himself seem jaded, familiar. Was the quarrel scene, in which she comes across as a completely undesirable woman, stuck in just ahead of her number to sabotage it? The other women in the movie keep their place; the saintly filmmaker may be putting Ronee Blakley in hers.

Sara Dylan has a flirtation scene with Sam Shepard that is like a *cinéma vérité* nightmare. She goes through womanly-wisdom routines while he plays the juvenile, and you feel it will never end. Slender and smiling, Joan Baez is pleasantly relaxed (except when she does an arch parody of a gypsy accent). She never takes what's going on seriously enough to be embarrassing; playing something called The Woman in White, she just seems to be humoring Dylan. But her slightly blank, ironic offhandedness makes the viewer feel a fool for watching, and she does more necking than singing. Part of Dylan's psychodrama here involves a triangle—hot revelations about his past life with Sara Dylan and Joan Baez. With the improvisational techniques he's using, what is revealed amounts to this: Baez has a soliloquy on the sound track about wanting somebody. (The women in this movie are very hard up.) Then she sings a song about her relationship with Dylan, and asks him, "What do you think it would have been like if we'd gotten married?" This is capped by her switching drinks with him; they're playing Hollywood lovers for us. Somewhere toward the fourth hour, Dylan and Sara Dylan are referred to as Renaldo and Clara, and a little later we sit watching while Sara Dylan gives Dylan a little soft pawing and Baez plays the rejected other woman. And in one howling moment, he stands between the two women and the camera moves down his torso, as if he were the oak tree of life. This triangle is the big number (Mailer having already played a love scene onscreen with *his* wife). Dylan tries an artistic-filmmaker device by having Sara Dylan ride in a carriage, and then step out and enter a building, to be replaced by Joan Baez, inside the building, wearing Sara's clothes. Only Dylan could imagine that either of the characters they're playing has enough identity to transfer. (And in visual terms, he picked the wrong woman for this transfer scene: in long shot, Joan Baez and Ronee Blakley look enough alike to confuse viewers.)

The pretense that Dylan is playing someone named Renaldo collapses when we see how he is received by the Tuscarora Indians. They're delighted and honored that Bob Dylan, the star, has come to visit them. And this star, who in his lyrics identifies himself with the "poet who died in the gutter" and the "clown who cried in the alley," reacts as if he were blessing them by his presence. (He wants to be buried in an unmarked grave. Of course. That's why he's made a four-hour movie about himself and his pilgrimage.) Is Dylan still so impressed by adulation? Doesn't he know that even fourth-rate actors in a TV series who rent themselves out to open a supermarket are received as if they were saviors?

[February 13, 1978]

Mythologizing the Sixties

Jane Fonda isn't playing a character in *Coming Home,* she's playing an abstraction—a woman being radicalized. The time is 1968, the place is Los Angeles, and she's Sally Hyde, the proper, repressed wife of a hawkish Marine captain (Bruce Dern). Sally has been married for several years but has no children and nothing to do after her husband leaves for Vietnam, so she volunteers for work in the veterans hospital. On the day she signs up, she crashes into Luke (Jon Voight), who was an athlete when she knew him in high school and is now a paraplegic in a rage of helplessness. She discovers that the men injured in Vietnam are embittered by neglect, and that the other officers' wives, frozen-faced, sitting in their club all groomed and primped, don't want to know about it. As she works among the men, her identification shifts away from the idle-class women. She trades her sexless, crisply laundered clothes for T-shirts and jeans; she stops straightening her hair and lets it frizz up and tangle. Dramatists have always had a terrible time showing their characters "growing," and have usually had to resort to speeches announcing the interior changes; movies can spread the transformation, more novelistically, over a period of months or years. Sally Hyde gradually (and entertainingly) loses her inhibitions, but she develops only to the level of doctrinaire awareness which has been reached by the people who put *Coming Home* together, and this means that the character has a hollow tone—the same inauthenticity that the home-front heroines had in Second World War movies. Fonda develops that sorrowing-woman smile. The other characters are playing abstractions, too. Voight, round-faced and blond-bearded, is like a Kris Kristofferson who studied acting. He handles the transition from rage to boyish romantic hopes with star magnetism, and he gives his scenes a sexual undercurrent that may help put the movie over at the box office. But his role (with scenes that appear to have been suggested by actions of the paraplegic anti-war activist Ron Kovic) could be a parody of the new sanctimoniousness. Luke is a feeling human being, gentle and firm— stuffed with grand compassion. He embraces the distressed and comforts them with thoughts such as "You have enough ghosts to carry around."

The measure of Voight's stature as an actor is that he very nearly gets by with his pontifical lines. Sally's friend Vi (Penelope Milford) is a miniskirted version of the smart, knowing, heart-of-gold working girl of thirties movies. She wises us up with her social perceptions; she explains that she went back where her home used to be but "they tore down my past and built a shopping center." Her salty, pithy, neo-Odetsian dialogue carries the label "gallant proletarian." We may not have had other movies with so much remorse about the Vietnam War, but we've been here before.

Coming Home started out to be about how the Vietnam War changed Americans, and turned into a movie about a woman married to a hawk who has her first orgasm when she goes to bed with a paraplegic. Sally Hyde's hospital collision with Luke is actually the only strong dramatic sequence, and the porny romanticism of their affair has a morbid kick to it. The musical prelude to the sex is reverential—moviemakers haven't found a slicker way of combining purity and eroticism since Marlene Dietrich unknowingly married a runaway monk (Charles Boyer). Viewers could go on fantasizing about this bedroom scene, except that Sally announces the obvious: "That's never happened to me before."

The politics of the film are extremely naïve, and possibly disingenuous. *Coming Home* doesn't oppose the Vietnam War on political grounds. The film embodies a pure-pacifist attitude toward Vietnam: the war is condemned on the basis that our soldiers are maimed and killed in it. Except for a sex scene or two, *Coming Home* is the sort of film a Protestant church group might put out—blandly humanitarian. Though it was shot by Haskell Wexler, a wizard of fast-moving strong graphics, it has a Waspy glaze to it—a soft, pastel innocuousness, as if all those involved were so concerned to get the message across without offending anyone that they fogged themselves in. Jane Fonda's face seems a little vague and pasty, as if she didn't want to stand out too much; her features seem to have disappeared. She's trying to act without her usual snap, and the result is so unsure she comes flutteringly close to a Norma Shearer performance.

The picture has a peculiar, anticipatory tension: you wait so long for something to happen you're ready to jump out of your skin. At first, it seems that the director, Hal Ashby, just has a drifting, dawdling approach to getting under way. Then you realize that this amorphous, inappropriately dreamy movie reflects Ashby's approach to the subject—maybe to any subject now. A former editor, Ashby is generally referred to as a meticulous craftsman; he took more than four months to shoot *Coming Home* and then eight months to supervise the cutting. Can it be that it's so sloppily made because he took so long over it? He plans in the sense of wanting to have enough to edit, and then he has too much. He must get overwhelmed by choices, and so far inside whatever he's shot that he loses the spine of the story. Ashby's two best-known films, *The Last Detail* and

Shampoo, had tightly structured scripts by Robert Towne, and Ashby, working within trim shooting schedules, stayed with those scripts. But he had greater control of his next picture, *Bound for Glory,* and he and his editor, Robert C. Jones, added explicit, messagey scenes and extended the film until it meandered into shapelessness. The *Coming Home* project, initiated by Jane Fonda, began with a script by Nancy Dowd. Then Waldo Salt was brought in for a rewrite, and the Dowd script was mostly discarded. And then when John Schlesinger, who was expected to direct, left the project, and Ashby was hired, he brought in his former editor, Robert C. Jones, who gets his first credit as a writer. The script that emerged from all this labor and God knows how many conferences is a mixture of undeveloped themes, and is so thinly textured that Ashby has filled in the dead spaces by throwing a blanket of rock songs over everything. (It's disconcerting to hear words like "strawberry fields forever" when you're trying to listen to what people are saying to each other.) The music isn't used for a strong beat or for excitement; it's more like a deliberate distraction, as if Ashby had got·bored with the movie and wanted to hear what was going on in the next room.

Ashby's mood scenes can be very personal and touching; a sequence with Luke on the hospital basketball court telling Sally that he's being discharged from the place and Sally on the other side of the fence telling him that she's going to Hong Kong to see her husband does everything it needs to do and more—the feelings spill over, and stay with us. The whole picture is evocative of that messy time; it's permeated with free-floating anxiety, and Luke's stricken eyes serve as an emblem of the country's guilty confusion. *Coming Home* idles, it goes from scene to scene intuitively, romantically, until Sally's visit to Hong Kong; after that the cutting is often like a door slamming in our faces, and, without any dramatic preparation, there's bam-pow crosscutting between simultaneous events. In one sequence, Vi's despondent younger brother Bill (Robert Carradine) is having a fit of depression at the hospital, and Luke, having been on the phone with him, realizes the condition the boy is in and rushes to his aid. We see Luke wheeling himself to his car, folding up his wheelchair and driving off, and then arriving at the hospital and racing through the ward. But in between we see the paraplegics at the hospital staring at Bill and halfheartedly calling out to him, instead of spinning down the corridor to get help. One's time sense is violated; movie crosscutting was more highly developed than this in D. W. Griffith's day. The plot device of having Luke and Sally under F.B.I. surveillance is introduced at such an unstrategic moment that we half expect the F.B.I. men to burst in on their big love scene and beat Luke up. The captain returns from the war limping from a leg wound—ignobly received—and overnight his limp is gone. And what is Sally doing in the scene in which she stands holding out her arms to her husband? Every time there's a cut to her, obediently playing statue, we can practically hear the director thinking, Time stands still; this moment is an eternity. Bad moments are the real eternity.

What the film shows us goes against the grain of what it asks us to accept. The captain is such a charmless, reactionary stiff that when he comes home and Sally says she loves him, we don't believe her. With Bruce Dern in the role, Captain Hyde—who is supposed to be driven mad by the war—looks buggy-eyed and crazily distracted even before he goes to Vietnam; when the war deranges him, who can tell the difference? It's a fatally wrong piece of casting. Everything to do with Hyde is false, creepy, awful—he's like a psychotic Andy Gump. We feel no regret over anything that happens to him; the director has so little imaginative sympathy for a war supporter like Hyde that we don't feel Hyde's bewilderment at the ugliness of what his men have been doing. *He* doesn't seem a casualty of war.

At the beginning, we see Sally's open eyes while she's enduring intercourse with her husband. Later, we watch her face during her orgasm with Luke; this scene is the dramatic center of the movie. The question in the viewer's mind is, What will she feel when her husband comes home and they go to bed? Will she respond, and, if she does, how will he react? The psychological structure of the situation practically demands that he discover her infidelity by the sexual change in her. His attitude would then help determine whether the marriage will become a real one or will end. Instead, he finds out by means of the F.B.I. eavesdroppers; we never learn how he would react to the new, responsive Sally, and Ashby has no ending—just a lot of cutting back and forth.

Allowing for the differences in the wars, *Coming Home* may be the post-Vietnam equivalent of the post–Second World War movie *The Best Years of Our Lives,* which also dealt with returning veterans in smooth, popular terms. Maybe, considering the squalor and disruptiveness of the Vietnam War, we can't expect much more than this depoliticized, melodramatic elegy with shame spreading in the sunshine. There's a pettiness of spirit here. People are judged too easily, and by class. Why are the other officers' wives shown as so coolly indifferent to the conditions in the veterans hospital? Mightn't some of them have been so insulated by their own lack of experience or so lonely and fearful of what could happen to their husbands that they dreaded the thought of the hospital? (And were there no officers among the seriously wounded?) There's a strong element of self-admiration in the film's anti-Vietnam attitudes. It's not enough that Hyde is wrong about the war; he's got to be a lousy lover, too, while the good war protester Luke—paraplegic though he may be—is so life-affirming that he brings Sally Hyde to life. Are liberals really such great lovers?

[February 20, 1978]

The Cotton Mather of
the Movies

*B*lue Collar has to be one of the most dogged pictures ever produced. Making his début as a director, Paul Schrader, the phenomenally successful young screenwriter, has approached directing as a painful, necessary ritual—the ultimate overdue term paper. He goes at it methodically, and gets through it with honors but without flair, humor, believability. *Blue Collar* is an exercise, an idea film in which each scene makes its point and is over. Hard pressed for money, three Detroit auto workers—two black, Zeke (Richard Pryor) and Smokey (Yaphet Kotto), and one white, Jerry (Harvey Keitel)—rob their union headquarters; their haul is only six hundred dollars, but they find a notebook with a record of loansharking transactions and they attempt to blackmail the union. They're small-timers, though, and no match for the operators they're up against, who systematically go about corrupting or destroying them. There's a subject buried here: that of three men whose lives are crud—who have nothing going for them but their camaraderie, and then lose that. But for Schrader their friendship and its destruction are important only as an illustration of the film's you-can't-win thesis.

Blue Collar says that the system grinds all workers down, that it destroys their humanity and their hopes. At the start, under the titles, there's the ominous, heavy rock beat of "Hard Workin' Man"—like the hammer of oppression. The music is calculatedly relentless. It's to make us feel the throbbing noise of the assembly line, so that we'll grasp how closed-in the men's universe is. Noise isn't just noise in this movie, it's fate. The meaning of *Blue Collar* is in its dark, neon tones, its pounding inexorability, its nighttime fatalism. There's no feeling of fresh air, and even the sunlight has a suggestion of purgatory. The *film noir* style of nightmare realism, which in the thirties and forties was used in high-strung thrillers about loners in the city or outlaws on the lam or prisoners threatened by brutal guards or innocents who got on the wrong side of the law and were hounded, is here applied to American blue-collar workers. When Jerry, thinking to escape from the blackmail mess, says "Maybe I'll go to Canada," he gets the classic *film noir* answer—"Wherever you go, they'll find you." Smokey, in the deep voice of a man who knows, spells out the conditions in the automotive industry: "Everything they do, the way they pit the lifers against the new boys, the old against the young, the black against the white, is meant to keep us in our place." And when at the end Zeke and Jerry raise their arms against each other it's the proof that they were pre-ordained to be victims and that the system has won. In all probability, the automotive industry wants to keep the assembly lines running, and doesn't want any dissension among the men which might slow the lines down. But this film's jukebox Marxism carries the kind of cynical, tough-minded charge that encourages people in the audience to yell "Right on!"

The entertaining *noir* movies usually had some neurotic tension; they revelled in sleaziness and shadows, in cheaters and femmes fatales and twisty plots. And they were marvellously well suited to black-and-white cinematography; the oppression had a sleek theatricality—jagged patterns, shivery contrasts, highlighting. The oppression here is really oppressive— blue and drab. Shot by Bobby Byrne, mostly in documentary locations, *Blue Collar* has a consistent dark, threatening scheme, and some of the sequences in the auto plant (particularly the opening montage) are strong and feverish. But several of the most critical dramatic scenes are weakly staged, with no visual energy: the actual robbery doesn't have an ounce of tension, and seems to be lighted with a fifteen-watt bulb. The shortcoming of Schrader's direction is that, with all the ominousness and threat in the percussive music and the visual design, there's no suspense. When the fatalistic style was used in crime thrillers, even with doom hovering in the air luck might change; there was a chance, a hope, some poetic radiance. (If there wasn't, the picture flopped.) Schrader doesn't yet know how to create that tingling sense of possibilities, or that suggestion of delirium, which might make his doominess vibrant and funny. What he's got is a mulish driving force. The script (which he wrote with his brother Leonard) is plodding in a shrewd, manipulative way, and he lets the dull story play itself out. That could be his swindling genius; he's a propagandist without a cause. In puritan tones, he tells us that the world is an ugly place and you can't change a thing. If you stick up your head, they chop it off. So you might as well be a flunky to the bosses and make things easier on yourself.

The risky astuteness is in having Richard Pryor's Zeke (rather than Harvey Keitel's Jerry) the one who's bought out by the union officials. Casting Pryor as the turncoat causes a little friction—our responses to him are destabilized. Zeke is lean, a lightweight griper and joker, boyishly corruptible. He's a brooder, but with a short attention span, and in some fundamental way he's not connected up right. Pryor plays the role close to the vest; you feel Zeke's affable tinniness, his gift for self-deception, and by the end he has mean little eyes that go with his calculations. In Schrader's thinking, to survive men either allow themselves to be used or

407

become users; Smokey, who balks at the first and is constitutionally incapable of the second, has to die. He's the only man of substance in the entire film, and Kotto gives a quietly beautiful performance. His burly, gentle Smokey is pleasure-loving, loyal to his friends, innocent, and deep. And the blending of the latter two qualities seems so natural that it becomes plausible that the bosses have to destroy him—he's a saint. Keitel, short and heavily muscled, has a convincing physique for the Polish welder Jerry Bartowski, but Jerry is the character the writers did the least for (even his motivation for taking part in the robbery—that his daughter needs braces for her teeth—is tacky, since the U.A.W. has a dental plan), and Keitel is glum. He doesn't seem to use his instincts, all we see is his determination to act with integrity. Could it be that he's interiorizing his emotions, in response to Schrader's conception of the emptiness of Jerry's life, and doesn't realize how little he's putting out? Keitel produces the veneer of someone who's meant to believe that his life is terrible; he holds on to the idea so hard his face is pinched in concentration. A looser, lighter performance might have covered the hole in the script—might have made us see qualities in Jerry that would explain his having two black men for his closest friends, and explain why they would feel at home with him. As it is, there's no interplay, nothing to suggest that there's a history to the friendship. All their responses to each other are so programmed they might have met the day before—they're pals because the movie needs them to be. In the same way, the three men have an accomplice in the robbery because an accomplice is needed to rat on them, and at the end Jerry goes back to his locker at the factory so there can be the confrontation between him and Zeke.

Harry Bellaver's portrait of a smooth, white-haired labor faker—Eddie (Knuckles) Johnson, the president of the local—is enjoyable, because Bellaver gives one the impression of effectiveness; you can see how Knuckles gets things done. It's too neat, though, that he knows just how to divide and conquer the three men, because he understands their characters perfectly. (He must have read the script.) Most of what happens in the movie has no intrinsic interest; it's for the sake of the plot. When there's an incident at the plant which doesn't serve the plot directly, such as George Memmoli's bit as a man enraged by a food dispenser that doesn't work, it's a relief. There's not nearly enough detail of what the men say and do at home or at the union meeting or the bowling alley or the beer tavern. No one ever talks about quitting; there's no indication of the rapid turnover of auto workers, of the fact that perhaps thirty per cent a year get fed up with the gruelling, noisy, hard work and leave (so that auto workers get younger all the time). If the film recognized that men can step sidewise in the society, can try to move on to something easier, or something that doesn't grind them down, its cosmic hopelessness would look overcooked.

In this movie, even the men's buying worthless things on the installment plan is part of the bosses' grand design. *Blue Collar* is about the malaise of the workingman, trapped in all his comfort. Schrader isn't interested in the men's lives; it's only the system—a symbol of evil—that quickens his blood. There's anger in this movie (there is in most of the films Schrader has had a hand in—that's what makes his scripts sell), and his hostile, melancholy tone unifies this amalgam of pilfered pieces of old pictures and ideologies. The big flaw in *Blue Collar* is that Schrader has imposed his personal depression on characters who, in dramatic terms, haven't earned it. He's given Zeke, Smokey, and Jerry no will but the will to destroy themselves. They embark on an ill-planned robbery; then they're caught and are full of self-pity. And when they blame the system for their own dumbness, we're supposed to agree with them. This is the old plot about thieves falling out, only it's the oppressors who are responsible.

People can be impressed by a movie this low in entertainment value; they can assume that it's thinking of higher things. But chances are that when Paul Schrader gets his bearings as a director he'll put his manipulative cynicism to more sparkling uses.

□ □ □

*T*he Betsy, an adaptation of a Harold Robbins novel, is also set in Detroit. Laurence Olivier, who plays the superabundantly sexed patriarch of an automobile dynasty, stands out with startling boldness, and one begins to perceive the secret of his greatness: Laurence Olivier dares to be foolish. He doesn't protect himself; he just goes right out there and takes the risks. In *The Betsy,* he keeps on acting after everyone else has given up. They all wilt and die, and there he is, supplying energy to his scenes, working up a Scottish-Midwestern accent, giving tautness to his flabby lines. He must be doing it for himself—for the sheer love of testing himself as an actor. The lines destroy the other performers; you see the sheepish faces and hear the dead fall of the words. How does Olivier manage to speak so that we absorb the sense without having the idiot dialogue ring in our ears? Partly by distracting us with his accent (the vowel sounds recall Tim Conway's Swede in his running series of skits with Carol Burnett) and partly by using the big, harsh voice he has developed in recent years, as if in defiance of natural processes, to blast through the film's largo style.

The director, Daniel Petrie, aims low and misses his target—maybe through taste and halfheartedness as much as ineptitude. The film announces its theme: the lust for success and power. Everything is explained to us; each sequence advances the three-generation plot—it's like a TV mini-series jammed together. Yet it has no momentum; it's tranquil trash. Petrie doesn't have the juicy vulgarity of soul which Harold Robbins requires—the film is like a reverie on the clichés of the Robbins genre, and the cinematographer, Mario Tosi, gives everything a dreamy calendar-art softness. When the actresses are stripped for their carnal numbers, you're embarrassed—not because they're nude but because they're nude and it isn't risqué, it isn't bawdy, it isn't titillating. They've taken off their clothes for nothing.

[February 27, 1978]

Empathy, and Its Limits

*E*rica (Jill Clayburgh), the heroine of Paul Mazursky's *An Unmarried Woman*, sleeps in a T-shirt and bikini panties. There are so few movies that deal with recognizable people that this detail alone is enough to pick up one's spirits. Erica works part-time in a SoHo gallery and lives in an East Sixties high rise, with her stockbroker husband (Michael Murphy) and their fourteen-year-old daughter, Patti (Lisa Lucas). She has been married for sixteen snug years when her husband tells her he's fallen in love with a girl he met in Bloomingdale's. Suddenly, she's on her own, like her divorced women friends, contending with loneliness and the comic horrors of the modern dating game. She's resentful, scared, dazed. And her sexual hostilities are so acute that when a man greets her with an ordinary, faintly leering hello she rasps out an obscene put-down. The audience breaks up in laughter at her expletive—which represents the truth of what she feels, and cuts right through to what's on his mind, too.

Jill Clayburgh has a cracked, warbly voice—a modern polluted-city huskiness. And her trembling, near-beautiful prettiness suggests a lot of· pressure; her face is a little off-key, quizzical and unsymmetrical, and too thin for her features. (Nature intended there to be cheeks where there are only hollows.) On the stage, she can be dazzling, but the camera isn't in love with her—she doesn't seem lighted from within. When Erica's life falls apart and her reactions go out of control, Clayburgh's floating, not-quite-sure, not-quite-here quality is just right. And she knows how to use it: she isn't afraid to get puffy-eyed from crying, or to let her face go slack. No other film has made such a sensitive, empathic case for a modern woman's need to call her soul her own, and *An Unmarried Woman* is funny and buoyant besides. It's an enormously friendly, soft-edged picture. Yet there's a lot of hot air circulating in it. Mazursky, who wrote the script as

410

well as directed, is a superb shaggy screenwriter and rarely less than deft, but he touches so many women's-liberation bases that you begin to feel virtuous, as if you'd been passing out leaflets for McGovern.

In dealing with social themes, movies are generally about five years behind books, and right now they're also two or three years behind TV. That may explain why Mazursky is a little ashamed to introduce Erica's consciousness-raising group, and passes it off as a club. Erica's clubmates are played by Pat Quinn, the Alice of *Alice's Restaurant,* as hardheaded, compromising Sue, in short hair with thick bangs; Kelly Bishop (who was known as Carole Bishop when she appeared in *A Chorus Line*) as Elaine, an alcoholic, brunette version of the old, Eve Arden pal; and Linda Miller as the glazed seductress Jeannette. We can't see what brought Erica and these coarse-grained types together; she went to Vassar and they're M-G-M, class of '39. But we know what they're doing in the movie: they illustrate the various humiliations to which aging women are subject, and they spell things out—loss of self-esteem, problems of identity. They're in the movie to raise *our* consciousness.

An Unmarried Woman may give Mazursky the popular success that his films *Blume in Love, Harry & Tonto,* and *Next Stop, Greenwich Village* should have given him; this is the only one to deal in marketable compassion. What may be disappointing to those who love his earlier work is that in crucial parts of this picture he seems to have suppressed his sense of satire. The analytic sessions in his *Bob & Carol & Ted & Alice* and *Blume in Love* were small masterpieces of comic timing: every pause made its point. Here Erica's two sessions with her therapist, Tanya (played by Dr. Penelope Russianoff), dribble on tentatively, in what feels like real time; they're lifelike in the worst sense. Potentially, the analyst-analysand relationship is just as funny as in his other movies—maybe funnier, since both doctor and patient appear to be unusually slow thinkers. But Mazursky seems so overwhelmed by the seriousness of the subject that he's unwilling to trim and heighten these conversations so that the banality would make us laugh instead of just leaving us to feel, Oh, God, this scene isn't working. He may be afraid of being cruel, yet there is no cruelty in the comedy of his earlier pictures—his heart and his wit are in the same place. In the second session, when the therapist (who dawdles like Stepin Fetchit) finally suggests that Erica "get into the stream of life, get back in there"—i.e., go out with men—it's a deliverance for the audience, because the picture needs to start rolling.

It does. Erica has a one-night stand with a wood sculptor, Charlie (Cliff Gorman), at his loft; the clotted hanging fern that she pushes aside when she leaves—it's like a long-haired wig that's growing—might be an emblem of their tussle. The whole movie is full of sexual anxiety; that's why it has such a prickly, contemporary feel. It's very consumer-culture-conscious and New York–conscious. The cinematography, by Arthur Ornitz, which features windows and skyline views, doesn't have anything like the sun-spangled vivacity that Gordon Willis brought to the New York of *Annie Hall* (a film with related states of anxiety). Ornitz is an inexpressive realist; he makes images "real" by sapping the life out of them. (There's no dynamism even when the camera moves.) But his work here is more delicately muted and less grungy than usual—the SoHo streets seem to spark him. The score, by Bill Conti (who did the *Rocky* music), is heavy on the saxophone—a blend of Gershwin and *Last Tango* that is maybe too expressive. It keeps crashing in, drenching us in symphony-of-a-city melancholy sex. Even when the sex is fairly cheerful. Erica's next encounter is with Saul Kaplan (Alan Bates), a bearded, bearlike painter who works in acrylics on huge canvases. (His studio and his paintings are those of Paul Jenkins, whose style suggests a more garish, sloppier, and less lyrical Morris Louis.) Bates works on a canvas lovingly: this is one of the rare occasions when a movie actor has simulated a painter so that you enjoy watching. In the first film Bates has made in this country, he gets a chance to be expansive and show his talent for comic mimicry. (He does great double takes using only his gleaming eyes.) Saul is another of Mazursky's men who are born husbands—an older Larry Lapinsky, a rounder Blume. When he comes to dinner at Erica's apartment to meet her daughter, Patti tries to be flip and knowing; she gets snagged in her feelings, recovers, and apologizes. The scene doesn't turn too poignant, because we take in Patti's shifts of emotion through Saul's what-have-I-got-into-here responses. He has scale and ebullience; he's so blissfully, demonstratively physical that the movie gives promise of turning into a happy love comedy. But Erica has been becoming more and more high-minded, under Mazursky's awed gaze. He's such a romantic that when he turns feminist he's the most romantic feminist of them all.

Is a princess fantasy any the better for being dreamed up by a man (and dedicated, in an end title, to his wife)? Erica leaves men groggy with admiration after they've been to bed with her. Her ex-husband, realizing the mistake he's made, asks to be taken back, but she's grown beyond him. (His tight face and anguished eyes show us that he accepts the justice of his punishment.) Erica is in a different class from her divorced clubmates. They can't land a decent, suitable, sexy fella; she casually snares the famous Saul Kaplan. But she's discovering so much about herself and the meaning of independence that she isn't ready for a commitment.

Jill Clayburgh's appeal to the audience is in her addled radiance; she seems so punchy that we're a little worried for her. And so when the movie provides Erica with a robust, worshipful man with good instincts (and he's even got money), and she hesitates and demurs and worries about her development, we lose interest in her. This attractive man with the most

412

honorable, protective intentions wants her (and her daughter) to come to his house in Vermont for the summer, and this woman who has nothing in particular she wants to do and nothing special she's interested in feels she has to stay in New York to continue finding herself. In New York in the summer? She appears to be a goofed-up spoilsport, who doesn't want Saul or herself or her child to have a good time. What is she going to find? That's what viewers may be asking. As a moviemaker, Mazursky is a stand-up guru, a manic psychologist; his gift is that he can be funny without telling jokes. But he seems afraid to kid the rhetoric of the quest for the self. This quest—a new kind of feminine mystique—Mazursky treats tenderly, respectfully.

There are probably a fair number of men who have become feminists out of love for a woman combined, perhaps, with a sense of justice and maybe a dose of guilt, but Paul Mazursky is the only one of them to have made a movie about it. His heroines, such as Nina in *Blume in Love* and Sarah in *Next Stop, Greenwich Village,* have been mysteriously, somewhat antagonistically unreachable, and his heroes have made bumbling attempts to understand them. Identifying with the heroes, Mazursky didn't stay away from making them fools. But here, trying to identify with Erica and tell the movie from a woman's point of view, he does shy away from having her look foolish. And because women are still mysterious to him, he takes refuge in the new women's rhetoric. His approach is benign, tentative— entangled in the craziness of this war in which you sleep with the enemy.

From the way Mazursky presents Erica, when she indicates to Saul that she isn't ready to live with him—that she needs more time—we can't tell whether she's struggling toward independence or embracing the generalized anxiety and dissatisfaction in the culture and sinking into it. Mazursky's underlying ambivalence may be partly responsible for the lack of inner strength and depth in Jill Clayburgh's performance. Erica has vague yearnings, while Saul, trying to hold on to her, despairing of ever getting through to her, is solid, alive, all there. The parts of the movie don't fit together. This nebulous tormentor Erica is not the same woman who was happily married for sixteen years; she was never happily married. She was never solid and all there. Mazursky turned away from his story about the tragicomic shattered lives of divorcées who can't find the emotional security of a new marriage toward the story of a woman who's looking for something—unformulated—in herself. He began in Dore Scharyland and then stumbled into the Red Desert. His ambiguous ending, which is a way of postponing *his* decision, suggests that he can't get through to his own creation. He doesn't know what's going on in Erica's head.

Despite Mazursky's conscious intentions, Saul has been made such a rich, loamy Father Earth figure that he overpowers the movie, and Erica seems puny and pale by comparison. Everyone is neurotic except Saul; the only way the comic balance could be restored would be if Saul were revealed to be a smothering fraud. Erica seems an idiot for resisting him—the picture leaves her turning in the wind, like a slightly gaga Mother Courage directed by Andrei Serban.

[March 6, 1978]

"What symmetrical digits!"

—W.C. Fields to Mae West as he lifts her hand
to his lips in My Little Chickadee.

*I*n *Fingers,* the first film he has directed, James Toback is trying to be Orson Welles and Carol Reed, Dostoevski, Conrad, and Kafka. The film is a howl of ambition, and you get the feeling that at least two-thirds of it is still locked up in the writer-director's head—that he simply did not have the experience, the cast, or the budget to get more of his exuberantly melodramatic fantasy onto the screen. Still, what's there has the wild self-dramatization that one associates with the young Tennessee Williams, or with Mailer when he gets high on excess. Insanity, violent bouts of sex, Jacobean revenge killings—nothing is too much for Toback in his exhilarated state. There's almost a swagger in the way he consciously goes beyond the rationally acceptable: he's looking for art in that beyond, wanting the unknown—the dangerous—to take over. It's a willed hysteria. We're used to it in the work of young poets and young novelists who are trying to feel as intensely and recklessly as possible, who want to be electrifying, but it's startling to see this hunger for extremes nakedly revealed on the screen. James Toback doesn't just risk self-parody in *Fingers*—he falls into it. Yet the film never seems ridiculous, because he's got true moviemaking fever.

All of us have probably had the feeling of being divided between what we got from our mother and what we got from our father, and no doubt some of us feel that we've gone through life trying to please each of them and never fully succeeding, because we have always been torn between them. *Fingers* takes these Oedipal facts of life and tries to treat them in classic, tragic terms within the structure of a gangster shoot-'em-up. Jimmy

414

(Harvey Keitel) has a father (Michael V. Gazzo) who's a Mafia loan shark and a mother (Marian Seldes) who's a concert pianist gone mad. The split carries through everything in his life. He's an artist with the soul of a violent hood; he makes his living as a strong-arm collector, but alone in his apartment he's a sensitive, dedicated pianist, and he longs to liberate that side of himself. Jimmy's father is an Italian Catholic, and his mother is Jewish. He's aggressively hostile toward women and takes them at their most passive, the way he secretly wants to be taken; he's victim and victimizer. Each half works against the other half, so that he's in torment.

As Toback has written the material, the jagged split in parentage doesn't dramatize Jimmy's conflicts, it merely explains them. Toback, who taught English at City College, lays these polar concepts of Jimmy's internal conflicts right out on the surface; he surveys them like elements in a literature course—the symmetrical patterning is perfect. But they don't *play*. Jimmy needs to be an exciting, violent, emotional man, a man who's at war with himself, who has so much going on that he's shooting sparks, hitting highs and lows. Then, maybe, we could experience the pianist/gangster split as a heightened, neurotic metaphor for Everyman—a Dostoevskian Everyman. If we're to feel that, Jimmy's torment must be *live*—torment with charm and magnetism. Harvey Keitel tries more unusual character touches in *Fingers* than he did in *Blue Collar,* and some of them have real audacity, but he seems scared of making a mistake; as a volatile gangster, he's like Richard Conte with a hump on his back—a thick book on the theory of acting. The role of Jimmy could have done with some of the flamboyant, hot-wire sexual awareness that Keitel had in his small parts in *Alice Doesn't Live Here Anymore* and *Taxi Driver.* Keitel doesn't use Jimmy's sexual confusion for bisexual seductiveness, he uses it as if it meant that Jimmy were paralyzed by misery. There's an idea behind the performance: Jimmy is robotized by his divisions. One never gets the sense that he loves his music or is transported by it; rather, he's striving for perfection. (Keitel may think him incapable of being transported, because he's cursed—his soul is dirty.) Alone at the piano, playing the Bach E-Minor Toccata, Keitel does a very creepy version of the tics and humming along of Glenn Gould and Erroll Garner and other musicians who have seemed to play the music in their heads. Jimmy has a nervous drive not just for classical music but for rock, too, and he carries around a cassette machine and plays pop music wherever he goes. When a man in a SoHo restaurant complains of the noise, he snarls, "This is The Jamies, man—'Summertime, Summertime'—the most musically inventive song of 1958. Do you mean to tell me that doesn't go with your shrimp?" Conceivably, a man could be jumpy and half crazed with tension and still feel the beat and get happy and forget everything else. But Keitel never allows him to forget a thing; Jimmy seems to be waiting for somebody to complain—he's playing his cassette to punish people. He does everything in his head, even making love. This scowling robot Jimmy is an actor's intellectualization that makes good sense, but it dampens the passion in Toback's fantasy, and it doesn't do anything for an audience.

Keitel is far more effective in Jimmy's funny scenes. At one point, some thugs set him up for an arrest, and he does a hipster routine, trying to talk the cop out of taking him in, and then, when he fails and is thrown in the tank, he sings the Bach Toccata to his cellmates. Stuck in an elevator on his way up to a crucial audition, he whacks the buttons furiously, with all his pent-up fear localized in his fingers; there's more tension in this pantomime than anywhere else in his performance, because his tightness works for him here. It works comically: there's a Mack Sennett side to his panic—he's a loser in a frenzy of losing. Gazzo, whose cheeks have filled out since his *Godfather II* days, comes on strong as Jimmy's loudmouthed, always hopped-up, sentimental father, but he's enjoyable; the picture needs his hammy all-out emotionalism. When Jimmy shows his love for his father by flattering the old man, telling him that other Mafiosi are frightened of him, Keitel has just the right desperate tenderness. Jimmy opens up here, and we can see layers in his character. But we needed to see more of Jimmy's capacity for feeling at the beginning, so that we'd care enough about him to want to know why he is what he is. If he were more open at the start—if the film built a dramatic curve—then the audition would have some suspense; his failing would be the catastrophe that puts him on a downward course, and his final closing in would have more horror.

There's an avidity for filmmaking in *Fingers*; in some sequences—such as one at a health club, moving the action around the swimming pool to Jimmy semi-raping a brunette vamp (Tanya Roberts) in the ladies' room, or a street scene with Jimmy comforting a weeping old woman—the director's pleasure at being able to work in this medium is palpable. The rooms look exactly right; the sound is unusually clean and natural; the camera setups are simple, yet inventive; the bit players (such as Georgette Muir, in the role of the father's girlfriend, Anita, a weary-but-still-trying old campaigner) are wonderful. The moviemaking itself doesn't seem forced or hyperbolic; there's a sureness—a sound instinct—in the pacing and the flow of images. The SoHo locations, where chic and crummy coexist, are metaphorically perfect. Toback doesn't establish the neighborhood, though; he takes it for granted. And he takes it for granted that we'll understand why Jimmy starts chasing Carol (Tisa Farrow), a painter with a druggy-angel look, and becomes fixated on her. When Jimmy says to her, "Don't you understand what's here . . . between us?" we can't tell if it's all meant to be on his side or if there really *is* something between them. It's as if what was in Toback's mind were so powerful to him that he assumed we must know all about it.

The fantasy element is most fully realized in the sequences involving Jim Brown as Dreems, a former world-champion prizefighter who now operates a café, where Carol hangs out. Toback (who wrote a book about Brown) idolizes Dreems, in a very special sense: Dreems is so completely knowledgeable about everything to do with sex that he takes one look at Jimmy and knows immediately what his hangups are. The black athlete Dreems is sexually psychic. And so another division is charted: between the frightened Jimmy and the utterly confident, sensual master. Dreems treats Carol and another angelically lovely girl, Christa (Carole Francis), as sexual slaves, and they're proud of the honor. There's a whiff of the dàrk-powers-that-we-whites-will-never-understand in the film's idolatry of Dreems; naïve in an almost comic-book way, this suggestion of a world out of the reach of the educated mind—a world more heated, where you're exposed to the ultimate danger—is the Conradian element of *Fingers*. In the script that Toback wrote for the Karel Reisz film *The Gambler,* the hero went to Harlem at the end as if he were voyaging into the Heart of Darkness, but in Reisz's film the sexual fantasy—the belief that the black man can see right through to your weakness—wasn't nearly as apparent as it is here. This film sees Dreems as a man without incapacitating divisions. Jimmy is hideously violent when he's on the rampage retaliating against his father's enemies (this part of the picture might be called *Piano Driver*). But the most shocking scene is that of Dreems disciplining Carol and Christa. (It has some of the I-can't-believe-this impact of the Coke-bottle scene in *The Long Goodbye*.) The shock is in the speed of Dreems' action: the film views him not as thinking fast but as not needing to think—as not being sicklied o'er with the white man's pale cast of thought. Dreems is scariest—hardest to interpret—when he's low-key and affable; he's what Jimmy is terrified of, and his world is what Jimmy aches to be part of. It's Jimmy's (or Toback's) fantasy that if he belonged to that world he could live as violently as he does without living in terror. He envies blacks because, as he might see it, "it wouldn't scare them to be me." But, being white, Jimmy can't escape from "civilization"; his own violence destroys him.

Fingers tries to create the screen equivalent of a tropical region of the mind; it's an educated man's high-powered masochistic fairy tale, the story of a descent into madness. Toback is trying hard for purgative effects; he wants to show us man stripped down to a cowering, naked animal waiting in the jungle. Normality doesn't interest Toback; he's playing the literary-adolescent's game of wanting to go crazy so he can watch his own reactions. And because he doesn't censor his masculine racial fantasies, his foolishness and his terrible ideas pour out freely. The movie is a true oddity: it could stand as a definition of the perils of the "personal" film. Yet its streak of euphoric humor suggests that Toback could take romantic screwball comedy to a new, high plane, where excess could become rhapsodic.

[March 13, 1978]

Shivers

There's an ecstatic element in Brian De Palma's new thriller *The Fury*: he seems to extend the effects he's playing with about as far as he can without losing control. This inferno comedy is perched right on the edge. It may be to De Palma what *The Wild Bunch* was to Peckinpah. You feel he never has to make another horror movie. To go on would mean trying to kill people in ever more photogenically horrific ways, and he's already got two killings in *The Fury* which go so far beyond anything in his last film, *Carrie,* that that now seems like child's play. There's a potency about the murders here—as if De Palma were competing with himself, saying "You thought *Carrie* was frightening? Look at this!" He's not a great storyteller; he's careless about giving the audience its bearings. But De Palma is one of the few directors in the sound era to make a horror film that is so visually compelling that a viewer seems to have entered a mythic night world. Inside that world, transfixed, we can hear the faint, distant sound of De Palma cackling with pleasure.

Most other directors save the lives of the kind, sympathetic characters; De Palma shatters any Pollyanna thoughts—any expectations that a person's goodness will protect him. He goes past Hitchcock's perversity into something gleefully kinky. In *Carrie,* he built a two-way tension between our hope that the friendless, withdrawn, telekinetic heroine would be able to sustain her Cinderella happiness at the school prom and our dread of what we feared was coming. De Palma builds up our identification with the very characters who will be destroyed, or become destroyers, and some people identified so strongly with Carrie that they couldn't laugh—they felt hurt and betrayed. *The Fury* doesn't have the beautiful simplicity of the Cinderella's-revenge plot of *Carrie,* and it doesn't involve us emotionally in such a basic way; it's a far more hallucinatory film.

418

The script, which John Farris adapted from his novel, is about two teen-agers, spiritual twins who have met only telepathically. They are superior beings; in a primitive tribe, we are told, they would have become the prophets, the magicians, the healers. In modern civilization, they become the prisoners of a corrupt government (ours), which seeks to use them for espionage, and treats them impersonally, as secret weapons. In the opening scenes, set on a beach in Israel, the psychic boy, Robin (Andrew Stevens), is captured by an agent, Childress (John Cassavetes). The picture deals with the efforts of Robin's father, Peter Sandza (Kirk Douglas), to find him. The search centers in Chicago, where Sandza enlists the help of the psychic girl, Gillian (Amy Irving). Douglas gives a creditable professional-powerhouse performance; his quest has a routine action-film quality, though, and doesn't affect us emotionally. Once again, the suffering center of a De Palma film is a young girl. Amy Irving (she was the chestnut-haired, troubled Sue Snell, the survivor of the prom, in *Carrie*) brings a tremulous quality to *The Fury*; she's lyrical in the most natural way. The script is cheap gothic espionage occultism; she humanizes it. Both Gillian and Robin have the power to zap people with their minds. Gillian is trying to cling to her sanity—she doesn't want to hurt anyone. And, knowing that her power is out of her conscious control, she's terrified of her own secret rages. There's a little of the young Sylvia Sidney in Amy Irving's apprehensive, caught-in-the-glare-of-headlights beauty. Her sense of alarm makes us feel that real lives are at stake. With her blue, heavy-lidded almond eyes, she can look like an Asiatic princess in a fairy tale or a mask of tragedy. Farris's complicated, rickety plot doesn't give Robin an opportunity to demonstrate his prodigious gifts before Childress corrupts them. And it doesn't develop the core relationship of Robin and Gillian, so that we'd feel her need to get to him (and to avenge him). This film's dark, symphonic terror might seem almost abstract if Amy Irving weren't there all the way through, to hold it together. De Palma's virtuosity and her unaffected performance play off against each other, to the great advantage of both.

There's a third major collaborator: Richard H. Kline, whose deep-toned, velvety cinematography keeps the whole movie vibrating. Kline, who shot *King Kong,* knows how to light to create hyperbolic imagery; scenes such as a telepathic vision on a staircase and gunfire on the streets at night have the luster of a binful of garnets, amethysts, cat's-eyes. The compositions have so much depth and heavy shadow that objects stand out as if they were in 3-D; one can touch the metallic sheen of the cars, respond to Robin as a sculptural presence. There's also a fourth major collaborator: John Williams, who has composed what may be as apt and delicately varied a score as any horror movie has ever had. He scares us without banshee melodramatics. He sets the mood under the opening titles: otherworldly, seductively frightening. The music cues us in. This isn't going to be a gross horror film; it's visionary, science-fiction horror. De Palma is the reverse side of the coin from Spielberg. *Close Encounters* gives us the comedy of hope, *The Fury* the comedy of cruelly dashed hope. With Spielberg, what happens is so much better than you dared hope that you have to laugh; with De Palma, it's so much worse than you feared that you have to laugh.

Obviously, De Palma was offered this project because Robin and Gillian have telekinetic powers, like Carrie's, and, just as obviously, although he uses some effects similar to those in *Carrie,* he's too original not to have embroidered them and turned them into something different. The violence is presented in such a stylized, aestheticized way that it transcends violence. When Peter Sandza is in a commandeered Cadillac at night in a pea-soup fog and the cars chasing him go up in balls of flame, the scene is so spectacularly beautiful that it hardly matters if one doesn't know why he sends his car flying into Lake Michigan; maybe he's just blowing off steam—having a destruction orgy because De Palma felt that this flourish was *visually* necessary to complete the sequence. There is a joke involving an amusement-park ride which is surely one of the great perverse visual gags of all time; one knows exactly what's going on, yet here, too, one is struck by the languorous richness of the scene. The joke itself has been aestheticized. Most directors are so afraid of losing our attention that if two people are sitting together talking we're not allowed to see what's happening around them. De Palma pans around the rooms and landscapes slowly—a Godardian ploy—to give us more and more to look at, and to key up our expectations. He doesn't quite make good on his promises: he doesn't provide the crucial actions—the payoffs—within the circling, enlarging movements. But the expansiveness is essential, because of the stodgy dialogue; he anticipates the boredom of the ear by providing excitement for the eye.

No other director shows such clear-cut development in technique from film to film. In camera terms, De Palma was learning fluid, romantic steps in *Obsession*; he started to move his own way in *Carrie*—swirling and figure skating, sensuously. You could still see the calculation. Now he has stopped worrying about the steps. He's caught up with his instructors— with Welles in *Touch of Evil,* with Scorsese in *Mean Streets.* What distinguishes De Palma's visual style is smoothness combined with a jazzy willingness to appear crazy or campy; it could be that he's developing one of the great film styles—a style in which he stretches out suspense while grinning his notorious alligator grin. He has such a grip on technique in *The Fury* that you get the sense of a director who cares about little else; there's a frightening total purity in his fixation on the humor of horror. It makes the film seem very peaceful, even as one's knees are shaking.

The Fury isn't tightly structured; there are rising and falling waves of suspense, and De Palma's visual rhythms outpace the story. (Sometimes the characters talk as if they hadn't noticed that the movie has gone past what they're saying.) Randall Jarrell once quoted some lines from Whitman and commented, "There are faults in this passage and they *do not matter.*" The visual poetry of *The Fury* is so strong that its narrative and verbal inadequacies *do not matter.* No Hitchcock thriller was ever so intense, went so far, or had so many "classic" sequences.

Carrie Snodgress returns to the screen in the role of Hester, Peter Sandza's lover and confederate; she's so pale and thin-faced that she's unrecognizable until one registers her eyes and hears that purring, husky voice of hers which seems to come out of furrowed vocal cords. Her plaintive, low-pitched normality helps *The Fury* to touch the ground now and then; fortunately, she goes out of the picture in a tense, slow-motion death-knell sequence that does her full honor. Fiona Lewis, who plays the woman Childress assigns to watch over Robin and satisfy his sexual needs, is not so lucky; she goes out of the picture in perhaps the most gothic way that any beloved has ever been dispatched by her lover. Her exit is topped only by that of Childress, and this is where De Palma shows his evil grin, because we are implicated in this murderousness: we want it, just as we wanted to see the bitchy Chris get hers in *Carrie.* Cassavetes is an ideal villain (as he was in *Rosemary's Baby*)—sullenly indifferent to anything but his own interests. He's so right for Childress that one regrets that there wasn't a real writer around to provide dialogue that would match his gloomy, viscous nastiness. He's been endowed with a Dr. Strangelove dead arm in a black sling (and there's a nice touch: his dead arm hurts), but only his end is worthy of him. This finale—a parody of Antonioni's apocalyptic vision at the close of *Zabriskie Point*—is the greatest finish for any villain ever. One can imagine Welles, Peckinpah, Scorsese, and Spielberg still stunned, bowing to the ground, choking with laughter.

□ □ □

*I*n the early fifties, a Cleveland disc jockey, Alan Freed, built a following of black listeners by playing rhythm-and-blues records produced by small companies for the "race" market; the driving beat and shouting, screaming, raving voices caught on with white teen-agers, too, and his nightly "Moondog Rock 'n' Roll Party" became a key element in the youth subculture. Freed is generally credited with having invented the term "rock 'n' roll"; in fact, he successfully filed a copyright on it. In 1954, New York's WINS decided to feature rock, and signed him up. Freed introduced the new mixture of rhythm-and-blues with country-and-Western to thousands of teen-agers in the late fifties, and they flocked to the three films he appeared in and to the live, interracial shows he produced and m.c.'d, which were generally staged in movie palaces. He became the kingpin in the world of selling rock 'n' roll records to teen-agers.

In *American Hot Wax* Alan Freed (played by Tim McIntire) is presented as a martyr to the cause of rock 'n' roll. He's so righteous he's Buford Pusser in the world of pop music; the picture might have been called *Spinning Tall.* The moviemakers—the director, Floyd Mutrux; the producer, Art Linson; the screenwriter, John Kaye—should have had more trust in the fifties-rock milieu and in their own talents, because everything about the movie *except* this pious morality-tale aspect of it is cheerfully, trashily enjoyable. That includes McIntire's performance. He creates a layered character inside the myth. Freed is weary, omniscient, and slightly uninvolved—a man who sacrifices himself because he doesn't care enough to save himself; he's tinny and self-pitying in the show-biz manner of obnoxious, depressing comedians. What makes *American Hot Wax* so entertaining is the unashamed tackiness of a milieu in which people's minds aren't violated by ideas. The fast-talking lapel grabbers who rush in and out simply want success and fun. (It's what used to be a B-movie milieu.) Mutrux has a feeling for the crass, pop surfaces of things, for the energetic seediness and the too bright smiles of the singers and agents and managers and promo men and assorted hangers-on who clamor for Freed's attention. They surround him at the radio station, at the recording studio; they gang up on him in hallways and outer offices, and they wait for him on the street. The supplicants run the gamut of show-business types; there's even a sisters act, and the younger girl—she looks like an eight-year-old Gilda Radner—is so dead set on stardom she won't stop belting out her music when the audition is over.

Freed's unabashedly shrill secretary, Sheryl (Fran Drescher), is in the middle of the congestion—noisily adding to it. (Jean Harlow might have been her voice teacher.) Sheryl has a blank, open, pretty face with nothing in reserve; she swings her full skirts and proudly explains how she coördinates her clothes for work (she picks them out the night before). Sheryl's happy ordinariness runs along the edges of Freed's maudlin martyrdom, and the edges are the life of the film. Fran Drescher, who played the bit part of Connie in *Saturday Night Fever,* was born in 1957 and was first runner-up to Miss New York City Teenager of 1973, when she was fifteen. As Sheryl, she suggests a nasal fifties version of the appealingly vacuous friend-of-the-heroine parts that Lucille Ball used to play in the mid-thirties. But Sheryl isn't contrasted with a middle-class ingenue who speaks in dulcet tones. She's the only love interest in the movie, and Mookie (Jay Leno), Freed's shovel-faced driver, who doesn't know how to court her except by teasing her, keeps her shrieking in outrage; the two of them flirt and bicker constantly—this solves the problem of how to have a love story without conventional romantic scenes. She's all perfect curls, and he's got his slicked-down Presley ducktail. The way Jay Leno plays

Mookie, he's like a dogface soldier who's done his basic training in coffeehouse comedy.

The film toys with the conventions of musicals, good-naturedly, half parodistically. The standard earnest young composer who is discovered and set on the path to success is replaced by Laraine Newman as Teenage Louise, a bobby-soxer composer. Newman's stylized emphatic way of speaking her lines gives them a comic twist, and when Louise teaches a song she's written to four young black men she meets on the sidewalk outside the radio station, and they start to harmonize on her material, the song turns into a spoof of countless "improvised" routines in earlier movies. At other points, such as in dealing with a twelve-year-old boy (Moosie Drier) who's president of the Buddy Holly Fan Club (five thousand members), Mutrux dances on a satirical tightrope. He's helped by John Kaye's dialogue; Kaye (who also did the script of *Rafferty and the Gold Dust Twins*) writes a subtle form of verbal slapstick—people having normal conversations sound as if they'd shorted a few circuits.

Mutrux has worked with the same cinematographer, William A. Fraker, on three pictures now, and they must have a good accord, because Fraker does less of his usual lyric blur; the contrasts are sharper, and there's more going on within the frames. Fraker keeps *American Hot Wax* from having the drabness of the old B musicals centering on the world of radio. When Freed is in the outer room of the recording studio listening to a group cutting a record, we see the group through a glass wall, with the responses of Freed and his entourage reflected on it. In the last part of the film, when Freed puts on a big rock 'n' roll show at the Brooklyn Paramount (it was actually shot in L.A. at the Wiltern Theatre, with its signs changed), the backstage activity and the numbers are shot in such high spirits that the intrusion of the story line seems an insult.

Up until the big show, the editing has been fast and snappy, and the short scenes have been just long enough. But during this show, when the music should mount in excitement, the editing style doesn't change, and the great performers are edited into short sequences just like everybody else. Chuck Berry, singing "Reelin' and Rockin'" and doing his duck walk while playing his guitar, is followed by the raunchy white Louisianian Jerry Lee Lewis punching the piano and singing. The kids in the audience at the Paramount are dancing in the aisles by now—happy interracial dancing—and backstage the head villain, the D.A. (John Lehne), is about to close down the show, because in his view Freed is making the kids "behave like animals." And Freed delivers these saintly lines: "Look, you can close the show. You can stop me. But you never can stop rock 'n' roll." Wearing this jive halo, he rushes into the pandemonium that follows the D.A.'s action, scoops up the little president of the Buddy Holly Fan Club, who is about to be trampled, and carries him to safety. The sham is so obvious that viewers may enjoy the hokiness, but the moviemakers must have gone past what they could stomach; they tossed in an abrupt ending—a few *American Graffiti*–style titles indicating that Freed was taken off the air. They flubbed their heartbreak finish. But it's a super B movie.

□ □ □

*E*lizabeth Taylor may be generous enough to forgive the director Harold Prince and the cinematographer Arthur Ibbetson for what they've done to her—out of the innocence of incompetence—in *A Little Night Music*. But she may not be able to forgive herself for the sad fact that she can't get by in the role of a famous stage actress—not with her little-girl-with-a-cold-in-her-nose voice and her sloppy carriage. How is *A Little Night Music*? Well, it's a cut above *Song of Norway* and *The Blue Bird,* but it's in that general sylvan-settings category. The film is an adaptation of the Broadway show *A Little Night Music* (also directed by Harold Prince), which was a reworking, with music and lyrics by Stephen Sondheim and a book by Hugh Wheeler, of Ingmar Bergman's *fin de siècle* love roundelay *Smiles of a Summer Night.* What was lyrical farce in the Bergman film has now become clod-hopping operetta. The attempt at stylization results in pale-pink interiors that look like rooms in a doll's house, and there's a dear sweet young girl with a voice that's a piercing reminder of Julie Andrews.

The camera angles weren't planned in terms of how the film could be edited, and whoever put the scenes together seems to be yelping in despair. The images jump back and forth, from one humiliated frozen face to another. The actors' flesh tones recall Marlon Brando's alternately yellowish and grayish-pink complexion in *A Countess from Hong Kong* (also shot by Arthur Ibbetson). This picture has been made as if Harold Prince had never *seen* a movie. Two of the performers survive: Diana Rigg, because even though her comedy expertise sticks out a little too much in the crawling, dragging scenes, she has great chest tones in her whoops and honks; and Lesley-Anne Down, who is so lusciously, ripely beautiful in her peach-blond wig that her trained, accomplished acting suggests an intelligent form of self-respect. Rigg and Down actually manage to get a performance rhythm going in a few of their scenes. But you know what you're in for near the beginning when the hero (Len Cariou) is greeted with "Good afternoon, Lawyer Egerman." Do people really enjoy Stephen Sondheim's sour sentimentality—songs like "Every Day a Little Death"? The punks are cheerful by comparison.

[March 20, 1978]

424

PART FIVE

Fear of Movies

Are people becoming *afraid* of American movies? When acquaintances ask me what they should see and I say *The Last Waltz* or *Convoy* or *Eyes of Laura Mars,* I can see the recoil. It's the same look of distrust I encountered when I suggested *Carrie* or *The Fury* or *Jaws* or *Taxi Driver* or the two *Godfather* pictures before that. They immediately start talking about how they "don't like" violence. But as they talk you can see that it's more than violence they fear. They indicate that they've been assaulted by too many schlocky films—some of them highly touted, like *The Missouri Breaks.* They're tired of movies that reduce people to nothingness, they say—movies that are all car crashes and killings and perversity. They don't see why they should subject themselves to experiences that will tie up their guts or give them nightmares. And if that means that they lose out on a *Taxi Driver* or a *Carrie,* well, that's not important to them. The solid core of young moviegoers may experience a sense of danger as part of the attraction of movies; they may hope for new sensations and want to be swept up, overpowered. But these other, "more discriminating" moviegoers don't want that sense of danger. They want to remain in control of their feelings, so they've been going to the movies that allow them a distance—European films such as *Cat and Mouse,* novelties like *Dona Flor and Her Two Husbands,* prefab American films, such as *Heaven Can Wait,* or American films with an overlay of European refinement, like the hollowly objective *Pretty Baby,* which was made acceptable by reviewers' assurances that the forbidden subject is handled with good taste, or the entombed *Interiors.*

If educated Americans are rocking on their heels—if they're so punchy that they feel the need to protect themselves—one can't exactly blame them for it. But one can try to scrape off the cultural patina that, with the aid of the press and TV, is forming over this timidity. Reviewers and commentators don't have to be crooked or duplicitous to praise dull, stumpy movies and disapprove of exciting ones. What's more natural than that they would share the fears of their readers and viewers, take it as a cultural duty to warn them off intense movies, and equate intense with dirty, cheap, adolescent? Discriminating moviegoers want the placidity of *nice* art—of movies tamed so that they are no more arousing than what used to be called polite theatre. So we've been getting a new cultural puritanism—people go to the innocuous hoping for the charming, or they settle for imported sobriety, and the press is full of snide references to Coppola's huge film in progress, and a new film by Peckinpah is greeted with derision, as if it went without saying that Bloody Sam couldn't do anything but blow up bodies in slow motion, and with the most squalid commercial intentions.

This is, of course, a rejection of the particular greatness of movies: their power to affect us on so many sensory levels that we become emotionally accessible, in spite of our thinking selves. Movies get around our cleverness and our wariness; that's what used to draw us to the picture show. Movies—and they don't even have to be first-rate, much less great—can invade our sensibilities in the way that Dickens did when we were children, and later, perhaps, George Eliot and Dostoevski, and later still, perhaps, Dickens again. They can go down even deeper—to the primitive levels on which we experience fairy tales. And if people resist this invasion by going only to movies that they've been assured have nothing upsetting in them, they're not showing higher, more refined taste; they're just acting out of fear, masked as taste. If you're afraid of movies that excite your senses, you're afraid of movies.

*I*n his new book *The Films in My Life*, François Truffaut writes, "I demand that a film express either the *joy of making cinema* or the *agony of making cinema*. I am not at all interested in anything in between; I am not interested in all those films that do not pulse." Truffaut's dictum may exclude films that some of us enjoy. You couldn't claim that *National Lampoon's Animal House* expresses either the joy or the agony of making cinema. It's like the deliberately dumb college-football comedies of the thirties—the ones with Joan Davis or Martha Raye—only more so; it's a growly, rambunctious cartoon, and its id anarchy triumphs over the wet-fuse pacing, the blotchy lighting, and the many other ineptitudes. In its own half-flubbed way, it has a style. And you don't go to a film like *Animal House* for *cinema,* you go for roughhousing disreputability; it makes you laugh by restoring you to the slobby infant in yourself. (If it were more artistic, it couldn't do that.)

But that sort of movie is a special case. Essentially, I agree with Truffaut. I can enjoy movies that don't have that moviemaking fever in them, but it's enjoyment on a different level, without the special aphrodisia of movies—the kinetic responsiveness, the all-out submission to pleasure. That "pulse" leaves you with all your senses quickened. When you see a movie such as *Convoy,* which has this vibrancy and yet doesn't hold

428

together, you still feel clearheaded. But when you've seen a series of movies without it, whether proficient soft-core porn like *The Deep* or klutzburgers like *Grease,* you feel poleaxed by apathy. If a movie doesn't "pulse"—if the director isn't talented, and if he doesn't become fervently obsessed with the possibilities that the subject offers him to explore moviemaking itself—it's dead and it deadens you. Your heart goes cold. The world is a dishrag. (Isn't the same thing true for a novel, a piece of music, a painting?)

This pressing against the bounds of the medium doesn't necessarily result in a good movie (John Boorman's debauch *Exorcist II: The Heretic* is proof of that), but it generally results in a live one—a movie there's some reason to see—and it's the only way great movies get made. Even the madness of *Exorcist II* is of a special sort: the picture has a visionary crazy grandeur (like that of Fritz Lang's loony *Metropolis*). Some of the telepathic sequences are golden-toned and lyrical, and the film has a swirling, hallucinogenic, apocalyptic quality; it might have been a horror classic if it had had a simpler, less ritzy story. But, along with flying demons and theology inspired by Teilhard de Chardin, it had Richard Burton, with his precise diction, helplessly and inevitably turning his lines into camp, just as the cultivated, stage-trained actors in early-thirties horror films did. Like them, Burton had no conviction in what he was doing, so he couldn't get beyond staginess and artificial phrasing. The film is too cadenced and exotic and too deliriously complicated to succeed with most audiences. But it's winged camp—a horror fairy tale gone wild, another in the long history of moviemakers' king-size follies. There's enough visual magic in it for a dozen good movies; what the picture lacks is judgment—the first casualty of the moviemaking obsession.

What Boorman has in surfeit is what's missing from *Heaven Can Wait*: there isn't a whisper of personal obsession in the moviemaking. The film has no desire but to please, and that's its only compulsiveness; it's so timed and pleated and smoothed that it's sliding right off the screen. This little smudge of a movie makes one laugh a few times, but it doesn't represent moviemaking—it's pifflemaking. Warren Beatty moves through it looking fleecy and dazed, murmuring his lines in a dissociated, muffled manner. The film has to be soft-focussed and elided—a series of light double takes—because if Beatty raised his voice or expressed anything more than a pacific nature, the genteel, wafer-thin whimsy would crumble.

There's no way I could make the case that *Animal House* is a better picture than *Heaven Can Wait,* yet on some sort of emotional-aesthetic level I prefer it. One returns you to the slobbiness of infancy, the other to the security of childhood, and I'd rather stand with the slobs. I didn't much mind *Heaven Can Wait* when I saw it. Some of the lines have Elaine May's timorous, unaccountable weirdness. (Those jokes of hers come at you like wobbly cannonballs; you're never sure which ones will hit.) And in their marginal roles Dyan Cannon (a frenzied, lascivious bunny) and Charles Grodin (a discreet lizard) play off each other like cartoon confederates. It wasn't bad. Why, then, does it offend me when I think about it? Because it's image-conscious celebrity moviemaking; Beatty the star (who is also the producer and the co-director and even takes a co-writing credit) wants to be a nice guy, the same way Burt Reynolds does in *Hooper*. They go soft on themselves and act on one cylinder. They become so *dear*—Beatty the elfin sweet Jesus, and Reynolds the macho prince who hides his saintly heart—that they're not functioning as artists; they've turned into baby-kissing politicians.

As Hooper, Reynolds risks his life and injures himself in order to protect a little mutt, and afterward, while in pain, he's bawled out by a huffy official from an animal-protection society who doesn't recognize his devotion to dogdom. But *we're* sure not kept in the dark. In this slapstick celebration of the "real people" in Hollywood—the stunt men—the director, Hal Needham, lays out the gags for us as if we were backwoodsmen, and when it's time for him to show his stuff by staging the breathtaking stunts that the movie keeps telling us about, he fumbles every damn one of them. The camera is always in the wrong place; it's as if Needham had a tic that made him turn his head at the crucial moment. And it's almost a sickness—the repetition mania, the falling back on exhausted conventions. The hero has a live-in girlfriend (Sally Field) who is an irrelevant drag on the action, just like the worrying wives of old. As Hooper goes off to perform the most dangerous stunt of his life, she delivers the line that emerged from the compressed lips of generations of movie wives: "I won't be here when you get back." Was there ever one of them who carried out the threat? (The alternative was the John Ford woman, who said, "Matt, be careful.")

Reynolds has a faithful audience for pictures in which he doesn't attempt anything he hasn't done before. A half-cocked piece of moviemaking like *Hooper,* with its neo–John Wayneism (we red-blooded men who aren't afraid of risking our bodies are the true chivalrous knights of America, the only ones you can trust), is accepted as "a kick." The public has genuine affection for Reynolds' West Coast wise-guy swagger, and it doesn't seem to matter to people that in *Hooper* his merriment often seems a tired reflex. (That moon face crinkles on call.) Even if the press treated *Hooper* or a Clint Eastwood picture as contemptuously as it did *Convoy*, those pictures might not be hurt at box offices.

It's no accident that the directors who have an appetite for the pleasure and complexity of moviemaking are so often abused in the press. Their films are likely to grip people, and in impolite ways. These directors can't resist subverting the old forms that give comfort to audiences. And, given the hell of dealmaking and the infinite number of things that can go wrong during a production, a director who cares about the rhythm and texture of his imagery is likely to turn into a mixture of pompous bore, master strategist, used-car salesman, maniac, and messiah—in short, a major artist. And yes, he'll try for too big an effect, or he'll upset the balance of a neatly structured pipsqueak script. The pressures of deal-making squeeze the juice out of him, but still, in his sheer burning desperation to make movies, he'll try to turn a dud into *something*. And maybe he'll sustain that drive for only a part of the picture and he'll let the rest of it go to hell. How can moviemakers sustain their energy? How can they believe they should give the public of their best when the kids want to get Greased over and over and the literate adults go off to their cozy French detective comedy? Whom can they make movies *for*? They have every reason to be bitter and confused. (And they are, they are.)

Audiences hiss the sight of blood now, as if they didn't have it in their own bodies. They hiss those bloody scenes that have the power to shock them, even when the blood isn't excessive. Bergman gets away with shocking effects; in *Cries and Whispers,* he even shows vaginal blood, and no one dares hiss. But in *Eyes of Laura Mars,* where the first flash of bloodletting comes right at the beginning, and in *The Fury,* where the bloodshed is stylized, hyperbolic, insane, audiences who seem hypnotized by the urgency in the moviemaking still hiss the blood. They seem to be saying, "I don't need this!" They hiss the blood as if to belittle it, to make it less menacing. And these movies are treated with condescension.

Movies have upset repressive people right from the start, but the old Hollywood studio heads learned to appease pressure groups by keeping a lid on sacrilege and eroticism, and by making sharp moral distinctions between the violent acts committed by good guys and those committed by bad guys. Probably the movie that did the most to overturn all this was *Bonnie and Clyde,* in 1967. Lingering sensuously on violent imagery, the director, Arthur Penn, brought our hidden, horrified fascination into the open. Eisenstein had plunged us into violence, and so had Buñuel and Kurosawa and many others, but this was an American movie made by an American director—in color—and it was saying, "Don't turn your head away, there's something horrible and rapturous going on." Louis B. Mayer and the old Hollywood simplicities were finally undermined. In 1969, Peckinpah's *The Wild Bunch* came out—a traumatic poem of violence with imagery as ambivalent as Goya's. And as the Vietnam War dragged on and Americans became more and more demoralized and guilt-ridden, our films splattered blood at us—so much blood that going to the movies was often a painful, masochistic experience. The lurid didacticism was generally hypocritical: every crummy action-adventure picture that didn't know how to keep the audience's attention except by piling on massacres pointed to the war as a justification. And people became particularly incensed over the balletic, slow-motion scenes; although there's a psychological rationale, as well as an aesthetic one, for this "eternity in an instant" treatment of falls and accidents and horrors, it began to seem a mere device to force us to stare at gruesomeness.

People had probably had it with movie violence long before the war was over, but they didn't feel free to admit that they really wanted relaxed, escapist entertainment. Now that the war has ended, they talk about violence in movies as if it would plunge us back into that guilty mess. There's a righteousness in their tone when they say they don't like violence; I get the feeling that I'm being told that my urging them to see *The Fury* means that I'll be responsible if there's another Vietnam. During a brutal fight in *Who'll Stop the Rain,* there were cries in the audience—on the order of "O.K., enough!"—and applause for the cries. These weren't the good-natured catcalls that are heard at stupid movies; it was an escape from the power of the fight. It's a way of closing off what you feel. I think I first became conscious of this audience mechanism back in the mid-forties, when I saw *Dead of Night* on its opening day in a crowded theatre and the audience laughed raucously during Michael Redgrave's greatest—most terrified—moments. The tension had got too much for them, and they turned philistine, rejecting their own emotional immersion in his performance. That's what people are doing now, on a larger scale. Maybe it's partly because they want to put the war behind them, but there's more to it: they're running away from flesh and blood on the screen. They have lost the background of security that used to make it easy for them to respond to suspense stories. Now, when they're always conscious of the violence in the society and are afraid that it's going to be coming at them when they leave the theatre, they don't want to see anything frightening on the screen. They've lost the hope that things are going to be better—that order will return. So they go to the movies to be lulled—to be gently rocked to sleep. (*Heaven Can Wait*—the acclaimed movie of the summer—is a lullaby.) What may be behind all this is the repression of the race issue. People feel that there's violence out there, and they want to shut it out. Movies, more than any other form of expression, are capable of bringing us to an acceptance of our terrors; that must be why people are afraid of movies.

*W*as *Convoy* punished because of the blood Peckinpah has made us look at in the past? It got the bum's rush, though it's a happy-go-lucky ode to the truckers on the roads, a sunny, enjoyable picture, with only ketchup being splattered (in a mock fight in a diner). The lighting suggests J.M.W. Turner in the American Southwest, his eyes popping with surprise. Seeing this picture, you recover the feelings you had as a child about the power and size and noise of trucks, and their bright, distinctive colors and alarming individuality. Peckinpah uses the big rigs anthropomorphically. Each brawny giant in the procession has its own stride; some are

432

lumbering, others are smooth as adagio dancers, while one bounces along and its trailer shimmies. At night, when a frightened driver pulls out of the line to go off alone in the darkness, the truck itself seems to quaver, childishly. The trucks give the performances in this movie, and they go through changes: when the dust rises around them on rough backcountry roads, they're like sea beasts splashing spume; when two of them squeeze a little police car between their tanklike armored bodies, they're insect titans. The whole movie is a prankish road dance, and the convoy itself is a protest without a cause: the drivers are just griped in general and blowing off steam. They want the recreation of a protest.

Sam Peckinpah talks in code, and his movies have become a form of code, too. *Convoy* is full of Peckinpah touches, but you can't tell the put-on from the romantic myth; his cynicism and his sentimentality are so intertwined by now that he's putting himself on. He has a mocking theme here that's visual: the spaciousness of the land and the pettiness of men's quarrels. But the script doesn't play off this disparity, and so, when the spaciousness overwhelms the lawman's spite that set the convoy in motion, it's the plot (rather than mankind) that seems silly. The film barely introduces the characters, and one of the funniest, J.D. Kane's Big Nasty, who talks in a voice so deep it might be his mammoth truck talking, is lost sight of. And here, as in *Cross of Iron,* Peckinpah can't shoot dialogue; he doesn't seem to know anymore how people talk. (Also, the post-synchronization is so poor that the voices seem disembodied.) The visual music of the moving trucks is enough to carry the film for the first hour, but when the truckers stop for the night at an encampment, the movie stops; there's no narrative energy to keep it going.

The actor at the front of the convoy, Kris Kristofferson, isn't convincing as a horny trucker grabbing a sad-eyed waitress (Cassie Yates) and hopping into the truck for a quickie; Kristofferson lacks the common touch that might have given the movie some centrifugal force. But, with his steely blue eyes, and his hair and beard blowing in the wind, he's as majestic as the big trucks, and his reserve is appealingly heroic. Kristofferson doesn't overact, and his charm is so low-key and easy that even the disembodied sound doesn't damage him—it goes with his faintly detached personality. The sound is rough on the other performers, though; they seem not quite there. Kristofferson is partnered by Ali MacGraw, who has never seemed anywhere, and some of the resentment directed against the film may be because of her. She is a truly terrible actress, of the nostril school. (Did she study under Natalie Wood?) As the camera comes closer, the nostrils start flexing—not just for anger, for *any* emotion. Her role makes her seem soft and spoiled and rich, and she doesn't react to a situation, she comments on it, in a hideously superior way. When she's really working hard, she adds a trembling lip (reminiscent of Jackie Cooper as a child) to her tiny repertory of expressions. She isn't around a lot, though, and Kristofferson doesn't pay much attention to her (which saves him).

It isn't clear whether Peckinpah walked away from *Convoy* after presenting his first cut, or was barred from the final editing, or how much Graeme Clifford, who finally put it together (he was the editor on Nicolas Roeg's *Don't Look Now*), is responsible for. But there are lovely editing transitions and fast, hypnotic rhythms and graceful shifts of stationary compositions. Sequences with the trucks low in the frame and most of the image given over to skies with brilliant white clouds are poetic gestures, like passages in Dovzhenko. The film has a springiness of spirit, and a lust for drifting white desert sand; it's so beautiful (yet funny) that often you don't want the camera to move—you want to hold on to what you see. Probably Peckinpah intended to make a simple action movie, but something in him must have balked at that. He saw the trucks and the skies and he kept shooting, like Eisenstein when he saw the faces of the Indians in Mexico.

No American movie this year has been as full of the "joy of making cinema" as Martin Scorsese's *The Last Waltz,* his film of The Band's Thanksgiving, 1976, concert in San Francisco. He shot it while he was still involved in *New York, New York*—which was full of the "agony of making cinema." In *The Last Waltz,* Scorsese seems in complete control of his talent and of the material, and you can feel everything going right, just as in *New York, New York* you could feel everything going wrong. It's an even-tempered, intensely satisfying movie. Visually, it's dark-toned and rich and classically simple. The sound (if one has the good luck to catch it in a theatre equipped with a Dolby system) is so clear that the instruments have the distinctness that one hears on the most craftsmanlike recordings, and the casual interviews have a musical, rhythmic ease. Why was it so hard to persuade people to go see it? Were they leery of another rock-concert film? Were they tired of hearing about Scorsese? All of that, maybe, and possibly something more. They swooned and giggled over *A Star Is Born,* but *The Last Waltz* is a real movie, and it must have given off some vibration that made them nervous. They couldn't trust the man who'd made *Mean Streets* and *Taxi Driver* to give them a safe evening.

The fun of a movie thriller is in the way it plays on our paranoid fantasies; we know that we're being manipulated and yet—if the manipulation is clever enough—we give over to it. But can people respond to this as entertainment if they're on such edgy terms with themselves that they're afraid of being upset? In the press coverage of *Eyes of Laura Mars,* the reviewers seem to be complaining that it's a thriller—or, rather, an effective thriller. Their being frightened seems to make them resent the film as immoral. *Eyes of Laura Mars,* Irvin Kershner's seductive whodunit, is up against attitudes that a comparable fantasy, such as Polanski's *Rosemary's Baby*—also about justifiable female paranoia—didn't have to face. *Laura Mars* operates on mood and atmosphere, and moves so fast, with such delicate changes of rhythm, that its excitement has a subterranean sexiness. It's a really stylish thriller, and Faye Dunaway, with long, thick dark-red hair, brings it emotion and presence, as well as a new erotic warmth. (Her legs, especially the thighs, are far more important to her performance than her eyes; her flesh gives off heat.) More womanly and more neurotically vulnerable—even tragic—than before, she looks as if she'd lived a little and gone through plenty of stress. She's glamorously beat out—just right to be telepathic about killings. Caped and swathed in clothing, with her glossy pale face taut against the lustrous hair (so thick it's almost evil), she's both Death and the Maiden. No Hollywood sex goddess has ever presented so alluring an image of kinky Death herself.

The scabrous is part of the elegant in this film; Laura Mars is a celebrity fashion photographer who specializes in the chic and pungency of sadism. The pictures she shoots have a furtive charge; we can see why they sell. Her photographic sessions, with burning cars and half-naked models strutting around their prey, are set up so that we get a sense of friction between the models, who are acting as killers and victims, and the buzzing, over-intense city, where everyone seems to be on a stage. Laura's pictures are, in fact, single-image versions of high-style blood thrillers, such as *Laura Mars.* The humor in the movie is in the mixture of people who drift through the celebrity-circus milieu. Models who in their poses look wickedly decadent may be just fun-loving dingalings; unself-conscious when they're nude, they put on their gaunt insouciance with their clothes. In this high-fashion world, decadence is a game. But the creepiness of the environment isn't. The frames are packed with abrasive movement, and we see the dreck right next to the glamour, the dirty fingers that handle the expensive photographs. In the rush and bickering confusion of Laura's work life, she's dependent on her scruffy, wild-eyed driver (Brad Dourif), who's into God knows what, and her agent-manager (René Auberjonois), who probably hates her, because he has to take care of all the technicalities of time and place and money while she's being "creative." She has no one to trust. And so the harassed, frightened Laura falls in love with a police lieutenant (Tommy Lee Jones), who comes from a different, working-class world and represents simple values, old-fashioned morality. In many ways, it's a subtle, funny movie. Laura's voice is heavy with emotion, the policeman's is light and high and boyish; they're as unlikely a pair of lovers as you would ever hope to see. With the help of Michael Kahn, who was the editor, Kershner glides over the gaps in the script and almost manages to trick viewers past the mediocre lighting. He gets us to experience the jangled, onstage atmosphere viscerally. Brad Dourif's excitable driver makes us laugh, because he epitomizes New York's crazed messengers and hostile flunkies; he's so wound up he seems to have the tensions of the whole city in his gut. The film has an acid-rock texture, while Tommy Lee Jones, with his cat burglar's grace, his sunken eyes, rough skin, and jagged lower teeth that suggest a serpent about to snap, takes us into the world of punk.

In *Laura Mars,* you barely see any violence; it comes across by suggestion and a few quick images. But it's violence of a particular kind (and this may explain the angry, moralistic reactions to the film): the danger is to the eyes. If the killer had gone for the throat, probably the movie wouldn't be so frightening and wouldn't be considered immoral. (Of course, it wouldn't have any point, either.) *Laura Mars* violates our guardedness about our eyes. The most dreaded thing that can happen to what many regard as their most sensitive organs happens in this picture; like *Un Chien Andalou,* it attacks what we're watching the movie with. *Eyes of Laura Mars* hasn't the depth of intention (or the art) to upset us profoundly; it doesn't go at the eyes like *King Lear* or *Oedipus Rex* or the *Odyssey,* it just touches lightly on our dread. But this movie has enough "pulse" to make us register how horribly vulnerable our bodies are. And people in the audience who are used to TV, with its car crashes and knifings and shootings that have no pain or terror in them, and no gore, feel violated: how dare a movie scare them, and how dare it attack their taboo about the eyes? Has their world become so close to a paranoid fantasy that they no longer experience any of the primal fun in being frightened?

One film has shocked me in a way that made me feel that it was a borderline case of immorality—Hitchcock's *Psycho,* which, because of the director's cheerful complicity with the killer, had a sadistic glee that I couldn't quite deal with. It was hard to laugh at the joke after having been put in the position of being stabbed to death in the motel shower. The shock stayed with me to the degree that I remember it whenever I'm in a motel shower. Doesn't everybody? It was a good dirty joke, though, even if we in the audience were its butt. I wouldn't have wanted to see *Psycho* that first time alone in a theatre (and I sometimes feel a slight queasiness if I'm by myself late at night somewhere watching a horror film on TV). But that's what a theatrical experience is about: sharing this terror, feeling the safety of others around you, being able to laugh and talk together about how frightened you were as you leave.

Those people who are trying to protect themselves from their own violence and their own distress by not going to see anything that could rock the boat are keeping a very tense cool. There's something crazily repressive in the atmosphere. They're rejecting the rare films that could stir them, frighten them, elate them. And they're accepting the movies in which everything happens affectlessly and even bloody violence can be shrugged off. Within a few years, everything has turned around. Violence that makes you feel afraid has replaced sex as what's offensive, exploitative, dirty; since the end of the war, particularly, this kind of violence has become pornographic—it's as if we thought we could shove muggers and urban guerrillas under the counter. Movie sex, meanwhile, has become trivialized—made casual. It's posh call-girl sex, *Playboy* sex; there's no hatred or possessiveness or even passion in it. (Imagine the sour rage and depth of desire a director like Peckinpah might show us if he made a movie about sex.) What does it mean when someone says to you in a prissy, accusing tone that he "doesn't like" violence? Obviously, he's implying that your ability to look at it means that you *like* it. And you're being told that you're made of coarser stuff than he is. He's found a cheap way to present his cultural credentials. There's something snobby in all this; sex is chic but violence is for the animals. The less worldly still ask, "Why can't they make movies about *nice* people?" It's the comfort of order that's wanted—everything in its place. It used to be that well-brought-up ladies were not expected to be able to stand the sight of blood; they were expected to be so protected from sex and blood and flesh and death that they would faint if exposed to what the common people had to learn to look at. It was considered an offense to them to bring up certain subjects in their presence. Now the same sort of delicacy is once again becoming a mark of culture and breeding. Squeamishness—surely with terror and prurient churnings under it?—is the basis of this good taste.

*T*he people in Woody Allen's *Interiors* are destroyed by the repressiveness of good taste, and so is the picture. *Interiors* is a puzzle movie, constructed like a well-made play from the American past (such as *Craig's Wife*), and given the beautiful, solemn visual clarity of a Bergman film, without, however, the eroticism of Bergman. *Interiors* looks so much like a masterpiece and has such a super-banal metaphysical theme (death versus life) that it's easy to see why many regard it as a masterpiece: it's deep on the surface. *Interiors* has moviemaking fever, all right, but in a screwed-up form—which is possibly what the movie is all about. The problem for the family in the film is the towering figure of the disciplined, manipulative, inner-directed mother (Geraldine Page). She is such a perfectionist that she cannot enjoy anything, and the standards of taste and achievement that she imposes on her three daughters tie them in such knots that they all consider themselves failures. Alvy Singer, the role Woody Allen played in *Annie Hall,* was just such a compulsive, judgmental spoilsport, and Allen's original title for that film was *Anhedonia*—the lack of the capacity for experiencing pleasure.

Among the many puzzling aspects of *Interiors*: How Can Woody Allen present in a measured, lugubriously straight manner the same sorts of tinny anxiety discourse that he generally parodies? And how intentional is most of what goes on under the friezes and poses? Are we expected to ask ourselves who in the movie is Jewish and who is Gentile? The characters are so sterilized of background germs that the question is inevitably raised, and one of the film's few overt jokes is an overheard bit from a television show in which an interviewer asks a boy, "What nationality were you at the time of your birth?" and the boy answers, "Hebrew." Surely at root the family problem is Jewish: it's not the culture in general that imposes these humanly impossible standards of achievement—they're a result of the Jewish fear of poverty and persecution and the Jewish reverence for learning. It's not the joy of making cinema that spurs Woody Allen on (as he made clear in *Annie Hall,* he can't have that kind of joy), it's the discipline of making cinema. The movie, with its spotless beaches, is as clean and bare as Geraldine Page's perfect house: you could eat off any image. The prints of *Interiors* were processed on a new film stock, and during the showings for the press and people in the industry in Los Angeles, Allen had the print returned to the lab after every screening to be washed. Which makes this the ultimate Jewish movie. Woody Allen does not show you any blood.

The father (E. G. Marshall) asks his wife for a divorce and then marries a plump, healthy, life-force woman (Maureen Stapleton), and so there are two mothers. The tall, regal first mother, an interior decorator (who places a few objects in a bare room), wears icy grays and lives among beiges and sand tones; the plebeian stepmother bursts into this hushed atmosphere wearing mink and reds and floral prints. This is the sort of carefully constructed movie in which as soon as you see the first woman caress a vase and hover over its perfection you know that the second woman will have to break a vase. The symbolism—the introduction of red into the color scheme, the broken vase, and so on—belongs to the kind of theatre where everything was spelled out. But under this obviousness there are the layers of puzzle. The two mothers appear to be the two sides of the mythic dominating Jewish matriarch—the one dedicated to spiritual perfection, the other to sensual appetites, security, getting along in the world, cracking a few jokes. It's part of the solemn unease of the film that no one would want either of them for a mother: they're both bigger than life, and the first is a nightmare of asexual austerity, the second an embarrassment of yielding flesh and middle-class worldliness. If the two are warring for control of Woody Allen, the first (the *real* mother) clearly has him in the stronger grip. She represents the death of the instincts, but she also represents art, or at least cultivation and pseudo-art. (As a decorator, her specialty, like Woody Allen's here, seems to be the achievement of a suffocating emptiness.) Maureen Stapleton, the comic life force, lacks *class.* The film might be a representation of the traditional schizophrenia of Jewish comics, who have had the respect for serious achievement planted in them so early that even after they've made the world laugh they still feel they're failures, because they haven't played Hamlet. Groucho Marx talked morosely about not having had the education to be a writer, and said that his early pieces for the *New Yorker* were his proudest achievement. For Woody Allen, the equivalent is to be the American Ingmar Bergman.

The three daughters represent different aspects of the perfectionist neurosis. The oldest (Diane Keaton) is a well-known poet, determined, discontented, struggling with words while unconscious of her drives; the middle one (Kristin Griffith) is a TV actress, dissatisfied with her success, and snorting cocaine; the youngest (Marybeth Hurt), who looks like a perennial student, rejects sham and flails around, unable to find herself. In plays, the youngest is generally the one who represents the author, and whenever you see a character who's stubbornly honest you know that you're seeing the author's idealized vision of some part of himself. With Marybeth Hurt, if you have any doubts all you have to do is look at how she's dressed. (You'll also notice that she gets the worst—the most gnomic—lines, such as "At the center of a sick psyche there is a sick spirit." Huh?) She's unsmiling—almost expressionless—closed in, with specs, hair like shiny armor (it says hands off), and schoolgirl blouses and skirts. She's like a glumly serious postulant, and so honest she won't dress up; determined not to be false to her feelings, she actually dresses down for her father's wedding to the "vulgarian," as she calls her. (She's there under duress, and her clothes are an implicit protest.) She's the Cordelia, the father's favorite who refuses to lie, even to the mother, whom she alone in the family truly loves (she guiltily hates her, too).

The men's roles are relatively minor; Sam Waterston's part, though, is the only one that's unformed in the writing and doesn't quite fit into the formal plan. Geraldine Page is playing neurosis incarnate, and the camera is too close to her, especially when her muscles collapse; this failure of discretion makes her performance seem abhorrent. But Maureen Stapleton livens things up with her rather crudely written role. Hers is the only role that isn't strictly thematic, and you can feel the audience awake from its torpor when she arrives on the scene and talks like a conventional stage character. Diane Keaton does something very courageous for a rising star. She appears here with the dead-looking hair of someone who's too distracted to do anything with it but get a permanent, and her skin looks dry and pasty. There's discontent right in the flesh, while Kristin Griffith, the TV sexpot, appears with fluffy hair, blooming skin, and bright white teeth—the radiance that we normally see in Keaton. This physical transformation is the key to Keaton's thoughtful performance: she plays an unlikable woman—a woman who dodges issues whenever she can, who may become almost as remote as her mother.

For Allen, who is a very conscious craftsman, it is surely no accident that the mother's impoverished conception of good taste is sustained in the style of the film. But what this correlation means to him isn't apparent. *Interiors* is a handbook of art-film mannerisms; it's so austere and studied that it might have been directed by that icy mother herself—from the grave. The psychological hangups that come through are fascinating, but the actors' largo movements and stilted lines don't release this messy material, they repress it. After the life-affirming stepmother has come into the three daughters' lives and their mother is gone, they still, at the end, close ranks in a frieze-like formation. Their life-negating mother has got them forever. And her soul is in Woody Allen. He's still having his love affair with death, and his idea of artistic achievement (for himself, at least) may always be something death-ridden, spare, perfectly structured— something that talks of the higher things. (If this, his serious film, looks Gentile to people, that may be because for Woody Allen being Jewish, like being a comic, is fundamentally undignified. This film couldn't have had a Jewish-family atmosphere—his humor would have bubbled up.) The form of this movie is false, yet it's the form that he believes in, and the form of *Interiors* is what leads people to acclaim it as a masterpiece.

People like Woody Allen for a lot of good reasons, and for one that may be a bummer: he conforms to their idea of what a Jew should be. He's a younger version of the wise, philosophic candy-store-keeper in *West Side Story*. His good will is built partly on his being non-threatening. He's safe—the schlump who wins, without ever imposing himself. People feel comfortable with him; the comedy audience may even go to *Interiors*—to pay its respects to the serious Woody. Woody Allen's repressive kind of control—the source of their comfort—is just what may keep him from making great movies. *Interiors* isn't Gentile, but it *is* genteel. He's turned the fear of movies—which is the fear of being moved—into a form of intellectuality. If only it were all a put-on.

[September 25, 1978]

Forty-eight Characters in Search of a Director

Why is there a pastel haze in the interiors of *A Wedding*? The film is so soft-focus it's always on the verge of a dissolve, but with no other image coming in. Robert Altman's movies have been showing less attention to visual style for several years now, but this is the only one that opens like a blurry segment of "Masterpiece Theatre." The film takes place during one day, starting with a family-only Episcopal-church wedding and then moving from the church to the reception at the groom's family mansion, in a North Shore suburb of Chicago. The dusty murkiness in the church could be taken for clouds of incense, but what is it that's fogging up the atmosphere at the reception? Is the cinematographer, Charles Rosher, playing around with "flashing" techniques—with pre-exposed or post-exposed film? (The results look more like re-used film.) There's no depth in the imagery, and the film is lighted like a twenty-year-old issue of *House & Garden*. With forty-eight characters scrambling in and out of the rooms, it's a soft jumble. It takes most of the movie to spot the actors who are listed and to figure out who they're playing and what their relationships to each other are. This sorting-out process is about all you get to occupy your mind. When the picture is over, you still may not be too sure about a few of them. (The only reason for the proliferation of characters seems to be to double the ante on *Nashville*, which had twenty-four.) This picture is intended as a satirical farce, but the haze is like a scrim—it keeps you from getting a clear look at the characters. And their movements aren't timed and choreographed for farce; Altman merely reproduces the confusion of the household during a party that's going to pieces.

There's no way *into* the movie; it's like a busted bag of marbles—people are running every way at once. It's a succession of short scenes in which family members, servants, security guards, caterers, musicians, and wedding staff reveal their secrets—generally nasty—and/or make fools of themselves. The revelations are a standard set of scandals, foibles, sexual oddities, and addictions, with incest, epilepsy, nymphomania, and interracial love all treated pretty much on the same level. Then, toward the end, the storytelling method changes to a fast, overloaded narrative and finally to a rapid series of dramatic parallels and reversals. But the editing keeps stopping the picture cold; the film doesn't move forward, it hobbles about. And so we don't experience those last events as the fulfillment of the earlier scenes. *Nashville* was crowded, but it built into a shape, like an acrobats' pyramid. *A Wedding* stays flat and disorderly. And with all the talk—a constant battery of idle, compulsive babble—the dialogue lacks the crackling liveness of typical Altman overheards; it has an inert tone, and the sound level keeps changing. If there's any clear emotion that comes through the film, it's the director's impatience—perhaps even indifference. Actors seem to have become his only real collaborators, and they're running loose here.

Altman hasn't really recharged since *Nashville*. In *Buffalo Bill and the Indians*, he didn't appear to have the will or the strength to fuse the vignettes. There were concepts there (the lampoon of show-business celebrity, the contrast between the white man with his unsureness and the

Indian with his primal spiritual power), but they didn't come together and turn into something else—a mood, a vision. The film's Buffalo Bill (Paul Newman) didn't have the star dynamism to make us feel that he was the big lie we wanted. The role needed a strutter, a man with the stature of a fraudulent folk hero. (Newman is good at small blowhards who reveal the needs behind their transparent lies.) And the Wild West show itself didn't travel—it was stationary—and so it seemed disconnected, off by itself, in a mournful, metaphorical realm. When Altman succeeds, he magically pulls a picture out of his hat. When he fails, it looks as if he never had anything in that hat. Yet it's likely that he was close to something big in *Buffalo Bill*, and that somehow it was lost in the editing process. The movie seems to dribble away, scene by scene.

After that, Altman made *3 Women*, a smaller failure. He had earlier switched from beautiful, vital, often dazzling cinematography (generally by Vilmos Zsigmond) to the serviceable cinematography of *California Split* and *Nashville*; in *3 Women*, a dream film, he employed a consciously rhapsodic style, and the whole film is smooth, graceful. But he lingers on his own artistry. He seems to love setting the scenes (he's great at it), but he doesn't get much action going, and he holds on to those flowing scenes after whatever action there is is over. *3 Women* might have been a success if it had been *2 Girls*, because almost everything to do with Shelley Duvall and Sissy Spacek in the first hour had affection and humor. You could feel his love of these actresses (and the assurance they drew from it), and he showed his feeling for the comic beauty in pop and trash and kitsch (a feeling he shares with Godard); it was lovely, fresh sociological comedy about two working girls from Texas. But the paintings under the titles and the electronic score gave intimations of aesthetic howlers to come, and they arrived with a Jungian thud after Sissy Spacek's suicide attempt and her dream within the larger dream structure—a mistake so mood-shattering that one never regained confidence that the director knew what he was doing. The film was stunted by the archetypal female mysticism of the second hour; it was an act of devotion to sit through it. Still, both *Buffalo Bill* and *3 Women* were honest, risk-taking failures, and you could see a major filmmaker at work in them. With *A Wedding*, you can't. It's as if Altman had set out to prove that those who couldn't see the innovative greatness of his earlier films were right. It seems to have been made by an Altman imitator.

A Wedding, which opened the New York Film Festival on September 22nd and began its theatrical run the next day, isn't as listless as Altman's last two films; it has a tittering countercultural tone, and there are laughs in it. But they're laughs of recognition of Altman's type of humor rather than of the accuracy of the jokes. Maybe Altman shouldn't have gone to the Midwest (where he comes from) to make this movie. He doesn't like the characters on the screen; he's taking potshots at them, but he doesn't show

442

us what he's got against them. We can barely see what he's shooting *at*; he hasn't bothered to make the target exist. Probably Altman had an idea when he got involved in this project: probably he'd always hated these country-club Wasps—the kind of people Douglas Sirk made classy soap opera about in the fifties (*Magnificent Obsession, All That Heaven Allows*). He must have meant to be savage. The musical score, with its pompous irony—the trumpets and fanfares that attend the empty vows of the promiscuous teen-agers and the arrival of the only guest who shows up for the reception (Bert Remsen, as a wedding aficionado)—suggests that he intended to point up what a mockery the monied classes' rituals are. But you can stay mad for only so long. Chances are that as Altman got closer to the subject he got bored with his own smoldering resentment. These people don't reach him now (they may even be his admirers); he's flailing away, half-heartedly, at Babbitty shadows from the past.

The wedding is supposed to represent a union of new money with old money; it's the entrance into the Midwestern élite of a Louisville, Kentucky, girl whose father, once a truck driver, is now a big-time trucker. Yet the movie is singularly lacking in social nuances. It isn't clear what brought the mousy bride (the gifted young comedienne Amy Stryker) and the crumbum-stud groom (Desi Arnaz, Jr.) to the altar, and we don't have the chance to see how the socially untutored Southern family would be received in "society." We're given to understand that the Wasp suburban-ites who were invited didn't come because they're so bigoted they have never accepted the groom's Italian father (Vittorio Gassman). The economic underpinnings are also slighted. People who have been to these affairs say that the presence of the guards makes you acutely conscious of all the reasons for their presence. But here, on an isolated estate, with no barrage of guests or gate-crashers, there's no visible necessity for the large security staff guarding the gifts and the premises, and the guards are used as bumbling fools in a series of messy low-comedy scenes. The only characters who are exempted from the film's contempt are the Italian father, who is spiritually still a foreigner, with his own culture; a black servant (Cedric Scott) of such distinction and noble bearing that he's clearly the superior of all the whites (has Robert Altman sunk to this cowardly sentimentality?); and the groom's grandmother (Lillian Gish). She's the only one in the film who has her own space—she keeps her dignity. (The cuts to her in bed often seem to be misplaced tributes to Miss Gish herself.) The film appears to be in awe of what this matriarch represents. Has Altman fallen into the trap of respecting *old* money? All the other money on the screen is bad money.

The movie has moments: a red-headed teen-age cousin of the bride (Mark R. Deming) talking about *The Fly* and about Ray Milland in *Frogs*; the bride's lopsided, slightly fiendish grin of triumph at having snared her stud, and the mixture of practicality and furtiveness which marks her as her mother's daughter; a romantic interlude between that mother (Carol Burnett) and the groom's uncle (Pat McCormick), who are like Shakespearean clown-lovers together. But the good bits slip away; they don't seem to count for anything. Though Pat McCormick's beatific quiet as he clutches Burnett to his capacious bosom stays in the memory, the film doesn't really set up the scene. If we had had a glimpse of the exact moment when he was smitten, then his gathering his beloved in his arms would be much funnier. Carol Burnett is more relaxed about acting for the big screen than she has been before, and she shows her gift—the quick, pure looks her face can shoot out, those precisely overdone emotions of happy surprise, helpless heat, second thoughts. Carol Burnett brings out the insanity within sane people better than anybody. She looks as if she's made of ordinary rubber, but when she tells off her nosy sister-in-law (Peggy Ann Garner), her screeching voice could kill. It's the director who muffles what could have been one of her best scenes: her confusion about which of her daughters she has just been told is pregnant by the groom. And it's clearly the director whose timing is off in the longer scenes, such as the one in which a family group watches while the bride's father (Paul Dooley) grills the bride's pregnant sister (Mia Farrow, looking like a teen-ager, and more blissfully fey than ever)—a teasing nymph who is mute and feeble-witted. All the way through, there are incidents and lines that are potentially funny but are flubbed. The script, by John Considine, Patricia Resnick, and Allan Nicholls (who are all in the film), and Altman, may not be bad—just unrealized. There's a running gag about the groom's family doctor (Howard Duff), who can't be around a young girl without copping a feel. But Duff doesn't have the manner of an impotent old lech, and instead of our registering his sneakiness out of the corner of an eye, so that we'd have to do a double take to be sure, we are given a full, dull view. The camera can't seem to stay away from the groom's beautiful, ravaged addict-mother (Nina Van Pallandt), tense and strung out until she gets her shot and then nodding off graciously, in her best hostessy manner; the closeups of her become little editorials on leisure-class decadence.

Surprisingly, the director gets almost nothing out of most of the "name" players. Geraldine Chaplin as the lesbian wedding coördinator, Lauren Hutton as the woman in charge of making a film record of the occasion, Ruth Nelson as the groom's great-aunt, and Vittorio Gassman and Howard Duff could all be eliminated without loss, and the elimination of Viveca Lindfors, who is a Swedish caterer twirling feverishly in blue chiffon, would be a definite gain. (Lindfors has now attained to such a state of bravura bad acting that her self-dramatizing womanliness gives women a bad name.)

The eccentricities of Altman's characters have usually been likable; their crotchets and buggy pretensions were tipoffs to other surprises they had in them. Here most of the forty-eight people are reduced to their eccentricities, and we're supposed to see that because they're American mercenaries that's all there is to them. Their heartlessness might be funny if it were stylized. But it isn't—it's just soggy and unconvincing. Altman has always had some bad-boy iconoclasm in him; there was a spunky, goading side to his work. The spunkiness is missing in *A Wedding*.

It's possible that *Nashville* was a pivotal point for Altman—that since then his wanting to make movies has become more a nervous reflex than a creative drive. The way he works, his feelings come right through, and when he isn't fully engaged in a subject the film lacks mood and substance. *A Wedding* is flimsy. There's a great difference in texture between the work that Altman did with Vilmos Zsigmond as cinematographer and Lou Lombardo as editor (and Leon Ericksen as production designer) and what he's doing now. Their work together was really jazzy—it had a feeling for the possibilities in lighting and rhythm and design. And it didn't hurt when there was a writer's script—something with some layers in it—if only to depart from. Altman is depending too much now on the actors, and on himself. The actors do many charming things in *A Wedding*, but the movie is bitter in a concealed, dry, facile way; the joking almost seems private. At the end, the people seem to have been chopped up, as if by a pixieish yet rancorous comedian.

□ □ □

Many novelists have been influenced by the movies, but probably no "serious" novelist has absorbed into his writing what movie audiences want the way that Richard Price, the young author of *Bloodbrothers*, has. (He was twenty-five when he wrote the book.) He describes the action—bam-pow—and tells the story through the dialogue; the effect is like that of a classic novel speeded up. It's a childish approach to the novel, but that of a TV-age child aware that he's competing with movies and TV for your attention and determined not to lose you for an instant. (Book reviewers responded with such praise as "It will tear your heart out" and "*Bloodbrothers* is a kick in the spine.") He also writes fast and carelessly, as if, like a TV writer or a screenwriter, with other projects waiting, he was punching an inner time clock. But Price has a talent for profane humor, and that redeems almost everything—the passages repeated for emphasis, the textbook explanations, the characters who are developed and then lost sight of, the mixture of didacticism, sensationalism, and pathos. His story of a brawling Italian Catholic family living in Co-op City, in the Bronx, should have made a striking tragicomic movie; it practically *is* a movie. But it was adapted by the wrong screenwriter (Walter Newman), directed by the wrong director (Robert Mulligan), and miscast in every major role. The movies that inspired Price were not the movies of Robert Mulligan. Though Mulligan may seem to have the right background (he's the son of a

New York police officer and once studied for the priesthood), Price acknowledges *Mean Streets* as the specific influence on the novel. Mulligan is the man who gave us *To Kill a Mockingbird* and *Summer of '42.*

Trying for something crude, powerful, volatile, Mulligan has made a film that opens like an ABC Movie of the Week. It has Sears, Roebuck imagery—you order it from the catalogue. And he and the writer (probably with the encouragement of the producer, Stephen Friedman) have turned the book completely around. Price's story is about a blocked rite of passage; it's about how the eighteen-year-old Stony De Coco is bound to his father and uncle (both electricians, who work on construction sites) by ties of love and gratitude, and because of that love, never breaks free to develop the possibilities in himself. It's about why Stony will turn out to be a frustrated, boozing, skirt-chasing, braggart hardhat just like them. The movie, however, is an ethnic variant of all those the-summer-the-adolescent-became-a-man pictures. The sensitive, imaginative Stony (Richard Gere) breaks free of his generous father (Tony Lo Bianco) and his doting, childless uncle (Paul Sorvino) and goes off to save himself, and his little brother (Michael Hershewe) as well. Stony is John-Boy Walton, but from a family that talks dirty and doesn't understand him.

There are exploitation messagey movies that are badly made but succeed at the box office because they have some hook—the idea behind the movie, publicity about a new star, whatever. *Looking for Mr. Goodbar* was one. *Bloodbrothers* (which showed at the New York Film Festival on September 25th and 26th and opens in theatres on the 27th) could conceivably be another. The characters tell anecdotes that are really their life stories, and Annette (Marilu Henner), the girl Stony turns to for understanding, gives us a fat hint of what the moviemakers want us to carry away with us when she says, "Life can hurt. It's made me feel close to all those doin' the hurtin' dance." The movie has got this heartfelt hurting glop going for it, plus an Elmer Bernstein score emoting like mad, swooping in with beery passion for the deep scenes and making sure you never miss the pity of it all, and performers pouring on Mediterranean sensuality and playing at their highest pitch. People laugh with hysterical heartiness in this movie. The book's obscenities are no longer funny, though: what's supposed to account for them and redeem them kills them. "I may be the town pump," Annette tells Stony, "but at least I'm not afraid to face the truth." And she isn't meant to be obnoxious; she's supposed to be a model of courage for the still indecisive hero. When Stony worries about what will happen in his family if he leaves, Annette is ready with metaphorical wisdom: "Worry about your own ass. Theirs is out of reach."

The actors are working on different levels, and Mulligan brings their performances up when they should be taken down. There's only one performer who seems to know how to get inside his role—Kenneth

McMillan, in the minor part of Banion, the crippled barkeeper. McMillan (he was Sergeant Rooney in the New York production of *Streamers*) listens to other actors without overreacting, and his calm, expressive style here allows us to see into Banion's distrustful nature and read his rapid, angry shifts of feeling. McMillan's quiet saves him in a cast in which everybody else seems to have been goosed just as they got within camera range. Tony Lo Bianco is reaching so frenziedly for patriarchal, hot-tempered, large-scale emotions that he seems three feet off the ground, and Paul Sorvino must equate hardhat with wide-eyed simpleton—he's playing Lennie in a tank-town *Of Mice and Men*. Lo Bianco and Sorvino don't look or act like brothers; they just laugh together a lot.

The film's chances at the box office probably depend almost completely on the public response to Richard Gere. He is one of those performers—Susan Sarandon is another—who seem to achieve total inauthenticity in every role. This doesn't necessarily destroy their careers: Susan Sarandon has physical attributes to offset her blank-faced hyper-eager, tongue-twister line readings. Pure plastic is not without its appeal. And people notice Richard Gere. His imitative style made him stick out in *Looking for Mr. Goodbar*, and it does in *Days of Heaven*, and here, too. Gere might be competent in smaller roles, but when he has an important part he doesn't seem to have enough resources of his own to draw upon, and so he dips into the performances of actors he admires—De Niro and Brando, mostly. *Days of Heaven*, which is set in the period before America entered the First World War, is all visual bombast; it has no center and is full of dissociated silent-movie emotions. Gere, with his post-fifties acting style and the overtones it carries of Brando and Dean and Clift and all the others who shrugged and scowled and acted with their shoulders, is totally anachronistic in it. And the one basic emotion he needs to show—sexual avidity for his former companion, now another man's wife—seems quite beyond him. In *Bloodbrothers*, he's better off, because the adolescent Stony is within the range of hurt-boy emotions that the post-fifties actors established, and Gere has models for everything he does. But his performance is all mannerisms—defenseless, sunshiny grins and juvenile torment. Stony is trying to find himself, all right—Gere is ransacking *On the Waterfront*, *Rebel Without a Cause*, *East of Eden*, and *Mean Streets*, and trying to come up with a self. The eyes squinch dutifully while the camera closeups keep alerting us, "Look how lovably he suffers—our new prince." But the intensity that we're told to feast on isn't there. Gere is to De Niro and Brando what the singers in *Beatlemania* are to the Beatles.

[October 2, 1978]

Furry Freaks

*U*p in Smoke, which stars Cheech and Chong (who also wrote it), is an exploitation slapstick comedy, like *The Groove Tube*; this piece of stoned-hippie foolishness is also crudely done but is more consistently funny. Pothead viewers may think that they're laughing at inside jokes, but you don't have to be an insider to see the humor in dopers' single-minded, never-ending quest for great grass. What makes this an exploitation picture, rather than a family picture, like *Blazing Saddles* or *High Anxiety*, is that it's dirtier, wilder, and sillier. (It's also better paced.) *Up in Smoke* gives us the sunny side of the drug culture; it's a pot-party picture—the flip side of the coin from *Who'll Stop the Rain*. Giggly, happy insanity is always the goal. The humor is like dogface underclass humor, but without the resentment of the officers. And Cheech and Chong are so gracefully dumb-assed that if you're in a relaxed mood you can't help laughing at them.

Cheech Marin, who plays Pedro, is a Mexican-American born in East Los Angeles; he wears a gigantic droopy mustache and is frisky and hopeful. His partner, Tommy Chong, who plays Man, as in "Hey, man," is a Canadian-born Chinese; he wears glasses low on his nose, a full beard, and a red headband holding back a mass of hair, and is amiably slowed down. Cheech and Chong have been working together since 1969, and became nationally known in 1972, when their albums, produced by Lou Adler (who directed this movie), began to sell in the millions. They're sleepy-eyed naturals in front of the camera, and so perfectly attuned to each other's physical movements that, in the film, when they meet for the first time it seems preordained. At the opening, Pedro decides to take a break from his bawling kids in the barrio; he does an anticipatory jerky little dance of freedom around his lowrider sedan as he polishes it, and he's tootling along the Coast highway, listening to the Fiestas, with the ball fringe on his fur upholstery swaying, when he sees what he thinks is a sexy girl hitchhiker. It's Man, who has left his well-heeled parents' home and is hauling all his gear and a set of drums. Pedro, it turns out, is the lead singer with a new Chicano rock band that needs a drummer. Even with Man on the drums, though, the band can't play without grass, and that starts Pedro and Man on a search that takes them to Tijuana and back. On the way back, driving a van that is made of Fibreweed (i.e., pure marijuana), they pick up two women hitchhikers. One is a cheerful busty blonde (Anne Wharton), who satisfies Pedro's lecherous dreams, while the other (Zane Buzby), who is skinny and toothy and blank-faced, with long dark-red hair hanging like a rag mop, takes charge of Chong. She talks amphetamine style, with a British accent, pouring out sympathy while dispensing uppers and downers from a plastic medicine chest. This speed-freak earth-mother Vampira knows everybody in L.A. and everything that's going on. The girls tell their heroes about a contest open to all rock bands which is being held that night—the Rock Fight of the Century—and when Pedro decides to enter and phones his Chicano band to meet them at the contest site, the redhead practically carries Man to the stage. The film loses its satiric tone during the footage of the competing rock groups, which seems almost like a documentary. But the lapse is brief. Just as the Chicanos' turn comes, the van outside catches fire. High on the delicious fumes, Man goes at his drums like a conquering hero, and Pedro, dressed in a pink tutu, sings and jumps like a cross between Mick Jagger and Jerry Colonna, but he's more ecstatic than either. He does stiff-bodied, wild dance steps, with a few Chuck Berry kicks, while shouting gibberish doggerel: "Mama papa talka to me / Try to tell me how to live / But I don't listen to them / 'Cause my head is like a sieve."

Once *Up in Smoke* gets past obtrusive reaction shots of Edie Adams (as Man's mother) in the opening section, it's fairly smooth, despite places where you feel you must have missed something. Probably the supervising editor, Lou Lombardo (who co-produced with Adler), achieved the smooth, quick pace by cutting some scenes short—such as one in traffic court—and chopping out the really dull scenes, even if that left us without a number of plot connections. There are still too many pitiful dumb jokes mixed in with the good dumb jokes, and some gags are a little askew, so that we only half get them. As a narc sergeant, Stacy Keach, with his square head and crewcut, has a comic-strip look but can't quite find the laughs in his routines, and his three narc stooges have no rhythm in their bungling; this whole part of the plot is uninspired. It's possible that Cheech and Chong don't know how to write for anybody but themselves; with the exception of Zane Buzby, whose deadpan stoned soliloquy is so satirically accurate you're sure you've run into her a few times, and two people with great bits (June Fairchild as a woman who snorts Ajax, and Otto Felix as a motorcycle cop who grows lyrical from the van's exhaust), the other performers seem to have standard-buffoon material. Adler's directing is often wobbly and sometimes sure in just the wrong ways, but at least he is an appreciator of comic performers and he doesn't butt in when Cheech and Chong get their act going. Some of the best scenes are of just the two

449

of them in a car, having an incoherent rap, lighting a joint the size of a stick of dynamite or a joint so teeny it has to be stuck on the end of a pin.

What a piece of semi-satiric salesmanship for Mary Jane. *Up in Smoke* is the *Blue Bird* of the dope culture—the quest for the happiness weed. Everybody who sniffs the van's fumes finds heaven on earth.

□ □ □

*I*n Farrah Fawcett-Majors' first movie as a star—*Somebody Killed Her Husband*, a romantic suspense comedy—her teeth flash automatically, and she speaks in a thin, girlish voice. It sounds like a made-up voice—how she thinks she should talk, with a tinkle. When she's impersonally sweet, she gets by, and we're relieved. It's a respectable performance. The director, Lamont Johnson, has shielded her, softened her plastic TV image; he presents her as your gentle, friendly dream girl. Yet there's something rigorous about this girl; you can see the years of training that it takes to turn yourself into an artifact. She gives herself away as an actress only when she has to show anger or when she cries. These emotions are so far outside the range of her impersonality that after her passable opening scene, when she discovers her husband's corpse and starts to sob and whimper, the narrative flow is completely blocked. It can't start up again until she stops making those tinny sounds of simulated grief and shock. Later, when she screams in anger, the movie has another awful intermission. As a model, Farrah Fawcett-Majors has a public personality with no affect, and when she fakes it here the movie is frozen in embarrassment.

Did the screenwriter, Reginald Rose, pull the script out of a filing cabinet where it had rested for decades? There's a caterpillar motif. (Caterpillars were box office in the forties, when one co-starred with Cary Grant.) This caterpillar, the hero of a children's book, is—I don't know if I'm strong enough for this—ecology-minded. Set in New York in winter, *Somebody Killed Her Husband* resembles the pictures that Ginger Rogers did in the late thirties—the ones about ordinary, pleasant people falling in love and getting into farfetched scrapes—and it attempts the same sort of casual, wisecracking, everyday good humor. But when this dishy blonde walks through the toy department of Macy's with her toddler son in a stroller and spills a bag of pretzels, and a clerk (Jeff Bridges) rushes to her assistance and looks into her teeth and it's love at first sight, everything seems a little custardy and congealed. Her overpowering niceness faintly suggests Mary Hartman, Mary Hartman, but without even neurosis underneath. Farrah Fawcett-Majors is the ideal stewardess; stewardesses are nice because they're paid to be nice. Hers is an invitation to which no response is possible—which may explain her enormous popularity, especially with teen-agers. She projects a foggy desirability: look but don't touch, don't spoil. Working next to her, Bridges probably does better by the dated romantic badinage than anybody else could have done. His way of giving a line a slight deëmphasis that makes it *his* and funny helps to lend the film some semblance of contemporaneity. His inflections bring out any possibility of comedy; if you say his lines over to yourself you can't understand how he did it. He makes the movie semi-watchable, but he's overdoing big-father-bear likability. His loose, slouchy gaucheness is getting a little too practiced. Bridges' hair seems thicker than ever before, and he's also wearing a full beard (probably to conceal his round cheeks); his hairy face might look fine if he didn't show us his hairless chest—one part of his body doesn't know what the other part is growing.

John Wood and Tammy Grimes appear briefly as nosy neighbors—and he wears what must be the narrowest shoulder tailoring that has ever appeared on the screen—but they're trying for a stylish, arch ghoulishness without having the witty lines that are needed to support that style. John Glover does better by his role as the dead man's secretary; Glover manages a pinched-face, amused craziness—he's enjoying himself frightening people, in a great movie tradition. Though corpses begin to stack up, the picture isn't frightening enough for suspense or funny enough for macabre comedy. But no doubt many people will find Farrah Fawcett-Majors' hair and teeth satisfyingly romantic. It's not an unpleasant movie, it's just awkwardly synthetic—like the Christmas tree in the heroine's apartment. The apartment itself seemed so deliberately gloomy that I kept waiting for the heroine to account for the ugly décor by pinning it on her dead husband's terrible taste. And I wished that she would stop hauling her toddler around, like a pet. She's enough of a pet.

□ □ □

When veteran American actors are cast too strongly against type, they look ridiculous. Who could accept John Wayne or James Stewart—or Gregory Peck—as a Nazi sadist? Peck strides into *The Boys from Brazil* with stiff black hair, beady little eyes (one squintier than the other), a chalky complexion, and a thin mustache that seems to be coming out of his nose, and when he speaks in an arch-villain's sibilant German accent you can't keep from laughing. In this large-scale version of Ira Levin's 1976 novel, he plays the monstrous geneticist Dr. Josef Mengele, who in his jungle hideaway is still carrying on the experiments he began in the death camps, staring into the future as he walks unconcernedly among the zombie mutants he has created. Charles Laughton was genuinely clammy and terrifying when he did this mad-genius-among-his-mutants number in 1932, in *Island of Lost Souls*, but Peck hasn't it in him to inspire primitive terror. His effects are all on the surface, and he looks particularly bad because he's playing opposite Laurence Olivier, who is the aged hero, Ezra Lieberman, a famous Nazi-hunter (and a fictional counterpart of Simon

Wiesenthal). Olivier does a mischievous impersonation of aged, hammy actors, such as the late Albert Basserman and Felix Bressart, with their querulous whiny voices and their fussiness—their way of seeming almost helpless yet resourceful, sagacious, and totally *good*. He takes off on this cloying humanistic style just enough to be very funny; if an actor to whom this falsetto came more naturally had played the role, Lieberman would probably have been as tiresome as the other characters in the movie take him to be. Only Olivier, with his daring flirtatiousness, could make this old bore enchanting. In the prison sequence, when he sits across a table from a convicted war criminal (Uta Hagen) and must control the loathing that makes the encounter physically painful to him, and, later, at the end of a discussion about cloning with a scientist (Bruno Ganz), when he realizes what the ninety-four "boys from Brazil" are, he rises above his Viennese singsongy charm. He demonstrates that the harmless-old-bore act of the aged can be a way of saving oneself for the things that count.

This picture is another of Lew Grade's international blockbuster packages (such as *Voyage of the Damned* and *The Cassandra Crossing*); the deals are worked out in terms of story elements that will sell and of performers with followings in as many markets as possible. The films are *assembled*. Lord Grade (known in film circles as Sir Low Grade) must exact a pledge from his directors that they will use no art and no imagination and will do their level best to forget whatever they know of technique. But he didn't need a pledge from Franklin J. Schaffner, who directed *The Boys from Brazil*. A thriller demands pace, dread, eerie concealment, surprise; Schaffner is so honest and aboveboard that he shows you the thumbscrews instead of applying them. We should be hurtling along, identifying with cagey old Lieberman's lonely struggle to outwit the Nazis; Schaffner, as he demonstrated in his most recent pictures (*Patton, Nicholas and Alexandra, Papillon, Islands in the Stream*), has become too logy and literal-minded for suspense.

And too inefficient. *The Boys from Brazil* is misshapen, like Schaffner's other recent films. He doesn't seem to have a sense of proportion about telling a story. His scenes are the wrong length: there are long scenes that should be short, and sometimes the first hour should be a half hour, or an eighth of an hour. By the time Schaffner gets a story started, the audience is snoring. As soon as he became successful enough to command large budgets, his camera began to linger on broad avenues, palatial rooms, entranceways and exits, big men standing against the horizon. In the first sequence of *The Boys from Brazil*, the camera moves sweepingly from an open-air café in Paraguay past a bullring, with a fight in progress, and through the streets to a palace and then to an airfield. There's no particular reason for all this visual pomp, since nothing in the sequence takes place on a large, public scale. But when we get further into the film, to Lieberman's tracking down of the components of the Nazi plot, the action seems almost desultory: a matter of knocking on a few doors. After all the ceremonial foreplay, we're desperate for some tension and movement, and what finally, do we see? Talking heads and two old actors wrestling on the floor, pretending to maul each other. When Schaffner gets to a climax, he brushes past it (as in *Islands in the Stream*) or else just stumbles through it, as he does here. Directors who don't have an instinctive sense of structure generally compensate for that lack by thinking their stories through. But Schaffner seems more concerned with the set decoration and the actors' grooming. His long-winded openings and sluggish scenes give his films a dilapidated grandeur. They're expensive ruins.

Although Peck appears to relish his fling at villainy so much that he doesn't recognize that his performance will go down in the annals of camp, James Mason, who plays a colonel (the security officer for the Nazi plotters), knows—oh, how he knows. In the swacked paranoid fantasy of *Mandingo*, Mason managed to have an uproarious good time, but when he's conversing with Peck, in a room stocked with mementos of Hitler and with tropical birds in their cages, while the zombies wander about outside in the jungle (specially constructed in a lagoon twenty-five miles south of Lisbon, with fifty thousand dollars' worth of imported tropical plants), an infinite weariness seems to settle over him. This is the sort of deal movie in which the actors should be wearing price tags; Mason shows a bland contempt for what he's got himself into. Olivier doesn't experience shame; he has no need to. Now more than ever, he has the power to find something he's never done before, in any role. Rosemary Harris, in her few minutes of screen time, matches her style to his. Playing a recently widowed German woman, she has a gleaming-eyed rapport with him: as Lieberman and the widow talk together, their decorous smiles and coy pauses parody—ever so sweetly—the vaudeville of European politesse. Lilli Palmer does not fare as well. As Lieberman's solicitous, doting sister, who frets over his health, she gets to show her famous ravishing smile—that's all.

The picture is almost belligerently sexless, and even its hyperbolic gothic touches come to nothing. When the colonel arrives, with his aides, to remove traces of Mengele's hideaway, and sets the buildings on fire, there are no shots of the exotic birds being released from their cages or of the mutants running away into the jungle. And the plot itself is left dangling. If the film wants to be taken as a cautionary fable—another one!—about the ever-present dangers of Nazism, then it should leave viewers with a sense of the menace that Mengele's "boys from Brazil" constitute. Instead, we get Lieberman's fuddy-duddy humanism and vague assurances that the boys are not really dangerous. And this is supposed to be a *movie*. We never get the vision we expect of the ninety-four boy Hitlers. Maybe the moviemakers were afraid that it would look as if Mengele had set out to breed a marching band.

It's such a dumb idea to start with, this notion that Hitler's closest associates—whom he dragged down with him—would want him cloned. Nazism has become comic-book mythology, a consumer product. Movies like this aren't making the subject more important, they're making it a joke. They're cloning Hitler to death.

[October 9, 1978]

Bertrand Blier

The French writer-director Bertrand Blier has an authentic, lyrical impudence in *Get Out Your Handkerchiefs,* which was shown at the New York Film Festival on September 29th and 30th. This is the third in his series of male erotic fantasies. Blier, who is a novelist and the son of the well-known plump character comedian Bernard Blier, started to direct movies in the sixties, and then in 1974 made *Going Places* (the original title is *Les Valseuses,* French slang for testicles), and in 1976 *Calmos* (it turned up, without publicity, in New York last year under the title *Femmes Fatales* and disappeared almost immediately). Perhaps *Handkerchiefs,* a more subdued, deeper variation on the themes of those two films, will make it easier for audiences to respond to what he's about and to look at his earlier work without becoming incensed. When *Going Places* was released here, in 1974, it was variously described as "sordid," "loathsome," and "disgusting," and just this past March it was taken off the Home Box Office schedule because of complaints from affiliate stations. What is the picture's crime? Probably that viewers find themselves laughing at things that shock them. At one point, the two young roughneck protagonists (Gérard Depardieu and Patrick Dewaere) board a train and observe a beautiful, pure-looking young mother (Brigitte Fossey) nursing her baby in an otherwise empty car. They offer this madonna money to give them a sip and, apparently terrified of refusing, she accedes. When she gets off the train, her husband, a scrawny, pasty-faced soldier on furlough, is waiting, and as she walks to join him she has a silly, happy grin on her flushed face.

Audiences have come to accept the dirty joking in Buñuel films; the years, the honors, the press have given it a pedigree. But Blier's joking is so unself-conscious that it makes Buñuel's seem preconceived, almost pedantically outrageous. Blier gives us the kind of joke that can't be done by implication or symbolically—that has to be absolutely literal. This kind of joke has found only verbal form before, yet Blier visualizes it—as if that were the most natural thing in the world to do. The two roughnecks act out their sex reveries—in which, no matter what a woman says, she's really begging for it, so they're doing her a favor if they force themselves on her. And people watching this may be so fussed about the disreputability of what excites them that they can't accept the humor of their own situation. *Going Places* is an explosively funny erotic farce—both a celebration and a satire of men's daydreams—and some people find its gusto revolting in much the same way that the bursting comic force of the sexual hyperbole in Henry Miller's *Tropic of Cancer* was thought revolting.

Going Places shakes you up and doesn't seem to leave you with anything to hang on to. It's easy to find it upsetting and degrading. But that's part of what makes it funny. The two men's crude energy is overwhelming, grungy, joyous. Life to them is like a big meal: they go at it like hungry workmen tearing at a carcass of beef, with greasy fingers. They aren't hippies rejecting middle-class materialism; they have none of the sanctimonious counterculture glamour of the pals in *Easy Rider*. They're closer to the joyriding lowlifers in *The Wild One*. These two pals talk in rough lower-class accents and don't fit into modern urban France, with its homogeneous middle-class culture. They're outsiders without jobs or money who want to live the life of the rich and satisfy their appetites. So they help themselves to things: they snatch purses, steal cars, pilfer shops, and make passes at almost every woman they get near. They're not professional criminals; they just rip people off. They harass shopkeepers and work them up into a rage, but, in terms of the film, this is the only excitement the smug, bored shopkeepers get, and it's way in excess of any damage that the boys actually do. The atmosphere is that of classic farce, as in Ben Jonson: these two are no worse than the respected members of the bourgeoisie, they're just less skillful in their methods. It takes a half hour or so before a viewer grasps that the two pals (one is twenty-five, the other twenty-three) are guileless raw innocents and that almost everything they do backfires on them.

The tone of *Going Places* is startling, both brutal and lyrical. The men are barnyard characters with the kind of natural magic that the kids have in Vigo's *Zero for Conduct* and that Jean Renoir's Boudu has; there's a poetic logic in what they do. They pick up a compliant scraggly-blond waif, a beautician (Miou-Miou), who is so used to being treated as something inanimate—as garbage—that she thinks she is garbage. The two guys beat

455

her up and abuse her. Yet they also like her, and they take turns trying to bring her to orgasm—one of them even encouraging and coaching the other. But she remains sad and frigid, and they become furious with her. In between their heterosexual episodes, Depardieu jumps Dewaere (he yelps); he has also suffered the indignity of being shot in the groin, sustaining what the doctor calls "an abrasion of the left testicle." After the failure with Miou-Miou, the two go off to find an experienced older woman who will feel something; they wait outside a women's prison, confident that discharged prisoners will be sex-starved, and a middle-aged woman (Jeanne Moreau) who has spent ten years inside emerges. They treat her royally, with food and attention, and she gives them a great night of sexual maternal passion. But in the morning she kisses them both as they sleep and commits suicide by putting a gun to her vagina. Shocked by this first encounter with real madness and pain, they go back to their frigid little beautician; they weep and she comforts them, and then, out of a sense of responsibility to the dead woman, the three of them travel to another jail to await the release of her son. He turns out to be physically unappealing and not quite right in the head, but when the four of them are off in the country at a hideaway and the two pals are fishing they hear their frigid girlfriend, who is in bed with the crazy jailbird, making cries of sexual arousal, and in a minute she rushes out, radiant, to tell them the happy news of her first orgasm. (They pick her up and dunk her in the river.) Once aroused, she is always eager, and the two pals keep swapping places in the back seats of stolen cars.

The social comedy in Blier's work is essentially sexual comedy: sex screws us up, we get nicked in the groin or jumped from behind, idiots make out better than we do, and some people are so twisted that no matter what we try to do for them they wreck everything. And sex between men and women is insanely mixed up with men's infantile longings and women's maternal passions. Sexually, life is a Keystone comedy, and completely amoral—we have no control over who or what excites us.

Going Places was perhaps the first film from Europe since *Breathless* and *Weekend* and *Last Tango in Paris* to speak to us in a new, firsthand way about sex and sex fantasies; it did it in a terse, cool, assured style influenced by Godard, yet with a dreamy sort of displacement. (Godard achieved something similar in the postcards sequence of *Les Carabiniers*— also a two-pals movie.) When Blier's two pals are not in movement, they're disconsolate; they can't think of what to do with themselves from day to day. The landscapes without other people, the deserted places they go to, suggest a sex-obsessed dream world. These are cavemen who give women what in their exuberant male fantasies women want. The dialogue is slangy, the mood buoyant—flagrantly funny in a special, unpredictable way. You have no idea what may be coming. The distinctive aspect of

Blier's method of work is that although his scripts are completely written in advance of the shooting—and he doesn't improvise—he writes in an improvisational manner. Most scenarists, like dramatists, think out their structure in terms of the development of a situation—with conflict and resolution. They instinctively plan it out and know where they're going. Blier writes psychological picaresques: he begins with a group of characters and a certain tone, and then he may veer off and go wherever his subconscious takes him. Where he ends up probably surprises and partly mystifies him, as it does us. But generally he's right to trust his impulses, because they take him somewhere we might not have got to in any other way. Crazy connections get made—things unexpectedly tie together. And there is, finally, an underlying set of themes which emerges, and it's much richer than if he'd stuck to a conscious plan. The limitation—if one chooses to regard it as that—of Blier's go-with-your-subconscious method is that, naturally, his films all have the same themes. But he has the wit to treat his own subconscious as a slapstick fantasy land.

*B*lier's method worked in *Going Places,* and it works in *Handkerchiefs,* but something went wrong in his sexual extravaganza *Calmos* (and the picture failed, even in France). The first half hour or so of *Calmos* is a hilariously scandalous dirty-boy romp. Blier has such economy that he goes right into the comedy; there are no preliminaries, no waste—you're laughing before you've settled into your seat. There are two pals again, but now they're forty-year-old boulevardiers who look like wax grooms on a stale wedding cake. One is a gynecologist (Jean-Pierre Marielle), and the other a baby-blue-eyed pimp (Jean Rochefort). The doctor can't bear to look at women's genitals anymore; the pimp is exhausted by women's sexual demands—he feels women are chasing him even in his sleep. When the doctor's wife (Brigitte Fossey), hoping to tantalize him, offers herself for bondage—tells him she's ready for *anything*—he asks for foie gras. It's a dumb joke, but her nudity and his uncontrollable disgust make it lewdly, visually funny. The comedy is derived partly from a banal premise, a reversal of women's saying they have a headache. But the men's satiation—their demonstration of revulsion against sex—has real comic conviction. The two men run away together into the countryside, to a village where they eat and drink and wear old clothes and begin to stink. Calm, that's what they want. Eating is the only thing they can get excited about. They sit at a Rabelaisian feast, along with the local curé (Bernard Blier) and his helper, in an old house, and the cinematographer, Claude Renoir, makes the house, the food, the landscape sinfully beautiful. This opening is an inspired exploitation porno fantasy, with Renoir's images (and the music, by Georges Delerue) providing a feeling of grandeur and folly. But then the story enlarges and takes a science-fiction turn. It shifts from the lunacy and regressions of these two men to the sexual revulsion of men en masse. Blier and his co-scriptwriter, Philippe Dumarcay (who also worked on *Going Places*), lose the flavor and the characters, and the picture falls back on the stored-up debris of mass culture. The two men are joined by other escaping men; women demanding gratification come after them with guns, and it's a full-scale tedious war of the sexes until, finally, the two pals, old men now and shrivelled in size, are dropped out of a cloud onto an island, where they walk through the pubic hair of a giant black woman and slip into her vagina just as her giant black lover arrives to deflower her, and crush them. *Calmos* is an overscaled back-to-the-womb satiric fantasy—a male daydream about the impossibility of escape from the sexual wars.

How much distance does Blier have from his characters' foolishness? Well, at least enough to make us laugh at them. In a sense, *Calmos* is about sex rather than about women. A couple of guys coming out of a bar late at night might talk like this—about wanting to go home just to sleep but knowing that there's a woman waiting up for them, and not being able to face it. It's about the demands of sex on men who spent their youth chasing women and now—jaded—want a break from it. There's no macho in the male bonding of the Marielle and Rochefort characters; they just want to be left alone for a while—they want to go off and live like pigs. It's a funny idea, and though *Calmos* abandons it, there are still things to look at all through the picture. It was a stroke of genius to use Renoir and Panavision: the images have clarity, depth, richness, sweep, and the color is deeper even then Decae's. Early on, there's a streetcar full of avid women—a not too bright idea that is given a redemptive comic intensity by Renoir's lighting. Throughout, the women are made repellently beautiful—they have a neon voraciousness. Brigitte Fossey, a blond cat with a perfect tiny mouth, is like sensual porcelain. The light on her is so metallic and cold that her makeup seems to be dry ice. Any man would fear to come to her: who could live up to the glittering desire in her cat eyes? And even the idea of the giantess (shot on a beach in Guadeloupe) is almost redeemed by Renoir's use of Eastman color and Panavision. No one but Blier has matched such raunchiness and such visual beauty; you have to have a true respect for raunchiness to do that.

The title *Get Out Your Handkerchiefs* suggests a mockery of such movies as *Love Story,* but it also carries another suggestion—that we *should* be prepared to weep at the perplexities of love. It's a gentler, more refined comedy than either of the others; our laughter is never raucous. The wildness of *Going Places* hasn't disappeared, though—now it's underneath. The impression that the film gives is of freshness and originality, and of an unusual serenity. Feelings are expressed that haven't come out in movies before, and in a personal voice of a kind we think of as novelistic, yet nothing is wasted in the shots. Everything is to the point, and so we sit trustingly as things drift along and work themselves out. Here, as in the two other pictures, we never know where the story is going, and there's a considerable shift of direction midway, but this time it's all reassuringly quiet. The music is by Mozart, by Delerue (writing in the spirit of Mozart), and by Schubert, and this has an additional modulating, controlling effect. The style is almost chaste.

The two protagonists are played by the stars of *Going Places*, Depardieu and Dewaere (it was written with them in mind), but they're not the boors they were before—there's no violence in them. They're polite, harmless workingmen—Depardieu a driving-school instructor, Dewaere a playground supervisor. The picture opens at Sunday lunch in a Paris café. Jug-faced and serious, the powerfully built Depardieu is eating robustly while his lovely dark wife (Carole Laure) pecks at her food. Suddenly, he begins expostulating; he explains to her that she doesn't eat because she's sick of his face. He says that he loves her and wants to make her happy, so he'll bring her the man sitting opposite her whom she's been staring at and wants to go to bed with. There's something Neanderthal about his clumsiness; he's telling her of his consideration for her while making a public spectacle of her misery and their sexual failure. He goes over, introduces himself to the bearded stranger (Dewaere), propositions him, and says, "If you get her to smile, you'll be my pal." From this first scene—which is as deft and quick and funny as scenes in Sacha Guitry's comedies, such as *Lovers and Thieves*—Blier is playing with his characters and with us. The wife certainly looks bored and depressed, but we don't see her eying Dewaere—who wears glasses, and looks rather vague and self-absorbed. He accepts the invitation, though, and becomes the wife's lover, and the men then take turns trying to impregnate her—it being their theory that she is silent and morose because a woman needs a child. What we do see once the two men become pals (without Dewaere's getting her to smile) is that neither one makes any emotional contact with her. Dewaere has the complacency of a literate simpleton. He owns five thousand of the Livre de Poche paperback classics; reading them and listening to Mozart are his life. And he proselytizes, and converts Depardieu to his interests, while the wife scrubs and knits. When a neighbor (Michel Serrault, the star of *Lovers and Thieves*) bangs on their door at night to complain of the sound of a Mozart record, Depardieu sits him down and converts *him*.

So far, it's an enchantingly quirky sex comedy. The situation of the sterile wife and the rattled husband has its classic-farce overtones; the cuckolded husband is generally rich and decrepit, of course, but this is a classic farce in modern slang, with a barrel-chested, virile young husband who cuckolds himself with complete casualness, on the spur of the moment. Yet the film's texture is soft and sensual; there's a velvety underlayer to the scenes. Jean Penzer's cinematography suggests another world—like something shot from a diving bell. Because of Blier's method, nothing is ever explained. It's clear the two men are chumps. But if they don't have any idea what's going on in the wife's mind, neither do we. And the secret of the film—its essence—is that Blier doesn't, either. Carole Laure, with her neat little choirboy head and her slender, sinuous body, is treated as an object throughout. But never with contempt. And Carole Laure is a wonderful reactor. Her elusive, doleful shades of feeling delight us, even though we can't be sure what they mean; we can't tell if her knitting is a way of escaping the men's idiocy or if her mind is blank, or both, but we enjoy entertaining the possibilities. Are the men right to think she will be happy only if she has a child? Maybe so, but they go about trying to give her one without ever getting through to her. Their obtuseness—their clumsiness—may be the reason they can't reach her, but then perhaps it's her unreachability that makes them so clumsy. She has the natural, yielding grace of a sapling.

In the second half, the classical elements vanish, and the picture becomes more mysterious, leisurely, and meditative. In all three of these films, the movement is from the city to the country—to the primeval wilderness—and it's always the men's propulsion. This time, the two men decide that the wife they've been sharing needs country air, and the three of them go off to be counsellors at a summer camp for the underprivileged. The camp has one wealthy child, a thirteen-year-old boy (the child who plays the part is billed only by his nickname, Riton, to protect him from notoriety); he has been sent there by his parents to obtain experience of the underprivileged, whom he will be dealing with when he takes over the family's industrial enterprises. He's a smart brat, with a genius I.Q., though he looks unformed; there is no suggestion of horniness about him, and the first time we see him, when the other children are picking on him, we might easily take him for a girl. But he's far more clever than the two pals, and he hasn't had any reason to feel that he's clumsy; he has his child's guile and seductiveness. He says and does the shrewd things that thirteen-year-olds must want to say and do but don't have the courage for, or the knowledge, except in their dreams. He uses entreaties drawn from Cherubino in *The Marriage of Figaro*. And he gets through to the wife. The men were right: she wanted a child.

The woman takes this little boy to her bed, and can't live without him, even if that means he must be kidnapped. When he has been sent away from her to boarding school, and is in the dorm at night telling his awed fellow-students the story of his conquest, and the woman herself tiptoes in and, in full view of all those boys, kisses him, we're watching a mythological romance. There are all the obstacles, such as the boy's parents, to be taken care of, but the two men (who turn into her clown attendants) help her, though it lands them in jail. How can they not help? The boy prodigy is like their Mozart. The film goes off in this weird direction, yet it all seems uncannily logical and prepared for. At the end, the woman has her child lover and is pregnant as well.

It's bewildering yet mysteriously right, satisfying, down to the pensive sounds of Schubert at the end. There's a gravity to this film—to Blier's generous, amused giving in to a sense of defeat. At some level, he has the feeling that what women want men for is to perpetuate the species—that they really want a child. And he has compounded this fantasy by having a child father the child, thus eliminating the need for men altogether. *Handkerchiefs* is a farce that turns into a fable. Now we recognize why everything about the young wife is so ambiguous—that melting look in her eyes, her shimmering beauty. Now we can understand Dewaere's double take when he was spending a night with her and said he wondered what her husband was doing, and she said "Who?" This is a sleeping-beauty fable, but told from the point of view of a man's erotic fears. This woman is to be awakened not by a prince but by a princeling. At the moment that her child lover is seducing her, in the sleeping quarters at the summer camp, the two chumps come down the hallway, pause outside her door, and discuss whether to go in. They decide that there's no reason to worry—the boy is too young. It's a funny moment, yet there's poetic tension in it, and the hallway has a palpable sensual beauty. They're losing out forever.

All three of these films are about two pals who don't really understand women—and their not understanding women is part of their bond. The teamwork of the actors is the true marriage. Depardieu, with his beautiful long jaw and his loping walk, and Dewaere, with his nearsighted vagueness (he's like a more delicate Timothy Bottoms), move together rhythmically. Marielle and Rochefort twitch and grimace and drop their eyelids in perfect counterpoint; their show of revulsion at women is the flirtation dance of impotent roués. The pal teams in these movies have intuitive rapport. They hang loose when they're together.

In *Handkerchiefs*, Blier's fantasy themes seem to turn against the male fantasist. There's pain along with the humor. The thirteen-year-old who arouses the wife is a variation of the jailbird who aroused the beautician, but, once aroused, the lovely wife does not want the men—she wants only the child. The two men who were so happy with the mother figure played by Moreau, and who wanted to be suckled on the train, are now rejected by the mother. Marielle and Rochefort at least found their way back to the womb, but Depardieu and Dewaere seem to be locked out. All they've got is each other, and at the end they're going off together, maybe to live happily like pigs. But that's not how it looks. Discharged from jail and carrying their belongings, Depardieu and Dewaere peer through an iron gate into the window of the solid, rich home where the wife they have lost sits contentedly knitting baby clothes, and then disappear down the road.

Blier's poetic logic is so coolly, lyrically sustained in *Get Out Your Handkerchiefs* that nothing that happens seems shocking. You feel you understand everything that's going on. But only while it's happening—not afterward. Afterward, you're exhilarated by the wit, and by your own amusement at how little you understand. What does the woman respond to in the child? His need? His foxiness? His strength? His childishness? It's a mystery. Sex is emotional anarchy.

Blier doesn't attempt to present a woman's point of view; he stays with the man's view of women, and that gives his films a special ambience. For a woman viewer, seeing *Handkerchiefs* is like a vacation in a country you've always wanted to visit. Reading a book such as *From Here to Eternity*, a woman enters an area of experience from which she has been excluded; seeing a Blier film, a woman enters a man's fantasy universe stripped of hypocrisy. Blier's films have no meanness about women; the wife in *Handkerchiefs* isn't neurotic—just elusive. Women are simply seen as different. A man friend of mine used to say, "If the first Martian who lands on earth is a male, I'll have more in common with him than I do with all the women on earth." Blier's is an art of exaggeration: he takes emotions and blows them up so big that we can see the things people don't speak about—and laugh at them. *Get Out Your Handkerchiefs* makes you feel unreasonably happy.

[October 16, 1978]

Detectives—The Capon and the Baby Bowwow

Agatha Christie wrote perfectly controlled ensemble work in her novel *Death on the Nile*; the story is told almost entirely in dialogue, and the voices of her characters are so cleverly orchestrated that there's never a wrong note that isn't deliberately wrong. Her detective, Hercule Poirot, is a living, walking lie detector; he can sense the best-concealed flickers of emotion, and hear the pause before a falsehood or the slight tonal evasiveness of someone who isn't telling all he knows. The book, first published in 1937, moves along like a movie with a lot of talk (you cast it in your mind), and, though it's too drawn out, it's a model of escapist engineering. Reading it is a pleasant form of oblivion.

The salaries and availabilities of actors with box-office appeal being a form of international roulette, the movie of *Death on the Nile* can't possibly achieve the novel's ensemble perfection. The goal of the movie is "all-star" ensemble work (i.e., a showcase, in which everyone has his turn), and, like its predecessor, *Murder on the Orient Express* (both were produced by the English team of John Brabourne and Richard Goodwin), it's shaped to satisfy the audience's nostalgic longing for extinct forms of idle-class travel. Once again, it's the thirties; this time we travel by steamer. The script, by Anthony Shaffer, has wit and edge and structure—too much structure, as it turns out, for the methodical pacing of the director, John Guillermin. His directing here is languid, depleted; he rouses himself now and then, when he gets a chance at a big outdoor scene, such as an attempted murder in the Theban ruins at Luxor, but he sinks right back.

The novel centers on two beautiful young women who have known each other from their convent-school days in Paris. Jacqueline de Bellefort, the recently impoverished daughter of a French count, has fallen passionately in love with a penniless Englishman, Simon Doyle, and goes for help to her best friend, Linnet Ridgeway, who is an American heiress and one of the richest girls in the world. Linnet, who has always had everything she wanted, is in England remodelling an ancient estate she has just bought, and Jacqueline asks her to hire Simon as estate manager, so that they'll be in a position to get married and go off for a honeymoon in Egypt. Jacqueline takes Simon to meet Linnet, and within a month it's the two of *them* who are off honeymooning in Egypt. In a single-minded rage over her betrayal, Jacqueline follows, turning up wherever they go, making scenes and spoiling things for them. The married lovers hope they've got away from her when they board the steamer Karnak, which will take them for a luxury cruise on the Nile, but Jacqueline shows up on board, among a collection of tourists who almost all have reasons to hate the imperious Linnet. The only clear-cut exception is Poirot (on vacation, naturally).

The movie is fatally perfunctory about emotion, atmosphere, suspense. We never really see Jacqueline's total love for Simon, which sets the story in motion, or feel the shock of the honeymooners when she first confronts them, or the guilt that envelops them. The movie's first mistake is the casting of Lois Chiles as Linnet Ridgeway; in a movie where nuances should be exact, here is an actress so inept you can't even tell that she's meant to be American. Lois Chiles (she was Jordan Baker in *The Great Gatsby*) has a low voice that doesn't seem to be coming from her at all—she always sounds dubbed or vaguely ventriloquial, like a transsexual. And she hasn't the style for arrogance. She looked smashing in her brief scene in *Coma* (as the heroine's friend who was having an abortion), but more of her is less. She's so inexpressive that her beauty does not make her enticing. The only time she lives up to the demands of the role is when she's seen from the back, dancing in a low-cut gown. It's a sly touch that Linnet and her full-lipped, overeager bridegroom, Simon (Simon Mac-Corkindale), look matched by nature: dark, lusting, unpleasantly sensual—and with big, long chins. But, even made up to resemble the young Rita Hayworth, Lois Chiles is much too crude to be an heiress favored by the gods; she's more like the tough young wife of a Texas used-car dealer. The casting of Mia Farrow as the jilted Jacqueline is damaging in a different way. Mia Farrow is an increasingly skillful actress, and her pale-pink eerie sprite face takes the light as delicately as any face in movies. She is never dull in this role—she may be incapable of dullness. Nor is she a wispy sweet ingenue here; she does suggest Jacqueline's scorn for self-preservation. But the story is calculated around the pity that the other characters feel for Jacqueline, and Mia Farrow is too exquisitely perverse for pity—she's the carrot-haired daughter of Morgan le Fay. When she attaches herself to the honeymoon, she seems to be amusing herself rather than abasing herself. So there's no fiery passion, with its suggestion of evil, at the center of the plot. What's there is more like malice. Perhaps Shaffer intended it this way, but it's a little parched. (Why Jacqueline's French name is retained when there is no other suggestion that she is French seems a puzzling oversight in a movie in which so much of the comedy relates to the characters' nationalities.)

Death on the Nile is a flop of a very special kind. I don't know that I've ever seen a movie with so many clever things in it which was yet so disappointing. Shaffer has an ear for high-style romp, and the details are knobby and funny. There's invention in the relationship between the rich old pearl-freak, Mrs. Van Schuyler (Bette Davis), and Miss Bowers, her nurse-companion (Maggie Smith). It's the thin-nosed, neat-looking nurse, in her insanely correct nurse-companion ensembles (they're like military drill suits), who has the upper hand—who sneers at her employer's attempts to give her orders, and grabs the old lady, jerks her arm, and hustles her around rudely. Maggie Smith is so fast you can't keep track of her hands. Bette Davis's timing is off, and she never gets into her role (she seems much too vigorous for her old-dowager clothes), but she uses her distinctive style of vocal emphasis to get her few laugh lines across, and her teammate Maggie Smith—Our Lady of the Wrists—takes care of the action. Maggie Smith plays her part with nippy, spinsterish angularity; Miss Bowers' brooding, furious bad temper about the injustice of her subservient position keeps flaring up in a quick angry movement, a sudden flush, or a burst of pinched-face resentment. Her boiling point is her normal body temperature. It's a small role, but so triumphantly mannered that you have the pleasure of seeing a great actress at work. Though I came out of this movie feeling down, I can easily imagine myself watching it again, when it turns up on Home Box Office—to see the Maggie Smith scenes, and Angela Lansbury in her war paint, and Peter Ustinov's chickeny bachelor Poirot.

Angela Lansbury does a superlative caricature of a wreck of a vamp—Salome Otterbourne, a trash novelist whose steamy blend of sex, fate, and the mystery of the East has become passé. Lansbury doesn't walk; she slouches and lists (and not because she's on a boat). She's whooping it up one moment and sagging from booze the next. She's all curves, satin turbans, amber beads that hang to her crotch, and drizzling clouds of chiffon and fringe. Lansbury does a Margaret Rutherford, but with visions of satyrs in her bulging eyes. Talking out of the side of her gargling, sloshing mouth, she bats Fuller Brush eyelashes. (She must have swiped them from Louise Nevelson.) You feel she needs a derrick to lift her lids. It's a glorious piece of eccentric excess, right down to the love bracelet on the ankle. Lansbury could use some comic foils, though. When she twists and sways her concave body in the ecstasy of a tango, all she's got for a partner is David Niven (as Poirot's colleague, Colonel Race), and he doesn't bring much to the party. It must certainly have been the disappointment of David Niven's life that he didn't grow up to be C. Aubrey Smith. (Smith was the rock foundation of the British Empire; when he died, it was the end of the Empire.)

Ustinov is an ideal fatuous, vain Poirot. An inspired mimic, he does the accent so easily that he can relax and do what other Poirots haven't been able to: he gives us layer upon layer of fatuity and vanity, and Poirot acquires depth—or, rather, thickness. Sherlock Holmes was smart about everything, but, as Ustinov demonstrates, it's possible to be a great detective without being a great intellect—it can be a craft, like knowing how to make boots that fit. His Poirot is an essentially ponderous man—that's what makes him funny. And Shaffer has provided conceits, such as a shaggy-cobra story, in which Ustinov can show us Poirot in moments of mortification. But, since Ustinov is playing a moldy fig and is on the screen fairly steadily, he suffers the most from the director's failure to vary the rhythms of the scenes. And when Poirot gives us his hypotheses of how each of the surviving passengers could have committed the murder, and these hypotheses are visualized for us, we should be enjoying the comedy of Poirot's arch pedantry—his need to stretch things out. Instead, the film itself seems to stretch out, as each suspect is seen huffing and puffing down the deck into the victim's cabin and out again.

There are fine bits. As the helplessly grinning obsequious Indian manager of the cruise ship, who talks through protruding teeth, I.S. Johar does the kind of racial comedy that is often frowned on (as if every racial joke were really a racist slur); it's like Mickey Rooney's Japanese photographer in *Breakfast at Tiffany's* and Ernie Kovacs' Cuban in *Our Man in Havana*, or one of Peter Sellers' Indians. Except that for Johar it's Indian self-satire. Jon Finch is personable as the rich Bolshevik on board, who dresses like a volunteer for the Abraham Lincoln Battalion, though he falters in his last scene (in beret and open shirt), when he looks much too effete to be pairing off with Salome's serious-minded daughter (Olivia Hussey). Playing a medical quack, the head of a Swiss clinic, Jack Warden seems out of his element (he looks as if he should be in the boiler room), and his New York accent sometimes comes through his German accent, but he has one scene with Ustinov in which their comic impersonations commingle—it's like a duet for bugles. From moment to moment, the film is never less than engaging (it's easy to blot out people like George Kennedy, who gives his usual blustering, overscaled performance, this time as a thieving lawyer), yet the over-all effect is drab. You sit in your seat disconsolate, whimpering for a little moviemaking flair.

□ □ □

*I*n *The Big Fix*, the first movie Richard Dreyfuss has appeared in since he won the Academy Award for *The Goodbye Girl*, he acts like a puppy surprising his master with little tricks he's thought of all by himself; you feel he wants petting after each scene. When Dreyfuss appeared in *The Apprenticeship of Duddy Kravitz* and jiggled impatiently and sweated and scratched, it was in relation to the other people in the story; Duddy's drive for success was a comic passion. Here, when Dreyfuss hops and grins and pirouettes, he's not doing it for the people in the frame—it's for us. He's grandstanding. It's the grandstanding of a kid who's the best actor in the acting class—the one the other kids think is going to make it. He acts as if the camera were a mirror, and preens in front of it. He does too much: every shot is another entrance, another chance for him to see what he can come up with. He's trying gestures on for size. When he tells off some F.B.I. agents who are grilling him and walks down the hall grinning and evoking Bogart, he looks as if he couldn't resist it. When he registers deep emotion by lifting his head, closing his eyes, and giving his head a fast shake to clear away the pain, all he shows us is an enormous amount of boyish self-consciousness.

There's often something likable in the self-consciousness of show-off kids—we respond to their eagerness to please. But not after they've begun to count on our response. In *The Goodbye Girl*, Dreyfuss started to give up acting for being loved. His role, like many other roles written by Neil Simon, was both more and less than an opportunity: it offered a chance for opportunism. As soon as he stuck his head in the door of Marsha Mason's apartment, we in the audience asked how long it would take for her to realize how wonderful he was. And once Dreyfuss had played wonderful he must have lost his heart to himself. In *The Big Fix*, he smooths and perfects everything he did that got a simpering response in *The Goodbye*

Girl. He's so endearing, he acts with such cherubic self-satisfaction, that he should be billed as Richard "Cuddles" Dreyfuss.

This is a potentially major screen actor settling for "love-me" star acting. He still has moments: when, as Moses Wine, a private investigator, he discovers the body of the woman he's been dating, we're moved not by the sight of the body but by the shock to him. There are still glimmers of the range of expressiveness of a real actor. But the whole production (and he's the co-producer) is shaped to set off his darling-little-Jewish-boy angst and humor, and to mythologize them, giving them roots in the student-protest movement of the sixties. *The Big Fix* is based on Roger L. Simon's adaptation of his own 1973 detective novel, which was originally commissioned by *Rolling Stone* and its subsidiary, Straight Arrow Books, and is a counterculture roman à clef. The film's nostalgia for the great days of Berkeley in the late sixties—for the sit-ins, the strikes, the anti-war demonstrations—is like a form of intellectual mildew. Everything that has happened to the characters since is a fall—a compromise or a sellout. The movie uses "Berkeley" the way Stalinists used "Spain": to set off waves of guilt and sadness. Moses Wine isn't merely the usual cynical, down-at-the-heels private eye; he's warm and Jewish and disillusioned, with two small sons to support from a failed marriage (to Bonnie Bedelia). This is a private eye so full of love it oozes out of him; he's creamy. There's a scene that may be a touchstone for viewers' reactions to the film. Moses Wine is in his pad, and one of his sons phones and says he can't sleep, and Moses sings him a children's song—"I Went to the Animal Fair." This could have been an affecting scene if the director, Jeremy Paul Kagan, had simply cut away from it. But the camera pulls back as Moses sings, calling our attention to how small and isolated and lonely he is—a man who has lost everything he believed in, and is separated even from the children he loves. If you aren't bothered by that editorializing camera movement, chances are you'll enjoy *The Big Fix*.

The publicity for the film stresses the youth of the filmmakers and their shared background of sixties demonstrations. (It's the background of just about anyone now in his late twenties or early thirties who went to college.) But *The Big Fix* looks like a sloppy old-man's movie. This is Kagan's second theatrical feature. Earlier, he made several films for TV—*Unwed Father*, *Judge Dee*, and *Katherine*, the last with Henry Winkler, and with Sissy Spacek as a member of the revolutionary underground. His first feature, the amateurish *Heroes*, starring Winkler as a whimsically disturbed Vietnam veteran, was an exploitation of counter-cultural attitudes—a naïve, earnestly romantic film, with mushy love for its own purity and kookiness. (Do moviemakers who begin this way ever get the mush out of their skulls?) *The Big Fix* isn't as dismal as *Heroes*; the author's mixture of hard-boiled private-eye wisecracking and leftist politics is at least a new brand of pop manure. There are laughs in the picture. But

Kagan's work as a director has got even worse. *The Big Fix* has a much more complicated story than *Heroes*, and nobody is holding on to the plot threads. It looks as if the director had abdicated, or had never taken over. Dreyfuss dominates the picture the way actor-directors do when they have become sentimental about their own acting, and the scenes are imprecise, mottled. Often you can't tell where the story is taking place (it's set in locations in the Los Angeles area) or exactly what is going on; you figure the scenes out after they're over. There's virtually no indication that anyone connected with the film had any interest in visual composition, and the images are uniformly underlit, without contrast or emphasis. The whole movie seems to have been photographed through sludge.

In the messy flux of each of Kagan's films, there's an authentic piece of acting. In *Heroes*, it's Harrison Ford as an anxious, emotionally burned-out veteran. The performance is startlingly plain. You can believe this vet went through combat; it didn't turn him baby-talk whimsical, it left a blank space in his good nature. In *The Big Fix*, it's F. Murray Abraham as Howard Eppis, an Abbie Hoffman–like sloganeering radical and the author of *Rip It Off*. We see him first in newsreel footage from Berkeley in the sixties, and he's bouncing up and down gleefully, out of sheer kinetic high spirits. And when we meet him we can see that all the shouting and demonstrating were a physical outlet for him—that he's still dancing with energy, still maniacal and shallow. On the stage, Abraham probably gives audiences as much joy as any American actor of his generation, and some suggestion of his gift comes through in this small part. His satirical version of a student leader who has grown older and changed his ideas but is still all hopped up feels completely right, because his body is in character. He has stepped past his other self—the one that might be self-conscious.

The plot of *The Big Fix* involves someone's attempt to sabotage the campaign of the liberal candidate for governor of California by dirty tricks—distributing flyers that associate him with Eppis's bravado. Moses, who once knew Eppis, is hired by the campaign organization (the workers include Susan Anspach and John Lithgow) to find out what's going on. (When Dreyfuss and Susan Anspach are on the screen together trading big smiles, they seem to be competing for the Miss Congeniality Award.) It would certainly help if the director had drawn our attention to the vital plot elements—if there were enough visual design and clarity for us to see who is in the scenes, so we could tell who is chasing whom (even if we were still never to know why). It would also help if we cared; that is, if we had some stake in the liberal candidate's being elected, if he represented the ideals of the sixties radicals (as was the case in the book, where his opponent was fascistic). But, possibly for the sake of taking a hard line—i.e., nothing good can come from working within the system—the liberal candidate has been made a droning dullard and a phony. In the movie, it doesn't matter who gets elected, so not only do we not have a rooting interest in the candidate but we can't even see any reason the reactionaries are out to get him. If I read the situation right, the moviemakers are so fearful of being accused of having turned into liberals that they've destroyed their own plot. The movie has no core. But they've kept their purity.

[October 23, 1978]

Saint Dorothy

Diana Ross's determination to play Dorothy in the film version of the black Broadway musical *The Wiz* is possibly the chief example in all movie history of a whim of iron. Doom-laden as the idea was, something might still have been saved if Joel Schumacher, who was hired to write the script for this Diana Ross *Wiz*, had conceived an adult Dorothy who was ready for anything, and funny. That way, the thirty-four-year-old star might at least have sung some hot songs and shown off her icy glamour and salacious imp's smile. But, in the tradition of those actresses of the past who made their reputations as sirens and courtesans and then decided they had to play a saint or a nun, Diana Ross approaches the role like a reformed sinner. Her Dorothy, a kindergarten teacher in Harlem, is implacably virtuous and too shy to go out with men. She wears a demure, high-necked, pale-lavender blouse and a white skirt with a touch of orange at the waist, and a frightened look. Fervently wet-eyed, she sings songs of preachy uplift, in relentlessly slow arrangements. Each time she starts glowing for a number, it's like a nightmare version of "Sesame Street."

When a picture is packaged with elements that don't really belong together, almost everything that can go wrong generally does. The director, Sidney Lumet, who took on the job after John Badham quit (rather than accept Diana Ross in the lead), is known as a man who comes in under budget. In a business in which it's notoriously difficult to hold to a shooting schedule, he probably has had the best record of any director. But, just as in the contemporary legend it's the good, quiet boy who climbs up to the tower and starts shooting, Lumet, the director least likely to run over budget, exploded into extra time and extra money until the cost of *The Wiz*, which Universal, in association with Motown, had budgeted at the frighteningly high figure of eleven million dollars, rose to somewhere between twenty-seven and thirty-five million dollars (exclusive of advertising). Shot entirely in the refurbished Astoria Studios and on New York locations, *The Wiz* is easily the most expensive film ever made here; it is also the most expensive film ever made with a black cast and, in fact, it is the most expensive movie musical ever made. Only a half dozen or so musicals (*The Sound of Music, Saturday Night Fever, Grease, Mary Poppins,* and a few others) have ever brought in as much money as *The Wiz* cost.

Lumet's feeling for New York is his strength in some films (as in *Dog Day Afternoon*), but his decision that Manhattan would be the fantasy land of Oz turns the movie into a garbled "I Love New York" commercial. The script hasn't been thought through in terms of the adult heroine or of the city, and the film has no imaginative logic, no consistency. Dorothy and her Aunt Em (Theresa Merritt) live in a house with a handsome exterior (inside, somebody has gone berserk with fudge-colored paint), but from what they say they don't seem to know whether it's in Harlem or Brooklyn, or whether the party they're having is for Thanksgiving or Christmas or for somebody who has a new baby. This opening sequence appears to be an elaborate preparation for Aunt Em's nudging of Dorothy, telling her that it's time for her to get out in the world and find a fella. It seems that Dorothy, because of her "shyness," has never ventured below 125th Street. Schumacher, who must be one of the most maladroit screenwriters of all time, has dear old Em tell Dorothy she should stop teaching kindergarten and teach high school instead. Is old Em suggesting to Dorothy that in a high school she could pick up a boyfriend, or just that high school would be closer to "life"? After this bizarre conversation, Dorothy rushes out into the snow, chasing her little dog, Toto, whereupon a tiny cyclone whisks them both off to the land of Oz. Although Oz is meant to be Manhattan, it includes locations in Queens, the Bronx, and Brooklyn, and after Dorothy accumulates her travelling companions, they have to go over a couple of bridges to get to the Emerald City (the capital of Oz), in lower Manhattan. Geographically, we're thoroughly dislocated. When Dorothy first arrives in Oz, she's in a dark-bluish playground with graffiti-covered walls. The cyclone seems to have tossed her around the corner. When she's in a rubble-strewn lot and we expect her to say "Damn, it looks just like home," she dithers "Where am I?"—as if she'd never seen a burned-out block in Harlem. Since the movement of the film parallels that of *Saturday Night Fever*—away from the drabness and into the big city—it would make sense if this adult Dorothy loved what she saw of the great world. But all she does is moan about wanting to be home with Aunt Em—she seems quite pathological. Even L. Frank Baum, the author of *The Wonderful Wizard of Oz*, got bored with returning his child Dorothy to Kansas, and in the later books in the series he moved her Aunt Em and Uncle Henry to Oz with her. Baum's Dorothy was a very grown-up, matter-of-fact little girl; the original W.W. Denslow illustrations show a child of about six. (She gets a few years older in the later books.) The Dorothy of this movie is a woman who behaves like a little girl—a case of arrested development.

The "classic" M-G-M, Judy Garland version of 1939 wasn't the first time the story had been filmed: in 1925, Dorothy Dwan played Dorothy, with Larry Semon as the Scarecrow and Oliver Hardy as the Tin Woodman, and back in 1910 there was a film version that looks highly imaginative in photographs (a little Gustave Moreau, a little Edward Hicks). The book itself is a magical vaudeville. Baum had spent his youth in the theatre: he joined a touring company when he was nineteen, and was in a New York hit when he was twenty-two. While he was still in his mid-twenties, he wrote a musical comedy and toured in it, but the sets and costumes were destroyed by fire, and, with a growing family to support, he had to go to work as a travelling salesman. It wasn't until he was past forty, and had run a store and then a newspaper (both failed), that he began to publish the fairy tales he'd been improvising as bedtime stories for his four sons. *The Wonderful Wizard of Oz*, which came out in 1900, was the most successful children's book of the Christmas season, and Baum immediately set about dramatizing it and writing lyrics. His musical-comedy version opened in Chicago in 1902 and played on Broadway for a year and a half, and its two stars—Fred Stone as the Scarecrow and David Montgomery as the Tin Woodman—toured with it off and on for almost a decade. In 1906, Baum himself, a popular lecturer by then, went on the road with a "fairylogue" of Oz—hand-colored movies and slides.

When I read the Oz books as a child, I loved their plainness. The fairy tales that we inherited from Europe were usually translated and adapted in fancied-up styles that didn't resemble how Americans talked. But there were no poetic embellishments in Baum—it was magical prosiness. A child could feel he was being talked to straight. And in the Oz series the magic itself had an ordinary, everyday quality; the things that were endowed with personality were ridiculous domestic objects—a sawhorse or a lumpy old sofa. There was a basic topsy-turvy egalitarianism: animals, children, inanimate objects, witches, and fairies all talked the same simple Yankee language. It wasn't until I began reading the books aloud to my own child that I realized how much showmanship there was in them: the characters were vaudeville comics, the jokes were stage patter, and there was an acceptance of the corny enjoyment in puns and parodies. Even the outsize toys that came to life were like the "transformations" in stage shows for children. (In the new film, there's a suggestion of this in a robot camera and especially in a walking mike that looks like a Grandville lithograph.) Probably all these common stage devices were part of what I had experienced as blessed plainness. With the illustrations as a guide, a child reads along and projects himself into this funny, amiable vaudeville show; that may be part of why those of us who loved the books (and we were legion) had a special identification with them. We, too, joined a touring company. When I'd read ten or eleven of the books aloud and my daughter was ready to read the rest of the series by herself, I felt as if I'd been dropped along the road.

Baum's material is so essentially theatrical and unserious that it's adaptable to the song-and-dance gifts of almost any culture, and, in fact, white viewers can easily accept Michael Jackson as the Scarecrow, Nipsey Russell as the Tinman, and Ted Ross as the Lion. They give their roles black show-biz equivalents of the musical-comedy and burlesque styles that Ray Bolger and Bert Lahr, in particular, brought to the 1939 film. As far as the performers are concerned, the only problem is the insufferable Dorothy, who's some sort of superstar neuter, smiling through tears, with her arms always raised to the heavens. And she doesn't have the face of a dreamer. Judy Garland, with her fleshy vulnerability, provided a contrast to her three companions, but Diana Ross is as much an artifact as they are. And without her slinky costumes and her glamour makeup, she looks anorectic and forlorn. If *The Wiz* were a great black vaudeville show—a jazzy, satirical version of the fantasy story, with magic, songs and dances, and jokes—it could really be joyous. And even if it just had half a dozen cheerful numbers and a good spirit, a viewer probably could forgive everything that went wrong. But you come out of this film asking, "Couldn't twenty-seven million dollars buy one good song?" Charlie Smalls' score for the Broadway show has been padded out with some new music, and adapted by Quincy Jones, but only a few of the songs are even tolerably pleasing, and some of these few are staged in ways that make us uncomfortable.

After the stiffly proper scenes in Harlem (the one in Brooklyn), the show finally livens up a little when Dorothy, in Oz, sees the Scarecrow. Only nineteen when the film was shot, Michael Jackson is a very young Scarecrow, and a sweetness comes through his Pagliacci makeup. His lack of experience as a screen actor works partly to his advantage; his ingenuousness is touching, though there are too many reaction shots of him being self-consciously dear, and you want to yell "Cut!" to the editor (Dede Allen). As a child, Jackson was a soprano in the Jackson Five, and he sings "You Can't Win" in his lovely high tenor voice. But he's not just stuck on a broomstick, like an ordinary scarecrow; he's crucified on a TV antenna, and so there's a masochistic edge to his sweetness, and the four black crows who dance around him aren't funny tormentors whose fast high stepping and bouncy rock dancing we can enjoy—they're making him suffer. He's hanging there. None of this is the actor's fault, or the fault of the dancers, either. It's the result of the crudeness of the moviemakers— reaching for an immediate "powerful" effect, and not considering what this bathos does to the spirit of the whole production. When Dorothy helps the Scarecrow down, the scene is hopelessly static: she looks solicitous and merciful, and he's moving on his knees as if he were about to sing "Bess, you is my woman now." When he begins to pull out bits of his paper stuffing and read homilies by great thinkers—Bacon, Confucius, Shakespeare, and so on—each one is a dead moment. Nobody has provided any zingers from black thinkers or jazz musicians.

The one performer who is able to ride right over the messy carelessness is Nipsey Russell. In the 1939 version, Jack Haley's Tin Woodman was the weakest of the major characters—though hardly in a class with the sugary inanity of Billie Burke's Glinda, the Good Witch. Nipsey Russell is a vast improvement; his first lines are funny, and he gives them rhythm and beat, and though the lyrics of his song "What Would I Do If I Could Feel?" are unbelievably feeble ("What would I do / If I could suddenly feel / And to know once again / What I feel is real?"), he sings them in a Dapper Dan night-club style—like a suave carnival barker—and on a nearby carousel the painted heads of three girl angels provide a backup chorus. (It's probably the most charming bit in the film, yet we see the angels only in cutaways; there isn't a single frame with the Tinman and the girls in the same composition—which is what we're dying to see.) This song and his second one, "Slide Some Oil to Me" (performed in the Fats Waller manner)—both relatively simply staged—are the film's best numbers. Like Ray Bolger and Bert Lahr in the 1939 version, Nipsey Russell understands that the roles are vaudeville-comedy turns. And, though his tap-dancing is unexciting, he shows here that all his years of playing the inoffensive black entertainer in front of white audiences haven't softened him as a performer; he has the true pro's integrity of style. His performance is marred only by a special effect. When Dorothy and the Lion have been drugged, the Tinman's tears falling on their faces wake them up. But instead of a magical teardrop Lumet gives us a faucet in full flood. We get an obscene twinge from this attempt at boffo humor.

Ted Ross has a smily scat humor in that awakening scene, and his lion costume may delight small children, but the "I'm a Mean Ole Lion" number is plodding (and this lion certainly could have used an Afro). As the con-man Wiz, Richard Pryor begins entertainingly, but his role peters out. And the film's negligence is bewildering: the big head that is an indispensable part of the Wiz's illusions is suddenly seen lying on its side, as if the Wiz had become demoralized and discarded it. (Pryor, with his spooked look, which gives a tension to whatever he does, seems such an obvious choice for the Cowardly Lion that the casting appears a little off.) Except for Michael Jackson's song and the two songs by Nipsey Russell, the only number that has any real fun to it is the hot, jumping, growly "Don't Nobody Bring Me No Bad News," sung by the Wicked Witch, Evillene (Mabel King). Wearing a heavy jewelled armature—a dress encrusted with knickknacks—and made up as a female ogre, with a headdress like a Carmen Miranda bowl of fruit that's sending out sinister

473

tendrils, she yet manages to be a Kewpie doll. This sequence is staged in the most striking set in the movie—a huge, long sweatshop with patterned skylights, like something out of Manchester at the time of the industrial revolution—and, although the dancers do too much rushing up and down its length, the choreography is more clearly structured than it is in the other sets. (This may be the first musical number by Friedrich Engels.)

This film brings out all of Sidney Lumet's weaknesses as a director and almost none of his strengths. Style, sensitivity, attention to detail, a fine ear—these are what he gets along without in his commercial successes. His gift—and it's not a minor one—is for urban animal energy, for drive. But in a musical the energy springs from style. Lumet has worked for two years and employed the talents of hundreds of people to produce a film that looks rushed and cheap. The singing is eerie: superbly recorded dead, empty sound. There's none of the ambience of the city in these clear, post-synched tones. Visually, the film is static, rhythmless, chaotic. The big production numbers are free-form traffic jams. They're shot the way a fagged-out TV crew arriving at the scene of a riot in the streets might grab whatever it could from behind the police barriers. Was Lumet trying to get the whole block in every shot? Our eyes scan the rows of dancers, trying to sort out what we're meant to be looking at, but the dancers are photographed at such a distance, and with such low-key photography, that we don't really see a dance—just vast quantities of people milling around. Models parading in swishy designer clothes are merely part of the bedlam. And, though they're wearing red and then green and then gold, it's all really dun-colored. The big sequences seem dark and flattened out. In filmed-dance terms, *The Wiz* is a regression to the days when cameramen stood at the back of the theatre and shot the Ziegfeld Follies straight on.

The whole film has a stagnant atmosphere; there's never a breath of air or a relaxed sense of space. When a troupe of dancers appears (like the sirens on Poppy Street), we don't know where they've come from or where they disappear to. The production designer, Tony Walton (who also did the costumes), doesn't transform the New York locations—he doctors them. Walton's New York, with its Congoleum yellow brick road with imprinted bricks, is like your old high-school gym festooned with crêpe paper for the junior prom. This is not to suggest that the sets in the 1939 version were ideal; they had the vacuously literal M-G-M look. But at least they weren't confusing, and they didn't overwhelm the actors. Walton uses graffiti paintings for an almost Haitian urban-primitive effect, but the yellow brick road doesn't beckon us on, and the film has no over-all visual design to bind it together. Many of the sets in *The Wiz* seem designed only for long shots and don't work at all for middle-distance scenes. There's a pleasant matte of Manhattan with five Chrysler Buildings, and there are charming, slightly miniaturized yellow Checker cabs that suggest Red

Grooms, but then when Dorothy and her companions arrive to see the Wiz at the Emerald City and it's the World Trade Center Plaza, you think, My God, that's where King Kong died. Many of the early scenes in Oz are underexposed, and the effect isn't mysterious, it's depressing. You have the feeling that the cinematographer, Oswald Morris, is trying to blur the edges of bum sets. There's so little visual differentiation in the scene in front of Walton's New York Public Library that stone and air melt into each other. There doesn't seem to be any sunlight or radiance in this Oz. With hundreds of dancers gyrating, it's Hades-on-the-Hudson.

And then, at the end, Lena Horne has her number. Surely the moviemakers should have learned from the mistakes of the M-G-M team and made Glinda a sexy Good Witch; Lena Horne could certainly have played her that way. Instead, she's done up like Elizabeth Taylor in *The Blue Bird*—in lyrical glitter. Shining down on us from the stars, and dressed like a blazing blue-and-silver Christmas tree, she says "Hello, Dorothy" with a condescension that leaves you breathless. After that, she makes a speech that sounds like a sermonette for the human-potential movement, and sings a gospel version of "Believe in Yourself" with an orchestration that suggests Mahalia Jackson. She's in beautiful deep voice, but gospel isn't what we want from Lena Horne, and it doesn't go with the tight muscles in her face. The first time there's a cut from her to a closeup of a black baby angel, it's amusing, but then there's another fat baby face, and another. Only the energy and anger emanating from Lena Horne—and cutting through the cloying effects—save her. Movies have sometimes succeeded in mixing satire and sentimentality, but this movie tries to mix satire and uplift.

The story is told as if the screenwriter had had no access to the book and had written the screenplay from disjointed memories of the 1939 film, seen on television. Once again, Dorothy's companions go off with her in order to ask the Wizard to give them what they believe they lack: brains for the Scarecrow, a heart for the Tinman, courage for the Lion. But in this movie, the Wizard doesn't give them the tokens that convince them that they now have what they needed. Dorothy lectures them instead, and after we've seen her call into the blank hole where the Tinman's heart should be and heard an echo, what are we to think when she tells him that he's had a heart all along? *The Wiz* doesn't give us the fairy-tale pleasure of seeing the pieces of the story fit into place. When Pryor's Wiz, who is young and, unlike Dorothy's other friends, completely human, tells her of his loneliness and pleads with her to keep him company, we half expect them to get together. Aunt Em has clearly implied that Dorothy needs sex, and if a romance with the Wiz would get her to stop kissing her dog and crying all the time, we'd certainly be for it. But Diana Ross's Dorothy is too nunlike to come out of Oz with anything but an improved character: she has learned not to be afraid. As for the poor Wiz, she tells him he has to "find himself." With all the talk about fulfillment and the endless lyrics about "feeling," *The Wiz* is like a month of Sundays in church.

[October 30, 1978]

Tentacles

*I*n Ingmar Bergman's *Autumn Sonata,* a spiritually distraught, dowdy woman of perhaps thirty-five or forty, the wife of a pastor in rural Norway, invites her majestically worldly concert-pianist mother, whose longtime lover has recently died, to come for a visit. The introverted Eva (Liv Ullmann) greets her celebrated mother, Charlotte (Ingrid Bergman), whom she hasn't seen in seven years, with a humble show of affection. But within a few hours this recluse, in her frightened-schoolgirl's Peter Pan collar and shapeless dress, precipitates a crisis for herself. After mentioning that she's the church organist and practices every day, she plays a Chopin prelude for her mother—plays it so falteringly, so inhibitedly, that it has no musical quality. Then she insists that her mother show her how it should go, and, as her mother performs, explaining her interpretation as she moves along, Eva is transformed by irrepressible rage. Sitting on the piano bench, with her face next to her mother's, her tightly braided long hair plastered across her head, her creepy weak eyes staring from behind wire-framed glasses, she's a half-mad blob. She has sought her own humiliation, and her thick lips part slightly in hatred and in ugly anticipation. That night, she goes at her mother with the impacted rage of a lifetime, accusing Charlotte of having deserted her when she was a child by going off to give concerts, and of never loving her. Charlotte's crimes, as Eva cites them, include forcing her to have an abortion when she became pregnant at eighteen, and being responsible for the degenerative spastic, inarticulate condition of Eva's younger sister, Helena (Lena Nyman). As Eva's rancor boils over, we see in flashbacks the childhood rebuffs she describes, and right in front of us we have the evidence of Charlotte's guilt: the emotionally crippled Eva, who cannot respond to her husband's love, and the physically crippled Helena, whom Eva has taken out of the institution that Charlotte had put her in. Even as Charlotte tries to justify herself to Eva, the helpless Helena has a seizure, tumbles out of her criblike bed on the top floor, and writhes on the staircase landing, making strangled sounds, calling "Mama, come," like an infant, to the mother who doesn't hear her—who, symbolically, has never heard her.

The picture, which spans roughly twenty-four hours, presents Eva's charges—that she was full of love for her mother, was rejected, suffered, and was destroyed—as the truth. Not just the truth as she nearsightedly sees it but the truth. Charlotte is resentful of Eva for having Helena in the house, because it means she'll have to go in to see Helena. As she stands over Helena's bed, we are shown her barely controllable revulsion and the collapse of Eva's hopes that her mother might have changed. One visit to Helena's bedside and Charlotte wants to get away from this house as soon as she can without losing face. She talks to herself when she's alone, and the thoughts she expresses are all about her own loneliness and her own comfort. In bed that night, she adds up the vast sums she has in the bank, like a child clutching a Teddy bear. Her fortune is her peace of mind; she can coddle herself and put her two children out of her life. This may be the first time in any seriously intended piece of dramatic literature that a character's soliloquies are designed strictly to confirm someone else's accusations. As Ingmar Bergman has conceived the artist-mother Charlotte, she is a compartmentalized character: she admits to closing herself off from all emotion except what she can feel and express within the formal protection of her music. (The explanation offered is that her own mother never gave her any love—this is like a new form of predestination.) Charlotte is a successful concert pianist and recording artist, but the film never suggests that she's a great pianist; she's in demand, that is all—she's the star she wanted to be.

Ingrid Bergman has always had a great throaty, sexy voice; now, at sixty-three, she uses it for power, and she has the commanding presence to go with it. Her aged demimondaine in the 1976 *A Matter of Time* was also startlingly strong—and was far more poetic—but the film was a shambles and few people saw it. Her role here suggests an older version of her natural-looking Hollywood heroines (and, in fact, in 1939 she played a pianist in *Intermezzo*, her first movie in English, which was a remake of a 1936 Swedish film she'd appeared in). Her face hasn't been surgically tightened; it's a plain on which emotions openly war with each other, and age itself helps determine the course of the battle, and the outcome. Charlotte is the villainous straw woman of the piece, the shallow, self-obsessed concert star, and Ingrid Bergman plays the role to the hilt. Unfortunately, some of the scenes that are played to the hilt are written too broadly. In a long telephone talk with her agent, in English, Charlotte is loud and hearty and childishly greedy for money—a tough old theatrical bird. And Ingrid Bergman beats her wings too much. Elsewhere, though, her freshness and energy make one laugh with pleasure. Her humor when she's talking to herself gives the movie its only leavening; she's the one likable performer.

Sven Nykvist's compositions have a rich depth: the simple interiors seem heavy, weighted. Visually, Nykvist's work is peerless—technically, that is. In expressive terms, the look of the film is less satisfying. The air is thick with a familiar misery—mannered misery. This time, Ingmar Bergman's use of space turns the compositions into a stage frame: the characters shift around and deliver monologues, and when they take over the screen in closeup their slightest movements assume great significance. When Ingmar Bergman first used giant double closeups, with the two actresses in *Persona*, there was something unfathomable in the graphic seepage—those giant faces melding into each other seemed to hold the hidden meaning of the movie. In *Autumn Sonata*, the closeups (again of women: here it's Eva and Charlotte, and, in one scene, Eva and Helena and Charlotte) are used like a spotlight calling attention to people on the stage—to emphasize the importance of what is being said or revealed. It's just a giant attention-getting device, a way of billboarding the big emotions: we're told that what Eva is going to say now is so revelatory that nothing—no other movement or detail—must be allowed to distract us. And so when what Eva says (she does most of the talking) doesn't seem worth listening to, the effect is shattering. We lose confidence in Ingmar Bergman.

Eva's pipe-smoking, fiftyish pastor husband (Halvar Björk) opens the film with a dry, stagy speech, addressed directly to us; he talks about wanting to turn and tell his wife how completely she is loved but being unable to—he has never been able to find the right words. He's so sober-minded he's like a Scandinavian version of Herbert Marshall in *The Little Foxes*. In the background, we see the wounded frump, Eva, sitting at her desk, writing the letter of invitation to her bereaved mother, and it's hard to suppress a groan. Of all Ingmar Bergman's heroines, Eva is the least appealing. Liv Ullmann's performance can hardly be faulted. Or can it be? Bergman's *The Passion of Anna* and *Face to Face* didn't hold together except for the intensity Ullmann brought to them; we were obsessed by her while we were in the theatre—afterward, the pictures fell apart. But she's playing a dependent woman this time. Her work seems utterly extraordinary; here, even more than in those two films and in *Scenes from a Marriage*, she goes so far into the character she's playing that it hardly seems acting at all—it's more like a self-transformation. She seems to be mesmerized—to go into a hypnotic state and become a different person. This may be very great screen acting, of a type we've never had before, but her performance doesn't have the beauty and clarity that her work had earlier, in Bergman's *Shame*, or in Jan Troell's *The Emigrants*, and we don't receive the understanding of the character that we usually get from proficient actors. There's a growing helplessness about her work for Bergman—a lack of shape, of completeness. When she plays a psychotic or a slug, we watch fixated, horrified—as we would watch the real thing. She is that person. What she does is like a highly refined form of the amateurism of someone who plays a drunk by getting drunk. Why do we need a painting of a cityscape when we can look out the window? Obviously, for the interpretive shaping that we get from an artist. And that's what we don't get from Liv Ullmann as Eva. She enters into Ingmar Bergman's disturbed emotions and puts them on the screen, just as he desires; neither of them does the shaping job of an artist in *Autumn Sonata*—their collaboration has become a form of *folie à deux*. As Eva, Ullmann spares herself nothing: she gets so far inside this dullard that there isn't a shred of beauty in her face or body; she moves in anxious little steps, and there's wormy sanctity in her smiles. Eva is weak, dim, remote—yet clinging. Liv Ullmann is a virtuoso at this soft-throated suffering. (But it may bring out the wolf in you.)

Does anybody really believe a word of this movie? It's like the grievances of someone who has just gone into therapy—Mother did this to me, she did that to me, and that and that and that. Eva is vengeful and overexplicit and humorless; she takes no responsibility for anything. Without any recognition of the one-sidedness, Ingmar Bergman lays it on so thick—makes it all so gruelling—that we have to reject it. "I saw that you loved me," Charlotte admits, "but I was afraid of your demands." That is supposed to convict Charlotte, but who wouldn't be afraid of Eva's demands? Eva is such a mewling total victim she's a worthy successor to Shelley Winters in *A Place in the Sun*. She and Helena up there on the landing are so grasping that the film should have been called *Tentacles*.

Much-married—once to a concert pianist, whose Chopin is dubbed in for Charlotte's—and many times a father, Ingmar Bergman must feel accused of having deserted his children. (And he wrote the mother's role for Ingrid Bergman, who shares his name and whose own children have grown up on different continents.) But he's also a man of sixty who still rages publicly—on television—about how his parents mistreated him. Throughout the film, he accepts guilt as the accused and yet identifies with the accuser; he's beating himself with a stick while yelling, "Hit harder, he has to be punished for what he did to me!" The parent-child conflict of raw nerves and frayed memories might be very different if it were actually dramatized by Eva. The daughter who feels wronged would probably reveal the absurdity of her excessive demands for love (as Kafka did in his crazy—undelivered—letter to his father). Then we could see the give-and-take of nuttiness, and how the daughter turns herself into a soft, squalid victim in order to be a living accusation of her Sherman tank of a mother. In the film, we're not convinced by what Eva says: we don't even feel that we're getting *her* truth, and we keep waiting for the turnaround—for the mother's answering taunts and the kind of mutual savagery that Strindberg gives us. (Can one imagine Kafka's father receiving that maniacal letter intended to prove that it's his fault that his son is a failure, and bowing his head in grief? More likely, he'd howl with rage or shout insults, or even cackle at the comedy of a grown man who's still nurturing the injuries of his childhood.) *Long Day's Journey Into Night* is about a houseful of emotional wrecks, too, but it's a balanced, dramatically structured view of family infighting, and it's painfully funny. There's no testing, no resilience in *Autumn Sonata*—none of the comedy of squabbling for love, or the comedy of love's blindness. Charlotte listens to her daughter's chronicle of victimization, accepts the guilt, and can only ask for forgiveness.

Ingmar Bergman's psychological movies have always mixed the clinical and the gothic, and he uses one to reinforce the other. So that there will be no way for Charlotte to be let off the hook, there's the deformed Helena upstairs, that twisting, helpless torso, like something out of *Freaks*. Helena does not figure in the childhood flashbacks; there's no indication that she and Eva might have kept each other company while their mother was away. Helena seems almost a gaudy afterthought—an Expressionist representation of Eva's yearning, warped soul. Helena is there to make us wallow in the mother's guilt and in the evil in her unconscious. (It's a mercy that Helena's crib wasn't put in the basement.) Charlotte is meant to be evil, all right. Eva's face is right next to Charlotte's—the two big heads filling the frame for another of the film's many moments of truth—when Eva asks, "Is the daughter's misfortune the mother's triumph? Is my grief your secret pleasure?" Lines like this, and the realization that you're watching a gothic thesis movie, make you start bickering with Ingmar Bergman. You notice that he plays Freudian games, but only when it suits his convenience. There is no suggestion that when Charlotte went off on tour and Eva was left at home with her father the little girl might have been able to satisfy her dearest fantasies of replacing her mother—or that some of her hatred of her mother could be jealousy. And why is it that Charlotte is indicted for Helena's crippled condition but no one accuses Eva, whose only child has died by drowning, of any complicity in that death? And how can Eva be so certain that Charlotte's absences from home were the cause of Helena's condition, which looks like multiple sclerosis? (This leap beyond medical knowledge seems alarmingly cruel to people in the audience who have similarly afflicted children.) If we could become spastic from rejection, we'd all be spastic—there wouldn't be a smoothly functioning person around.

Just when Americans seem to be getting over that fifties craziness of children's blaming everything on their parents, we're getting it back from Ingmar Bergman. *Autumn Sonata* appears to be made by a parent so eager to do penance that he grossly simplifies the case, and a son who can't get beyond his own accusatory anger. This is raw guilt and anger, not fully transformed by thought, or by art. There's artistry in the filmmaking craft—in the image of the hand that slips into Charlotte's hand while she sleeps, and then clutches at her throat; in the graceful integration of the flashbacks. But the flashbacks themselves are a key to the movie's falseness. They're romanticized: the little girl Eva (Linn Ullmann) isn't aggressive or foolish or whiny; she's sweet-tempered and well-behaved.

The mother is represented as an emotionally niggardly monster. Yet even with the soliloquies in which she briefs us on her selfishness Charlotte does not seem a worse mother than many whose children grow up to have an easy enough relationship with them. The question that *Autumn Sonata* never raises is that of Eva's grossly inflated expectations—of her inhuman refusal to accept her mother for what she is and to make the best of it. As Eva recites her litany of childhood wrongs—her anger when her mother went away and her unsatisfied longing for attention when her mother was at home—she seems a born drip, or at least a self-made one. She complains that when Charlotte stayed home she was full of pent-up energy and tried to make Eva conform to her own ideal vision. This is like Brooke Hayward's complaints in *Haywire*; the mothers are convicted for not caring, or for caring the wrong way. (Children want parents to conform to an ideal vision, too.) With the full authority of the picture behind her, Eva tells her mother that people like her should be locked away, and Charlotte acknowledges the justice of this lunacy. The mother's crimes are selfishness and hypocrisy—and they're treated here as hanging offenses. Charlotte never points out that the love Eva says she feels for her is a form of leeching—that it's a pain. We look at Eva, who has invited Charlotte there to torture her, and think, Imagine having a daughter like this muffled, damp creature whose gray husband talks of the gray film over their married life.

After the rough night with Eva, Charlotte cancels her visit and makes her escape. In a hasty epilogue, we're told that Eva has been purged of her rage—that somehow because of this visit, and hours that Eva has spent in the parish cemetery communing with her dead child, she can write her mother a letter of forgiveness. This device is like the mawkish reconciliations at the end of bad silent movies: nothing has prepared us for Eva's change of heart. Isn't it more probable that, having driven her mother away, Eva would write to her out of fear of losing her? When Bergman is on top of his material, questions like this aren't likely to occur to viewers.

[November 6, 1978]

Enfant Terrible

Macabre farce with a high polish—Grand Guignol with the Lubitsch touch. That's clearly what Peter Stone had in mind when he wrote the screenplay for *Who Is Killing the Great Chefs of Europe?* Stone doesn't write in a high style, exactly: he imitates the derivatives of Oscar Wilde—from the snooty insolence of Noël Coward down to the self-congratulatory archness of Alexander Woollcott. But he's an inventive gagman, and if some of his epigrammatic repartee seems to be just a professional wit's nervous reflex, most of it (including the food-sex double-entendres) is at least clever, and a fair amount of it is very funny. The script, adapted from the 1976 novel by Nan and Ivan Lyons, has the kind of irresistible-gimmick plot that several of the most memorable English comedies of the fifties had, and the film could have been played in the debonair slapstick manner that Audrey Hepburn and Cary Grant brought to Stone's script for Stanley Donen's *Charade.* It has been gummed up: the timing is off. The director, Ted Kotcheff, can't seem to get a rhythm going, and everything is pushed and bumpy. Kotcheff simply doesn't have the reserve for elegant ghoulishness. The visual movement is smoother than in his other films, though, and John Alcott's airy pastel cinematography gives the images a soft, innocently decadent pastry-shop sensuousness. And, bad as the film is, it's spirited, it's fun. The plot provides enough impetus to hold it together even when we're just marking time with the romantic leads, Jacqueline Bisset and George Segal, and waiting for the next scene with Robert Morley.

He plays Max, the editor of a London-based gourmet magazine called *Epicurus,* which has featured the "world's most fabulous meal," prepared by four of the greatest masters in Europe. Max's doctor tells him that he's eating himself to death and must lose half his weight, and someone starts picking off those chefs, murdering them in the style of their specialties— the dishes that Max celebrated. The entire film is a series of food references and food jokes; there were lots of them in *Charade,* too— Audrey Hepburn kept eating. But the joke there was how skinny she was, and the joke here is the opposite. Morley's legs, his arms, and even his head are appendages of his stomach: he enters a scene, as he enters his British Airways commercials, by pointing his gut and then following it—the legs are a distance behind, holding it up. (Stone wrote the role knowing that Morley—who not quite coincidentally was once the restaurant critic for *Punch*—was the only one who could play it.) Max is childishly unreasonable, and his greedy pleasure in eating is as openly expressed as an infant's. His palate may be refined, he may be wickedly articulate about the culinary arts, but all he really wants is to ingest. As the editor of *Epicurus*, he has converted his greed into a profession. If the role had been played by a once-handsome actor who had grown corpulent with the years, it wouldn't have worked; we would regret what had happened to him, and wonder why he didn't get back in shape. But we've never known Morley any other way (his chins drooped onto his chest in his film début, as Louis XVI in *Marie Antoinette*, in 1938), and with him as Max we can see that, whatever fatness does to Max's health, it fulfills his personality and gives him pomp and authority. Max is an imperious child, ruling the world of haute cuisine. What separates him from the people around him is that he eats without guilt. He's a more primitive carnal organism than they are. They consider superb food one of the pleasures of life—and, perhaps, an aphrodisiac. For him, it is all of life. Guilt-ridden, diet-conscious American audiences may be in a unique position to laugh at the food fixation of this movie. *Great Chefs* comes at a time when the generation that protested Vietnam has become health-food-minded and their younger siblings are becoming vegetarians. Guilt about ingestion has become a national political issue, and here is the superbly tailored Max walking with his belly in front of him and patting it like a pet. "I'm a masterpiece," he says—and it sounds better coming from him than from Arnold Schwarzenegger.

At seventy, Morley is clearly overjoyed at having this chance to play an enfant terrible. It's a completely controlled debauch: he knows the precise effect of his pendulous scowl, his sagging lower lip and trembling jellyfish chins; he knows that his eyes are so close together that when he knits his bushy brows the wiry hairs commingle and he's a cartoon. He's so convivial an actor and so sure in the way he uses his face and body that we can laugh without embarrassment: we never feel that he's mocking himself. He's got great acting equipment, and he also has the best nasty lines in *Great Chefs*.

George Segal has the brash ones. He plays Robby, an American fast-food entrepreneur whose infidelity has lost him his wife, Natasha (Bisset), Max's favorite dessert chef. Robby pursues her from London to Venice to Paris, with a murder taking place in each (while Kotcheff makes the mistake of trying to amuse us with the comic confusion of Robby and Natasha dashing in and out of luxurious restaurants). There's a deliberate sexual innuendo in the idea of the American as a fast-food man, but the scriptwriter may be less conscious of the irony in his having given the

English and the Europeans far more elegant turns of phrase. Robby (the robot?), in his big cowboy hat, is so crudely off-key that he's like an American played by a European in a foreign film. There isn't a clue to what Natasha sees in him. The life has been steadily draining out of George Segal's performances, and by now when he mugs cheerfulness we don't believe it; his face is a mask of misery, and his smile is more like a wince—he seems to be passing us something agonized. Segal has technique to fall back on when he butts in on Natasha's date at a Venetian restaurant; and in a sequence in which he's trying to prevent a murder that's scheduled to take place during a live television show and he rushes around the studios, barging into the wrong shows, the gag itself carries him along. But he looks as if he hadn't slept for four years, and, in the burnt-out distressed state he appears to be in, he just can't be accepted as a romantic funnyman hero. Leering sexlessness isn't funny. You wonder why people in the movie don't ask, "What's wrong? Are you in pain?"

Jacqueline Bisset is somewhat livelier than usual, and anyway, her soulless beauty (has anyone ever had such ravishingly blank sea-blue-green eyes?) isn't a problem in a comedy in which she isn't expected to be anything but superficial. For no evident reason, she's been swathed in ostentatious clothes that don't do justice to her special tactile decorativeness. (A dinner dress with a gigantic floral print is such an atrocity that you expect a gag to be played off it.) Her scenes with Segal show Kotcheff at his worst—they're like parts of his *Fun with Dick and Jane*—but she is delectably relaxed in her comic-erotic eating scene with Jean-Pierre Cassel, as Louis Kohner, a famous Swiss chef. (His specialty is baked pigeon in crust.) Louis's frenzied fear of something going wrong when he's cooking a meal in the kitchen at Buckingham Palace—his distraction from anything in the world but this one anxiety—is a heightened form of something that everyone who cooks has probably experienced. And his changed personality afterward—his bubbleheaded jauntiness as he dances off from bed with Natasha, bare-assed in his chef's apron—provides the only sexual grace note in the film.

Every time you give up on *Great Chefs*, it recoups with an imaginative flourish, like the black cat's glowing eyes that alert us to the presence of a killer, or the headwaiter who seats the guests at a murdered chef's funeral. The Henry Mancini score has some deft weightlessly ominous passages. And there are a lot of experienced performers to keep things going: Madge Ryan as Max's secretary, who's like a disciplinarian mother to him; Stefano Satta Flores as a bottom-pinching Italian chef whose specialty is a lobster dish (Flores has a profile so much like Segal's that when they're in the same frame it's as if they were impersonating each other); Philippe Noiret as a chef whose specialty is pressed duck; Jean Rochefort (though he's not well used) as a chef who is quite mad even by the standards of a profession where paranoia is the norm; and John LeMesurier, Daniel Emilfork, Kenneth Fortescue, and many others. Even after you think Morley is finished, he comes back with a royal hiccup. The memory of it can sustain you through the stupid romantic wrap-up. All babies are sybaritic, but when this one pouts about being deprived of the pleasure of food he has more than three hundred pounds of piteousness behind it. Max isn't happy when he has lost weight: he's spiritually diminished.

□ □ □

*C*omes a Horseman, a Western set during the Second World War, opens on a vast plain, under sullen skies, at the burial service for a cattle baron's son who has been killed while he was fighting for his country. We wait to discover the dead man's connection to the story: Is Ella (Jane Fonda), who is the only person at the funeral who doesn't offer sympathies to the bereaved father (Jason Robards), perhaps the soldier's sweetheart or widow? But no one offers Ella condolences, so that can't be right. We never learn anything more about the dead man; he isn't mentioned during the rest of the movie. Why, then, does the picture open with this big mournful number? As far as we can tell, it's to get us down, right from the start. Over the mantel in the main room of the cattle baron's manse there's a gold-framed oil painting of a landscape, and when, at the end of a scene, the camera moves in on that painting and there's a dissolve to events taking place in the actual landscape, we wonder, Is this something that happened in the past—something that explains why the picture is in such a prominent place in the baron's house? It turns out that the events are going on now, and that the actual landscape isn't even part of the baron's landholdings. The only reason for the painting to be over his mantel is that somebody thought the transition would be "cinematic." *Comes a Horseman*—the title is from Gordon Lightfoot's "Don Quixote" ("Comes a horseman wild and free")—is so self-conscious about its themes that nothing in the storytelling occurs naturally.

The director, Alan J. Pakula, wants the movie to have the primitive appeal of old Westerns, and basically the story is a variant of the evil land-grabber who is determined to take the land of the honest, hardworking rancher: now the honest rancher is a woman. But the melodrama here is smothered under the lowering Colorado skies, and how can you get involved in the conflict between the good guys and the bad guys if you can't even see them? A couple of men ride up on horses and talk together, with their faces just brown shadows under their cowboy hats. After a while, you figure out that one of them is James Caan, but, the way he is photographed, United Artists could have economized by hiring him for a couple of weeks of closeups and using a stand-in the rest of the time. Has Pakula become perversely artistic or is it that he let his cinematographer, Gordon

Willis, get carried away? Every time there's a cut to Robards, the baron, at home, he comes out of deep shadows; the house doesn't appear to have any windows. (It doesn't have an exterior, either—every time we return to the house, we're tossed right inside, into the gloom.) Willis has lighted the movie for an audience of bats. This is an outdoor picture, yet it's much darker than the two *Godfather* films. The sky is always overcast, with a poisonous grainy mist coming down. Is there a refinery over the hill? There's more smog in this picture than there is in L.A. And the interiors, even of Ella's house and barn, are like Don Corleone's study, except that here you don't see black as distinguished from the other dark tones—it's all muddy dark. There's an explanation: When Willis developed his style of lighting from above, leaving dark patches, he was working in the finest Technicolor. The colors were dyed onto the film stock in a process known as I.B. (imbibition); you could get a black that was distinct from even the darkest brown, and these colors wouldn't fade. This was what made it possible for Pakula and Willis to achieve the shadowed terror effects of *Klute*—a *film noir* in color. But *Godfather II* was the last American movie to be made using Technicolor's I.B. process before the company shut down its special dye-transfer operation. *Comes a Horseman* is made in a less expensive process that fades and doesn't allow for the same subtle contrast of black and darkness, yet Willis hasn't adapted his technique. (The picture looks the way the two *Godfather* films did when NBC ran them, after transferring them to tape.)

You can't see this movie, and you don't have much to listen to, either, except Michael Small's mood music. The screenwriter, Dennis Lynton Clark, must be under the impression that, in this part of the West, when you were born the gods gave you a certain number of words and when they were used up you died. That would explain why Ella's old ranch hand, Dodger (Richard Farnsworth), utters each syllable so painfully. (There are at least forty minutes that should be cut, but how do you cut between the words of a sentence?) Farnsworth's likable performance is a major feat, considering that he's playing a role in which he's affectionately addressed as "Old Man." (Dodger calls Caan, whose name is Frank, Buck.) Farnsworth is also subjected to symbolism: Dodger's horse rears up and throws him because of the sound of the blasting for oil on the baron's land. Once again, we're being told that the times they are a-changin'. Dodger is brought back home, but the sentimental music on the track must tell him he's dying, for he struggles to his feet and climbs up on his horse (as if to go off and pose for *End of the Trail*), and dies outdoors under the stars. It's typical of this film's inability to achieve even a simple, calculatedly noble effect that when we see him stretched out on the ground in a freeze frame there's a lap dissolve coming through the freeze and a little Ford pickup is running off his thigh. Farnsworth is in luck, though, compared to Robards, who has nothing to work with. He's photographed so often from low angles while he's staring silently that he looms up like one of the figures on Easter Island, and his infrequent lines seem to be rejected by the microphone—we can't make out what he's saying. This is a film of few words, and the sound recording mangles about a quarter of them.

Jane Fonda looks great in her tan weather-beaten makeup and tight jeans, but her acting is disappointingly constricted. This woman rancher is more taciturn even than the Westerners of Gary Cooper and Clint Eastwood, but where their silence was entertainingly heroic, hers is a matter of repression and man-hating. When Ella's neighbor, Frank, is shot, she puts him on a cot in her barn, on dirty pillow ticking. He lies there in his bloodstained underwear, and all she does for him is leave some canned food nearby. When he gets better, she informs him that he owes her for the food and that she expects him to pay the debt by working on her ranch (Hostile Acres?). Eventually, Dodger reveals that her (now dead) father raised her as the son he never had. That wheezing line—it used to account for why a heroine wore pants or didn't ride sidesaddle—doesn't explain much. Why would being raised as a boy prevent her from keeping a wounded man clean? The movie turns into a cow-country version of *Summertime*: eventually, the patient, long-suffering Frank defrosts the tight, spinsterish Westerner. Caan holds his own with strong women (as he demonstrated in *Funny Lady*); he does it with dignity and without strain, using his smaller screen presence as a foil to their strength. He's much more effective in these character roles than when he tries to enlarge himself to dominating-star status. Obviously, he enjoys the effects he can get out of a quiet drawl; he gives his lines here wryly humorous readings—it's a well-calibrated performance. Caan's modest manner would be more appealing if it weren't for the suggestion of arrogance—or perhaps explosiveness—right under the surface. He's not all of a piece as a performer: he's never quite himself—you feel he's concealing himself rather than revealing a character. And what you feel about him relates more to this subtext than to his proficiency.

Fonda and Caan ride and rope with convincing assurance, but the roundups are surprisingly brutal. The way that the panicking running animals are roped and come crashing down on their heads may be authentic, but it works against the film's liberal and ecological theses. We're supposed to see that Ella's dedication to ranching preserves the land, while the nearby areas are being dynamited in the quest for oil. Yet it's hard for us to work up much sentiment for this pair of honest ranchers who are tossing cows into back flips before sending them off to be slaughtered. The big sequence is a cattle stampede on a stormy night. It's dramatically beautiful, in its dark-blue way, but the visual conceit of this picture really gets to you. The dark, overblown pictorial style works against the exhilaration possible in the Western genre. (This night-on-the-range movie is going to be a real puzzler on television.)

Comes a Horseman doesn't invite us in; in fact, it doesn't brief us on the rudiments of who is who and what's going on until it's half over—and by then we don't care. When there's a killing, there's no investigation. When Ella and Frank are selling off their herd, and the buyer offers them five cents (a pound), we think they're being insulted until we discover that what they're really hoping for is six cents; couldn't the script have planted a simple line about the market price at that time, so we'd understand what's going on? Jane Fonda stays in her monotonously hard-bitten "realistic" character, yet there's viper music on the track to alert us that the baron is lurking around, and when the gentle, soft-spoken Frank goes into a bar and is harassed by two big brutes, he pummels them in the manner of John Wayne brushing off flies. In the finale, Frank and Ella are trapped inside a burning building; he has been beaten and she's bound and gagged. They free themselves and then pause to look out the window at the baron, who set the fire, and his two ruthless-killer cohorts, and this triumvirate isn't hightailing it out of the area, as one would expect, but, inexplicably, riding toward the fire, like three of the Four Horsemen of the Apocalypse. Frank and Ella jump off the roof, run for weapons, and dispatch all three of them. This sequence is a succession of howlers, but the picture doesn't have enough snap for us to laugh.

Maybe one of these days somebody will be able to make a good Western again, but it's not going to be done by a director whose head—like Pakula's—is full of theories. It will be by somebody who isn't trying to rehabilitate the genre.

[November 13, 1978]

Rocky's Knucklehead Progeny

Rocky, a piece of innocent shamelessness, was written by its star, Sylvester Stallone, and directed by John G. Avildsen. Now they're both back, with more urban folklore drawn from the movies: Stallone with *Paradise Alley*, which he wrote, directed, and stars in (he also sings the theme song, "Too Close to Paradise"), and Avildsen with *Slow Dancing in the Big City*, on which he was director, co-producer, camera operator, and editor. These two movies, both set in New York, are so simplistic and unsophisticated that when you enter the theatres you enter the Dark Ages.

488

The art of narrative has progressed a little since the Celtic bards, but no word of that has reached Stallone or Avildsen.

Stallone plays a loudmouth in *Paradise Alley*, and we're never allowed to forget it. His Cosmo is the middle one of three Italian brothers who share a basement apartment—a Dickensian dump—in Hell's Kitchen, and he shouts his entire overwrought performance at us, projecting to the deafest person in the audience even when he's talking to his brothers and they are near enough to touch. Stallone doesn't seem to know about restraint, or what can be accomplished by understatement. He writes, directs, and acts in a form of Esperanto—a basic, reductive approach to human possibilities. Everybody in the movie has one thing to express, and the only development is that midway Cosmo and his older brother, Lenny (Armand Assante), swap their things. (It's like a Jekyll-and-Hyde trade-off.)

The characters hold expressions, so that we'll have time to recognize what they're thinking. There's a studied dumbness about the people—a knot of muscle between the ears. *Paradise Alley* could do for the Italians what generations of Polish jokes have done for the Poles. The dialogues are acting-class exercises about deprived, "limited" people with a spark of illiterate poetry in them. *Golden Boy* and half a dozen other Odets plays have filtered into this movie, along with *Dead End*, *Winterset*, *Of Mice and Men*, boxing pictures such as *Body and Soul*, and the Depression according to Warner Brothers. It's an actor's baroque version of the lower depths, compounded of dime-a-dance girls, cripples, beggars, floozies, a good-hearted whore, a gentle giant who talks to a pet canary named Bella, and a Damon Runyonesque assortment of crooks and thugs. Not a single one of them seems capable of walking the two or three city blocks that would get him out of Hell's Kitchen; instead, they all dream about escape, or hatch near-impossible plans. The time is 1946, the year of Stallone's birth, which he has romanticized back to a yellow-gaslight look. The moody, embittered Lenny, whose leg was injured in the Second World War, drags himself around hopelessly; the only work he can find is in a mortuary that's like something from the Paris sewers of *Les Misérables*. Didn't anybody point out to Stallone that the veterans of the Second World War were better treated than the veterans of any previous war in our history—that they received educational benefits and federally guaranteed housing loans, and that they were regarded as heroes?

What is all this early-thirties left-wing poetry of defeat doing in *Paradise Alley*? (Even the title is a neo-Odetsian irony.) It's the heritage of the Group Theatre, and it's there because it's the only poetry that American actors are trained in. The joke is that Stallone sets up the situation with the defeatism of the politicized Depression plays and movies, and so we get the simple dreamers—Cosmo's hulking younger brother, Vic (Lee Canalito), and Vic's Chinese girlfriend, the outcast

Susan (Aimee Eccles)—making plans for the houseboat in Jersey they're going to have someday, with the disillusioned Cosmo sounding the warning note: "Guys like us, we don't live on houseboats." But as a moviemaker Stallone has this post-*Rocky* conviction: "There's a definite formula in reaching audiences—provide them with heroes and heroines who pull themselves up by the bootstraps and out of the depths of despair. You can just hear the audience saying, 'My God, that's the kind of person I want to be.'" And so all the gloom and the dramaturgic signals that Vic's hopes will be blighted turn out to be red herrings. Vic, who is the Rocky of this film, becomes a wrestler, and though we're warned repeatedly that his few brains are being smashed—and we have the figure of a battered, aging black wrestler, Big Glory (Frank McRae), to presage Vic's fate—he seems, if anything, to get a little smarter. Early on, Cosmo angers a gangster leader (Kevin Conway), and we're alerted to expect reprisals, but nothing happens. The heroes must triumph. Stallone wants everybody to go out happy and tout the picture.

At first, the cinematography, by Laszlo Kovacs, is imposing, because it's so controlled and richly picturesque—the shots are like a collection of choice stills. But the galumphing heaviness of the imagery begins to be oppressive. Kovacs seems to have lost interest in looseness and fluidity and clear, bright color; his recent pictures (*Harry and Walter Go to New York*, *Nickelodeon*, *New York, New York*, *F.I.S.T.*) have been so visually alienating that when you come out of the theatre you want to shake them off. Here, even the footage shot on the New York streets seems tightly enclosed. (Eightieth Street between Broadway and Amsterdam and an alley near the Brooklyn Navy Yard double for the old Hell's Kitchen area.) You can't find any way to locate yourself in reference to this movie. There are times when it suggests an early Expressionist film about Berlin in the twenties; shot by shot, it looks like an Edward Kienholz—a Dead End set, with plaster effigies in clotted color. The faces are rubberoid. The people look stuffed and glazed, like the brown-green elves and gnomes sticking out from the walls in German taverns. And once Vic, managed by Lenny and trained by Cosmo, gets into his wrestling career, huge, greasy-looking faces are twisted and gouged out of shape right smack in front of us. People are meat in this movie. As Vic becomes more successful, we expect larger arenas, crowds, some distance. But there is no variation: the matches are all shot in the same ring, with brutally ugly Silly Putty wrestlers' faces being rammed at us over and over. A montage of Vic's bouts seems designed to punch our eyes out. As a director, Stallone shows no more feeling for visual modulation than as Cosmo he does for vocal modulation. In all his capacities here, he's trying to get a hammerlock on our emotions. You feel he'd reach out from the screen and grab you by the throat if he could. It's nightmarish having these bulging, sweating titans clawing at each other with their hooklike arms and groaning and writhing in front of us; in the

490

final wrestling match, the two mountainous forms clash ponderously, in slow motion, in water that has flooded the ring. This movie was made by a Wagnerian gorilla.

You don't get a sense of the whole film; from the way it feels, it could have been shot over seven years. When Cosmo and Vic first go to visit Big Glory, in the rat-infested basement he bunks in (this picture is very big on basements), he talks about all the money that his manager is saving for him, and we get the feeling that he's being screwed and doesn't know it. Later, it turns out that he knew all the time that he had nothing. This isn't the actor's fault: Frank McRae is a skillful performer. It's the fault of the writer-director, who arranges each scene for the point he wants to make at that moment, and doesn't keep the whole work in mind. (There are never several dramatic components working together in a scene.) A large chunk of the picture is given over to an arm-wrestling contest that Cosmo puts Vic through in order to win a dancing monkey that Cosmo wants, and the monkey—who looks ancient, has a nasty, chattering grimace, and suggests real hostility—gives the one authoritative (and affecting) performance in the movie. But then he disappears without a word of explanation from anyone. And though Terry Funk, a former world wrestling champion, who plays Franky the Thumper, the man Vic beats in this contest, makes us understand the pain of losing, Stallone doesn't develop this theme. He has one idea only: winning.

A friend of mine who was watching the comedian Robin Williams in his one-man show on Home Box Office said, "It's the media outpourings of the past fifty years put into a duck press." Williams expects his audience to be quick enough to get his thirty-second allusions; what he parodies is what Stallone is still doing straight. Stallone lays every little thing out for you (and then forgets it himself). As a writer, he's a primitive mining the mass media, without any apparent awareness of how stale his ideas are. Doesn't he know that there are a lot of us who have seen the same plays and movies he has? Aren't we even expected to remember *Rocky*? Stallone tries to work our emotions again in exactly the same ways, and there's no surprise to the shamelessness this time. (Rocky pounded sides of beef; Vic wears a vest of salamis. Rocky talked to his turtles; Vic talks to his canary—that's already a step down.) As a director, Stallone tries to recapture the melodramatic dynamism of those old movies in which tarnished ladies flung up their heads defiantly as they leaned back against a jukebox, and crooks had comic eccentricities: he comes out with a catalogue of Hollywood's excesses. It's tumescent filmmaking. Inadvertently, he has made many of his performers ridiculous, by having them play in antique styles. Anne Archer is dumbfounding as Annie, the head-flinger, with her red hair tucked behind one ear, like Lana Turner; she also sculpts, like Lola Albright in *Champion*. And Joyce Ingalls, the tall blond model who used to do those "Fly Me" commercials, is bewildering as Bunchie, a Hell's

Kitchen whore in a crummy walkup; Bunchie is so clearly equipped for a better address that we keep waiting for the explanation. Is she a moron? (No, merely a saint.) The enormous Lee Canalito, a twenty-four-year-old, six-foot-five, two-hundred-and-fifty-five-pound prizefighter from Houston, makes his movie début as Vic. He's mild-mannered and personable, with a young-Brando grin and a handsome, classic profile. But the movie pauses every time he has to speak a line. He isn't a bad actor—just a slow, inexperienced one. As Lenny, Armand Assante has a different problem: Lenny is an Anthony Zerbe role—the guy who gets his hands on a little money and is immediately diabolically corrupt. Assante turns into Mr. Slime and has such an educated actor's diction and polish that we can't imagine how Lenny grew up as the brother of two palookas. (The three have completely different accents.) Cosmo, who wanted Vic to become a wrestler, later wants him to stop, and Lenny, who was against it, eggs Vic on. Nothing is made of this reversal; it's simply there. And Lenny casts off his girlfriend, who doesn't like the change in him, with the thirties gem "I'm climbin' now, and you don't like heights."

It's not as if Stallone didn't have some talent. When he's very soft—when he's hesitant and uncertain of himself—as in most of *Rocky* and in the courtship sequences in *F.I.S.T.*, the contrast between his uncouth presence and the gentle emotions he exposes makes everything he says touching, comic. And in both those movies he had actresses—Talia Shire in one and Melinda Dillon in the other—who knew how to bring out his more delicate shadings. Melinda Dillon had a beautiful mixture of lyricism and strength in *F.I.S.T.*, and in her and Stallone's early scenes (which he reportedly wrote), when he kidded his own tough manner and played off it, they got something really distinctive going. (It was the only live part of the movie; we never got to see their funny formality with each other break down—never got to see what developed once they were married.) But after three starring roles Stallone's limitations as an actor have become very apparent. For one thing, his voice is toneless in the low registers, and his staccato way of talking makes the words come out like a series of belches. He couldn't begin to suggest the spellbinding oratory that made the hero of *F.I.S.T.* a great union leader, because he couldn't speak three sentences without getting a logjam in his sinuses, and snorting.

The role he's given himself in *Paradise Alley* is probably a fantasy version of himself: the scam artist without a mean bone in his body, a man full of love and humor, with the soul of a poet tucked inside that roughneck's body. Cosmo wears one gold earring and long hair, as a tipoff that he's the François Villon of the New York slums. Stallone specializes in the wit and poetry of illiteracy: if a character can barely say hello—if he says dese and dem and dose—and then comes out with a joke or a lyrical flight, it's supposed to be taken as an authentic expression of the human spirit. This linguistic triumph (which is an exact analogue of what's going on in the rest of the movie) is Stallone's chief resource. He works a comic-strip version of Odets: to express how hurt he feels, Cosmo says, "I hope I catch ammonia." Once the plot gets going, Cosmo, whose worries are all about Vic's getting hurt, never actually does anything: he doesn't even try to persuade Vic to stop wrestling. He's just on the sidelines of the action, but in frequent closeup, shouting ineffectively, and moping, like Cary Grant in Odets' *None but the Lonely Heart*. Having failed to give himself anything to do, Stallone is still trying to charm us. He's playing to us, not to the other characters. And it's typical of his whole misconception that he overscales the charm.

He gives a blowhard performance, and he's a blowhard director, too. It's Stallone's belief that he has discovered the secret of success, and the secret is that puny old-industry formula of having people with everything against them prove themselves winners. It's "I shall overcome." He's grotesquely eager to move the audience; he pounds you so hard that you come out feeling you've been slammed on the head with a two-by-four.

□ □ □

*I*n Avildsen's *Slow Dancing in the Big City*, the message about becoming a winner is the same, but the bird talked to is a parakeet and the Rocky is a young ballerina, Sarah (Anne Ditchburn). The parakeet's name is Orville Wright, and, in case you don't get it, Sarah explains, "One day I'll get to the tropics and set him free. He shouldn't be in a cage." What happens in the film is roughly this. In four days, Sarah is going to perform her first starring role at Lincoln Center, in a ballet conceived for her, and with a whole company that has been built around her. Restless and anxious, she gets up at five-thirty in the morning to work out; she thrashes around passionately (though suffering from cramped thigh muscles) in a mixture of rock and ballet styles, to Carole King's "I Feel the Earth Move Under My Feet," which is playing full blast. She's like the Patti Smith of ballet, pouring sweat and suffering ecstatically for her art. Then David (Nicolas Coster), the rich businessman she lives with, wakes up and interrupts her. Later that day, she finds an apartment for herself in a brownstone; she rents 3-A, and her neighbor in 3-B is Lou Friedlander (Paul Sorvino), a Jimmy Breslin–like columnist who works for the *News*. Sarah speaks in the damnedest prissy little-girl voice and is so clenched and glum and haughty that her name should be Anastasia; Lou, a heavyweight macho sentimentalist, looks at her, his eyes bug out, and, sure enough, he starts calling her "Princess"—but in tribute. He arranges to do a story on her starring début and starts following her around, giving her inspirational encouragement— most notably, by comparing her to a mayfly, which has to give its all and soar because it has got only a few hours before it dies. He doesn't know how apt his metaphor is—doesn't know about her tragedy: her legs have been giving her such torture during rehearsals that her dance partner, Roger (Hector Jaime Mercado), insisted on her seeing a doctor, and she has just been told that she must have surgery immediately, and that she will never be able to dance again; it's the doctor's opinion that if she goes ahead with the opening at Lincoln Center she may never walk again. On Halloween, Sarah and Lou have dinner together in a warm, friendly Italian-family restaurant (it's like a Mamma Leone's commercial), where the owner's child looks at Sarah with starstruck eyes and decides that she wants to be a dancer when she grows up. (Nobody tells her that it's already almost too late.) This film has its Odetsiana, too: Sitting there at the table, Lou says, "I'll tell ya. If we can beat the odds in New York, we can do anything—walk on the stars, kiss the moon, turn the garbage into roses." Sarah leans forward into his face and says, "You're a poet," and he leans forward and ripostes, "You're be-yootyful." Lou's devotion spurs Sarah on to have the moment of stardom she has worked for all her life; she keeps rehearsing, spinning around at night on the brownstone's tarpaper roof, with only Orville Wright for company, until Lou finds her there and they dance slowly together. It's Marty meets Pavlova. (The ads explain, "Slow dancing is falling in love.") The generous Lou has also been giving inspiration to a Puerto Rican child drummer (G. Adam Gifford), whom he wrote a column about; the boy—a baby junkie—plays with two wooden spoons. On the big night, Lou goes to meet the kid, to take him to Sarah's première, but the kid isn't at the meeting place—he's in the hospital. Lou rushes over and finds that the child has OD'd. The nurse offers him the kid's belongings, and he takes the spoons. As he's leaving, the nurse, who has read his column, asks, "Could he really play the drums with those things?" And Lou, his back to the camera, pulls in his breath as he says, "He never had any drums." Meanwhile, backstage at Lincoln Center, Sarah is waiting anxiously for Lou's arrival; she doesn't know whether she can dance if he doesn't get there. He's running, running from the hospital to get to her, but she has to start before he arrives. She remembers the mayfly, though, and that saves her: she goes out and wows the audience. Lou is running, muttering, "Don't be over, don't be over, please God, don't be over," and he gets there in time to see how great she is. The audience is applauding wildly. It's time for her to take a bow, but she has collapsed backstage. It's all right: big, burly Lou picks her up and carries her onstage, and, safe in his arms, she acknowledges the cheering crowd, which gives her a standing ovation.

In the old boxing movies, the hero was going to fight just once more and risk everything (as Vic does); *Slow Dancing in the Big City* is a boxing ballet movie. Lou even explains to Sarah that she isn't a champion because she's a dancer—she's a champion inside. This picture is small, and it moves along. But Avildsen, in his own way, is much more shameless than Stallone. The screenwriter, Barra Grant, is the daughter of Bess Myerson and is primarily an actress; her script (which attracted interest at United Artists because of the company's success with *Rocky*) is a feminine fantasy, yet it's inspired by the tough-guy-with-a-soft-heart school of journalism. And, like the bad newspaper writing that inspires her, Barra Grant feeds a special brand of New York chauvinism—belief in the creative vitality of crumminess, aggression, noise. *Slow Dancing* aims for our hearts with brass knuckles, in the Breslin manner. But it never once lands on target. Avildsen, who now claims Frank Capra as his favorite director, said in a recent interview, "My pictures are about people who have dreams, because I'm prone to fairy tales." This condition seems to have afflicted him since he won the Academy Award for Best Director of 1976 for *Rocky*. (Before that, he was best known as the director of *Cry Uncle* and *Joe*.) But that doesn't mean that Avildsen is being cynical here; on the contrary, the film suggests that he's capable of treating this material absolutely earnestly. He has simply swung the gross credulity of his approach in *Joe* over to romantic, uplifting stories. If the emotional tugs in *Slow Dancing* seem funny, it's not because Avildsen is too slick—it's because he isn't slick enough.

The casting is suicidal. Sorvino is still carrying over the sweet-eyed simpleton's manner he affected in *Bloodbrothers*. He can't play a rambunctious personality-kid columnist who identifies himself with the big city: there's no street-smart energy flow from Sorvino. He's a loud, sad-sack oaf, with an idiot smile—a patsy. He's the bumbler a girl feels sorry for and then wants to be rid of. When Sorvino means to look infatuated, he's so smirkingly camera-conscious that he just looks foolish. And, as an actress, Anne Ditchburn, a leading dancer and a choreographer with the National Ballet of Canada, is the greatest discovery to hit movies since Ingrid Boulting, of *The Last Tycoon*. It's hard to believe that Sarah's leg condition would be incapacitating, since she does most of her dancing with her waving arms. (The choreography is in the international-schlock style of Béjart.) About the only performer who isn't all tensed up trying to act is Hector Jaime Mercado, who talks like a normal person.

When almost all the actors in a movie seem to be impaled by the camera, it's not just the casting that's at fault—it's the director. Avildsen has given more care than usual to the look of the film, and to its rhythm and pacing, but his mind doesn't seem to function on the level of what the characters are doing and saying. Does he blank out and not hear what's going on? When Sarah's rich lover comes to see her and says, "I'm flying to Munich tonight," she asks, "On a plane?" In the course of editing the film, Avildsen must have listened to this exchange dozens of times—didn't it occur to him to cut it? Avildsen doesn't have a sense of embarrassment about gaucheness and naïveté. His shamelessness is awesome: *Slow Dancing* fails as romance but succeeds as camp. Avildsen quite clearly wants to be taken for a poet and thinks that mayfly talk is poetry. He has a rare gift: it takes an Avildsen not to know.

[November 20, 1978]

Movie Yellow Journalism

Midnight Express* puts the squeeze on us right from the start. First, there are titles explaining that the movie is "based on a true story" that began in 1970 in Istanbul. Before we see anything more, we hear ominous percussion music: the thump thump of Billy Hayes' heart. We're inside this college boy's chest, pulsating with his panic as he straps two kilos (about four pounds) of hashish around his torso and goes out to the airport to catch the flight that will take him home to New York. By the time he gets to customs, he's sweating in terror and his chest is about to burst, and then, at the very moment of boarding the plane, he is apprehended.

For the next two hours, this innocent American is subjected to the most photogenic brutalization that the director, Alan Parker, and the screenwriter, Oliver Stone, can dream up. The "true story" of Billy Hayes—that is, the relatively simple account given in the book by Hayes and William Hoffer, which was probably already somewhat heightened—is used merely as a taking-off place for the moviemakers' sadomasochistic and homoerotic imaginations. Parker and Stone pile on the horrors, and, together with the composer, Giorgio Moroder, and his synthesizer, jack them up to a frenzy. The film is like a porno fantasy about the sacrifice of a virgin. When he's arrested, Billy (Brad Davis)—the beautiful male ingenue, with his well-fed, muscular American body—is stripped, in a smoky room, for the delectation of the cruel Turks. He's cast as Lawrence of Arabia, for the roughest of rough trade. Surrounded by these garlicky, oily men with hairy nostrils who talk in their incomprehensible language, like members of another species, he's isolated with his fear, and the pounding in his chest is joined by electronic buzzing and heavy bell sounds. He's thrown in jail and, on his first night, he's hung up by the ankles and clubbed—and there's the strong suggestion that he's also sodomized—by the head guard, Hamidou (Paul Smith), a huge, sadistic bullock of a man with great clumps of hair growing from the rims of his ears, like outcroppings of lust. When Billy meets another American inmate, Jimmy (Randy Quaid), a hothead whose thoughts pop like firecrackers, he says, "I'm Billy Hayes—at least, I used to be."

We watch him deteriorate as the film rushes from torment to torment, treating his ordeals hypnotically in soft colors—muted squalor—with a disco beat in the background. The prison itself is more like a brothel than a prison; the film was shot mostly in a nineteenth-century British barracks in Malta, which was turned into a setting worthy of this de Sade entertainment. (It even has a flooded catacomb.) When you see Max (John Hurt), a drugged-out, emaciated English prisoner, caress a kitty, you wait for something terrible to happen to it; it does, and you get to see that, plus Max's stricken face. When you observe that there are child prisoners, you brace yourself, and, sure enough, they're cold-bloodedly tortured. Yet this picture, which presents itself as an unsparingly realistic, hard-hitting view of the brutalities of prison, has an interlude to tease us. Suddenly, a steaming sauna appears in a patch of sunlight in the middle of this foul dungeon, and an amiable Swede is giving Billy a lyrical scrubdown. The Swede kisses Billy solemnly and the music rises for a triumphal wedding celebration, but the marriage isn't consummated: with a Madonna smile, Billy gently—one might say with polite regrets—declines the offer. That's the only overt sexual advance in the movie; you'd think sex among prisoners meant whimsical, tender friendships—among Westerners, that is. (The dirty Turkish prisoners are sodomites, who also keep knifing each other.) This Billy-the-pure scene is part of the director's preparation for his big number. Billy is so lacerated by deprivation and torture that his mind snaps and he goes wild and attacks a Turkish informer, chasing him back and forth, beating him, and then grabbing him for what at first appears to be a horrifying, harsh kiss. Billy bites the Turk's tongue off and, in sensuous slow motion, triumphantly spits it out. By that time, the electronic hype has been so effective—the audience has been coiled so tight—that there are people in the theatre cheering this insane revenge. Billy's gleeful bloody madness—his face drips gore—marks a new, stepped-up phase. He's dragged off to the section for the criminally insane, where the misery is so decorative it's almost Felliniesque. When his girlfriend, Susan (Irene Miracle), comes to see him in this Turkish snake pit, he is a gibbering, whimpering animal, masturbating with desire for her. It's five years, all told, before he escapes.

Midnight Express is single-minded in its brutal manipulation of the audience: this is a clear-cut case of the use of film technique split off from any artistic impulse. Parker seems almost vindictive in the way he prods the viewers—fast, efficiently, from one shock to the next. You get the feeling that what he and his team set out to do was to take this darling American boy Billy and subject him to the most garish tortures they could without running into an X rating. The moviemakers are British, but with virtually no film industry in Britain now, they're working with American financing and with Peter Guber (of *The Deep*) as executive producer; they're demonstrating that they can be vivid and ferocious enough for the international "action" market. There's a mean-spiritedness in this fake-visceral movie which has got mixed together with the cause of imprisoned young pothead smugglers like Billy Hayes.

It's symptomatic that the director's control is least effective with the actors. Brad Davis's Billy is a standard young actor's imitation–James Dean performance, without much assurance. There's a heroism of physical force in most of the powerfully built American men stars; Davis—unlike the actual resourceful Billy Hayes—exudes weakness. This may be what attracted the moviemakers to him; their Billy is conceived as a victim—they deify weakness. But Davis isn't a strong enough actor to hold the screen when he plays scenes with Quaid or Hurt. And the director damages both of them by zeroing in on them as soon as they're introduced; he seems to be saying, "Perform." Quaid grabs attention simply by his usual overacting, which he tries to pass off as Jimmy's nuttiness; it isn't until late in the movie that we respond to the way Jimmy's one-cylinder high-combustion mind works and feel the comedy in the doggedness of his attempts to escape. Hurt, however, as he demonstrated on television—as Quentin Crisp in *The Naked Civil Servant*, and as Caligula in *I, Claudius*—is a truly great interpreter of eccentrics; he has such inner force that he can play the most passive of roles, as he does here (he barely moves a muscle), and still transfix the audience. Hurt has some good lines as Max, and he delivers them in a dry deadpan, like a wasted English Buck Henry. Max is so spiritually exhausted that he doesn't have the emotional energy required for facial expressiveness: he's an almost burned-out light bulb with just a few dim flashes of the filament left. Yet he's the most moving character in the film.

The director works in xenophobic, melodramatic terms: the Americans, the Englishman, and the Swede are civilized and sensitive, and the Turks are bestial, sadistic, filthy. There are no ambiguities, there is no depth. Alan Parker doesn't waste his sympathy on Turkish prisoners, and his idea of irony is to have the hairy-eared Hamidou (the actor is actually an American with degrees from Brandeis and Harvard) whipping Jimmy with a leather belt while the Turks are at their prayers to Allah—Jimmy's yells of pain provide the melody to the praying chorus. The film is a crude rabble-rouser: like a wartime atrocity movie, it keep turning the screws to dehumanize Billy's jailers, and even his lawyer, who's a fat nose-picker. At the same time, it's sanctimonious about Billy's victimization: he writes florid, high-toned letters to Susan which we hear him read, and, worse, at a hearing he makes a messagey speech to the court, lecturing it on the meaning of crime and punishment and mercy, and denouncing the Turks as "a nation of pigs." The facts of Billy Hayes' case as presented in the book (which is by no means as anti-Turkish as the movie) make a solid, strong claim on our feelings: sentenced to four years and two months for possession of hashish, he had almost completed his term and was awaiting release when he was sentenced to an additional term of thirty years for smuggling—all for the same two kilos. But the film's cheap grandstanding—indicting a whole people on the presumption that the brutality of prison guards represents the national way of life—destroys those feelings. (It is not made clear that it was the American government which put the pressure on the Turks to keep dope from being smuggled into the United States: we gave them an assistance program in criminology and trained their customs officials. The Turks have been trying to oblige us.)

Why are people lining up at theatres to see this picture? I assume that there are others besides me who felt squeezed so much that they grew to hate the picture more and more. (I didn't hope for Billy and his friends to escape—just for the movie to be over.) But *Midnight Express* may be something close to an all-purpose fantasy. For those who are part of the drug culture (which is by now almost the national culture), it can serve as a confirmation and extension of their fears. This movie is being sold as a journalistic exposé—the ads say, "Walk into the incredible true experience of Billy Hayes. And bring all the courage you can." And even if people who have read the book know that most of the juiciest episodes in the movie were invented, they can still respond to it emotionally, because it's what they want to see—the worst that could happen, and the depths to which they could be driven. What could be more satisfying to students and young dopers than this intoxicating view of the horrible pitfalls of smuggling dope—an ultimate romantic horror show. (The Billy of the movie doesn't just go biting-tongue-off mad; he also becomes a murderer.) Confinement in foreign prisons constitutes the martyrdom of the drug culture, and it's about the only part of that culture which the movies had missed until now. This story could have happened in almost any country, but if Billy Hayes had planned to be arrested to get the maximum commercial benefit from it, where else could he have got the advantages of a Turkish jail? Who wants to defend the Turks? (They don't even constitute enough of a movie market for Columbia Pictures to be concerned about how they're represented.)

And this picture is not only a full-scale fantasy for the drug culture but the cautionary tale that parents have been waiting for. Here, at last, is the movie that puts Vietnam behind us. It has been a long time since middle-aged people could say to their kids, "You don't know how lucky you are to be Americans, safe and protected." Billy's shame when he writes to his parents for help rehabilitates the shame that disobedient children used to feel in movies of the twenties and thirties. In prison, Billy feels totally abandoned, forsaken, left to rot. The love that fills his being when his father (Mike Kellin) comes to try to help him is so traditionally boyish that it recalls Lon McCallister in his doughboy uniforms, and Van Johnson waving to Mom as he went off to war. Billy is never more James Dean–like than when he weeps and his father weeps. There hasn't been this kind of reconciliation-between-the-generations scene in many years. (It recalls *East of Eden*.) When Billy's father says that his bowels are running because of the Turkish food he ate, and that for the rest of his stay "I'm not takin' any more chances—I'm gonna eat at the Hilton every night: steak and French fries and lotsa ketchup," he's making the fundamental point of the movie (as older people will see it). Stay out of Turkish jails, don't do anything you shouldn't, eat right, this is what can happen to you if you're not a good boy. *Midnight Express*, with its sadistic sexual current, is a there's-no-place-like-home story, of a very peculiar variety. Hysterically sensual on the surface but with basic honor-thy-parents-and-listen-to-them glop at the center, it manipulates cross-generationally.

This fantasy even has a special appeal to liberals: the package is presented as social protest, as a modern *J'Accuse*. There's a final crawl title: "On May 18th, 1978 the motion picture you have just seen was shown to an audience of world press at the Cannes Film Festival . . . 43 days later the United States and Turkey entered into formal negotiations for the exchange of prisoners." And ringing upbeat music—exaltation music, like slow disco Muzak—accompanies this remarkable piece of journalistic self-congratulation. The producers sell this prison rhapsody as an example of bold muckraking that had immediate results—so, in a sense, the film claims that it has already proved its worth. Actually, the United States and Turkey have been talking about a prisoner-exchange agreement for several years, and last January the United States sent a draft proposal to Turkey, which is still under negotiation; no prisoners have yet been transferred. (What happened in forty-three days? Nothing.) The music that says "Rise and salute our accomplishment" is really telling us to salute bunko artists.

The actual Billy Hayes, who has been out flacking for the film on the talk shows, was quizzed about that accomplishment in a recent interview in the *Los Angeles Herald Examiner*. Here are his answers:

> HAYES: I believe, and certainly hope that to some degree, how great or how small is very hard to say, that [the film] *Midnight Express* has been instrumental in making this prisoner-exchange treaty happen.
> QUESTIONER: Did you have anything to do with that?
> HAYES: No, I don't think I had anything to do with it, directly. But I think anybody who's spoken about it, who's tried to spread an awareness of the fact that there are people who are being beaten,

tortured, and thrown into prison for years for what is not even a crime in some places, had something to do with it. If *Midnight Express* does nothing else, it's making people aware that this kind of thing happens.

It's wonderful—isn't it?—that there are young dopers coming along who have already mastered the politician's art of squirming off a hook and floating in a sea of generalizations.

[November 27, 1978]

Taming the Movies

Movie Movie is a dum-dum title for a pair of skillful parodies that were written by Larry Gelbart and Sheldon Keller under the provisional title *Double Feature*. The idea is to stir up our happy memories of early talkies—especially the Warners fight pictures and musicals, with their tenement-born heroes and heroines who conquered the big city. Movies of that period commonly ran about seventy minutes and were double-billed, but these two—*Dynamite Hands*, in black and white, and *Baxter's Beauties of 1933*, in color—run their full course in about fifty minutes each. The lines are stylized, cryptic: the dialogue of the thirties has been compacted into its essential clichés, which the characters innocently mismatch, so that the feelings they express go askew. And the way the characters say each other's names, as if to remind the person they're talking to of who he is, has a ritual quality—like the latest celebrity paying homage to Carson by answering his first question with "Actually, Johnny, you're the reason all this has happened to me." Stanley Donen, who directed, gives the material some of the magical Warners resilience: the characters define themselves instantly and completely—they're flash-card characters—and they're played by performers who pop out at us, through sheer acting energy. The two "features," which give chances to a lot of new people, have some of the zest that the brash, intrepid performers fresh from the stage brought to early talkies. Harry Hamlin, the night-school-law-student-turned-boxer of *Dynamite Hands*, and the Broadway dancer Ann Reinking, who plays Troubles Moran, the grinning blond gangster's moll who corrupts him, are both making their film débuts. Barry Bostwick, the Dick Powell–like singer-composer of *Baxter's Beauties of 1933*, is relatively new to the screen, and this is the first film of Rebecca York, who plays the Ruby Keeler innocent who inspires him. What keeps a viewer happy throughout is the performing gang; even the old-timers seem to be on their toes, responding to the fresh talent.

The star of both features is George C. Scott. In the first, he's a white-haired old geezer—Gloves Malloy, a manager-trainer who devotes himself to young Joey (Hamlin). And in the second—a parody of backstage musicals, based principally on *42nd Street* (1933)—he's slick-haired Spats Baxter, a Broadway impresario, like Warner Baxter in that film. The writers have tied the two features together by having them open at the same crossroads and by giving Scott parallel final scenes—both real rousers that he does full justice to—and also by giving him a helper (Red Buttons) who serves exactly the same function in both. So we get the feeling of the way the films of a particular studio used to resemble each other. And the crack young art director, Jack Fisk, tips us to the economies of thirties moviemaking by using the same huge, duplex Art Deco set for a gangster's lair in the first and a Broadway star's white, overscaled dressing room in the second. Perhaps the greatest compliment that can be paid to Stanley Donen's skill with the actors here is to point out that Red Buttons—Red Buttons!—never milks a line, and that Eli Wallach, who also appears in both, doesn't become obnoxious. Wallach usually has irrelevant energy pouring out of him, and doesn't do anything *plain* anymore—he's always busy being in character. Somehow, Donen has restored him to simplicity, and as Vince, the dead-faced, mean-eyed gangster, in the first, and Pop, the stage doorman, in the second, he's more likable than he has been in many years. There's also Art Carney as a doctor in both features; it's easy to forget him, because he's the kind of good actor who does things so instinctively that you don't see any actor's tension or control—he just plays his part, as if there were nothing to it.

All the casting in *Dynamite Hands* is successful. As Joey, the law student with the knockout punch, Harry Hamlin has a dark, puffy-lipped handsomeness that he uses for a straightforward, open-faced effect. He can reject the suggestion that he turn prizefighter with the reproof "These hands are for reading books" and get his laugh without ever tipping you off that he knows a laugh is coming. He manages to make Joey totally earnest, and yet do it lightly, buoyantly. As Joey's corrupter—the night-club performer who wriggles and kicks while she sings—Ann Reinking out-Ann-Margrets Ann-Margret. Her number is a little too naked for thirties torchiness, which was slow and slinky; with her big, frizzy blond wig, she looks like a Berlin dandelion—more Paramount Continental than Warners Manhattan. But Reinking is exuberantly likable on her own; she has her angles and curves so completely in control that she carries the concept of sexpot to abstract heights. And she's stylized in her acting scenes, too:

502

she's funny in a bemused, metallic way. Donen has the performers playing not in thirties style but, rather, in a seventies style that includes just a shade of comment on the thirties, and Kathleen Beller, as Joey's sister Angie, who needs an operation to keep from going blind (that's what sends Joey into the prize ring), and Michael Kidd and Jocelyn Brando, as Joey's and Angie's parents, have also mastered it. It's just a slight distension of innocence—the shallowness is built into it, so that the characters' emotions don't last beyond the scenes in which they're aroused. As the ingenue—Joey's faithful librarian girlfriend—Trish Van Devere is a little mature and mock-ingenuous, but she shows some of the tickling charm that she had in her first picture, *Where's Poppa?* When she's feeding her pigeons and speaking in her cultivated voice, she has comic style; she can discuss those pigeons ("Socrates is dead; Plato's very lonely") with a mournful precision that is all her own.

But she can't play the boozing old vamp of *Baxter's Beauties of 1933*. In a raven wig and a red satiny negligee, she's a self-conscious lunk, like Julia Child dressed up as a Polynesian hooker, and she's a dead weight right at the center of the story. When you watch someone playing a drunken Broadway star, you expect to see what made that person a star; with Trish Van Devere, you know that it's only casting—Miss Van Devere is also Mrs. Scott. And the Scotts overdo things when they play together: they were too arch with each other on the stage in *Sly Fox* (written by Gelbart), and they have detracted from each other's performances in several movies and in their TV *Beauty and the Beast*. Their scenes here turn into limp farce. In the days of touring companies, husband-and-wife teams could be forgiven a lot, but viewers of a movie like this one may feel that there's an impropriety—and an injustice to all concerned—in the star's wife's being cast in a role for which she's clearly unsuitable. And because spoofing thirties musicals has become a light industry, this casting failure takes a larger toll than it might in more original material. Trish Van Devere's role has a lineage: Bebe Daniels played it in *42nd Street*, which was loosely based on the 1929 Technicolor musical *On with the Show*, in which Betty Compson played it; Gladys George did a variation as the besotted, self-pitying star in *The Hard Way* (1943), and more recently Glenda Jackson did a wry takeoff in *The Boy Friend*. It's a part that demands hardness—pungency—and Van Devere, with her pure, school-mistressy diction, is amateurishly soft.

Scott himself isn't at his ease in this backstage story; he doesn't look right in Spats Baxter's dapper toupee—you're uncomfortably aware of his bulk, and he seems to be acting down. It's a ponderous performance. One of the sources of the public's joy in thirties movies was that everybody was always in a hurry, and Scott lacks that manic urgency. This whole second feature lacks it, except when Barry Bostwick is on the screen. He has that wonderful Dick Powell candied-yam cheerfulness, and there's six feet four of him falling all over himself. He's called Dick, and his true-blue, unruffled Ruby Keeler is Kitty. (Were Gelbart and Keller doing a little homage to the progenitive *On with the Show*, in which Sally O'Neil, who played the part, was called Kitty? Or is it just an accident, or perhaps an unconscious homage—a little kickback of memory?) Rebecca York's Kitty is played with a charming, youthful straightness. York isn't nearly as clunkish as Ruby Keeler; she's a trifle more toothy and saucer-eyed, but, if anything, she's less dopey. And as her aging-cutie roommate, Trixie the trouper, Barbara Harris, with bee-stung lips and a curly reddish-blond wig, looks more like a wacked-out barmaid than ever. She has such knowing eyes and such a perfect sad pout it's a pity she doesn't have more lines; she's the petite essence of all the hard-luck girls who pined for men who never gave them a tumble.

Movie Movie is almost terrific, but it's also a little flat. Some of the timing is off, and the second feature sags, but the problem goes deeper than these lapses. Watching the two linked features, we know that all our guesses about what's coming are going to be right—the authors aren't going to take the potentialities in the archetypal stories and throw a curve with them. They're going to stick to little jokes—and do exactly the same thing in both features. And Donen hasn't given this rather limited approach much visual help. Early Warners talkies were shot in a fairly basic style, but the camera in both these films jumps all over the place, and the indifferent lighting doesn't suggest the thirties, either. The humor is almost all verbal, and though the fouled-up clichés are entertaining, you begin to wish that there had been a few additional gag writers brought in, to break the pattern of facetiousness and jump off from it. *Movie Movie* doesn't have the Dadaist mania that sometimes exploded in the movie satires Carol Burnett did on her show: when she was playing the Bette Davis twins in "A Swiped Life" and turned herself into a foghorn, or when she played Scarlett O'Hara and came on in her finery to greet Rhett Butler with the drapery rod across her shoulders. And *Movie Movie* could use some of that golden hysteria of taking the situations in old movies to a logical extreme, as Charles Ludlam does with the Ridiculous Theatrical Company, putting viewers' secret wild fantasies about the stars and the plot situations right into the story. Clearly the moviemakers wanted to avoid sophistication, satire, and camp, and one can appreciate why. Their simple comedy-parody approach holds us for the length of *Dynamite Hands*. But *Baxter's Beauties of 1933* is so cautious that we don't feel the thirties excitement of shrill voices backstage telling the dancers to get out there faster, faster, and we don't have the elation of the final "hit," when the lovable unknowns stop the show. Having decided to be comedic but to avoid camp, the moviemakers and Michael Kidd, the choreographer, don't know what to do about Baxter's show, which turns out to be a few fragments of watered-down Busby Berkeley, and not nearly as surreal as what is being parodied.

The film opens with a pathetic prologue in which George Burns, still wearing the nimbus of *Oh, God!* (from a Gelbart screenplay), explains what we are about to see, as if double features belonged to the prehistory of man. He tells us that thirty, forty years ago "everything was black and white, except when they sang sometimes it came out in color"—which makes no sense, because that doesn't happen here and it belonged to the pre-thirties anyway. Why is it assumed by the very people who love movies that movie history is so trivial that it doesn't matter what they give God to say? And then there's the rollicky music (it recalls the score for Mel Brooks' *Silent Movie*) to assure us that the picture is going to be harmless. *Movie Movie* is friendly and funny and enjoyable, but it also gives you a sense of the timidity of moviemaking now, and of how talented people who have been working in television, such as Larry Gelbart and Sheldon Keller, internalize the censorial pressures and restrictions. When they get a chance to work in movies, their own conventionality runs very deep. *Movie Movie* takes fewer chances than Gelbart's "M∗A∗S∗H" series has taken. Movies were never really this tame: Burnett and Ludlam get closer to the true happy dirty madness.

□ □ □

*B*ernard Slade's two-character, one-set play, *Same Time, Next Year*, is about an accountant, George (Alan Alda), and a housewife, Doris (Ellen Burstyn)—both in their twenties and both more or less contentedly married—who meet by chance in an inn on the Northern California coast, have a one-night stand, and resolve to meet the following year. They meet for twenty-six years in all, and the play (or film—it makes no difference) invites us in to share their anniversaries every five years. The time span is from 1951 to 1977. The gimmick is the way that social changes and fashions in dress and ideas are reflected in these two, and the single joke is that adultery can be regulated and celebrated, just like marriage. Of course it can be, if you remove every ounce of passion and sexual tension from it, which is what Slade and the director, Robert Mulligan, do. This is cozy adultery, between two ciphers who are devoted to each other. I've sensed more physical attraction between two neighbors gossiping across the back fence than there is between George and Doris. And the neighborly gossip had lustier language than there is in Slade's blanched-out dialogue; he's a TV writer (the creator of "The Flying Nun"), and you hear it in every line, except that without a laugh track these sitcom lines sound slow and reverential. Mulligan's contribution seems to be to make the film soggy in every detail, and he has the best-qualified helpers. Marvin Hamlisch's chord progressions are like flowered wallpaper, and the cinematographer, Robert Surtees, lights the movie for an effect of monochromatic gentility that makes his gentility in *The Turning Point* seem savage. If someone you make the mistake of caring about insists on your going to this movie, take a small flashlight and a book.

How are the performances? Well, on the stage a time span of twenty-six years can give veteran actors a chance to show off their skills, including mimicking youth. But the camera ruthlessly exposes this kind of mimicry, and the exposure is almost all we can think about. The actors begin to seem older than they are. For Doris at twenty-four, Ellen Burstyn lightens her voice to a sprightly little-girlishness, and she glows for all she's worth—she achieves a state of radiant waxiness. She doesn't let up on that glow until the end, when she's playing a faded fifty in foggy focus (and acting more like seventy). She plays nicey-nice, and you've never seen so much wise womanly understanding. She doesn't really act in this movie— she apes movie emotions. Alda's performance isn't willfully self-contained and off-putting, like Burstyn's. It's more tragic. Alda, whose understanding of TV is probably as acute as Cary Grant's understanding of movies, has been able to sustain his easygoing appeal in every light-comedy TV appearance. He knows just how to pace himself and project on TV, but he must long for the opportunities that only movie stardom can provide. He's an actor of extraordinary resources: late last year, in a television show called *Kill Me If You Can*, he played Caryl Chessman, and, in the totally unsentimental two-hour performance, which was more abrasive, riskier than what any star except De Niro has attempted in movies of recent years, there wasn't a gesture or an intonation that was familiar from the Hawkeye character on "M*A*S*H" which he has played weekly from the start of the series. (It's now in its sixth season.) He may be our only great actor who has, up to now, proved himself only on television. Others (such as Jonathan Winters and Carol Burnett) have proved their greatness as comedians, but no one else I know of has demonstrated the full acting range that Alda has. Yet he hasn't found the director and the role that would enable him to show what he can do on the big screen. (Olivier had to wait for William Wyler to teach him how to adapt his stage technique; perhaps a comparable movie director could sense what Alda's problem is, and free him so that he could fill the screen.) His performance here is underscaled, and he makes the kind of mistake that an actor with too much integrity is likely to make: George is hung-up and fatuous—he's a schmuck—and Alda stays in character. He never releases his full charm or personality, in the way that a movie star needs to (especially in a two-actor movie), and neither does he have the nervous comic inflections of a specialist in schmucks, like Charles Grodin (who first played the role on Broadway, opposite Burstyn). Alda just seems uncomfortable and emasculated, and in the scenes of farcical panic, when the innkeeper knocks on the door, or when Doris suddenly goes into labor, he is stupefyingly bad.

He might at least have saved face if he had just stayed on the surface and used some tricks, but he's trying to give a searching performance, and the material is actually much worse than "The Flying Nun"—it's totally neutralized. This is the sort of movie in which, when Doris's marriage is falling apart, George patches it up by talking to her husband, on the pretense that he's a priest—the sort of bland, sickly-sweet movie in which, as soon as George tells Doris that he hasn't been able to cry for his son who was killed in Vietnam, you know he's going to break down in the next instant and start sobbing in her arms. It's not surprising that writers should tell lies for profit; what's surprising is that they can make a profit out of the same old lies. *Same Time, Next Year* features the teasing concept of adultery while preserving total asexual respectability; that's what kept it going on Broadway for three and a half years—it shows that people can lead double banal lives. At the end, George and Doris are both soft and beige; they could be posing for a beige valentine. Didn't Alda recognize that his material is like kapok? It's like wadding for your mind—and Alda is trying to find some truth in it.

[December 4, 1978]

Manic/Depressive

In Goin' South, a barnyard comedy set in the old West, which Jack Nicholson directed and stars in, his face is given over to full-time ogling: he bats his eyelids, wiggles his eyebrows, and give us his rooster-that-fully-intends-to-jump-the-hen smile. When movie actors also direct, they're rarely able to bring anything new to their own performances, but with Nicholson it's not just that we don't get anything new—we get the old in an unrestrained form. In most of his roles, Nicholson saves his grin for a few devastating flashes; each time we see it, it's a revelation of the demon he's got bottled up. Here there's nothing hidden and nothing hell-bent or sinister; he grins all the time—he's just a fatuous actor, a leering leprechaun. He looks shorter than usual, because he stands in a semi-squat, with his britches riding low. As a director, he's so generous with views of his backside you'd think he was taking pictures of a starlet; he likes it so much he's named for it—Henry Moon. Hauled back from across the Rio Grande by a posse, Moon is about to be strung up, but the Texas border town he's in has an unusual ordinance: a condemned outlaw can escape the noose if a woman of property agrees to marry him. A virginal young Miss Muffet type (Mary Steenburgen), who needs a man to work her gold mine, claims him, and the film is about their squabblings and misunderstandings until they find love—it's a mixture of *Blazing Saddles* and *The African Queen*.

Nicholson didn't appear in the 1971 *Drive, He Said*, the only other film he has directed; it was perhaps the most ambitious, chaotic, and daring of the counterculture films—it had a deranged, dissociated vitality. Though Nicholson couldn't pace it or bring it together, he did seem to have control of the actors, and you knew that nobody was just trying to charm you—they were all trying to get something new onto the screen. This time, Nicholson is out to charm us; there's nothing the matter with that, but, not having had any serious intentions, Nicholson seems to have had nothing to restrain his hammiest impulses: he's like a young kid pretending to be an old coot, chawing toothlessly—the new Gabby Hayes. He talks as if he needed to blow his nose—this must be his idea of a funny voice. Nicholson's prankish performance dominates the movie, and, with his prankishness also coming out in the casting and the directing, the movie hasn't any stabilizing force; there's nothing to balance what he's doing—no one with a straitjacket. Henry Moon bays at the moon; he runs around in a stocking cap; he plunges into mud and hops up looking as gleaming-eyed as Old Nick. He stiffens his neck and turns his head slightly so that we can see those cartoon eyes, squinched up dementedly. With spiny tufts of hair sticking out from his head and beard, he's a crested cuckoo bird—he's got everything but tail feathers. Yet the other characters don't seem to notice anything odd about him; even his wife, who's meant to be sensible and practical-minded, appears to accept his cackling, scratching, horny, mangy slob as a normal fellow. *Drive, He Said* featured Karen Black, perhaps the most oral of actresses, and now, as Henry Moon, Nicholson keeps working his mouth, with the tongue darting out and dangling lewdly; he's like a commercial for a porno film. (What a hard-core comedy team he and Black would make.) He's so busy being raunchy he neglects to make any romantic contact with the heroine. Mary Steenburgen, in her film début, seems vague and recessive, but this could be because the script (there are four writers listed) doesn't do anything to reveal her character, and this inexperienced actress doesn't know how to project and reach out to us. Her small, flat, nasal voice isn't much help. She has a delicate, distinguished face, with a resemblance to Anjelica Huston, but she also suggests a twitchy, tremulous Olive Oyl, and she seems to clutch her character to herself, like a recluse. Her not being quite there may make Nicholson feel he should have enough personality for two—so he gives us enough for two dozen.

Nicholson must have selected most of the rest of the cast for how grotesque they could be made to appear, then egged them on to overact, and instructed the cinematographer, Nestor Almendros, to get in as close as he possibly could. The faces often seem to be squashed against the lens. There's no aesthetic distance in *Goin' South*: Nicholson doesn't even leave enough space between himself and us for us to care about him. The camera angles are eccentric and overbearing in almost every shot that has dialogue in it. Near the beginning, when Moon is in the jailhouse and the members of his old gang come to see him, the sequence appears to have been photographed in the hold of a slave ship; the outlaws' heads press in on us, with their faces so distorted that even the sexy girl among them (Veronica Cartwright) has bulging eyeballs. Throughout the film, the sequences don't give us a feeling of a visual progression—they're like random views pieced together. The effect is very similar to that of Terrence Malick's *Days of Heaven*, which was also shot by Almendros. What we're getting isn't cinematography—it's just photography. In *Days of Heaven*, I got the impression that the director had constantly broken into the dialogue flow—that he had become dissatisfied with the scenes and didn't let them play out naturally—but I didn't get the impression that there had ever been a *visual* flow to disrupt. It may be that both these directors didn't know what they were after and left too much to the famous cinematographer, who made his reputation by working with directors who knew exactly what they were after. Or it could be that Malick wanted fastidious photographic-plate imagery—stills to be revered—and wasn't interested in the more instinctive aspects of moviemaking, such as tempo. But when Nicholson hires Almendros and turns him loose on a burlesque Western that has reworkings of Hal Roach slapstick routines, Almendros falls back on the austere dark-toned lighting that he's known for, and the jokes go into a classy deep freeze.

John Belushi made his movie début in *Goin' South* (though his second film, *Animal House*, was released first); he plays a Mexican-American deputy sheriff. Clive James, in his television column in the London *Observer*, recently distinguished between the Mexican characters in earlier American movies: "There were two kinds of Mexican, bad-teeth and straight-teeth. The bad-teeth Mexican, who usually had a name like Gonzalez Gonzalez Gonzalez, said: 'Hey gringo, you throw down the gon and we no hort you.' The straight-teeth Mexican wore tailored suits and said: 'Senorita, since you have come to our hacienda I feel lightness in my heart for the first time since my sister was trampled by her horse.' " Belushi does a takeoff of one of the most jagged-toothed of them all—Alfonso Bedoya, of *The Treasure of Sierra Madre*—but Nicholson has stolen his thunder; by comparison, poor Belushi is a model of mandarin refinement. The only performer who has a dynamic presence—who isn't just acting crazy—is Veronica Cartwright. She has the kind of talent that Nicholson has when he isn't thinking with his rump. Wasn't there anybody on the set (in Durango, Mexico) who could tell Nicholson to give it a rest? An actor-director who prances about the screen manically can easily fool himself into thinking that his film is jumping. Nicholson jumps, all right, but *Goin' South* is inert.

□ □ □

Watching Anthony Hopkins perform as the star of *Magic* is maybe about as close as one can get to watching the formation of a geological stratum. He is so toned down in his passive desperation that he's funereal: you look at him and you don't expect anything good to happen. And since he has no light or happy range and doesn't show a capacity for joy, there's nothing at stake when things go wrong for him. This Welshman is bewilderingly miscast as Corky, an American vaudevillian—he's the least corky of actors, and maybe the least like an American and the least like a vaudevillian, too. It's true that Corky is meant to be sweating and anxious—a performer who hates the audience. But the gloomily withdrawn Anthony Hopkins of this movie has no vulgarity in his soul—nothing that suggests any connection with the world of entertainment. At first, when Corky, who's a card-trick magician, is unable to make contact with his audience, we don't feel his suffering, because Hopkins is unable to make contact with us. A year later, Corky has a new act: he's still doing card tricks, but he has also become a ventriloquist, with a scatological dummy called Fats, who keeps putting him down with standard cheap sex jokes. This act looks just as hopeless as the old one, but we're told that it's a wow, and Corky's agent, Ben Greene (Burgess Meredith), books Corky and Fats on the talk shows—Mike Douglas, Johnny Carson, and the rest. (There's no explanation of how this "X-rated dummy" functions on TV.) Corky's new act is such a big hit that he's about to sign a contract for a network special that could lead to his having his own show—as soon as he takes the routine physical examination that the network requires. But Corky balks at this; having a great deal more faith in doctors than the rest of us, he seems to think that in the course of a routine physical a doctor will detect that he's schizophrenic—that he's being dominated by Fats. (The moviemakers don't leave anything to the imagination: the dummy, who looks like a lascivious caricature of Hopkins, has a larger head than he does; we can see at once who's in command.) In terror of the network's physical, Corky leaves New York and goes to a lonely spot in the Catskills, to find the cheerleader he had a crush on in high school, fifteen years earlier; she's right where she used to be, and he rents a cabin from her. Once he heads into the country, there aren't enough things going on in the story: there's nothing for Corky to do but deteriorate, and the film shuts down. William Goldman received a million plus for his novel and adaptation, yet the script is so thin and the cast is so small (with Ann-Margret as the girl and Ed Lauter as her husband) that *Magic* seems to be a made-for-TV movie—the kind with people going mad in isolated settings, where moviemaking is cheapest.

The only hope for a film with this subject is that it tease us—that it keep us in suspense about whether it's a psychological thriller, in which Fats is the hostile, violent side of Corky, or an occult horror story, in which Fats is a devil doll. But Goldman, having specialized in brotherly buddies and now having simplified that theme down to a split personality, merely prolongs and vulgarizes the Michael Redgrave schizophrenic-ventriloquist sequence in *Dead of Night,* and he seems to have scarcely bothered to polish his script. (Does the producer, Joseph E. Levine, just wait for something to come in with Goldman's name on it, and then rush into production?) When we first see Corky, we aren't given any indication of where in him this hate-filled demon might have sprung from, and after Corky has split he seems no different—he's still the same bundle of smothered angst. Hopkins leaves all the emotion to the dummy. Probably nobody dared point out to Goldman that card tricks are not terribly photogenic, but, once Hopkins had been cast, couldn't the moviemakers at least have asked Goldman to write a few lines changing the character from a Borscht Belt American to a transplanted Englishman? Hopkins expends all his effort on trying to sound American; the result is that Corky has a dulled-out, from-nowhere way of talking, while Fats sounds like a Limey tough. The director, Richard Attenborough, grinds along so seriously that there's no suspense, no ambiguity—just the unpleasantness of watching most of the tiny cast being eliminated. Each piece of bad news arrives on schedule. There's nothing much to look at, unless one enjoys watching the microphone hover at the top of the frame when Corky and his newly found cheerleader sit in her house in front of the fireplace; a few minutes later, he returns to his cabin and leans back against the door, and the mike drops down as if to clunk him on the skull—which isn't such a bad idea. *Magic* is an atrocious-looking movie; the cinematographer, Victor Kemper, makes every interior look like a cold latrine. When Corky and his agent meet for the lunch at which the agent tells him about the network special, it's a celebration lunch at The Four Seasons—surely one of the most spacious and elegant restaurants in the country. Lighted by Kemper, it looks like a Burger King.

[December 11, 1978]

The God-Bless-America Symphony

A "magnificent hermaphrodite born between the savage and the civilized": that's how Balzac described Hawkeye, the Deerslayer— the idealized frontier hero of James Fenimore Cooper's Leatherstocking Tales. The steelworker hero of Michael Cimino's *The Deer Hunter* is the newest version of this American "gentleman" of the wilderness, and the film—a three-hour epic that is scaled to the spaciousness of America itself—is the fullest screen treatment so far of the mystic bond of male comradeship. It is steeped in boys' adventure classics, with their emphasis on self-reliance and will power, and their exaltation of purity of thought— of a physical-spiritual love between men which is higher than the love between man and woman, because (presumably) it is never defiled by carnal desire. The American wilderness of our literature is (as D.H. Lawrence wickedly put it) the boys' Utopia. *The Deer Hunter* is a romantic adolescent boy's view of friendship, with the Vietnam War perceived in the Victorian terms of movies such as *Lives of a Bengal Lancer*—as a test of men's courage. Yet you can feel an awareness of sex just under the diffused sensuality of the surface. The whole movie, with its monumental romanticism and its striving for a symphonic shape, is sexually impacted. It takes the celibacy of football players before the big game and attaches it to Vietnam. The hero, Michael (Robert De Niro), and his friends—Nick (Christopher Walken) and Steven (John Savage)—are as chaste as Norman Rockwell Boy Scouts; they're the American cousins of hobbits.

Cimino, who is thirty-nine, has directed only one previous film— *Thunderbolt and Lightfoot*, with Clint Eastwood and Jeff Bridges, in 1974, which he also wrote. He's a New Yorker and a Yale M.F.A. in graphic design who went into the Army and was a medic attached to a Green Beret unit training in Texas. When his interest turned to movies, he worked in documentary film and in commercials before he was able to use writing as a way to break into directing. His first credit was on *Silent Running*, in 1971; then he (and also John Milius) worked on the script of *Magnum Force* for Clint Eastwood, who had already arranged to give Cimino his chance on *Thunderbolt and Lightfoot*. His new film is enraging, because, despite its

512

ambitiousness and scale, it has no more moral intelligence than the Eastwood action pictures. Yet it's an astonishing piece of work, an uneasy mixture of violent pulp and grandiosity, with an enraptured view of common life—poetry of the commonplace.

When we first see the three men, it's 1968 and they are in a steel mill, on the floor of the blast furnace; at the end of the shift, they go from the blazing heat to the showers. It's their last day on the job before they report for active duty, and the other workers say goodbye to them. Then they move through the casual sprawl of their hilly mill town, Clairton, Pennsylvania, to their nearby hangout—Welsh's bar—to guzzle a few beers and loosen up. Each step of their day is perceived in ritual terms. The big ritual is to come that night: Steven's wedding at the Russian Orthodox Church and then the celebration at the Clairton chapter of the American Legion, which is also the farewell party for all three. We spend about three-quarters of an hour in the church and the hall; the moving camera seems to be recording what's going on in this microcosmic environment—to be giving us an opportunity to observe people as they live their lives. The long takes and sweeping, panning movements are like visual equivalents of Bruckner and Mahler: majestic, yet muffled. Because of the length of this introductory section, and because it isn't dramatically focussed, we feel an anticipatory ominousness. Derivative as this opening section is (it's easy to see the influence of Coppola and Visconti, and probably Minnelli, too), it conveys a very distinctive love of rootedness and of the values of people whose town is their world. (It's the sort of world we used to see in French films of the thirties, with Raimu.) Cimino brings an architectural sense into his collaboration with the cinematographer, Vilmos Zsigmond, whose style here recalls his smooth long takes in *Deliverance* but has a crisp vitality, like his more recent work in *Close Encounters*. There may be a touch of *National Geographic* in the first views of the beautiful, gaudy interior of the Byzantine-primitive church, yet Cimino and Zsigmond take the curse off the usual limitations of Panavision and the heightless wide screen by panning down, down, slowly. They provide such an illusion of height that it's hard to believe the screen is the same shape that George Stevens once said was good only for high-school-commencement pictures. In the church, we see the faces of people we have already met; our eye is caught by John Welsh (George Dzundza), the cherub-cheeked bar owner, singing in the chorus. Here and in the Legion hall, there are uninterrupted panning movements in which we see people singing and dancing, flirting and fighting, and moving from one group to another. And it has a detailed clarity: we feel that we're storing up memories. There's something nostalgic about this ceremonial view of ordinary American community life even as it's going on. This town of Clairton is actually a composite of a number of locations, most of them in Ohio, but it becomes a clear geographical entity for us, and even the double mobile home that Michael and Nick share feels so accurate that it, too, seems rooted. Nothing was shot in a studio.

Cimino's virtuoso staging has a limitation: the brilliance of his panoramic ensembles sometimes gives us the idea that in seeing so many things so quickly we have come to know these people. They don't actually reveal much more than the convivial crowds in a beer commercial do, yet we're made to feel that what we see is all they are. (A great director would plant doubts in us.) And even with the dozen or so principal characters, the casting and the actors' physiognomies and intuitive byplay do most of the work of characterization; the dialogue is usually just behavioral chatter. When Cimino wants to make a point, it's usually an outsize point—a portent or an omen that reeks of old-movie infantilism. Someone draws Michael's attention to a nimbus around the sun, and he explains what the Indians used to say this formation meant. (Is Cimino invoking the mythology of Hawkeye and the great chief Chingachgook?) Steven and his bride, who is pregnant but not by him, are served wine in a double-cupped goblet, by the priest, who tells them that if they drink it down without spilling a drop they will have luck all their lives, and we see the small stains forming on the bride's white lace bodice. (Here it's *Smilin' Through* that's invoked.) Nick, the best man, makes Michael promise that, whatever happens to him, he will be brought back to this place, these trees. A grim-faced Green Beret just returned from Nam comes into the Legion bar during the party; the men ask him "What's it like over there?" and he replies with an obscenity. And so on. Cimino's talent is for breadth and movement and detail, and the superlative mix of the Dolby sound gives a sense of scale to the crowd noises and the voices and the music; we feel we're hearing a whole world. But Cimino doesn't know how to reveal character, develop it, or indicate what's going on in a human relationship. When Linda (Meryl Streep), one of the bridesmaids, catches the tossed bridal bouquet, and Nick asks her to marry him and she says yes, we don't know if she's in love with him or with Michael, with whom she exchanged glances earlier, or what Michael feels. Probably, Cimino doesn't know; he may think it doesn't matter. Michael keeps his distance from people, and he seems too pure to have anything particular in mind when he looks at Linda; he's saving his vital juices for chivalry.

After the party is over and the bride and groom have left for their weekend honeymoon, Michael and Nick and their pals—John Welsh and skinny, dark Stan, played by John Cazale, and huge, bearded Axel, played by Chuck Aspegren—climb into Michael's white '59 Cadillac with tail fins and drive to the mountains, for a last, ritual hunt before Vietnam. A couple of the men are still wearing their rumpled tuxedos, but Michael, who is the leader of the group yet also a man apart, emotionally hidden, and with a compulsive orderliness that makes the others uncomfortable, has stripped down and dressed for his date with the deer. Unlike such makers of epics as Coppola and Bertolucci, Cimino doesn't seem to want his themes to rise to our full consciousness (or perhaps even to his own), but he can't resist eroticizing the hunt—it's a sexual surrogate, a man's-man wedding. Michael climbs to the top of a virgin mountain and, with a snowcapped peak behind him and a male choir in the sky singing a Russian Orthodox liturgical chant and rain clouds swirling about him, stalks a buck and fells it with one clean shot. That's his consummation.

The five hunters drive back down to Welsh's bar, and there follows a scene that is possibly too clever: fat, baby-faced Welsh plays a Chopin nocturne, and the others listen attentively. It's a moment of communion before the parting of the ways. The music is lovely, and if one of the men—the amiable nonentity Axel, perhaps—had only fallen asleep this scene might have been as great as it wants to be. But with all of them demonstrating their innate sensitivity, showing us that beer sloshers' savage breasts are soothed by music and that their inarticulate feelings go far beyond what they talk about, it's too much like those scenes in which roomfuls of Hitler's lieutenants all swooned to Wagner. And it's just a shade too effective, too theatrical, when Cimino cuts from this solemn grace to the noise and hell of Vietnam.

It's in the contrast, though, between the Clairton sequences, with all those people joined together in slowly rhythmed takes, and the war in Vietnam, where everything is spasmodic, fast, in short takes, with cuts from one anguished face to another, that Cimino shows his filmmaking instinct and craft. But also his xenophobic yellow-peril imagination. It's part of the narrowness of the film's vision that there is no suggestion that there ever was a sense of community among the Vietnamese which was disrupted. We are introduced to Asians by seeing a soldier (North Vietnamese, or, perhaps, Vietcong—we can't be sure) open the door of a shelter, find women and children cowering inside, and then thoughtfully lob in a grenade. Michael, a Green Beret Ranger in an advance reconnaissance unit, spots the soldier machine-gunning a fleeing woman and her child, yells "No!," and hits him with a flame thrower. The impression a viewer gets is that if we did some bad things over there we did them ruthlessly but impersonally; the Vietcong were cruel and sadistic. The film seems to be saying that the Americans had no choice, but the V.C. enjoyed it. Michael meets up with Nick and Steven again, and the three are taken prisoner and are tortured strictly for their captors' pleasure. The prisoners are forced to play Russian roulette in teams while the Vietcong gamble on which one will blow his head off.

The Vietnam War—and, more particularly, Russian roulette—serves Cimino metaphorically as the Heart of Darkness; Michael, the disciplined Deer Hunter, doesn't succumb. He has the will and courage to save the three of them. These prison-camp torture sequences are among the finest-edited action scenes that I know of; they are so fast and powerful—

and so violent—that some people will no doubt be forced to walk out. They are the very center of the film—the test it was preparing for. Although Michael, the superman who forces his friends to develop the will to survive, belongs to the boys'-book world of grit and sacrifice, the sheer force of these pulp atrocity scenes takes over one's consciousness. I say "pulp" because the Vietcong are treated in the standard inscrutable-evil-Oriental style of the Japanese in Second World War movies and because Russian roulette takes over as the ruling metaphor for all the action scenes in the rest of the movie, even in the later episodes in Saigon and back home. Why is Russian roulette used this way? Possibly because it goes so completely against the American grain—it's like a metaphor for the General Westmoreland theory that Asians don't value human life the way we do. But also because it has a boyish vainglory about it: does one have the guts to pull the trigger? It's a boy's kicky idea of courage.

If *The Deer Hunter* had been a serious consideration of boys'-book values, it might have demonstrated that they did not apply in the mechanized destructiveness of modern warfare—that Michael was basically as vulnerable as everybody else. But the fact is that Cimino believes they do apply, and so Michael is put up against curs and sadists; he's in a Victorian test of manhood. And no doubt many people will go along with the film and accept Michael, the superior being, as a realistic hero, because of the general understanding that comradeship and depending on your buddies and helping them is finally all that you can believe in when you're in the midst of war. Cimino, who believes in those Hemingwayesque one-clean-shot values that Michael (whom he has obviously named for himself) represents, has framed the whole war in terms of that kind of courage. Everything that happens appears to be the result of the atrocities of the Vietcong. Yet the film's point of view isn't clear. The American helicopters are like Walpurgisnacht locusts coming down on your head, and no one who believed that the Americans behaved honorably in Vietnam would have staged the evacuation of Saigon as Cimino has done, with thousands of Vietnamese abandoned and despairing. And, although Michael proves himself by performing extraordinary feats of valor, he is not ennobled by them, as movie heroes used to be. *The Deer Hunter* is Beau Geste-goes-to-Vietnam, all right, but with a difference: when Michael returns to his home and goes up to the mountain peaks again, and the male choir chants, he has the deer in front of him but he doesn't kill it. Cimino has made a film that vindicates the boys'-book values (without them, Michael and his friends would not have survived the prison camp) and then rejects them.

This movie may offend conventional liberal thinking more by its commitment to parochial, "local" values than by any defense of the Vietnam War—for it makes none. Neither does it take any political position against the war. But the film's very substance—the Clairton community in contrast with the Asian chaos—is the traditional isolationist message: Asia should be left to the Asians, and we should stay where we belong, but if we have to go over there we'll show how tough we are. This parochialism may be the key to why some people will reject the film in toto—even find it despicable in toto. Although cosmopolitan values were actually the ones that got us into Vietnam (the government planners weren't small-town American Legionnaires; they were Harvard men), it has become the custom to pin the guilt on the military "hawks." Michael is not a liberal hero, like the Jon Voight character of *Coming Home*; we can feel (without being told) that he's grounded in the rigid values of people who are suspicious of science and world affairs and anything foreign. Cimino is as careful to leave controversy out of his idealized town as Louis B. Mayer used to be. Clairton is abstracted from even those issues that people in beer joints quarrel about; no one ever asks what the Americans are doing in Vietnam, there are no racial jokes, and there isn't as much as a passing reference to strikes or welfare, or anything else that might show dissension, anger, or narrowness. And, of course, there are no homosexuals in the town (or even in the war); if there were, the film's underpinnings would collapse, and its eerie romanticism would become funny. In this film, evil itself is totally unsexual; Russian roulette is the perfect solution—Nick, who has had his soul burned out by it, goes AWOL and disappears into the dives of Saigon, where civilians play that game. Without sharing the implicit God-and-country, flag-on-the-door political assumptions of *The Deer Hunter*, one can see, I think, that, even with its pulp components and the racism of its Saigon dens-of-vice scenes and its superman hero, it is not merely trying to move people by pandering to their prejudices—it is also caught in its own obsessions. And, because it plays them out on such a vast canvas, it has an inchoate, stirring quality. Audiences can project into *The Deer Hunter* in a way they couldn't with such male-comradeship films as *Butch Cassidy and the Sundance Kid*, because it gives us the feeling that it's got a grand design lurking somewhere in those sensual rhythms and inconsistent themes.

In traditional American literature—in Mark Twain, say—the boys with pluck run away from proprieties, restrictions, manners, chores. Women represent the civilization that must be escaped. But in *The Deer Hunter* women are not even that much: they exist only on the margins of the men's lives. Steven's mother (Shirley Stoler, in a poor, mostly one-note performance) is a virago, his bride is a sallow weakling, and the bridesmaids are overly made-up and have too many curls; they're plump—stuffed with giggles. The only woman we see in Clairton who could attract a man of substance for more than a quick fling is Meryl Streep's Linda, who works in the supermarket; Streep has the clear-eyed blond handsomeness of a Valkyrie—the slight extra length of her nose gives her face a distinction that takes her out of the pretty class into real beauty. She doesn't do anything standard; everything seems fresh. But her role is to be the supportive woman, who suffers and endures, and it's a testament to Meryl Streep's heroic resources as a mime that she makes herself felt—she has practically no lines. There were three writers on this project in addition to Cimino (Deric Washburn, Louis Garfinkle, and Quinn K. Redeker worked on the story with him, and Washburn did the screenplay), but Linda is a presence rather than a character. She's a possibility glimpsed, rather than a woman, or even a sex object—least of all, a sex object. Michael and Nick, the two central characters, both have some sort of commitment to her, without our knowing what either of them feels for her—it's a very limp triangle. She is the film's token of romance, and Cimino's unwillingness to go beyond Victorian tokenism muddies the film when Michael returns from Vietnam and his relations with Linda consist mostly of the exchange of unhappy, solicitous looks. Does he love her but feel that she's pledged to Nick, who he thinks is dead? (There's no clue to why he would think Nick was dead.) Michael shows no physical desire for Linda. They lie on a bed together, he fully clothed—should we know what they're thinking? We don't. And when, for one night, they're under the covers together, without their clothes, and he rolls over on top of her, the scene is deliberately vague, passionless. He never even kisses her—would that be too personal? He was hotter for the deer.

Finally (and improbably), Michael learns that Nick may still be alive, and goes back to Vietnam to find him and pull him out from the Heart of Darkness. The scenes in Vietnam, with all those people clamoring to survive, and with him going back in there to rescue a man who doesn't care to live, are so sweeping yet so slick that they're like Coppola without brains or sensibility. Exotic steaminess is pushed to the melodramatic limit, as Michael, looking for his friend, passes through the inferno of war and enters Saigon's sin city, operating in the midst of flames and human misery. The film's last hour, in which it loses its sure progression and its confident editing, would have been far less wobbly if Michael had not come home until after he had made this rescue attempt. As it is, he returns from Vietnam twice, and during the period when he's home for the first time the story weaves back and forth, with fumbling scenes of Michael trying to make up his mind whether he should go see Steven, who's in a hospital. This period is unformed; it lacks resonance and gives us the impression that we're missing something—that pieces of the plot have been cut out.

It's possible that Cimino grew as an artist during the years of making this film (the production costs doubled, to thirteen million) but was locked into certain fantasy conceptions, and was never able to clarify the characters without violating the whole deer-hunting mystique he'd started with. And even after he'd shot the sequences that re-created the obscenity of the evacuation of Saigon, he was still committed to the gimmickry of the roulette game of life and death. *The Deer Hunter* is a small-minded film with greatness in it—Cimino's technique has pushed him further than he has been able to think out. His major characters don't articulate their feelings; they're floating in a wordless, almost plotless atmosphere, and their relations aren't sharp enough for us to feel the full range of the film's themes. Too many of the motifs are merely symbolic—are dropped in rather than dramatized. At times, we feel that we're there to be awed rather than to understand. We come out knowing the secondary characters—John Cazale's weak Stan (who hits women and kills deer sloppily) and George Dzundza's music-loving Welsh and John Savage's simple-hearted, ingenuous Steven—far better than we know Michael or Nick.

This isn't because De Niro and Walken don't do their jobs. Walken seems completely authentic one minute and totally false the next, because he has so little that's definite to project that he's straining. Yet he has never been so forceful on the screen, and when he's feverish and wet in the Vietnamese jungle and his hair is plastered down on his head, his large eyes, sharp chin, and jutting cheekbones suggest Falconetti in *The Passion of Joan of Arc*; he has a feminine delicacy without effeminacy. He's right for his part, but his rightness for it is all that the part is. And this is true of De Niro. He's lean, wiry, strong. Physically, he's everything that one wants the hero to be. (The only thing that's unheroic about him is that he's still using the cretinous grin he developed for *Bang the Drum Slowly*.) He fails conspicuously in only one sequence—when he's required to grab Nick's bloody head and shake it. You don't shake someone who's bleeding, and De Niro can't rise above the stupidity of this conception; even his weeping doesn't move us. We have come to expect a lot from De Niro: miracles. And he delivers them—he brings a bronze statue almost to life. He takes the Pathfinder-Deerslayer role and gives it every flourish he can dream up. He does improvisations on nothing, and his sea-to-shining-sea muscularity is impressive. But Michael, the transcendent hero, is a hollow figure. There is never a moment when we feel, Oh my God, I know that man, I am that man.

[December 18, 1978]

Pods

I *nvasion of the Body Snatchers* is more sheer fun than any movie I've seen
since *Carrie* and *Jaws* and maybe parts of *The Spy Who Loved Me.* The
scriptwriter, W.D. (Rick) Richter, supplies some of the funniest lines ever
heard from the screen, and the director, Phil Kaufman, provides such
confident professionalism that you sit back in the assurance that every
spooky nuance you're catching is just what was intended. It's a wonderful
relief to see a movie made by people who know what they're doing.
They're also working with a deliciously paranoid theme: trying to hang on
to your human individuality while those around you are contentedly
turning into vegetables and insisting that you join them. The film takes off
from the 1956 *The Invasion of the Body Snatchers,* directed by Don
Siegel—a low-budget Allied Artists movie (about $350,000) that has an
honored place in film history, because of its realistic atmosphere (it's set in
a drab, isolated small town that seems to close in on the characters) and the
solid, frightening theme, which is essentially the idea that Ionesco
developed in *Rhinoceros.* (Americans seem to have better luck when they
treat surreal paranoid ideas in low-down science-fiction form.) Siegel's
version was subjected to executive bowdlerizing: most of the humor was
excised, and a prologue and an epilogue were tacked on to provide a
hopeful resolution. Even so, it's a tight little economy-package classic. The
new version is wilder and more fantastic, with perhaps the best use of
Dolby stereo yet—the sound effects have you scared and laughing even
before the titles come on. This Phil Kaufman version is so sumptuously
made that it looks very expensive, even though it was done on what is now
considered a small budget (under three and a half million, with a sizable
chunk of that going into the post-production work on the sound.) The
pre-title rumbling roar suggests how God might have started the Creation
if only He'd had Dolby. The first images, which are of diaphanous
gelatinous spores wafting upward, have a spectral comic beauty; it's like
being in a planetarium while something awesomely, creepily sexy is taking
place. This is a full-scale science-fiction horror fable, a realization of the

potentialities of the material. For undiluted pleasure and excitement, it is, I think, the American movie of the year—a new classic.

The story is set in San Francisco, which is the ideally right setting, because of the city's traditional hospitality to artists and eccentrics. Probably nowhere else have people considered so many systems of thought and been through so many interpersonal wars; San Franciscans often look shell-shocked. The various outcroppings of the human-potential movement have had an unexpected result: instead of becoming more individual, people in therapeutic groups get so self-absorbed in their various quests that they appear dulled out. And so when the gooey seeds from space come down in the rain over San Francisco and cling to leaves and establish root systems and blossom, and each flower pod develops into a fetus that grows large enough to replace an individual as he sleeps, while the old body crumbles into a small pile of garbage, it is not surprising to hear the reborn flower people proselytizing for their soulless condition as a higher form of life. "Don't be trapped by old concepts," one of them says. The story simply wouldn't be as funny in New York City, where people are not so relaxed, or so receptive to new visions. There are no a-priori rejections in San Francisco.

The hip-idyllic city, with its gingerbread houses and its jagged geometric profile of hills covered with little triangles and rectangles, is such a pretty plaything that it's the central character. The movie itself is like a toy; it's all filigree, in the way that *The Manchurian Candidate* is. As the malignant growth sprouts brilliant-red blossoms, we hear the film's first words: in the bland, bored tone of someone who's trying to fill up the time, a teacher who's out with her class says, "There's some more flowers, kids. Go pick them." That has got to be a famous first line. For the opening third of the picture, almost every scene has a verbal or visual gag built into it, and throughout there's a laciness to the images—to the way the interiors include exterior views of the whimsical, Victorian-dollhouse architecture, and the bright-colored sanitation trucks gobbling up waste matter.

Elizabeth (Brooke Adams), who works at the Department of Health, picks one of the carnal red flowers on her way home. When she gets there, Geoffrey (Art Hindle), her laid-back lover, is sprawled out watching basketball on TV; he kisses Elizabeth without taking off his earphones and gets excited only when he hears a terrific play—he pushes her aside so he can see it. Geoffrey, who's a dentist, is so quintessentially laid back you don't know what keeps him vertical, or in such good shape. He just seems to have been manufactured with muscles: that's the model. The flower is left near his side of the bed, and in the morning he no longer goes with the flow; he gets up with a stolid sense of mission, dresses up as if he were a Rotarian huckster, and takes a bundle out under his arm and tosses it into a waiting garbage truck. And as he goes about the city he makes eye contact with other people, who all know what's on each other's minds—it's as if they were governed by Muzak. (Watching the clear-faced, neatly dressed, upstanding Geoffrey, you suspect that Werner Erhard was the original spore.) Scared by the change in him, Elizabeth tells her boss, Matthew (Donald Sutherland), that Geoffrey isn't Geoffrey, that "something is missing." But then she goes to a cocktail party celebrating the publication of a new how-to-be-happy book by Dr. Kibner (Leonard Nimoy), the city's leading chic psychiatrist, who suavely explains that she thinks Geoffrey has changed—has become less human—because she's looking for a chance to get out of their relationship. (Kibner is as smug as the psychoanalyst in *Cat People* explaining to Simone Simon that she only fantasizes turning into a leopard.) And Elizabeth, who knows she's beginning to have romantic urges toward her boss, half accepts Kibner's explanation.

In most science-fiction movies, the stalwart characters would have nothing to lose to the pod people; they have already been vegetablized by the lack of imagination of the filmmakers. But Kaufman and Richter have managed to give substance to the fear of losing one's individuality, by creating believable, likable characters. Brooke Adams doesn't have the sullen-washerwoman look she had in *Days of Heaven*; her turned-down mouth has an odd attractiveness, and her Elizabeth is smart and resilient, with a streak of loony humor. (She spins her eyeballs, like the great Harry Ritz.) Even her flat voice is funny here: she uses vocal affectlessness as a deadpan, and rings trick low notes on it. (The women in this movie are every bit as strong and sharp—and foolish—as the men, without any big point being made of it.) As heroes go, Sutherland may not be a world-beater, but at least he's plausible and stays in character. And the other leads play genuine San Francisco weirdos. Jeff Goldblum, who knows enough to disregard his handsomeness, and to stick with a huffy, distracted timing that is purely his own, is Jack Bellicec, a furiously angry poet who is proud of taking six months to decide on a word, and Veronica Cartwright is his wife, Nancy, who works in their Turkish-bath establishment—Bellicec Baths—as desk clerk and masseuse. Veronica Cartwright has such an instinct for the camera that even when she isn't doing anything special, what she's feeling registers. She doesn't steal scenes—she gives them an extra comic intensity. When Nancy Bellicec greets someone by scrunching up her face, her whole goofy soul is in her expression. What the film catches with this devoted pair is their domestication of nuttiness—they wouldn't love each other so much if they weren't both a little cracked. San Francisco is a city full of people who are sure they could write better than the successful writers in their midst, and probably could, but they're too busy living and griping to try. Jack's contempt for the best-selling Dr. Kibner is the contempt of a writer who doesn't put anything on paper for the fraud who does. Phil Kaufman (who makes his home there) and Rick Richter (who was on the locations throughout the shooting) have got the conversational tone of the culture down pat. The Bellicecs must protect their eccentricity: it's the San Francisco brand of humanity. This film is almost like a surreal variant of Simone Weil's thesis that the people who resisted the Nazis weren't the good, upright citizens—they were the dreamers and outcasts and cranks. There's something at stake in this movie: the right of freaks to be freaks—which is much more appealing than the right of "normal" people to be normal.

There are some amazing special effects: the plant tendrils that sneak over sleeping people, and the fetal pods that bleed when they're crushed, and a dog joke that is perhaps a nod to *The Fly* and *The Mephisto Waltz* and the famous dog in *Yojimbo* but is also pure Dadaism. *Invasion of the Body Snatchers* gives the impression of a supernatural and fantastic visual style, though the cinematography, by Michael Chapman, is very straightforward. This may be because of the unusual delicacy of his work. The daylight scenes, with sharp primary colors that aren't posterish in the Godardian way, because of a softening use of secondary colors, emphasize the orderly movements of the pod people, which are so at odds with the iridescent bauble of a city. At night, of course, the city is theirs. Much of the photogenic power of the material (it's based on Jack Finney's early-fifties *Collier's* serial *The Body Snatchers*) comes from the fear of night and sleep: if a character closes his eyes, he may not be himself when he wakes up. When the first version was made, the filmmakers thought of calling it *Sleep No More.* Chapman has a special feel for night subjects, as he demonstrated in *Taxi Driver* and *The Last Waltz,* though his work on Kaufman's *The White Dawn* was also eerie and mysterious. He shows a gift here for bringing out the personality of the city locations; there's a finely drawn, cluttered grace in his San Francisco, and it intensifies the horror, in the same way that the characters' idiosyncratic styles of humor do. When the four principals run down Telegraph Hill, with a phalanx of pod people in pursuit, and dash to the Embarcadero, they cast long shadows, like figures in one of de Chirico's almost deserted piazzas. Parts of this film have a hellish beauty, like Cocteau's *Orpheus* and, more recently, *The Fury.*

There are small disappointments. Elizabeth tells Matthew of the conspiratorial meetings of the pod people before we actually see them meet. And Matthew has a sequence of racing from one telephone booth to another which is charged with meaningless tension and has no particular payoff. Perhaps the scenes in which pods are being dispatched to other cities are not as elegantly staged as they might be. And there may be a few times when the generally dazzling score, by Denny Zeitlin, the jazz pianist turned San Francisco psychiatrist, overpowers the action, but the music is a large contributor to the jokes and terrors. There is also a truly inspired electronic effect, devised by the sound expert Ben Burtt: the pod people make a shrieking, warning cry that suggests an inhuman variant of the rhythmic trilling-screaming sounds of the women in *The Battle of Algiers*. In that film, it was a cry for freedom; here it's a cry for conformity.

There's a great entertainment-movie tradition of combining high jinks and artistry, and this film belongs to it. Michael Chapman, the cinematographer, can be spotted in a corridor, leaning against a mop, and Robert Duvall, who played Jesse James in Kaufman's first major studio film, *The Great Northfield Minnesota Raid,* is visible as a priest on a playground swing. (As a benediction for the movie?) Don Siegel turns up, playing a cabdriver. And there's a reënactment of what is generally remembered as the end of the 1956 version (it's how the movie would have ended if the studio hadn't slapped on the "Get me the F.B.I." epilogue), with Kevin McCarthy, the star of that version, once more banging on car windshields. He yells, "They're here! Help! They're here!" But this time he isn't saved—he's finished off. There are also fog-enshrouded shots of the Transamerica pyramid. (Transamerica is the parent company of United Artists, which financed this picture.) *Invasion of the Body Snatchers* doesn't take itself too seriously, yet it plunges into emotional scenes with a fast, offhand mastery. At night, Matthew stands on the terrace of his apartment, where he and his three friends have holed up, and looks down at the four adult-size fetuses that are almost ready to replace them. He wants to smash those bodies, but he can't destroy the ones of his friends, because they're so close to human that it would be like killing people he loves. He can smash only his own reproduction. This set of variations on the 1956 film has its own macabre originality; it may be the best movie of its kind ever made.

[December 25, 1978]

The Package

Christopher Reeve, the young actor chosen to play the lead in *Superman,* is the best reason to see the movie. He has an open-faced, deadpan style that's just right for a windup hero. Reeve plays innocent but not dumb, and the combination of his Pop jawline and physique with his unassuming manner makes him immediately likable. In this role, Reeve comes close to being a living equivalent of comic-strip art—that slang form of simplified storytelling in which the visual and verbal meanings can be totally absorbed at a glance. But *Superman,* one of the two or three most expensive movies ever made, and with the biggest *event* promotion yet, is a cheesy-looking film, with a John Williams "epic" score that transcends self-parody—cosmic fanfares keep coming when there's nothing to celebrate. The sound piercing your head tells you that you should remember each name in the euphoric opening credits. That's where the peak emotion in the film is: in the package.

Superman gives the impression of having been made in panic—in fear that "too much" imagination might endanger the film's appeal to the literal-minded. With astronomic sums of money involved (though not in ways perceptible to viewers), the producers and the director, Richard Donner, must have been afraid even of style—afraid that it would function satirically, as a point of view (as it does in the James Bond pictures). Style, to them, probably meant the risk of camp, which might endanger the film's appeal to the widest audience. Several modern directors (most notably Godard) have been influenced by the visual boldness of comic-strip art—by the primary colors, unfurnished environments, and crisp, posterish sophistication—and the Pop artists who did blowups of comic-strip frames made us conscious of the formal intelligence in those cartoons, but *Superman* hasn't been designed in terms of the conventions of Pop. It has no controlling vision; there's so little consistency that each sequence might have had a different director and been color-processed in a different lab. Visually, it's not much more than a 70-mm. version of a kiddie-matinée serial. *Superman* carries a dedication to its cinematographer, Geoffrey Unsworth, who died a few months ago, but this poorly lighted and, for the most part, indifferently composed film is not a fitting tribute to the man who shot *Cabaret.*

The immediacy of comic strips has a magical effect on kids. The plot is socked to them, with exclamation points. And we go to *Superman* hoping for that kind of disreputable energy. But it isn't there, and you can feel the anticipatory elation in the theatre draining out. Donner doesn't draw us in and hold on to us; we're with him only in brief patches—a few seconds each. The plotting is so hit or miss that the movie never seems to get started. It should, because there's a marvellous, simplistic fantasy in the story of Superman: a superior being from another planet who is so strong that he can take care of the problems afflicting ours with his bare hands, but who must not reveal himself, and so goes among us in disguise as Clark Kent, a timid, clumsy, bespectacled reporter. Jerry Siegel and Joe Shuster, the Cleveland teen-agers who developed the idea and began trying to market the strip in 1933 and finally succeeded in 1938, provided a metaphor for the troubles and conflicts of boy dreamers: hidden inside the fumbling, fear-ridden adolescent is the all-competent giant. The divided hero is both a ninety-seven-pound weakling and Charles Atlas, but, unlike human beings, with their hope that the clown will grow into the hero, Superman is split forever. He can perform miracles, but he remains frustrated: as Clark Kent, this lonely stranger cannot win the woman he loves—the girl reporter Lois Lane—because she is in love with Superman. (Like the Scarlet Pimpernel and a number of other mass-culture heroes, he is his own rival.) This tragicomic figure might have provided a great central character for a space-adventure picture—a supremely human non-human hero—if only the moviemakers had trusted the idea of Superman.

The story has been updated from the thirties to the seventies, but not modernized, not rethought—just plunked down in the seventies. In the era of Al Pacino, Dustin Hoffman, and Woody Allen—a time when people acknowledge the humor and good sense in cowardice—might not the girl reporter (Margot Kidder) find herself drawn to Clark Kent's unsureness and feel some conflict in her swooning response to Superman? (She might even prefer Clark Kent.) And, in an era in which urban corruption and decay are deep and widespread, Superman's confident identification with the forces of law and order, and his thinking that he's cleaning up Metropolis (New York City) when he claps some burglars and thieves in jail, might be treated with a little irony. (It would be more fun to see him putting out a fire while kids threw stones at him, or arresting a mugger and being surrounded by an angry, booing crowd, or tackling the garbage problem.) The Superman who announces "I'm here to fight for truth, justice, and the American way" needs a little ribbing. But the film doesn't bring any ambiguity into this portrait of an outsize F.B.I. man from space. It doesn't risk new sources of comedy. It sticks to dumb jokes about spelling, and low-comedy scenes between Lex Luthor (Gene Hackman), the criminal mastermind who makes his home under Grand Central Station, and his bungling helper (Ned Beatty), with Luthor's floozy (Valerie Perrine) looking on. You can see that Hackman likes the idea of dressing up in what must be Liberace's castoffs and playing a funny maniac, and when he has a halfway good line he scores his laugh. But he's strenuously frivolous, like a guest villain on a late-sixties "Batman" show. Most of the time, he and Beatty are doing deliberately corny material—a kiddies' version of the kind of burlesque routines that Roy Kinnear does in Richard Lester movies—and the director can't seem to get the timing right.

Probably the moviemakers thought that the picture would sell on its special effects—Superman's flying, and his rescues, and the disasters and cataclysms. The special effects are far from wizardly, though, and the editing often seems hurried and jerky just at the crucial moments. The biggest effects (such as Superman's zipping up the San Andreas fault) are truncated—a couple of quick shots and out. In the early scenes on the planet Krypton, where the infant Superman lives, we're acutely conscious of the lack of elegance in the design, because Krypton, which is supposed to be more advanced than Earth by thousands of years, has plastic-chandelier décor, like a Vegas lobby. There is only one truly elegant trick effect in the Krypton footage: three revolutionary "traitors" who are expelled from the planet become reflections trapped in a fifth-dimensional object that suggests a flying mirror. The conversation of the advanced beings on Krypton isn't very stimulating, either. Mostly, it's just the infant's father, Jor-El (Marlon Brando), delivering ponderosities. Brando has begun to look like an Indian chief, and he confers a distinguished presence on his scenes. His magnificent head is topped with white hair, and he does a straightforward God the Father performance, with perhaps a trace of Claude Rains in his intonations. Jor-El packs his plump, bright-eyed infant off to Earth, in a little star-shaped spaceship, just before Krypton is destroyed. It's a husky three-year-old with an impish expression who lands in a farming area, in a sequence of considerable charm. Glenn Ford is an inspired choice for Pa Kent, the farmer, who, with Ma Kent (Phyllis Thaxter), adopts the boy—Ford's resources as an actor having contracted to the point where he has become a comic-strip version of the simple good American. Photographically, this farmland section, with almost motionless clouds hovering over wheat fields that stretch to infinity, and one or two looming figures, has a look that's related to Pop enlargements, but it's the enlargement of Andrew Wyeth or Peter Hurd. It doesn't have the stylish crude strength of cartoons—its strength is softer, more genteel. Though visually striking, this section is weakened by a choice that makes almost no sense: instead of going directly from the child actor to Christopher Reeve and letting him play the eighteen-year-old Superman, the film introduces another actor (Jeff East), who doesn't look like the little boy or like Reeve. This intermediate figure is very inexpressive, and something about him seems all wrong—is it just his pompadour, or is he wearing a false nose?

Part of the appeal that has made Superman last so long is surely in the quasi-religious feelings that children develop about him: he's the savior myth of their very own subculture. Although this film tries to supply an element of mysticism (the box-office lesson of *Star Wars* and The Force has been learned), it's Superman in the form of the joyless interim actor who goes to the North Pole to commune with his psychically still alive father. Jor-El informs him of his mystical mission to serve "collective humanity," and Brando shows a gleam of amusement as he instructs the youth in the capacity for goodness of the people on Earth, and says, "For this reason above all—their capacity for good—I have sent them you, my only son." The sequence takes place at the Fortress of Solitude, which constitutes itself out of the ice for Superman. This should be the magical heart of the film, and surely a building that materializes out of ice might do so with occult symmetry? But the mystic fortress looks like a crystal wigwam that is being put up by a stoned backpacker.

The film rallies when Reeve takes over—especially when he gets out of the drably staged scenes at the offices of the *Daily Planet*, gets into his red cape and blue tights, flies over Metropolis, and performs a string of miracles. Yet after the first graceful feat, in which he saves Lois Lane, who has fallen from a helicopter that crashed on a skyscraper, and then steadies the falling chopper (with the injured pilot inside) and gently lifts it to safety, the other miracles don't have enough tension to be memorable: each one wipes out our memory of the one before. And the insufferable shimmering metallic music—as congratulatory as a laugh track—smudges them together. When Superman takes his beloved up for a joyride in the sky, the cutting works against the soaring romanticism that we're meant to feel, and, with Lois reciting Leslie Bricusse lyrics to convey her poetic emotions, even the magic of two lovers flying hand in hand over New York City is banalized. Lois Lane has always been one of the more boring figures in popular mythology: she exists to get into trouble. Margot Kidder tries to do something with this thankless part, but she's harsh-voiced, and comes across as nervous and jumpy; she seems all wrong in relation to Reeve, who outclasses her. He's so gentlemanly that her lewdness makes one cringe. (We aren't given a clue to what our hero sees in Lois Lane. It might have been more modern fun if he hadn't been particularly struck by her until she'd rejected his cowardly Clark Kent side for his Superman side—if, like any other poor cluck, he wanted to be loved for his weakness.)

Superman doesn't have enough conviction or courage to be solidly square and dumb; it keeps pushing smarmy big emotions at us—but half-heartedly. It has a sour, scared undertone. And you can't help being aware that this is the sort of movie that increases the cynicism and sense of futility among actors. In order to sell the film as star-studded, a great many famous performers were signed up and then stuck in among the plastic bric-a-brac of Krypton; performers who get solo screen credits, with the full blast of trumpets and timpani, turn out to have walk-ons. Susannah York is up there as the infant Superman's mother, but, though Krypton is very advanced, this mother seems to have no part in the decision to send her baby to Earth. York has no part of any kind; she stares at the camera and moves her mouth as if she'd got a bit of food stuck in a back tooth. Of all the actors gathered here—all acting in different styles—she, maybe, by her placid distaste, communicates with us most directly.

[January 1, 1979]

Simon & Ross —
The Compassion Boys

David Hockney's views of Los Angeles as a new Riviera are softened into decorator art for the opening titles of *California Suite*. The movie—Herbert Ross's transcription of the four Neil Simon playlets that opened in Los Angeles early in 1976 and on Broadway later that year—is color-coördinated with the Hockneys. Most of it takes place in mockups of rooms at the Beverly Hills Hotel, and the cinematographer, David M. Walsh, has given the whole production a cooled-out look: the performers are smartly accented against whitened interiors. Stylization was clearly Ross's goal. Part of the hell of filming stage material is that it usually has nothing but foreground, and Neil Simon, who writes arguments between couples, rarely even provides intervention by subsidiary characters. So Ross bleaches the space around the pairs of combatants, to get rid of it as tastefully as possible. This look of sunstruck swank is appropriate to two of the plays—the clash between Jane Fonda and Alan Alda, and the duel between Maggie Smith and Michael Caine. Though Neil Simon still pays tribute to his New York conscience, and Jane Fonda, as a caustic *Newsweek* editor, jeers at Los Angeles, the visual style of the film conveys its message of upward mobility: there's an attempt here at rich artistic chic. The writing in these two plays is also bleached out, and as it happens, the two couples are Wasps.

These Wasp plays represent the serious side of Neil Simon, which turns out to be surprisingly close to Noël Coward—not good Coward but mawkishly bittersweet Coward, in which gallant people use bitchy wisecracks to conceal their breaking hearts. In texture and attitude, these plays might be something Simon dug up that was buried in London during the blitz. The entire point of the bickering between Jane Fonda, the intellectual snob, and Alan Alda, as her screenwriter ex-husband, who accuses her of never having had "an honest emotion," is how vulnerable she is. The entire point of the anguish exhibited by Maggie Smith, as an English actress who has received an Academy Award nomination, and Michael Caine, as her antique-dealer husband, who accompanies her to the awards ceremony, is that, though he is homosexual, they really love each other. And each playlet reaches its climax when the mask of sophistication is dropped and we see the suffering face. The plays are stripteases: brittle, glittering "successful" people are brought down to ordinary humanity.

California Suite is such an acute embarrassment because Herbert Ross directs as if he thought there were depth in the lines, when what he has got Jane Fonda, Maggie Smith, and Michael Caine bringing out is the sentimentality in them. When Laurence Olivier does his virtuoso turns in pictures such as *The Betsy* and *The Boys from Brazil*, we can see that he isn't deceived about the quality of the material but that he's enjoying himself acting anyway. Jane Fonda and Maggie Smith are anxious and straining, as if they thought there were something more in the material, which was eluding them. They do extraordinarily well by it, but they're not fun to watch, as Olivier is. You may find yourself flinching at the toads that leap out of their mouths.

Jane Fonda plays Hannah, one of those career-centered, woman-of-distinction roles left over from the forties: a veneered cold bitch, a boss lady. Hannah has come to Los Angeles to reclaim her daughter from her ex-husband, Bill, to whom the girl has fled. Bill seems meant to represent the mellow, suntanned spirit of L.A., but Alan Alda is too self-conscious. Wearing bangs like a Roman emperor, and with his eyes made up to look bigger and bluer, he has a hangdog look. He gives such a flabby, insecure performance that Bill doesn't seem to be a full person, and Hannah's attacks on him appear gratuitously spiteful; when he mildly remarks that perhaps he should get a lawyer to help him retain custody of their daughter, Hannah slams down the information that the Attorney General is a good friend of hers. It isn't just that Hannah is more than Bill's match—Fonda is more than Alda's match. She's whirring around and hitting emotional peaks in a vacuum; it might be better if she just ran the gamut of emotions from A to B rather than race from A to Z. Jane Fonda is so tensely eager to act that she puts out too much. Her comic edginess, her emotional precision, the heat rising in her cheeks, even that slender, wiry body primed for movement are too electric for her to be taking cheap shots at L.A. (while her heart is breaking). The only time I heard myself laugh was at a line that probably isn't meant to be funny: when she says of her current lover (who hasn't long to live) that "he has the second-best mind I've ever met since Adlai Stevenson." And she describes her daughter as "a bright girl with an intelligent mind." Herbert Ross is on record as believing that Neil Simon is a "classicist" on a level with Molière and Shaw. I may go out of my intelligent mind.

Maggie Smith and Michael Caine have a more evenly balanced sparring match. Maggie Smith plays *as if* her situations and lines were witty, and she makes them so by the distancing device of eccentricity. She goes beyond cleverness: it's a succinct performance—each gesture is an epigram. Yet there's a cost: when an actress triumphs in great material you can often feel the joy she takes in the material that is bearing her aloft; here, with Maggie Smith triumphing *over* her material, you can see the tiny frown lines, the doubt. Michael Caine performs like a professional who is used to doing the dramatist's job for him. He creates a decent, wary character out of his own flesh: the sagging and thickening of the muscles in his face suggest the husband's defensiveness and pain. Together, Maggie Smith and Caine waltz through the most ridiculous Wasp glitz dialogue with their heads held high and every syllable producing a satisfying click. It's a class act, or would be if it weren't marred by the author's and the director's hunger for the higher banalities—for shoving the couple's suffering in our faces. The husband accounts for their marital problem by referring to "biological discrepancies"—as in a daring drawing-room tragedy of 1925. And, as if all this tony torment weren't enough, Maggie Smith is obliged to play one of the most degrading of all scenes: a woman pleading with a man—who does not desire her—to make love to her. This is Neil Simon's idea of the moment of truth, and Ross brings the camera in for a tight closeup of Maggie Smith's desperation as she begs, "Tonight, Sidney, let it be me." Ross insists on our seeing the couple's style as a lie, a concealment; what makes people human in a Herbert Ross movie is always their weakness, their vulnerability, their need. Finally, he reduces everything to pop lyrics: people need people. For him, that's truth—that's classicism.

The two other playlets are low-comedy relief, and in them the chaste, whitening effect results in a loss of vitality. Abstracted from the everyday sitcom jumble of domestic furnishings, these playlets seem drained, bloodless. Walter Matthau has come out for his nephew's bar mitzvah a day ahead of his wife; his brother (Herbert Edelman) presents him with a pert blond hooker, and in the morning, with his wife due any minute, he can't wake the girl up. As an earnest, panicky shlump who has never before cheated on his wife, the tall, lean Matthau tries to look small and flustered and despairing; he mashes up his face and smacks his lips as if he were toothless, and puts on *"Oy, gevalt!"* Yiddish intonations, which keep slipping. As the wife, Elaine May could be Dracula's daughter. She's pale, with woebegone eyes and lank hair—a supplicant with meagre expectations. Yet her oddness is endearing, and her underplaying is in such contrast with Matthau's twittering hysteria that she piques the viewer's curiosity. Ross seems apathetic, though. He gives reverent care to the pacing of the Wasp segments, but here almost every vaudeville gag collapses, and even the physical-comedy bits (such as Matthau grabbing May's ankle) have no snap.

In the other slapstick playlet, Richard Pryor and Bill Cosby are vacationing doctors from Chicago who, with their wives (Gloria Gifford and Sheila Frazier), get into a mixed-doubles brawl. On the stage, this material—in which the actors squabble, turn belligerent, and have a knock-down-drag-out fight, from which they all emerge battered and bandaged—was played by white actors. But, since these are the only misfits in the hotel, when the roles are played by black actors the skit seems to be saying that the men may be doctors but they're still uncontrollable, dumb blacks who don't belong in a rich, civilized atmosphere; and the recessive whitened décor turns them into tar babies. When they don't know how to handle cars, when they stumble around a flooded room, crash into each other, step on broken glass, or, even worse, when Cosby bites Pryor's nose, it all has horrifying racist overtones. If Pryor and Cosby were at their comic ease, they might be able to redeem the situation by giving it a satiric edge—or even just by being funny. But Ross seems so dedicated to the immaculate preservation of Neil Simon's diction that he hasn't allowed them to work up their own comic rhythm. They're impaled on each line.

California Suite would seem to give offense to just about everyone: it goes from confirming the stereotypes of repressed, glamorously unhappy Wasps to confirming the comic stereotypes of henpecked baggy-pants Jews and of blacks who act like clowning savages. And one could hardly claim that it was well made. The four plays have been scrambled and intercut, but the players from one never appear in a frame with players from another; they never meet in an elevator or even cross paths in a corridor. And, though most of them leave L.A. at the same time, there isn't even the fun of having Jane Fonda stick her hand across the aisle of a plane to Maggie Smith and say, "Do you remember me? We met at the Attorney General's party." Several scenes are "opened out"; that is, they go outside the hotel rooms. Fonda and Alda sit down in a restaurant, and then zip—they're at the beach. But nothing happens at the restaurant, because Simon didn't invent dialogue for the opened-out scenes. We're most sharply aware of the stagebound nature of the material when we see Maggie Smith and Michael Caine go in to the Academy Awards presentation; the crucial part—her not getting the award, and her reaction to losing—is denied us. After it's over, we rejoin them and are told what happened. Neil Simon has made a fainthearted attempt to tie the four plays together into a *Grand Hotel*; what this comes down to is that the individual plays reach their unmistakable curtain lines and—in dramatic terms—end, but then an anti-climactic scene or two is tacked on.

Yet why does instinct tell one that this clumsy, chopped-together movie may be a hit? The secret of the popular success of the Simon-Ross combination (*The Sunshine Boys, The Goodbye Girl,* and now this) could be that pathos is their goal—that they have no emotional range beyond it. The audience doesn't get restless, because the contestants keep whacking each other with insults. But at the end there's always the loneliness, the fear, the reconciliation. No doubt Simon and Ross see wisdom in this, and probably many in the audience do, too. Simon and Ross weep for us. They succeed by turning vaudeville into mush.

[January 8, 1979]

Doused

The opening sequence of the Australian film *The Last Wave* could have made a classic three-minute short. In an outback township, hailstones come down from a clear blue sky; schoolchildren who have been playing outdoors are called into the school for safety. The huge icy stones crash a window, and a child is cut and bloodied. There is, suddenly, no safety anywhere; nature is freaking out. The director, Peter Weir, has apparently studied Nicolas Roeg's allusive, portentous films—especially *Don't Look Now,* with its angled shots and doomy noises and retarded tempos. But Roeg himself doesn't seem to know what to do with his fractured-time-and-memory techniques, and the self-serious occultism of his pictures is only partly redeemed by their unisexy languorousness. Weir's occultism isn't even faintly erotic, and except for the first sequence *The Last Wave* is over-deliberate; the camera movements are ominous as if by habit.

Visually, the film is active until the first shot of Richard Chamberlain, who plays the protagonist, a Sydney corporation lawyer. Every time he appears, the camera seems to hold on him—and the film croaks out. This lawyer has water gushing from his car radio, water trickling down the carpeted stairs in his home, and water in his premonitory dreams. At the request of a legal-aid society, he becomes involved in a murder case—a young aborigine has been found dead, and a group of five aborigines are accused of killing him. The lawyer, with his orderly life thrown off course by a black rain falling on the city and by his encounters with the aborigines, discovers that he is some sort of spiritual throwback to a primordial race of seers, whose "sacred place," with its artifacts still intact, is in the grottoes near the sewage tunnels of Sydney. In this ancient underground temple, he finds his own mask, and the painted hieroglyphs on the wall tell the story of the hailstones, the black rain, and his apocalyptic destiny. This plot is also a throwback—to the B movies of the thirties and early forties. The dialogue (by Weir and two co-scriptwriters, Tony Morphett and Peter Popescu) is vintage R.K.O. and Universal. The police doctor, who can't determine the cause of the aborigine's death—it was the result of a shaman's pointing a "death bone" at him—finishes the autopsy, looks up, and says, "There's something about this. . . ." After the lawyer meets the group of defendants, he tells his wife (Olivia Hamnett), "They're keeping something from me." His wife asks why he thinks that, and he replies demurely, "Just a feeling."

Weir provides apparitions holding sacred stones, frog noises in the night, shadows in slow motion, and the kind of haunted-house acting that many of us have a certain affection for—the actors' sense of hopelessness is so disarming as they deliver a line and then try to find a suitable expression to go with it. But *The Last Wave,* which at its best recalls *I Walked with a Zombie,* is hokum without the fun of hokum. Despite all its scare-movie apparatus, the film fairly aches to be called profound. The lawyer, who has been visited in his dreams by one of the murder defendants, invites the young man to dinner and earnestly asks him, "What are dreams?" The aborigine answers, "A dream is a shadow of something real," and the film treats this as Revelation. Pitying the lawyer, the aborigine tells him that it's *he* who is in trouble—"You don't know what dreams are anymore." When the lawyer's clergyman stepfather comes for a visit, the lawyer, in torment, cries, "Why didn't you tell me there were mysteries? . . . We've lost our dreams and then they come back and we don't know what they mean." This infernally sluggish movie is about the white man's burden of alienation—and nobody could be whiter than Richard Chamberlain, with his porcelain cheekbones and tired, empty blue eyes.

The maudlin hysteria in the film links it to some of the Hollywood movies of the late-sixties-early-seventies period. (This may help to account for the respectful tenderness with which it has been treated in much of the press.) It's the kill-us-because-we-deserve-to-die syndrome. Instead of seeing the victims of expansionist drives and colonial policies—the aborigines or blacks or Indians—as people whose rights were violated and must be restored as quickly as possible, these movies romanticize the victims. They are seen in terms of what whites are supposed to have repressed. A few generations ago, whites saw the victims of white civilization (as racist bigots still do) in terms of sexuality and savagery; now the victims are seen in terms of magic, dreamspeak, nobility, intuition, harmony with nature. The white bigots saw them as mentally inferior; the modern, guilt-ridden whites see them as spiritually superior. In neither case are they granted what is their plain due: simple equality.

It's implicit in *The Last Wave* that the crime against the aborigines is what alienated the whites from their dreams, and that because of this crime a Biblical flood is coming—punishment and purification. It doesn't seem to matter that the flood will flush away the aborigines as well. This film is so infatuated with white guilt that the aborigines are created in our lost self-image. The lithe, graceful Chris (Gulpilil, the star of Roeg's *Walkabout*), who's on trial, and the dignified, wily shaman, Charlie (Nandjiwarra Amagula), are what self-hating whites emotionally need them to be: our betters. Aborigines who cling to their tribal rites are seen as uncorrupted, and the shaman, like an old Indian chief, is revered because he's such a photogenic custodian of our consciences. (We all know that, in order to survive, many people of oppressed races have developed inner strength, but this strength also shines forth in many white faces—in the inhabitants of Appalachia, for example—or in almost any group at a time of crisis.)

The decadent white race is represented by the sickly paleface lawyer, and surely there isn't an actor with less natural rhythm than Richard Chamberlain. But if the filmmaking team hired Chamberlain with malice aforethought why didn't anybody explain to him that he needn't wear himself out acting? Chamberlain has got by in a few roles—as Aramis in Richard Lester's *The Three Musketeers,* because he could be in motion, and in the TV *Count of Monte Cristo,* when he was bearded and dashing. But throughout this film we listen to vaguely alarming distant sounds on the track while the lawyer muses about his intimations that things aren't . . . quite right. And Richard Chamberlain is not an actor you want to spend quiet moments with. He can't stop quivering his lips to connote sensitivity and contracting his nostrils for apprehensiveness and pulling in his cheek muscles for ineffable sorrow. He keeps us conscious that he's acting all the time. His toes act in his shoes.

Like a number of other modern directors, Weir doesn't seem to know what actors are for; he uses them only as visual objects. Olivia Hamnett gets some tension going in her scenes, but she's defeated by the way her role is written. In the midst of torrential days and nights, she murmurs absently to the children, "Yes, it's been raining, hasn't it? Very hard," as she looks worriedly at her husband. The writers have conceived her in the mold of the devoted wife: she barely notices the crazy flooding waters; she's only worried because her husband seems unduly disturbed about his dreams. Weir doesn't develop any characters, so if all the people are to be killed the viewer has no particular cause for regret. Or even for much interest, because the film has worn us out with all its forebodings. Weir has reversed the techniques needed for audience involvement. Instead of starting with the ordinary, getting us to care about the characters, and building to a hallucinatory climax, he uses his dislocating tricks right at the start, and keeps using them in the Sydney streets and rooms. Nobody in the lawyer's home can pick up a toothpick without the scene's being invested with dread. But when Weir gets to the mystic big number—the journey to the "sacred place," where the lawyer reënacts the whites' primal crime against the aborigines—he might be shooting a documentary of everyday events. He's prosaic just when he needs to be imaginative to pull the movie together.

The aborigine actors, with their deep-set eyes, are by far the most vital element in *The Last Wave,* yet they're kept on the margins and used as supernatural forces. In the one great Australian film that I have seen—Fred Schepisi's *The Chant of Jimmie Blacksmith,* from the Thomas Keneally novel—they are at the center, in conflict with themselves and with the whites. In theme, Schepisi's epic suggests an Australian *The Birth of a Nation* seen from the side of the blacks. I hope that someone shows this movie before Americans get the idea that pictures such as Phil Noyce's *Newsfront* and *The Last Wave* are the best that Australia has to offer.

□ □ □

Hot Tomorrows is an *extremely* low-budget film, written, directed, produced, and edited by Martin Brest; it was shown at the 1977 New York Film Festival and will play at the Entermedia Theatre in New York this month as part of the American Mavericks series. Brest made this seriocomic movie, with macabre musical numbers, for $33,000, plus some deferments. If economy dictated the use of black-and-white stock, Brest turns this to his advantage in stylized *film noir* effects. It's a typical young-filmmaker's film, in the sense that it's movie-obsessed, but Brest's obsession takes a baroquely original form: to him, old movies—Hollywood musicals, in particular—are memento mori. His hero, Michael (Ken Lerner), an aspiring writer from the Bronx who is living in Los Angeles, is sorrowfully in love with Laurel & Hardy and the other dead entertainers whom he watches on the screen. Michael's childhood friend Louis (Ray Sharkey) is out visiting him, and as they pal around Hollywood on Christmas Eve—the glum intellectual Michael suggesting Oliver Hardy, and little Louis, who just wants some action, suggesting Stan Laurel—everything they encounter reminds them that life hangs by a thread. Each reminder has a quirky unexpectedness—from a radio announcer's predictions of holiday traffic fatalities to a cadaverous combo at the Paradise Ballroom, with a mock-Dietrich vocalist (Marie Elfman) singing the mournful "Jonny," and a man (Danny Elfman) singing "St. James Infirmary." There has never been a movie so comically centered on death in life and life in death. Brest writes easy, naturalistic dialogue that comes across as a series of riffs; whatever the characters start to talk about, death always enters in, and the impossibility of avoiding the subject gets funnier all the time—like a good, broad burlesque-house joke.

Hot Tomorrows has such a distinctive, fluky temperament I wish that it didn't miss—I wish it were really a knockout. It doesn't have much shape, though; there are listless scenes, and the part of Michael is underwritten; at times he seems just to have been born tired—a depressive stick-in-the-mud. Michael's sedentary impassivity must have been intended to play off against Louis's scroungy restlessness—the domineering Ollie against the ever-willing Stan—but Ken Lerner doesn't have enough charge to hold his own with Ray Sharkey. All our interest shifts to Louis, who, as Sharkey plays him, is both a punk and an innocent. Sharkey has a bantam-cock, scat style of acting, and, though he sounds friendly, even familiar, he sounds abrasive, too. He's full of energy, and his face takes the camera, the way the young Cagney's did. ("Sharkey" might have been a good nickname for Cagney.) Louis's eagerness for experience—his aliveness—is matched only by that of the spry elderly women who appear in roles or do bits in an old-age-home sequence. Brest has given these women gag lines that we don't anticipate, and they deliver them so expertly that jokes about death seem to be pelting us from all directions. In the finale, Louis, the angelic vulgarian, gets to tap-dance to "42nd Street" in a tacky-lavish production number, which somehow ties the living and the dead together. It's Busby Berkeley with a maggot in his brain.

The talent that Martin Brest brought to this ambitious first feature is sizable, and his drive must have been, too. He got his $33,000 from diverse sources: $10,000 was a grant from the American Film Institute (on the basis of a script for a short); $8,000 he and his cinematographer/associate producer, Jacques Haitkin, begged and borrowed; and a last-minute-reprieve gift of $15,000 came from Warner Brothers, after two of its executives saw the footage. Brest, who got his training at N.Y.U., was twenty-four when he shot this film (in three and a half weeks) but twenty-six by the time he'd got enough money together to put the sound track on. He's now twenty-seven and at work on his second feature, *Going in Style,* with a budget of $5,000,000. That is both a success story and a terror story. When studio heads are impressed by what a filmmaker does for thirty-three thousand and, with (economically sound) Alice-in-Wonderland logic, back him to the tune of five million, he may feel—in some corner of his mind—that the world is saying to him, "We'll show you that you're not as smart as you think you are."

[January 22, 1979]

Steam Engines

Michael Crichton's *The Great Train Robbery,* which is set in mid-Victorian England, has a golden, plummy look. It's not often now that we get this "civilized-entertainment" sort of costume picture—handsomely mounted and slightly stiff. The year is 1855, and the hero (Sean Connery) is a thief masquerading as a wealthy businessman in order to gather the information he needs to steal the gold bullion that is being shipped by train in double-locked safes to pay the British troops fighting in the Crimean War. The film is a fictionalized version of this theft, which, according to Crichton, was the first train robbery. (Trains themselves had been in existence for only a few decades, and such aids to safecracking as dynamite were yet to be invented.) Although Crichton has made two other movies (*Westworld* and *Coma*), this is the first time he has been in a position to adapt one of his own novels to the screen and direct it; the result is an evenly paced suspense movie with laconic, dryly funny flourishes. There's a total absence of personal obsession—including moviemaking obsession—in the way Crichton works. He never excites us, emotionally or imaginatively; when he shows the poverty and cruelty that went along with the overstuffed Victorian poshness, we never feel threatened, never identify with those who suffer. *The Great Train Robbery* could almost be a textbook demonstration of bourgeois moviemaking: there are painstaking re-creations and restorations of the Crystal Palace, the trains pulled by coal-burning steam engines, Newgate Prison, mansions and slums, but the camera rarely moves. We seem to be looking at pictures of the past, with people moving around in them. The film has a satisfying tame luxuriousness, like a super episode of "Masterpiece Theatre."

Though Crichton's attempt to whet our curiosity about how an elaborate robbery was carried out more than a hundred years ago has an antiquarian charm, the problems to be solved aren't clear and the narrative is a bit of a cheat. The film concentrates on relatively simple matters, like how keys are duplicated, and leaves us in the dark about bigger questions. Who is this thief? How has he acquired the manners and the social knowledge of a gentleman? (Was he born a gentleman?) We don't find out how he got into the exclusive men's club where he learns details vital to the robbery, or even such smaller points as how he manages to take over the operation of a fashionable bordello for a night and stage a police raid. In the book, Crichton speculates about questions such as these and then skillfully ducks them by the ruse that he is dealing only with the known facts; in the movie, he never raises them at all—leaving the viewer puzzled about why we're given what we're given when so much that would seem to the point is left out. But Sean Connery gives the movie something of his own substantiality. Though his character seems practically unwritten—a carry-over from Crichton's literary conceit about working only with the historical records—he makes the thief what used to be called a fine figure of a man. Dandified, with light-brown hair and a darker beard, Connery plays his role close in and makes his smallest changes of mood register. He's the film's animating force, and the other actors—costumed to the hilt, and set off the way they are in those British TV series—are very agreeable.

As the thief's devoted doxy, the lushly pretty Lesley-Anne Down gives an overeager, literal-minded performance. There's one scene in which the script must have called for her to pace in agitation; she paces back and forth as dutifully as a boy acting a soldier in his first school play. You can see her calm face under her energetic efforts, but she gets by with this childish, let's-pretend acting because of her warm blue eyes and her rolling, eiderdown softness and her desire to please. Her bad acting complements her physical presence—makes her more appealing, more accessible. (She's so beautiful that if she were also a good actress she might be forbidding.) She and Connery share the film's two most visually facetious—and best—moments. The first comes at the start, when the thief is sitting up in bed, and she peels off her black net stockings and her merry-widow corselet and joins him by climbing in under the covers at his feet, with her pert round behind to the camera. (The thief gets part of the action, the audience the other part.) In the second, she's leaning over his head, scraping his neck with a straight razor, as he tells her something that gives her pause; it's a fine tableau—the two heads and the hand with the razor. In narrow-tailored clothes, the tall Donald Sutherland is a stork-legged pickpocket: a scarecrow of a man. Limbering his cadaverous fingers and cracking his knuckles, Sutherland provides flighty, eccentric contrast to Connery's resourceful leader with his feet on the ground. Two English character actors do more than create the environment for the robbery— they *are* the environment. As a plump-faced bank manager, Malcolm Terris fairly quivers with lust; he's like a horny pudding. And as a Scotland Yard inspector, Robert Lang carries his share of bureaucratic anxieties and works on the case in a Victorian way—doggedly, intuitively. It's also a graceful touch that Gabrielle Lloyd, who plays the marriageable daughter of a bank president (Alan Webb), is made out to be perky, as if she had learned to overcome her plainness by her acuity in turning a phrase.

Crichton miscalculates, though, in his handling of Wayne Sleep as Willy, the human fly who, having got word in Newgate that the thief wants his help, scales the prison walls and escapes; Willy's tight little Cockney face is too masklike, and his role (which relates to a minor aspect of the robbery) is too melodramatically conceived—it throws the movie slightly off balance.

The Great Train Robbery was the last film that the cinematographer Geoffrey Unsworth completed before his death, and, like *Superman*, it is dedicated to him. But, unlike *Superman*, this picture has the subdued richness that one associates with Unsworth's lighting. His formality has nostalgia built into it; the images have gravity—they seem both perfectly controlled and ripely sensuous. It's too bad that Crichton doesn't direct with a more fluid sense of movement, but with Unsworth's images to look at, watching Connery and the others move in and out of the shadowy frames, as if they were entering and leaving a series of stages, has a pleasant, ceremonial aspect. The settings recall the photographs of the marvels of the new industrial age in the rotogravure sections of old newspapers; the London Bridge Station is a particular beauty. (It is actually the Heuston Station in Dublin, and most of the other locations are also Irish.) Viewers may even feel grateful that the director's attempts at suspense fail: without pressure on your nervous system, you can enjoy the well-behaved crooks, their finely tailored dupes, the deft Jerry Goldsmith score, and the many teasing touches. And though the dialogue, which often seems on the verge of being witty, doesn't quite make it—Crichton's Shavianism is gummy, it has no bite—the actors convey an illusion of wit. This poorly plotted movie is told in such a deceptively orderly manner that the effect is very relaxing. There's a subtle flattery in bourgeois entertainment: sitting back in your seat, you feel like a person of taste.

□ □ □

*F*or its first hour, Visconti's 1976 film, *The Innocent*, based on the 1892 D'Annunzio novel, is a steamy comedy of manners that seems an almost perfect preparation for a tragicomedy of jealousy. Tullio (Giancarlo Giannini), a freethinker and atheist, an aristocratic liberal who believes in his own intellectual distinction, has become sexually indifferent to his innocent, round-cheeked, country-mousy wife (Laura Antonelli). He has turned to a liaison with an ardent and experienced countess (Jennifer O'Neill), a slim, glittering beauty—a sexual woman of fashion. Visconti shows us Tullio's dilettantish character from an amused distance, in a series of shapely ironic sequences; he's an Italian male peacock whose modernist ideas are displayed like tail feathers. Tullio is so spoiled and so unthinkingly cruel that he doesn't only talk about his mistress when he's at home with his wife—he complains about her to his wife. But when his mistress mentions to him that his wife is having an affair with a novelist, she sees from his change of expression that her careless words were a blunder. Tullio may have begun to regard his modest, fair-complexioned wife as a sister, but, alerted by his mistress's remark, he becomes excited by the sensual emanations this gentle woman is suddenly giving off. He falls passionately in love with her.

Though the red-damask décor, with its furs and patterned-silk couches and heavy draperies, provides the setting for an Italian opera, and Jennifer O'Neill, with her skin darkened, has the imperiousness of a diva, the camera glides smoothly among the rich at their social rituals, and the tone is almost that of Viennese light opera. The film recalls an earlier movie about the tragic consequences of passion among shallow people: Max Ophuls' *The Earrings of Madame De* . . . —which, like this one, was set at the turn of the century. The 1953 *Madame De* . . . , with its expressive décor (lace and gauze, chandeliers and staircases) and its distilled passions, also dealt with aristocrats who were protected against almost everything in life but their own emotions. Visconti points up his indebtedness to Ophuls in a musicale at the home of a princess (Marie Dubois), where the virginal-looking young wife, who has seen the novelist among the guests, feels a touch on her shoulder and for an excited instant thinks it is his hand, then looks up and sees her husband. She is listening to the "Che faro senza Euridice" aria from Gluck's *Orfeo ed Euridice* during this scene, and she goes on humming the tune at home. It's the same aria that Ophuls featured in the opera sequence of *Madame De* . . . Like Ophuls, Visconti shows a richly ambiguous joy in evoking the past and in demonstrating that love can be a form of damnation which cancels out good sense even among the sophisticated. Both films, with their attention to the customs and manners that the most privileged people in a society can violate and those they can't violate, show the influence of the greatest of all studies of passion and shallowness—*Anna Karenina*. (D'Annunzio is said to have been under the sway of Russian literature when he wrote *The Innocent*.) Tullio is a male variant of Anna, and, like Anna and like Madame De, he becomes rash and destroys himself.

If the second hour, in which the tone of Tullio's jealousy deepens, moved along like the first, *The Innocent* might be a masterpiece, but the film becomes so ponderous that the characters begin to seem used up. Visconti did not live long enough to complete the editing, and, though his pictures have often maundered (*Death in Venice* ends over and over again), I wonder if those who prepared this cut may have exaggerated the flaws in the script. He has clearly planted the clue to the structure: the wife's lover (Marc Porel) writes popular romances, and the joke on the husband, who is contemptuous of this trash, is that passion turns his own life into a cheap novel. Tullio's newfound ecstasy with his wife is marred when he discovers that she's pregnant by the novelist. A devout Catholic, she cannot be persuaded to have an abortion, and when the child is born Tullio sees her attentions to it as confirmation of his jealous fears that she still loves the novelist.

Giannini is far from ideally cast; his Tullio, who is such a foolish, limited man from the beginning, doesn't have enough intellectual stature for the film's delicate mockery of him to make its fullest impact. But Giannini seems acceptable until he remembers to act. In the second hour, he's all over the place acting. And with him staring into mirrors for moody closeups and wandering about looking stricken and rottenly atheistic, while his rejected mistress raises the issue of women's rights and also suggests that the novelist transmitted a venereal disease to his child, the movie seems to be poking into all the family closets. Instead of turning out to be a tragicomedy about a man who is in torment because his wife doesn't love him, it becomes a melodrama that truckles to Catholicism: being an atheist, Tullio does not value human life—he commits infanticide without remorse, and finally he has no reason to go on living. This Hollywood-style attitude toward godlessness is an ingredient of the movie from the start, but could Visconti have intended it to function so moralistically? Surely he meant it to serve more elegantly—as the coup de grâce, perhaps?—that Tullio is destroyed by all the things he doesn't believe in. The wife uses her piety as the stratagem by which she clings to the child of the novelist, whom she does indeed still love. But as the film stands, Tullio seems to be destroyed by his immorality (rather than by jealous passion), and the film loses its ironic balance. Toward the end, the charges and recriminations between the husband and wife have no force, because we haven't been shown the turns and twists they're arguing about, and the picture has long since run out of steam. What we're left with are images: of the gentlemen's gym where Tullio and his rival fence, of Tullio's holding fire tongs in a blazing fireplace at the moment his wife's infant is delivered by forceps, of Antonelli herself. She's like a placid ingenue in a Russian movie, except that she has furtive yearnings—naughty thoughts. Laura Antonelli doesn't act, exactly, but she behaves amusingly, and she builds up sexual suspense. When she's finally nude, in bed, and aroused, she heaves and writhes so prodigiously she's like a storm-tossed sea. It's the kind of passion you learn in a circus: she's a horizontal belly dancer. If only W. C. Fields were there to comment on the undulations of her succulent flesh.

[February 12, 1979]

No Contest

Paul Schrader has powerful raw ideas for movies, but he attempts to function as a writer-director without ever developing his ideas or his characters. In his new film, *Hardcore,* the protagonist, Jake VanDorn (George C. Scott), who is a Grand Rapids furniture manufacturer and a member of the Dutch Reformation Church, waves goodbye to his only child, Kristen (Ilah Davis), a quiet, dark, teen-age girl, who is going off to California with her Sunday-school classmates, in a chartered bus, to a Calvinist youth convention. A few days later, the father gets a phone call: during the group's visit to Knott's Berry Farm, Kristen disappeared. Jake goes to Los Angeles and, on the recommendation of the police, hires a private detective (Peter Boyle), and then he goes back home to wait. After several weeks, Boyle comes to see him, bringing an 8-mm. hard-core movie with Kristen in it. Jake leaves his secure fundamentalist environment and for the next several months searches through the porno-prostitution world for his daughter. This might be a great fiery subject if we could feel what the girl was running away from and if the father were drawn into experiences that scared him, sickened him, shook him up. In old movies that warned viewers about the vices lying in wait for their daughters (white slavery, prostitution, drugs), there was something to attract the audience: the thrill of sin. Even when the cautionary aspect of the films was just a hypocritical ploy, there was something at stake; the temptations of the Devil were given their due. In *Taxi Driver* (which Schrader wrote but which Martin Scorsese directed), the protagonist, Travis Bickle, had a fear and hatred of sex so feverishly sensual that we experienced his tensions, his explosiveness. But in *Hardcore* Jake feels no lust, so there's no enticement—and no contest. The Dutch Reformation Church has won the battle for his soul before the film's first frame.

Jake, a loner who sticks to his convictions, is Travis Bickle as a daddy, but a Travis Bickle who stayed in Grand Rapids and kept his sanity. Schrader, who has said that Jake is modelled on his father, doesn't explore the possibility that it's what Jake, in his firm religious morality, denies and excludes from his life that drives his daughter to sexual degradation. In this

543

film, there's nothing between fundamentalism and licentiousness—no forms of sexual expression or pleasure that aren't degraded, and no way to have any sexual freedom without going to porno hell. The script was inspired by the 1956 John Ford film, *The Searchers*, in which John Wayne spends five years tracking down his niece, who has been abducted by Comanches. Like *The Searchers, Hardcore* is woodenly acted and methodical. The story is set up as a demonstration of the superiority of fundamentalist moral values over pornographic laxness. Jake is above sex. He hates porno the way John Wayne hates rustlers and Commies.

Schrader shot in actual porno bookshops and massage parlors and peep shows, yet he missed out on the atmosphere—there's none of the pulsation of sleazy dives, no details strike our imaginations. Schrader doesn't enter the world of porno; he stays on the outside, looking at it coldly, saying, "These people have nothing to do with me." The girls are displayed like pieces of meat in a butcher's counter, under fluorescent glare. And since the film doesn't regard these girls as human there's no horror in their dehumanization—only frigid sensationalism. It has never been difficult to feel out the psychological mechanism of how pimps draw and hold runaway teen-agers: the girls are brutalized in the porno world, yet they also get the attention they've always wanted, and any attention can seem better than none. *Hardcore* treats them as if they weren't worth attention. The only person who attempts to reveal something of her feelings is Niki (Season Hubley), a young girl who guides Jake in his search. Niki's poorly written dialogue makes her seem realistically self-aware—she has no illusions to sustain her, no psychological defenses against the truth of her situation. She's very straight, and Schrader leads us to expect that she will get through to Jake—warm him up, change him, make him human. At the end, when Niki is brushed aside and we're told that she belongs where she is, we feel completely baffled and cheated. Jake will go on being the same self-contained moralist whose daughter ran away, but because, like the hero of *The Searchers,* he single-mindedly pursued Kristen, found her, and took her home, we're supposed to see him as a man whose principles have triumphed.

Scott seems Midwestern, and without condescending to it; he endows Jake with a pained dignity and moments of depth, and at least one of his rampaging explosions—his picking up a table lamp and bashing a porno-film stud who has worked with his daughter—is quite terrifying. But Schrader creates effects, not characters; there's nothing for Scott to hang on to and develop. Jake looms up in scenes like Frankenstein's monster, and he's constantly pounding people—smashing them and beating them up. He even slaps Niki (which is so ugly you feel yourself wincing). Jake's rage provides the action in the film, yet it's never treated as having any relation to his solitary way of life or to how he raised his daughter. There's something a little batty about the way Jake strides through hell swinging his fists, like a Calvinist John Wayne. This movie considers violent physical confrontation as the efficient way to fight the Devil. Jake is a can-do guy.

The tone of the film is cautious and maddeningly opaque. There's no feeling of suspense, because the characters are all prejudged and they stay the same from scene to scene while Schrader holds the camera on them for an extra instant to make them look empty, or plays with photographing them from different angles. He seems to like the sinister possibilities of Peter Boyle's big bald head and beady eyes and domineering physique. Boyle is photographed head-on so much he seems to be attempting to stare us down, and when he talks to Scott the camera cuts back and forth between the two, with so many overpowering closeups of Boyle that we assume that something overpowering is being signified. There may never have been another American director as lacking in spontaneity as Paul Schrader. The Europeans, such as Bresson and Dreyer, whose methods have been deliberate and studied (and whom he emulates) have achieved their effects through rigorous design. But Schrader doesn't have that control and precision. There is no radiance to the color in *Hardcore,* and there's no indication of a visual plan. Every now and then, there's a shot with an exact kind of garish density—a travelling shot of the equipment in a sex shop, or a mirror image. But it just seems an effect applied to a scene—it isn't integral. The film can't resist such gaudy pulp flourishes as the white-suited Ratan (Marc Alaimo), who materializes in order to provide a last-minute shoot-'em-up ending. Ratan, we're told in awed tones, deals in pain and produces "snuff" movies; the implication is that Kristen might be the next victim. (A few years ago, publicists pumped up business for an exploitation film by starting the rumor that its murder scenes involved actual murder—that it belonged to a decadent new genre, the snuff movie—and editorial writers leaped to the bait.)

It's not merely that Schrader went to porno places and missed them—he went home to Grand Rapids and missed that, too. There are lovely shots of the downtown area and of Christmas snow scenes, but they're edited in a random way that dulls the effect, and we feel as alienated from the family life there as we do from the porno environment. It's hard to distinguish between the furniture in Jake's factory and the family members he sits down to dinner with. They don't inquire after Kristen once she has vanished, and don't show any anxiety about what might have happened to her. When Jake's brother-in-law, Wes (Dick Sargent), follows him to Los Angeles to make sure he's all right, he doesn't even ask if Jake has had any word of Kristen. Sargent, who purses his mouth every time the camera is on him, plays the role as a TV wimp.

Who *does* matter to this director? He presents everyone in the same detached, affectionless way; even the sound is hollow. His scenes are so inexpressive that it could be he simply doesn't have enough interest in other people's emotions to loosen up the performers and bring something out of them, and doesn't have an instinctive sense of film rhythm. There's the same determined ploddingness in this movie as in his 1978 *Blue Collar,* but it's much worse here. The possibility also comes to mind that the porno world is Schrader's metaphor for show business, and that, in some corner of his mind, he is the runaway who became a prostitute. He has sometimes said that he regards working in the movie business as prostitution, and *Hardcore* looks like a film made by somebody who finds no joy in moviemaking. (Paul Schrader may like the idea of prostituting himself more than he likes making movies.) Several veteran directors are fond of calling themselves whores, but, of course, what they mean is that they gave the bosses what was wanted. They're boasting of their cynical proficiency. For Schrader to call himself a whore would be vanity: he doesn't know how to turn a trick.

□ □ □

Once in Paris is a moderately engaging romantic movie about a married American screenwriter (Wayne Rogers) who arrives alone in Paris to doctor the script of a film going into production. Rogers knows how to make fun of himself, in pantomime. The hero's flickers of egotism about his writing are very quick, and so are his pangs of desire each time he sees a sexy woman: he looks surprised and hurt—almost stricken. Frank D. Gilroy, who wrote and directed, shows somewhat more film craft and a better sense of pacing than he did in his first two pictures (*Desperate Characters* and *From Noon Till Three*), but he thinks small, and in fifties terms. He's always a few steps behind where the movie needs to be. The picture is a middle-aged man's fantasy—a bittersweet brief encounter. The hero falls in love with an Englishwoman (Gayle Hunnicutt) who's staying at his hotel, and makes a friend of his chauffeur (Jack Lenoir), who has a shady past, and they're all three terribly kind and considerate of one another. *Once in Paris* might have more substance if Hunnicutt weren't such an expensive-looking, high-toned sex object. She has a luxuriant cloud of dark hair, an exquisitely thin nose with incredibly refined nostrils, and a large, generous mouth. She's groomed to perfection even in bed, and when she plays footsie under a table with the hero she has the highest arches you've ever seen. Her acting is groomed, too. She drops her eyelids to indicate the pain of giving him up, and in a bed scene she has been directed to turn her back to her lover and hide her emotion from him while turning her face to the camera, so we'll understand how nobly she's suffering. Her suffering looks like something she bought in a swank shop, to match her bracelet.

The more serious the screenwriter gets about this woman the less likable he is; love turns him into a jackass. The palship of this innocent American and his worldly, illusionless French driver is all that keeps the movie from sagging completely. Lenoir (who actually was Gilroy's driver when Gilroy worked on *The Only Game in Town* in France) suggests an aging matinée idol—an old pro—though he's never acted in a movie before. He has a slight sullenness and complication under his charm; he could play spookily untrustworthy characters. This trace of grime saves him when Gilroy gives him French wisdom to spout. The driver explains to the American that a man must be unfaithful to his wife in order to save his marriage; it's a swinger's line, presented as paradoxical oo-la-la. Gilroy sets the two men to quarrelling, and then has to turn the plot every which way to get things to come out happily. The film is like a padded short story, and the color isn't as bright as you might want it to be—it's modest, like almost everything else about this movie.

□ □ □

John Carpenter, who made the low-budget scare picture *Halloween*, has a visual sense of menace. He quickly sets up an atmosphere of fear, and his blue night tones have a fine, chilling ambience—the style is reminiscent of the Halloween episode in Minnelli's *Meet Me in St. Louis*. But Carpenter isn't very gifted with actors, and he doesn't seem to have any feeling at all for motivation or for plot logic. *Halloween* has a pitiful, amateurish script (by Carpenter and his producer, Debra Hill). An escaped lunatic wielding a kitchen knife stalks people in a small Midwestern town (Haddonfield, Illinois), and that's about it. There's no indication of why he selects any particular target; he's the bogeyman—pure evil—and he wants to kill. The film is largely just a matter of the camera tracking subjectively from the mad killer's point of view, leading you to expect something awful to happen. But the camera also tracks subjectively when he isn't around at all; in fact, there's so much subjective tracking you begin to think everybody in the movie has his own camera.

As a doctor from the lunatic asylum that the killer has escaped from, Donald Pleasence is solid and forceful; enunciating in the impeccable tradition of Lionel Atwill, he delivers idiotic exposition about e-vil. Sometimes you think he's going to have to cross his eyes to keep a straight face. Carpenter doesn't seem to have had any life outside the movies: one can trace almost every idea on the screen to directors such as Hitchcock and Brian De Palma and to the Val Lewton productions. It may even be that Carpenter selected Jamie Lee Curtis to be his pure heroine—the teen-age babysitter, Laurie—because she recalls the serious-faced little blond girl in *The Curse of the Cat People*. The daughter of Janet Leigh and Tony Curtis, Jamie Lee Curtis has a hoarse, low, rather inexpressive voice and a plaintive Lauren Bacall–ish look and an attractive gaucheness. For no discernible reason, the bogeyman (who is masked) zeroes in on her near the start of the picture, but he keeps being sidetracked. He has no trouble picking off the teen-agers who "fool around"; only Laurie has the virginal strength to put up a fight.

There's one really neat effect: near the beginning, when the madman is driving past, the more brash teen-age girls jeer at him, and the car pauses for an instant, as if the masked figure inside were deciding whether to dispatch the girls right then or bide his time. But Carpenter also wrote the score himself—all four bars—and he's devoted to it. With the seductive tracking shots and the repetitive music, the film stops and starts so many times before anything happens that the bogeyman's turning up just gets to be a nuisance—it means more of the same. Carpenter keeps you tense in an undifferentiated way—nervous and irritated rather than pleasurably excited—and you reach the point of wanting somebody to be killed so the film's rhythms will change. Yet a lot of people seem to be convinced that *Halloween* is something special—a classic. Maybe when a horror film is stripped of everything but dumb scariness—when it isn't ashamed to revive the stalest device of the genre (the escaped lunatic)—it satisfies part of the audience in a more basic, childish way than sophisticated horror pictures do.

[February 19, 1979]

The Altman Bunker

Allegorical poetic films never do work. Worse, they're somehow all the same, and yet many directors seem to have one in them, and they struggle for years until they raise the money to realize their vision. When they finally get to it, they seem to forget most of what they knew about movies and all of what goes under the heading of common sense. Art empties their minds. The peculiarity of Robert Altman's *Quintet,* which is set in the future, in a new ice age, is that it's not his first allegorical poetic. He was already into his Jungian phase in the Janice Rule section of *3 Women* (and there were yearnings for the abyss in both *Brewster McCloud* and *Images*). When Altman enters this phase, he goes into his own fugal version of dreamtime, which means, in practice, that he puts the audience in such a depressed state that people are fighting to stay awake even before the titles come on. I'm not quite sure how this effect is achieved, but electronic sounds and a lot of white on the screen may be part of the secret.

It also helps to have the camera travel with one person trudging along in the snow, offering views of nothingness for our admiration. You get a sense of eternity fast.

Quintet seems to be shot through a hole in the ice—the perimeter of the frame has been blurred. This iris shape adds to the delicate dreaminess of some of the snow imagery, but also adds to the monotony of the clammy, greenish interiors. In this post-apocalypse age, the scattered survivors of a highly technological society live without hope in decaying, vandalized structures that suggest public housing designed by a drunken spider. The interiors were shot in the remnants of Expo 67 in Montreal, with the "Man and His World" photo-murals still visible—a black child and his mother, and other faces from the past. (These murals enrich the visual texture in an accusatory way; we're made to feel vaguely guilty.) To alleviate the boredom of survival, the last men and women play a death game called Quintet, which appears to be an elaborate form of Arctic roulette. (You wouldn't think that survival in subfreezing cold would be so easy that people would be bored, but let it pass.) The corpses of the losers are tossed outside into the frozen waste, to be devoured by packs of Rottweilers. Sleek and black against the snow, these Rottweilers are a death image—vultures, only more so.

The game of Quintet has, as anyone who has ever seen an allegorical poetic will expect, more than one metaphoric meaning. It is the game of life—life being, as one of the players, who is named St. Christopher (Vittorio Gassman), explains, the interruption in the void. And Grigor (Fernando Rey), the adjudicator, explains the game's excitement: the rush of adrenalin after you've killed is what tells you you're alive. (It helps you keep your sanity at this point to think of *Quintet* as a Mickey Spillane movie set in the far future: this place is a jungle. Or you can try thinking of it as an ice-age Sicily.)

There's also a metaphoric meaning signified by the caption that is lettered across Paul Newman's solemn headgear in the ads for the picture: "One man against the world." Newman plays Essex the seal hunter, who appears to be the last potent man left. At the beginning, he and his fresh-faced pregnant companion, Vivia (the French actress Brigitte Fossey), arrive at the ruins where the game is being played. The other, older women touch Vivia's stomach, wonderingly: she is probably the only woman alive who can still bear a child. Brigitte Fossey is lovely, and she's one of the few performers in the movie whose accents don't cripple them; this is her first English-speaking role, and she's enchanting. So, of course, Vivia is killed almost at once. After she's gone, we have nothing at stake. The noble Essex, in despair, hangs around and plays the game for a while; he's a winner, and he's also gracious enough to go to bed with Ambrosia (Bibi Andersson). This provides a brief respite from the script's enigmatic, fuzzily epigrammatic discourse. Throughout the film, people talk in semi-abstract generalizations, but Ambrosia is permitted a monologue about a dream she had of her mother in a green hat on a train, when there were still trains. Bibi Andersson does wonders with it: for a minute, we have the illusion of being involved in a movie. Eventually, Essex wearies of the ugly game and leaves, heading north. Why north? Well, the North Pole is the top of the world, and Newman appears to be a mythologized version of Robert Altman the moviemaker. In *Buffalo Bill and the Indians,* Newman was the showman aspect of Altman, and here he is the man who leaves other people (the studio people?) playing their rotten games and heads off into the unknown. Essex is the life force, the humane man in an inhuman world—in fact, everything an artist should never think of himself as.

In case critics don't know that they're not fit to have opinions of the movies made by northward-bound heroes, Altman and his team of writers give us Grigor, that adjudicator who wants the rush of adrenalin he gets from killing. Actually, critics may get a rush of misery from watching Fernando Rey, a great actor in French- and Spanish-speaking roles, work his mouth around words like "adrenalin" and overact so much that he seems a fool. Altman's magic now seems to be used up on the set, in convincing the actors that they're part of something great, masterly. They have the fun, and we get *Quintet.*

This picture enlisted the help of the cinematographer Jean Boffety and the designer Leon Ericksen, but to no great avail. The bombed-out décor, with its partitions and girders and dripping icicles, has zigzag effects reminiscent of *The Cabinet of Dr. Caligari,* and it bisects what's left of the frame after the edges have been blurred. You feel cramped; you have to squint your eyes as well as your mind. In a number of scenes, the actors lurk about like the conspirators in Eisenstein's *Ivan the Terrible.* Tom Pierson's ominous, dissonant score, which has the incantatory quality of medieval music, gives the film some lift, though it sounds too spacious for the cubbyholes of this futuristic flophouse. It also recalls the pealing and clanging of the bells in the *Ivan* score. *Quintet* might be *Ivan the Terrible, Part III*—the film no one was waiting for.

Altman has reached the point of wearing his failures like medals. He's creating a mystique of heroism out of emptied theatres. (A woman near me who thought she had lost a glove moaned, "A double disaster.") He's giving weight to scenes that he would have treated as comedy skits only a few years ago—like the comics who have had their gags explained to them by academics. There's a dialogue scene played by two people who are sitting on either side of a loser in the game (Nina Van Pallandt) who has been skewered to death. You can't listen to a word they're saying: you're watching to see if she blinks. In another scene, a woman (Monique Mercure) widowed by the game holds her hand over a fire until it is charred and bursts. (Did Altman run out of marshmallows?) Actors in medieval and Renaissance hats sit around swathed in pyramidal layers of cloth and fur arguing in assorted European accents about some game we don't understand. And with dialogue such as the diabolical Gassman's "Hope is an obsolete word," contrasted with the inspirational music as Newman presses on northward, it's like a Monty Python show played at the wrong speed.

□ □ □

Vanessa Redgrave has a luminously loony quality in *Agatha*; she's playing a distraught Agatha Christie, and when the goddess-tall Vanessa is distraught there's all that wavering height—she seems more fragile than ordinary people, more exposed to the elements. Dressed in clinging twenties shifts, with jewel-like Art Nouveau embroidery at the neck, she looks so eerily sensitive that your mind may easily drift to the terrible (true) accounts of how people on the street sometimes laughed at Virginia Woolf—she looked so odd to them. Vanessa Redgrave endows Agatha Christie with the oddness of genius. But the people who made *Agatha*— Kathleen Tynan, whose script initiated the project; Michael Apted, who directed it; and a slew of producers and additional writers—haven't come up with enough for their sorrowful, swanlike lady to do.

The movie proposes a solution to the "mystery" of what might have happened during the eleven days back in December, 1926, when Agatha Christie, whose husband wanted a divorce so he could marry his mistress, disappeared, and then was found living in a hotel in Harrogate, a Yorkshire spa, using the mistress's name. (There is, of course, no "mystery"—only an obvious and painful nervous distress. Mrs. Christie, who was upset over her mother's recent death as well as the breakup of her marriage of twelve years, left home on a Friday and by Tuesday her brother-in-law had received a letter from her explaining that she had gone to a Yorkshire spa for rest and treatment.) The movie attempts—very tentatively— to treat Agatha Christie as one of her own characters, and to invent a plot in the manner of one of her detective novels. But the situation is locked in: except for those "lost" days, her life is fully accounted for. So this fictional Agatha can't kill anybody or commit suicide; she can't even embark on a lasting love affair, since it is well known that she went back home with her husband and, after a discreet interval, gave him the divorce that enabled him to marry his mistress, and that a few years later she married the archeologist Max Mallowan and went on to lead a busy, productive life right up until she died, at eighty-five. How do you make a whodunit when nothing happened? *Agatha* pretends that something *almost* happened—it's about a death scheme that is foiled.

The movie has a lulling tempo and a languid elegance. When the story dawdles (as it does while Agatha is settling in at the spa), the director seems willing to let the cinematographer, Vittorio Storaro, take over, and we idly observe the lush closeups of women's profiles under their cloches, the décor, and the rays of diffused light. There can't be a primary color in the whole production; it's all in subtle, faded tones—in pale gray-greens, shimmery silver-grays, old rose. The rooms look smoked, and everything is in soft movement. This is the rare movie that is *too* fluid—perhaps partly as a result of trying to conceal the seediness of the hotel in which much of the film was shot. (It's the hotel that Agatha Christie actually stayed at.) Some sequences suggest a series of orange-toned pre-Raphaelite paintings of the golden-red-haired Agatha floating by; she's always caught on the wing, trembling. She's a transcendently lovely swirling object—a living Burne-Jones and a poetic essay in neurasthenia—but where is her core of sanity? Where is the Agatha Christie who wrote the hundred and five books and plays—the woman who entertained herself and the world by devising complicated riddles? In the film, we see Agatha only when she isn't herself. The movie, too, lacks a core: it has a general air of knowingness, and some of the incidental dialogue is clever, but it seems to be missing the scenes that would explain why it was made. *Agatha* doesn't have a story—it's from a musing.

The something-*almost*-happened crime plot that has been devised is feeble, but the character who foils this plot is played by Dustin Hoffman, and he's far from feeble. He's furiously theatrical in the role of Wally Stanton, a star journalist from America who trails Agatha to the spa and falls in love with her. Hoffman's lively-eyed, self-aware Wally Stanton has such a preening grand manner that you almost hear the drumroll each time he appears. Last year, when Hoffman played the paroled robber of *Straight Time,* he made the character mean and unyielding—a man with closer psychosexual relations to people from the prison world than he could ever have with outsiders. Hoffman gave a daring, stretching, self-testing performance. Though Wally Stanton is just a concoction of a role, Hoffman gives the impression of trying to find something unyielding here, too. What comes across is a crabbed intensity in the actor. Hoffman has grown into his older-man's head, which looked a little anomalous when he played youthful roles. Yet he's even less relaxed now and more stage-actorish: you feel that in *Agatha* he has an image of the character in his mind and he's impersonating it. Sometimes he has images of so many characters that he's impersonating a whole gallery of people; at other times, there's nobody there. The faintly smiling Wally Stanton explains his presence at the spa by claiming to have a constipation problem, and Hoffman seems to take his cue from that. Wally is physically tight and immaculately groomed, and has a mechanical-man clipped voice—he out-clips the British. What makes this performance seem miscalculated is that Hoffman's Wally is also intelligent, generous, and good-humored, and he falls in love with Agatha because of her sensitivity. So they seem meant for each other. But because of the locked-in situation nothing can come of it. If Wally were more simply and more broadly drawn, as a shallow, show-offy yellow journalist with a taste for luxury, or possibly as an envious writer, the movie might make more sense—there'd be a reason for the romance to be doomed.

Agatha invades the privacy of Agatha Christie and then gets fixated on her imaginary suitor. Hoffman never blends into the atmosphere; his performance is the cocky kind that doesn't allow you to take your eyes off him. (Someone in the audience referred to him as José Ferrer, Jr.) Yet he brings some fun into the movie, and it's his tough confidence that enables us to believe that Wally would court a woman a head taller than he is without giving it a moment's thought. Hoffman's confidence makes possible a series of scenes with an emotional forward movement: Wally teaching Agatha to swim, Wally the suitor gravely dancing with her, and the climax—when the swan Agatha responds to Wally's (previously denied) request for a kiss by coiling over and down to reach him. It's sculptural, blissful—one of the great romantic moments in movies.

As the adulterous Colonel Christie, a First World War combat pilot, Timothy Dalton suggests a man exhausted by the wounded look and the high-powered sensitivity that Wally admires. For the Colonel, living with Agatha must be like being under emotional siege. When he asks her for a divorce and she literally throws herself at him, you're aware of what a towering big girl she is. (Elsewhere, she seems weightless.) Wearing a trim mustache, Dalton looks like the young lounge-lizard Olivier of early 1930s films, with a slight trace of Laurence Harvey besides. He's a strong, funny actor. His Colonel Christie is tense from the strain of being civil when he wants to explode. You can see exactly why the woman he falls in love with (played by Celia Gregory) should be an utterly common sort: her vulgarity is like an ocean breeze to him. There's also a performer in a small part who makes you wish she could take over the movie—Helen Morse, as Evelyn, the friendly woman Agatha meets at her hotel. An Australian actress with a curly mouth, Helen Morse is such a vivid dimpled charmer that she makes you aware of how muted the film is.

Michael Apted's talent seems to be for the tactile, the plangent, the indefinite. Though he has a feeling for large-scale imagery, as he shows in the scene of thousands of people combing the countryside searching for the missing Agatha (and as he also showed in the grandiose rock-music film *Stardust*), his big scenes are so ambiguous and undeveloped that they're slightly frustrating. When he has to make a simple dramatic point, he becomes crude. (When Wally performs a last-minute rescue, the staging and editing are disastrous; when Colonel Christie holds a press conference to answer questions about his wife's disappearance, we can't tell how we're supposed to interpret what goes on at it, and the post-synched hubbub on the sound track is an embarrassment.) Yet the unattached bravura of Apted's directing has a gentle pull to it. His work suggests a becalmed Ken Russell.

[February 26, 1979]

Rumbling

*T*he *Graduate, Easy Rider, Five Easy Pieces, Little Big Man,* and other American films of the late sixties and early seventies which rejected middle-class values had a special appeal for middle-class college students. The anti-draft, anti-Vietnam counterculture took up movies in such a big way that it was sometimes called the film generation. By now, it's the "Masterpiece Theatre" generation. Some of the biggest recent hits have once again expressed—as movies did up through the fifties—the needs and fantasies of the people at the bottom of society. Tony Manero and Stephanie, of *Saturday Night Fever,* wanted to escape the coarseness and limitations of working-class life; they hoped to achieve the middle-class prerogatives that the college-educated anti-war audience held in cynical contempt (while, of course, enjoying them). And now, in *The Warriors,* the heroes are so far down in the social scale they can't even aspire to middle-classness—they envy it and hate it. What Tony and Stephanie are leaving behind is luxury compared with these heroes' welfare-gutted lives. With Walter Hill's *The Warriors,* movies are back to their socially conscious role of expressing the anger of the dispossessed. But this picture isn't a melodrama; it's a fantasy spectacle that has found its style in the taste of the dispossessed—in neon signs, graffiti, and the thrill of gaudiness. *The Warriors* enters into the spirit of urban-male tribalism and the feelings of kids who believe that they own the streets, because they keep other kids out of them. In this vision, cops and kids are all there is, and the worst crime is to be chicken. Paramount opened the picture in six hundred and seventy theatres, without advance press screenings, promoting it as an exploitation film, via a thumping TV commercial. Probably the assumption was that the audience for this picture doesn't read reviews. But the literate shouldn't miss out on it. *The Warriors* is a real moviemaker's movie: it has *in visual terms* the kind of impact that "Rock Around the Clock" did behind the titles of *Blackboard Jungle. The Warriors* is like visual rock.

At the opening, a lighted subway train—a many-eyed monster—moves toward us out of the darkness. The Wonder Wheel—the complicated old Ferris wheel at Coney Island—forms a pink-and-white pattern against black skies. The subway system is the central nervous system of the movie. Deserted subway stations are mysterious, cavernous, terror-filled places, with graffiti-covered trains pounding in and out. The film's atmosphere suggests the decadent nighttown feeling of Vienna in *The Third Man,* but in purplish tones. *The Warriors* is mesmerizing in its intensity. It runs from night until dawn, and most of the action is in crisp, bright Day-Glo colors against the terrifying New York blackness; the figures stand out like a jukebox in a dark bar. There's a night-blooming, psychedelic shine to the whole baroque movie. The story, which has a classic shape and suggests the Odyssey, is actually Xenophon's Anabasis retold in modern urban terms, and compressed, so that, like rock, it never lets up. The heroes—nine members of a Coney Island youth gang called the Warriors, wearing red-brown leather vests over bare skin—journey by subway to a foreign terrain, the Bronx. There, in a park amphitheatre, nine delegates each from a hundred youth gangs converge—every group in its own colors. Cyrus (Roger Hill), the head of the biggest of the gangs, the close-cropped paramilitary Riffs, has declared a truce for the purposes of this assembly, and the Riffs, in their orange karate jackets, patrol the meeting. Cyrus, his gold-and-burgundy robe gleaming in the moonlight, tells the crowd of his plan: that the gangs should organize their full membership of sixty thousand into a single gang and take over one borough at a time until they run the city, which has a police force of only twenty thousand. (Actually, twenty-four thousand.) To the boys yelling and waving their arms in approval, Cyrus seems inspired. But a psychotic—the head of the Rogues—shoots him, and the Warriors are mistakenly thought to be responsible. Pursued by the other gangs and by the police, they fight their way home through the city, which is laid out in primitive tribal patterns. Encountering one gang after another, they dart in and out of subway trains and stations while a rock-music d.j. on an all-night show broadcasts the word that they should be stopped.

In Sol Yurick's 1965 novel, on which the movie is based, the youngest of the heroes carried a comic-book version of Xenophon's account of how the Greek warriors, whose leader was killed in Persia, had to make their own way home. The movie is that comic book seen through the young reader's eyes: it's a slum kid's vivid fantasy of the hardships and adventures of a group of boys who have to prove their courage, their discipline, and their fighting skill to survive the night. The Warriors' torments are modern, mythic, surreal. Running from the Turnbull A.C.s—skinheads in overalls—they make it to the elevated; when they get to the Ninety-sixth Street station, there's the horror of realizing that the train is being held. Each time they have outwitted or fought off one gang, another turns up, in its colors and with its favored weapons. When the Baseball Furies—who have harlequin-painted faces (like the rock group Kiss) and are wearing baseball uniforms and carrying bats—catch up with them, it's a paranoid nightmare. Three of the Warriors are invited to party with some girls, then discover that these girls—so sensuous, so enticing—are the Lizzies, who are out to get them, too. A Warrior alone in the Union Square station sees a boy on skates who whizzes around, watching him, and we hear synthesized, high-pitched music; these Carol Reed–like touches presage the arrival of a switchblade-wielding gang. The Warriors have their losses (they don't all make it back), but they're tough, quick, resourceful fighters, who look after each other. If at the start of the picture they look like punks, by the end they're heroes.

Their long trip home is, however, tinged with a pathos that isn't comic-strip classical—it's Sol Yuricky. The members of each gang may fight to defend their own turf, but on a deeper level they know they don't own it. They don't own anything. This is an Anabasis of the despised, the lumpen. Like the novel, the movie endows their fighting with an existential rationale. Fighting means *more* to them than if they were actually defending their own land or property: fighting is its own reward—it ennobles them, and this macho pride is all they've got. And so the movie expresses something that's international: why the poorest boys of so many countries form disciplined, loyal tribal units and attack other boys as poor and scared and powerless as themselves. When the Warriors are told that they will be allowed to pass through an area without being attacked if they take off the vests that identify them, they refuse. Without that token of membership, they would have no proof of their manhood.

The physical action is so stylized that it has a wild cartoon kick to it, like *Yojimbo* and the best kung-fu movies. The fighting is exhilaratingly visceral, and so contrapuntal in the Oriental-martial-arts-dancing manner that you have no thought of pain or gore. The director, Walter Hill, is a fantasist, of a peculiarly violent yet abstract kind; each battle is different—spatially and kinetically—and tops the one before. Lighted in a different style, this movie might have been merely romantic pulp: it's the color itself that's violent. The purplish cheap-thrill color is as deep and strong as what cinematographers used to get when Technicolor was still Technicolor, and it gives off a hot glow against the darkness. Working with a ritualistic story, and in collaboration with the cinematographer, Andrew Laszlo (who also did the highly stylized work on the TV mini-series *The Dain Curse),* Hill achieves poetic power for the whole length of the movie. The Warriors run through a park that is all blackness except for the green trees and grass. When they run into a subway station through the territory of a gang called the Orphans, the streets are like wet greenish-black velvet. (About five minutes into this movie, you realize that it has the folkloric quality that *The Wiz* was trying to get at: the sleazy city as magical city, urban fear mythologized.) Hill's gift is for translating spectacle into action. His staging of the park assembly and then its disintegration into a riot, with the gangs swarming in all directions, is reminiscent of the Babylonian scenes of D. W. Griffith's *Intolerance*; his calling the head of the Riffs Cyrus (which is not the name Yurick used in the book but goes back to Xenophon) may also be an homage to Griffith's Cyrus the Great, who conquered Babylon. Hill's choreographed fights are certainly indebted to Peckinpah, for whom he wrote *The Getaway*; some of the tumbling, crashing bodies suggest variations on the fast cuts of fighting aboard the phantom fleet in Peckinpah's *The Killer Elite*.

Walter Hill is one of the rare American directors who function better in abstract, patterned scenes than they do in conversational ones; in *The Warriors*, there's almost a formal break between the two. The camera doesn't move around in the action scenes to include what the characters say; instead, there's a cut to someone speaking—the dialogue has the effect of inserts. Most of the film was shot on New York locations at night, but the performances seem to be taking place in the void of a studio (which may in fact be the case). We never feel that we're just overhearing the Warriors; they're not talking to each other—they're talking to us, and, at the opening, one at a time. There's another, bigger problem: While Hill's martial-arts Expressionism suggests something that has never been seen before—a blending of Fritz Lang and kung fu—the characters take us back to the Dead End Kids and all their brothers in the socially conscious movies of the thirties, and to *The Wild One* and the other delinquency movies of the fifties. Hill doesn't allow the actors to overdramatize themselves in fifties style—to clown or be too ingratiating. On the contrary, he cools them out—keeps them at a respectful distance. They're handled like dancers; their faces are slightly impassive, and when they talk it's a little impersonal, like dance recitation. But they seem almost redundant—it's as if Hill's vision were complete without them, and he put them in just so we'd have some people on the screen to identify with. Since the characters don't seem integral to the conception, we aren't particularly drawn to them. As Swan, the blond war chief for the Warriors who takes command when the group's leader is killed, Michael Beck leaves us unsure whether Swan is meant to be as stoic and tight-mouthed as he's played. Swan lacks spirituality, and it takes a while to respond to him. With his broad, muscular neck, he's like a Joe Dallesandro who keeps in lean, fighting shape—a mixture of turn-off and turn-on. The other Warriors— white, black, Hispanic—are less forbidding, and we come to accept them all. Marcelino Sanchez, who plays the youngest, Rembrandt—named for his dexterity with a spray can—has an easy, natural manner; at the other extreme, David Harris, who wears a headband and a turquoise necklace, is such a fine-boned camera subject that he functions almost purely in graphic terms.

Even in the scripts Walter Hill wrote before he turned director, he didn't think in terms of character, and in his two earlier movies as a writer-director (*Hard Times* and *The Driver*) the motivation was primarily visual. As a director, he's like an addict hooked on visual effects—not a bad addiction for a movie director, but it can alter a novelist's conception in surprising ways. Hill shows only a half-hearted interest in the psychology of youth-gang members and in the psychology of violence itself, which are Yurick's primary concerns. The novel is like a description of a movie, but not necessarily this movie. Yurick's gang members are just kids, full of fear. They strike out with their fists and weapons before they can be struck. In the book, it's not a single psychotic who shoots the Cyrus-gangster-messiah figure; psychotics abound, and the discipline of staying quiet for Cyrus's speech is too much for almost everyone. A boy slaps at a mosquito; a fight breaks out; it turns into a general brawl. And when the prowl cars come toward the field and the boys hear the sirens, they don't know the way out, and they blame the orating messiah for trapping them. "From all around the field they aimed their guns at the circle of light. They fired." And in the panic of the police-car headlights and spotlights pouring down on them, they "pounded at one another, not only at enemies, but at friends, as if only terrific motion could make them feel less frightened." What the movie does is to shape gang warfare into a fantasy fulfillment: the Warriors become true warriors. (The title of the book is ironic and full of pity: the novel is a study in volatility—a man on the street who happens to look at one of the gang members in a way the boy doesn't like is stabbed and slashed by all of them.) The book is about real violence; the movie is about dissociated, comic-book violence. That may be why the characters' emotions, which are integral to Yurick's vision, seem an excrescence here—as if they were stuck in for redeeming social value.

There *are* attempts at characterization: As the psychotic assassin, David Patrick Kelly, who has the pointed nose and jutting square chin of a Mephisto, suggests a degenerate, comic version of Vic Morrow's villain back in *Blackboard Jungle*; when he beats out a rhythm with three bottles on his fingers, like castanets, he's a real manic cuckoo. And as a girl who joins the gang, Deborah Van Valkenburgh seems at first no more than an affected actress with twisted, pouty-smudgy lips, but her performance grows in quality; she even survives a sentimentalized confrontation of the haves and the have-nots in the subway when she looks at some dressed-up kids returning from a prom, and is conscious of her own deprivation and trampiness. Walter Hill, who had been in New York only a couple of times for brief visits before coming to start work on *The Warriors,* has a goof in this scene: prom kids wouldn't make eye contact with street punks. But maybe it's partly because Hill isn't a New Yorker that he is able to sustain the jumping excitement of this vision: he's seeing the city in his head. And his editor (David Holden) and art directors (Don Swanagan and Bob

Wightman) seem to know exactly what he's after. Many objections could be raised to the script (by David Shaber and Hill)—to devices such as that of the witness who arrives to tell the Riffs who really killed Cyrus, to the way the role of a policewoman is written (she gives the false impression that she will turn out to be a man in disguise), and to many overexplicit lines of dialogue. But the acid-rock score, by Barry De Vorzon, with its electric, third-rail sound, seems perfectly rhythmed to the images. I have just one small complaint about the music: when the d.j. (we only see her great red-lipped mouth) puts on "Nowhere to Run," couldn't it have been the original, by Martha and the Vandellas?

If there's one immutable law about movies, it may be that middle-class people get hot and bothered whenever there's a movie that the underclass really responds to. And there's also a reason for them to get upset: as Yurick indicates, when the underclass gathers, there's so much restlessness and psychosis that a mosquito can cause a murder. There have been violent incidents in theatres showing *The Warriors,* as there were in the fifties at *Blackboard Jungle,* and as there frequently are at theatres that run action movies. I saw *The Warriors* at an 11:15 P.M. show in a Broadway theatre, and the audience was so attentive to the movie it was hushed; it may have been the quietest late-night Broadway audience of my experience in recent years. I'm told that at theatres where the audience is all teen-agers they participate happily and noisily. But there's bound to be trouble in some places when a movie comes along that's bursting with energy and is set in the imaginary kids-and-cops city of youth.

[March 5, 1979]

Index

Guillermin, John (*cont'd*)
  238; *Waltz of the Toreadors,* 238; *Guns at Batasi,* 238; *The Blue Max,* 238; *The Bridge at Remagen,* 238; *Skyjacked,* 238; *Death on the Nile,* 462–466
Guinness, Alec, 171, 286, 295, 353
Guitry, Sacha, 167, 233, 355, 459; dir., *Lovers and Thieves,* 459
Gulag Archipelago, The, 299
Gulpilil, 535
Gunga Din, 17, 18, 19, 23, 29, 107
Guns at Batasi, 238
"Gunsmoke," 114
Guthrie, Arlo, 226, 397
Guthrie, Woody, 224–230
Guzmán, Patricio, 384–388

Hackett, Joan, 171
Hackman, Gene, 45–46, 106–107, 199, 526
Hagegård, Håkan, 75
Hagen, Uta, 452
Hail the Conquering Hero, 213
Haitkin, Jacques, 537
Haldeman, H. R., 263
Haley, Jack, 473
Halloween, 547–548
Hamilton, Gay, 102
Hamilton, Margaret, 210
Hamlin, Harry, 501–502
Hamlisch, Marvin, 149, 151, 505
Hammer Films, 331
Hammerstein, Arthur, 12, 15
Hammerstein, Oscar, II, 12
Hammerstein, Reggie, 12
Hammett, Dashiell, 123, 305, 306, 308, 309
Hamnett, Olivia, 534, 535
Handle with Care, see *Citizens Band*
Harbach, Otto, 12
Hard Times, 40–42, 558
Hard Way, The, 503
"Hard Workin' Man," 406
Hardcore, 543–546
Harding, Ann, 16
Hardwick, Michael, 111
Hardy, Oliver, 471, 536, 537
Hardy, Thomas, 47
Harewood, Dorian, 165–166
Harlan County, U.S.A., 249–253
Harlow, Jean, 15, 422
Harper, Jessica, 156
Harper, Valerie, 359
Harris, Barbara, 504
Harris, David, 557
Harris, Julius, 66, 282
Harris, Leonard, 133
Harris, Richard, 158, 197
Harris, Rosemary, 453
Harrison, Cathryn, 82
Harry & Tonto, 128, 129, 411

Harry and Walter Go to New York, 490
Hart, Moss, 13, 22
Hartman, Elizabeth, 210
Harvest, 144
Harvey, Laurence, 553
Haskell, Molly, 138
Hasso, Signe, 123
Hauben, Lawrence, 85
Hauser, Kaspar, 51
Having Wonderful Time, 370
Hawks, Howard, 17, 18; dir., *Bringing Up Baby,* 3, 8, 16, 17, 18, 29; *Only Angels Have Wings,* 3, 4, 18, 30; *His Girl Friday,* 4, 16, 18, 19, 23; *Twentieth Century,* 6, 16, 141; *I Was a Male War Bride,* 30; *The Big Sleep,* 262; *To Have and Have Not,* 281, 282
Haydée, Marcia, 347
Hayden, Sterling, 325, 326, 328, 330
Hayes, Billy, 496–501
Hayes, Gabby, 508
Hayes, Helen, 16
Hayward, Brooke, 481
Hayward, Louis, 49
Hayward, Susan, 166
Haywire, 481
Hayworth, Rita, 3, 261, 464
Head, Edith, 109
Hearst, Patty, 223
Hearst, William Randolph, 373
Hearts and Minds, 176, 251
Hearts of the West, 45–49
Heaven Can Wait, 427, 429–430, 432
Heaven Has No Favorites, 302
Hecht, Ben, 18
Hegel, Georg Wilhelm Friedrich, 306
Hellman, Lillian, 304–310
Hemingway, Ernest, 91, 278–283, 308, 516
Hemingway, Margaux, 236
Hemingway, Mary, 282
Hemmings, David, 282
Henner, Marilu, 446
Henreid, Paul, 116
Henry, Buck, 498
Henstell, Bruce, 41
Hepburn, Audrey, 3, 5, 32, 61, 157–159, 214, 345, 482
Hepburn, Katharine, 3, 7, 16, 17, 18, 19, 20, 28, 29, 61, 62–64, 157, 201, 209, 233
Heroes, 467–468
Herrmann, Bernard, 134, 352
Hershewe, Michael, 446
Herzog, Werner, 51–55; dir., *The Mystery of Kaspar Hauser* (*Every Man for Himself and God Against All*), 51–55; *Signs of Life,* 54
Hesse, Hermann, 258
Hester Street, 79–82
Heston, Charlton, 178, 179, 198
Hewitt, Mary, 368
Hicks, Edward, 471

Milius, John, 42, 196, 203, 512; dir., *The Wind and the Lion*, 42, 196; *Dillinger*, 116, 196
Milland, Ray, 8, 30, 218, 443
Millar, Stuart, 62–64; dir., *Rooster Cogburn*, 62–64, 197
Miller, Arnold R., 249–250
Miller, Henry, 182, 455
Miller, Linda, 411
Miller, Marilyn, 12
Minnelli, Liza, 61, 106–107, 167, 193–194
Minnelli, Vincente, 192–195, 513, 547; dir., *The Bad and the Beautiful*, 61; *The Band Wagon*, 177; *A Matter of Time*, 192–195, 477; *On a Clear Day You Can See Forever*, 193; *The Cobweb*, 373; *Meet Me in St. Louis*, 547
Miou-Miou, 181, 182, 455–456
Miracle, Irene, 497
Miracle of Our Lady of Fatima, The, 354
Miranda, Carmen, 473
Misérables, Les, 489
Missouri Breaks, The, 427
Mr. Blandings Builds His Dream House, 21
Mr. Deeds Goes to Town, 48
Mr. Klein, 396
Mr. Smith Goes to Washington, 48, 227
Mitchell, Millard, 13
Mitchum, Robert, 218
Mobil Oil, 150, 386
Modesty Blaise, 94
Molière, 530
Molina, Angela, 365–366
Molly Maguires, The, 170
Monogram Pictures, 291, 379
Monroe, Marilyn, 3, 39, 219, 316
Monsieur Beaucaire, 336
Montand, Yves, 153–155, 223
Montenegro, Conchita, 364–365
Montez, Lola, 50
Montgomery, David, 471
Montgomery, Robert, 27
"Moondog Rock 'n' Roll Party," 421
Moore, Mary Tyler, 224
Moore, Terry, 291
Moreau, Gustave, 471
Moreau, Jeanne, 56, 94, 143–147, 155, 218, 230–233, 456, 461; dir., *Lumière*, 230–233
Morgan!, 258
Morley, Robert, 482–483, 485
Moroder, Giorgio, 496
Morphett, Tony, 534
Morricone, Ennio, 331
Morris, David, 253
Morris, Garrett, 188
Morris, John, 100
Morris, Oswald, 108, 190, 338, 475
Morrow, Vic, 558
Morse, Helen, 553

Mostel, Zero, 171
Motown Records, 60, 469
Movie Movie, 501–505
Mozart, Wolfgang Amadeus, 72–76, 459, 460, 461
Mucha, Alphonse, 205
Muir, Georgette, 416
Muller, Jorge, 386
Mulligan, Robert, 445–447, 505–507; dir., *To Kill a Mockingbird*, 368, 446; *Bloodbrothers*, 445–447, 495; *Summer of '42*, 446; *Same Time, Next Year*, 505–507
Muni, Paul, 206
Murder by Death, 188
Murder on the Orient Express, 192, 194, 463
Murphy, George, 13
Murphy, Michael, 170, 410
Murphy, Rosemary, 305
Murphy, Walter, 368
Murray, William, 114–115
Murrow, Edward R., 220
Mussolini, Benito, 137, 178, 310, 311, 312
Mutiny on the Bounty (1935), 15
Mutrux, Floyd, 421–424
My Darling Clementine, 328
My Fair Lady, 8, 177
My Favorite Wife, 3, 18, 19
My Little Chickadee, 414
"My Man," 244
My Man Godfrey (1936), 141, 236
Myers, Dave, 287
Myerson, Bess, 495
Mystery of Kaspar Hauser, The (Every Man for Himself and God Against All), 51–55

Naked Civil Servant, The, 498
Naked Truth, The (Your Past is Showing), 246
Namath, Joe, 359
Napier, Charles, 321, 322
Napoléon, 324
Napoleon I, 25, 380–382
Napoleon III, 55
Nashville, 136, 143, 202, 204, 227, 259, 267, 276, 284, 322, 400, 441, 445
Nasty Habits, 262–266
National Ballet of Canada, 495
National Enquirer, 209
National Geographic, 513
National Lampoon's Animal House, 428, 429, 509
Navigator, The, 136
Nazimova, Alla, 335–336
NBC, 149, 284, 486
"Need a New Sun Rising," 400
Needham, Hal, 430
Negro Ensemble Company, 188
Nelson, Ricky, 291
Nelson, Ruth, 261, 444
Nero, Franco, 140

590